DATE DUE

~~MR 10 99~~ ~~MY 13 04~~			
~~AP 21 99~~			
~~MY 8 99~~			
~~NO 14 00~~			
~~JE 11 04~~			
~~DE 1 8 03~~			
~~NO 27 06~~			

Exceptional Individuals

AN INTRODUCTION

Exceptional Individuals

AN INTRODUCTION

Bill Gearheart
University of Northern Colorado

Robert C. Mullen
Rangely Public Schools

Carol J. Gearheart
University of Northern Colorado

Brooks/Cole Publishing Company
Pacific Grove, California

Brooks/Cole Publishing Company

A Division of Wadsworth, Inc.

© 1993 by Wadsworth, Inc., Belmont, California 94002.

Printed in the United States of America

10   9   8   7   6   5   4   3   2   1

Library of Congress Cataloging in Publication Data

Gearheart, Bill R. (Bill Ray), [date]
    Exceptional individuals : an introduction / Bill Gearheart, Robert
C. Mullen, Carol J. Gearheart.
        p. cm.
    Includes bibliographical references and index.
    ISBN 0-534-14274-5
      1. Special education—United States.   I. Mullen, Robert C., [date]
      II. Gearheart, Carol J. (Carol Jean), [date].   III. Title.
LC3981.G43   1992
371.9′0973—dc20   92-11900
                                                  CIP

Sponsoring Editor: *Vicki Knight*
Editorial Associate: *Heather L. Graeve*
Production Editor: *Marjorie Z. Sanders*
Manuscript Editor: *Pamela Evans*
Permissions Editor: *Marie DuBois*
Interior and Cover Design: *Katherine Minerva*
Cover Photo: *Lee Hocker Photography*
Art Coordinator: *Lisa Torri*
Interior Illustration: *Precision Graphics*
Photo Editor: *Larry Molmud*
Photo Researcher: *Gail Meese*
Typesetting: *Graphic World Inc.*
Cover printing: *Lehigh Press Lithographers/Autoscreen*
Printing and Binding: *Arcata Graphics/Hawkins*

We dedicate this book to the parents, teachers, exceptional students, and college students who have been and continue to be a source of inspiration.

Bill Gearheart
Robert Mullen
Carol Gearheart

This book is about *people*. To help the reader better understand those who have disabilities or who are gifted or talented, we have described some of their unique characteristics, focusing on their educational and social development. In doing so, we've used terms such as *learning disabilities, mental retardation, behavior disorders,* and *hearing impairments* — but our concern is always with *individuals*.

Chapters 1 and 2 provide an overview of the field of special education and of its historical, legal, and financial foundations. Chapter 3 offers an optimistic look at the future by describing the role that technology can play in meeting the needs of exceptional students. We believe that the potential of technology may have been overlooked by educators. These three chapters are the basis for more meaningful consideration of the exceptionalities addressed in Chapters 4 through 11.

PREFACE

Chapters 4 through 10 contain definitions, prevalence data, characteristics, causal factors, and educational interventions as they relate to mental retardation, learning disabilities, behavioral disorders, communication disorders, hearing impairments, visual impairments, and orthopedic disorders and health impairments. In all instances, our emphasis is on individuals' special needs that may be generated by those disabilities. Chapter 11 is about students who are gifted, talented, or creative and their unique needs to realize their full potential.

Chapter 12 reviews the importance of early intervention in the lives of infants and children with special needs. The critical nature of the need is discussed, along with strategies to meet that need. Chapter 13 points out the various transitions that individuals make throughout life and the reasons why individuals with disabilities may require additional assistance at those times.

Chapter 14 enumerates the variables that must be considered when planning for students from diverse cultural or linguistic backgrounds. Careful consideration of the special education, bilingual, and bicultural interface is essential in identification and in planning appropriate educational interventions. We stress the importance of educators understanding the potential influence of cultural factors. Chapter 15 discusses the role of the family with respect to gifted students and those with disabilities. Not only parental but also sibling and extended family relationships have the potential to harm or help the development of exceptional students.

Although our primary focus throughout this text is on preschool and school-age individuals, we also provide information about exceptional adults. This reflects our belief in the importance of planning for the entire life span.

Special Features of This Text

- Vignettes at the beginning of each chapter help to set the tone and provide initial insight into the content of the chapter.

- Feature boxes titled "People Who Make a Difference" describe people who have made unique contributions leading to improvements in the lives of persons with disabilities or to a better understanding or acceptance of those individuals.
- Terms included in the Glossary are printed in boldface the first time they are used in significant discussion in the text.
- Appendix A offers a comprehensive listing of sources of additional information on individuals with disabilities and the organizations that advocate on their behalf.

Supplementary Aids

Various supplementary aids are provided for the instructor, including an instructor's manual with a chapter overview, key terms and concepts, chapter outline, questions and issues for class discussion, suggested special activities, and related readings. Also included are 118 transparency masters, developed from and coordinated with 15 chapters. These are provided on computer disks so that instructors can easily modify them, if desired, to meet specific instructional goals. A separate test bank is provided on disk and in hard copy.

Acknowledgments

We gratefully recognize the contributions of many individuals in the completion of this text. The coordinated efforts of our managing editor, Vicki Knight, and our production editor, Marjorie Sanders, are greatly appreciated. The questions, suggestions, and constructive criticisms of our copy editor, Pamela Evans, were most valuable. We also recognize and appreciate the assistance of reviewers, contacted by and responsible to our editor, who provided valuable suggestions about additional concepts that should be included and additional ideas that we believe have made this a truly comprehensive introductory college text. Those reviewers are John Beattie, University of North Carolina, Charlotte; Hazel B. Cobb, University of Alabama; Gerard Giordano, New Mexico State University; Anita L. Hermann, University of Wisconsin, Milwaukee; Eric Jones, Bowling Green State University; Elliot Lessen, Northern Illinois University; Peter Matthews, Lock Haven University of Pennsylvania; Susan Meyers, San Jose State University; Gerald Spadafore, Idaho State University; and Barbara Wasson, Moorhead State University.

We also acknowledge with appreciation the contribution of ideas and assistance from the following special educators: Joe Bocke, Earl Brabandt, Milo Henkels, Tom Jeschke, Gaylen Kapperman, Earl Owens, Madeleine Humbert Poole, Ron Rubadeau, Tom Sileo, Dean Tuttle, Naomi Tuttle, and Joan Wolf. Colleagues who voluntarily provide such assistance to others' professional efforts are much more than colleagues—they are true friends. In addition, Bob Mullen would like to acknowledge the support he received from his wife, Celest.

Finally, we must attribute the motivation to complete this text to the encouragement of college students who, over the years, have commented on, critiqued, complimented, and complained about texts we and others have authored. They told us what they want and why they want it. They explained what makes a text interesting and challenging, yet readable and understandable. We have tried to listen to and respond to their comments.

This book promises the reader a general understanding of exceptional individuals, their unique characteristics, and how we may ensure their successful participation in family life and in their community. It should also give the reader a basis from which to make more meaningful decisions about further investigation into this exciting and rewarding field of specialization.

Bill Gearheart
Robert Mullen
Carol Gerheart

BILL GEARHEART   Bill Gearheart is Professor Emeritus of Special Education at the University of Northern Colorado. At UNC he directed the Special Education Administration Program, the Doctoral Program in Special Education, and the Navajo Education Program in Utah, Arizona, and New Mexico. His previous experience was as a teacher, principal, director of special services, and assistant superintendent of schools in the public schools.

ABOUT THE AUTHORS

This is the 15th college textbook he has authored or coauthored; several have been translated into Spanish, Japanese, or Chinese. In addition, he has contributed a chapter to a pediatric textbook, provided written evaluations to state legislative bodies and the federal government, and served as an evaluator of federal research projects. Dr. Gearheart has served as a consultant to numerous local educational agencies in the United States and Canada. One of his primary interests is the way schools organize their systems so that all exceptional students have optimal opportunity for maximum personal development.

ROBERT MULLEN   Robert Mullen is presently Superintendent of Schools in Rangely, Colorado. He previously served as director of the Rio Blanco Board of Cooperative Educational Services, during which time he was responsible for special education services for Rio Blanco County. He held a similar position as executive director of Reno County Education Cooperative in Hutchinson, Kansas. Dr. Mullen was executive director of the Alaska Treatment Center for Crippled Children and Adults in Anchorage, and prior to that director of the ACCA Speech and Hearing Center in Fairbanks.

Robert Mullen entered the field of special education as a speech-language pathologist in Iowa and has since worked in the development or supervision of programs for all areas of exceptionality. He has filled such diverse roles as special educator to isolated village schools in the Alaskan ''bush,'' the first hearing officer in Alaska for Public Law 94-142, and president of a variety of state advisory boards in Kansas and Colorado. His major interest is in providing effective educational programming for all students.

CAROL GEARHEART   Carol Gearheart is Professor of Special Education at the University of Northern Colorado, where she has had primary responsibility for teacher training programs in the areas of behavior disorders and learning disabilities. She has also directed programs related to early intervention.

Dr. Gearheart has authored or coauthored five college textbooks and contributed chapters to several others. She has conducted research in the areas of behavior disorders and learning disabilities and worked with the Colorado Department of Education in an attempt to put the results of that research into practice. Carol Gearheart has been a classroom teacher in the regular class, a principal, and a demonstration teacher in a special education laboratory school setting. She has served as an educational consultant to numerous local educational agencies and to the Bureau of Indian Affairs. Her major interest is helping teachers implement more effective educational strategies for students with disabilities.

Bill Gearheart

Robert Mullen

Carol Gearheart

BRIEF CONTENTS

CONTENTS

10 *Physical or Health Impairments*   307

Exceptional Individuals

AN INTRODUCTION

1940 *Mike's parents knew before he was 2 years old that he was "slow." He had trouble learning to talk and understanding what others expected of him. He could not do at age 6 what their other children could do by age 3. Mike did not enter school until he was 7 (the compulsory attendance age), and even then he couldn't keep up with the other kindergartners. After six unsuccessful, frustrating years in school, Mike was officially classified by school personnel as "uneducable"; his parents were told that they must make other arrangements for him. They eventually enrolled Mike in a private, special school, for which they had to pay tuition.*

1950 *Joe's parents were very concerned about his difficulty in controlling emotional outbursts, which seemed to be a reaction to authority figures. After nine years in school Joe was still in the fifth grade and "failing." His parents were called to school regularly about his behavior. Finally, in a meeting with school officials, they were told he would be permanently expelled from the regular school program. There was a special class in a public school on the other side of the city in which he might be enrolled on a trial basis, if Joe's parents could arrange transportation.*

1960 *Mary was a well-behaved girl but was, according to her parents, "not nearly as quick as the other kids." Mary spent two years in first grade and two years in fourth grade. One day when Mary was 12, her mother went to school to take her a coat, because the weather had suddenly turned very cold. But Mary wasn't in the classroom in which she had been since September. The teacher said, "Oh, I'm sorry. Mary is now in the special class. You'd better go see Mr. James." The principal, Mr. James, told her he was sorry that the note they*

CHAPTER ONE

The Foundations of the Education of Exceptional Students

had sent about the move to the special class had not gotten home with Mary. He told her that Mary had been tested and found to need special help. He added that the special class would be much more beneficial for Mary. Mary's parents had not known that she was being evaluated for possible special class placement and had not been asked for information about her early development or health history. They had not been consulted about the change in educational program, and the special class had never been mentioned in their various school conferences.

Today a broad variety of programs and services is provided for exceptional students in the United States. There is variation between states and within states with respect to both quantity and quality of programs, but the provision of appropriate, comprehensive educational programs for exceptional students is accepted in principle. This has, however, not always been the case. The legal right to a free, appropriate, individually planned program for students with disabilities was not established until 1975, and there is still no national legislative mandate for special programs for gifted and talented students.

In this text we will consider the recognized exceptionalities and the variety of ways in which students with special needs are educated today. The current stage of development of programs and services for exceptional students has evolved over the past 300 to 400 years, the more rapid changes occurring since about 1950. Information about this evolution and the factors and forces that gave it momentum is of considerable value in understanding the nature of educational programming today. The information may also provide insight into possible future trends. We will consider this evolution in relation to several major, overlapping forces or influences; however, we will first review and attempt to clarify some of the basic terminology that will be used in this text and that may be used in any related publication.

Our basic concern is with exceptional students and how they may be most effectively educated. Exceptional students require special educational programming or services; thus, some authors prefer the term *students with special needs* to that of *exceptional students*. We feel that both terms are quite acceptable. But who are these exceptional or special needs students? We will consider two major categories: those with **impairments** or disabilities and those who may be called gifted, **talented,** or creative. We will provide, in separate chapters, information about students with mental retardation, learning disabilities, emotional or behavioral disorders, communication disorders, hearing impairments, visual impairments, physical impairments or health conditions, and students who are gifted, talented, or creative. As we consider these exceptionalities, we will discover many alternative terms that may be used with respect to each.

Other terms of major importance include ***mainstreaming,*** which some define as education in the **least restrictive environment** in which effective education may be provided, and others define as education in a regular class. Another set of terms—such as *resource teacher, resource room teacher, consul-*

■ One goal of legislation on behalf of individuals with disabilities is to prevent situations like this. ■

■ Many individuals with disabilities contribute at the same level as nondisabled peers. ■

tant, specialist, collaborative consultant, and *helping teacher*—may refer to persons with exactly the same job description and duties or, in different school districts, to persons with quite different roles and responsibilities. In spite of the variations in meaning, in almost all cases these titles refer to teachers with specialized training who in some manner cooperate or collaborate with the regular classroom teacher in educating students with special needs.

As for such terms as **handicap,** *disorder, impairment,* and *disability,* Table 1.1 provides an overview of their evolution. This evolution has progressed from a disembodied emphasis on the handicap, disorder, or disability itself to a humanistic one on the individual with the handicap, disorder, or disability. In fact, the

Table 1.1 The evolution of terminology relating to individuals with disabilities

Federal Legislation Influencing Terminology	Education of All Handicapped Children Act (1975)	→	Americans with Disabilities Act (1990) Individuals with Disabilities Education Act (1990)
Terms Used in Education-Related Disciplines	Handicapped children →	Children with handicaps →	Children with disabilities
	Special education students	Special needs students	Students with special needs
Terms Used in Medicine-Related Disciplines	Disorder, disease, impairment (with reference to specific conditions)	→	Disorder, disease, impairment Developmental disability

term *handicap* has been for the most part replaced by *disability*. As may be seen in the table, those in medicine-related disciplines have tended to use the terms *disorder, impairment,* or *developmental disability*. Educators more often use *disability* but will also use *impairment* and *disorder,* as appropriate. Other potentially confusing terminology exists; we will attempt to point it out when appropriate throughout this text.

The Origins of Present-Day Programs

The early history of the treatment of individuals with disabilities is primarily one of abuse, mistreatment, or willful ignorance of such individuals' existence. Historical records mention "the blind," the "deaf and dumb," "idiots and imbeciles" (probably individuals with mental retardation), and "witches" or those possessed by "evil spirits" (probably persons who were mentally ill, or perhaps epileptic). Because such conditions appeared to be abnormal, and "normal" was equated with "right," most of these individuals became societal outcasts. The less fortunate were imprisoned; still others were burned at the stake; in a few cases, the disabled were made court jesters, to amuse the nobility.

Between early Christian times and the 16th century, some advances were made toward a scientific understanding of persons with disabilities, but such temporary advances were regularly counteracted by superstition and the fear of what could not be fully understood. The spread of Christianity brought with it an ethic of service to the less fortunate, from which some persons with disabilities benefited; however, during this same period church doctrine recognized demonology and witchcraft and promoted the idea that the forces of evil caused what we now call mental illness. In a notable case in 1584, Reginald Scot effectively argued in writing that some of the "witches" of the day were actually mentally ill; King James I of England personally condemned Scot's position and ordered his book seized and burned (Coleman, 1976).

Persons we would now recognize as having mild or moderate disabilities were simply ignored. People who were "slow" mentally did more menial work or perhaps begged, existing at an even lower economic level than those around them. It appears that the majority of those students for whom we now provide special educational services would have been ignored through the 16th century, unless they were sons or daughters of the aristocracy.

■ Schools and Residential Facilities

During the last half of the 18th century, a number of special schools for persons who were deaf or blind were established in France, Germany, and England. These were followed in the early 1800s by similar schools for persons with mental retardation. Some were "day school" institutions, for those who could continue to live with relatives, but most evolved into residential facilities. These were not national efforts—that is, national governmental attempts to meet the needs of persons then recognized as having a particular disability. Rather, they were launched by individuals who believed that persons who were deaf, blind, or mentally retarded could benefit from education and training. Usually the head of such a school was a medical doctor, and the effort was supported by wealthy individuals who believed in the potential of such a program. Programs for persons with mental retardation apparently included quite a mixture: those whom we would still consider mentally retarded, others who were mentally ill, some who were severely hearing impaired, and others who fit none of those classifications but who for some reason were not able to learn and otherwise function in what was considered a normal or near-normal manner. This development of programs in Europe provided the basis for those that would evolve in the United States.

■ Early Efforts in the United States

By the early 1800s residential programs for persons who were deaf or blind began to develop in the United States. The first school for individuals who were deaf was the American Asylum for the Deaf, established in West Hartford, Connecticut, in 1817. The term *asylum* was adopted from terminology in use in France at that time. In 1831 a school now known as the Perkins School for the Blind was opened in Watertown, Massachusetts, by Samuel Gridley Howe, a Boston physician. He also played a major role in establishing a number of residential institutions for persons with mental retardation. At that point, the establishment of such facilities was an accepted sign of a state's growing maturity and was vigorously promoted by state leaders (Gearheart & Litton, 1979). In contrast with early residential facilities in Europe, these institutions were state-sponsored and funded.

Another pioneer of note was involved in the establishment of treatment facilities for a group of individuals that had either been completely ignored or inaccurately classified as mentally retarded and that had thus received inappropriate help. Dorothea Dix, a retired schoolteacher, vigorously pursued her conviction that persons who were mentally ill were among the most mistreated members of our society. Between 1841 and 1881, Ms. Dix was instrumental in the establishment of 32 modern mental hospitals (Zilboorg & Henry, 1941). Along the way she had an opportunity (in 1848) to roundly chastise the U.S. Congress, and she lectured various state legislatures with equal vigor.

By the end of the 19th century, many persons who were blind, deaf, mentally retarded, or mentally ill were receiving some recognition and treatment, primarily in residential settings. By the turn of the century, programs in the United States had for the most part caught up with their counterparts in Europe with respect to both **classification** procedures and treatment programs.

■ The Era of Special Classes

In 1898 Dr. Alexander Graham Bell made a radical recommendation to the National Education Association (NEA) at the closing session of its national convention. He recommended that programs for children with disabilities should become

> an annex to the public school system, receiving special instruction from special teachers, who shall be able to give instruction to little children who are either deaf, blind, or mentally deficient, without sending them away from their homes or from the ordinary companions with whom they are associated.

His recommendation, backed by his considerable stature both within and without the educational community as well as by a small number of school systems that had tried out this concept, led to the special education class. Very quickly, the most popular special class became that established for the **"educable mentally retarded,"** meaning those students with IQs between approximately 50 and 75. "Special education class" came to mean, in much of the nation, "class for the educable mentally retarded." Unfortunately, because there were few classes for students with other disabilities, many students whom we would today classify as having learning disabilities or behavioral disorders were placed in those classes as well, even though they did not really meet their educational needs. Most such classes were full-time; students spent all day with the special class teacher, with the possible exception of recess or lunchtime. Even though these students mixed with their age peers in their neighborhoods, they were almost totally segregated in school.

Although local special education classes were developed on a national basis for students with mental retardation, state-run schools for the visually or hearing impaired were the norm during this period. Students in the latter typically went home during major holidays and the summer but lived in the state school for the remainder of the year. Some parents moved to cities where state schools were located so that their children could come home each day. Public school–based classes or programs for students who were visually or hearing impaired did begin to develop somewhat later in the century.

Another type of special class began to appear in the public schools starting in the late 1920s and throughout the 1930s. These were classes for students with physical disabilities such as heart defects, crippling conditions, or asthmatic conditions, and were called variously classes for the physically handicapped, the health impaired, or the "delicate." Such programs became increasingly popular in the 1940s and 1950s, and were seen, like the institutions for persons with mental retardation in the late 1800s, as an indication of the progressive status of a city or school district. Separate buildings with special adaptations such as ramps, elevators, special doors, desks, and bathroom facilities were built, often with funds given by some local philanthropist. They were usually much larger than the need dictated, and by the mid-1960s it became evident that some students were placed in those buildings simply to fill up the space. Many could have, and should have, stayed in their original buildings, with minimal adaptations.

One other disability began to be recognized by the 1950s. Earlier, many larger cities had established classes for "delinquent" students, but these could not be properly equated with classes for students with behavior disorders. By 1960 it became clear that assistance must be provided to students with behavior disorders, and such programs were initiated.

A different type of service, initiated during the first half of the 20th century, was a program of itinerant aid to students with speech problems. A few programs existed during the 1920s and 1930s, but speech therapy—as it was called then—was not a regular part of special education programs until the 1950s and 1960s. This was not a special class program, but rather a service in which speech therapists (now more commonly called speech/language pathologists) took small groups of children out of regular classes for intensive therapy. Although in 1940 relatively few students were served by speech therapists on a national basis, by 1960 more students were so served than by any other component of special education.

During the latter half of the 1950s and throughout the 1960s, events were taking place that were rapidly changing the face of the United States and that were to have a profound effect on the manner in which students with special needs would be educated in the public schools. These events were related to a growing awareness within the majority White population of how racial segregation had oppressed African Americans and other minorities, how those born in poverty had little real opportunity to escape it, how women had often been relegated to second-class citizenship, and how governmental agencies and bureaucratic policies and practices often contributed to the continuation of these inequities. Coupled with the growing understanding of these injustices was an increased acceptability of more militant protest, advocacy, and legal action on behalf of the wronged or the oppressed. Persons with disabilities—both children and adults— are one significant minority group in this nation, and advocacy on their behalf became an important part of this movement to right past wrongs.

There were demonstrations and protests on behalf of persons with disabilities, but the major tools in the fight to obtain more complete, appropriate educational programs for them were litigation and legislation. Parents complained to local school boards, but they soon found that a lawsuit was often more effective than a conference with the superintendent or members of the school board. They also soon realized that state legislators were interested in reelection, and that organized parent groups backed by politically powerful **advocates** might be able to change state law or at least get state education officials to change their interpretations of current law and regulations. These efforts to influence legislators were later applied at the national level. Parent groups that had been quiet advocates for their children in the past became noisy advocates, and their numbers grew. Attorneys who believed in such advocacy—and who also welcomed the visibility that working with advocacy groups provided—joined in the effort. A "new age" in the education of students with disabilities was dawning.

In this chapter we will review some of the more important litigation and legislation that has shaped present programs and services for students with special needs. It is difficult to say which came first, litigation or legislation, in part because some litigation had direct effects in only one state, whereas other litigation had more broad-ranging influence. In addition, the chronology of cause and effect with regard to litigation is particularly difficult to determine. Suits are filed on one date; temporary injunctions are issued on another; and final settlements are reached on yet another. Which is the pertinent date to use, when litigation in different suits lasts for different durations? We will review only federal legislation, though legislation related to this movement was taking place in all 50 states. We will cover litigation and legislation separately, even though it would appear that litigation led to legislation, which led to more litigation, which led to more legislation, and so on. Whatever the sequence, the cumulative influence of litigation in a variety of jurisdictions around the nation was a major factor in the passage of the most important legislation of all, Public Law 94-142, the Education of All Handicapped Children Act in 1975. However, this act and the regulations implemented to promulgate it led to considerably more litigation. In the following section we will review litigation that appears to have played a major role in shaping special education—the total program of identification procedures, classes, and other services for children and youth with disabilities—as it exists today.

Litigation has played a major role in establishing the rights of persons with disabilities. This litigious influence has affected many areas of life, including architectural barriers, assessment and classification, commitment (to residential facilities or treatment centers), custody of children, employment, the right to education, guardianship, sterilization, the right to treatment and to protection from harm while under treatment, voting rights, and zoning (of group homes for persons who are mentally retarded or mentally ill). We will focus on litigation affecting classification practices and the right to a free, appropriate education.

Litigation continues to shape how education is provided for students with special needs and how it is funded. In our consideration of legislation, we will see that the question of who pays for special educational programs and services has played a major role in the development of present-day programs for students with special needs.

■ Litigation Related to Classification or Labeling

Two cases, *Diana v. State Board of Education* (1970) and *Larry P. v. Riles* (1971), both in California, are often cited as establishing the pattern for later cases, rulings, and eventually for the regulations later included in Public Law 94-142. The first alleged the use of biased tests in placement procedures that assigned children of Mexican-American and Chinese ancestry to classes for students classified as educable mentally retarded. *Diana* was settled through a consent decree, in which the state of California agreed to modify the language used in testing for eligibility for special education services. It also agreed to develop tests that would be less "Anglocentric," including questions to reflect California's various minority cultures. In addition, the state agreed to reevaluate all students then enrolled in classes for the educable mentally retarded. Although California agreed to do these things, changes failed to occur in a timely manner, so the plaintiffs had to initiate contempt proceedings later to hold the state to its promises.

Larry P. v. Riles (Riles was then California Superintendent of Public Education) was similar, essentially an extension of the *Diana* case. It included African-American children who spoke English but were not a part of the White, middle-class culture that served as the norm for most tests, whereas *Diana* covered only bilingual students. Eventually the court ruled that public educators must use tests that account for varied cultural backgrounds. It further required school districts to provide a great deal of information to the plaintiffs, including the percentage of African-American children in total enrollment and the percentage in classes for students classified as educable mentally retarded. The plaintiffs also gained access to lists of all IQ tests used in each district, and information about how those tests and testing procedures in use took into account the cultural background and experiences of African-American children.

These two cases set the stage for cases in other states relating to assessment and classification practices, particularly as applied to students not a part of the White, middle-class culture. For all practical purposes, all such cases were eventually decided in the same manner, but only after several years and the expenditure of hundreds of thousands of dollars in legal costs to the various state or local education agencies.

■ Many of the rights of individuals with disabilities were won as a result of litigation. ■

■ **The Right to a Free, Appropriate Education**

Many cases relating to students' rights to an appropriate education at public expense have been litigated and settled, but two are generally recognized as landmark cases. They were simultaneous with *Diana* and *Larry P.* but took a considerably different direction. Whereas *Diana* and *Larry P.* involved the question of possible overplacement in special classes, in these cases parents were demanding the right for their child to *be* in special classes and to receive an appropriate education there. These cases involved a considerably different student population than did *Diana* and *Larry P.*

The Pennsylvania Association for Retarded Children (PARC) v. The Commonwealth of Pennsylvania (1972) was a suit directed at policies and practices followed in Pennsylvania that led to the denial of an appropriate education, at public expense, for many school-age children who were mentally retarded. Pennsylvania had public school classes for students classified as educable mentally retarded, but this case involved children who were, in general, of considerably lower intellectual ability. Pennsylvania had compulsory attendance laws, but pro-

Table 1.2 Litigation that has influenced special education

Court Case	Summary of Ruling or Consent Decree
Brown v. Board of Education (1954)	Educational segregation based solely on race deprives children of equal educational opportunities and thus violates the equal protection clause of the Fourteenth Amendment to the U.S. Constitution.
Hobson v. Hansen (1967)	Grouping in the schools ("tracking") based on standardized tests that are not relevant to the experience or culture of many students violates the principle of due process and the equal protection guarantees of the Fourteenth Amendment.
Diana v. State Board of Education (1970)	The state of California agreed to change evaluation practices with respect to the language used in testing Mexican-American and Chinese students and to eliminate certain test items that were not appropriate to their culture or experience. California also agreed to reevaluate all such children in classes for students classified as educable mentally retarded and to develop tests that more closely reflect the students' cultures.
Larry P. v. Riles (1971)	In California, the *Larry P.* case extended the classes of plaintiffs included in the *Diana* case to include African-American children and led to results similar to those in *Diana*.
Pennsylvania Association for Retarded Children v. Commonwealth of Pennsylvania (1972)	The Commonwealth of Pennsylvania agreed to provide a free, appropriate education to children with mental retardation. Such education must include preschool programs when such programs were offered to other children in a given school district. "Education" was expanded to include a variety of activities that the state had maintained was not "educational."
Mills v. D.C. Board of Education (1972)	The District of Columbia agreed that students cannot be excluded from school on the basis of behavioral problems, mental retardation, and so on. Students must have a hearing before exclusion or placement in a special class.

visions in the Pennsylvania School Code permitted local school authorities to ignore the needs of these children. Many parents, particularly those active in the PARC, were involved in private school programs that were costly and difficult to staff and manage. Others had children in state residential facilities that were shown—in the litigation that followed—to be totally inappropriate. The thrust of the *PARC v. Pennsylvania* case was simple. The PARC maintained that the state had a responsibility to provide an appropriate program for all children in the state, regardless of their level of intellectual ability. PARC attorneys set out to establish three main points: (1) children with mental retardation can learn if an appropriate program is provided, (2) "education" must be viewed more broadly than just the traditional academic program, and (3) early education is essential to maximize later educational potential. The *PARC* case was typical **class-action litigation**, filed on behalf of 14 specifically named children and all others of a similar class now residing in the state, plus all children similarly situated who will be living in Pennsylvania in the future.

The *PARC* case was settled through a consent agreement, resulting in an overwhelming victory for PARC. The state was ordered to provide free public education appropriate to the learning capabilities of children with mental retardation. A framework for the implementation of this very detailed plan was established, and two "masters" (experts in the field of education of children with mental retardation, who were not employees of the state) were appointed to oversee the entire process.

Court Case	Summary of Ruling or Consent Decree
	All students have a right to an appropriate education. In essence, the case extended the *PARC* case to include all disabilities.
Stuart v. Nappi (1978)	Expulsion for disciplinary reasons may constitute a denial of the opportunity for appropriate education. In such cases, due process procedures must be followed.
New York State Association for Retarded Children v. Carey (1979)	Children who are mentally retarded and have hepatitis B, a containable disease, cannot be placed in self-contained programs solely because of the disease.
Board v. Rowley (1982)	The parents of a student who was deaf, receiving some special education services, and achieving at an academic level above average for age peers in her class demanded specific additional services. The Supreme Court upheld the board of education's denial of these services, stating that the law supported comparable, appropriate educational opportunity—but not necessarily maximum opportunity— for each child with a disability.
Roncker v. Walters (1983)	A proper continuum of placement options must be provided, but the cost of services for one student with a disability may be weighed against its potential for depriving another student of appropriate services.
Burlington School Committee v. Department of Education of Massachusetts (1985)	Parents may be eligible for reimbursement for the cost of private schooling in which a child was enrolled without school approval, *if* the court ultimately rules that the private school placement was appropriate.
Honig v. Doe (1988)	Students classified as having a disability cannot be expelled for behavior that is a manifestation of the disability. Shorter-term suspensions may be appropriate if used in a reasonable manner. Students with disabilities *may* be expelled if the behavior leading to their expulsion is not a manifestation of their disability.

Mills v. D.C. Board of Education (1972), in the District of Columbia, was the second case of far-reaching importance. Its unusual significance derived from two major factors. First, it applied to *all* children with disabilities. Second, it was decided by a court judgment (rather than a consent agreement) and was based on a constitutional holding. Thus it provided a stronger precedential base for future decisions than did the *PARC* case. The decision of the court, however, was patterned after that of *PARC,* including the appointment of masters to oversee its implementation. Like the *PARC* case, it emphasized the right to a free, appropriate education.

Thus school districts and state education agencies, which had seldom been sued successfully, were now the target of litigation brought by parents and advocates for students with disabilities. They were forced to rethink both their practices and their programs. These cases led to a flood tide of similar cases. Some simply affirmed that a principle also applied in other states, but others expanded the scope and findings of earlier cases. Table 1.2 summarizes the major cases that have shaped programs for students with disabilities. We will comment further on only one case, because of its unusual relationship to all the rest.

Brown v. Board of Education (1954) has had a greater influence on other aspects of education than on the education of students with disabilities. It addressed school segregation on the basis of race and was decided by the U.S. Supreme Court. The Fourteenth Amendment of the U.S. Constitution states that it is unlawful to discriminate against a class of persons for arbitrary or unjustifiable reasons. In his ruling on *Brown v. Board of Education,* Chief Justice Earl Warren wrote, "In these days it is doubtful that any child may reasonably be expected to succeed in life if he is denied the opportunity of an education. Such an opportunity, where the state has undertaken to provide it, is a right which must be made available to all." This ruling, which applied to African Americans, has obvious application to students with disabilities and was cited in later litigation on behalf of those students.

Legislation and Its Role in the Education of Exceptional Students

Legislation on behalf of exceptional students can take many forms, on both the state and the national level. Local educational agencies provide programs and services on the basis of laws passed by the legislative bodies of their particular state. There is some degree of local control and autonomy, but education is primarily a function of the state and varies considerably from state to state. Therefore, the manner in which exceptional students are served throughout the nation also varies. We will focus here on federal legislation and how it has "encouraged" the states to modify the way they provide educational programs for

**Box 1.1
Selected
Federal
Legislation
Relating to
Exceptional
Individuals***

1965 Elementary and Secondary Education Act (PL 89-10): assistance to local educational agencies to better serve educationally deprived or disadvantaged students

1968 Handicapped Children's Early Education Assistance Act (PL 90-538): experimental preschool programs

1970 Gifted and Talented Education Assistance Act (PL 91-230): programs for the gifted and talented and the learning disabled (amendments to the Elementary and Secondary Education Act)

1973 Vocational Rehabilitation Act Amendments (PL 93-112): Section 504, the Bill of Rights for the Handicapped

1974 Education of the Handicapped Amendment to the Elementary and Secondary Education Act (PL 93-380): basis for the passage of PL 94-142

1975 Education of All Handicapped Children Act (PL 94-142): establishment of the principle of a free, appropriate education for all children with disabilities in the least restrictive environment; rights of parents, of due process, to appropriate assessment, and to a fair hearing and appeal process

1978 Gifted and Talented Children's Act (PL 95-561): funds to state education agencies for planning and improving programs for gifted and talented students

1983 Amendments to the EHA (PL 98-199): incentives for services to children from birth to age 3 and for planning the transition of secondary students

students with special needs. Box 1.1 briefly characterizes some of the laws discussed in the next pages, along with others not covered in detail.

Federal involvement in education was minimal until the 1950s. It was considered unacceptable—and, in fact, a violation of the U.S. Constitution—for the federal government to "interfere" with or attempt to regulate education. Education in the various states was financed by both state and local educational agencies, with no federal monies. Education was a matter reserved for the states to plan and manage.

In 1954, a departure of sorts was signaled with the U.S. Supreme Court's *Brown v. Board of Education* ruling. This decision regarding racial segregation in the schools was based on the Constitution, and many reluctantly agreed that it was a matter of defending the rights of persons—of prohibiting indefensible discrimination—rather than an invitation for the federal government to become involved in education. It was not then seen as a matter of legislators passing laws that would infringe on the constitutional rights of the states. But in 1958 two laws were enacted that would signal a new era in the federal government's involvement in education. One was the National Defense Education Act, providing considerable "incentive" funds to encourage school districts to provide better programs in mathematics and the sciences as well as providing universities with funds to prepare or retrain teachers. This was a result of the Soviet Union satellite launching, which appeared to indicate that the United States was losing the space

(continued)

1986   Amendments to the EHA (PL 99-457): new incentives for early intervention for infants and toddlers (from birth through age 2) and services for children from ages 3 to 5 with disabilities, even in states that do not provide public education for other children of these ages

1990   Americans with Disabilities Act (PL 101-336): employment (not education) provision for persons with disabilities, paralleling PL 94-142 in many ways. Employers may not use disabilities as a basis for hiring or firing and must provide specialized equipment as required by workers with disabilities. Applies to all employers with 15 or more employees

1990   Amendments to EHA, renamed the Individuals with Disabilities Education Act (IDEA) (PL 101-476): substitution of the term *disability* for *handicap* throughout the EHA and in many related acts

1990   Carl D. Perkins Act (PL 101-392): vocational education assistance stipulating that individuals who are members of "special populations" must have equal access to the full range of vocational education programs available to individuals who are not members of special populations

*Although this listing does not include all federal legislation relating to individuals with disabilities, it does include the major, significant legislation plus samples of special-purpose legislation that, in total, demonstrates the thrust of all such legislation since 1965.

race. The National Defense Education Act was hailed by most Americans, for it was designed to help regain national pride and prestige. The other legislation was Public Law 85-926. It received little general publicity; however, it was the first in a series of legislative enactments that, along with the litigation discussed earlier, was to radically change the scope of special education and the way services were provided to exceptional students—especially those with disabilities.

Public Law 85-926 (1958)   This legislation provided funds, in the form of direct grants, to state governments and institutions of higher learning to encourage the education of college instructors who would in turn train teachers of students with mental retardation. This established the principle of federal support of students in institutions of higher learning as part of the pursuit of national educational objectives. It also established the principle of categorical support for persons with a specific disability.

Public Law 88-164 (1963)   Called the Mental Retardation Facilities and Community Mental Health Centers Construction Act, this legislation went far beyond what its title would seem to indicate. Earlier amendments to PL 85-926 had led to its expansion to include education of instructors to train teachers of students with hearing impairments. PL 88-164 expanded this concept to include grants for college-level training of instructors who would teach teachers about various disabilities, and for a variety of research and demonstration projects. These facets of the legislation were in addition to funds for assistance in building mental retardation facilities and community mental health centers. As with PL 85-926, funding was tied to categories of disability.

Public Law 89-10 (1965)   The Elementary and Secondary Education Act (ESEA) was the first broad-scale education act to be enacted by Congress. There was considerable opposition from many quarters, but the law was written to offer "something for everyone," including private schools. It was difficult to argue with the avowed purposes of this enactment, as its primary focus was on improving the educational opportunities of educationally disadvantaged children. Though not deliberately aimed at children with disabilities, it provided massive amounts of money compared with any earlier education-related enactment, some of which was used to initiate programs for students with hearing impairments, mental retardation, physical disabilities, and so on. In fact, in some school districts the entire amount of money received under Title I of PL 89-10 (the major section of the law, based on the number of low-income families in the district) was spent on programs for students with disabilities. This law had additional facets, perhaps the major one being the granting of funds to local school districts to pay teachers' salaries.

Public Law 91-230 (1970)   The Elementary and Secondary Act Amendment consolidated all existing legislation related to students with disabilities into one section, Title VI, which was then called the Education of the Handicapped Act. It also recognized a new condition, learning disabilities, and included legislation that had been proposed for some time but never enacted in law. This new area of emphasis (not a part of Title VI) was gifted and talented students. It was important recognition that such students also should be assisted, because they too had a right to an appropriate education. The rationale differed considerably from that

■ Following litigation and the advocacy efforts of many individuals and organizations, laws have been enacted that establish the rights of persons with disabilities. ■

of earlier federal assistance for gifted and talented students, which was based on national defense needs rather than those of the students.

Public Law 93-112 (1973) The Rehabilitation Act of 1973 included a section that has often been referred to as the Bill of Rights for the Handicapped. Its section 504 had complex, far-reaching implications and covered both school-age individuals and adults. In fact, so many difficulties in spelling out the regulations for this act emerged that it was not until April 1977 that they were implemented. By that time, Public Law 94-142 (discussed throughout this chapter and Chapter 2) had been passed and implemented, covering many of the more important features of this act as they applied to school-age individuals. However, features in this act—such as guarantees of nondiscrimination in employment practices and program accessibility—were of importance to students with disabilities.

Public Law 93-380 (1974)   This amendment to the Elementary and Secondary Education Act was an umbrella act affecting almost all aspects of education. It directed the states to plan for children with disabilities, to protect the rights of children and their parents during assessment and classification, and to provide as much of their education as possible in regular classes rather than in segregated settings. It was the forerunner of Public Law 94-142, and in fact, when PL 93-380 was passed, much of what would become PL 94-142 was already written. PL 93-380 was important in that it "set the stage" for PL 94-142 one year later.

Public Law 94-142 (1975)   This enactment was the culmination of all the efforts of the previous 15 to 20 years. It reflected legislation already passed and took into account court rulings relating to the rights of students with disabilities. It provided a blueprint for determining eligibility for services, planning an appropriate program, and implementing that program.

Public Law 95-561 (1978)   The Gifted and Talented Children's Act of 1978 was a part of PL 95-561 and provided funds to state education agencies to assist in planning and improving programs for gifted or talented students. It also provided funds for the Office of Gifted and Talented (at the federal level) to distribute as discretionary grants.

Public Law 98-199 (1983)   This act, a series of amendments to the Education of the Handicapped Act, included encouragement for programs to better prepare secondary school-age students for transition out of public education as well as incentives for local agencies to establish services for children from birth to age 3.

Public Law 99-457 (1986)   These additional amendments to the Education of the Handicapped Act provided for services for children from 3 to 5, even in states that provide no public education for other children of that age. It also provided new incentives for early intervention programs for children from birth through age 2.

Public Law 101-336 (1990)   This law, the Americans with Disabilities Act, primarily affected adults but reflected a continuing concern with the rights of persons with disabilities. It was important to children with disabilities in that it helped assure them a fairer chance of employment after they completed their schooling. This law required that all businesses with 15 or more employees provide needed specialized equipment for workers with disabilities (readers for workers who are blind, special desks and ramps for physically disabled persons) and that disability not be used as a criterion for hiring or firing.

Public Law 101-476 (1990)   The amendments to the Education of the Handicapped Act of 1990 renamed it the Individuals with Disabilities Education Act (IDEA), reflecting the greater acceptability of the term *disabilities.* The amendments also abrogated states' immunity (under the Eleventh Amendment to the Constitution) from suits brought in federal courts for their violation of the act. This made it possible for parents and other advocates to sue the states more successfully for nonconformance.

Other legislation   The laws described here represent only a fraction of the legislation covering individuals with disabilities passed during this time, but they do suggest the targets of such legislation. Almost every year since 1975 amendments have added, deleted, or changed the emphasis of some related legislation. In general, legislation has expanded the scope of federal involvement in the education of students with disabilities, despite the ongoing efforts of some politicians to reduce federal involvement, federal funding in particular. Though federal involvement has not been reduced, funds have. The status of some federal offices that administer programs has also changed, leading to variation in the power and ability of federal officials to monitor and enforce federal guidelines. Overall, however, the original and continuing impact of federal legislation has been significant in the evolution of programs and services for students with disabilities. The legislation has had somewhat less impact on programs and services for gifted and talented students.

Catalysts, Initiators, Agitators, and Organizers

The litigation and legislation just outlined provided the impetus for dramatic changes in the ways students with disabilities were served in the public schools and greatly broadened the range of special needs that were served. But litigation and legislation do not "just happen." Attorneys do not just suddenly say "I think I'll sue the state of California." Lawmakers do not just decide, on Wednesday morning at 10:00 A.M., that they will write complex legislation to ensure the rights of students with disabilities. They happen because parents, committees from some advocacy group, or representatives of some professional group raise the issue. These are the initiators and agitators; they may also serve as catalysts or organizers. They are the all-important advocates for persons with disabilities. Their role is crucial, both in initiating litigation and legislation and in following through to make certain that directives resulting from litigation are followed, that legislation is not diluted by additional legislation or negated by lack of funding.

■   Parent Groups

Parent groups in the United States have a long historical tradition. According to Cain (1976), they have been a part of our nation's history since the establishment of the colonies. Though there were earlier, informal groups, the first national parent group organized on behalf of children with disabilities was the National Society for Crippled Children, founded in 1921. In it, as in most earlier organizations of this sort, professionals from the field of medicine played a major role in providing organizational impetus. Such groups emphasized primarily physical and medical (as opposed to educational) needs, but they eventually moved toward a much greater concern with educational needs. The two parent groups that appear to have had the major impact on early federal legislation for students with disabilities were the National Association for Retarded Children (NARC), which later became the National Association for Retarded Citizens, and the United Cerebral Palsy Association (UCP). These and similar groups enlisted the aid of those who were not parents of children with disabilities, but their strength and dedication was due to the very personal need felt by parents. A third group, organized somewhat later, was the Association for Children with Learning Disabilities, now the Learning Disabilities Association of America. They organized in the early 1960s and wielded a great deal of influence with respect to both federal and state legislation.

■ Professional Groups

Many professional groups have also played a role in the process through which litigation and legislation have changed the field of special education; one, however—the Council for Exceptional Children (CEC)—welcomes and represents all educators who work with students with disabilities. The CEC has divisions representing all the major disabilities, the gifted, and related areas of interest such as assessment. Over the years it has developed a power base in Washington, D.C., and is the only professional group to have some basis for claiming to represent all

People Who Make a Difference

CAROL HUNTER AND HER BOOK Carol Hunter had a great idea. She loved the outdoors, valued outdoor life, and wanted to write a book about nature areas accessible to persons with disabilities. But she immediately ran into a problem: there were very few such areas. So she decided to develop one near her home.

Her first project was Yeoman Park, a mountain meadow area near Eagle, Colorado. With the help of newspaper editor Cliff Thompson—an avid fly-fisherman who is paraplegic—a plan was developed, volunteers organized, and additional help provided by the White River National Forest Service and the Vail Rotary Club. Various individuals and local businesses donated materials, and Beaver Creek Hyatt Hotel allowed paid time off for its employees to work on a multifeature nature trail.

Yeoman Park is an ongoing project that now includes tent platforms for campers with physical disabilities, modified restrooms that would accommodatewheelchairs, an all-weather fishing dock designed for wheelchair use, and tactile interpretive material at archeological sites for persons with visual impairments. The nature trail was given special attention, and as Hunter says, it is really for families—"for small children, for your grandfather who had a stroke, your brother in a wheelchair from Vietnam, and your aunt with cataracts."

Yeoman Park was an immediate success, and word quickly spread throughout Colorado and adjacent states. It became the prototype of accessible design and demonstrated how such projects could be completed at minimal expense, primarily with volunteer help. As a result, PAW (Physically Challenged Access to the Woods) was formed, located in Empire, Colorado, and is now a national organization. PAW volunteers conduct accessibility evaluations, act as an information clearinghouse, provide a public education function, and coordinate the contribution of materials and labor to make other areas accessible and meaningful to persons with disabilities. Carol Hunter wanted to write a book. Instead, she found a way to open the outdoors to persons with disabilities.

■ Signs of the times. From garden descriptions in Braille to special handicapped access, more attention is being given to people with disabilities. ■

aspects of special education. It has been of some assistance in litigation, but its major role has been in working with congressional representatives in developing new legislation and amending existing legislation. It has also actively assisted representatives of the federal government and state agencies in carrying out the mandates of legislation.

Money — the Mortar

If our historical legacy, as expanded and reshaped by litigation and legislation, is the foundation for current programs and services for students with special needs, then it is money that holds the foundation together. To fully understand and appreciate existing programs for exceptional students, one must understand how they are funded. Some of the changes the past 50 years have witnessed did not require additional funding, but most did. Serving an 8-year-old student in a special program (smaller classes, consultative assistance, assessment personnel, special furniture or equipment, special transportation, and so forth) costs more than, for example, placement in a regular third-grade classroom with no special help. The same applies at all age and grade levels. The salaries of personnel such as school psychologists, speech or language pathologists, and similar specialists add significantly to the cost of operating a school district. Serving students with severe disabilities costs more than serving those with mild or moderate disabilities. Most of these are "excess costs," something superintendents and boards of education try to keep to a minimum.

As our historical review indicated, prior to the 1950s the major special programs were special classes for students with disabilities and speech therapy. In most states, much of the cost of the personnel to staff these programs was reimbursed to the local school districts by the state. Each of the 50 states has its own system of financing schools, but most utilize some combination of local property taxes and general state support. Special education has usually been financed on an excess cost basis by the state, as an incentive to get programs started and keep them going. School officials had become accustomed to some higher-cost programs for students with special needs, with the state paying most of the bill, but they were not ready for the greatly increased costs of all of the programs dictated by PL 94-142.

As federal initiatives on behalf of exceptional students emerged, they usually included some related, additional federal funding. These funds, however, have been regularly reduced, leaving the states and local school districts to pick up the bill. In commenting on the effect of lessened federal support for programs for the gifted and talented (brought about in part by some "shuffling" in the way federal dollars were forwarded to the states), B. Clark observed that "while in the 80s the United States federal government all but abolished its role in supporting or even encouraging the appropriate education of its most able children, advocacy groups, including national organizations for the gifted, began to form in an attempt to meet some of those needs" (1988, p. 181). It is somewhat easier for the federal government to reduce funds for programs for the gifted and talented, because local school districts do not have a federal mandate to provide such programs. But reductions of assistance to programs for students with disabilities have also occurred. In such cases, the state or local school districts must somehow "find" the additional money; sometimes they simply reduce programs or services, claiming that they can provide just as effective a program through some alternative plan.

Most educators support programs for students with disabilities. State legislators and local superintendents and school board members do not harbor ill will toward special education programs, but they are relatively expensive and therefore tempting targets for needed budgetary reductions. There is likely to be a continuing need for advocates of special education programs, if their present status is to be maintained.

Summary

The history of the treatment of individuals with disabilities may be traced from early practices reflecting misunderstanding and mistreatment to the present level of acceptance and emphasis on inclusion in the least restrictive environment. Litigious efforts were a major influence in the establishment of the principles on which today's educational programs are based, and they continue to shape both principles and practices.

Legislation that provided the framework for provisions to students with disabilities preceded, accompanied, and followed litigation. Federal legislation began with the acceptance of limited federal responsibility in the field of education, progressed to the encouragement of additional efforts on behalf of students with specific disabilities, and culminated in Public Law 94-142, the Education of All Handicapped Children Act. PL 94-142, enacted in 1975, was all-inclusive legislation, bringing together various earlier enactments and formalizing what the courts had said with respect to individual cases. Amendments to PL 94-142 have expanded its influence and clarified the manner in which it must be applied. In its present stage of development, it is called the Individuals with Disabilities Education Act.

The efforts of many catalysts, initiators, agitators, and organizers have contributed to this total endeavor: individual parents working alone, parent advocacy groups, professional groups, and legislators. But the "mortar" that bonds the foundation stones of programs for students with disabilities, thus holding these efforts together, is money.

Sam and Lucille were going to a school meeting in which their 8-year-old son's future educational program would be discussed. The teacher had told them that it was an IEP conference, and though they knew they would be discussing the special program Sam, Jr., was to enter, they weren't sure what IEP stood for. So they asked a neighbor, Mary Krause, whose son was already in a special needs program. She told them that IEP stood for Individualized Educational Program. She also said they must take an active part in the conference: providing information, asking questions, and disagreeing with school officials if they thought their plans were not right for Sam, Jr. Mary said this kind of information and interaction was what the school people wanted, and that they must speak up, for Sam, Jr.'s sake.

CHAPTER TWO

The Provision of Programs and Services

But they weren't sure whether they would feel comfortable with all those professionals. They were still discussing how they could encourage each other to speak up as they got out of their car to go into the school.

Everyone acknowledges that some programs and services should be provided for exceptional students, but many questions remain about the scope and nature of such services. How different should they be from those provided for other students? Which teachers should offer them? How should students be identified as eligible for such services? In what settings should these services be provided? How should parents be involved? How often should these special programs be reviewed? To what extent should the students be involved in planning their own programs? These are just some of the questions that must be asked. We will explore the answers in this chapter—but keep in mind that program provision for exceptional students is far from static. It has changed considerably in recent years and apparently will continue to do so.

Observers in some other part of the world might say "in the United States they provide . . . " — naming some particular program or service for exceptional students. Or they might describe the quality of programs for exceptional students "in the United States." Such statements can be quite misleading. Although Public Law 94-142 is a federal law, considerable variation remains in the scope and quality of services for students with disabilities, both between and within states. Even more variation exists with respect to programs for the gifted and talented. Of course, there are also many shared features, which will be our major focus in this chapter, but we will first explore the determinants of scope and quality of programs and services at the level of the local educational agency.

At least three sets of legislation or regulations determine local educational agencies' provision of programs and services for exceptional students. The first set is the regulations promulgated by the passage of Public Law 94-142. These were not an actual part of the legislation but rather guidelines for its implementation, spelled out by members of the executive branch of the federal government and published in the *Federal Register*. Yet these regulations have, for all practical purposes, the full force and legal impact of law.

The second set is state law and its related regulations. Though state laws differ, particularly in terminology, they share many, many similarities, primarily because of PL 94-142.

The third set comprises the various local educational agency policies and regulations. These are generally consistent with state regulations and mandates, but variations can exist, due to the flexibility of interpretation permitted in most states.

In addition, a number of other factors help determine the nature of the programming in any given local educational agency. Note that the *interaction* of the factors shown in Figure 2.1 determines quality and scope. They will be addressed in detail following our discussion of Public Law 94-142, the Education for All Handicapped Children Act. We will not attempt to discuss state legislation that parallels PL 94-142.

■ **The Basis for Programs and Services**

PL 94-142, the Education for All Handicapped Children Act, changed the face of special education. Though not all advocates for students with disabilities approve the evolution of the law's implementation, all probably approve its stated goal, that

> all handicapped children have available to them . . . a free appropriate public education which emphasizes special education and related services designed to meet their unique needs, to assure that the rights of handicapped children and their parents or guardians are protected, to assist states and localities to provide for the education of all handicapped children, and to assess and assure the effectiveness of efforts to educate handicapped children.

■ **Children to Be Served**

To ensure that there be no question about which disabilities were included, PL 94-142 regulations, as amended by PL 101-476 in 1990, stated that the term

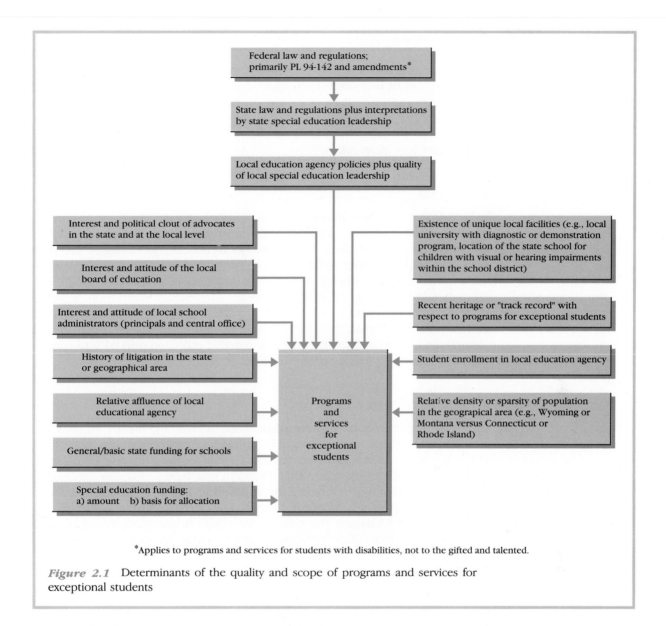

Federal law and regulations; primarily PL 94-142 and amendments*

State law and regulations plus interpretations by state special education leadership

Local education agency policies plus quality of local special education leadership

Interest and political clout of advocates in the state and at the local level

Interest and attitude of the local board of education

Interest and attitude of local school administrators (principals and central office)

History of litigation in the state or geographical area

Relative affluence of local educational agency

General/basic state funding for schools

Special education funding:
a) amount   b) basis for allocation

Existence of unique local facilities (e.g., local university with diagnostic or demonstration program, location of the state school for children with visual or hearing impairments within the school district)

Recent heritage or "track record" with respect to programs for exceptional students

Student enrollment in local education agency

Relative density or sparsity of population in the geographical area (e.g., Wyoming or Montana versus Connecticut or Rhode Island)

Programs and services for exceptional students

*Applies to programs and services for students with disabilities, not to the gifted and talented.

Figure 2.1   Determinants of the quality and scope of programs and services for exceptional students

included children "(A) with mental retardation, hearing impairments including deafness, speech or language impairments, visual impairments including blindness, serious emotional disturbance, orthopedic impairments, autism, traumatic brain injury, other health impairments, or specific learning disabilities; and (B) who, by reason thereof need special education and related services" (104 Stat. 1103). Though the specific terminology for these disabilities has changed over time, often corresponding to earlier legislation that legislators have chosen to continue, the intent of the newer legislation is clear.

If the goals of PL 94-142 and its subsequent amendments are to be realized, several steps must be followed with care. The first is to identify students in need of special education services. A review of the litigation discussed in Chapter 1 reminds us that inaccurate identification will only lead to legal difficulties. Yet identification of students who need special assistance is essential, and the process often begins with **referral.**

■ Referral

Referral of students for evaluation of their specific needs may be done by parents, physicians, or community agencies, but it most often originates with a teacher. The teacher may already have tried a number of educational strategies that have been successful with other students in the past, to no avail. Hence, referrals often result from a teacher's sincere desire to assist a student to learn combined with his or her frustration and feelings of failure. Whatever its motivation, a formal referral will normally lead to an assessment process that is costly in terms of both student and professional time and resources and that may be traumatic for students and parents alike. Therefore, a practice called prereferral intervention has been adopted by many school districts.

■ Prereferral Intervention

Advocates of **prereferral intervention** make several arguments. Perhaps the most frequently mentioned advantage is that needless assessment can be avoided, and with it the implicit suggestion that a given student has a disability. With some teachers and parents, just a hint that a student may have a disability can lead to premature classification or labeling. Such **labeling** may have negative connotations for parents, teachers, or other students. Prereferral intervention also encourages educators to examine the educational needs of the student and to try a variety of alternatives before initiating a formal referral. Another argument is that this intermediary step is a cost-saving measure.

Prereferral intervention is usually spelled out in local educational agency guidelines as comprising at least the following four steps:

1. The teacher requests prereferral assistance within the school.
2. A conference is held with whatever person or committee is assigned to respond to such requests. The educational problem is outlined and intervention strategies are suggested.
3. After the suggested strategies have been tried for some specified time period, another conference is held. This conference determines whether to continue the same strategies for a set period, modify existing strategies, or try new ones.
4. If, after trying a variety of strategies, the problem persists, a formal referral will be made.

It is important that these steps be recorded so that they can later be reviewed, if necessary. If prereferral intervention does not achieve the desired results, this record of interventions that has been tried will be helpful later in developing the individualized education plan.

■   Cooperation among teachers is essential for effective intervention.   ■

Graden suggests that prereferral intervention should be redefined as "intervention assistance: collaboration between general and special education" (1989, p. 227). She believes that its roots are in the principle of collaborative consultation and wishes the term *prereferral intervention* had never been used. She does, however, believe that we should continue to search for alternatives to the more traditional referral practices in special education. In the meantime, Graden suggests that regular and special educators work to provide a stronger base for collaborative consultation.

■ Completing the Assessment

When prereferral intervention strategies are effective and the student's educational needs are met, no assessment for purposes of planning special education programming is necessary. When they are not effective, assessment procedures must be initiated in accordance with the following evaluation guidelines.

State and local educational agencies shall insure, at a minimum, that:

(a) Tests and other evaluation materials:
   (1) Are provided and administered in the child's native language or other mode of communication, unless it is clearly not feasible to do so;
   (2) Have been validated for the specific purpose for which they are used; and
   (3) Are administered by trained personnel in conformance with the instructions provided by their producer;

(b) Tests and other evaluation materials include those tailored to assess specific areas of educational need and not merely those which are designed to provide a single general intelligence quotient;

(c) Tests are selected and administered so as best to insure that when a test is administered to a child with impaired sensory, manual, or speaking skills, the test results accurately reflect the child's aptitude or achievement level or whatever other factors the test purports to measure, rather than reflecting the child's impaired sensory, manual, or speaking skills (except where those skills are the factors which the test purports to measure);

(d) No single procedure is used as the sole criterion for determining an appropriate program for a child, and

(e) The evaluation is made by a multidisciplinary team or group of persons, including at least one teacher or other specialist with knowledge in the area of suspected disability.

(f) The child is assessed in all areas related to the suspected disability, including where appropriate, health, vision, hearing, social and emotional status, general intelligence, academic performance, communicative status and motor abilities.

Comment. Children who have a speech impairment as their primary handicap may not need a complete battery of assessments (e.g., psychological, physical, or adaptive behavior). However, a qualified speech-language pathologist would (1) evaluate each speech impaired child using procedures that are appropriate for the diagnosis and appraisal of speech and language disorders, and (2) where necessary, make referrals for additional assessments needed to make an appropriate placement decision (*Federal Register,* 1977, pp. 42496–42497).

Before initiating such an evaluation, **due process** requires that parental permission be obtained (see Table 2.1). In some cases, as with a visual or hearing impairment, the impairment is obvious; then the purpose of the assessment is to gather more data so as to plan the best possible program. In other cases—for example, if mental retardation, learning disabilities, or behavioral disorders are suspected—the situation is considerably more complex. Factors to be considered include whether or not the student fits the state's definitions and how to proceed given the student's unique educational needs. Language background and other sociocultural factors must be carefully considered in these cases.

Gearheart and Gearheart (1990) indicate that special education assessment usually involves "(a) initial assessment to determine eligibility for special program provisions; (b) additional assessment to assist in developing an **individualized education program (IEP)** and in making meaningful program placement decisions; (c) regular, ongoing assessment to monitor program effectiveness and

Table 2.1 Basic elements of due process*

Parental Consent	Parents must consent to initial evaluation.
	Parents must consent to placement in special education program and may revoke consent at any time.
	Parents must consent to substantial changes in program.
Evaluation	Parents have right to appropriate, multidisciplinary evaluation, in their native language.
	Parents have right to an independent educational evaluation.
Records	Parents have right of access to all of the child's records.
	Parents have right to request amendment of records.
	Parents have right to expect confidentiality of records.
	Parents have right to request that no-longer-needed records be destroyed.
Notice	Parents have right to prior written notice of any meeting relating to their child (following evaluation or reevaluation, development or modification of the IEP, anticipation of change of placement, etc.).
Hearing	Parents have right to hearing before impartial hearing officer if they believe their due process rights have been denied.
	School officials have right to impartial hearing if they believe parents' objection to school's proposed course of action amounts to unfair treatment of the child.

*Due process of law is guaranteed under the Fifth and Fourteenth Amendments to the U.S. Constitution. The goals of due process, stated in PL 94-142, are fair treatment, mutual accountability, a balance of power (between parents and the school), and a focus on the rights and needs of students, parents, and professionals (Turnbull and Turnbull, 1990).

provide a basis for program modifications, if needed; and (d) assessment required by IEP review regulations, to determine whether the program is meeting the student's needs, and whether continued special education services are warranted" (p. 11).

The initial assessment to determine eligibility may not include all of the information needed to plan the IEP. For example, in the case of suspected learning disabilities, only one academic area may have been pursued in depth. This is because a significant discrepancy between intellectual ability and actual academic performance must be documented in only one academic area to satisfy this part of the learning disability classification and eligibility criteria. To facilitate planning an appropriate, effective program, all academic areas should be assessed. This provides a more complete picture of the student's strengths and weaknesses and may offer clues to how difficulties in one basic skill or academic area are influencing learning in others.

Misclassification is always possible and must be avoided. Specific assessment techniques and tools are appropriate when certain conditions are suspected, but the details of such assessment are beyond the scope of this chapter. Perhaps it is sufficient to say that great care must be exercised to be certain that assessment tools are appropriate and properly administered, that classification is accurate, and that all possible data are gathered to provide a basis for meaningful educational planning. Many arguments can be made for and against classification. In "real life," a child or adult with a visual impairment does not become eligible for a number of free supportive services such as large-print materials without being classified as legally blind. In this instance, these services have nothing to do with the requirements of PL 94-142. Similarly, a veteran does not become eligible for certain VA benefits and services without being classified as a veteran. They are both classifications, and relate to eligibility for some benefit or service provided through legislation and related regulations. Services for students with impairments or disabilities are in many ways quite similar. *But educators must be certain that classifications are accurate and that as a result of classification the student receives concrete benefits, not simply the classification.*

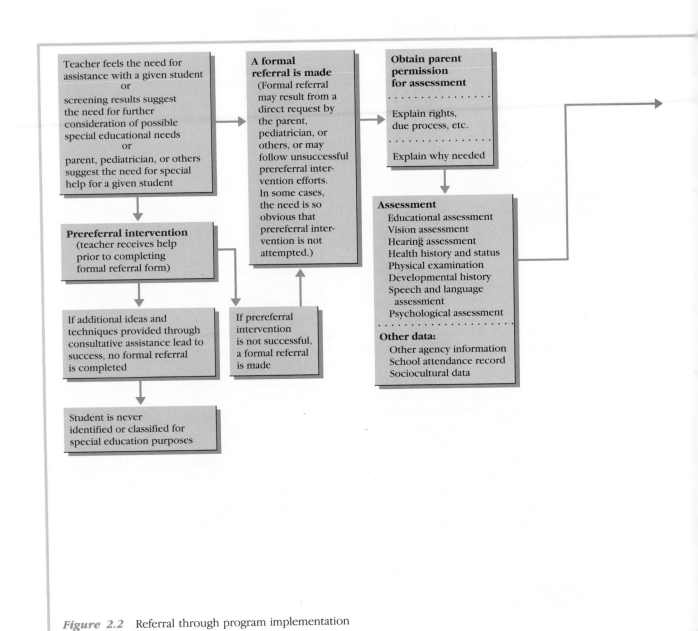

Figure 2.2 Referral through program implementation

Federal regulations establish a number of major principles and requirements that guide educational planning and placement. These include the individualized education program (IEP) that must be developed for each student, the requirement that a full **continuum of placements and educational services** be available, and the principle of the least restrictive placement alternative, popularly called *mainstreaming*. We will now consider these three topics and their influence and role in the total process. Figure 2.2 is a visual representation of the sequence of events in this total planning process, beginning with the referral.

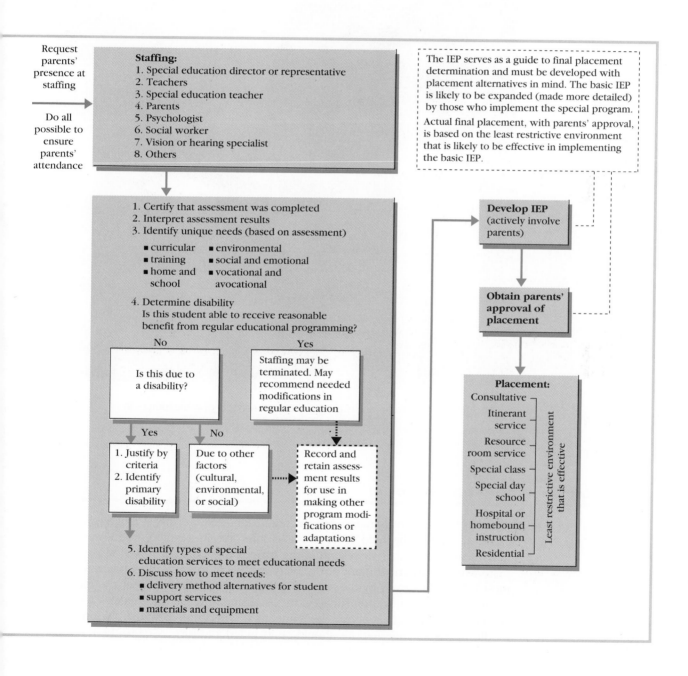

■ Individual assessment is part of the total process of evaluation. ■

Developing an Appropriate Program

After the assessment is made, federal regulations require that a meeting—often called a staffing—be held to review and interpret its results. At this meeting, parents and personnel representing the various disciplines involved must determine whether an impairment or disability exists and the way the student may be most effectively served by the school. If the student does not meet the requirements for special education services, the assessment results and reasons why the student was not eligible should be summarized. Recommendations for program modifications and adaptations should be included and forwarded to the teachers and administrators responsible for the student's continuing program. Parents should also receive a copy of these recommendations.

If the student's educational difficulties are determined to be due to a specific impairment or disability qualifying him or her for special education services, the planning process will continue, following the principles and requirements established by federal guidelines.

■ The Individualized Education Program (IEP)

Federal regulations specify the participants for the staffing at which the preceding decisions will have been made. When the student appears to be eligible for special education services, those participants often develop the IEP at that same meeting. The staffing includes, at a minimum, the following:

1. A representative of the public agency (other than the student's teacher) who is qualified to provide or supervise special education
2. The student's teacher
3. The student's parents
4. The student, when appropriate
5. Other individuals who have pertinent information or who serve to further represent the student, at the request of either the parents or the public agency

In addition, when a student is first evaluated, at least one member of the team must be familiar with the evaluation tools and techniques that were used and qualified to interpret the results.

At this meeting, opportunities are provided for all members to discuss, question, and clarify the implications of the assessment and the various educational strategy and placement alternatives. Parents are encouraged to provide input, the student's unique needs are identified, and various ways in which those needs may be met are discussed.

The basic components of the IEP are also established in federal regulations. They include the following:

1. Statement of the student's present levels of educational performance
2. Statement of annual goals, including short-term educational objectives
3. Statement of special education and related services to be provided and the extent to which the student will participate in regular education programs
4. Projected dates for initiation and duration of services
5. Objective criteria and evaluation procedures and schedule for determining, at least annually, whether short-term objectives are being achieved
6. Statement of needed transition services, beginning no later than age 16 and annually thereafter

The regulations also clearly state that the IEP, once developed and approved by the parents, is a set of goals and objectives to guide the program, *not* a legally binding contract. That is, a goal, such as the attainment of a specific reading level, does not become a legal requirement. The school district does, however, have a legal responsibility to provide the services stipulated in the IEP—for example, specific assistance from a speech or language pathologist or from an occupational therapist. If it does not provide those services, the parents have legal recourse.

Note that we've now reached the third major step in the series of events that lead to special education programming, in which the law specifies that parents must be intimately involved. The first was the initial request for parental approval

Table 2.2 A representative individualized education program (IEP)

1. A procedural checklist, including dates of the multidisciplinary evaluation report, eligibility determination, IEP meetings, and required reviews
2. Student's name, birth date, sex, primary language, parents' names, address, telephone numbers
3. IEP committee members' names and functional titles
4. *All* assessment information, formal and informal
5. Related information: medical, health history, historical
6. Statement of annual goals and how they will be evaluated
7. Statement of short-term objectives and how they will be evaluated
8. Specific educational services to be provided
9. Educational placement recommendations, including time in and rationale for each placement
10. Time frame for special services, including dates of initiation, and duration of services
11. Statement of needed transition services (for students 16 and older)
12. Persons responsible for providing (or ensuring provision of) each significant element of the total program
13. Signatures of IEP conference participants or IEP developers, plus parents' signatures indicating acceptance or rejection of the various elements of the program

for assessment or evaluation. The second was the staffing, or meeting, that determined the student needed special help and could be classified as having a specific disability. This third step, the development of the IEP, requires the parents' signatures. The IEP is of great importance as a starting point for determining who will provide services, what they will be, how long they will last, and other related questions about the total program. Table 2.2 describes and Figure 2.3 exemplifies the average IEP.

A Full Continuum of Placement and Service Alternatives

Figure 2.4 is a simplified representation of the full continuum of placement and service alternatives. This continuum ranges from instruction in the regular class, with consultative or collaborative assistance from specialized personnel, to instruction in a separate day school or residential facility. However, placement in the least restrictive peer environment consistent with the student's special needs is mandated by PL 94-142.

Figure 2.4 includes five placement alternatives; note that in any of them the student may be receiving additional specialized services such as speech therapy, physical therapy, or psychiatric counseling. In practice, many combinations of placement and service are common.

■ Instruction in the Regular Class with Consultative or Collaborative Efforts

When other interventions (whether or not they are called preintervention strategies) are deemed insufficient, and after a student is classified as eligible for and in need of special education services, the most desirable, least restrictive place for such service to be provided is in the regular classroom. However, such service will neither be effective nor meet the student's special needs without close consultative assistance from—and preferably collaborative efforts in conjunction with—

Student name _____   Referral by _____
Parent names _____   Reason(s) for referral _____
_____   _____

D.O.B. _____ Grade ___ School _____   _____
Address _____
Phone (home) _____ (work) _____
Primary language _____

Assessment Information — Summary/dates | ATTACH WRITTEN REPORTS TO IEP PACKET |
vision _____ hearing _____
general physical exam _____
test _____ date _____ summary _____
_____
_____
_____

Summary — *Current Levels of Performance* (physical, social, educational and developmental, psychological, communicative)
| ATTACH WRITTEN REPORTS TO IEP PACKET |
Strengths _____   Weaknesses _____
_____   _____
_____   _____
_____   _____
_____   _____
_____   _____
_____   _____

Certification of Eligibility — The following disabilities exist that prevent this student from obtaining an appropriate education without special education services.
_____
_____
_____

Certification of disability(ies) Yes _____ No _____

Special Services to be Provided
Nature of Service   Where provided/by whom   Hrs. per wk.   Init. date   Duration
_____
_____
_____
_____
_____

Annual Goals and   Objective Criteria &   Date or   Personnel and
   Related, Prioritized, Short-Term Objectives   Evaluation Procedures   Timeline   Resources Required
_____
_____
_____
_____
_____

(In an actual IEP, two to six pages may be required for goals and short-term objectives)
_____
_____
_____
_____
_____

IEP Participants' Signatures   Approve IEP   Do not approve IEP   Date
Parent/guardian _____   _____   _____   ____
Spec. ed. tchr. _____   _____   _____   ____
LEA adminis. _____   _____   _____   ____
Student _____   _____   _____   ____
(_____) _____   _____   _____   ____

Figure 2.3 An individualized education program

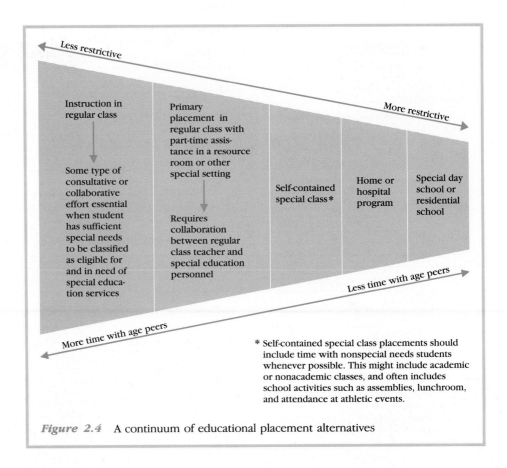

Less restrictive

More restrictive

Instruction in regular class

Some type of consultative or collaborative effort essential when student has sufficient special needs to be classified as eligible for and in need of special education services

Primary placement in regular class with part-time assistance in a resource room or other special setting

Requires collaboration between regular class teacher and special education personnel

Self-contained special class*

Home or hospital program

Special day school or residential school

More time with age peers

Less time with age peers

* Self-contained special class placements should include time with nonspecial needs students whenever possible. This might include academic or nonacademic classes, and often includes school activities such as assemblies, lunchroom, and attendance at athletic events.

Figure 2.4   A continuum of educational placement alternatives

the appropriate educational specialist. The nature of this collaborative effort is determined by the student's needs and will in most cases be detailed in the IEP and related documentation. This may involve little more than regularly scheduled conferences between classroom teacher and specialist in which ideas are shared, the student's efforts reviewed, and strategies devised. This of course must then translate into differentiated assignments, special materials, motivational techniques, and other aspects of individualized instruction for the student. With appropriate record keeping, the specialist may be able to assist the teacher to monitor educational progress and keep the program on track with little or no direct contact with the student. The amount of specialist contact with the student may or may not be specified in the IEP and documents developed concurrently with it.

In other cases, the special educator may work in the classroom part of each day or on specified days each week. This may be done with individual students or in small groups. Small group work can include the targeted student and other classified special needs students, or simply other students who need additional help. It also might comprise the targeted student and one or two others who work as peer tutors at other times during the day or week. In some states, the degree to which the special educator works with other students may be regulated in some manner. It is critically important that the classroom teacher and the

■ One-to-one assistance is one aspect of special education programming. ■

special educator function as co-workers, especially in this setting. The special educator should not be viewed as the "authority," the person with all the answers, but rather as someone with ideas and experience to share with the classroom teacher, who knows the student better and can provide daily progress information.

■ **Resource Room Programs**

For some time, the **resource room** has been a common placement for students eligible for special education services (see Table 2.3). Although the term *resource room* is used somewhat loosely throughout the United States, it most often means a separate classroom, staffed by a special education teacher and perhaps an aide. Strickland and Turnbull describe a resource room as "a separate special education instructional setting that provides an opportunity for the student to

Table 2.3 Percentage of students served in six educational environments (school year 1988–1989)

Environment	Age			
	3–5	6–11	12–17	18–21
Regular class	42.19	41.02	19.33	14.19
Resource room	16.17	34.71	44.94	34.98
Separate class	26.36	20.48	28.12	31.51
Separate school	12.88	3.09	5.14	14.64
Residential facility	0.43	0.38	1.17	3.26
Home/hospital	1.98	0.33	1.30	1.41

SOURCE: From the *Thirteenth Annual Report to Congress on the Implementation of the Individuals with Disabilities Education Act* (Washington, D.C., 1991).

receive specially designed instruction, for various amounts of time, in an environment removed from the activity of the regular classroom, while still receiving the majority of her instruction in the regular program" (1990, p. 292).

The resource room may provide special instruction according to a variety of models: (1) individual instruction, (2) small-group instruction organized by disability, (3) small group instruction organized by age or grade level, (4) small group instruction organized by academic or behavior management need, or (5) some combination of these and other variables. Generally, all students in the resource room come from the school in which the room is physically located, but at times one room and one teacher (or teacher and aide) may serve two or more schools. The program usually involves daily instruction, but some students may be given special instruction only two or three days per week.

The resource room model permits students who require specific assistance to remain in the regular classroom most of the day. However, in some cases a student may be assigned to a resource room for most of the day, in which case it becomes—for that student—a self-contained special class program. Strickland and Turnbull (1990) note that the resource room is the least restrictive of the "pull-out" programs, because the student usually spends more time in the regular class and because it is similar to other pull-out programs such as remedial reading or math and certain programs for the gifted or talented.

Resource room models have been used for students in all of the disability categories, but some, such as those for the hearing impaired or visually impaired, are more often organized for that one specific disability. This, of course, reflects the unique instructional needs of students with impairments of hearing or vision. In such programs, students may be bused to attend a regular class in a school that also houses a special resource room. In other cases, they may attend school in their regular attendance area and be bused to the building in which the resource room is located. In a few instances, school districts have organized a resource room program offering specialized assistance for students with disabilities as well as for those who are gifted and talented, all in the same class setting. In programs of this type there are generally at least two certified teachers (one with special certification relating to specific disabilities and one with special training or interest in the gifted and talented) and an instructional aide. Such programs are unusual, but they illustrate the flexibility and versatility of the resource room concept.

■ At times, itinerant special education services may be provided in sparsely populated areas through the use of a mobile classroom. ■

■ The Self-Contained Special Class

As we noted in Chapter 1, the **self-contained special class** for students with disabilities was the model for many years, except for students who required only speech therapy. The special class was also inextricably involved in many of the early court cases reviewed in Chapter 1. Today, the special class model is the service vehicle for perhaps 20% to 30% of all special education placements (see Table 2.3), and the percentage is slowly decreasing. However, it remains a viable program alternative for some students, especially those with more severe disabilities or who definitely need an alternative curriculum for most or all of the school day.

In practice, the self-contained special class may be full-time for most students, except for some nonacademic classes and whole-school activities such as assemblies, athletic events, and lunchroom. However, some type of modified self-contained program may be appropriate for some students. In all cases, each student's program must be individually planned.

Students who might require a self-contained program include those with severe emotional problems or severe mental retardation. It may be impossible to follow the type of curriculum required in the regular class and include severely emotionally disturbed students; in addition, some of the more disruptive students might prevent the nondisabled students from learning. For the more severely mentally retarded, it is often absolutely essential to provide an alternative curriculum, usually one that stresses functional living skills. For students with moderate mental retardation, a program directed toward basic job skills and improvement of adaptive behavior may be required for a considerable part of the day, particularly at the high school level. In addition, many of these students may spend much of the school day working in the community during their last two or three years in school. However, continuing contact with age and grade peers should be scheduled whenever consistent with other program needs.

■ Home or Hospital Programs

Students with chronic health conditions that require long-term hospital treatment may require special instruction from **itinerant special education teachers** or through special electronic equipment. Similarly, those who cannot leave their homes for an extended period of time may require such assistance. The nature of the program depends on the student's age, ability, level of achievement, prognosis, and projected date of return to school.

A number of different means may be used to provide such instruction, including two-way communication systems that employ telephones or videophones to reduce the student's isolation and provide continuing interaction with classmates. For other students, a teacher who calls at the home on a regular basis, working with both the student and the parents, may be best. Some hospitals in larger cities include on-site educational facilities and teachers; however, the teacher may be paid by the school district and thus technically be a school district employee.

Home instruction, like hospital-based instruction, is an important service to students who cannot attend school, whether the need is temporary or permanent, but it is not an acceptable solution to the dilemma posed by, for example, a disruptive student who could be served at school.

■ Special Day Schools or Residential Schools

In a very few cases, the IEP committee may decide that a separate facility will be required to accomplish the goals established for a given student. This could be a private day school in the community or a 24-hour residential facility. The residential facility may be local, but it may also be elsewhere in the state. In more sparsely populated states, the nearest appropriate special needs program may be located in another state. In such cases, it is normally the responsibility of the school district to pay for the cost of this program, including room and board. In some instances, however, a student may be placed in a residential facility by another community or state agency, and the school district may then be responsible only for educational costs. These types of highly specialized interventions are rarely required but must be provided when they are the most appropriate placement.

The Least Restrictive Placement Principle

Public Law 94-142 requires that the least restrictive appropriate placement be made. It does not require that every student be educated in a regular classroom; in fact, as we've seen, it requires that alternatives such as private, separate

CLARISSA HUG, AN ORGANIZER WITH A PURPOSE

How do national awareness weeks get organized and started? Often they come about through the tireless efforts of one individual. Clarissa Hug is one such person.

Clarissa began her career as a physical education teacher and director of after-school and Saturday recreation programs for the Chicago public schools. She soon realized the value that the study of drama could play in recreational activities, and she returned to college to receive her credential in that area. She then began producing children's plays.

In the 1940s a polio epidemic rendered many children unable to attend school. Clarissa was asked to develop materials and methods for teachers to use in instructing these homebound children. Clarissa had no special training in teaching exceptional children, but she knew how to develop materials and procedures that would ensure children high-quality instruction. She quickly became involved in promoting the cause of all exceptional students. Thus began a long commitment to special education.

One of Clarissa's efforts culminated in the establishment of Exceptional Children Awareness Week. She had learned that the superintendent of schools in Chicago was considering eliminating educational programs for exceptional students because of their costs. This was before such children were protected by PL 94-142, so such decisions were sometimes made by superintendents and boards of education. As president of the Chicago chapter of the Council for Exceptional Children, Clarissa reasoned that, if the public were more aware of exceptional students' potential when afforded appropriate education, there would be such an outcry that it would be politically impossible to eliminate such programs. So she began organizing a variety of activities highlighting existing special education programs. These culminated in "Exceptional Children Awareness Week." This special week "just happened" to coincide with the meeting of the school board to discuss elimination of these programs.

Clarissa's ambitious campaign included numerous newspaper articles, signs in public buses, special exhibits in public areas and businesses throughout Chicago, acquiring space at no cost for a public rally, obtaining the volunteer services of prominent people of the time such as Danny Kaye, and staging a pageant of over 600 exceptional children displaying their dramatic and musical accomplishments. She flooded the media with information about exceptional children, focusing on their achievements and potential, and made the public so aware of the value of such programs that no superintendent or school board would dare to terminate existing programs. Her plan worked! Clarissa's program was a success. Special education in Chicago was saved.

Exceptional Children Awareness Week became an annual event in Chicago and was soon held throughout the state. Mayors and governors set aside a week in May for it, and it is now nationally celebrated — all as a result of Clarissa Hug's campaign to make Chicagoans aware of the needs of exceptional children.

Today in Illinois, one day during Exceptional Children Awareness Week is designated as "Hug" day: a day to acknowledge the contributions of all those who support exceptional children. School secretaries, businesspeople, volunteers, members of the press, bus drivers, and anyone else who supports exceptional children receive a "hug" for their efforts. It is in the spirit of Clarissa Hug to acknowledge and thank all those who are aware of and already recognize the achievements and potential of exceptional children.

A further recognition of Clarissa's contributions is the "Clarissa Hug Teacher of the Year Award," which is given by the International Council for Exceptional Children. The plaque has been awarded since 1985 in recognition of one teacher's imagination, creativity, innovation, and ability to inspire. Its recipients are following in Clarissa's footsteps.

schooling be provided, if that is the *most appropriate placement* to achieve the educational goals of the IEP. However, soon after the passage of PL 94-142, the term *mainstreaming* became so popular that it became a synonym for least restrictive placement. Turnbull, in a discussion of the underlying beliefs and values in right-to-education laws, stated that "the doctrine of integration/least restrictive alternative/mainstreaming really is three separate concepts rolled into one . . . the legal doctrine of least restrictive alternative placement in education attempts to maximize the disabled student's education as well as the opportunity to associate with nondisabled students and adults" (1986, p. 255). The principle of the least restrictive alternative placement "allows removal from such settings (regular class settings) and placement in special classes, separate schools, or other separate activities only if the nature or severity of the handicap is such that education in regular classes, even with the use of supplementary aids and services, cannot be achieved satisfactorily" (ibid., p. 147).

We should note that the term *mainstreaming* does not appear in PL 94-142, nor in the regulations related to the law, but it quickly became so common that school districts trying to discourage its use in favor of the more accurate terminology—least restrictive placement—soon gave up. Instead, they provided a definition of mainstreaming that was actually a definition of the least restrictive alternative placement.

There is little question that maximum integration of students with disabilities within the mainstream of education is desirable. The question is when, where, with whom, and to what extent they are integrated. If *all* students could function successfully in a regular classroom all of the time it would certainly be best, but special education programs and services were established because some can't. PL 94-142 recognized this fact with the requirement for a full continuum of placement options, and educators are called upon to choose the most appropriate program (the first and most basic requirement), in the least restrictive environment in which it can be provided. The principle of the least restrictive placement (or least restrictive environment, or mainstreaming) is clear. When educators follow the requirements of appropriate, multidisciplinary assessment and program planning, utilize input from parents and all other potential sources of information, apply good professional judgment, and realize that all placements are subject to change, the least restrictive placement principle is viable and practical in application.

Other Determinants of Program Quality and Scope

Figure 2.1 outlined the major factors that influence the quality and scope of programs for exceptional students. The factor listed first, PL 94-142 and its amendments, directly influences only the education of students with disabilities. All other factors shown may influence programs for students with disabilities, but may also affect gifted and talented programs. For example, the interest and political clout of advocates for any specific program can bring about changes at both the state and local levels. The interest and attitude of the school board will influence funding of special needs programs, which certainly can have a great effect on both scope and quality. If the school board does not have sufficient interest and a positive attitude, powerful and motivated advocates can influence its members or work to elect others who will be more positive.

It is difficult to overemphasize the importance of the interest and attitude of local school administrators. It is important to have a superintendent who believes in the value of a good program for special needs students, but this alone is not enough. Unless building administrators believe in quality programming, they may do little to promote the needed cooperation between regular and special educators. Without this cooperation, even the best-funded program suffers.

Figure 2.1 included three factors related to funding: (1) the relative affluence of the local educational agency, (2) general, state-level funding for the total school program, and (3) special education funding—both its amount and rationale. In total these factors determine the amount of money available for special needs funding and the manner in which it must be spent. There are exemplary special education programs in states where state funding—both for the regular program and for special education—is poor; but this is the exception. In general, more dollars and a flexible policy for dispensing them translate into better programs.

One factor over which local educational agencies have little control is assistance from unique local facilities for special needs students. For example, a university with a special diagnostic program, a child development clinic, demonstration programs related to the training of special education teachers, and unique programs for gifted and talented students can add much to the "richness" of local special education services. Another possibility is a state-funded facility for students who are visually impaired, hearing impaired, or emotionally disturbed. It can be of great value in local planning and programming—as long as students are not improperly referred to it exclusively rather than being served directly by the school district. Again, the principle of the least restrictive placement alternative must be followed.

Two final factors of significance are the numbers of students in the district and the relative density or sparsity of population in the geographical area. These are of particular significance with respect to low-incidence disabilities—for example, students with very severe behavior disorders—and to children with multiple disabilities. It is much easier to plan and staff programs if more than one student with a given set of special needs lives in the school district.

Whatever the status of these individual variables in a given school district, the interaction of their effect determines program scope and quality. Some of these variables (such as population density) cannot be changed, but others can, and the end result can be an improved program.

The Regular Education Initiative

The Regular Education Initiative (REI) is the name given a movement initiated by special educators (not by regular educators, as the title might seem to indicate) that recommends a restructuring of the relationship between regular and special education. It became a topic of considerable discussion within the leadership ranks of special education after publication of an article by Madeleine Will, then Assistant Secretary for the Office of Special Education and Rehabilitative Services of the U.S. Department of Education (Will, 1986). Will's proposal advocated "a shared responsibility" between regular and special education and made a number of proposals.

Special educators have interpreted Will's comments in various ways and have disagreed about the readiness of many regular educators to assume added responsibilities in educational programming for students with disabilities (Algozzine, Maheady, Sacca, O'Shea, & O'Shea, 1990; Braaten, Kauffman, Braaten, Polsgrove, & Nelson, 1988; Heller & Schilit, 1987; Jenkins, Pious, & Jewell, 1990; and Lieberman, 1990). A direct result of the REI proposal has been considerable reexamination of the present relationship between regular and special education.

One product of this discussion was a report issued by concerned special education leadership personnel who convened specifically to analyze the REI initiative. At that meeting, a list of assumptions felt to be essential to the success of the REI was developed. The list covered the following: (1) student rights, (2) support from the education community, (3) partnership, (4) attitudes, (5) student grouping, (6) curriculum, (7) instruction, (8) classroom structure, and (9) assessment (Heller & Schilit, 1987). Conference participants supported Will's call for greater shared responsibility, but expressed the belief that it was "important to acknowledge that special education cannot seek institutional solutions to individual problems without changing the nature of the institution. . . . The nature of school organization is what must fundamentally change" (ibid., p. 6). Other special educators were also concerned about possible misperceptions of the REI. For example, a Division of Learning Disabilities Position Paper sought assurance that "services to students with specific learning disabilities will not be diluted or diminished by remedial or compensatory programs for students with problems in learning due to other causes" (McCarthy, 1987, p. 75). Others urged that the populations of students to be served be more clearly defined.

Very different points of view were expressed by other special educators, however. Some advocated a merger of special and regular education that would effectively eliminate separate special education programs (Stainback & Stainback, 1987). Others, concerned about the dual system of education that now exists, apparently foresaw fewer possible negative effects of the REI (Lilly, 1988; Wang & Wahlberg, 1988). Some contended that the present dual system actually inhibits the integration of students with disabilities. But all special educators agree with Will's concern for students who "fall through the cracks" and support efforts to promote a greater degree of cooperation and coordination between regular and special education.

Special Education Programs for Students Who Are Gifted, Talented, or Creative

Most of the questions that may be raised about appropriate educational programs for students with disabilities also apply to programs for students with unusual intellectual ability, talent, or creative potential, though they are seldom articulated with the same urgency and frequency. This difference in stress is due to a number of factors. The major ones are that for the latter (1) there is no strong legal pressure, less threat of litigation, and in many states little legislative encouragement; (2) there is much less parental activism; (3) most of them do not "stand out" as students with disabilities may; and (4) it is difficult to create sympathy for their exceptional needs; not many people are likely to pity "that poor little highly intelligent kid." These four factors are interrelated, and additional factors also come into play. The end result is that gifted, talented, and creative students may receive very little special attention except when their talents

■ Gifted students need special opportunities to allow them to reach their full potential. ■

relate to athletics, or in some cases to music. Fortunately, there are notable exceptions to this situation, as we will see in Chapter 11.

Though on a national basis the special needs of students with unusual gifts, talent, or creative potential are not being met to the same degree as are those with disabilities, it is noteworthy that the factors identified as determinants of the quality and scope of programs for students with special needs (see Figure 2.1) apply equally to programs for gifted, talented, and creative students. The only exception is that PL 94-142 does not apply unless a student is both gifted and disabled (one who is intellectually gifted and also blind, for instance). This, of course, is an exception of major importance, but advocates for gifted, talented, and creative students may analyze and utilize or attempt to influence any of the other factors outlined in Figure 2.1.

How Many Students Need Special Education Services?

There is no real agreement on the number of exceptional students in the United States, and no absolute way to determine how many students need special education services. Here is one example of why this is so. At one time, soon after learning disabilities were recognized by the federal government, certain leaders in the Association for Children with Learning Disabilities (now the Learning Disabilities Association of America), the leading advocacy group for such children, were talking about the "fact" that 20% or even 25% of all students had learning disabilities. In support of their efforts, high-visibility politicians echoed those percentages on television. Publishers of learning materials used this information to sell their products to schools—and to individual parents via the trade book market. The general public, including many teachers who were well informed about their own areas of expertise but poorly informed about students with learning disabilities, began to think in terms of 20% or 25%. What is the true percentage of students with learning disabilities? That depends on how learning disabilities are defined; a similar problem exists with respect to mild levels of mental retardation and behavioral disorders.

Another potential source of confusion is the two different ways to estimate the numbers of students who need special education services. Data may be collected on either prevalence or incidence, and though these are sometimes used interchangeably, they are not the same. Prevalence means the number of individuals in a given population who exhibit the same condition at a given time.

People Who Make a Difference

BONITA BERGIN AND CANINE COMPANIONS FOR INDEPENDENCE In 1975, Bonita Bergin had an idea destined to change the lives of many individuals with disabilities. While teaching in Asia, she had seen people with disabilities using burros to guide them about the city streets. After her return to the United States, she began to think about the possibility of training dogs to do what burros did in Asia—and much, much more. She established Canine Companions for Independence (CCI) to provide such training. The first Canine Companion was placed in 1976 with a woman who was quadriplegic. Since that time, hundreds of Canine Companions have brought independence to their disabled masters. Headquartered in Santa Rosa, California, CCI currently provides four types of specially trained dogs.

Service dogs are trained to assist persons who are physically challenged by turning light switches on and off, pushing elevator buttons, retrieving dropped items, and pulling wheelchairs. Service dogs typically help persons disabled due to cerebral palsy, muscular dystrophy, spinal cord injury, or stroke.

Signal dogs alert persons with hearing impairments to sounds such as the ring of a telephone, the doorbell or knock on a door, an alarm clock, a smoke detector, or the cry of a child.

Social dogs work primarily in institutions with individuals such as the developmentally disabled or those who are autistic. They provide what is often called Pet-Facilitated Therapy through their loving, nonjudgmental interactions.

Specialty dogs are custom-trained to meet the needs of individuals with multiple disabilities. For instance, as a companion to someone who is both physically disabled and deaf, a specialty dog must have the skills of both the service dog and the signal dog. At one time, some questioned whether such complex training was possible, but it has proved to be highly successful.

CCI was the recipient of the 1987 Distinguished Service Award presented by the President's Commission for Employment of the Handicapped. Bonita Bergin's idea has been of inestimable value to many individuals with disabilities and has provided a model for similar programs throughout the nation and the world.

Table 2.4 Theoretical prevalence of exceptional children in the United States

Exceptionality	Percentage of Population
Learning disabled	2.0–4.0
Speech handicapped	2.0–4.0
Mentally retarded	1.0–3.0
Emotionally disturbed	1.0–3.0
Hearing impaired (includes deaf)	0.5–0.7
Multihandicapped	0.5–0.7
Orthopedically and health impaired	0.4–0.6
Visually impaired (includes blind)	0.08–0.12
Gifted and talented	2.0–3.0

SOURCE: From various U.S. government publications between 1980 and 1990.

Incidence means the number of new cases of some condition in a given period of time—usually one year. In this text we will limit ourselves to prevalence estimates.

Tables 2.4 and 2.5 both address the prevalence of exceptional students in the United States. The first table reflects the theoretical prevalence, based on estimates utilized by various agencies of the federal government and recognized authorities in the various fields of specialization. Table 2.5 indicates the number of exceptional students actually receiving some type of special education service. It displays one column for the percentage of national public school enrollment (total data for the 50 states) and another for the percentage range, as reported by individual states. It is interesting to note that some states apparently identified, and were serving, ten times as many students as other states with respect to the same impairment or disability. Some feel that, as a middle-of-the-road definition of each of the exceptionalities, Table 2.5 provides the best estimate. Even there, however, using a range of prevalence seemed appropriate.

Prevalence figures are important in projecting the need for trained personnel, facilities and equipment, and funds to pay the cost of these programs. Some have

Table 2.5 Exceptional children (ages 6–21) receiving services

Exceptionality	Percentage of National Public School Enrollment	Percentage Range (as Reported by the Fifty Individual States)
Learning disabled	3.62	1.69–5.80
Speech handicapped	1.72	0.62–2.97
Mentally retarded	0.97	0.30–2.65
Emotionally disturbed	0.67	0.04–1.66
Hearing impaired (includes deaf)	0.10	0.02–0.23
Multihandicapped	0.15	0.00–1.56
Orthopedic and other health impaired	0.17	0.05–0.50
Visually impaired (includes blind)	0.04	0.02–0.09
Gifted and talented	no comparable data on a national basis	

SOURCE: The *Thirteenth Annual Report to Congress on the Implementation of the Individuals with Disabilities Education Act* (Washington, D.C., 1991). These data reflect children served under Chapter One of the Elementary and Secondary Education Act and the Individuals with Disabilities Education Act.

■ Learning social skills is an important aspect of the total educational program. ■

criticized special education leadership for its inability to provide prevalence data that are acceptable to all and that stand the test of time as students are identified and provided with services. Our point of view is that services must be provided no matter how many students in a given area need special educational services. And we wish those services to be timely, sufficient in scope, consistent in quality, and provided in the least restrictive placement appropriate to the student's special needs.

Summary

Many interrelated factors determine the quality and nature of programs and services provided for students with disabilities, including federal and state laws; local education agency policies; the presence of unique local facilities; and the interest and support of the school board, parents, school administrators, and local advocates. The federal definitions of the various disabilities largely determine the scope of programs, for they are the basis for determining which students are to receive special education services under the provisions of PL 94-142.

The process for identifying students with special needs is outlined in PL 94-142, and since its passage a move to emphasize prereferral intervention has gained wide acceptance. Various cautions during assessment, emphasizing the requirements of due process, must be observed, and local educational agencies must provide a full continuum of placement alternatives, programs, and services. These include regular classes with collaborative efforts, resource room programs, self-contained special classes, home or hospital programs, special day schools, and residential schools. An Individualized Education Program (IEP), which identifies the needs of the student, the goals to be achieved, and the services provided to meet those goals, is essential and is required by PL 94-142. The principle of the least restrictive placement consistent with effective educational intervention is central to the concept of free, appropriate educational services for students with disabilities.

Special provisions for students who are gifted, talented, or creative are provided in some states, but there is no consistent national pattern for this type of education. Such programs enjoy only limited support and encouragement, and there is no requirement for them at the federal level unless a student who is gifted or talented also has a disability.

The federal government has estimated the prevalence of exceptional students in the United States, and there is also general acceptance of theoretical prevalence data. However, the percentage of exceptional students (those with disabilities and the gifted or talented) receiving services in the 50 states varies widely. Factors such as different definitions and identification procedures in the various states limit the validity of national totals of the data reported by them.

Imagine a school classroom in which a student studying the life of John F. Kennedy gets to watch news clips from his administration and hear him give the speech that launched our NASA program to the moon; in which a student studying civil rights is able to see news clips of Martin Luther King, Jr., and hear him give his "I Have a Dream" speech from the Lincoln Memorial.

Imagine a school in which the student-to-computer ratio is two to one, each teacher has a personal computer, and students have instant access to the library card catalog and to encyclopedia software. In this school, teachers use integrated learning systems to individualize students' assignments and monitor their progress.

A student giving a report on recent volcanic eruptions pauses, and at the touch of a button demonstrates the important points by displaying an actual volcano erupting on the classroom video wall.

Imagine a national network of teachers linked to each other and to education researchers by computer, exchanging concepts and improving student learning—all for the cost of a telephone call.

Imagine high school students collecting real agricultural data and using computers to analyze and assist in agricultural production in their community.

These are not visions from the 21st century, but rather actual examples of the impact of technology on schools today (Geiger, 1991).

CHAPTER THREE

Technology and Special Education

Technology is quickly changing society and—because education reflects society—the way we teach, the way students learn, and the way schools are organized. The examples mentioned here are realities at Silver Ridge Elementary School in the Central Kitsap School District, near Seattle. Models such as Silver Ridge and other technologically advanced school systems are proving that technology can assist all students to become independent learners and problem solvers. It can also help teachers become true facilitators of learning.

The Philosophy of Technology in Special Education

One of the measures of the greatness of a society is how it uses its technology (Hannaford, 1987). For the past few decades, those with disabilities and those working to assist them have explored the potential of technology for this field. These studies have revealed several implications of profound impact to the field of special education.

Technology has made available powerful tools that can enhance students' ability to learn and to make maximum use of their educational time. It is continuing to make possible specialized adaptive devices that assist those with physical and sensory disabilities in overcoming many of the challenges they face. The combination of these two implications has had a synergistic effect, narrowing the gap between those with and those without disabilities. In addition, adaptive devices designed principally for those with one type of disability but useful for those with another (for example, devices utilizing speech synthesis to "read" to those with blindness also assisting the learning disabled) are causing a "blurring" of categorical boundaries.

The effective use of technology calls for untraditional teaching styles that emphasize nonlinear thinking and roles that foster student facilitation and exploration. Not only must we use technology to more effectively educate students with disabilities, but we must also educate them to use technology if we wish to prepare them to participate in a technological society. For example, in what were once considered minimum skill-level jobs—requiring only basic reading, arithmetic, and writing skills—computers are now extensively used. Students employed in such jobs will be required to use computers, read printouts, and input data.

All of this underscores the fact that special education is now in a phase of informed decision making regarding when, where, and how this new technology can best be used. For informed decisions to be made, it is imperative that careful study and thought be given to this subject and that the necessary database of knowledge be compiled. It is our view that current and emerging technology are the harbingers of a new revolution—one that has already begun and that will have such a profound and pervasive impact on society and education that it, as well as the legal and legislative parameters we discussed earlier, will become the foundation of change in all areas of special education.

Technology's Impact on Society

There can be no doubt that the industrial revolution brought profound changes to society. That revolution was based on mechanical innovations that extended, multiplied, and leveraged our physical strength.

Concepts such as the assembly line process, yoked with these enhanced mechanical abilities, produced a partnership that increased production to a previously unthinkable level. This revolution led to a reduction in labor-intensive industry, and, though jobs were lost in certain areas, more new jobs directly linked to expanding industrialization were created. The revolution also had a great impact on why and how we educated our children. To fit the workplace of the 21st century, American industry will need a new kind of worker, one who can be easily trained. Given the projected increase in the speed of technological advances, workers with skills that make them good learners will be in demand. D'Ignazio (1990) has characterized those skills in the following way.

- Strong basic skills, including both written and verbal communication, practical math, estimation, and computation
- An ability to adjust to new technologies and to use them to achieve organizational goals
- An ability to be an independent learner, self-directed and self-motivated
- An ability to foster learning on the part of peers and colleagues
- An ability to work cooperatively in a high-performance, team-oriented environment
- An ability to adjust to fluid, evolving, and ambiguous situations, in which problems must be solved quickly using incomplete information and experience

These skills are a far cry from the traditional industrial skills the present school system was designed to instill. A popular educational axiom can be paraphrased as follows: "It's not that we're doing a bad job of educating students compared with the past; it's that we *are* educating them for the past!" The use of technology and training in the use of technology will be crucial skills for this time of social and educational change.

The presence of such changes in our society indicates that we are now in the midst of another revolution, this one based on machines that will extend, multiply, and leverage our mental abilities. As Raymond Kurzweil points out,

> This new revolution, based on machines that expand the reach of our minds, will ultimately have a far greater impact than the revolution that merely expanded the reach of our bodies. It promises to transform production, education, medicine, aids for the handicapped, research, the acquisition and distribution of knowledge, communication, the creation of wealth, the conduct of government and warfare. The cost-effectiveness of the key ingredients in our new technological base — computers and related semiconductor technology — is increasing at an exponential rate. The power of computer technology now doubles (for the same unit cost) every 18 to 24 months. (1990, p. 8)

We are no longer so much a country rich in industry as a nation rich in information; our future industrial strength rests more on our effective use of computer-based technologies such as robotics and computer-aided design (Martinez & Mead, 1988).

In today's modern office, microcomputers have all but displaced the typewriter and are used not only for word-processing letters, memos, and reports, but also for tasks associated with inventories, distribution of lists, storage of vital data, financial projections, and budgeting. Their graphic capabilities are being used for desktop publishing in offices as well as for professional magazines and newspapers. Networking has seen an increase in the use of the computer as a primary communication tool, sending and receiving messages, graphics, and files of information across the occupational spectrum. In today's marketplace, the secretary must have the skills to use technology for data entry and word processing. The designer, architect, or engineer must be able to use graphics software and computer-assisted design. Both the librarian and the auto parts clerk must be able to access and search large data bases. The mechanic must be able to use complex diagnostic machines to repair computer-based ignition systems.

In medicine the impact of technology has been astounding. Magnetic resonance imaging (MRI), ultrasound, and CAT scans allow interior views of the body that are noninvasive and that provide physicians with valuable diagnostic information. Advances in gene splicing allow some direct intervention in genetic-based disabilities.

Leisure opportunities have also expanded due to the use of current technology. Computers are used to help keep personal financial records, store recipes, and stay current with correspondence. Children use software for a variety of activities, from video games to the composition of music. Compact disks provide music of remarkable clarity and are programmed for any sequence of desired music. All of these exist in concert with the pervasive context created by television, radio, and video games that influences students' personal world views. Such advanced information technology, through its generation of artificial realities, helps shape the ways in which students view their physical and social environments (Dede, 1990). Such potential can be utilized either for greatly expanded learning and communication opportunities or for the dissemination of propaganda.

Researchers and inventors such as Kurzweil are expanding technology's frontiers in the areas of artificial intelligence (AI) and intelligence amplification (IA). Their work is complementing human creativity and flexibility by creating empowering environments that use a great variety of technological media (hypermedia). Their work on roboticized applications includes the installation of tutoring and coaching operating systems—or "expert systems"—that cross human expertise and greater data resources with neutral, endlessly patient machines. We will explore in this chapter some of the astounding technologies that AI and cognitive science will bring to the specific areas of education and special education in the 21st century.

Technology's Impact on Education

Kurzweil's (1990) conclusions on the impact that technology and intelligent machines will have on society and work rest to no small extent on education and its pivotal role in shaping the future world economy. This led him to consider technology's impact on education itself. While other media such as television, cinema, and recorded music have had a great influence on education, so far, computer-based technology has had only a modest impact. In 1985, a report from the U.S. Office of Education predicted that educational technology would lead to the transformation of the public school. Although there has been a significant increase in the number of computers—an estimated 2 million plus in the classroom (O'Neil, 1990)—hence lower student-to-computer ratios (see Figure 3.1), little evidence of an "educational transformation" can be seen (Holden, 1989).

Although a great number of computers are used in schools, even more are in place in the home, along with video games and a host of consumer electronic products using digital technology. But in spite of this technology, the content and

Figure 3.1 Computer-to-student ratios

process of education remains unchanged and the computer revolution, which is radically transforming work in the office and factory, has not yet made its mark in the schools (Kurzweil, 1990).

Eisele and Eisele (1990) suggest that such slow progress in technological transformation may be related to educators' limited training in the use and selection of those technologies. O'Neil (1990) reports that the influx of computers in the schools has neither sparked a broad revolution in learning nor faded away. He suggests that computer use is in a holding pattern until the organizational climate in the schools changes enough to allow educators and students an opportunity to take advantage of their potential. He indicates that computer-based technology is not being used systematically across the curriculum, and that those attempting to use computers in the classroom face several barriers. These include sporadic and limited opportunities for training, shortages of quality hardware and software, and little time allowed for planning how to use computer-based technology to optimize learning.

Some have suggested that many educators and administrators see this technology as just another methodological fad and are not willing to expend the effort to acquire the in-depth skills they need to utilize it fully (Dede, 1990; Eisele & Eisele, 1990). Dede (1990) has gone on to list four "misconceptions" that he feels have resulted in educators' passive attitude toward educational technology.

1. *Misconception of consolidation:* The wave of innovation is almost over, and we know now what these devices can and can't do. Now we need only consolidate and refine that knowledge. In fact, the opposite is true. The pace of emerging newer and more powerful tools and devices is increasing, and we lack the strategies to maximize these new discoveries. The real impact of technology on education is only now beginning.

2. *Misconception of literacy:* Information technologies are primarily a me-

dium for manipulating and communicating symbols similar to language or math. In fact, the emerging intelligent devices are more like potential intellectual partners. Our goal should not be student mastery of the mechanics but rather a complementary relationship between learners and intelligent technologies that are more than objects but less than human.

3. *Misconception of power:* Students need less powerful devices than people in the workplace. In fact, students need computers that are more functional than upper-end work stations, and our current base of computers is far too underpowered to support the next generation of instructional applications.

4. *Misconception of timing:* We need to wait until the new types of applications and their supporting hardware and software are widely available. In fact, adequate preparation of teachers and schools to take advantage of the emerging technologies will take years. We will be able to utilize the full effectiveness of these powerful tools and work stations only if the organizational infrastructure to support their use is already in place before they are purchased.

■ A History of Technology in the Schools

Reviewing the history of technology in the schools can be helpful from at least two perspectives. First, many people think of technology in schools as just computers

---

Box 3.1 Computer Usage

- Students in private schools have greater access to computers than do those in public schools.
- Some 28% of Americans over age 17 used computers at home or in school in 1989. This is an increase of 18% since 1984.
- Some 46% of Americans between 3 and 17 used computers at home or in school in 1989.
- There are racial demographic differences in computer usage, as indicated by the following graph.

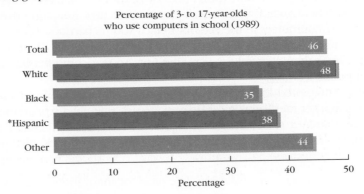

Percentage of 3- to 17-year-olds who use computers in school (1989)

	Percentage
Total	46
White	48
Black	35
*Hispanic	38
Other	44

*Persons of Hispanic origin may be of any race.

SOURCE: U.S. Bureau of the Census, 1990.

with no preceding events and, without understanding the antecedents, can mistakenly look to one technology to provide all solutions. Second, knowing this history may help us understand the emerging technologies of the future and learn from past mistakes (Eisele & Eisele, 1990).

The term *information revolution* or *information explosion* has been used to characterize our current age. We have discussed the new revolution brought about by emerging technology and the age of the "intelligent" machine. This same concept of the history of technology as a series of revolutions was used effectively by Ashby (1967). Such revolutions included the revolution in communication represented by cave drawings, which used some of the first symbols for written communication. This was followed by a revolution in the written word as communication, through the recording of important manuscripts and documents such as the Bible. The availability of written documents changed what had been a totally oral presentation mode in education. It enabled society to shift the responsibility for educating the young from parents in the home to teachers in a school setting.

The revolution created by Gutenberg's printing press in the mid-15th century had such a profound impact on education that its effect is still felt today; schools still use the printed book as the primary tool in establishing curriculum and through it educational practice and instructional procedures.

Yet another revolution was sparked by the invention and use of electronics. Beginning with more basic inventions such as the light bulb, telegraph, and telephone, this revolution influenced education and set the stage for future developments such as television, calculators, and computers.

Molnar (1990) has reviewed the history of technology from a unique educational perspective, summarized here.

* The first large-scale computers ever made were designed and built on campuses of American universities: Harvard's Mark I in 1944 and the University of Pennsylvania's ENIAC in 1946. The ENIAC was the first all-electronic computer, and is often considered the beginning of the first generation of computers. Both devices were demonstration projects designed to show the potential of the computer.

* The first working computer was created by the University of Illinois in 1959 and called PLATO® (Programmed Logic for Automatic Teaching Operations). It was the first computer used for instructional purposes.

* In July 1976, with urging from President Johnson, the National Science Foundation established the Office of Computing Activities, to study the potential of computers in education.

* In 1954 there were only 12 computers in the United States. Commercial investors were uninterested, and those "in the know" said the market would not exceed a dozen. By 1990 it was estimated that there were over 2 million computers in the schools and another 2 million, including work stations, in colleges and universities. Many universities now require that incoming students have a computer; two-thirds of them provide financial assistance to help students purchase computers.

* National commissions have elevated computing to the position of a new basic skill, on a par with reading, writing, and arithmetic.

Eisele and Eisele (1990) have supplemented these historical views by adding two other areas for consideration as historical "revolution" phases in technology. The first is the developments that led to the use of television in the classroom, including closed-circuit television. Although criticized for its early reliance on the "talking head" mode (just televising a teacher teaching in the classroom), the technology advanced with applications such as *Sesame Street,* a children's television production based on the educational principles of its time. The second area of revolutionary impact on education has been the development of microcomputers. Advances in technology have allowed a continual reduction in size of computer components and circuitry and eventually enabled them to be imprinted on small silicon chips. Steven Wozniak and Steven Jobs (cofounders of Apple Computers, Inc.) can be singled out for their specific impact on computer usage in the schools. Through their efforts, many educators became acquainted with computers for the first time, had affordable hardware to purchase themselves or through their schools, and had software developed for educational purposes.

By the end of the 1980s schools were utilizing increasingly more powerful computers, had monitors with better resolution and color, and were networking to provide integrated learning systems (ILS) that allowed an articulated and individualized approach to assessment, diagnostic and prescriptive teaching, management, and evaluation.

Box 3.2 *Historical Influences*

Dr. John Kemeny, who had been a research assistant to Dr. Albert Einstein at Princeton, worked with Tom Kurtz at Dartmouth to give birth to a new computer language called BASIC. The new language, along with time-sharing and operating systems that supported small programs and simple interfaces, took computers out of the hands of research specialists and extended them into classrooms and dormitories.

Dr. Donald Blitzer at the University of Illinois used the PLATO IV to demonstrate its potential for "distance" learning. He proposed systems that could serve several thousand student stations and teach several hundred lessons simultaneously. In 1989 he designed a new, more powerful system called NovaNet '89. The system uses satellite communication and hardware that allows 8000 terminals to be used interactively. Blitzer's vision is to scale up computer-based education to serve millions of students at a cost so low that educators can't ignore it.

Dr. Seymour Papert of MIT demonstrated that, given the proper tools and a supportive educational environment, children are able to perform tasks and utilize computers in ways usually expected of much older students. With Wallace Feurzeig, he created the computer language LOGO, a simple version of BASIC that enables even young children to program computers. He endorses the view that learning is a reconstruction rather than a transmission of knowledge and extends this idea by postulating that the most effective learning takes place when the student is creating a meaningful project. With that in mind, Papert is working on projects that help children use LOGO to program his electromechanical "turtle," robots, and "factories" made of interconnecting plastic blocks. He's also teaching them science principles by using sound-, touch-, and light-sensitive cybernetic toy creatures (Molnar, 1990).

In their discussion of the definition of technology a number of authors in the field (Eisele & Eisele, 1990; Gagné, 1987; Percival & Ellington, 1988; and Spencer, 1988) have pointed out that the term is often used to convey two different concepts. The first relates more to what Percival and Ellington would call "technology *in* education," the second to the "technology *of* education." Both of these concepts are addressed in the widely quoted definition issued by the Commission on Instructional Technology.

> Instructional technology can be defined in two ways. In its more familiar sense, it means the media born of the communications revolution which can be used for instructional purposes alongside the teacher, textbook, and blackboard. . . . The pieces that make up instructional technology [include]: television, films, overhead projectors, computers, and other items of "hardware" and "software" (to use the convenient jargon that distinguishes machines from programs). . . . The second and less familiar definition of instructional technology goes beyond any particular medium or device. In this sense, instructional technology is more than the sum of its parts. It is a systematic way of designing, carrying out, and evaluating the total process of learning and teaching in terms of specific objectives, based on research in human learning and communication, and employing a combination of human and nonhuman resources to bring about more effective instruction. (1970, p. 21)

Parette (1991) has pointed out that the federal government also has clearly expressed the importance of technology for the disabled and coined its own definition of the term with the passage of PL 100-407, the Technology-Related Assistance for Individuals with Disabilities Act of 1988. Within the context of this legislation, technology is "any item, piece of equipment, or product system, whether acquired commercially off the shelf, modified, or customized, that is used to increase, maintain, or improve functional capabilities of individuals with disabilities" [29 U.S.C. 2202, Sec. 3(1)].

Whereas the federal definition fits within the first category of the Commission on Instructional Technology's definition, we must realize the more profound nature of the second and broader category of that definition. In part, our lack of success in achieving the predicted transformation of education by technology has been due to a lack of attention to broader questions of curricula and the nature of learning. The classrooms and computer labs of ten years ago were influenced by the theories of B. F. Skinner, who viewed education and learning as a stimulus-response type of relationship. Computer use, and particularly computer-assisted instruction (CAI), reflected this view in its question-response-feedback format. Mageau points out that more recent research—indicating that children learn better actively, nonlinearly, visually, and cooperatively—is now reflected in technology such as laser discs and CD-ROM technology that allows teachers and students to randomly select thousands of visuals. It would seem that changes in our understanding of learning coupled with emerging technologies will increasingly lead us toward the broader definition of technology.

All too often in the schools, the term *educational technology* is synonymous with computers. Although we'll discuss computer-based technology at greater length than we will other technologies, keep in mind that technology is more than just computers. We will briefly discuss some of the more popular technologies and their use. (A list of basic terms and definitions relating to computer systems is provided in Box 3.3.)

Several additional technological developments relate to the input-output functions of the computer and use its base for a variety of functions affecting education.

■ Modems

While not as new as many other technologies, modems are the backbone of many of the networking uses of the computer, particularly in the area of what is called distance learning. Modems (modulating-demodulating) units translate the digital information sent by a computer into electrical waveforms that can be transmitted

---

Box 3.3
Computer
System
Terminology

Although computer systems can be very complex and have a large number of devices (called peripherals) connected to their central components, there are only four primary components of a system:

1. The central processing unit, or CPU
2. Memory
3. An input device
4. An output device

CPU The central processing unit of the computer is often considered its "brain." It can receive information, decipher it, and carry out the instructions. It directs the flow of information throughout the system and controls all the operations. It also performs arithmetic functions such as addition, subtraction, multiplication, and division, and carries out certain logic functions.

MEMORY To a large extent, the amount of memory determines the capabilities of the computer. The memory's storage capacity is measured in bytes. A byte can be defined as one character (such as an alphabetic letter, number, or symbol). When talking about computer memory, we normally use the scientific symbol K for each thousand bytes, so a computer that has 128K is able to store 128,000 bytes, or characters. The new, more powerful microcomputers used in the schools have a memory capacity measured in megabytes, or millions of bytes, microprocessors such as Intel's 80386 (which may soon power a new generation of microcomputers) have a storage capacity of 4 gigabytes, or 4 billion characters (Hannaford, 1987).

Computer memory can be classified in two ways: primary and secondary storage. Primary storage contains both permanent information needed to run the basic systems of the computer itself—called ROM, or read-only memory—and memory to be used by the individual while working with specific programs or applications—called RAM, or random-access memory. RAM is used when the teacher or student is writing a letter, drawing a graphic, or using some other application or software program. Secondary memory devices store information that the user needs to save but that can't be kept in RAM. The most common secondary storage devices are "floppy" disks and hard disks. These disk formats are also used to input data into the computer.

over telephone lines or broadcast over the air. Another modem at the remote site then translates the data back into digital information that can be used and stored by the computer and displayed to the other user. Such capabilities can greatly supplement program planning for hospitalized or homebound students. Modems transmit information at speeds expressed in terms of bits per second, or baud rates: those that transmit and receive at a baud rate of 2400 are able to send or receive approximately 240 characters per second.

■ Optical Disks

Optical disks (or discs) are one of the newer storage options for data used in computer-based applications. This technology utilizes a metal disk much the size

(continued)

INPUT   The third essential element in a computer system is some type of device to enter information into the computer. The most common input device is the standard keyboard. Several other input options offer some important advantages to most users and could be essential to an individual with a disability. The "mouse" is a small, boxlike unit that controls movement of an arrow or cursor on the screen of the computer; the user can send commands to the computer by pressing on a raised bar on the mouse. A track ball functions in a similar manner, but is set within a box that remains stationary or that is built into the side of the keyboard.

A light pen allows users to draw images on the screen that will be entered into the computer's memory, as well as to issue commands by pointing the light at objects on the screen. Graphic tablets provide a similar type of input by allowing users to draw on a palette or tablet with a kind of stylus connected to the computer. It, too, can call up programs and issue commands.

Touch-screen technology enables the user to enter commands and interact with the computer by touching the screen of the monitor or CRT. Optical scanners allow computers to scan information that is handwritten, typed, or printed (including graphics) and translate it into information that can be reproduced and edited by most word processors.

Game paddles and joysticks also offer options to interact with the computer and input information. These devices were originally designed for use in computer games, but by allowing the user to input commands through pushing knobs or pressing buttons, they have offered speed and flexibility to individuals with disabilities who are unable to use the standard keyboard.

OUTPUT   Some type of device to display the information stored and retrieved from the computer's memory is also essential. The primary device in use today is the cathode-ray tube, or CRT, which forms the main component of television and computer monitors. In this text we will refer to the CRT as the monitor or computer screen. Another primary output device is a printer. The printer enables the user to produce paper or "hard copies" of the work displayed on the screen. Plotters are another type of output device that can use pens of different colors to receive data from the computer and print or trace them on graph or regular paper.

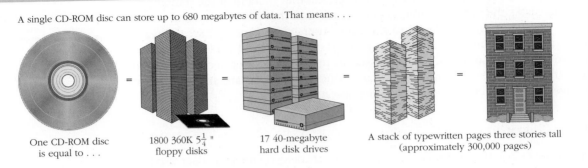

A single CD-ROM disc can store up to 680 megabytes of data. That means . . .

One CD-ROM disc is equal to . . . = 1800 360K 5¼" floppy disks = 17 40-megabyte hard disk drives = A stack of typewritten pages three stories tall (approximately 300,000 pages)

Figure 3.2   Storage capacity of a CD ROM

SOURCE: *Drew A. Kaplan, DAK Industries. 8200 Remmet Ave., Canoga Park, CA 91304. Page 14. © 1991. Used with permission.*

of a record album, or a small metal compact disk (CD), on which an intense beam of laser light writes information. The information is later "read" by the computer and displayed as text, photographs, or video. The two current major types of optical disks are videodiscs and CD-ROMs (Mageau, 1990).

Videodiscs   The key educational advantage to videodiscs has been that teachers can control any of 54,000 frames of high-quality video. These video sequences can be linked to such devices as touch screens, providing video answers or examples linked to the user's inquiry. This type of technology is now frequently seen in shopping malls, airports, and other public places in which customers need orientation or guidance.

The educational uses are varied and include a number of interactive video and computer programs to help students explore information in depth and permit the teacher to provide actual pictures and videos of historical, scientific, and other events. (Remember the video of the volcano erupting earlier in this chapter?) Programmed software can guide teachers and students through useful sequences; or they can sequence their own programs. The effectiveness of such complex measures tends to depend on the software used to access the videodiscs (Mageau, 1990).

CD-ROM (Compact Disk Read-Only Memory)   This is another type of optical disk, but it provides what is described by Hannaford (1987) as "fantastic storage capacity"; it's able to store over 680 million characters of information. As illustrated in Figure 3.2, such capacity allows the storage of whole libraries of data and is already radically changing the way in which data is presented and stored in the schools. Schools such as those in the small, isolated town of Rangely, Colorado (population 2500) are using CD-ROM and computers for a variety of tasks, from teacher and student data searches to exploring the geography and history of the world. Using an interactive CD-ROM system, middle school students with disabilities learn to conduct searches, find remote counties or cities, and read articles from the visual atlas or encyclopedia, illustrated by pictures and video clips. Words difficult to understand are underlined and the student can hear the word pronounced by the computer and see (and sometimes hear) it defined. The same process can be used for studying the human body in science. The students can read, get on-screen help and hear difficult words, and actually see videos demonstrating how a "hinge joint" (or other anatomical part) moves.

Continuing advances are expected within the optical field, with digital video interactive (DVI) and compact disk interactive (CDI) vying to expand storage, quality, and use far beyond today's capabilities (Hannaford, 1987; Mageau, 1990).

■ Speech Recognition and Synthesis

Speech recognition and synthesis enables computers to recognize human speech and to produce synthetic speech. Although currently in the research and development phase, it is nonetheless impressive and available.

Computer-based speech recognition programs allow the computer to follow spoken commands and carry out those functions. The process follows several steps (Hannaford, 1987). By means of a microphone, spoken words are translated into digitalized components and stored by the computer. Installed software programs guide the computer's actions as it "studies" these digitalized speech patterns and links them to particular program or operating system commands. A system vocabulary is developed by the computer, and this vocabulary allows the user to command and control the computer's programs and connected peripheral devices.

What Kurzweil (1990) calls automatic speech recognition (ASR) has been used commercially for several years in fields in which users' hands and eyes are otherwise occupied. For example, in laboratories, technicians may be busy examining an image through a microscope or working with other instrumentation; but they can speak into the microphone of an ASR system. Other fields are beginning to use ASR to automate routine business conducted over the phone: credit card verification, banking, sales orders, and accessing data bases or inventory records. It can recognize computer commands from input devices other than keyboard entry. It's also an important feature of robotics that aids those with physical disabilities (Kurzweil, 1990), allowing those without effective use of their arms or hands to interface with a variety of computer-based systems.

At a recent international conference of business and corporate leaders held in Europe, a respected American educator and expert on the vocational needs of the future completed his speech. After congratulating him, one of the members assisting with the meeting asked if she could distribute copies of his speech. The speaker replied that he would like to grant the request, but that the speech he had given was not written. Smiling, the conference member motioned to some people in the back of the room, who began to distribute printed copies of the speech given approximately 90 seconds before, not only in English but in several other languages. The astounded speaker had witnessed the amazing capabilities of speech recognition and automatic translation. This combination of computer-based technology and artificial intelligence was then only in the research and development phase, but it promises exciting possibilities in future technology.

Box 3.4
No Longer the
Future

Computers can also be used to synthesize sound patterns into a semblance of human speech. Speech synthesizers produce this artificial speech in the following manner. The computer is programmed to "read" words it has stored in memory and to translate combinations of the letters into phonemes, or sounds. Complex software programs then make the sounds resemble human speech. The software also assists the computer in combining and sounding out the phonemes, either individually or in combination, to make words (Hannaford, 1987).

Raymond Kurzweil's reading machine was first introduced in 1976, primarily for the use of those disabled by blindness. It used an optical scanner to input the print from a book or other written material and then produced synthetic speech to "read" the material to the user. Kurzweil has combined speech recognition with artificial intelligence technology to create a voice system that recognizes 10,000 words. This system can be modified by special programs so that radiologists or physicians in emergency medicine can automatically generate written text, using their specialized vocabulary, by dictating. Not forgetting his commitment to those with disabilities, Kurzweil is working on upgrades of these systems to allow those with severe physical paralysis or impaired use of the hands to create text and better control their environment. His long-term goals include a sensory aid that would allow deaf persons to "see" what is being said on the telephone as it is being spoken (Kurzweil, 1990).

■ Telecommunications

In a discussion of innovations in telecommunications, a wide variety of transmission and communication media are at work to meet the diversity of learning environments and their varied instructional delivery requirements.

Educational television   Since the first educational television station went on the air in 1953 (KUHT, in Houston), educational television, with models such as those presented on *Sesame Street,* has moved to dramatization, documentaries, and video magazine formats. Increasing production costs have led to a movement toward tape-lending libraries and consortium projects such as the Agency for Instructional Technology in Bloomington, Indiana.

Videotape   The 1960s and 1970s saw a dramatic increase in the number of videotape recorders used in the schools. This device allows the teacher to show prerecorded tapes as well as to program the recorder to tape live television programs in nonclass hours and play them back whenever appropriate. The system lets small student groups work with facilitators who guide discussion and problem solving in coordination with taped lessons, programs, or specific segments. This can be effective with many students with disabilities. Students with speech or language disorders can be videotaped in rehearsed or in real-life situations to practice effective therapy techniques and assist in transferring skills from the classroom to the "real world." In a similar manner appropriate behavior can be modeled on tape and studied by students with behavior or other disorders.

Instructional Television Fixed Service (ITFS)   ITFS is an over-the-air broadcast system that operates on frequencies higher than those used by regular television. Although users do not need cable to get ITFS systems on their regular television set, they do need a converter box. This can be an effective delivery system in densely populated areas (the signal has an approximate range of 20 miles), where it can be a cheaper alternative to regular television broadcasts and can function much like a closed-circuit system. Both colleges and public schools have utilized the system, sometimes with additional two-way communications that allow student-teacher interaction during live teaching and offer instructional options for homebound or hospitalized students. It is receiving additional commercial study because it can attract a cablelike audience in the urban home setting without the expense of installing cable wires or microwave dishes.

Audiographics   Microcomputers are used with graphic tablets, modems, speakerphones, and videocameras to communicate over standard phone lines. Regional networks may output videos—including prepared graphics, digitalized video, and "live-freehand" graphics—prepared by teachers and students in separate locations. Audiographic systems are being used to bring college classes to students in remote communities. Video/computer networks are yet another possibility: students view videotapes and then participate in directed activities, using interactive computer software that supports concepts on the videos. Students interact as they work on computers. These audiographic capabilities offer exciting options to teachers in more remote areas who work with disabled students. Such options include opportunities for consultation, interactive lessons, and in-service training from specialized consultants.

■ Artificial Intelligence and Expert Systems

The age of the "intelligent machine" is sparking debate and discussion over traditional definitions of thinking and intelligence (Dennett, 1990; Minsky, 1990; Waldrop, 1990). In today's market we see increasing examples—such as some of those cited in Box 3.5—of emerging technologies in artificial intelligence, or AI. Another example is the growth of what are called expert systems. While we have discussed the computer's ability to retrieve requested data, that presupposes that users know what they are searching for. Expert systems have been programmed to question the user and to use the answers to help them supply data the person needs to make a decision (Underwood & Underwood, 1990). These expert systems have stored vast amounts of specific knowledge in certain areas of human expertise; they then combine the facts supplied by the user and rule-based procedures to suggest a solution to the problem presented (Stefik et al., 1983). Such an approach has potential for a variety of applications in areas of specific knowledge and has been referred to as "knowledge engineering" (Hayes-Roth, Waterman, & Lenat, 1983). It has already been used in medical diagnoses. Hannaford (1987) described special education programs in which expert systems could help make administrative decisions such as classifying students with various disabilities. Such a system could function as a computerized assistant to the director of special education—providing prompts regarding appropriate data needed, bringing up pertinent legal considerations, and suggesting treatment options while recording progress. Direct services to individuals with disabilities are another possibility, because similar programs could provide a variety of prompts to assist in decision making and to suggest appropriate options for effective daily living.

Robotics   Current applications of robotics are in the fields of industry, music, crime prevention, hazardous waste removal, and assisting disabled individuals. Robots disarmed mines during the aftermath of the war with Iraq and are now capable of the following: assisting with some brain surgery, beating humans in table tennis, and picking up and cracking eggs to make an omelette. One Japanese-built, humanlike robot can engage people in simple conversation and, with its camera eye, read and play sheet music with its ten fingers, automatically adjusting to the key of the singer. In a joint project of the University of Utah and MIT, researchers are now working with a robotic arm that will be able to shave, brush the teeth of, feed, and retrieve food and drink for patients who are quadriplegic or challenged by other physical disabilities such as cerebral palsy or muscular dystrophy (Hannaford, 1987; Kurzweil, 1990).

It is the very essence of today's technology that whatever is written about it will be outdated before it is read. The emergence of optical computers that use

**Box 3.5
Technology
and
Education in
the 21st
Century**

By the end of the 1990s we will have a personal computer that will provide a powerful work station for every student. It will be a portable laptop device the size of a large book or the new "notebook" computers. It will be wireless and include high-resolution screens that are as easy to read as books. Its input devices will include a track ball and keyboard, and it will support high-quality two-way voice communication, including natural language understanding. Users will find it extremely easy and "intuitive."

New computer-assisted instruction models will diagnose the student's thinking and learning patterns in specific areas and then devise a strategy to upgrade them to the desired level. They will then provide entertaining and engaging experiences to carry out the remedial strategies.

Students will use the wireless network capabilities to share courseware, submit papers or exams, and send mail and other types of communication. They will have access to an international network and to all the great libraries of the world, with their own intelligent software assistants to assist them in quickly finding the desired information.

Though some aspects of this scenario are available, others will only emerge by the end of this decade. Given the current lag in educational applications of existing technology (about ten years), such applications will reach the "critical mass" for enactment near the year 2010. By the second half of the century, these technologies will be as widespread as our video technologies are today, and high school students may be able to participate in the Constitutional Convention of 1787 and debate the Founding Fathers over the separation of powers between the branches of government. A student assigned the role of trying to negotiate a better deal for the executive branch concerning war powers would submit an actual debate with one of the Founding Fathers. The teacher would watch this debate just as the student developed it, in a totally realistic three-dimensional holographic environment. The Founding Fathers would be extremely lifelike artificial people programmed to hear, understand, and respond to the student (and programmed to tolerate this interruption in their deliberations and to understand the student's modern-day language use), just as the true Founding Fathers might have (Kurzweil, 1990).

laser light to replace silicon and electrical operations, the development of more powerful and speedy computers that use a chemical transmission and storage of information, and the possible development of biological computers composed of living matter and capable of implantation and growth in the body are vivid examples of this fact. The remarkable technologies that currently exist can assist us to make a more confident assessment of Kurzweil's view of what the 21st century will be like for the disabled (see Box 3.6).

Technology and Special Education

Special educators must use the technology at their disposal to keep pace with the dramatic advances in such areas as medicine, technology, and learning. Judging when and how to utilize new technologies to assist student learning will require study and training.

At the very least, the skills needed in an increasingly technological workplace force us to give our attention to vocational preparation of students with disabilities. Not only must *we* learn how to use these technologies to more effectively assist students; *they* must also acquire the necessary technological skills to be competitive in the job market.

D'Ignazio (1990) cautions that, in order to accomplish such goals and utilize technology and multimedia effectively, teachers must become collaborators and facilitators with students as they explore knowledge. If classrooms are to model the workplaces of the future, technology must be combined with opportunities for students to take responsibility for their learning, collaborating and working cooperatively to explore and solve problems. In such a classroom teachers have a dual role: they are both leaders of and collaborators with their students.

In discussing the specific use of computer technology in the schools, Carter (1990) postulated six lessons that must be learned.

1. Technology for technology's sake does not work; technology for education's sake does.
2. Computers can be a great "equalizer."
3. While technology can't guarantee increased student achievement, schools with solid implementation plans, adequate resources, and staff training are reporting exciting results.
4. Computers in schools can initiate the "rethinking" of instructional methodology.
5. Successful change requires effective staff development.
6. Change is constant in educational technology.

Lewis and Doorlag (1991) offer several general advantages that computers as a medium for instruction give the special educator. A discussion of these advantages follows.

• *Individualization of instruction.* Personal computers are specifically designed to be used by one individual at a time. Given enough computers, each student in a class of 25 could be learning practical skills in 25 different content areas. Or they could all be working in the same content area, at 25 individual paces. Programs now allow teachers or students to adjust the pace of instruction; and expert systems guide the student to remedial or advanced steps, as appropriate.

• *Student motivation.* Novelty is motivating in its own right; but most software programs also personally address the student or employ a game format to make learning fun. (Some caution is necessary: students who are distracted by extraneous noise and movement might find typical game formats less effective for learning academic skills [Semmel & Lieber, 1986].) One motivating factor, particularly for students with special learning needs, is the nonjudgmental response of many programs to errors; for example, "Not quite, Johnny. Try again."

• *Promoting new learning and new ways to accomplish old tasks.* Teachers are able to use computers to present a variety of learning experiences not usually available in more traditional classrooms. Simulation programs can allow students to manage a lemonade stand, track a spy through the world, command troops in the Civil War, or conduct a series of scientific experiments—all experiences difficult to create in the traditional classroom. This promotes active student involvement in "real" activities that call for integrating knowledge in a variety of subject areas, such as math, geography, and science. New ways to accomplish old tasks can be demonstrated by the use of the word processor for writing assignments. Students can use the capabilities of the computer to modify, correct, edit, and change their production's format in many ways. They can add graphics and desktop publishing programs to produce newsletters, reports, and booklets. All of these options provide a more rewarding and richer writing environment for the student. A number of schools are using this technique—through their own pro-

**Box 3.6
Technology
and the
Disabled
Entering the
21st Century**

In the early 21st century, the lives of persons with disabilities will be greatly different. Individuals with visual impairments or reading disabilities will carry pocket-sized devices that will "read aloud" not only text but signs and symbols with essentially perfect intonation and a broad variety of vocal styles. These devices will describe pictures and graphics, translate in several languages, and serve as a wireless means of access to knowledge bases and libraries.

The visually impaired will also have navigational aids that will perform the tasks of Seeing Eye™ dogs, but even more intelligently. Ultimately, compact devices will be built that combine those navigational aids with the ability to scan and describe what is going on in the visible world. The device will respond to questions or requests for information and may be built into the frames of glasses to see in all directions, with greater acuity than the human eye.

Early versions of speech-to-text aids for individuals with hearing impairments should appear by the end of the 1990s. These devices will eventually translate forms of auditory information, such as music and natural sounds, into modalities such as touch and vision.

Progress will be made in restoring sight and hearing; it is even possible that new suitable channels of communication directly into the brain will be found.

Continued progress in experiments to directly stimulate the muscles of those paralyzed, thereby emulating the control link that was broken by spinal cord damage, can be expected. Exoskeletal robotic and power orthotic devices, put on like a pair of tights and controlled by finger, head motion, or speech (and eventually thought), will free those in wheelchairs and allow them to walk and climb stairs (Kurzweil, 1990).

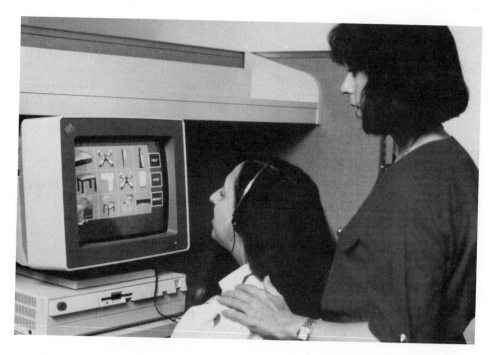

■ Various forms of technology can enrich the lives of persons with disabilities, compensating for their disabilities. ■

grams or through purchased programs such as IBM's® "Writing to Read"—to convey to preschoolers, kindergartners, and first-graders the joy and excitement of communicating experiences to others through written language. Such approaches appear to be more motivating than a traditional study of grammar, punctuation, and phonics to foster the love of writing and reading.

 · *Assisting special students in bypassing or compensating for their disabilities.* As we will see more specifically later in this chapter, computer-based technology can help children with physical or sensory disabilities bypass some of their limitations through input and output modifications. Students who are paralyzed can nod their heads or use a light beam or joystick to have the computer answer questions and thereby participate in the classroom discussion. Students who are blind can have their braille work converted into regular print for the teacher. Students with learning disabilities can use the word processor to compensate for poor spelling and grammar. Interactive programs that use pictures, video, and voice synthesizers can promote better understanding and learning by their combination of presentations.

Although technology can greatly extend and expand our options, the solutions to the problems faced by those with disabilities will be the result of human thoughtfulness and a knowledge of human needs. With such thoughts in mind, Hannaford (1987) generated some guidelines for deciding whether to use technology to assist those with special needs.

 · Although computer and other technologies are rapidly expanding, there are still technological and practical limits.

- Our focus must be on the needs of the individuals who will be using the technology.
- We must know how to utilize the technology so that it will do what needs to be done. This requires careful analysis and specification of what is to be done, by whom, when, under what conditions, and with what effect.
- The technology must be integrated into effective instructional, managerial, and adaptive systems.

■ Specific Applications

Redefining the textbook   The definition of a textbook in some states has been expanded to mean any instructional materials that meet curricula requirements (Mageau, 1991a). This redefinition appears to be a significant step toward the adoption of technology for basal curriculum instruction. For students with mild to moderate special needs, this trend could foster more active learning environments rich with multimedia and opportunities to learn in varied and more true-to-life situations. Opportunities to apply basic skills in recognized and creditable situations should benefit many such students. Current capabilities of presenting interactive lessons utilizing video discs or CD-ROM drives have opened new vistas of learning that offer the student with milder disabilities distinct advantages.

Integration of interactive programs can assist in a number of curriculum areas. Higher levels of literacy for adolescents and adults is the aim of some interactive programs, such as IBM's Alphabet Literacy System. Using a videodisc, InfoWindow® display, and a computer, this program is embedded in a fable of two kingdoms that need to invent an alphabetic system to prevent a war. Students learn how combining the 26 letters of the alphabet enables them to write every word in the English language. Phonics and other approaches are combined with an interesting story line and dramatic graphics. Janda (1990) has discussed using Macintosh® platforms and hypercard and videodisc combinations to explore themes in American democracy. Students can explore, study, and answer guided questions on such subjects as Watergate, presidential popularity, Vietnam, and civil rights. In the process they view, discuss, and study video clips from news programs, and listen to President Roosevelt address Congress after the attack on Pearl Harbor.

Although technology is challenging traditional printed textbooks, it may also make possible customized textbooks. Two technologies—"intelligent" documents and "hydra" machines that combine CD-ROM's storage of text-based material with a copying machine that can store images and text—let users specify the content of their textbooks. A request for material in line with the school's curriculum objectives can result in an appropriate data base. A search is made through the CD-ROM for all pertinent material, graphics, and documents. The "hydra" machine then uses high-speed laser printing and binds the user's book in a matter of minutes. Some major publishers have already begun to use this technology in their college divisions and are now considering it for the elementary and secondary markets (Mageau, 1991b). Aligning books with specific goals and objectives in the curriculum through such customized texts, and the possibilities of adjusting them to students with specific special needs, will afford more options and challenges.

Telecommunications and distance learning   The Los Angeles County School District has launched what it calls the nation's first satellite education project specifically for disadvantaged students, their parents, and teachers. And the weekly Telecommunication Education for Advances in Mathematics and Science Education program beams basic math and science programs, in both Spanish and English, to schools in Boston, Washington, D.C., Detroit, and Los Angeles. Project officials indicate that those districts serve nearly half of the nation's at-risk children. Both projects train staff to work in partnership with the on-camera instructor; programs include family health and multicultural, multidisciplinary math units (Thrasher, 1991).

ILS (Integrated Learning Systems) In 1990 public education spent an estimated $200 million to purchase ILS systems (Mageau, 1991b). The systems normally comprise custom packages of computers, data storage devices, and instructional software. They allow students to interface with computers and participate in hundreds or thousands of hours of instruction delivered in 10- to 15-minute periods that are sequenced and individualized by a centralized microcomputer-based file server. Most systems contain functions that diagnose individual needs, select appropriate programs, analyze and record progress, and adjust lessons accordingly. These individual progress records can be aggregated with class results and reports for administrators, teachers, or parents.

■ General Applications

More familiar computer-based applications for students with mild to moderate disabilities offer general assistance in a number of areas. Students with difficulty in editing their work visually can utilize word processing and grammar and spelling checkers to find and correct errors and verify the information they have entered. Speech synthesizers can assist them by "reading" the text they have entered; they can also perform the same service for students unable to read commands or text. Color, graphics, motion, and highlighting built into programs can assist in figure-ground problems or in reading lines of text. This can improve learning skills needed for employment or for better job performance. Similar improvements in communication on the job and in school can be attained by using computer-based programs to relay messages. Students can be trained to use data bases to store things they need to remember for school and job settings, and then shown how to search and retrieve the information. The structured environment and the graphics and sound can lengthen some students' attention span. Earphones can be used to reduce distracting noise.

Available software is pertinent to skill building at various levels. Frequent repetition, unending patience, and student self-pacing are characteristics that benefit students having more cognitive delay. Programs addressing survival skills can use sophisticated or simplified simulations to provide practice and guidance.

Computer-based programs also can provide opportunities to practice or simulate situations in which cognitive strategies are employed. Behavioral options can be explored that are helpful to those with behavioral difficulties. For these students the structured, consistent, unthreatening, unemotional, and motivating tasks and the simple and direct interaction between child and computer may be advantageous (DLM, 1988). Socialization skills can be encouraged by utilizing the computer and appropriate software in small groups. Most students with disabilities don't need programs labeled LD, MR, or BD but rather well-designed programs that motivate them to work and attain necessary skills. For these children, "computers can make a difference, enabling them to work by themselves with dignity, yet publicly share their triumphs" (Furst, 1990, p. 42).

Computer-based speech recognition systems convert speech into text and

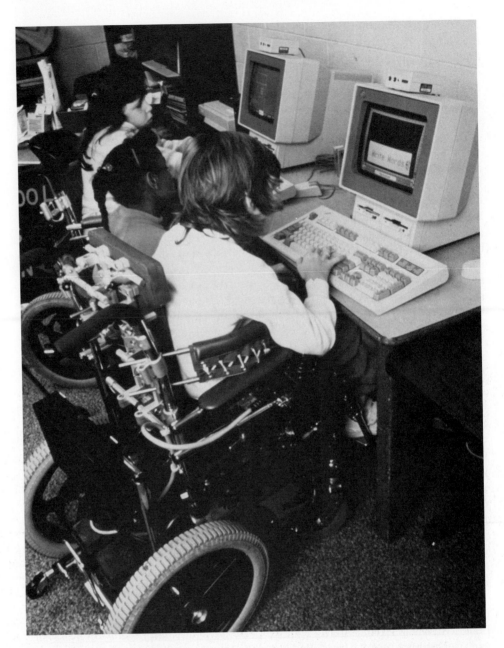

■ Increased capabilities of computer-related programs can greatly enhance the educational process. ■

display it on screen. The work of Ross Stuckless in real-time graphic speech display at the National Technical Institute for the Deaf in Rochester, New York, is only one example. The system uses a court stenographer to enter speech sounds, in a type of phonetic shorthand, into a microcomputer. The computer then regenerates the input into English and displays it on a television monitor for students. Hard copy can be handed out following the sessions (Esposito & Campbell, 1987). These devices, which continue to evolve toward the "real-time" devices envisioned by Kurzweil (1990), offer exciting opportunities for those with hearing impairments.

Computer-based programs are used by speech-language pathologists to provide visual displays of speech in speech training. The programs allow the specialists to monitor speech characteristics such as pitch, loudness, and intonation. Software programs using fingerspelling and sign systems exist to assist individuals with hearing disabilities as well as those wishing to communicate with them. See Chapters 7, 8, and 9 for more information on technologies relating to communications.

Telecommunication advances have seen the rise of closed-caption programs for those with hearing impairments and telecommunication devices for individuals who are deaf (TDDs). Computers that connect voice synthesizers with touch-tone phones and other assistive listening devices allow visual alerting (bright or flashing lights) or tactile vibrating devices (see Chapters 8 and 9). Interactive videodisc presentations with signing, captions, or live interpreters have also been used effectively as a teaching tool (Oska, 1987).

Students with mobility disorders can use technology to overcome the challenges they face due to their physical impairments. Electric battery-powered wheelchairs and carts are controlled by a variety of switches powered by puffs or

People Who Make a Difference

HUGH HERR, MOUNTAIN CLIMBER Hugh Herr, the youngest of five children, spent his boyhood summers climbing mountains. It was a family passion, and by the time he was 11, Hugh was leading other climbers.

While climbing Mount Washington in the White Mountains of New Hampshire when he was 17, Hugh and a friend were caught in a "whiteout," an extremely severe snowstorm. The two struggled in 70-mile-an-hour winds; the temperature, with wind-chill factor, was −40° F. Throughout the night they huddled together to share their body heat. The next morning, after wandering in circles, they were rescued—but not before they had suffered frostbite. Hugh's doctor tried to save his legs, but gangrene set in and both had to be amputated 6 inches below the knee.

Hugh says of his first attempts to use his artificial feet, "There was incredible pain, but I knew I was healing and I knew I had to climb again." He made sure that the artificial feet would fit his climbing boots before he was even able to walk on them.

Hugh now drives, dances, climbs, and can do anything except run. However, he has a goal of running in a marathon. While planning for that, he is not idle. Hugh has engineered an artificial foot with a bladelike front for climbing areas with cracks and another type for climbing on ice. He has eliminated the heel, because "climbers don't need it," and has invented an artificial limb socket that inflates to adjust to the normal swelling and shrinking of the amputee's stump. He also graduated from college summa cum laude and is studying mechanical engineering.

"There's this attitude that if one should lose a leg or whatever, he should accept it. That's grotesque," says Hugh. "The correct attitude is, if there's a problem, let's solve it."

■ Persons with artificial legs can now "feel" through sensors inside the artificial limbs, allowing full physical activities. ■

sips of air and by movements of the hand, arm, foot, or chin. Advances in robotics, to date too expensive or sophisticated for general use, are enabling robotic arms (following voice commands) to push wheelchairs as well as assist in other self-help skills.

Orthotic advances allow stronger and lighter materials to be used for braces, and prosthetic devices utilizing microprocessors to improve mobility and motor control are coming in the future.

Environmental control for other tasks, such as turning on a TV, adjusting heat, turning appliances off and on, operating a telephone, and operating motorized drapes or doors can be accomplished through computer-based operating systems. Electronic page turners assist readers in school or at home.

Esposito and Campbell (1987) have selected several examples of computer-based usage along with instructional objectives for each one. They are shown in Table 3.1.

Adaptive technology can be a great equalizer for students with a physical disability; it enables those who can't manipulate a keyboard or mouse to use

Table 3.1 Selected examples of computer usage and instructional objectives

Instructional Objective	Use of Computers
Signal for adult attention	Teach switch activation skills (to use to signal for attention)
Increase receptive language	Software (with voice synthesizer and switch activation), e.g., First Words (Laureate Learning Systems)
Perform independent recreation or leisure skills	Computer games
Assess developmental milestone skill level	Software (such as Discover Your Baby, BTE systems)
Teach motor coordination	University of Washington software and computer games (with use of switch)
Teach switch activation	Software (such as Ontario Crippled Children's Program) with switch interface
Teach academic skills	Computer-assisted instruction software
Enhance academic abilities	Computer-assisted instruction software
Teach problem-solving skills	LOGO, robotics, with switch or Koala pad
Allow for expressive "oral" communication	Communication software programs (with or without voice synthesis)
Allow for expressive written communication	Word-processing software (with required adaptations, such as keyboard emulator, switch interface)
Perform business-oriented vocational skills	Business software (with required adaptations)
Teach environmental control	Software systems that allow for multiple functions through direct access and/or voice input/output

Source: Reprinted with the permission of Merrill, an imprint of Macmillan Publishing Company, from Esposito and Campbell (1987), "Computers and severely and physically handicapped individuals." In Jimmy D. Lindsey (Ed.), *Computers and exceptional individuals* (p. 112). Copyright © 1987 by Merrill Publishing Company.

computers along with their classmates. Access and efficiency are the two key factors in adaptation. Access lets the student input data into the computer through rearrangements of the work station, minor keyboard modifications, or alternative input devices. If a student can use a keyboard or alternative input device but spends 3 hours on a task others can complete in 20 minutes, the issue becomes one of efficiency.

Access   Usually the first level of keyboard modification for those with physical disabilities is a key guard, consisting of an overlay that fits over the keyboard to prevent drag and multiple key pressing. These systems often include a toggle key that locks keys that normally must be held down—for example, the shift or control keys (Shell, Horn, & Severs, 1989).

■ Voice-activated laptop computers are a valuable tool for individuals with disabilities. ■

Some keyboard software enables users to enter commands in a sequential order rather than hold down two keys simultaneously. It further allows the automatic key repeat function to be turned off, thereby reducing accidental key presses. These programs can also redefine the keys on the keyboard, to bring commonly used functions within easy reach and to allow frequently used sequences to be typed with one or two keystrokes. This "remapping" can also adapt the keyboard for one-handed typists.

Similar adjustments can be made by replacing the keyboard itself. Many keyboards come in preadapted versions: one-handed layouts, Dvorak arrangements (in which the most commonly used keys are the closest), and other easy-to-switch layouts. And some expanded keyboards feature large, flat, membrane-covered boards with large, touch-sensitive squares. These squares can be assigned—individually or as a group—a single function or character; when pressed, they respond appropriately. Jim Henson's Muppet Learning Keys™ is a much simplified alternative with similar advantages, for use with young children or those with lower functioning levels.

Keyboard emulators are most often used by those unable to take advantage of the foregoing options. These devices bypass the keyboard entirely; they usually display on the screen a picture of a keyboard, an array of numbers or letters, or special function keys. Using direct-selection software, the student can move the cursor across the screen with a device such as a mouse, joystick, Morse code signals, or head-mounted optical pointer. Once the cursor is in the desired location, the student selects by pushing a button, moving a knob, or blowing air into a ''puff switch'' mounted on a headset. Scanners are also used that automatically travel across and down or up the rows on the display, stopping when a signal is given by the user.

Voice input is another adaptive means of access to the computer. Most applications require that the student speak clearly and have good pronunciation; however, with increasingly sophisticated devices, students are able to use single-word utterances to issue one or a series of commands to the computer. Students can create multiple vocabularies with these programs to use with specific applications. Adaptive computer cards can program computers to use these devices, as well as slow down interactive programs for slow-responding children. The cards assist the teacher or user in setting up the applications through a series of computer prompts.

Efficiency Because the alternative input models are slower than regular keyboard entry, software has been developed to increase the speed and efficiency of input. These programs utilize word prediction and abbreviation and expansion techniques. Word prediction programs may respond to a message that begins with *I* by offering a list of the most commonly used verbs that might follow—such as *will* or *don't*—and await the user's choice. If none is chosen, but the first letter of the word is entered, the program immediately updates the choices to include only those beginning with that letter. In a similar fashion, some programs use rules of predictability to offer the words most often used by the student in his or her past work. Punctuation and spacing can also be added.

Abbreviation and expansion software allows operations such as the user entering initials only and seeing the full name typed out from previously stored information. Other abbreviations can trigger whole computer sequences, such as selecting software applications or logging on to the computer system.

Technology for those with visual impairments has focused primarily on devices to enhance mobility or otherwise help them meet their physical challenges. Electronic mobility aids such as the laser cane, sonic guide, and sonic pathfinder are of great utility. New explorations in technology are moving toward visual recognition and speech synthesis, so that devices may scan and describe what they perceive (Kurzweil, 1990). Audio aids often use compressed speech to relay books and other taped material to the student. Talking calculators and simple recorders can effectively record, review, and capture auditory data. Talking touch pads are being developed to facilitate interactions with the computer.

The Kurzweil reading machine and other computer-based reading programs translate information from the computer into synthesized speech or into braille. For individuals with low vision, large print and enlarged displays of computer screens, magnification screens on the monitor, closed-circuit camera displays, or hand-held magnifying devices are available. Chapter 9 provides more detailed information regarding the design and use of these adaptive aids.

Computer applications for people with communication disorders generally fall into three basic categories: (1) teaching good speech habits, (2) monitoring speech attempts and providing feedback, and (3) producing a means of communicating other than by speech. Software programs have been developed to assist people with these disabilities to develop articulation skills, appropriate voice

■ Technology can provide unique access to learning that was previously unavailable to people with disabilities. ■

quality, and language skills. Programs have also been designed to be used with speech disorders related to deafness, stuttering, and immature speech development. A program to increase fluency for a stutterer might, for example, emphasize speech rhythm and control and keep a record of progress in fluency. Such programs assist in the assessment of speech and language, eliciting responses and providing feedback about their quality.

Software treating more cognitive aspects of language—such as memory, categorization, sequencing, and association—helps retrain language functions in those whose impaired language is due to stroke or brain injury. These individuals may also utilize synthetic speech or a program of augumentative communication. Such systems can be as simple as pointing at a prepared "language board" or pressing a button on a device that will "talk" for the individual. Any communication success is particularly important, as success in one form of communication may stimulate increased efforts to try other methods.

Language growth can be fostered by programs that motivate children to create and tell stories; these aim for improved structure, increased vocabulary, and pragmatic language skills.

Studies of the effectiveness of technology for students with special needs are still relatively limited and primarily focus on the use of the microcomputer and its accompanying software in the classroom (Ellis & Sabornie, 1986; Semmel & Lieber, 1986).

Ellis and Sabornie examined the "promises" of computers in the classroom and concluded that microcomputers may be used effectively across a wide range of instructional applications with students who are mildly disabled. They point out that computers can assist with instruction and review of content, fact, skills, strategies, and problem solving. Promises regarding simulations, drill-and-practice, and word processing appear to be on their way to being fulfilled. These researchers explode the myths that computers are best used for drill and practice, to reward student behavior, or to present games that have no instructional content.

But effective use of this technology requires that special education teachers focus on attaining their own academic, motivational, and social goals for students, according to Semmel and Lieber (1986). These researchers found that working together on problem-solving tasks facilitated achieving social goals, which are particularly crucial for children who are disabled and who may not be accepted by other students. This suggests that, though teachers tend to group students with disabilities together in these type of projects, more benefits may accrue in heterogeneous groups. Random grouping also has advantages in computer-based work designed to develop and apply higher-order cognitive skills, which allows questions to be answered and hypotheses about the most effective strategies to be discussed. Learning within a group appears to be most effective when material is at the acquisition stage.

Hannaford (1987) has presented information regarding parallel findings of computer research studies with students who were disabled and nondisabled.[1]

- When computers are used, students tend to learn the material in less time.
- The use of computers seems to result in increased attention, motivation, and time on task.
- The general effects of computer instruction are similar regardless of the type of software used. This does not imply that the quality of individual software is not a factor, but rather that one category of software has not consistently been found to be superior to others.
- Exceptional as well as nonexceptional learners tend to view the computer in the instructional setting quite positively.
- Drill and practice are the most frequent type of programs used. These programs are most useful with lower ability students.
- Higher ability level students appear to benefit the most from use of computers in terms of the amount and diversity of learning attained. This would appear consistent with the learning characteristics of this group.
- Using computers appears to more easily provide education to students who have typically been difficult to reach and teach.
- Computers are helpful in reviewing previously learned material. This may be a very significant factor in mainstreaming settings.

---

[1] Reprinted with the permission of Merrill, an imprint of Macmillan Publishing Company, from Hannaford, A. E. (1987), "Computers and exceptional individuals." In Jimmy D. Lindsey (Ed.), *Computers and exceptional individuals.* Copyright © 1987 by Merrill Publishing Company.

- The most effective use of computers is when they are used to supplement other instruction.
- Use of computers leads to better social interaction when students work jointly than when they work in isolation or when they work in traditional ways with traditional instruction. (p. 8)

Technology and Special Education Teachers

Word processing, test assessment, and data management for the teacher are all applications in current use. Computer-generated information packets can be used to highlight the nature of a child's disability and provide home activities that are easily and quickly tailored to the individual needs of students and their families (Masterson, Swirbul, & Noble, 1990). More sophisticated programs that provide more specific assistance in diagnosis, classification, and difficult management decisions are being developed.

The new technology will challenge teachers to stay informed and to seek training to utilize it effectively. Telecommunications can offer staff development and distance-learning opportunities not available at the local level. Data-based searches and access to such educational research sources as ERIC are increasingly possible through local school libraries, and media centers and video libraries provide coursework or actual instruction. User groups designed to give teachers computer assistance can be helpful resources. Special-Net™, a network specifically created for computer access, updates a variety of bulletin boards containing information on issues crucial to the field; it can also assist in data searches.

A variety of resources is available on the use of technology in educating individuals with disabilities. As much of this technology has a very broad application, the special educator may want to contact regional and state educational technology organizations. Journals such as the *Journal of Special Education Technology* and newsletters such as *The Catalyst* from the Western Center for Microcomputers in Special Education can be helpful. Two major commercial computer-based companies, Apple and IBM, have produced excellent guides to technological and particularly computer-based resources for those with disabilities. Both companies have established support and information centers for students and teachers alike.

Trends

Throughout this chapter reference has been made to the technology of the 21st century. New and innovative technologies continue to appear and have an impact. Advances in medicine and technology are creating new frontiers, with a corresponding impact on education. That impact may blur many of the special education categories, as technologies compensate for differences between those with and without disabilities. As miraculous as much of today's and tomorrow's technology may seem, its real promise lies in combating attitudes toward the disabled. As Kurzweil has stated,

If the handicaps resulting from disabilities are significantly reduced, if blind people can read and navigate with ease, if deaf persons can hold normal conversations on the phone, then we can expect public perceptions to change as well. When blind and other disabled persons take their place beside us in schools and the workplace and perform with the same effectiveness as their nondisabled peers, we shall begin to see these disabilities as mere inconveniences, as problems no more difficult to overcome than poor handwriting or fear of public speaking or any of the other minor challenges that we all face. (1990, p. 443)

Summary

Technology has influenced and directly affected public education, but not to the same extent as it has transformed work in the office and factory. This may be due to educators' misconceptions about, and limited conceptualization of, technology. In recognition of the potential of technology-related assistance for individuals with disabilities, Congress passed legislation in 1988 that encouraged the use of technology to "increase, maintain, or improve functional abilities of individuals with disabilities."

Technology has provided tools that can contribute to making maximum use of educational time as well as adaptive devices that can narrow the gap between individuals with physical or sensory disabilities and those without disabilities. However, it may be equally important to teach students with disabilities to *use* technology (especially computers) as it is for us to use technology to enhance their educational opportunities.

Computer-related technology is a major element in education, but many other advances also may benefit education. For example, there is great potential in various telecommunication systems and in applications of artificial intelligence. Technology may provide specific assistance to individuals or general instructional assistance to students from each of the recognized areas of exceptionality, including the gifted and talented. Its greatest contribution may be to reduce the differences between persons with disabilities and their nondisabled peers, thus leading to a change in public perception of disabilities and full acceptance of persons with disabilities.

THEN   *A baby girl is born; the doctor tells her parents that she is mentally retarded. He suggests that they may want to consider placing her in an institution. They decide not to. When she is 6, they search for an appropriate class or school for her, finding one only after a long search. As she grows older they must search for other schools; they are successful, but must pay tuition and transport her each day. When she reaches the age of 21, the school officials say the program is no longer appropriate for her. Thereafter she spends most of her time at home watching TV.*

NOW   *A baby girl is born; the doctor tells her parents that she is mentally retarded. He also tells them that, unless they object, he will inform the local Association for Retarded Citizens (ARC) so that someone from that group can visit them.*

The next day parent members from ARC arrive with information and firsthand experience to share. Personnel from the Early Childhood Program also visit and within a few weeks have developed, with the parents, a stimulation program for the new baby. Later the daughter attends a preschool that includes as many children with as without disabilities. At the local grade and high school she has an educational program designed specifically for her, implemented in both school and community. She learns to use the bus, to make and keep friends, to manage money, to take care of her clothing, and to cook. She develops a variety of skills that will enable her to be employed. By the time she is 21, she is working at a local fast-food restaurant. She plans to move into an apartment by the end of the year.

CHAPTER FOUR

Mental Retardation

In centuries past, **mental retardation** was probably considered a disease or possession by a demon. More recently it has been referred to as a condition or as a concept. The person on the street has some idea of the nature of mental retardation, but it is probably based on very limited information and experience.

Mental retardation has been described and defined from many different points of view, some professional and others very personal. Perhaps Heward and Orlansky are right in claiming that it is "above all, a label" (1988, p. 83).

In this chapter we will consider the historical origins of services for persons who are mentally retarded and how that history has influenced the educational interventions provided today. We will examine the major causes of mental retardation, different classification systems, and the forces that continue to change the outlook for persons with mental retardation. Major trends in planning programs and services for this population include providing programs and interventions that emphasize and encourage normal life activities via classroom environment or community participation; defining mental retardation more narrowly; and offering more special services to persons with severe to profound mental retardation.

Historical Background

■ In the Beginning . . .

According to Barr (1913) and Lindman and McIntyre (1961), both the Greeks (in 1552 B.C.) and the Romans (in 449 B.C.) made specific reference to persons with mental retardation in official records. These writings often referred to them as "fools" or "monsters"; they were thought of as nonhuman and treated accordingly. Until at least the middle of the 19th century, mental illness and mental retardation were poorly distinguished, so those earlier references may have described either or both.

Christianity provided some hope that the situation would change. As early as the 4th century A.D., St. Nicholas Thaumaturges urged giving care to the feeble-minded, the term in use at that time (Kanner, 1964), and beginning in the 13th century churches began to provide asylums for persons who were mentally handicapped (Kott, 1971). However, for the most part they were mistreated, kept in chains or cages, and even put to death. This was particularly likely if, in addition to mental retardation, the individual had obvious physical deformities.

■ The Institutional Movement

The few monasteries and asylums that did provide for persons who were mentally retarded were a great improvement over the treatment provided in early Athens and Sparta, which advocated drowning or throwing "fools" and "monsters" over cliffs and abandoning infants who were physically deformed or appeared to be mentally retarded. However, most church-sponsored asylums did little other than provide sanctuary from society. Then in 1798 three men who were hunting near Aveyron, France, made an unusual discovery. They found a naked boy, apparently 11 or 12 years of age, searching for acorns and other edibles on the forest floor. This "boy-savage" was captured and taken to Abbe Sicard Bonnaterre, a professor of natural history at Aveyron. Bonnaterre named him Victor, pronounced him an incurable idiot, and sent him to Paris for further observation and study.

In Paris, Dr. Jean Marc Gaspard Itard, chief medical officer for the National Institute for the Deaf and Dumb, observed Victor and concluded that his condition was not incurable or irreversible. He ascribed his condition to social and educational neglect and began a program of planned sensation training. Itard's efforts with Victor, who came to be known as the "Wild Boy of Aveyron," were documented in 1801. Though Victor did not respond as Itard had hoped, the scientist's description of his teaching methods led to much more successful efforts on the part of his pupil, Edouard Seguin. In 1850 Seguin emigrated to the United States, where he played a major role in establishing residential facilities for individuals with mental retardation in Pennsylvania, New York, Massachusetts, Ohio, and Connecticut. These early institutions, in both Europe and the United States, were established in the hope that mental retardation might be remediated and patients returned to the community. Though mostly that goal was not realized, Western society had established the principle that the mentally retarded were human beings who should be trained or educated, if possible. Seguin's efforts became the basis of public school classes for students with mental retardation, the next step on the road to present-day services.

■ The 20th Century

Special classes for students with mental retardation became an established part of the public school program in the first half of the 20th century. These were segregated, self-contained classes, and — particularly prior to the development and standardization of the Binet individual test of intelligence in the United States in 1916 — many questions arose about how students should be identified for them. (Of course, some questions still remain.) The early efforts did not, however, include public school programs for individuals with more severe mental retardation.

The period following World War II, when U.S. leaders became fully aware of the details of Hitler's extermination of mentally retarded persons in Nazi Germany and the plight of those in the United States who could not attend public school became evident, brought a number of efforts to change the situation. President Kennedy appointed the National Panel on Mental Retardation in 1961; in 1966, President Johnson appointed the President's Committee on Mental Retardation, and a national movement was under way. The result has been that many individuals with more severe mental retardation who were formerly in institutions are now in the local community, and the public schools play varying roles in their education. More of those students who were called the educable mentally retarded are now in regular classes; there are fewer special classes; and there are more attempts to provide for students classified as mildly handicapped through alternative educational strategies. Above all, we've seen a significant movement toward accepting persons with mental retardation as citizens who require understanding and increased opportunity to live their lives in the most normal possible environment.

Definition and Classification of Mental Retardation

The most widely used definition of mental retardation was developed by the American Association on Mental Retardation (AAMR):[1] "Mental retardation refers

[1] This may be called either the AAMR definition or the AAMD definition, as it was provided in a manual titled *Classification in Mental Retardation* (Grossman, 1983) published by the American Association on Mental Deficiency. In 1987 the AAMD became the AAMR; hence the two possible designations.

EUNICE KENNEDY SHRIVER AND THE SPECIAL OLYMPICS

What brings royalty from Spain and England, First Ladies of a dozen countries, hundreds of Hollywood stars, and thousands of children and adults with mental retardation into one place for fun and games? The Special Olympics.

Eunice Kennedy Shriver recalls that the Special Olympics actually started in her backyard. Some neighborhood children could not go to camp because they were mentally retarded. "We decided to do something with the large backyard we had," she said, adding, "We could teach them to swim, play games, and enjoy the benefits of outdoor exercise similar to that of the other children who were allowed to go to camp. And I decided to see what was being done about encouraging the physical development of people with mental retardation." She found that little was being done and that many thought physical activity for persons with mental retardation was unnecessary. People failed to consider that physical activity requires the mind to develop concepts of discipline and time as well as an awareness of distance and directions. Mind and body work together to benefit both.

Eunice got an opportunity to remedy the situation in 1967. The Chicago Park District considered holding a track meet specifically for persons with mental retardation and contacted her, as vice president of the Joseph P. Kennedy Foundation, for financial support. This was just the type of event she had envisioned. The competition would be patterned after the Greek Olympics but widened to include events such as swimming. It would draw national attention to the athletic accomplishments of the participants—who happened to be mentally retarded. The public would see these individuals in terms of what they could—rather than couldn't—accomplish.

Reactions to the plan were mixed and frequently negative. People assumed that the competition would be too much for the athletes, that they would be fearful and confused in new and crowded surroundings, and that participants who lost would become depressed. Even though she disliked public speaking, Eunice spoke to various groups, encouraging participation. She also arranged for fanfare such as the lighting of the John F. Kennedy Flame of Hope, the participation of bands, parades of the athletes, the raising of the Special Olympics flag, and the release of thousands of balloons— all to highlight the athletes' accomplishments. Special medals were designed for the winners and patches provided for all participants so that no one would go home empty-handed.

Amid the hoopla, Eunice Shriver managed to emphasize an important point: "These games have not been organized as a spectacle. They are not conducted just for fun. The Special Olympics proves a very fundamental fact. The fact that exceptional children—retarded children—can be exceptional athletes. The fact that through sports they can realize their potential for growth. Our purpose here today is to secure a pledge that *all* retarded children will have this chance in the future." She further announced that the Joseph P. Kennedy Foundation would support local, state, and regional Special Olympics and continue to support the International Special Olympics, to be held every two years.

Shortly after this first competition, Special Olympics, Inc., was established; Eunice Shriver was president. Under her direction the Special Olympics has developed into an event in which over 500,000 children and adults from 15 foreign countries participate and to which over 150,000 volunteers contribute time and energy. She has enlisted the help of scores of entertainers and professional athletes. Using her status as the sister of former President John F. Kennedy, she has gained the support and attendance of heads of government.

Eunice Shriver is often asked whether having a sister who is mentally retarded influenced her efforts. She responds that it only made her more determined to do something. "These people are special and you must realize you can't mainstream everyone but give them something with which to find their own dignity and lifestyle. That's what we are trying to accomplish."

Eunice says that, as she travels around the country promoting the Special Olympics, teachers are often in awe of her as the sister of JFK—but the children are more excited because she is the mother-in-law of Arnold Schwarzenegger!

■ A *winner* in Special Olympics. An accomplishment like this adds immeasurably to a person's self-esteem and motivation. ■

to significantly subaverage general intellectual functioning resulting in or associated with concurrent impairments in adaptive behavior and manifested during the developmental period" (Grossman, 1983, p. 11).

"General intellectual functioning" means one's ability to reason, to understand the consequences of one's actions, to make generalizations, to deal with abstractions, and other related abilities thought to reflect "intelligence." For the purposes of applying the AAMR definition, results obtained by one or more of the recognized, individually administered tests of intelligence are ordinarily used to verify the level of intellectual functioning. "Significantly subaverage" is defined as an IQ of 70 or below, but permits clinical judgment to extend this as far as 75. "Impairments in adaptive behavior" means the degree to which an individual meets "the standards of maturation, learning, personal independence, and/or social responsibility" expected for his or her age level and cultural group (Grossman, 1983, p. 11). This may be determined by clinical assessment, which if possible should include the use of a standardized scale. "Developmental period" means the time between conception and the 18th birthday. Note that according to this definition there must be *both* subaverage intellectual functioning *and* impairments in adaptive behavior, and both must have been manifested prior to age 18.

Classification systems for mental retardation often reflect the purpose for such classification and thus tend to reflect the thinking of various professional groups. The two most common classification systems are (1) by degree of severity and (2) by medical etiology. Various versions of the degree-of-severity systems are

Table 4.1 Classifications of mental retardation according to level of intellectual functioning (IQ)

Level	Classification Source	
	American Association on Mental Retardation (1983)	American Psychiatric Association (1987) World Health Organization (1978)
Mild	50–55 to 70–75	50–70
Moderate	35–40 to 50–55	35–49
Severe	20–25 to 35–40	20–34
Profound	Below 20–25	Below 20

used in the public schools and by state agencies that work with persons with mental retardation. The AAMR classification system uses the terminology *mild, moderate, severe,* and *profound.* Table 4.1 lists IQ limits recommended by the AAMR for this system, the comparable limits recommended by the American Psychiatric Association in their *Diagnostic and Statistical Manual of Mental Disorders—Revised* (DMS III-R, 1987), and by the World Health Organization in their *International Classification of Diseases* (1978). Each of these systems specifies related impairments in adaptive behavior. All three systems share similar classification guidelines.

Public schools also classify by degree of severity; however, they utilize a variety of systems having different terminology. Utley, Lowitzer, and Baumeister (1987) reported the results of a study in which the AAMR definition, eligibility criteria, and classification system were compared with those used by state departments of education; they noted wide variations. One of their more interesting findings was that nearly half (44%) substituted some other terminology for *mental retardation.* The upper limits for a classification of mentally retarded (or for any state's version of this term) also varied considerably. This meant a student could be classified as mentally retarded in one state but not another.

As programs developed in the public schools, the more commonly adopted degree-of-severity terms became *educable mentally retarded* (EMR) and *trainable mentally retarded* (TMR). Until the 1970s public schools had very limited contact with individuals with severity levels below the TMR level; if they did, they were often referred to as having severe or profound mental retardation, mirroring the AAMR classifications. Table 4.2 is a summary of the educational classifications established by common usage compared with the AAMR classifications.

Another system of classification, that of medical **etiology,** may be in greater use outside of the education profession. This system relates to causes of mental retardation and assumes that much is due to disease or biological defects. Because educators must work with physicians, social workers, and related professionals who are likely to refer to this system, they should be familiar with it. The ten major classifications, as discussed in *Classification in Mental Retardation* (Grossman, 1983), are described in Table 4.3.

Table 4.2 Educational classification compared with AAMR classifications

Educational Classification	*AAMR Classification*	*General Description of Functioning*
Educable mentally retarded (EMR) IQ range usually 50 to 70–75 (in some states, as high as 80)	Mildly mentally retarded IQ range from 50–55 to 70 (clinical judgment may raise higher than 70)	With appropriate educational opportunities, can learn basic academic skills. Can maintain themselves independently in the community; however, may require minimal assistance. May not be identifiable, when adults, as mentally handicapped.
Trainable mentally retarded (TMR) IQ below 50 (minimum often not specified) Eligibility for programming may depend on other types of functional assessment	Moderate level of mental retardation IQ range from 35–40 to 50–55	Will be limited in achievement of academic skills. Can learn to function successfully in some work settings, with supervision. May require continued community-sponsored assistance and supervision throughout life. Greater variation between individuals at "top" and "bottom" of this classification than in other classification levels.
Many labels used, relating to severe, profound, dependent status as viewed by school	Severe level of mental retardation IQ range from 20–25 to 35–40 Profound level of mental retardation IQ below 20–25	Will require supervision and assistance in almost all aspects of daily living.

Prevalence

How many individuals are classified as mentally retarded? How many should be so classified? How many would be classified as mentally retarded if appropriate identification procedures were initiated nationwide?

The data of Table 2.5 in Chapter 2 indicate that in the *Thirteenth Annual Report to Congress on the Implementation of the Individuals with Disabilities Education Act* (1991), 0.97% of the national public school enrollment, ages 6 to 21, was classified and served as mentally retarded. Perhaps as many as 0.1% to 0.2% more individuals (primarily those classified as severely and profoundly mentally retarded) in this age range were served through some other public or private agency. However, when we look at the data provided by individual states, we find that the state reporting the highest percentage served 2.65% of its age 6 to 21 population as mentally retarded. The state reporting the lowest percentage served only 0.30%.

Table 4.3 Major classifications of mental retardation

Infections and Intoxications:
Prenatal infections such as rubella and syphilis, postnatal viral or bacterial (cerebral) infections, fetal alcohol syndrome, lead poisoning, toxemia of pregnancy

Trauma or Physical Agent:
Prenatal injury, mechanical injury at birth, perinatal or postnatal anoxia

Metabolism or Nutrition:
Tay-Sachs disease, phenylketonuria, Wilson's disease, hypothyroidism

Gross Brain Disease (Postnatal):
von Recklinghausen's disease, tumors, Huntington's disease

Unknown Prenatal Influence:
Microcephalus, hydrocephalus (congenital), cerebral malformation

Chromosomal Anomalies:
Down syndrome, Edward's syndrome, cri-du-chat syndrome, Klinefelter's syndrome, fragile X syndrome

Other Conditions Originating in the Perinatal Period:
Extreme immaturity, slow fetal growth, fetal malnutrition, maternal nutritional disorders, disorders related to long gestation and high birth weight

Following Psychiatric Disorder:
psychosis, other psychiatric disorders as specified

Environmental Influences:
psychosocial disadvantage, sensory deprivation

Other Conditions:
defects of special senses, unknown or ill-defined etiology

Individuals with moderate, severe, or profound levels of mental retardation are more likely to be identified, so it would appear that prevalence data for those levels are more reliable. A review of 20 studies, using an IQ of 50 or below as the criterion, found 3 to 4 per 1000 persons (McLaren & Bryson, 1987).

If we utilize the AAMR definition of mental retardation, which requires an IQ score two standard deviations below the mean, and intelligence tests that relate to the normal curve or standard deviation concept, between 2.5% and 3% of the population could qualify. However, unless those persons exhibited concurrent impairments in adaptive behavior prior to age 18, they would not be classified as mentally retarded.

Grossman (1983) suggests that improvements in adaptive capacities that may develop with age and maturity may account for the reduction of prevalence in the adult community. He further notes that if the real issue is giving assistance to those who need it, we must consider reports indicating that from 10% to 30% of school-age children in very poor rural communities and urban ghettos may fall within the retarded range, whereas in affluent communities, where retardation is more likely to have a biological basis, prevalence rates are much lower. Our conclusion is that the actual occurrence of mental retardation, for all age groups and all degrees of severity, ranges from 1% to 3%.

Major Causes and Potential for Prevention

The medical etiological classifications of mental retardation listed earlier were presented in the sequence utilized by the AAMR classification manual. They summarize the potential causes of mental retardation, but do not speak to the

■ Students with mental retardation participate in aspects of the academic program. The trend among educators is to maximize that participation.   ■

frequency with which each might be found — nor of possible prevention. Causes will be discussed in the following sections in an order that more nearly reflects frequency and includes the potential for prevention.

■ Environmental and Psychosocial Influences

The largest group of individuals identified as mentally retarded are classified as mildly mentally retarded. For most of these individuals there is no known cause, no known organic damage, no recognized medical syndrome. They do not "fit" one of the first eight AAMR medical etiological classifications, and thus must be accounted for by the ninth or tenth causes listed: environmental influences or other conditions. At one time, many of these individuals would have been placed at school age in special classes for the educable (mildly) mentally retarded and have limited contact with other students in the school. After completing whatever schooling was available, they would enter the adult world and many, perhaps most, would marry. Most would have considerably lower-than-average incomes. Some would remain regularly employed, but many would be unemployed a great deal of the time. Today, a larger number of these students will spend much, perhaps all of their time in school in a regular class with nondisabled peers. They may receive special assistance in a resource room, or their teacher may be assisted through the collaborative efforts of a specialist. How different their status in adult life may be has yet to be determined, but it appears that it will be at least somewhat better.

Environmental or psychosocial influences leading to mild mental retardation may be one or a combination of the following: impoverished environment, inadequate diet, inadequate medical care, low birth weight, a history of infectious diseases, atypical parent-child interactions, subnormal intellectual functioning in at least one parent, or other related factors (Grossman, 1983). The most effective prevention is to change as many of those factors as possible. Chapter 12 includes a discussion of early intervention steps that may be taken to prevent or ameliorate mild mental retardation. Chapter 10 includes a discussion of maternal substance abuse–related conditions such as **fetal alcohol syndrome** and damage to the fetus due to the use of cocaine, "crack" cocaine, heroin, or other drugs that may lead to mental retardation or other disabilities. Efforts to provide parents with more information about child care and early childhood development, how to provide a more stimulating environment, and the importance of that environment are viable preventive steps. Better prenatal health care and more widespread availability of genetic counseling (particularly for low-income or low-educational-level parents) will reduce the number of children identified as mildly mentally retarded.

In their discussion of psychosocial factors, Patton, Beirne-Smith, and Payne (1990) note a host of environmental correlates of retardation. They believe that it is essential to focus on this whole cluster of potentially debilitating factors. Among them are low parental educational level, inadequate or inaccurate information about child development, low family income, authoritarianism or inconsistency in parenting practices, lack of intellectual stimulation, excessive or inappropriate stimulation (noise and confusion), health problems, and lack of appropriate health care. These factors overlap, and the presence of one—or several—of them does not mean that mental retardation will result. However, they are proven correlates of mental retardation. Unfortunately, "whether our society is willing to devote the necessary resources to breaking the poverty cycle and altering the effects of psychosocial causes with the goal of reducing the prevalence of retardation is still an unanswered question" (ibid., p. 192).

■ Infections and Intoxications

Infections and **intoxications** are among the major causes of mental retardation; they can lead to mild, moderate, or even severe levels. The extent of retardation is determined by the extent and location of the brain cell damage. Damage may occur during either prenatal or postnatal periods of development, and preventive measures for this cause are relatively straightforward.

Efforts to prevent mental retardation caused by **rubella,** a viral disease, are among the more successful in this arena. Though rubella was recognized as a disease in 1815, its relationship to birth defects was not understood until the early 20th century. Investigations initiated during the 1964 rubella epidemic in the United States highly correlated illness during the first trimester of pregnancy not only with mental retardation but with deafness, heart disease, cataracts and glaucoma, and various neurologic defects.

An effective rubella vaccine has been available since 1969; through its use rubella-related birth defects have been greatly reduced. However, a number of outbreaks of the disease on university campuses in the late 1980s indicates that

■ Despite mental retardation, these girls are able to contribute to society as hospital volunteers. ■

continuing efforts must be made to eliminate the effects of this relatively easy-to-control cause of mental retardation.

Rh incompatibility problems (as when the fetus has an Rh-positive blood type and the mother an Rh-negative) are also a potential cause of mental retardation. Sensitization between the mother and the unborn child may develop, destroying the red blood cells of the fetus; bilirubin is then secreted and deposited in the nerve cells of the basal ganglia of the brain. This process is a bit deceptive in that it may take more than one pregnancy for the sensitization to develop. It is therefore essential to determine the potential for Rh incompatibility.

Remedies include (1) induction of early labor, (2) providing massive amounts of oxygen during and after labor, (3) injections of Rh hapten to prevent antibody formation, (4) blood transfusions to the newborn, and (5) fetal blood transfusions before birth. When Rh incompatibility is suspected, Rh gamma globulin injections can be given to the Rh-negative mother after the birth of her first Rh-positive child, or following a miscarriage. This prevents initial sensitization and thus the formation of destructive antibodies.

Poisons of two general types are recognized causes of mental retardation. One type may be represented by lead poisoning. Fortunately, Congress's passage of the Lead-Based Paint Poisoning Prevention Act (PL 91-695), and related efforts in the early 1970s, have greatly reduced its effect. As older buildings are destroyed, eliminating the hazard of old, lead-based paint, this problem may eventually disappear. In the meantime, we must be alert for other hidden hazards such as manganese, arsenic, and mercury, which may be unrecognized components of other mixtures or compounds.

A second category of poison has become much more visible since about 1980: deliberately ingested poisons such as alcohol, drugs, and narcotics. Maternal substance abuse can lead to a variety of disabilities, including mental retardation, in the child. Problems related to this pattern are discussed in more detail in Chapters 10 and 12. Unlike most other causes of mental retardation, this one results from deliberate actions, taken with limited knowledge and apparently little concern for the possible effects.

■ Trauma or Physical Agents

Several types of **trauma** or physical agents may cause mental retardation, but we will focus on two. **Anoxia** (shortage of oxygen available to the blood) may lead to damage of brain tissue and is one potential cause. Prenatal anoxia, such as that caused by a twisted umbilical cord, and postnatal anoxia, which is more often the result of very high body temperatures, perhaps due to an infection, are both dangers. Either of these—or any event that results in a continuing shortage of oxygen supplied to the brain—may lead to mental retardation due to permanent brain cell damage. Prevention requires an awareness of this possibility and prompt action, for example to reduce high body temperatures.

Perinatal physical damage to the head of the fetus through the improper use of forceps can also cause mental retardation. Sadly, postnatal damage through child abuse may be a cause of increasing significance. Authorities are not in complete agreement about whether physical child abuse is actually on the increase, but Scheerenberger, in a review of growing issues in the medical treatment of mental retardation, refers to an "unparalleled, unjustified, and unequivocal explosion in the incidence of child abuse" (1987, p. 58). Earlier, Brandwein (1973) had estimated that there were as many as 170,000 cases of permanent brain injury annually resulting from child abuse; if there has truly been the explosion suggested by Scheerenberger, this is an increasing major cause of mental retardation. Mental retardation caused by physical abuse is ordinarily due to head injuries. Prevention requires awareness, prompt reporting of suspected cases, and appropriate action by authorities responsible for child protection in the local community.

■ Disorders of Metabolism or Nutrition

Disorders of metabolism or nutrition include some of the better-known conditions, many of which are subject to prevention. Hypothyroidism is the most prevalent of the metabolic disorders. Replacement of the thyroid hormone reduces the symptoms of hypothyroidism; without such treatment, "most hypothyroid newborns would become severely mentally retarded" (Scheerenberger, 1987, p. 63). Early identification, with appropriate treatment begun within weeks after birth, can greatly reduce the potentially devastating effects of hypothyroidism.

Phenylketonuria (PKU) is a second well-known metabolic disorder. Phenylalanine is an essential, naturally occurring amino acid (protein) found in many foods but particularly in milk. When an infant with this disorder receives a normal milk diet, levels of phenylalanine rise rapidly and can be detected as early as within two days. PKU is detected through a simple **screening** procedure now mandated in most states. With early detection, treatment often completely eliminates the otherwise serious effects. Treatment consists of a phenylalanine-restricted diet that creates a balance between essential amino acids. PKU received considerable national attention in the popular press once the condition and successful prevention diets for it were discovered, so most hospitals now screen newborns for both PKU and hypothyroidism. The general public may be familiar with the word *phenylalanine* because of the relatively prominent warning on most cans of diet soda, reading "phenylketonurics: contains phenylalanine." This kind of labeling reflects our growing awareness of the influence of various foods, chemicals, and especially food additives on our health.

Koch et al. (1988) report that all 50 states screen for PKU and hypothyroidism but that only about 20 have a mandatory, statewide screening program for all of the metabolic disorders that can be detected by existing broad-screen techniques. When metabolic disorders are discovered later, due to other symptoms, it is usually too late to prevent mental retardation.

■ **Chromosomal Anomalies**

Down syndrome is the most common of the chromosomal abnormalities that may cause moderate to severe mental retardation (Epstein, 1988). It is also the syndrome connected with the outward appearance that much of the general public relates to mental retardation. The physical characteristics are as follows:

> The back of the head is often flattened, the eyelids may be slightly slanted, small skin folds at the inner corners of the eyes may be present, the nasal bridge is slightly depressed, and the nose and ears are usually somewhat smaller. . . . The hands and the feet are small and the fingerprints are often different from chromosomally normal children. (Manfredini, 1988, p. 1)

About 95% of individuals with Down syndrome have trisomy 21, meaning that an extra chromosome is connected with chromosome 21 (that is, rather than a 21st *pair* of chromosomes, there are *three*—thus the designation *tri*somy 21). Some cases are genetic in origin, but other factors such as maternal viral infections, exposure to radiation or chemicals, or the absence of a mechanism for spontaneous abortion of a damaged fetus are possible causal or related factors. Some have estimated that in 20% to 25% of all cases the father contributes the extra chromosome (Abroms & Bennett, 1980), but others have questioned this (Carlson, 1984).

Down syndrome was first described by Dr. John L. Down in 1866, but it was not until 1959 that the chromosomal abnormality associated with the syndrome was discovered (Manfredini, 1988). According to Epstein, "Approximately one in

Table 4.4 Occurrence of Down syndrome according to age of mother

Mother's Age	Occurrence
Below 25	One in every 1500 to 2000 births
Over 35	One in every 400 births
Over 45	One in every 40 births

800–1000 newborns is born with this condition and, with improved medical care and social management, a large fraction of these individuals will survive well into their adult years" (1988, p. 35). This is in contrast to much shorter life spans just a few decades ago.

Manfredini indicates that "Down syndrome is the most common clinical cause of mental retardation in the world" (1988, p. 1). She also provides estimates of the likelihood of occurrence according to the mother's age, the most significant predictor of Down syndrome in the general population (see Table 4.4).

The most common prevention for Down syndrome is **genetic counseling,** sharing information such as the fact that the mother of a child with Down syndrome has a 1-in-25 chance of having another.

Because it is a common cause of mental retardation, and because it is easy to diagnose (with obvious early physical characteristics), a great deal of research has been done with individuals with Down syndrome. Advances in health care, particularly the advent of antibiotics, have tended to lengthen dramatically the life span of individuals with Down syndrome. Educational programs at the very early childhood level have led to the development of higher levels of intellectual functioning than was considered possible, but prevention efforts have not been particularly fruitful. A better understanding of the mechanisms of chromosomal imbalance seems to offer the greatest hope (Epstein, 1988).

A second chromosomal anomaly, more recently identified, is the fragile X syndrome (de la Cruz, 1985). This may account for the cause of some cases of mental retardation that were previously inexplicable; it thus deserves continuing research and attention (Patton, Beirne-Smith, & Payne, 1990). Its physical characteristics include prominent jaws, long and thin faces, soft ears, fleshy hands, prominent foreheads, and enlarged heads. Fragile X syndrome is associated primarily with males having severe and profound levels of mental retardation.

The Relationship between Environmental and Organic Causes

Although an individual's mental retardation may be the result of a single cause, it is often the result of several. Typically, environmental factors such as poverty, the absence of proper prenatal care, or a lack of knowledge of child development or appropriate parenting practices lead to, combine with, or exacerbate organic causes. Lack of preconception preventive measures, inattention to prenatal care during pregnancy, lack of care during and immediately following delivery, and factors related to nutritional insufficiencies, lack of understanding of environmental hazards, or outright neglect or abuse during early childhood are all contributory factors.

■ Biomedical Prevention and Treatment

Prevention has been discussed with respect to specific etiological classifications, but it may also be grouped by interventions during preconception, during gestation, at delivery, and during early childhood (Patton, Beirne-Smith, & Payne, 1990). These interventions may be effective with respect to many different causal factors, but all require an awareness of the need for and availability of such measures.

Prior to conception, genetic counseling can provide information regarding the risk of occurrence or recurrence of genetic or chromosomal disorders. Counseling about the mother's nutrition, use of alcohol or drugs, and age in relation to risks may also be of value. Screening procedures can provide information about the possibility of recessive trait disorders, and blood tests can determine the presence of syphilis or other venereal diseases. All such information will help prospective parents make more informed decisions.

During pregnancy a number of preventive measures may be initiated. Using alcohol or drugs and exposure to radiation can be avoided. The general nutritional status of the mother is important, as is her protection from disease. In addition, the fetus may be analyzed for possible genetic or chromosomal disorders, through amniocentesis, chorion villus sampling, and ultrasound tests. In **amniocentesis,** amniotic fluid is drawn from the amniotic sac surrounding the fetus, permitting analysis of fetal cells. This procedure is of primary value in detecting chromosomal flaws, and is usually completed between the 14th and 16th week of pregnancy. In chorion villus sampling (CVS), chorionic tissue, or placental material, is sampled and analyzed for chromosomal or other biochemical anomalies. CVS can be performed after only nine weeks of gestation, thus providing earlier information than that available through amniocentesis.

Amniocentesis or CVS may assure the parents that all is well with respect to a variety of specific disorders, may confirm the existence of a disorder, or may suggest additional monitoring. When a specific disorder such as Down syndrome or Tay-Sachs disease is confirmed, this information can be used in counseling to permit parents to consider options such as elective abortion.

Ultrasound techniques project an image of the fetus and the placenta on a screen, thereby providing valuable early information with respect to limb anomalies, certain central nervous system disorders, or **hydrocephalus.** Ultrasound imaging also shows the exact location of the fetus, which is of value for amniocentesis.

During delivery, the most important factor may be adequate anticipation of potential problems. If the delivering physician is aware of risk factors—such as a history of stillbirths, previous children with birth defects, conditions such as diabetes in the mother, or blood incompatibility between mother and fetus—problems can be averted.

Prevention of mental retardation during early childhood depends on a knowledge of hazards in the child's environment (chemicals, lead poisons, and so on) and how to minimize their effects. It also requires an understanding of the need for proper nutrition, an avoidance of situations that might lead to head injuries, and proper care in the case of prolonged high body temperatures that could induce anoxia. If the child has a diagnosed metabolic disorder requiring a special diet, it is essential that the diet be maintained.

■ Any child who must live in environmental conditions such as these is at risk of diminished intellectual development. ■

Characteristics of Mental Retardation

Children with severe and profound levels of mental retardation are often "self-identifying." Their disability is obvious—in many cases within a few days after birth, and at least by age 1 or 2. Children with moderate mental retardation may be identified at an early age, particularly if the retardation is associated with a specific syndrome, but it is more difficult to generalize about their identification. Children with mild mental retardation are much more difficult to identify, especially at an early age. Once they attend school they will have difficulty making normal academic progress: learning to read, learning basic number facts, understanding content in subject areas, and so on. They may also have difficulty developing self-care skills and will have less-than-normal language competence.

The following are generalizations about characteristics of students with mental retardation. The degree to which these characteristics are present will vary greatly, according to the severity of the disability. Their presence does not necessarily indicate mental retardation, but it may indicate the need for further informal or formal assessment.

■ Personal and Social Skill Deficits

These are a leading characteristic of students identified as mentally retarded. Unless such "impairments in adaptive behavior" are present, as specified in the official definition (Grossman, 1983), an individual cannot be identified as mentally retarded. This may reflect an overall conclusion, based on multiple criteria, that the student is unusually immature. It may mean that when given a choice, he or she consistently plays or interacts only with younger children, may not be able to handle conflict situations, cannot take care of personal needs as well as his or her age peers can, cannot interpret social signals, and has other similar difficulties.

■ Lack of General Academic Performance

The most usual reason that children are referred for assessment regarding mental retardation is poor academic progress. If a 9-year-old girl in fourth grade were achieving at about the same level as other students in the class, she would not be classified as having mental retardation. If she were significantly retarded academically, she *might* be classified as mentally retarded, but her academic problems could result from many other factors. If, for example, her low academic performance was in reading but her achievement was normal in mathematics, it is highly unlikely that she would be classified as mentally retarded.

■ Memory Deficits

Research over the years indicates that, once they learn information, individuals with mental retardation are no more likely to forget it than anyone else (Polloway, Payne, Patton, & Payne, 1985). However, their short-term memory (information stored for only a few seconds to a few hours) appears to be considerably poorer than that of their normal peers (Borkowski, Peck, & Damberg, 1983; Ellis, 1970).

■ Below-Average Language Ability

This may be manifested in a limited breadth and depth of vocabulary, an inability to use more complex syntax, or a limited understanding of the nuances of meaning. Language ability will usually lag progressively behind that of age peers as students go through school.

■ Below-Average Ability to Generalize and Conceptualize

This specific characteristic of mental retardation may show up as difficulty in generalizing with respect to both academically oriented topics—such as mathematical concepts or those like justice or democracy—and personal or social skills—such as how to interact with others in a social setting.

■ **Limited Ability to Deal with Abstractions**

Difficulty in learning abstract concepts such as spatial ones (on, in, under, beside, top, middle) or size comparisons (longer, shorter, big, bigger, biggest) may lead to a variety of other difficulties. The abstract concepts involved in mathematics also pose problems. Most students with mild mental retardation will master the more elementary concepts, but will do so later than their age peers. Many mathematical concepts will never be mastered by individuals with severe or profound mental retardation. This limited ability to deal with abstractions leads to basic difficulty in spoken language development and reading, as well.

These six characteristics are almost certain to be found in students with mental retardation. In addition, Patton, Beirne-Smith, and Payne (1990) suggest the following deficits: (1) in observational learning, (2) in organizing information, and (3) in motivation, including the expectancy of failure.

Developmental Disabilities

A term that overlaps *mental retardation* and that in some cases has been used interchangeably with it is *developmental disabilities*. Grossman defines a developmental disability as "a disability associated with mental retardation, cerebral palsy, epilepsy, or another neurological condition of an individual that is closely related to mental retardation or requires similar treatment and that originates in early childhood, is likely to continue, and constitutes a substantial handicap to the individual" (1983, p. 168). A similar but more extensive definition was provided in Public Law 98-527, the Developmentally Disabled Assistance and Bill of Rights Act (1984):

> A severe chronic disability of a person which (a) is attributable to a mental or physical impairment or combination of mental or physical impairment; (b) is manifested before the person attains age twenty-two; (c) is likely to continue indefinitely; (d) results in substantial functional limitations in three or more of the following areas of major life activity: (i) self-care, (ii) receptive and expressive language, (iii) learning, (iv) mobility, (v) self-direction, (vi) capacity for independent living, (vii) economic self-sufficiency; and (e) reflects the person's need for a combination and sequence of special, interdisciplinary, or generic care, treatment, or other services which are of lifelong or extended duration and are individually planned and coordinated.

According to this federal definition, developmental disabilities is a somewhat more inclusive label than mental retardation, because technically a person could be developmentally disabled yet have only physical disabilities. The level of disability implied would effectively exclude individuals who are mildly mentally retarded, unless they had severe physical disabilities. In practice, almost all persons served under this and related legislation could also be classified as mentally retarded.

Many state programs for the mentally retarded are under the auspices of a state agency for the developmentally disabled; that is, the latter terminology is used rather than the former. This is probably the result of two factors: (1) some persons feel the term *developmental disabilities* is preferable to *mental retardation,* and (2) federal legislation referring to developmental disabilities (and providing dollars for such programs) has led some state-level personnel to adopt this terminology, even though the related legislation did not require such a change.

Identification of school-age students is likely to take place according to the process shown in Figure 2.2. Once formal, individual assessment is decided on, a variety of assessment instruments may be utilized; these must include an appropriate individual test of intelligence and a measure of adaptive behavior. (These will be discussed further in this section.) However, many children with more severe mental retardation will have been identified at the preschool level. In some instances, even before birth mental retardation may have been suspected—after amniocentesis or chorion villus sampling, for example.

In some cases, identification of mental retardation or of being **at risk** for it may be based on screening tests, including both chemical tests and surveys of physical characteristics. Or parents may make a tentative identification based on their knowledge of normal child development and have it verified long before schooling begins.

In addition several other diagnostic procedures—including neuroimaging (through ultrasound, digital radiography, nuclear magnetic resonance, and other procedures), which permit examination of the brain and its metabolism—are used at various ages, to better understand causation and decide on possible remedial measures (Menolascino & Stark, 1988). These procedures and others are important advances in the identification, understanding, and, in some cases, prevention of mental retardation.

■ **The Assessment of Intelligence**

Debate continues about almost everything concerned with the concept of intelligence, including whether it can or should be measured, whether existing tests are biased in favor of certain cultural groups, and whether existing tests measure aptitude, achievement, experience, capacity, or acquired knowledge. Early intelligence tests were based on the concept of intelligence as a single trait; more recently this has been generally discredited. But whatever the questions and concerns, a measure that provides some indication of level of intellectual functioning is essential to meet the definition of mental retardation. The two measures most commonly used with children and youth, and most generally accepted with respect to intelligence, are the Stanford-Binet Intelligence Scale (Thorndike, Hagen, & Sattler, 1986) and the Wechsler tests: the Wechsler Preschool and Primary Scales of Intelligence (Wechsler, 1967) and the Wechsler Intelligence Scale for Children—Revised (Wechsler, 1974). The Wechsler Adult Intelligence Scale—Revised (Wechsler, 1981) is the most widely used test for persons over 16.

McLoughlin and Lewis indicate that the WISC-R "is the individual test most often used to assess general intellectual performance of school-aged individuals" (1990, p. 192). The following summary of the subtests of the WISC-R will indicate what this test attempts to assess and how it does so. It also provides a fairly accurate picture of the nature of tests of intellectual ability. The WISC-R is divided into two major sections, a Verbal Scale and a Performance Scale.

Verbal scale

1. *Information.* Answers to these 30 questions require factual knowledge. They include questions reflecting formal educational experience as well as some related to general life experience.

2. *Similarities.* The test taker must indicate how 2 words in each of 17 word pairs are similar. Success presumably indicates logical thinking.

3. *Arithmetic.* These 18 practical arithmetic problems require a response without paper-and-pencil computation.

4. *Vocabulary.* The meaning of 32 words, taken from a master list arranged in order of increasing difficulty, must be stated. This reflects both school experience and the home environment.

5. *Comprehension.* The subject must have practical information and the ability to evaluate past experiences to solve 17 problem situations. This is thought to be a test of "common sense."

6. *Digit Span.* This "alternative test" may be substituted for others. A series of digits must be repeated both forward and backward after it is heard only once.

Performance scale

1. *Picture Completion.* For 26 incomplete drawings of common objects, the subject must identify missing elements. This may test the ability to differentiate between the essential and nonessential; in some respects it tests visual memory.

2. *Picture Arrangement.* The subject must place individual panels of cartoons into a logical sequence, so as to "tell a story." These 12 cartoon sets require the interpretation of social situations and are thus intended to measure one's ability to "size up" a total situation.

3. *Block Design.* Sets of blocks must be arranged to match pictures of designs. These 11 sets are believed to reveal an ability to analyze and synthesize information.

4. *Object Assembly.* Four jigsaw puzzles of well-known objects must be assembled. This permits observation of the subject's general approach to tasks and reaction to mistakes; it also demonstrates capability with respect to various visual and motor functions.

5. *Coding.* The subject must match numbers and symbols by referring to a code, which may be kept in view. This subtest is scored for both speed and accuracy.

6. *Mazes.* This alternative to the coding subtest requires the subject to "find the way out" of a maze. Success depends on planning and on the ability to follow a visual pattern.

The WISC-R is "the standard against which other measures of cognitive abilities have been judged for the last three decades" (Witt, Elliott, Gresham, & Kramer, 1988, p. 168). It is used extensively to determine eligibility for programs for the mentally retarded as well as for the gifted and talented. However, a low score on the WISC-R is not in itself sufficient for classification as mentally retarded. A corroborating measure of adaptive behavior must also be obtained.

■ **The Assessment of Adaptive Behavior**

The use or misuse of intelligence tests has played a major role in litigation over inappropriate placement in classes for the mentally retarded (see the discussion of classification- and labeling-related litigation in Chapter 1). However, most assessment authorities would agree that existing individual tests of intelligence are excellent compared with what we have to measure **adaptive behavior.** Grossman comments that "much more experience must be accumulated in the utilization of adaptive behavior scales and their scores for the same degree of confidence to be placed in them as is currently placed in the use of intelligence measures" (1983, p. 157). One of the more generous assessments, by Taylor,

PREPARATION FOR INDEPENDENT LIVING

Preparation for adult life for individuals with mental retardation begins early and includes instruction in social, leisure, and daily living activities. Skills related to employment are also of importance. With appropriate training, many adults with mental retardation can be gainfully employed. To be most effective, work-related emphasis and training should be initiated early in the public school program and should include maximum involvement in the community.

Volunteer work can provide an important learning experience.

Early participation in social and leisure activities leads to enhanced self-concept and greater enjoyment of adult life.

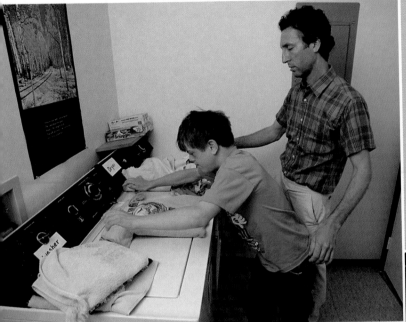

Learning to do the laundry is a step toward independence.

In addition to skills and competencies that are obviously related to various employment options, social skills are of great importance. Other essential learning includes understanding the role of the supervisor, how to follow directions, how to ask for assistance as needed, and how to get along with fellow workers. Individuals with mental retardation can, and do, learn specific job skills and become highly valued employees.

Weighing meat for a sandwich involves several important skills.

Ability to operate a computer can be of value in a variety of employment settings.

One critical area of learning relates to how to respond to various problem situations. Experience indicates that with proper instruction, specific responses can be learned. A number of restaurant chains have participated in cooperative training programs that have been highly successful in preparing individuals with mental retardation for competitive employment, and additional programs of this type are begun each year. In addition, restaurant owners and manufacturers have assisted local groups, such as the Association for Retarded Citizens, to establish training programs associated with sheltered workshops and work activity centers.

Any activity that promotes self-concept can be of value.

Learning to do things right can be fun. It can also require careful attention to the task at hand.

Contract work often involves sorting activities.

Contract work within a sheltered work setting can provide employment in relation to tasks such as sorting and packaging. Although not as beneficial to the individual as employment that provides more contact with nondisabled adults, it is certainly much better than the "warehousing" of individuals with mental retardation that was so common in the recent past. More discussion of preparation for the transition from school to adulthood may be found in Chapter 13 of this text.

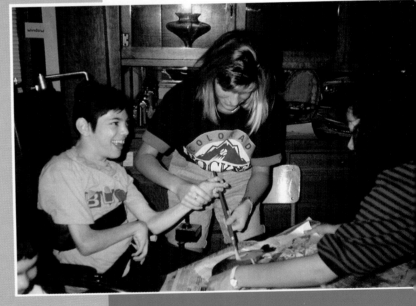

Preparation for participation in leisure activities is a key element in preparation for adult life.

notes that "[adaptive behavior] is a difficult construct to operationalize and subsequently, to measure" (1985, p. 1). Salvia and Ysseldyke list three "severe problems in the use of currently available instruments to assess adaptive behavior" (1988, p. 430). These are (1) the lack of a professional consensus about what constitutes adaptive behavior; (2) existing scales of adaptive behavior that require rating or completion by someone very familiar with the subject, thus introducing possibilities for bias ranging from ignorance to inaccurate statements; and (3) adaptive behavior scales that are typically poorly normed and of limited reliability.

Most adaptive behavior scales gather information from informants rather than by direct measurement. Teachers may be asked to complete a written questionnaire; parents are more often questioned through interviews. The areas included in the AAMD Adaptive Behavior Scale—School Edition (Lambert, Windmiller, Tharinger, & Cole, 1981), are shown in Table 4.5. This relatively all-inclusive scale demonstrates the types of concerns on which adaptive behavior scales focus.

Scoring procedures for this scale permit comparison with a normal population, a population of individuals considered mildly retarded, or one considered moderately retarded. The 21 domains are grouped into five major areas: personal self-sufficiency, community self-sufficiency, personal–social self-responsibility, personal adjustment, and social adjustment. As with other adaptive behavior measures, a great deal of the value of this assessment depends directly on the objectivity of the respondent.

Educational Programming

In the following discussion we mean education in its broadest sense, including activities that might be called training by some. All such activities require planning, careful implementation, and regular monitoring to ensure that IEP goals are met. Monitoring and reevaluation are also essential; they form the basis for planning and implementing any needed revisions.

■ Social Skills Instruction

As we have seen, deficits in personal and social skills are a common characteristic of students identified as mentally retarded. Some deficits exist regardless of the severity of retardation. As Sargent notes, "for most children and adolescents, social competence develops through incidental learning and intellectual maturation. Unfortunately, children and youth with cognitive delays are notoriously inadequate in their incidental learning ability" (1991, p. 3). Sargent further notes the many negative long-term consequences of the social rejection that often results from undeveloped or underdeveloped social skills. He strongly recommends proactive teaching of social skills rather than reactive treatment of social deficits. Consistent with this belief, Sargent developed a program of systematic instruction for children and youth with cognitive delays, which was originally published by the Iowa Department of Public Instruction. Due to its wide acceptance in the field, the Division on Mental Retardation—Council for Exceptional Children published a revised version (1991) that provides direct instructional techniques for various age levels, making this program available on a national basis. Sargent's program included suggestions for teaching in a number of major

Table 4.5 Areas assessed through use of the AAMD Adaptive Behavior Scale, School Edition

Domain 1. Independent Functioning
  eating
  toilet use
  cleanliness
  appearance
  care of clothing
  dressing and undressing
  travel
  other independent functioning
Domain 2. Physical Development
  sensory development
  motor development
Domain 3. Economic Activity
  money handling and budgeting
  shopping skills
Domain 4. Language Development
  expression
  comprehension
  social language development
Domain 5. Numbers and Time
Domain 6. Prevocational Activity
Domain 7. Self-Direction
  initiative
  perseverance
  leisure time
Domain 8. Responsibility
Domain 9. Socialization
Domain 10. Aggressiveness
Domain 11. Antisocial Versus Social Behavior
Domain 12. Rebelliousness
Domain 13. Trustworthiness
Domain 14. Withdrawal Versus Involvement
Domain 15. Mannerisms
Domain 16. Interpersonal Manners
Domain 17. Acceptability of Vocal Habits
Domain 18. Acceptability of Habits
Domain 19. Activity Level
Domain 20. Symptomatic Behavior
Domain 21. Use of Medications

SOURCE: Lambert, N. M., Windmiller, M., Tharinger, D., & Cole, L. (1981). *AAMD Adaptive Behavior Scale—School Edition.* Monterey, CA: CTB Macmillan/McGraw-Hill.

social skills areas, organized by primary, intermediate, middle school or junior high, and senior high levels. For example, for intermediate-level classroom-related skills, there are lessons on following classroom rules, cooperating with a work partner, ignoring distractions, staying with the task during desk work, completing work on time, participating politely in a classroom discussion, making relevant remarks during class discussion, following verbal directions, and following written directions. This type of social skills instruction is a basic part of any carefully planned program for students with mental retardation, regardless of its severity. However, certain generalizations about educational programming may be related to the level of retardation and merit separate discussion by level.

Many students with mild mental retardation are served primarily in the regular classroom with resource room support as required; however, 1988 to 1989 data reported in the *Thirteenth Annual Report to Congress on the Implementation of the Individuals with Disabilities Education Act* (1991) indicated that 58.9% of children age 6 to 21 with mental retardation were served in a separate class. Another 11.4% were served in a separate school. Though some students with more severe levels of mental retardation were undoubtedly included in the 58.9% figure, it would seem likely that most had mild mental retardation. We mention these specific data because general statements from a number of sources starting in the mid-1980s seemed to indicate that the majority of students with mild mental retardation were served in the regular class. All indications are that the trend is in that direction, but how soon such statements may be accurate remains to be seen.

A major complication has been that as the number of students classified as mildly mentally retarded has decreased—due to the lowering of the upper IQ

People Who Make a Difference

JERRY COLLINS, "THE COACH" Swimming, softball, volleyball, and basketball coach all rolled into one—that's Jerry Collins. Jerry teaches students with moderate and severe or profound levels of mental retardation at Ruby Van Meter School in Des Moines, Iowa. His instruction goes beyond teaching the usual skills associated with various sports. For example, he developed a device that, when fitted on students' heads, enables them to keep their heads down while swimming. When traditional flotation devices failed to work for some students with physical disabilities, he designed some from motorcycle inner tubes to meet their special needs.

Jerry saw the need for and instigated a booster club for his school, a public high school special education facility. The club raises funds for uniforms and other athletic equipment, just like booster clubs in the other high schools in Des Moines.

From Jerry's point of view, the Special Olympics is another opportunity for students to practice social skills and to build motivation and self-esteem. For example, the volleyball competition is held an hour's drive from Des Moines. Jerry takes the students to Ames the night before so that they can stay at a motel, eat at a non–fast-food restaurant, and see a college volleyball game. Funds from the booster club pay for the adventure.

To make all this work, Jerry has had to mow baseball fields because the city didn't, transport students to and from meets and practices when parents couldn't, wash uniforms, and give up his spring breaks because competitions take place at that time. Understanding that former students also value such experiences, he has helped establish a Special Olympics program for adults.

Attitudes are changing throughout the state as a result of Jerry's efforts. At the state basketball championships held at the University of Iowa, the high school teams attend a formal dinner each year. Another coach, when asked why his players were dressed in suits and ties for the first time, said "We saw the team from Ruby Van Meter School last year and we wanted to look like them."

■   Concrete materials are important.   ■

level for such classification—the overall functional level of students actually so identified or classified has also decreased. This has made the move toward mainstreaming, or more complete inclusion in regular classrooms, more difficult. In effect, some students who would in earlier years have been identified as educable mentally retarded have now been permanently mainstreamed and may receive no special attention or assistance. Reflecting on this phenomenon, Mac-Millan and Borthwick commented that "mainstreaming is feasible for only a very small percentage of the mentally retarded population when a restrictive definition is employed, such as is the case in California today" (1980, p. 158). Others have taken issue with this statement; the debate remains open. Much depends on the functional level of the students identified as mildly mentally retarded; given the considerable state-to-state variation, it is very difficult to generalize about or accurately predict the future.

Instructional needs are the same, wherever students are placed, but in practice certain types of instruction may be more effectively provided in certain settings. The setting—that is, the placement—must remain the least restrictive in which appropriate instruction can be provided. However, regardless of setting, certain generalizations can be made about the nature of instruction and related program planning. The recommendations that follow are based on the assumption that students need specific, individually planned interventions.

1. Attention must be given to opportunities for learning in nonclassroom settings. This would include, but not be limited to, the playground, cafeteria, hallways, school programs, and field trips.

2. All feasible possibilities for building motivation should be used.

3. Concrete rather than abstract instructional materials should be used whenever possible, particularly when introducing new ideas or improving basic skills.

4. Prompt and systematic feedback should be provided with respect to both academic tasks and social behavior.

5. Learning tasks should be analyzed for required readiness and ability levels. Learning tasks should not be initiated until readiness is achieved and unless the student has the requisite abilities.

6. The need to generalize or conceptualize in order to do any given task must be considered. If a student may not be able to handle that degree of generalization or conceptualization, the task should be reformulated at a simpler level.

7. A modified student evaluation and progress reporting system that is appropriate to both general instructional goals and actual instructional practice in the student's modified or adapted program should be used.

8. Individually designed **career education**–related efforts should be an important consideration in program planning. This should begin at the elementary school level.

9. Formal planning for the **transition program** must begin at least by age 16, often earlier. (Chapter 13 includes an expanded discussion of such planning.)

10. Work experience–type programming should be considered at the secondary level, providing an opportunity for students to work in various types of employment in the community.

11. Adapted instruction covering marriage and family responsibilities, citizenship, and related information with regard to life after graduation is essential.

Certain other guidelines for general curriculum emphasis are also applicable and should be observed in long-range planning of curriculum content, flow, and sequence. At the early childhood level, emphasis should be on experiences that provide for the maximum development of cognitive, psychomotor, and social skills. Those skills essential to success in kindergarten and the primary grades must receive special emphasis. Language experience is particularly important.

Basic academic skills must be emphasized throughout the formal educational program. Because of these students' predictable difficulty in adaptive behavior, their social interactions must be carefully monitored throughout the school years; in many cases, social skills that other students tend to learn automatically must be systematically taught to students with mild mental retardation.

At the secondary level it must be decided, on an individual basis, whether continuing emphasis should be primarily academic or functional—emphasizing work skills, money management, and the like. This decision will guide further educational planning. An additional need is for specific transitional planning, which is a required component of the IEP. Consideration must be given to local or state requirements for graduation, and for many students some type of supervised work program in the community will become a major facet of the last year or two of secondary programming.

These guidelines and suggestions are applicable to planning for all students with mild mental retardation. Additional, specific planning is needed to conform to the IEP developed for each student. The description of Susan and MariAnn in

**Box 4.1
Susan and
MariAnn, Two
16-Year-Old
Students**

Susan
Age: 16 years
Program: first year in senior high special program, with limited enrollment in adapted regular classes
Years in school: 11
Physical health: good
Full-scale WISC-R IQ: 65

MariAnn
Age: 16 years
Program: first year in senior high special program, with limited enrollment in adapted regular classes
Years in school: 11
Physical health: good
Full-scale WISC-R IQ: 66

Based on these data, Susan and MariAnn might be expected to be relatively similar in school performance. Each was referred as a result of significant academic problems near the close of the third year in school (second grade). At that time, Susan's IQ was recorded as 62, MariAnn's as 68. Measures of adaptive behavior supported identification of both girls as educable mentally retarded. Each was placed in a special program at the start of third grade. During their elementary school years, each spent approximately 2 hours each day in a special resource room and the remainder of the day in regular class.

Susan and MariAnn have lived in the same city throughout their 11 years of school attendance and have been in the same school and same resource room program since they moved to middle school. Other information indicates that the program quality in the two different elementary schools that they attended was essentially the same.

There are no known serious family problems in either family, and parents have been generally cooperative with school officials through the years. Both girls are from White, middle-class families.

But here the similarity ends.

Susan is reading at the upper fourth-grade level, according to standardized achievement tests. She can recognize the words included in the special program reading curriculum (relating to employment, voting, family responsibility, and practical, daily living skills), and next year will move into phase one of the work experience program with excellent preparation. She is successful in the adapted vocational education program taught by a regular class teacher and is as skilled as most other students in her school, including nondisabled students, in interpersonal relations. She has learned that she will be rejected or ignored by some students, but she does not

Box 4.1 illustrates the variation in program needs that often exists between two students who may on the surface appear to be quite similar.

■ Moderate Mental Retardation

It is generally accepted that students with moderate mental retardation can benefit from a program that will prepare them for semi-independent or supervised living and employment situations. Self-care skills like toileting, dressing, eating, and grooming receive primary attention, along with physical development and oral or signed communication (Patton, Beirne-Smith, & Payne, 1990). As the school program progresses, social behaviors and improving the quality of inter-

(continued)

make an issue of their behavior. Susan's speaking vocabulary is somewhat below that of other students her age but not notably so in most normal social situations. (This discrepancy would be noticeable if she were enrolled in some of the advanced classes in her school, but she is not.) In most respects, in the large school Susan attends, she does not appear different.

MariAnn is reading at the middle second-grade level, according to standardized achievement tests. She has difficulty in reading approximately 50% of the words included in the special program reading curriculum, and she will not likely be ready for phase one of the work experience program for at least two years. MariAnn experiences her greatest difficulty in the adapted vocational education program, where the teacher says, "She has difficulty reading our low vocabulary materials, but her biggest problem is understanding the concepts involved." MariAnn socializes with a few students in the special program but is not well accepted, even by many of the special program students. She has essentially no acceptance by nondisabled students. MariAnn's speaking vocabulary is very limited, and she has often attempted to become part of a conversation only to be rejected because her comments make her appear different. Even with specific suggestions from her teacher, she cannot seem to anticipate such situations.

Perhaps the most important understanding to be gained from the comparison of Susan and MariAnn is that students classified as EMR may perform very differently in regard to both academic achievement and social competence, regardless of similarity of test scores or other variables generally recognized as important. As such students progress through their educational program, projections of educational and social ability and success may become more reliable, but at ages 6, 7, and 8, predictions of future success may be inaccurate. Certain generalizations may be made based on valid test results and environmental and sociological data, but these are only generalizations. Variations in performance are undoubtedly just as great among students diagnosed as EMR as they are among the so-called normal student population.

SOURCE: Reprinted with the permission of Merrill, an imprint of Macmillan Publishing Company, from *The Exceptional Student in the Regular Classroom*, Fifth Edition, by Bill R. Gearheart, Mel Weishahn, and Carol J. Gearheart. Copyright © 1992 by Macmillan Publishing Company.

personal interactions are targeted, along with the development of functional academics such as recognition of signs relating to safety (Stop, Poison, Danger, Exit) or to successful community integration (Men, Women, Ladies' Room). Recognizing and writing one's name, address, phone number, and related information are also stressed.

Many authorities recommend developing a curriculum based on information collected from parents and other professionals in contact with the student, and on the specifics of the home and community environments in which the student is now and will eventually be expected to function. Such information should be systematically collected, recorded, and analyzed to permit the development of a meaningful IEP. In addition, information on current levels of performance in the various curricula is required to establish a useful summary of what students can presently do, what they can do with assistance, and what they must learn for a greater degree of self-sufficiency. A number of published adaptive behavior scales and behavioral checklists are helpful in this evaluation.

Throughout their school years, students with moderate mental retardation can benefit from interaction with their nondisabled age peers. Interaction is encouraged by matching them with nondisabled students who volunteer to be a friend or buddy, through school clubs, or through other, similar arrangements. In one-on-one arrangements, it is important that the nondisabled student be a volunteer and know in advance that he or she can discontinue the arrangement without recrimination from teachers. It is equally important that some information and orientation be provided these volunteers. Another avenue to promote interaction is peer tutoring. The nondisabled students should again be volunteers and must be taught how to teach students with moderate mental retardation. Usually a simplified program of prompting and reinforcement is utilized, following a task analysis. Research by Haring, Breen, Pitts-Conway, Lee, and Gaylord-Ross (1987) showed this type of effort to be successful, providing both learning dividends and social and attitudinal benefits similar to purely leisure-based programs.

As students continue through the school program, work habits, the ability to get along with co-workers and the boss, following instructions, and the like are emphasized. In addition, home-related skills such as making a bed, preparing meals, and using a washing machine are taught. Skills such as taking public transportation and ordering a meal in a restaurant are taught through instruction and role-playing at school combined with practice in the community.

Younger students may be instructed in some combination of regular and special classes, but as is clear from a description of the instructional content, this becomes less feasible as students progress through the formal educational program. At the secondary level, whenever possible they learn to move from class to class, following the same time schedule as other students. However, at that point students with moderate mental retardation usually spend most of their school day with similar students rather than in mainstream classes (Patton, Beirne-Smith, & Payne, 1990). They may be taught by both special educators and regular educators who have some training in adapted instruction. Considerable contact with nondisabled age peers continues to be desirable.

After these students complete the formal school program, participation in a supported employment program is the most likely step. Such programs may be provided through a variety of facilities but are not typically part of the public school program. When at all possible, individuals should be introduced to and have experience with these programs and facilities while still in the public school. The agencies that will play a role in this postgraduate program should be speci-

■   Adults with mental retardation can be gainfully employed.   ■

fied in the transition plan (part of the IEP), along with various other postgraduate options.

■   **Severe and Profound Mental Retardation**

Program planning for individuals with severe or profound mental retardation is different in most respects from that for individuals with moderate mental retardation. It is significantly different from that for individuals with mild mental retardation. It may take place in a 24-hour residential facility, a separate, publicly supported day program, a private program, or in the public schools. Placement options must be considered carefully when planning educational interventions, because certain placements will limit and others enhance program choices.

When educational interventions are provided in a public school, **integration** may be accomplished through special activities, part-time inclusion in the regular classroom, or peer tutoring under close supervision of the special education specialist. Individuals at this level of mental retardation often have related physical

113

■ These people, living in a group home, have learned to prepare
their own dinner. ■

disabilities and thus may require careful supervision and monitoring. They will require assistance throughout their life span, and early efforts to increase their potential and quality of life are of great value.

Before moving on to a discussion of more acceptable alternatives, we should mention residential facilities. The residential population—that is, the average number of individuals in 24-hour residential facilities—has decreased steadily since 1977 (Patton, Beirne-Smith, & Payne, 1990). As more individuals who were formerly served in large residential facilities are served through community services, the remaining institutional population has tended to comprise the elderly or very severely disabled.

Educational programs for individuals with severe or profound mental retardation require a specially trained teacher, and many such programs make effective use of trained paraprofessionals. The curriculum may appear similar to that for students who are moderately mentally retarded, in being organized by basic life skill domains. However, most individual goals will be much simpler. For example, in teaching self-care skills related to eating, it would be unlikely to assume that an individual would select the food to be eaten, prepare the meal, and then eat without assistance. A more realistic goal would be that an individual simply feed oneself. Self-care skills related to grooming would not include the whole cluster of skills: bathing, washing one's hair, face, and hands, combing one's hair, trimming fingernails and toenails, shaving, application of cosmetics, and so on. Rather, they might simply be wiping off one's hands before and after eating, wiping one's mouth after eating, and other relatively simple tasks. It is difficult to generalize, because of the range of abilities within the severely and profoundly retarded classification; skill goals must furthermore fit the individual.

Toilet training is one example of a goal for an individual who is severely or profoundly mentally retarded. The complexity of teaching such a skill may be illustrated by one of the better-known toilet training procedures developed by Foxx and Azrin (1973) and used in various revised forms by others since that time (Richmond, 1983). The Foxx and Azrin method includes the following: (1) increased liquid intake, to increase the likelihood of urination; (2) practice in walking to and from the toilet; (3) practice in taking down and pulling up pants; (4) a battery-operated urine-sensing device attached to the pants; (5) regular intervals on the toilet; (6) cleaning up when accidents occur; and (7) reinforcement for staying dry. This intense method includes day-long training sessions.

This toilet training procedure, and many others that help individuals with severe or profound mental retardation achieve a goal, requires that basic, prerequisite abilities be analyzed to be certain that the individual is ready to learn the procedure. For example, for this procedure children must be able to control their arm movements, have a developed grasp pattern, be able to maintain their balance and sit down and get up without assistance, and be able to communicate well enough to understand what the teacher wants them to do. If a child has learned to imitate in a variety of settings, this procedure is much easier to carry out; experience in responding to positive reinforcement is also helpful.

One final example of the specialized curriculum that may be necessary for students at this level relates to learning to communicate. Although many students will learn to use and understand speech, some may require alternative systems of communication. Picture systems, sign language, or both may be useful. The goal is successful communication, but the means to that goal may vary widely among children.

The unusual nature of the instructional methods required to achieve success with these individuals means that a special education teacher must provide most of the instruction. However, some interaction with nondisabled students is still of value, particularly with respect to social interaction skills.

Mental Retardation in Adults

Many adults with mild mental retardation become undistinguishable from the rest of the adult population. Others may require ongoing assistance from various community agencies in obtaining employment, managing their money, maintaining marital relationships, and other issues that concern nondisabled adults as well. For the most part, their needs and the ways in which they can meet them are quite similar to those of nondisabled adults. Therefore, our focus will be on adults with moderate, severe, or profound mental retardation, in two major aspects of their life.

■ **Employment**

Employment options may be envisioned as a continuum ranging from nonemployment to competitive employment. Individuals may move either way on this continuum; our target population generally has five options.

Permanent nonemployment   This may be a result of profound mental retardation and perhaps of related physical disabilities. It also may result from lack of motivation, from decisions made by parents or others, or by some combination of these factors. Temporary nonemployment may be the result of layoffs.

Unpaid employment   During a given time period, this may be the only option for some individuals. It can be volunteer work that is of value because it provides meaningful daily activity. It is also of value if it builds employment-related skills that lead to some period of gainful employment. In some instances it may reflect unfair treatment.

Sheltered employment   This option typically involves work in an activity center or **sheltered workshop.** Many of these provide some job training, and some continue education with respect to work and social skills. Some type of prevocational training often precedes employment in a sheltered workshop, and individuals are not paid for this training period. They do receive minimum pay (not the minimum wage) for work in the sheltered workshop. Brown et al. (1984) believe that there are several disadvantages to sheltered workshops: low pay, tolerance of behavior that will not be acceptable in competitive employment, and a tendency to keep on good workers (due to their contribution to production goals) rather than making efforts to move them to higher levels of employment.

Supported employment   This reflects an effort to move away from sheltered employment toward more integrated settings. One type of supported employment, work crew programs, may be established by local social service agencies. These may operate somewhat like any other small business and might include such work as window cleaning, house or small business cleaning, and lawn care. With proper supervision, individuals with mental retardation may be successfully employed in this type of job. Workers will generally be paid the minimum wage. Another type of supported employment is work as part of a small group of individuals with disabilities within a regular industrial setting. In this case, there will ordinarily be very close and continual support and supervision. In a few cases, supported employment may mean individual efforts at some regular job site. In all instances, planned support is essential. Supported employment is viewed as more desirable than sheltered employment because it involves work alongside nondisabled co-workers, and may serve as preparation for transition to competitive employment.

Competitive employment   This goal may be reached by individuals with moderate mental retardation and even by some with severe mental retardation (Rusch, 1986). Such employment may be part-time and will often involve unskilled labor such as lawn care or housekeeping tasks. It normally will require flexibility within the work environment. It is possible, however, and is indicative of the progress that may occur following changes in attitudes and increased expectations on the part of professionals who work to meet the needs of individuals with mental retardation.

Employment—that is, work—is a basic component in adult life, but where an individual lives and the living conditions there are equally important. The movement of individuals with mental retardation from large residential facilities to the local community has given rise to a variety of alternative living arrangements.

Some remain in the homes of their parents or other relatives. This can have both advantages and disadvantages, depending on the degree of the relatives' understanding of the needs of the individual, their willingness to permit a degree of autonomy, and their interest in promoting continuing self-development. If relatives are embarrassed during interactions with neighbors and thus restrict this essential element of home life, or if they don't permit the individual to participate, for example, in meal preparation, it is a less than desirable arrangement.

Intermediate care facilities for persons with mental retardation are the most restrictive of the various community living arrangements but may be appropriate for individuals who require 24-hour care. In theory, they are for those who need nursing or medical support or for those who cannot learn to move about the community with any degree of independence and cannot assist in meal preparation, housecleaning tasks, and the like. Despite considerable variation in the structure of such facilities, some may be little more than a mini-institution. Others are viable community facilities for individuals with more complex needs.

Group homes are the most common community living arrangements for adults with mental retardation (Patton, Beirne-Smith, & Payne, 1990). They tend to house relatively small numbers of residents—typically between four and eight—in a family-type dwelling situated in a primarily residential neighborhood (Heward & Orlansky, 1988). They also typically include an in-house staff and a relief staff. Group homes are often controversial, inspiring zoning laws in an attempt to bar their establishment in a given neighborhood.

Other protected community living arrangements may be made, of course. Boarding homes licensed to provide room and board for individuals needing minimal supervision, or care homes licensed to provide room, board, and personal care are examples.

Apartment living is the least restrictive living arrangement for individuals with mental retardation. In such programs, the degree of supervision and support advisable depends on individual needs. Variations of this arrangement include apartment clusters, living arrangements that pair individuals with mental retardation with nondisabled adults, and totally independent apartment living.

Issues and Trends

Issues already discussed to some extent in this chapter include the following.

1. The definition of mental retardation is controversial because of (a) the use of intelligence tests based on a particular construct of intellectual functioning with which not everyone agrees; (b) measures of adaptive behavior that are of questionable reliability; and (c) the influence of environment and the very high incidence of "functional mental retardation," especially in urban ghettos.

2. Debatable aspects of the prevention of mental retardation are (a) the use of procedures such as amniocentesis, which may lead to an abortion decision; and (b) the extent of governmental responsibility to initiate and pay for screening

procedures that determine potential mental retardation in newborns, and to provide for essential follow-up.

3. The role of the public schools in educating individuals with severe and profound levels of mental retardation has been questioned.

Other issues include the following.

1. How do we ensure the rights of individuals with mental retardation? A number of organizations, including the AAMR, have articulated those rights, but how they can be effectively attained, who will provide the most objective advocacy, and how nationwide advocacy efforts will be funded remain to be determined.

2. Which theories of human development hold the most promise for guiding future intervention and research in the field of mental retardation? For example, do the theories promulgated by developmental psychology provide a useful basis for planning interventions for mentally retarded individuals? Related questions are "What is the nature of mental retardation?" and "Is the two-group approach to mental retardation (cultural-familial plus organic etiologies) of value in researching and understanding mental retardation?"

3. Can any generalization be made about the possible overlap between mental retardation and learning disabilities?

Certain future trends seem apparent with respect to both programming for students with mental retardation and research on mental retardation. Here are a few.

1. More community-based facilities will appear for persons with moderate, severe, and profound levels of mental retardation, emphasizing a greater degree of independence.

2. More service will be provided in the public schools for individuals with severe and profound mental retardation.

3. Public recognition and acceptance of persons with mental retardation will increase.

4. There will be an increasing breadth and scope in research on the prevention of mental retardation.

Summary

The treatment of persons with mental retardation has evolved from fear, misunderstanding, and mistreatment. It has proceeded through the institutionalization movement and culminated in the present emphasis on living within the local community. Classifications of mental retardation emphasize differences in degree of severity (mild, moderate, and severe or profound) as well as in medical etiology. Estimates of the prevalence of mental retardation have decreased in recent years due to (1) a lowering of the upper IQ limit at which an individual may be considered mentally retarded, and (2) the requirement that there be concurrent impairments in adaptive behavior.

The major causes of mental retardation, according to a classification system advocated by the American Association on Mental Retardation, include environmental and psychosocial influences, infections and intoxications, trauma or physical agents, disorders of metabolism or nutrition, and chromosomal abnormalities.

There are established relationships between environmental and organic causes; a consideration of those relationships can contribute to the prevention of mental retardation.

Characteristics associated with mental retardation include personal and social skills deficits, low academic performance, memory deficits, below-average language ability, and limited ability to generalize, conceptualize, and deal with abstractions.

Educational programming varies according to the different levels of mental retardation but includes instruction in social skills at all levels. Educational planning is tailored to individual abilities and deficits and to the transition planned after formal schooling.

Employment options for adults with mental retardation range from competitive employment to nonemployment. Their living arrangements include apartment living, with or without limited assistance; group homes; boarding homes; and intermediate care facilities.

When Dean was in second grade, he and his parents were told that he had learning disabilities. During his grade school years he was given extra assistance in reading and writing. He had little difficulty in math, science, or social studies. His teachers recognized his difficulty in writing and gave him credit for his verbal contributions. When Dean entered high school he was still having difficulty reading and writing. His parents and teachers decided that he should enroll in vocational classes, so he took woodworking and auto mechanics. But when he graduated, so many other students had gone through the same classes that he couldn't find a job as a carpenter or mechanic.

Dean has much to say about what could or should have been done. "Why couldn't I have been taught to type instead of write? Why couldn't I have dictated and had someone transcribe it? Why didn't anyone encourage me to find my own way of reading instead of trying to teach me phonics, which I never did understand? Why didn't anyone teach me how to manage my time, knowing that it takes me longer to read something than it does everyone else? Why didn't anyone encourage me to go to college instead of deciding for me that I should be a carpenter or mechanic? I always wanted to teach, but no one listened. I am not as dumb as they made me feel."

Today Dean has graduated from college and has nearly completed his master's degree, with a double emphasis in biology and special education. He has received A's and B's throughout college (except for a C in poetry) and in his graduate program. Dean says, "I will teach, and I won't let my students feel as dumb as I was made to feel."

CHAPTER FIVE

Learning Disabilities

More students are evaluated by multidisciplinary teams in the public schools and determined to have **learning disabilities** than are those with any other disability. According to annual reports submitted to the federal government by the 50 states, more students are receiving special services due to learning disabilities than those with speech disorders, mental retardation, and behavioral disorders (the three next-highest disabilities of incidence) combined (see Table 2.5 in Chapter 2). This is of particular interest because "It is probably safe to say that in 1960 there were no public school classes for these children [with learning disabilities] except for remedial reading programs" (McCarthy, 1969). How this subarea of special education exploded into almost instant prominence, the controversies that continue to cause confusion and misunderstanding, and an overview of its present state of development will be the major topics of this chapter.

Historical Background

Unlike the history of conditions such as visual and hearing impairment and much of the history of mental retardation, for most of the history of learning disabilities the term itself was not even used. Most accounts of the historical development of this special education discipline credit an address given by Samuel Kirk on April 6, 1963, with the initial popularization of the term and the beginnings of a rush to provide services for students who had, in many cases, simply been overlooked by the public schools. This "birthday" of the definition of learning disabilities was when Kirk spoke to a group called the Fund for Perceptually Handicapped Children at its first annual meeting. He explained that terms such as *brain injured* or *aphasic* had little meaning from an educational point of view. He mentioned that he had recently been using the term *learning disabilities* to describe children who "have disorders in development in language, speech, reading, and associated communication skills needed for social interaction" (1963, pp. 2–3). He added that he did *not* include under this label children whose primary handicap was generalized mental retardation, hearing impairment, or visual impairment. Much of his address reflected his concern about parent and educator overdependence on labels; ironically, his speech led to the promotion of a new label, which was to become the most frequently heard in special education.

Parents and a limited number of educators who attended this convention were so inspired by his words that on the spot they organized the Association for Children with Learning Disabilities (ACLD). This organization was soon to become a major advocate—through legislative efforts and direct pressure on local educational agencies—for recognition of the concept of learning disabilities and for special educational services for students identified as having them.

What led up to this 1963 event? Where were these children prior to that time, and how were their problems and disabilities described? What led to this state of instant readiness among parents and educators? Here is the rest of the story.[1]

■ Prior to 1963

During the foundation period of investigations that would later be directly related to learning disabilities, a number of people, primarily physicians, worked with

---

[1] The following account is based primarily on information provided in *Historical Perspectives on the Education of the Learning Disabled* (Wiederholt, 1974) and in the various editions of *Learning Disabilities: Educational Strategies* (Gearheart & Gearheart, 1985, 1989).

individuals with known brain injuries that had led to language disorders. According to Wiederholt (1974), two of the first, Franz Joseph Gall and John Bouillaud, attempted to identify specific brain activities with specific parts of the brain. Gall presented a summary of his work in a letter published in 1802, and Bouillard affirmed his belief in many of Gall's theories in lectures in 1825, and in later years. Others were interested in visual perceptual problems that had apparently led to severe reading difficulties despite normal intelligence and accepted instructional methods. Just before the 20th century, three of those pioneers, James Hinshelwood, James Kerr, and W. P. Morgan, investigated what they called word blindness. The individuals they studied undoubtedly would have been identified as learning disabled today.

These early efforts prepared the way for other major researchers in the field that would come to be called learning disabilities. For example, Dr. Grace Fernald worked at the UCLA laboratory school with students who had normal or above-normal intelligence but were experiencing severe learning problems. Her efforts spanned the period between 1921 and the 1950s, and her text, *Remedial Techniques in Basic School Subjects* (1943), led to the popularization of a multisensory approach still in use today.

A second major contributor during this period, Dr. Samuel Orton, was a professor of psychiatry at the University of Iowa who in 1925 worked with a 16-year-old boy unable to read, despite normal intellect. Orton found others with similar disabilities; most seemed to have difficulty with reversals or other confusion of visual symbols. Orton coined the term *strephosymbolia* (twisted symbols) to describe this difficulty and popularized a theory of its neurological basis; his work led to the organization of the Orton Society. The Orton Dyslexia Society, as it is named today, is an active advocate for persons with learning disabilities; it provides educational materials, promotes legislation, and acts as a source of information and support for all who have an interest in learning disabilities.

Other contributors came to the field through their interest in children who had learning difficulties apparently caused by other factors. These conditions included actual brain injury, minimal brain dysfunction, **hyperactivity,** visual or auditory perceptual problems, perceptual-motor problems, and language disorders. Some of these children were in school, having serious academic difficulties and receiving little or no help. Others were exhibiting behaviors that led to expulsion from school. One thing they all had in common was learning difficulties, despite average or above-average intellectual ability. Although many had been referred for possible inclusion in a special education program, most were denied special service because they did not fit any recognized classification. For instance, though they may have achieved no better than a peer classified as educable mentally retarded, their IQ was too high for inclusion under that classification. In a few cases classification guidelines were ignored, and they were placed in such programs, but this was not an effective, appropriate placement. Then came Kirk's keynote address, and the stage was set for an unprecedented series of events launching the new field of learning disabilities.

■ From 1963 to the Present

Following Kirk's use of the term *learning disabilities* and the formation of the Association for Children with Learning Disabilities (now the Learning Disabilities Association of America), a number of events led up to the current prominence of programs for students with learning disabilities. The following were among the more important milestones.

1. A federally sponsored study was completed by the National Institute of Neurological Diseases and Blindness (NINDS), culminating in a report that included a better description of learning disabilities and an acceptable definition (Clements, 1966). This study emphasized the **minimal brain dysfunction** syndrome and the central nervous system causation of learning disabilities. It inspired much more interest on the part of physicians, but it was not particularly helpful to educators planning programs and implementation.

2. In 1968, the newly formed National Advisory Committee on Handicapped Children recommended that high priority, including federal funding, be given to the developing field of learning disabilities. Included in that recommendation was an educationally oriented definition of learning disabilities that became the basis for the later official federal definition.

3. In 1975, the Education of All Handicapped Children Act (Public Law 94-142) was passed; it included learning disabilities along with other handicapping conditions as eligible for federal funding.

4. In 1977, a federal definition of learning disabilities was published, to improve upon that in PL 94-142, which — as originally submitted to Congress — was so vague that the Bureau of Education for the Handicapped was told to develop a better one that spelled out more precisely how children would be identified. On December 29, 1977, that became the official federal definition.

As a result of efforts by parents and by organizations and individuals representing many disciplines, learning disabilities now had a nationally recognized definition and received federal funding. It had come into being as "a conglomerate of conditions grouped under one label, primarily for administrative convenience and to provide a focal point for advocacy efforts. Students who had previously been served, or denied service, under such labels as hyperactivity, brain injury, dyslexia, perceptual disorders, minimal brain dysfunction, aphasia, or **neurologic impairment,** were now 'learning disabled.' " (Gearheart & Gearheart, 1989, p. 12). Learning disabilities, as a recognized exceptionality, was here to stay.

Definitions of Learning Disabilities

Defining learning disabilities has not been simple. The fact that it began as an "umbrella" definition, deliberately structured to include a variety of conditions, led to several difficulties. Some have wanted a narrower, more precise definition, less susceptible to misuse and misunderstanding. Others have wanted precision and specificity so that more effective research could be carried out. Those in medically oriented disciplines would prefer a definition tied to cerebral or neurological dysfunction. Many educators, however, see great practical difficulties in the latter, both in identification (for example, the high costs of neurological screening, and the lack of qualified medical and neurological specialists, particularly in smaller communities) and in potential value as a guide for educational intervention. Most parents of children with learning disabilities are primarily concerned with having effective programs and services for their children. They will not support a definition that does not include their child, nor one that makes identification and eligibility for services unduly difficult.

Because parents called on educators to provide special education interventions for their children with learning disabilities, it became the responsibility of

■   Learning disabilities affect the educational progress of students with normal
or above-average intellectual ability.   ■

special educators to develop a definition that would apply to the educational
setting.

The federal definition published in the *Federal Register* (1977) provided a set
of criteria for identifying students with learning disabilities. The definition and
criteria follow.

"Specific learning disability" means a disorder in one or more of the basic psychological processes involved in understanding or in using language, spoken or written,
which may manifest itself in an imperfect ability to listen, think, speak, read, write,
spell, or to do mathematical calculations. The term includes such conditions as
perceptual handicaps, brain injury, minimal brain dysfunction, dyslexia, and developmental aphasia. The term does not include children who have learning problems
which are primarily the result of visual, hearing, or motor handicaps, of mental
retardation, of emotional disturbance, or of environmental, cultural, or economic
disadvantage.

Criteria for determining the existence of a specific learning disability
(a) A team may determine that a child has a specific learning disability if:
   (1) The child does not achieve commensurate with his or her age and ability
       levels in one or more of the areas listed in paragraph (a) (2) of this section,
       when provided with learning experiences appropriate for the child's age and
       ability levels; and
   (2) The team finds that a child has a severe discrepancy between achievement
       and intellectual ability in one or more of the following areas:
       (i) Oral expression;
       (ii) Listening comprehension;
       (iii) Written expression;

  (iv) Basic reading skill;
  (v) Reading comprehension;
  (vi) Mathematics calculation; or
  (vii) Mathematics reasoning.
(b) The team may not identify a child as having a specific learning disability if the severe discrepancy between ability and achievement is primarily the result of:
  (1) A visual, hearing, or motor handicap;
  (2) Mental retardation;
  (3) Emotional disturbance; or
  (4) Environmental, cultural, or economic disadvantage. (1977, p. 65083)

By 1984, enough doubts had developed among individuals at the federal level about the continued applicability of this definition that a national task force was established to investigate the matter. Members of this task force analyzed definitions then in use by the 50 state education agencies and reported as follows.

1. 22 states and the District of Columbia used the federal definition.
2. 11 states had developed their own definition.
3. 1 state used the federal definition supplemented by a definition proposed by the National Joint Committee for Learning Disabilities (NJCLD).
4. 2 states used a noncategorical approach, thus had no actual definition (Chalfant, 1985).

Five common factors surfaced in the various definitions: (1) a significant discrepancy between aptitude or ability and achievement, (2) academic difficulty, (3) psychological processes, (4) exclusionary factors (conditions or causes excluded), and (5) etiology. The diversity in definitions was outweighed by the similarities.

A second study of definitions in the 50 states indicated that three components in identifying learning disabilities—those relating to academic problems, exclusion, and discrepancy—had increased in significance since 1976. Three others—those referring to process, neurological involvement, and specific level of intelligence—were less often cited (Mercer, Hughes, & Mercer, 1985).

Though the federal definition and related criteria have considerable continued recognition, two other nationally recognized definitions are worthy of analysis. One is an updated version of the aforementioned NJCLD definition. The second is that adopted by the Learning Disabilities Association of America. These two definitions follow.

National Joint Committee on Learning Disabilities (NJCLD) definition (1989)
Learning disabilities is a general term that refers to a heterogeneous group of disorders manifested by significant difficulties in the acquisition and use of listening, speaking, reading, writing, reasoning, or mathematical abilities. These disorders are intrinsic to the individual, presumed to be due to central nervous system dysfunction, and may occur across the life span. Problems in self-regulatory behaviors, social perception, and social interaction may exist with learning disabilities but do not by themselves constitute a learning disability. Although learning disabilities may occur concomitantly with other handicapping conditions (for example, sensory impairment, mental retardation, serious emotional disturbance) or with extrinsic influences (such as cultural differences, insufficient or inappropriate instruction) they are not the result of those conditions or influences.

Learning Disabilities Association of America (LDA) definition (1985)
Specific Learning Disabilities is a chronic condition of presumed neurological origin which selectively interferes with the development, integration, and/or demonstration

of verbal and/or nonverbal abilities. Specific Learning Disabilities exists as a distinct handicapping condition in the presence of average to superior intelligence, adequate sensory motor systems, and adequate learning opportunities. The condition varies in its manifestations and in degree of severity. Throughout life the condition can affect self-esteem, education, vocation, socialization, and/or daily living activities.

Compared with the 1977 federal definition, these contain certain changes, additions, and deletions. The NJCLD definition includes increased emphasis on *presumed* central nervous system dysfunction and leaves out references to "basic psychological processes." It also notes that learning disabilities "may occur across the life span." The Learning Disabilities Association of America definition adds a phrase about "presumed neurological origin" and a sentence about lifelong influences on social and vocational performance. Like the NJCLD definition, it leaves out reference to "basic psychological processes."

We believe that all three definitions contribute to a better understanding of the nature of learning disabilities. It would appear that the only way to further avoid vagueness and ambiguity in these definitions would be to develop a precise, highly restrictive one that would greatly reduce interpretive questions. However, such a definition would also reduce the number of students identified and served in learning disabilities programs and would therefore alienate the parents who have played such a significant role in establishing the present programs. At least for the near future, it seems likely that we will retain some version of the 1977 federal definition, with perhaps some modifications suggested by the NJCLD or the LDA.

Prevalence

As we saw from Table 2.5 in Chapter 2, an average of over 3.6% of the students in the nation's schools have been identified and are receiving services for learning disabilities. At the time of the Thirteenth Annual Report to Congress (1991), the state serving the smallest percentage served slightly more than 1.5%, the state serving the largest percentage almost 6%. If we assume that some of those students will receive assistance for only a few years before achieving some degree of success without special help, this means that an even higher percentage will be identified and receive special educational assistance on the basis of learning disabilities at some time during their school years.

Senf (1987) said "There will never be consensus regarding the definition of LD because its meaning is embedded not in empirical fact but in the philosophy of education, the aspiration of parents for their children, the status of each profession and professional (on a variety of dimensions), personal well-being, and the deep-seated beliefs of each and every person involved as to what 'should be'" (p. 91).

Box 5.1
Something to
Think About

It may be that, when in doubt, evaluators tend to identify students as having learning disabilities rather than mild mental retardation. (For one thing, parents may more readily accept the learning disabilities classification.) In any event, the number of students served as learning disabled more than doubled between the school years 1976–1977 and 1986–1987, according to the Eleventh Annual Report to Congress on Implementation of the Education of the Handicapped Act, in 1989. However, the actual prevalence of learning disabilities can be determined only when the definition becomes more specific. Until that time, the 2% to 4% estimate seems reasonable.

Causes of Learning Disabilities

A significant factor in the debate over an acceptable definition of learning disabilities has been disagreement over and uncertainty about causation. However, because we currently have an umbrella definition, it seems reasonable to assume a number of potential causes. Note that the federal definition is an "effect-oriented" definition, as opposed to a "cause-oriented" one. That is, it emphasizes the difficulties in using language, and the criteria for identification relate to discrepancies between expected (for age and experience) and actual achievement in the various basic skills or academic areas. There is no reference to causation except to *exclude* any individual whose learning discrepancy is the result of other, named causes.

The NJCLD and LDA definitions refer to "presumed . . . central nervous system dysfunction" and "presumed neurological origin," and the federal definition states that conditions such as "brain injury" and "minimal brain dysfunction" are included under the term *learning disabilities.* This appears to provide a common starting point for considering one possible cause of learning disabilities, but none of the three definitions specifies one cause as essential to identification.

■ Brain Dysfunction

The idea that brain dysfunction is a cause of learning disabilities has a number of origins. Some of the higher-visibility educational programs that immediately preceded the earliest public school programs were primarily for children who had been identified as brain injured. In addition, most of the pioneers in this field (Cruickshank, Bentzen, Ratzberg, & Tannhauser, 1961; Strauss & Lehtinen, 1947) referred to brain injury, brain dysfunction, neurological dysfunction, or minimal brain dysfunction in their writings. More recent investigators have linked brain injury to learning disabilities in a variety of ways. For example, Spivak (1986) reported that approximately 20% of the students with learning disabilities in his study had a known prior brain injury. However, this would mean that approximately 80% did *not* have a known brain injury.

Clements, in his 1966 study that helped launch learning disabilities as a condition to be served in the public schools, referred primarily to minimal brain dysfunction and a "minimal brain dysfunction syndrome." In fact, his task force would have preferred this terminology to that of learning disabilities. Chalfant and Schefflin (1969), in a related review of research for the developing field of learning disabilities, titled their monograph "Central Processing Dysfunctions in Children." Their emphasis was not on actual brain damage, nor did they use the term *brain dysfunction* extensively, but they did stress central processing dys-

■ Fighting may result from social imperception, which is related to learning disabilities. ■

functions, and central processing takes place in the brain. It seems clear that, though brain damage can be related to learning disabilities, and though many persons who suffer injury or insult to the central nervous system exhibit the symptoms of learning disabilities, other individuals with the same problems have no verifiable indication of brain dysfunction.

■ Biochemical Factors

The assumption that biochemical factors cause learning disabilities has led to a variety of medical treatments. For our present purposes, we will consider any causal theory or assumption that has led to medical treatment to belong to a biochemical factor theory.

Gearheart and Gearheart (1989) considered pharmacotherapy, diet therapy, treatment of **hypoglycemia,** and orthomolecular therapy in their discussion of the medical–learning disabilities interface. According to Gadow (1986) and to Safer and Krager (1984), most of these treatments are controversial; however, of them, pharmacotherapy is the most widely accepted and commonly used.

Pharmacotherapy is the use of medications to alter behavior. Among students with learning disabilities, some type of hyperactivity is the most common target of drug therapy, and three stimulants—Ritalin®, Dexedrine®, and Cylert®—are most widely prescribed. According to Gadow (1986), Ritalin appears to be prescribed about ten times more than Cylert and Dexedrine combined. Though there are significant differences of opinion about the effectiveness of pharmacotherapy, and even more controversy over how to determine which children it will benefit, Kavale (1982), in a review of over 60 references, concluded that it might be an effective treatment for hyperactivity.

One of the major objections to stimulant pharmacotherapy is its potential side effects, some of which are insomnia, anorexia, headache, nausea, moodiness, stomachache, and irritability (Gadow, 1986). In a discussion of whether to use stimulant drugs with hyperactive children, Weiss suggested that it called for clinical judgment by the physician, based on multiple factors. He concluded, however, that "for hyperactive children with severe behavior problems the use of stimulants facilitates other treatment techniques such as remedial education and behavior modification" (1981, p. 390).

Diet therapy became popular in the mid-1970s, primarily as a result of the Feingold diet (Feingold, 1975, 1976). This diet was based primarily on the assumption that children are allergic to various food additives, and that in some children, that allergy is manifested in hyperactivity and learning difficulties. In a discussion of the Feingold diet, Mattes (1983) estimated that a total of 20,000 persons belonged to Feingold clubs at the time of his report. Feingold advocated a diet excluding the following: (1) foods containing natural salicylates (such as apples, cherries, oranges, tea, and tomatoes), (2) food containing artificial colors or flavors, and (3) items such as toothpaste and tooth powder and any compound containing aspirin.

A number of individuals, primarily medical doctors, have suggested other diet-related treatments. Powers (1974) related poor school performance, poor memory, and hyperactivity to an excessive intake of sugar, carbohydrates, and caffeine. Crook (1974, 1980) linked learning problems and hyperactivity with certain foods, including (in order of importance) sugar, food coloring, additives and flavors, milk, corn, chocolate, eggs, wheat, potatoes, soy, citrus, and pork. These physicians did not believe that all children should avoid all such foods, or even that all children who are hyperactive or have learning disabilities should avoid them. They believed that some children have a kind of allergic reaction to certain foods, which could lead to hyperactivity and learning problems.

The treatment of hypoglycemia is actually a diet-related treatment, too, but it is significantly different from those just discussed. Hypoglycemia, a recognized medical condition, is often associated with the narcolepsy complex (unusual, uncontrollable drowsiness). Hypoglycemia does not always result in learning difficulties; however, if a student were attempting to develop new basic skills or learn new material, it would certainly be a deterrent. Children with the narcolepsy complex may inexplicably take a nap while leaning against the school building during recess. Children with hypoglycemia may show signs of distress through symptoms such as nervousness, tremors, and rapid heart action. Hypoglycemia must be diagnosed by a physician; an appropriate diet will then be prescribed. Such a diet would likely eliminate table sugar and all foods containing simple sugar. It would be high in protein and include an adequate supply of fat. It would include more frequent snacks and might be supplemented with digestive enzymes that facilitate the utilization of proteins as a source of glucose. Lack of attention to hypoglycemia can lead to some rather serious physiological results in addition to learning problems.

Orthomolecular therapy, another medical treatment for learning disabilities, has also been called megavitamin therapy. Orthomolecular therapy is based on the assumption that there is a genetically based dysfunction in one or more of the brain's neurotransmitting processes, resulting in biochemical imbalances or abnormalities. Its advocates believe that neurochemical balance can sometimes be achieved through massive doses of certain vitamins. Dr. Linus Pauling, a biochemist who twice won the Nobel Prize for his scientific accomplishments, was an early advocate of orthomolecular therapy. His theories undoubtedly received more than ordinary attention because of his international stature. Following his lead, Dr. Allan Cott became a leading advocate of orthomolecular medicine; however, between his earlier advocacy and later publications (Cott, 1985), his recommendations have evolved from almost complete dependence on vitamins and minerals to a regimen in which a planned, modified diet plays a major role.

It appears that some learning disabilities may be related to biochemical imbalance or abnormalities, but these theories and their related therapies are certainly not accepted by all. Considerable research continues in this arena, but no clear trends, other than continued caution, are apparent.

■ Environmental Factors

Not all authors of basic texts on learning disabilities recognize environmental factors as a major cause. For example, according to Myers and Hammill, "Most professionals in the field maintain that true learning disabilities . . . are the consequence of central nervous system (CNS) damage, dysfunction, or structural anomaly" (1990, p. 17). Therefore, they limit learning disabilities etiology to CNS irregularities. However, they do list a number of "environmental factors that contribute to the severity of learning disabilities" (ibid., p. 22). According to these authors, such factors include insufficient early experience, behavior problems, cultural and linguistic differences, malnutrition, and poor teaching or lack of educational opportunity. Lovitt, in discussing who is learning disabled, provides a list of "common types of LD pupils" (1989, p. 4). In that list he includes the environmentally impoverished. His list of common types might be considered a list of characteristics, but the emphasis on environmental influences is clear.

Mercer lists environmental influences along with biochemical abnormalities, genetic or hereditary influences, and acquired trauma (insult or injury to the central nervous system) as the "four predominant medical etiologies of learning disabilities" (1987, p. 61). He lists exposure to lead and the influence of diet (which we have listed as a biochemical factor) as environmental factors. Mercer also notes that, though effective curricula and strategies exist for teaching students with learning disabilities, "when they are not practiced, the inadequate educational environment contributes to the number of students labeled learning disabled" (1990, p. 119).

■ Genetic Factors

Genetic studies of learning disabilities have taken quite varied approaches, but most suggest genetic or hereditary causes for some cases of learning disabilities. Many genetic studies have been done on dyslexia, a specific type of learning disability. Genetic theories seem to accrue more support from dyslexia research than from studies of nonspecific learning disabilities. For example, Decker and Defries (1981) provided convincing data on familial links in dyslexia, and earlier studies, such as one reported by Matheny, Dolan, and Wilson (1976), found a greater likelihood of shared learning disabilities between identical than between fraternal twins. Lovitt (1989) suggested that, to the extent that genetic endowment plays a role in determining a range of potential intellectual ability, it is also implicated in the genesis of some learning disabilities.

Despite the possibility of genetic links, so far these studies have not contributed much to the field. However, "recognition that certain children are at high risk for genetically influenced learning disabilities, whether it is because of a family history or a genetic syndrome, can ensure that diagnosis and appropriate remediation are not delayed. Thus genetics should be an important aspect in the multidisciplinary attack on learning disabilities" (S. D. Smith, 1986, p. ii).

■ Unknown Causes

As we've seen, learning disabilities became a part of the special education spectrum as a symptom-, effect-, or outcome-related disability as opposed to a cause-related one. There was a deliberate effort to separate the concept of learning disabilities from causal orientation for at least two major reasons. First, many felt that educators should focus on needed educational interventions, not on why the student had difficulties. Second was the variety of strongly held opinions about possible causes.

Since learning disabilities was accepted as a subarea of special education, there has been a gradual, general revival of the belief that central nervous system dysfunction is a related condition. However, even if there is a correlation, both the CNS dysfunction and the disability could be caused by a single "parent" factor. In the last analysis, these various hypothesized origins "are little more than alleged causes" (Lovitt, 1989, p. 5). We can only conclude that many, perhaps most, learning disabilities have unknown causes.

■ Alternative Conceptualizations

Depending on which definition of learning disabilities one accepts, and how one interprets references to central nervous system disorders, there may be three major ways to conceptualize causation or etiology.

1. All true learning disabilities are the result of CNS dysfunctions.
2. Learning disabilities are the result of relatively permanent CNS dysfunctions but also of more temporary dysfunctions, which may be remediated by correcting biochemical abnormalities.
3. Learning disabilities are the result of CNS dysfunctions—either relatively permanent ones or those that may be subject to interventions that correct biochemical abnormalities. In addition, some students' academic performance is similar to those who have a true CNS dysfunction, but is instead due to an impoverished environment or inadequate instruction.

Characteristics of Learning Disabilities

By definition, students with learning disabilities exhibit certain characteristics related to intellectual ability and academic performance. First, they are of average or above-average intellectual ability. Second, by definition and in accordance with identification criteria, they have significant single or combined difficulties in reading, mathematics, and written or oral language. "Difficulties" means that their achievement is significantly lower than would be expected for their age, intellectual ability, and school experience (or opportunity to have learned). Learning opportunities outside of school are also considered in this evaluation.

In addition to those characteristics, which are fairly measurable, are others that have traditionally been associated with learning disabilities and that may contribute to academic difficulties. According to Gearheart and Gearheart (1989), students with learning disabilities may demonstrate a variety of the following behaviors.

1. *Underdeveloped or unevenly developed learning strategies.* These include, but are not limited to, inappropriate strategies or a complete lack of strategies normally used by age peers. Examples are abilities to extract information from charts or maps, to learn through outlining or summarizing, to find key words or phrases in readings, to use note-taking skills during lectures, to develop appropriate scheduling and organizational habits, and to apply mnemonic devices.

2. *Disorders of attention.* Some examples are distractibility, hyperactivity, and **perseveration.** These disorders may inhibit the development of new skills, learning new information that must be related to previously learned material, or any learning task that requires sustained attention. Such disorders can also limit the ability to develop needed learning strategies.

3. *Poor spatial orientation.* A typical symptom is becoming lost in settings in which age peers have no unusual difficulty in orienting themselves to new surroundings.

***Box 5.2
Conceptual
Misunder-
standings***

Some children confuse the name of an object with the concept to which it is related. Mike Johnson, for example. He lived on an isolated farm. His father drove a Ford pickup and his mother drove a Ford Mustang. His grandfather drove a Ford sedan. His father sometimes called his vehicle "the pickup," and his mother often called hers "the Mustang." But sometimes they just referred to both as "Fords." His grandfather always called his car "the Ford." Mike soon learned that all three could be called Fords, but he later had difficulty understanding that other vehicles with motors and four wheels were not Fords. Because of his limited early experience (not a true conceptual deficit), Ford became Mike's name for the more abstract concept that included automobiles, pickups, and other transport vehicles. With a limited amount of additional experience and explanation, Mike learned to make sense of the various terms for automobiles, transportation, and related concepts.

Sam Pringle, on the other hand, had true conceptual deficits. He learned to recognize and recall the words for a highchair, a rocking chair, a lawn chair, and a kitchen chair. He also knew the name of the couch and the coffee table. But Sam could not relate all of these real objects to the concept of furniture. The concept was too far removed from the real objects. Sam required additional experiences and direct instruction to make the cognitive step from individual, concrete objects to an abstract concept. Abstract concepts such as patriotism, democracy, and freedom confused Sam even more. His conceptual difficulties led to a variety of problems in reading and in meaningful participation in class discussion.

Figure 5.1 Perceptual ambiguity. An observer with normal perceptual ability may see either a vase or two faces in this illustration. A child with the perceptual disorder of figure-ground distortion may experience continuous shifting of focus between foreground and background, which cannot be controlled. This may lead to a variety of problems in interpreting words or letters.

4. *Underdeveloped, inadequate-for-age time concepts.* This may include a lack of the normal time concept, continual lateness, and confusion regarding individual responsibility for time-related tasks.

5. *Difficulty in judging relationships.* Examples are confusion or difficulty in distinguishing concepts like big versus little, light versus heavy, and near versus far.

6. *Poor general motor coordination.* This may include poor balance, general clumsiness, poor coordination when attempting to complete simple physical tasks, and a tendency to fall.

7. *Poor manual dexterity.* This may be exhibited in difficulty in turning doorknobs, opening latches, manipulating pencils, or in any situation in which unfamiliar equipment must be used.

8. *Inability (not unwillingness) to follow directions.* Confusion when following even simple oral directions is the most common manifestation.

9. *Perceptual disorders.* Under this category fall disorders of visual, auditory, tactual, or kinesthetic perception—and combinations thereof (see Figure 5.1). Visual **perceptual disorders** are evident in an inability to accurately copy letters or to perceive differences between geometric figures. Related letter or word reversal is also common. Auditory perceptual problems may lead to difficulty in recognizing the difference between various consonant blends or in using phonic clues for word recognition. Perceptual disorders in tactual or kinesthetic

modalities may mean that the student receives faulty feedback about the shape of letters and thus loses potential tactual reinforcement of visual perception.

10. *Memory disorders.* Visual memory of word or letter sequences may be nearly nonexistent; some students may not be able to repeat a simple sequence of three or four words immediately after hearing it. Some may be unable to revisualize a scene (for example, their living room at home) when they are somewhere else. Lesser memory problems may be subtler and more difficult to recognize.

Box 5.3
Alfred, a
10-Year-Old
with Dyslexia

When Alfred was 10 years old, he described his situation in "plain English": "I can think okay. What's wrong with me is just my words. I forget them and I can't manage them."

WHAT IS A DYSLEXIC LIKE? How shall we recognize him, or less often, her? Alfred said, "I can think okay." The dyslexic's intelligence, vision, hearing, motor control and physical development are from very good to poor but mostly around average, as with everybody else. He has no more problems with home life, school attendance and emotional life than anyone else—except as they result from the frustration and discouragement caused by failure. "It's just my *words*," said Alfred.

- "I forget them." He cannot learn and remember whole words by sight so he has trouble with reading in the regular class. Perhaps he cannot remember letters, so he gets them twisted—*b* for *d,* and so on. Often he cannot call up the words he wants to say. "Oh, you know that thing you use to write with—." "Yesterday—I mean tomorrow—sometime or other."
- "And I can't manage them." The words come out wrong, "basgetti and cheese," or in the wrong order, "please up hurry!"
- Managing letters in spelling is even harder. He writes *p* for *b, was* for *saw, left* for *felt* and many others. Even in high school, what we call *nuclear* may be *unclear* to him.
- He may be clumsy in general, or he may have beautiful coordination except for the pencil so that his handwriting is irregular, slow, cramped and hard to figure out.
- He may have trouble with math. It is another language and its numbers take a lot of remembering and managing.
- The dyslexic finds organization, managing his life, difficult. His possessions, his homework instructions, his sense of direction or time may often get mixed up.
- It is quite probable that some other members of his family, through the generations, have found language hard to master, one way or another.

Dyslexia is not a "disease" to "have" and "be cured of," but a kind of mind. Very often it is a gifted mind—there have been many famous, productive, creative dyslexics. Every one of us is unique, different from everyone else, and people's ways of coming to terms with language are some of their normal differences.

SOURCE: What is dyslexia? *Unnumbered bulletin. (Reprinted by permission of the Orton Dyslexia Society, 724 York Road, Baltimore, MD 21204)*

■ Perceptual disorders may lead to serious learning difficulties. ■

11. *Social imperception.* Students may be unable to determine when others—students, the teacher, or parents—are becoming disturbed or angry, thus leading to conflict that could have been avoided. Much of this difficulty appears to relate to an inability to interpret body language, especially facial expressions.

We will now consider dyslexia and the attention deficit–hyperactivity disorder (ADHD). Some authorities consider dyslexia a separate disorder, but it is more commonly considered a specific type of learning disability. ADHD is a major

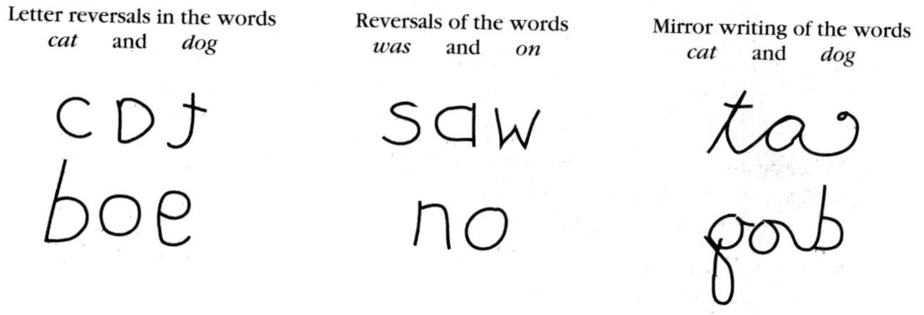

Letter reversals in the words *cat* and *dog*	Reversals of the words *was* and *on*	Mirror writing of the words *cat* and *dog*

Figure 5.2 Reversals and mirror writing. Reversals and mirror writing may be associated with reading disability and have been specifically associated with dyslexia. Note, however, that such confusion of symbols is normal for many younger children. For example, *b* and *d* or *was* and *saw* may be confused when children are learning to apply visual discrimination skills to the tasks of reading and writing.

learning disability syndrome. Each is a part of the total picture of learning disabilities and exhibits several of the characteristics in the foregoing list.

■ Dyslexia

Dyslexia is one of the "conditions" named in the federal definition of learning disabilities. It is a major type of learning disability and appears to be the one most often recognized and featured in the popular press. Some authorities on dyslexia might object to its characterization as a "type" of learning disability, maintaining that it is a unique condition or syndrome. It is essentially the same phenomenon Orton named strephosymbolia in 1925. A theory of specific dyslexia was developed by Katrina deHirsch (1952), a language pathology theorist in the early 1950s. Orton and his pupils recommended specific remedial techniques based on his theories of causation, but deHirsch suggested a more eclectic approach that responded to the unique needs of the individual student (Hallahan & Cruickshank, 1973). Lerner called dyslexia "an unusual type of severe reading disorder that has puzzled the educational and medical professions for many years" (1989, p. 349); Mercer stated that "dyslexia refers to a severe difficulty in learning to read" (1987, p. 374). According to Myers and Hammill, "dyslexia is an inability to read normally as a result of damage to the brain" (1990, p. 63), but this direct reference to brain damage is unusual and runs counter to many educational descriptions of dyslexia. As Kinsbourne pointed out, "despite numerous claims, it is not clear whether specific teaching programs for dyslexic children are any different than for children who are slow in learning to read" (1987, p. 69). He also commented that though there appear to be subtypes of dyslexia, it is unclear whether certain types of programs are better for certain dyslexia subtypes.

What are the characteristics of this puzzling condition? We believe the description of Alfred provided in Box 5.3 is the best way to answer this question. (See also Figure 5.2.)

■ Hyperactivity and the Attention Deficit–Hyperactivity Disorder

Hyperactivity was a symptom of many of the students whose educational needs led to the 1963 meeting discussed earlier in this chapter, in which learning disabilities got its name. The earlier efforts of Strauss and Lehtinen (1947) and Strauss and Kephart (1955) were with children diagnosed as brain injured and hyperactive. A survey of experimental programs that followed (Cruickshank et al., 1961) indicated their apparently equal effectiveness with students who were hyperactive and brain injured and with hyperactive students not believed to be brain injured. Hyperactivity and related distractibility were discussed and considered a part of the basic learning problems of the students with whom they worked by most pioneers in the field of learning disabilities.

In the 1970s, educators' references to this cluster of behaviors began to change to "attention disorders," "distractibility," "irritability," "impulsivity," and "low frustration tolerance." Extreme hyperactivity was not so often exhibited, in part because of much better control through medication.

Throughout this period debate continued within the medical field over the nature and etiology of hyperactivity. Most accepted that brain injury could result in hyperactivity—but what about the large number of children with similar symptoms who had no known brain injury?

In 1968 the American Psychiatric Association provided the first official diagnostic classification of hyperactivity in their *Diagnostic and Statistical Manual of Mental Disorders* (DSM II). It was called the hyperkinetic reaction of childhood and was characterized by overactivity, restlessness, distractibility, and short attention span. In 1982, with the revision of the *Statistical Manual* (DSM III), the condition became the attention deficit disorder (ADD), to emphasize that distractibility was the most salient component. In effect, hyperactivity was deemphasized; however, two types of ADD were recognized: one with and one without hyperactivity. By the next revision (DSM III-R), the term was changed to attention deficit–hyperactivity disorder (ADHD), reflecting a reemphasis on hyperactivity (American Psychiatric Association, 1987). That latest description follows.

> The essential features of this disorder are developmentally inappropriate degrees of inattention, impulsiveness, and hyperactivity. People with the disorder generally display some disturbance in each of these areas, but to varying degrees.

Box 5.4
The Evolution of Terminology and Concepts

The discussion of hyperactivity and the ADHD in this section illustrates how our understanding and use of a particular term and the concepts it represents can change over a relatively short period. Such change may be influenced by the way the term and concept are used by individuals in different disciplines. Those in the medical disciplines are more interested in description and diagnostic terminology acceptable to their field, in etiology, in amelioration or control through medication, and in the possibility of prevention. Those in education are interested primarily in how the condition may interfere with learning and in types of interventions that may reduce negative effects on both academic and social learning and development.

student—for example, attempting to improve attention span, memory, problem-solving abilities, and related learner skills and characteristics. Many cognitive approaches were earlier called "process" approaches. Perceptual-motor approaches (process approaches), popular following recognition of the field of learning disabilities in the 1960s, are now much less favored, except in some unusual cases. Approaches emphasizing learning strategies, cognitive behavior modification, and metacognitive strategies are now more widely used.

Behavioral approaches emphasize the influence of the environment on the learner. The teacher's task is to arrange and manage the environment to facilitate learning. Approaches in common use include data-based instruction and direct instruction.

Supporters of the ecological approach believe that within-student factors and external, environmental factors should receive equal consideration. This approach attends to both factors—and to the manner in which they interact. In fact, some call the ecological approach the interactional approach, reflecting its emphasis on the interaction of cognition and environment.

Mercer cites the importance of individualized instruction and a variety of

Box 5.5
Telling Time
and
Expressing
Time of Day

The ability to tell time and to express the time of day requires an understanding of the terms and concepts of past, present, before, after, and until. "Telling time" by the traditional clock with hour and minute hands also requires the ability to interpret spatial relationships.

For example, students must know that the following mean the same thing.

 and mean the same thing

They must also know that the time of day may be expressed in many ways:

* Forty-five minutes past two
* Forty-five minutes after two
* Fifteen minutes to three
* A quarter till three
* Two forty-five

The wide variety of ways in which we express time can be confusing to any child, but most children master these concepts. Children with learning disabilities may require additional, direct instruction on telling time and on the various ways in which time of day is expressed.

research supporting teacher-directed, systematic instruction. This should include "demonstration, controlled practice with prompts and feedback, and independent practice with feedback" (1987, p. 179). He also suggests placing continuing emphasis on academic instruction and using procedures and strategies that provide for motivation, success experiences, and a positive attitude on the part of the teacher. Finally, he stresses maintenance of attention as particularly essential for students with learning disabilities.

Lerner emphasizes clinical teaching, a process comprising assessment, planning, teaching, evaluation, reassessment, replanning, and teaching. She believes the clinical teacher must be a skilled "child watcher," noting both what students cannot do effectively and what they can do and actually do. She notes that student errors provide important clues to the nature of difficulties with reading, mathematics, thinking processes, and the like. Lerner also emphasizes ecological factors and their influence on learning. She suggests that remedial approaches may be classified as follows.

Approaches related to the analysis of the student
1. Cognitive processing approach
2. Stages of child development approach
3. Learning strategies approach

Approaches related to the analysis of the curricula
1. Mastery learning approach
2. Specialized techniques approach
3. Materials approach

Approaches related to the analysis of environmental conditions
1. Behavioral approach
2. Psychotherapeutic approach
3. Pedagogical approach

More research into the effectiveness of various academic interventions is needed. It has been impeded by the inconsistent application of learning disabilities identification guidelines as well as by the heterogeneous nature of the disorder.

Lessen, Dudzinski, Karsh, and Van Acker (1989) conducted a search of academic intervention research done with students with learning disabilities and published from 1978 through 1987. This search included eight major special education journals that were assumed to be widely read by special educators and that regularly reported applied educational research. A major purpose of this study was to learn what research efforts had to offer the learning disabilities practitioner with respect to effective educational interventions. The survey provided limited information about the effectiveness of interventions, but a notable finding was that fewer than 4% (119 out of 3106) of the articles addressed academic interventions with students with learning disabilities. It concluded that "if academic intervention research with learning disabled students is being conducted, it is not being published in special education journals that would communicate this information to practitioners in the field" (Lessen et al., 1989, p. 119). Until this situation changes, many questions will remain about the viability of the various educational approaches now being used with students with learning disabilities.

The goals established to guide the development of interventions for students

The many faces of learning disabilities.

■ Computer-based instruction may permit the student with learning disabilities to demonstrate talent that otherwise might not be demonstrated in the school setting. ■

with learning disabilities have a major influence on programming. Hecht, Badarak, and Mitchell (1990) summarize three alternative goals in current programs for students with learning disabilities in California. These are competing goals that cannot be achieved by the same programming elements. The staffing team must determine, for each student, which of the goals is most appropriate and then select instructional objectives consistent with it. The goals reported by Hecht and colleagues follow. Note that they refer to a "Resource Specialist Program"; this is the same thing we have called a resource room.

1. *The Resource Specialist Program should secure equal academic achievement outcomes for all students.*

Those who emphasize this goal argue that learning disabled students are capable of the same achievement as regular education students, given specialized services designed to help them overcome their learning disability. Measures of academic achievement, such as CAP test scores and High School graduation rates, are used to determine program success. High quality Resource Specialist services are expected to enable these students to attain CAP scores comparable to other students.

2. The Resource Specialist Program should overcome problems and give all students access to the same school curriculum.

Those who hold this position argue that learning disabled students have temporary problems which can be overcome by concentrated, but temporary, special education services. The goal is resolution of the disability and return of the identified learning disabled students to the regular classroom. If this goal be achieved appropriately, students should exit from the Resource Specialist Program with improved *academic* performance and be able to compete successfully with other students.

From this perspective, equality of educational opportunity means enabling all students to perform successfully without continuing specialized help. It would imply an emphasis on equalizing student capacity for school achievement and then exiting students from the learning disabled programs.

3. The Resource Specialist Program should provide specialized educational programs aimed at preparing learning disabled students to achieve a high quality of life in non-academic areas such as independent living, participation in community life, and holding productive employment.

Those who hold this position argue that learning disabled students are *not* able (or at least not likely) to achieve the same academic levels as other students. Hence, equality of educational opportunity does not mean reaching the same academic goals. Rather, equality means that students will have equally fulfilling and productive lives in areas that do not depend on academic skill levels. Adult life skills that lead to independence, productivity, and satisfaction are substituted for narrow school academic goals. (pp. ix–x)

Learning Disabilities and Juvenile Delinquency

Learning disabilities and juvenile delinquency[2] have been linked and studied by professionals from a variety of disciplines ever since learning disabilities became a recognized entity. A theoretical linkage is logical, given the similarity between the social problems that seem to develop as a result of or in relation to learning disabilities and those found in juvenile delinquents (Trapani, 1990). The prevalence of learning disabilities in adjudicated delinquents is from 26% to 73% (K. Larson, 1988). Whatever the actual prevalence among delinquents, it certainly is disproportionate to the prevalence among the general population.

Opinion varies regarding the influence of race and socioeconomic level (Trapani, 1990), but it is clear that youth with learning disabilities are more at risk to become adjudicated juvenile delinquents regardless of their race or socioeconomic level (Keilitz & Dunivant, 1986).

Several hypotheses or theories have been developed to help explain the relationship between learning disabilities and juvenile delinquency. Keilitz and Dunivant list five of them: (1) the school failure theory, (2) the susceptibility theory, (3) the differential treatment theory, (4) the sociodemographic characteristics theory, and (5) the response theory.

The school failure theory links juvenile delinquency with the negative self-image, negative labeling, and association with delinquency-prone peers that are associated with being part of a program for students with learning disabilities. The susceptibility theory postulates that the cognitive and personality characteristics

[2] A juvenile delinquent is here defined as a juvenile who has been legally determined to have violated existing law.

that are often part of learning disabilities (impulsivity, poor perception of social cues, and so on) increase the likelihood of delinquent behavior. The differential treatment theory assumes that students with learning disabilities lack strategies to avoid detection and that upon arrest they are more likely to be socially abrasive. As a result they are apt to be treated more harshly than their non–learning disabled peers. The sociodemographic characteristics theory holds that learning disabilities do not cause delinquency, even though there is a positive correlation between the two. According to this theory, factors such as parent ethnicity and education level contribute to juvenile delinquency equally, whether or not the student is learning disabled. The response theory proposes that adolescents with and without learning disabilities exhibit the same level of antisocial behavior, but that the non–learning disabled population "covers up" with faked, socially desirable behaviors, thus leaving the impression that students with learning disabilities are more delinquent.

The Learning Disability–Juvenile Delinquency Project was an effort conducted by the National Center for State Courts in Williamsburg, Virginia, from 1976 to 1983. Reports from this project seemed to verify the validity of the school failure, susceptibility, and differential treatment theories. They indicated that adolescents with learning disabilities had significantly higher rates of general delinquent behavior and engaged in more violence, substance abuse, and school disruption than their peers who were not learning disabled. This project also concluded that the link could be broken. Appropriate educational intervention was effective in improving academic performance and decreasing further delinquency on the part of youth who had been adjudicated (Keilitz & Dunivant, 1986).

Learning Disabilities in Adults

As national awareness of learning disabilities grew, and as the first children served in public school programs grew up, it became obvious that although some of the latter had developed sufficient skills to live normal adult lives, many needed continued assistance. The LDA reflects this fact in their learning disabilities definition, by including this statement: "Throughout life the condition can affect self-esteem, education, vocation, socialization, and/or daily living activities." The 1989 NJCLD definition also mentions that learning disabilities "may occur across the life span." The NJCLD had earlier developed a position paper titled "Adults with Learning Disabilities: A Call to Action" (1986), in which it noted the following.

1. Learning disabilities may persist throughout life.
2. Manifestations of learning disabilities may change over the life span.
3. There are few useful diagnostic procedures to assess the needs of adults with learning disabilities.
4. Adults with learning disabilities are often denied access to appropriate instruction, prevocational training, and counseling.
5. Few professionals are trained to assist adults with learning disabilities.
6. Employers are often insensitive to the needs of adults with learning disabilities.
7. Advocacy efforts on behalf of adults with learning disabilities are inadequate.
8. Funding from federal, state, and private agencies for programs for such adults are woefully inadequate.

This call to action constituted a status report of sorts, and only two significant changes seem to have taken place since then. First is an increasing awareness of learning disabilities in adults, promoted to a considerable extent by highly publicized television movies, documentary specials, and statements by high-visibility individuals about their personal experiences. Second is an increasing willingness to provide on-campus assistance to college students with learning disabilities throughout the nation.

In 1986, Buchanan and Wolf published a study of the characteristics of learning disabilities that persist into adulthood and of related implications for programming and service delivery. Its results were consistent with the NJCLD Call to Action statement; they verified that many problematic characteristics and behaviors of childhood persist into adulthood, but are often manifested differently due to changing environmental demands. Other studies indicate that although learning disabled adults may share many psychological, educational, and sociological characteristics with their adolescent counterparts, many are not fully aware of and do not understand their disability (Gearheart & Gearheart, 1989). A 1987 study of learning disabled adults, service providers, employers, consumers, and advocates concluded that adults with learning disabilities often have major social, academic, personal, and vocational problems (Hoffman et al., 1987).

Despite our increased information about the personal, social, and occupa-

People Who Make a Difference

CHER—"I NEVER READ IN SCHOOL" Cher—well known for her acting, musical talent, provocative gowns, independence, and visceral responses—was diagnosed as dyslexic at age 30. Now that she knows the truth, she can talk about the problems she faced as a child and as she gained fame as an actress and entertainer.

In school, Cher learned almost everything by listening. Her written work received low grades, and her report cards indicated that she was not achieving up to her potential. She dropped out of school in the 11th grade and did not finish a book until age 18.

In her career, she does not read cue cards while performing, and has been embarrassed when asked to do "cold readings" in auditions. She still

has trouble making change, reading numbers in the right order, dialing the telephone, and reading billboards. Cher was diagnosed when she took her daughter, Chastity, to a dyslexia center in Santa Monica, California, to seek the cause of Chastity's learning problems. Cher commented that Chastity's problems were just like hers. Further investigation revealed that both had dyslexia. Cher has now described her dyslexia-related problems in various interviews.

When asked how she feels now that the public knows about her dyslexia, Cher reportedly replied, "I could care less." However, her admission and discussion of her dyslexia are of value because she is so widely recognized. When successful, internationally known figures openly discuss a personal disability, it makes it more acceptable.

tional problems of adults with learning disabilities, this group is still largely overlooked as far as concrete assistance goes. Gerber (1986) reports that several European countries are considerably ahead of the United States in providing services throughout the life span for individuals with learning disabilities. The one U.S. arena in which significant progress has been made is that of provision for college or other post–high school educational opportunities.

An example of college programs for individuals with learning disabilities is the statewide system initiated in the California community college system in 1987. Learning disabilities programs for students in California community colleges were authorized in 1976 but encountered many problems in implementation. An effort to address those problems culminated in the California Assessment System for Adults with Learning Disabilities. This model established procedures for (1) intake screening, (2) measuring achievement, (3) measuring adaptive behavior, (4) determining intellectual ability and aptitude, (5) determining processing deficits, (6) determining aptitude-achievement discrepancies, and (7) making the final eligibility recommendation. If students are eligible, California community college programs provide such services as "registration assistance, academic advisement, test-taking and note-taking facilitation, transition assistance to 4-year college programs, and referral to other agencies such as vocational rehabilitation. Specific services and goals are identified for eligible students and recorded on an IEP" (Mellard, 1990, p. 76). During the 1987–1988 school year, approximately 11,000 students were reported as receiving learning disability–related services, a prevalence of almost 1% of the total enrollment.

The system developed in California may not be immediately applicable in many other states, but the manner in which it was developed can provide a model to be followed elsewhere. It represents an effort to recognize the needs of students with learning disabilities who can complete a high school program but who without help cannot successfully cope with a higher education system.

Every state has colleges or universities that provide some type of assistance to students with learning disabilities. Because Section 504 of the Rehabilitation Act of 1973 prohibits discrimination against college applicants on the basis of their disabilities, almost all institutions of higher education claim to make provisions for students with learning disabilities. In practice, however, a variety of service delivery models exists. Trapani indicates that there are three primary options: "(1) partially segregated resource programs, (2) walk-in diagnostic and tutoring services, and (3) general service programs for students with disabilities" (1990, pp. 97–98). She further notes, with respect to resource programs, that "a surcharge is often appended to the regular tuition for the provision of these intensive and specialized services" (ibid., p. 98). Extra payments by the student are not as likely to be required for diagnostic and tutoring service programs or for those that are part of a general program for any student with a disability.

Detailed descriptions of unique programs at various colleges and universities can be found in a variety of sources, but the most comprehensive national guide is *Peterson's Colleges with Programs for Learning Disabled Students* (Mangrum & Strichart, 1988). This guide provides information on over 900 four-year and two-year colleges that offer some type of service for students with learning disabilities. *Peterson's* distinguishes between comprehensive programs and those having special services but no specific program for students with learning disabilities. Careful, personal inquiry and investigation are essential to finding a program that will fulfill individual needs.

Much of this chapter has been devoted to issues in the field of learning disabilities. Professional journals tend to include articles about current problems, concerns, or issues, and basic texts discuss issues that their authors deem important, considering present needs and possible future trends. With this in mind, Addis and Lovitt (1987) conducted a survey that was limited to articles, chapters, or major portions thereof that "dealt specifically with recommendations and current needs" (Lovitt, 1989, p. 468). Their analysis led to the identification of several categories of concern in the field of learning disabilities.

1. The need for a more acceptable, unambiguous definition of learning disabilities
2. The need to better determine the efficacy and validity of a number of different theoretical approaches
3. The need for better (that is, less subjective, more precise, and more carefully controlled) research
4. The need for higher standards of recruitment and training and more rigorous instruction of future teachers of students with learning disabilities
5. The need for more accurate diagnosis — including better standardized tests — and more effective use of curriculum-based assessment
6. The need for more programs for adults with learning disabilities
7. The lack of an objective way to classify individuals as learning disabled
8. The need for research in specific areas: (a) longitudinal research on the long-term effects of various types of instruction, (b) the effectiveness of prevention and early intervention, (c) the effectiveness of resource rooms, (d) the operational differences between LD and non-LD students, and (e) a "catch-all" category of "other concerns"

An additional issue, that of the relationship between public policy and learning disabilities, has been highlighted by others. Note that, because it was a change in public policy (the recognition and funding, at federal and state levels, of programs for students with learning disabilities) that led to the unprecedented increase of such programs, public policy may have similarly sweeping effects in the future.

Finally, there is an unusually high degree of interrelatedness of *all* of the major issues in the field, as Figure 5.3 demonstrates. For most educators, the most important question is how to teach students with learning disabilities more effectively. The answers to this question depend to a great extent on the answers to other questions outlined in Figure 5.3.

Summary

Learning disabilities is the newest of the major disabilities. It received its name in 1963 and has experienced phenomenal growth since then. The federal government's definition of learning disabilities is the most commonly accepted, but it and all others suggested have potential problems or shortcomings. The prevalence of learning disabilities, which is highly dependent on its definition, is usually considered to be between 2% and 4%.

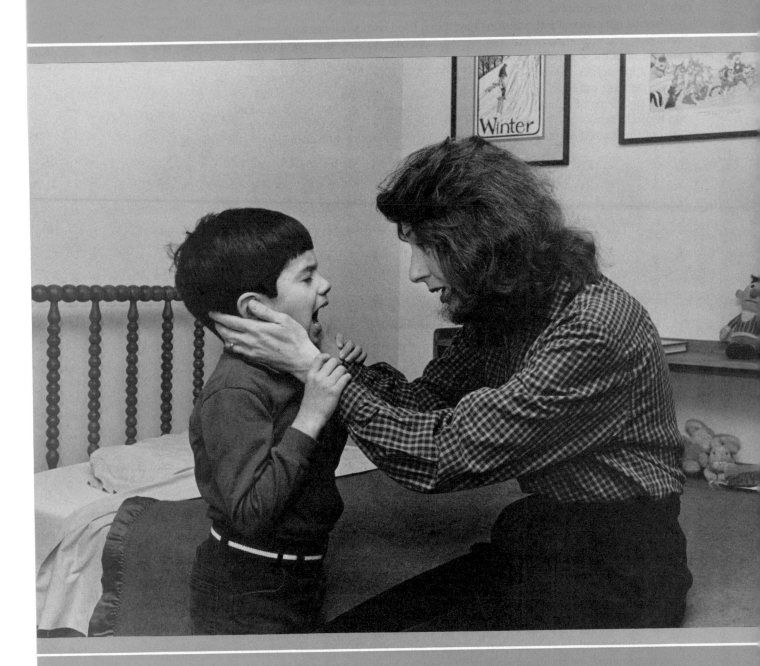

Assessment and identification of students with learning disabilities requires an individual measure of intelligence plus assessment instruments to document significant discrepancies between the apparent ability to learn and what has actually been learned. Environmental, cultural, and economic disadvantages must first be ruled out as possible causes of any educational discrepancy. There is a possible link between learning disabilities and juvenile delinquency; however, the two are not synonymous.

Various educational interventions have been used with students with learning disabilities: cognitive, behavioral, perceptual-motor, learning strategy, and ecological. Several of these overlap to some extent, and it appears that no one intervention or approach is universally effective; however, some have greater general acceptance than others.

The problems of adults with learning disabilities have received less attention than those of school-age students; it appears that several European countries are ahead of the United States in the provision of services to that population.

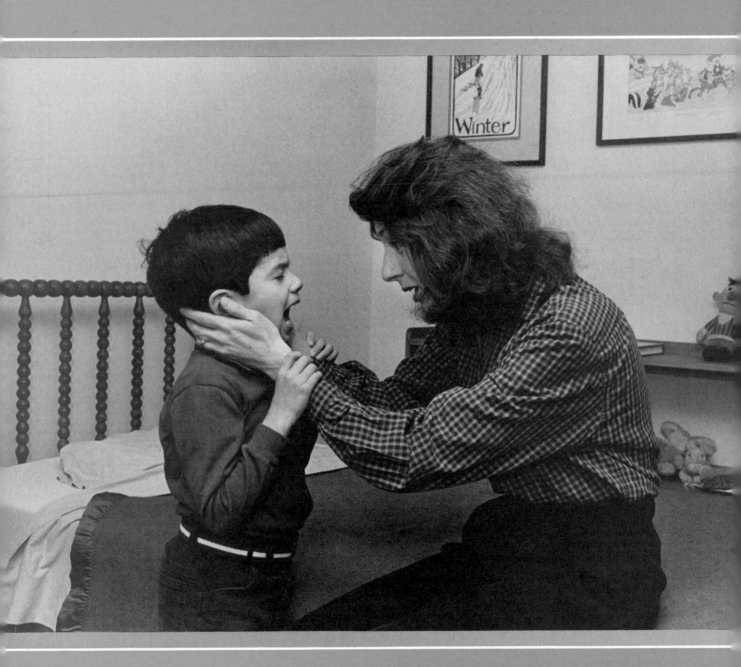

National Committee for Mental Hygiene. This organization encouraged early detection and prevention of mental illness, led the efforts to establish child guidance clinics, and is now recognized as having been the beginning of the mental health movement.

The intelligence and psychological tests developed in the 1920s and 1930s evolved into many of the assessment tools in use today. Psychologists were employed by school districts to administer and interpret the tests that were becoming more widely used to place students in special classes or to provide vocational guidance (Hoffman, 1974). This period saw efforts to establish classification systems, describe characteristics, and define emotional and behavioral disorders. The literature on children's behavior grew in size and quality (Baker & Stulken, 1938). Various educational plans were initiated, surveys of teachers' attitudes were conducted, and attempts to estimate the prevalence of children with behavior disorders were made (Wickman, 1929).

■ Notable Programs and Concepts in Recent Decades

In the 1940s New York City organized special schools, known as the 600 Schools because of the numbers they were assigned, for students who were emotionally disturbed or socially maladjusted. The purpose of these schools was to provide a therapeutic environment that would enable the students to return to nonspecial classrooms. The success of these schools was less than originally anticipated, but they represented an important start toward giving special assistance to students with behavior disorders.

Bruno Bettelheim established the Sonja Shankman Orthogenic School in 1944 for severely emotionally disturbed students; it implemented an environmental or "milieu" therapy. The environment was controlled in the sense that it was made as pleasant as possible for students and ensured that their need for gratification was met. For example, food was always available, because it was seen as a symbol of security. Less attention was given academic achievement than the emotional needs of the students. Bettelheim reasoned that the latter must come first, because learning could not take place until emotional difficulties were resolved (Bettelheim, 1950).

After studying Bettelheim's efforts, Fritz Redl and David Wineman established Pioneer House, a school for emotionally disturbed students based on psychoanalytic thought. It provided more specific techniques for teachers than did Bettelheim's program, perhaps the best known being the life space interview. The major goal of the life space interview was to change students' behavior through empathetic but directed discussions with them about their behavior (Redl & Wineman, 1952, 1954). Redl also emphasized the importance of the individual student's behavior *and* the group dynamics of any given incident. Modifications and adaptations of many of the teaching practices proposed by Redl are still in use today.

An **ecological approach** devoted to changing the environment rather than focusing on student change only was organized by Dr. Nicholas Hobbs in 1962. The Project Re-Education Schools (known as Project Re-ED) hypothesized that emotional disturbance was an educational problem more than an illness, and that through academic and social competence the student would gain control over the environment. Project Re-ED schools were residential during the weekdays; however, great emphasis was placed on readjusting the students' total social system, so school personnel involvement with families was intense (Hobbs, 1966, 1969).

In 1963 PL 88-164, the Mental Retardation Facilities and Community Mental Health Centers Construction Act, was passed. This legislation sought to provide federal money to develop local mental health centers, which were to service persons of all ages who were mentally ill. Part of PL 88-164 was a provision for training personnel to handle all recognized disabilities, including emotional disturbance. This greatly increased the number of trained personnel available, allowing more school programs to be developed.

The Council for Exceptional Children established a new division—the Council for Children with Behavioral Disorders (CCBD)—in 1964, responding to a recognized need for services for those students and for a forum in which research and promising teaching practices could be shared.

As the number of public school classrooms for students with behavior disorders increased, a variety of concerns surfaced. School administrators were uncomfortable with the therapy aspects of such programs, and teachers were reluctant to have students meet with psychologists during school hours. Both principals and regular teachers were troubled by the varied behaviors that special classroom teachers were willing to tolerate and by their teaching practices. The appropriateness of using different teaching methodologies to meet the special needs of these students was not yet fully appreciated—nor were the demands placed on the teachers. Their classrooms were frequently in separate buildings or in isolated rooms in the school building, and teachers lacked the supportive supervision available to general classroom teachers. Neither was there a system of support among teachers who taught similar students. The result was a high attrition rate among teachers of the behaviorally disordered.

Rising interest in behavioral principles led to their application in teaching students with behavior disorders. Frank Hewett (1967, 1968) designed an "engineered classroom" that emphasized the importance of the classroom environment, curricula designed to meet students' needs, and token reinforcement. The program became known as the Santa Monica Project and is frequently cited as a model of the behavioral approach.

If the 1950s and 1960s saw the development of programs for students with behavior disorders, the 1970s saw their application. A comprehensive study and analysis of theory, interventions, and delivery systems, the Conceptual Project in Emotional Disturbance created by William Rhodes and Michael Tracy (1972a, 1972b; Rhodes & Head, 1974) provided a three-volume reference.

A more holistic manner of thinking about students emerged in the late seventies and became known as cognitive behavior modification (Hallahan et al., 1983; Meichenbaum, 1977, 1979, 1983). The focus was on the interrelationship of affective and cognitive factors. This approach recognizes that teaching is cognitive in that it requires knowledge and information about child development, curricula, and classroom management; yet it is also affective because of the social interactions between teachers and students and among students.

Issues examined in the 1980s that are not yet resolved include the appropriate provision of services for students who are behaviorally disordered. In general the letter of Public Law 94-142 (see Chapter 1) is met, but the spirit may not be met with regard to students with behavior disorders. How to define "seriously emotionally disturbed" (from PL 94-142) also remains a subject of controversy. The term *emotionally disturbed* is the subject of another debate; efforts to change the term to *behavioral disorders* at the federal level have been unsuccessful. The latter is, however, widely used in the professional literature (Huntze, 1985; Kauffman, 1982; Kavale, Forness, & Alper, 1986).

■ A continuing pattern of isolation and rejection of social contact can be indicative of behavior disorders. ■

Definitions of Behavior Disorders

Federal definitions and regulations are meant to provide guidelines for the states. The states' definitions must be similar enough to the federal one to include the same type of student, but they may vary in terminology and characteristics. In turn, state definitions affect local practice. For example, if medical terminology is used, it may imply that medical rather than educational interventions are required. Hence, terminology may limit the types of students who receive services.

The field of behavioral disorders is still evolving its terminology and definition. The federal definition uses the term *seriously emotionally disturbed;* however, the CCBD, the largest professional organization representing educators working with such students, has urged that the federal terminology be changed to *behavioral disorders* (Huntze, 1985). The issue is a preference for terminology that reflects educational needs, that is not aligned with any specific theory of causation (historically, causation has determined the interventions), that allows for more flexibility in assessment procedures, and that has fewer negative connotations. State definitions and the professional literature in the field regularly interchange the following terms: *emotionally disturbed, emotionally disordered, emotionally handicapped, emotionally impaired, behaviorally disordered, behaviorally impaired, behaviorally maladjusted, behaviorally disturbed, socially and emotionally disturbed, socially and emotionally maladjusted, socially handicapped, emotionally and socially handicapped, emotionally and behaviorally disordered,* and *socially and emotionally impaired.* This list is not exhaustive but indicates the range of terminology purporting to describe the same population of students. The purpose of the CCBD proposal was to consolidate this terminology into one, more widely accepted, term.

According to PL 94-142, this is the definition of "seriously emotionally disturbed."

> A condition exhibiting one or more of the following characteristics over a long period of time and to a marked degree, which adversely affects educational performance:
>
> An inability to learn which cannot be explained by intellectual, sensory, or health factors;
>
> An inability to build or maintain satisfactory interpersonal relationships with peers and teachers;
>
> Inappropriate types of behavior or feelings under normal circumstances;
>
> A general pervasive mood of unhappiness or depression;
>
> Or a tendency to develop physical symptoms or fears associated with personal or school problems.
>
> The term includes children who are schizophrenic or autistic.[1] The term does not include children who are socially maladjusted unless it is determined that they are seriously emotionally disturbed. (*Federal Register,* 1977, p. 42478)

The federal definition uses the term *seriously* but does not elaborate on how to measure severity. Bower (1981) restated an earlier conceptualization of the following five levels of behavior disorder, on a continuum ranging from least (1) to most (5) severe.

1. Students who experience the usual problems associated with growing up, testing limits, and exploring alternatives
2. Students who develop some of the characteristics of emotional problems because of normal but difficult stresses of life, such as the death of a parent, serious injury, or perhaps losing a girlfriend or boyfriend
3. Students who demonstrate persistence in some or all of the characteristics beyond the normal expectation but who are able to function and manage their lives
4. Students who experience continual or persistently recurring characteristics but who with support can maintain school attendance and develop some personal relationships
5. Students who experience more continual and persistent characteristics, are unable to profit from school attendance, and who may be served best in residential settings

The difficulties of the students in the last three categories are not temporary, and many of the usual teaching strategies are not sufficient for those students.

The federal definition also states that the characteristics must be present over a long period of time and to a marked degree. Just what constitutes a long period of time is debatable. Some behaviors, such as assaulting the teacher or other students, cannot be tolerated over any length of time; however, they would seem to be included under the wording "to a marked degree." Physical violence is so different from normal that it calls attention to itself. On the other hand, some

---

[1] In 1990 the term *autistic* was removed from this definition and listed with other disabilities as a separate disorder.

behaviors such as withdrawal and isolation do not always come to the attention of parents or teachers. These behaviors may be noticed "over a long period of time." But that does not answer the question of what a long time is. Some school districts define it as 30 or 60 days, which is not meant to be a magical number but rather a guideline.

"Normal" behavior is often considered to be a range of behaviors along a continuum with subjective demarcations. Teachers and parents base their judgment of what is normal on environmental, cultural, and situational factors. What appears normal in one part of the country may not be considered normal in another. Similarly, what is normal for one ethnic group may not be normal for another.

The CCBD has issued a position paper on the federal definition and identification procedures used with students with behavioral disorders (Executive Committee of the CCBD, 1987). The paper critiques the inadequacy of the federal definition and urges a revision emphasizing an educational focus and including students who are socially maladjusted. It also recommends using educationally relevant data to determine whether a student is in need of special education services because of a behavior disorder. As we have no universally agreed-upon definition, it may be useful to consider several definitions to develop a better understanding of students with behavior disorders.

Bower developed an early definition that identified five significant characteristics. According to his definition, one or more of these characteristics must be present to a marked degree or over an extended period of time.

1. An inability to learn that cannot be explained by intellectual, sensory, or health factors
2. An inability to build or maintain satisfactory interpersonal relationships with peers and teachers
3. Inappropriate types of behavior or feelings under normal conditions
4. A general, pervasive mood of unhappiness or depression
5. A tendency to develop physical symptoms, pains, or fears associated with personal or school problems (1960, pp. 9–10)

As you may have noticed, the federal definition was based on Bower's; however, he has stressed that modifications of his definition evident in the federal definition "do serious damage to the integrity of the research and conceptual base from which the definition was drawn" (Bower, 1982, p. 55).

McDowell later defined disturbed behavior as follows:

The behaviorally disordered child is defined as a child whose behavior within the educational setting may be discordant in his relationships with others and/or whose academic achievement may be impaired due to an inability to learn utilizing the presented teaching techniques. The child's current behavior manifests either an extreme or a persistent failure to adapt and function intellectually, emotionally, or socially at a level commensurate with his or her chronological age. (1975, p. 2)

Algozzine defined as emotionally disturbed any person

who, after receiving supportive educational services and counseling assistance available to all students, still exhibits persistent and consistent severe to very severe behavioral disabilities that consequently interfere with productive learning processes. This is the student whose inability to achieve academic progress and satisfactory interpersonal relationships cannot be attributed primarily to physical, sensory, or intellectual deficits. (1981, p. 4)

Reinert and Huang, encouraging the use of the term *children in conflict*, defined that population as "youngsters whose behavior has a deleterious effect on their personal or educational development and/or that of their peers. Negative effects may vary considerably from one child to another in terms of severity and prognosis (1987, pp. 5–6).

Lambert and Bower suggested that "the emotionally handicapped child is defined as having a moderate to marked reduction in behavioral freedom, which, in turn, reduces his ability to function effectively in learning or working with others (1976, p. 95).

There are several common elements among the various definitions.

1. A behavior or combination of behaviors that poses a problem for the student, those around the student, or both
2. The persistence of problem behaviors
3. The severity of problem behaviors

In general, one or more of those factors leads teachers to refer a student for assessment.

Prevalence

The prevalence of behavior disorders is the number of students with behavior disorders at any given point in time. The *Thirteenth Annual Report to Congress* (1991) of the number of students identified and receiving services according to provisions of the Individuals with Disabilities Education Act (formerly PL 94-142, The Education of the Handicapped Act) indicates prevalence figures for individual states ranging from 0.04% to 1.66% and a national average of 0.67% (see Table 2.5).

Most authorities consider this low, considering the number of students who should be identified and receive services. When PL 94-142 was passed, the federal government predicted that about 2% of the school-age population would be identified as "seriously emotionally disturbed." In the 1980s this figure was revised downward to between 1.2% and 2.0%. According to Kauffman (1989), the government appears to prefer to revise its prevalence estimates rather than tolerate a wide discrepancy between its estimates and the number of students actually receiving services.

Other estimates of the prevalence of behavior disorders range from 1% to 45% of the school-age population (Cullinan & Epstein, 1986; Glidewell & Swallow, 1968; Rubin & Balow, 1978; Wickman, 1929). Explanations for such disparate estimates and the underidentification of students with behavior disorders are related to definitional controversy; negative attitudes toward behavioral disorders, resulting in a reluctance to label a student; the lack of available services; the lack of uniformity in identification procedures; and the exclusion of students who are socially maladjusted (although there *is* a recognized overlap with emotional disturbance). Another major factor is the tendency to identify students only when behavior is severe.

Characteristics of Behavior Disorders

The perplexing issue of definition remains unresolved; however, to provide teachers with practical referral and identification guidelines, many states have devel-

Table 6.1 Characteristics of behavioral disorders

Avoidance of contact with others	Inconsistency in friendships
Avoidance of eye contact with others	Lethargy
Behavior that is ritualistic	Lack of contact with reality
Chronic disobedience	Physical withdrawal from touch
Covert or overt hostility	Physical aggressiveness toward others or property
Disorganization in routine tasks or spatial orientation	Rapid or severe changes in mood
Temper tantrums	Denial of responsibility for actions
Disturbances of sleep or eating habits	Need for constant reassurance
Emotional isolation	Repetitive behavior
Exaggerated or bizarre mannerisms	Attention-seeking behavior
Few or no friends	Self-mutilation
Frequent or persistent verbalizations about suicide	Self-stimulation
Frequent unexplained illnesses	Severe reactions to changes in routine
Frequent unexplained crying	Sexual deviation
Low frustration level	Truancy
Hyperactivity	Unexplained "accidents"
Inability to complete tasks	Unexplained academic decline
Inability to concentrate	Lack of motivation
Inappropriate noises or verbalizations	Unreasonable or unexplained fears
Poor attention	Verbal aggression
Inconsistency in academic performance	Verbal disruptiveness

oped lists of characteristics that indicate some of the common behaviors demonstrated by students with behavior disorders. A composite of these lists may further our understanding of the concept of behavioral disorders (see Table 6.1). Note, however, that demonstrations of one or even several of those characteristics does not mean a student is behaviorally disordered. The degree to which the characteristics are exhibited, the length of time they are exhibited, and their resistance to the usual methods of amelioration must be considered. In addition, the context in which the behaviors occur, the student's age, sex, and level of development, and the degree to which adults in the student's environment are able to address the maladaptive behavior are all significant factors.

Lists of behavior disorder characteristics may be combined into broader categories. For example, Achenbach and Edelbrock (1981) condensed a variety of characteristics into two categories: *externalizing* behaviors—including various forms of aggressive, antisocial, and undercontrolled behaviors—and *internalizing* behaviors—comprising behaviors associated with fearfulness, withdrawal, immaturity, and excessive control. Quay (1979) suggested the following four broad categories.

1. *Conduct disorders,* which include characteristics related to physical and verbal aggression, lack of responsibility for actions, negative attitudes, and defiance of and conflict with authority
2. *Anxiety-withdrawal,* which includes such characteristics as excessive shyness, social withdrawal, abnormal fears, and sadness or depression
3. *Immaturity,* which includes characteristics related to passivity, short attention span, preoccupation, and daydreaming
4. *Socialized aggression,* including such characteristics as truancy, stealing, lying, and participation in a delinquent or gang subculture

■ Some defiant behavior is typical during adolescence. Excessive defiant behavior may be an indicator of behavior disorders. ■

Whelan and Gallagher (1972) compressed the characteristics into the two categories of *behavioral excesses* (the aggressive, acting-out types of behavior) and *behavioral deficits* (the immature and withdrawing types of behavior).

When behavior is very qualitatively and quantitatively different from normal it is often labeled psychotic. Lack of language, bizarre language, ritualistic or meaningless repetitive behaviors, lack of contact with reality, and unresponsiveness to others or to the environment are also characterizations of psychotic behavior. Two subcategorizations or labels are associated with such behaviors. The term *infantile autism* is used when the onset of those behaviors occurs at fewer than 30 months of age; *childhood schizophrenia* is applied for a later age of onset. These various classification systems enhance our understanding of the concept of behavioral disorders, but they also point to the elusiveness of a precise set of characteristics.

Identification

In our earlier discussion of the definition of behavioral disorders, we noted several concerns about its ambiguity. Those concerns directly influence procedures for screening and identification. The subjective nature of determining the presence and influence of any other disability, the degree to which deviant behavior must be present, and even whether the behavior is indeed deviant are some of the difficult issues of identification.

Chapter 2 contains a general discussion of the assessment practices and procedures dictated by PL 94-142. Those same principles and guidelines apply to students suspected of having behavioral disorders, with certain additional considerations. In 1987, the Executive Committee of the CCBD proposed a reduced reliance on the types of diagnostic systems used by psychiatrists, clinical or school psychologists, and other clinically oriented personnel. Its viewpoint was that such predetermined categories have little educational relevance. Further, some of the classifications provided in the *Diagnostic and Statistical Manual* (DSM III-R) of the American Psychiatric Association (1987) may be equated with social maladjustment, which is specifically excluded by PL 94-142—thus making students ineligible for services. To reduce the subjectivity of the assessment procedures, the full use of the *multidisciplinary* team and *multiple* sources of data were recommended (Executive Committee of the CCBD, 1987).

Using assessment data including health, vision, hearing, social and emotional status, motor abilities, intellectual capacity, academic performance, and communication abilities provides information from a variety of disciplines and helps ensure that no single criterion is used for identification purposes. In regard to the social and emotional status of the student, environmental and ecological data from multiple sources should be collected. Multifaceted data collection includes formal and informal observation in both academic and play or free time settings; discipline and attendance records; anecdotal reports; interviews with parents, teachers, and peers; checklists and rating scales; sociometric measures; social skills development measures; and documentation of strategies employed previously to modify the student's behavior. Ecologic assessments of the environments in which the student functions include examination of the materials, methods, and curriculum used in the classroom; teacher expectations; parental discipline practices; parent and family expectations; economic and cultural family status; and community expectations and standards for behavior (Executive Committee of the CCBD, 1987; Kauffman, 1989; McLoughlin & Lewis, 1990; Morgan & Jenson, 1988).

When such multifaceted data have been collected, the multidisciplinary team can use it as the basis for discussion to determine eligibility for services. For a positive identification to be made, there must be a high degree of congruence between these substantiating data and the perceived disordered behavior that was the basis for referral. Once identification is made, the abundance of collected data allows the multidisciplinary team to develop a useful IEP that addresses the disordered behavior as well as academic concerns.

The placement of students with behavior disorders ranges from consultative services to residential centers (see Chapter 2 for the complete placement options). As always, the emphasis is on the least restrictive placement for the individual student.

Causation and Related Interventions

Everyone has opinions about others' behavior and can explain why individuals behave as they do. Popular magazines frequently publish articles on child behavior problems and suggest methods to either correct the child's problem or deficiency or raise the parents' tolerance level. Various academic disciplines such as psychology, education, medicine, and theology have studied behavior, attempt-

Table 6.2 Approaches to treating behavioral disorders

Approach	Causes of Behavioral Disorders	Interventions
Biogenic or biophysical	chemical imbalance; genetic abnormalities; brain dysfunction	medication (stimulants, antidepressants)
Psychodynamic	unsuccessful negotiation of psychological stages; early traumatic experiences; inner conflicts	encouragement of free expression of feelings; reduction of limitations; accepting environment
Psychoeducational	negative self-image; anxiousness; undue stress; negative view of environment	support; reduction of stress; development of a realistic view of environment
Behavioral	learned inappropriate behavior that is reinforced; models of inappropriate behavior that are followed	reinforcement of appropriate behavior; modeling appropriate behavior
Social-Ecologic	interaction between student and various environments (classroom, school, home, community); interaction between student needs and demands of societal norms and responsibilities	adjustment of student, environment, or both; adaptation of environment; teaching alternative behaviors
Humanistic	depersonalized system of education; irrelevant curricula; individual depersonalization; authoritarian and rigid teachers	free, open educational system; emphasis on affect and interdependence; caring, supportive atmosphere

ing to define what constitutes abnormal behavior and what causes it. The true cause of a behavior disorder is seldom known; therefore, no discipline has been entirely successful in pinning it down. It appears that behavior—what one does and why—is too complex to be explained by a single factor or even prescribed sets of factors.

To understand the concept of behavioral disorders, however, it helps to appreciate the diverse explanations proposed by the various schools of thought. Each approach reflects its theory of causation and prescribes interventions intended to minimize the effects of the causative factors or eliminate them altogether. Some approaches are more relevant for teachers than others. Kauffman (1989) has suggested that teachers focus their efforts on factors related to the behavior disorder that they can alter. He also notes that, though causative factors may influence the behavior of the student, they are often buried in the past; realistically, teachers can do little about them. Only the present and future can be addressed in education.

The possible causes of behavior disorders and the typical interventions favored by each approach are summarized in Table 6.2 and elaborated here.

■ The Biogenic or Biophysical[2] Approach

As modern experimental science became prominent during the 19th century, our knowledge of chemistry, physiology, and neurology increased rapidly and led to a

[2] The term *biological* may also be used; either term is acceptable.

BEHAVIOR DISORDERS
TROUBLED YOUNGSTERS/ TROUBLING BEHAVIORS

Behavior disorders are among the most troubling of the disabilities for parents, teachers, and students. When a child obviously has the ability to learn but just won't learn, it is easy for adults to lose patience. When children are disruptive and interfere with the learning of others, it is even more difficult for all concerned. It is essential that the adult, who is troubled by the child's behavior, remember that the child is even more troubled.

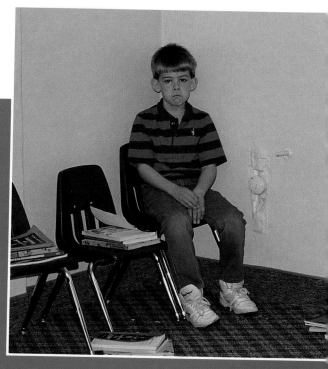

This is not a happy face. "The teacher hates me. This isn't fair."

This teacher must address this boy's behavior. What is the best way?

The face of innocence. "They slipped, I didn't throw them."

The parents' approach to managing their child's inappropriate behavior at home may influence the child's behavior at school.

Though aggressive, acting-out behavior is what is most often associated with students with behavior disorders, it is important to remember that withdrawn behavior, an unusual tendency to seek isolation, and inability to interact socially may also indicate a behavior disorder. Although such behavior doesn't receive as much attention as acting-out behavior (perhaps because it does not challenge the adults' authority or interfere with the learning of others), unusually withdrawn behavior is equally serious. And though it does not demand attention in the same manner as acting-out behavior, it deserves the same degree of attention.

For years, educators simply ignored the needs of students with behavior disorders, except to expel these students from school if the behavior was too disruptive. More recently, educators have recognized that some students with behavior disorders have legitimate special educational needs. Along with this recognition has come the realization that parent involvement is essential if effective programs are to be implemented.

Children may show a tendency toward behavior disorders through aggressive, acting-out behavior, or through an unusual isolation and inability to interact socially.

Teenage drug and alcohol abuse has increased in recent years. Although not necessarily an indication of behavior disorders, drug and alcohol abuse is often part of the overall picture. In a similar manner, it has been recognized that some teenage pregnancies cannot be accurately labeled "unwanted" or "accidental." In some instances, the pregnancy may be part of an attempt to find love and acceptance and to break away from parental and societal limits and restrictions.

Although not necessarily an indication of behavior disorders, drug and alcohol abuse is often associated with behavior disorders.

Drug use is a continuing problem and is often associated with behavior disorders.

Many students with behavior disorders drop out of school.

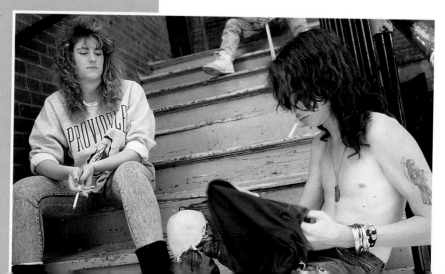

Behavior disorders remain a disability that is not fully accepted as "legitimate" by all experts. Some believe that if stricter discipline were in place, most of these students would no longer have a behavior disorder. These educators tend to ignore the possibility of a variety of serious, underlying causes. They also cannot explain the withdrawn student with this rationale. The undeniable fact is that behavior disorders exist, regardless of causation. It appears that behavior disorders may be a disability that is increasing in prevalence; the challenge to both parents and educators is obvious and will not likely diminish or disappear.

Teenage pregnancies may be part of an attempt to break away from limits and restrictions and search for love and intimacy.

Juvenile delinquents may have behavior disorders but the terms are not synonymous.

better understanding of the organic pathology underlying physical ailments. It was hoped that similar discoveries would link—in a simple cause-and-effect relationship—physiologic, neurologic, or chemical abnormalities with abnormal behavior.

William Greisinger published *The Pathology and Therapy of Psychic Disorders* in 1845; in it, he suggested that psychiatry should examine the physiologic aspect of mental disorders, which he felt were likely to be explained by brain pathology. Following a similar line of thought, Emil Kraeplin hypothesized in 1883 that mental disorders are diseases that follow predictable patterns, just like other known diseases of the time such as chicken pox or diphtheria. This led to speculation that specific organic causes for mental illnesses would be discovered, that illnesses would follow a predictable course, and that in time cures would be found. To some degree this kind of thinking guides researchers today who examine the relationship between physiologic functioning and behavioral disorders; their approach is often called **biophysical theory.**

Examples of the types of causal factors they examine are brain damage or dysfunction, CNS dysfunction, genetic or chromosomal abnormalities, and biochemical imbalances. Such abnormalities may occur prior to birth, during birth, or after birth.

Assessment of these types of abnormalities once consisted mainly of autopsies or examination of the electrical activity of the brain using electroencephalograms (EEGs). These did not provide sufficient information to draw definitive conclusions, however. More recent technology such as positron emission tomography (PET), which records the brain's chemistry and the interaction of neurochemicals within it; nuclear magnetic resonance or magnetic resonance imaging (MRI), which presents clear anatomical details of living organisms, including the brain; and the Tandem Scanning Reflective Light Microscope (TSRLM), which enables researchers to look at living brain tissue with reflected light, has opened up a new world of insights and information regarding the functioning of the brain and central nervous system.

Research into genetic or chromosomal abnormalities has focused on the location, organization, and regulation of the genetic materials on the chromosomes. More than 800 of the estimated 50,000 to 100,000 individual genes a person might possess have been mapped, and 200 of the 3000 disorders known to be caused by a single gene have been diagnosed (Menolascino & Stark, 1988).

Prior to the 1980s, research yielded inconclusive results when seeking biogenic or biophysical causes for behavior disorders, but it did indicate that individuals with behavior disorders show different brain structure and electrical activity than those without (Erickson, 1987; Rizzo & Zabel, 1988).

Researchers have located a specific gene that leads to the manic-depressive syndrome and have identified another four that may contribute to the development of the same disorder (Stark, Menolascino, & Goldsbury, 1988). The role of the environment in reducing or increasing the effects of such genetic abnormalities is less clear. Attention deficit–hyperactivity disorder (ADHD), associated with both behavioral disorders and learning disabilities, has been directly related to a specific metabolic abnormality. Using PET technology to measure metabolic activity in the brain of ADHD subjects, researchers found it to be lower overall than in non-ADHD control groups and significantly lower in two areas of the brain that regulate attention and motor control (Zametkin et al., 1990). (See Chapter 5 for a more extensive discussion of ADHD.)

The study of hormones, their role in body functioning, and how they interact with the brain is still in its infancy. However, researchers have found high levels of cortisol, noradrenaline, and thyroxine but low levels of testosterone in subjects diagnosed as paranoid schizophrenic or manic-depressive (Stark et al., 1988).

With increasingly sophisticated technology, researchers have gained access to information that until recently was regarded as unknowable. It appears that Rimland's assertion, made over 30 years ago, that biophysical or organic theories of severe behavior disorders were rejected because of our ignorance of organic and chemical functions of the human organism was more accurate than many believed (Rimland, 1964).

The effects of inadequate maternal nutrition during pregnancy, general inadequate nourishment, specific deficiencies in the diet, sleep habits, stress, temper-

---

People Who Make a Difference

PATTY DUKE—YOU DON'T HAVE TO BE ASHAMED Patty Duke won an Academy Award for *The Miracle Worker,* was nominated eight times for an Emmy, and won three Emmys for her TV performances. However, she was known in Hollywood as a "difficult" actress. She would be fine on the set for days or weeks at a time, and then would suddenly (as it appeared) get angry with the producer or script. Sometimes she would feel that the others were not working hard enough, fly into a rage, and leave work without telling anyone when she would be back. Her anger and frustration might last days or weeks. At other times she became so energized that she was angry because no one wanted to work as long as she did. She would accuse them of being lazy or of not caring about the production.

As an adult, she now describes her teenaged portrayal of Helen Keller in the stage version of *The Miracle Worker* as an "acting out" of her personal illness. In it, Helen has a fight with Annie Sullivan that lasts for 10 minutes on stage. Patty says, "One of the reasons I survived those awful years was that I could be on stage every night and beat the bejesus out of an adult and have people applaud me and think I was a brilliant actress. Now I know that it was a way to let out my feelings of anger. Now I know they were there because I didn't understand why I couldn't control my life."

At age 36, Patty was diagnosed as manic-depressive, a disorder characterized by periods of depression alternating with manic activity. After psychotherapy and medication (lithium), she said, "my whole life is changed and that feels like a miracle." Though acknowledging the difference that lithium has made, she adds, "It's not a panacea. All it does is correct a biological imbalance that's already present in your body's biological systems."

This "miracle" did not happen until after Patty had lived much of her life in what she describes as torture. Her autobiography, *Call Me Anna,* details her suicide attempts during depressive episodes, her angry outbursts at her children, and her periods of intense activity: shopping sprees in which she bought four cars in one week or flew anywhere just to be on the move, insomnia, and running until she collapsed. She now realizes that her behavior was all a part of the disorder.

Patty Duke has chosen to speak out about the manner in which manic-depressive disorder can affect lives when not treated, thereby giving hope to others. She has been president of the Screen Actors' Guild, which she regards as proof of the esteem of her peers, and received the first Eleanor Roosevelt Award for her political activities. She says, "These activities give me additional opportunities to speak about mental disorders and to let people know they don't have to be ashamed. When treated correctly, people can live full lives."

■ Fighting may reflect normal behavior or may be part of a pattern of behavior disorders. ■

ament types, and other similar factors will require additional study in the light of information and research techniques now available.

Interventions   Interventions based on the biogenic or biophysical approach are both medical and educational. Medical interventions include psychotropic drugs, which alter moods or thought processes, and various behavior or dietary modifications. Biofeedback can give individuals information that helps them control their behavior. When medical interventions are prescribed, the teacher's role is to monitor and record the student's behavior and provide that information to the parents and physician. In the field of pediatric psychopharmacology, the teacher is regarded as a member of a multidisciplinary team, all of whom are directing their efforts toward assisting the student (Gadow & Poling, 1988).

Educational interventions may require the teacher to attempt to provide a modified environment. More structure and reduced visual or auditory stimulation characterize such environments. Teaching may emphasize small, sequenced increments with ample drill and practice. Often behavior modification principles of reinforcement and reward are "borrowed" from that approach and implemented in conjunction with either medication or a modified environment.

■ **The Psychodynamic Approach**

The psychodynamic (or the psychoanalytic) approach is based on Sigmund Freud's conception of the id, ego, and superego. These psychic constructs interrelate to form the personality, and imbalances among them result in behavior often viewed as inappropriate.

According to Freud, the maturing child undergoes a series of psychosexual stages of development before reaching adulthood. These stages (oral, anal, phallic, and latency) represent biologic maturational stages as well as development phases in the sexual and aggressive instincts that play a critical role in shaping the personality. Each stage of development places demands on the individual that must be met and triggers conflicts to be resolved. If those demands are not met and conflicts not resolved, personality development is inhibited, and the individual may become fixated at a particular stage. For example, adult fixation at the oral stage may be exhibited by excessive eating or drinking.

Anxiety and its results are also focal issues. Anxiety is painful; to alleviate the pain, the individual takes some corrective action. If the ego is sufficiently strong, it can cope with fears or perceived dangers using rational measures. Students with behavior disorders rarely have strong egos, so they take irrational protective measures known as defense mechanisms. These alleviate pain but distort reality. Persons who feel inadequate or worthless and who are unable to rationally examine the reasons for their feelings may turn to fantasy, imagining themselves performing great feats or living satisfying lives.

The role of the unconscious is critical to this approach; it consists of all the hurtful memories, forbidden desires, and unpleasant experiences that have been excluded from consciousness. Usually the individual is unaware of them; nevertheless, they seek expression, often through dreams and fantasies, leading to maladaptive behavior. According to psychodynamic constructs, this unconscious material must be made conscious for the individual, integrated into the ego structure, and successfully resolved.

Advocates of this approach emphasize the influence of parents and siblings and of early traumatic events. Behavior disorders are viewed as symbolic attempts to address unresolved conflicts or unnegotiated stages. This approach to behavior disorders was the predominant therapy during the 1950s and early 1960s (Walker & Shea, 1988).

Interventions Interventions based on the psychodynamic approach include those from the disciplines of psychology, psychiatry, and education. Psychologists and psychiatrists may provide individual, group, or family psychotherapy that seeks to gain insight into the psychic conflicts. The assumption is that the insights gained thereby will help the individual return to normalcy and either solve or eliminate the conflicts causing the disordered behavior.

Teachers who are proponents of this approach strive to build warm, trusting relationships and to provide a permissive classroom atmosphere. They may also use variations of play therapy that have as a goal the expression of inner conflicts. Theoretically, once these conflicts are revealed they may be addressed and resolved. The major task of the teacher is to be a caring, understanding, accepting adult in the life of the child.

■ **The Psychoeducational Approach**

The psychoeducational approach is an educational extension of the psychodynamic approach. Its focus is on creating an accepting and understanding environment that fosters students' abilities to function appropriately. Teachers recognize that their appearance, behavior, and attitudes are critical because they are a significant adult in the lives of their students, who will unconsciously identify with them. The academic aspects of school are viewed as secondary; however, the

■ A student with behavior disorders who is in a regular class may not participate in classroom activities. ■

limits imposed by socialization in groups contribute to the growth of the ego. Disturbed students react to stress in immature ways such as lying, stealing, running away, and denial; it is the responsibility of the adult to act maturely in the face of such behaviors. Students who act out their feelings through behaviors such as withdrawal, hyperactivity, or passive aggression can draw adults into displaying similar behaviors, thus establishing a self-fulfilling prophecy. This perpetuates the behavior and increases resistance to change. Teachers who understand this conflict cycle and how the students' emotions are related to those behaviors will be better able to support students and encourage behavioral change (Long, Morse, & Newman, 1976).

Interventions   Interventions consistent with the psychoeducational approach are varied but have a common theme. The "life space interview" is designed to assist students in gaining insight into problem behaviors and personal motivations, in recognizing the consequences of their actions, and in planning alternative behaviors (Redl, 1959). In times of unusual stress, an interview may be used to provide the student with emotional first aid in the form of frustration reduction, restoration of disrupted communication, reinforcement of behavioral limits, and emotional support. The interviewer should be an adult who plays a significant role in the life of the student and should perceive his or her role as that of a facilitator.

Art, music, and dance activities that may encourage expression of both positive and negative feelings are consistent with this approach. Students who are not highly verbal and have difficulty in expressing emotions may find in such activities a socially acceptable avenue of self-expression. The therapeutic benefits include group participation with few limitations, relaxation during stress, motivation, externalization of personal feelings, self-exploration, and creativity (Chace, 1958; Cheney & Morse, 1972; Hibben & Scheer, 1982; Williams & Wood, 1977; Yell, 1988). These activities are not intended to directly change behavior, but rather to encourage the insights the student may gain. It is believed that those insights will then lead to behavior change.

■ The Behavioral Approach

The behavioral approach is based on B. F. Skinner's principles of operant conditioning. His conclusion that the most understandable determinants of behavior lie outside the individual and can be manipulated to change behavior is a cornerstone of Skinnerian thought (Skinner, 1953). Proponents of **behaviorism** assume that behavior is learned and reinforced rather than a result of emotions, thoughts, drives, or feelings. As such, behavior is subject to change if the principles of **reinforcement** are consistently applied. Alberto and Troutman (1990) have summarized those principles as the following.

1. Reinforcement is applied *after* the desired behavior is demonstrated.
2. Reinforcement is applied as *soon as possible after* the desired behavior is observed.
3. Reinforcement must be individualized and powerful for the individual.
4. Frequent, small rewards are better than infrequent larger ones—more is better.

Maladaptive behavior may also have been acquired through **modeling** (Bandura, 1973). Models of maladaptive behavior may have been provided by other students, teachers, parents, the media, or friends and peers in the neighborhood and observed and imitated. If behavior formed this way is to change, appropriate models of behavior must be available for observation, and sufficient reason (that is, powerful enough reinforcement) must be provided for students to emulate those models.

Interventions   Interventions used by proponents of the behavioral approach follow five steps.

1. Identifying target behaviors
2. Observing and recording baseline data
3. Identifying appropriate, powerful reinforcers
4. Implementing the intervention, observing and recording data related to it
5. Evaluating the effects of the intervention and making modifications if the desired change is not taking place

If the intervention is successful in obtaining the desired change, a scheduled reduction of the reinforcement is initiated. If the intervention does not produce the desired response, the target behavior or the reinforcers are reexamined and modified, thus beginning the five-step cycle again.

Teachers using **behavioral modification** are aware that reinforcement of maladaptive behavior can come from a variety of uncontrollable sources, such as the family and other students and adults in the school or community. They are also aware of the influence of their own behavior in reinforcing the student's, as well as of their potential for modeling appropriate behavior.

■ The Social-Ecologic Approach

Sociology as a field of study investigates the development, behavior, and interaction of groups of humans. Sociological study in an educational setting focuses on the social forces that affect individuals and groups within and without the organization known as school. Ecology is the study of interrelationships between an organism and the environment. Applied to education, that study inquires into the reciprocal relationships between a student, groups of students, and the many environments with which they interact. These two fields of study incorporate theories from psychology, anthropology, and community psychology. Their focus on the social forces affecting individuals and groups and on the reciprocal relationships between them may offer the most encompassing perspective on behavioral disorders.

Students are involved in many complex environments in which there are reciprocal relationships, both acting on the environments and being influenced by them. Among this school of thought's explanations for deviant behavior are anomie, social disorganization, and labeling. Anomie means a lack of the social rules that serve as inhibitors of deviant behavior. In rapidly changing societies, rules are neither sanctioned nor institutionalized rapidly enough to enable individuals or groups to meet their needs and attain their desires. This results in frustration and conflict (DesJarlais, 1972; Durkheim, 1951). Social disorganization theory evolved from studies of urban environments in which researchers found higher rates of delinquency, crime, mental illness, and breakdown of family units. They related these phenomena to the lack of educational opportunities, recreational facilities, availability of employment, and other services usually offered by organized communities. Within disorganized communities the fundamental needs of the individual are not met, resulting in disorganized life patterns and often maladaptive behavior (DesJarlais, 1972; Hawley, 1950). Labeling theory is based on the reciprocal relationship between those who label and those who are labeled. Individuals who are labeled gradually adopt the behaviors perceived as typical for the label. In addition, those who know of the label expect its characteristic behaviors, so the labeled individual conforms to this expectation. The interaction between being labeled and assuming the behaviors corresponding to the label has been and still is a matter of concern to all special educators, not just to those working with behavior disorders.

Every individual participates in a variety of ecosystems. When the rules, expectations, and demands of the ecosystem and the individual's responses to them are in harmony, there is goodness of fit, according to the ecologic perspective. Disharmony, or lack of goodness of fit, is attributable to the faulty interaction, not to the individual alone nor the environment alone.

Interventions Basic assumptions of those who practice the social-ecologic approach and its related interventions include the following.

- Disturbance is a consequence of the influence of the environment or the interaction between the environment and the individual; it is not the exclusive property of the individual.
- Each interaction between the student and that particular environment is unique.
- Interventions should focus on the individual, the ecosystems, and the interaction between the two and result in ramifications for all those elements.
- Interventions may produce unexpected results because of the complexity of the individual, the environment, and the reciprocal relationship (Swap, Prieto, & Harth, 1982).

Interventions may be child centered, environment centered, or exchange centered (Wagner, 1972). Child-centered interventions include remedial efforts to enhance students' abilities. The resultant heightened self-esteem and recognition of their increased abilities should reduce the antisocial behaviors. A related intervention manipulates the school environment to reduce the stress on the individual. Various tenets of the behavioral approach may also be applied in child-centered interventions. Environment-centered interventions focus on the physical surroundings that influence behavior and on family counseling or therapy. Exchange-centered interventions redirect existing natural groups (gangs or neighborhood groups) or establish artificial groups such as residential schools and Big Brother or Big Sister programs. Milieu therapy (Redl, 1959) provides a total environment designed to promote ego development through therapeutic group processes; Project Re-ED (Hobbs, 1969) exemplifies such a program, in that the environment is specifically designed to re-educate students. Group processes such as discussion groups, class meetings, problem-solving discussions, and role-playing intended to reduce conflict and achieve goodness of fit between the individual and various environments are interventions of the social-ecologic approach.

■ The Humanistic Approach

The social and political movements of the 1960s and early 1970s and humanistic psychology have been identified by Rhodes and Head (1974) as the "counter theory" approach. Schools were viewed as dehumanizing, and maladaptive behavior was seen as an adaptation to an unhealthy school environment. Proponents of the humanistic approach reject the behavioral approach as manipulative; instead, they emphasize the diversity and uniqueness of the individual. Self-direction, awareness of personal values and experiences, self-evaluation, and free choice among educational opportunities characterize the humanistic approach. A common thread of theory is difficult to discern; rather, the commonality appears to be dissatisfaction with the school system.

Interventions Few specific interventions are an outgrowth of the humanistic approach, but there are diverse specific suggestions from various individual proponents. Alternative schools, free and open schools, and open education are proposed. Classrooms should be affectively oriented, nontraditional, and allow students to be participants in their destiny (Hentoff, 1977; Holt, 1972; Melton, 1975). Teachers with a humanistic philosophy want to be viewed as facilitators

■ Busted! Students with behavior disorders may find acceptance through membership in a gang. ■

rather than imparters of knowledge or authority figures; they strive to make the classroom atmosphere free, open, personal, and accepting. Humanistic classrooms deemphasize traditional content areas to allow for the inclusion of materials and methods relating to affect, emotions, interdependence, and interpersonal relationships. Humanistic proponents believe that the students themselves, given sufficient support and care, will devise solutions to any problems that arise.

Educational Programming

Although we have presented the conceptual models as if they were distinct, each one leading to specific types of interventions, few teachers rigidly adhere to one model and implement only interventions associated with that model. Teachers tend to be more eclectic, considering the unique needs of each student and evaluating the merits and limitations of each model. They then design a program to enhance social development and decrease maladaptive behaviors. They monitor the student's behavioral changes and modify the interventions accordingly, selecting those most likely to ensure continued growth.

Teachers, together with the other members of the multidisciplinary team, should have a clear picture of the disordered behavior and the interrelationships between the student and his or her environments. This affords them pertinent information on which to base their selection of interventions. Teachers may use a combination of behavioral techniques and provide art or music activities to

Box 6.1
When Nothing
Goes Wrong

I had an exceptional day with my class last Monday. It led to an even more exceptional week. The kids were actively involved in the activities, no one told me to do things with my body that were anatomically impossible and they all turned in their homework. No, this is not a dream sequence. But why am I writing this "Pollyanna" version of life in a behavior disordered classroom? Perhaps to remind myself, and others, that we sometimes forget about all the good days we have with our kids—those days that make going back to work something to look forward to; those days when the kids respond to what we teach and show some excitement about what they are learning.

Let me recap my day. I teach in a junior high school behavioral disordered program and have several different classes in English, social skills and resource room. For the past eight weeks, we have been reading George Orwell's *Animal Farm* in one of my English classes. This is a large class, about 30 students, many of whom are labeled behaviorally disordered and all of whom are "at risk." We have discussed plot diagrams with rising and falling action, character analysis and comprehension questions all in cooperative groups. The groups have stayed together for the entire unit and have become adept at getting work accomplished and at understanding the concepts.

Today's activity involved an interview show, starring Sally Jessy Raphael, a.k.a. Lynne Schroeder, our drama teacher. Each student had the part of an animal from Orwell's book and each was asked questions about their identity, what they did and who they represented in Russian history. These kids knew the material and it showed! We invited an audience, including people from our Central Administration Office who are interested in kids and our principal (who is the best). He sent us a note after the performance, praising the students and their hard work. I copied the note and was amazed at how many of the copies disappeared to show parents, friends and fellow teachers about our success.

The following week, we developed our own country, much like the pigs did in *Animal Farm*. This was a joint project with Scott Bendler, our social studies teacher, who was teaching a unit on socialism and capitalism (socialism may be fading in Eastern Europe, but it is alive in junior high). Our classes again rallied to the cause and presented a program on their "new" countries to local newspaper staff—who thought this was a class for gifted children! (It is.)

My next class was studying *Slake's Limbo*, by Felice Holman. This is a book about the homeless and we are creating homes in class much like Slake does in the book. For those not familiar with this work, Slake is a 13-year-old boy who has no home and finds a space under a motel by the New York City subway lines to live. His space is about the promote expression of feelings and emotions. Or they may be aware of a biogenic cause for the behavioral disorder and administer medication prescribed by a physician, employ behavioral techniques, adapt the physical environment to facilitate behavioral change, and engage the student in group discussions of feelings or emotions. In each case the selection of interventions is based on knowledge of the student. Consideration must also be given to the academic performance of the student. Improved academic performance in reading, writing, mathematics, and other content areas may alleviate the behavior difficulties (Epstein, Kinder, &

(Continued)

size of a refrigerator box, and we have replicated his home in our classroom. We have discussed issues such as free meals, laws for kids under the age of 16 and the art of graffiti, but most importantly, we have learned how difficult life is for people in our own community who are homeless. We are planning to visit areas in our town where homeless people live, such as shelters, missions and assorted hiding spots. These visits will include reading to kids at a local shelter, serving in a soup line and making beds, etc. By reading articles and talking to homeless people, we have explored the despair of losing everything you own and having no dreams to carry you through. As a result of these activities, the class has put together a poetry book with some unbelievable insights into the plight of the homeless.

This class also has a cooperative project with a group of kindergarten students. Together, they are writing children's books to donate to their class library. We hope to write more books to donate to a shelter for homeless children as part of our new unit.

My seventh-graders are heavily into cooperative learning and the study of mythology. We have been reading and studying about Greek and Roman gods, goddesses and heroes, as they pursue their quests and adventures. Today, we played Jeopardy with questions about their reading and I was amazed at how much they knew and retained. (Although one student did ask if we got to draw the "Methodist" characters after we were done studying them.) Things clicked along in my other two student centers — kids brought in work and actually spent time completing assignments.

Granted, it is March, and classes should be well into "school behavior," but that doesn't always happen. Maybe this reflection is just to remind myself of these bright, talented kids, who manage to get into programs and do change, do make progress, do grow. When they have finished proving themselves to be "bad" and letting us know their limits and begin to be responsive to teachers, they become just a group of kids who come into your classroom to learn.

(P.S. Just to let you know that not all my weeks go this way — the following week we went on a field trip and my kids were so obnoxious that the bus driver refused to let them get off the bus . . . oh well, variety *is* the spice of life!)

Poems on the Homeless

Diamante
Home
Security, warm
Loved, wanted, cared for,

Bursuck, 1989; Morgan & Jenson, 1988). Writing poetry and stories, keeping journals, and similar activities may serve a dual purpose: to increase skills in written communication and to provide for the expression of feelings that the student has difficulty expressing otherwise. Similarly, bibliotherapy may be used both to enhance reading skills and increase the enjoyment of reading and to develop greater personal understanding through identification with fictitious characters or problem situations. Remedial academic instruction may also be necessary and may be specified in the IEP.

(Continued)

Family, children, bagwoman, bum
Penniless, unwanted, unloved
Lonely, cold,
Streets

Cinquain
Homeless
Out on the streets
Without food and home
No place to go, no place to stay
Sadness

Homeless
Out on the street
No home
No food
No shelter
No one to take care of them

Acrostic
Helpless
Outsiders
Meet
Everyday
Like
Examples of
Sad
Statues

—by eighth grade English class,
Culler Junior High School

SOURCE: *Barbara Peterson, "When Nothing Goes Wrong," Beyond Behavior 2 (Fall 1990) pp. 3–4. Copyright 1990 by The Council for Exceptional Children. Reprinted with permission. Barbara Peterson teaches students with behavior disorders at Culler Junior High School in Lincoln, Nebraska.*

Educational programming for students with behavioral disorders must be based on appropriate, accurate assessment data, and the interventions selected must be those most effective in facilitating academic and behavioral growth.

Depression

Although the federal definition of emotional disturbance includes as a characteristic "a pervasive mood of unhappiness or depression," until recently little research was conducted to differentiate between childhood and adult depression (Forness, 1988; Kaslow & Rehm, 1985). There appears to be a general consensus that depression in children and adolescence is characterized by poor academic performance, extreme lethargy, social withdrawal, and loss of interest in events and activities (Costello, 1981; Harris & Ammerman, 1987). Adult depression, in contrast, is manifested in a loss of interest in productive activity, which results in interpersonal relationship problems.

The DSM III-R (1987) lists the following behaviors, four of which must be present for at least a 2-week period, for a diagnosis of clinical depression.

- Disrupted sleep patterns
- Appetite or weight changes
- Inability to experience pleasure or happiness
- Excessive or severely reduced motor activity
- Feelings of guilt or lack of self-worth
- Excessive fatigue or lack of energy
- Indecisiveness, lack of ability to concentrate
- Thoughts about, threats of, or attempts of suicide

Theories about the causes of depression are varied. There are indications that the death of a significant person in the life of the individual may lead to clinical depression and that there is a correlation between the depression of parents and their children (Harris & Ammerman, 1987). It is unclear whether the latter is the result of genetic factors or whether depressed parents model depressed behavior, lack effective parental skills, establish a home environment supportive of depression, or reinforce depressed behavior in their children (Ferster, 1973; Forehand, McCombs, & Brody, 1987; Strober, 1983).

Treatment of depression in children and adolescents may take several forms, depending on the presumed cause. Antidepressant drugs are effective in some cases when the presumed cause is biogenic. If undeveloped social skills seem to have led to reduced pleasure in social interaction or to reduced interactions, social skills training is implemented. When depressed youth engage in self-depreciation and self-defeating thoughts or actions and seem to concentrate on negative events or circumstances, training attempts to develop their ability to view events and themselves more realistically. Some depressed youth may have developed, early in life, a persistently negative view of life and subsequently modified reality to fit their negative perceptions. If this is believed to be the case, cognitive and behavioral interventions to change belief systems and negative views are indicated. If they seem to believe that they are responsible for all the negative events that happen to them—as well as those affecting the larger society (hunger, poverty, war)—interventions would help them realize that they are less responsible than they think but that they can control much of what happens to them and reduce the negative aspects of life.

The more generic term *psychotic* is often used to include both infantile autism and childhood schizophrenia. All three are severe disabilities that are both qualitatively and quantitatively different from normal behavior. **Autism** and childhood schizophrenia are differentiated mainly by the age of onset according to the DSM III-R, though there are other differences in how each is manifested.

Infantile autism was first described by Leo Kanner (1943), though it was not until later that the disorder became known as autism (Kanner, 1957). Children with autism may have extraordinary skills in certain areas (music, science, mathematics, memory for dates, and so forth) without formal education or training. Yet they may not be able to perform routine tasks such as matching their clothing or managing an allowance.

Not all persons with autism display extraordinary skills (Gerdtz & Bergman,

**Box 6.2
Stephen
Wiltshire**

Though no longer a child, Stephen Wiltshire has been called the "child Picasso" of Great Britain.

At the age of 4, Stephen had not begun to talk, was withdrawn, and often had temper tantrums. His mother, a widow of one year, was told he was autistic. She enrolled him in London's Queensmill School for children with severe and complex disabilities.

By the time he was 7 Stephen was talking—but only when he drew. He was also astounding his teachers with his drawings. After field trips to St. Paul's Cathedral or to Parliament buildings he would draw them from memory with amazing accuracy and artistic flair. He included the correct number of windows and floors (although he could not and still cannot count them), a variety of architectural details, and showed unusual artistic interpretative ability. One of his teachers said, "He brings out the essence of something new to him." Stephen is still able to draw almost every building he has ever seen but cannot describe them.

Now nearly 20, Stephen has been to the United States and plans to come again. He says America is his favorite place and refers to it as "the great brand new." Three books of his drawings have been published in Great Britain; one was at the top of the best-seller list for several weeks. His book *Floating Cities* was published in the United States.

Stephen is known in the educational and medical disciplines as a savant. He has extraordinary capabilities in one area but extraordinary disabilities in others. His language is stilted and repetitive, and he has a great deal of difficulty communicating. He is unable to carry on a conversation but often recites lists of things, such as makes and models of cars (a passion of his, although he cannot drive), 20th-century earthquakes, or the complete dialogue from scenes in movies he has seen.

Stephen's mother says that the money he receives from the sale of his books is invested in a trust because he is unable to count or manage money. She adds, "I don't think he will ever be able to live independently, so we need to be sure he will be taken care of."

1990). They do all share some common characteristics, though. Four categories of behavior, according to Gerdtz and Bergman, are consistent with autism.

1. Difficulties with social relationships, marked by a lack of involvement with others and a lack of apparent pleasure in interactions or associations with others.
2. Severe deficits in language, including meaningless repetition, echolalia, and part/whole confusion. About half of all children with autism remain without speech through adulthood (Wing & Atwood, 1987).
3. Severe deficits in communication that are more than a language deficit. They seem not to understand the pragmatic functions of language, nor do they understand nonverbal communication such as body language and facial expressions.
4. A variety of other, associated behaviors: intense attention to small details, self-stimulation, excessive fantasizing, perseverative behaviors, intense attachment to an object, peculiar hand or finger movements, and so on.

For a diagnosis of autism the characteristic behaviors must be exhibited prior to 30 months of age. Many parents of children who are autistic report that they noted differences in behavior from the day of birth.

An increasing number of children are diagnosed as having infantile autism; the true prevalence is difficult to determine due to the great heterogeneity exhibited in this group. It does appear, however, that more males than females are so identified. Autism does not appear to be linked to genetic inheritance factors, but may be due to genetic abnormalities or the result of an injury to or dysfunction of the central nervous system (Folstein & Rutter, 1977; Gerdtz & Bergman, 1990).

Kanner's (1943) early descriptions of children who were autistic led many to believe that they were highly intelligent but either could not be tested or did not demonstrate their potential. However, although it was originally believed that most autistic children had normal intellectual ability, at least half of them are also mentally retarded and display both the developmental delays and deviant behaviors associated with mental retardation (Sigelman & Shaffer, 1991).

The characteristics of childhood schizophrenia are similar to those of infantile autism but may include hallucinations, delusions, and distorted thought patterns and perceptions not present in autism. Behavioral characteristics of autism are pervasive, while those of schizophrenia may be episodic, alternating with periods of complete normality. When the age of onset is later than 30 months, a diagnosis of childhood schizophrenia is made.

Studies seeking a genetic cause for schizophrenia seem to indicate a genetic link or predisposition: having a relative with schizophrenia increases the possibility of developing the condition (Nicol & Erlenmeyer-Kimling, 1986; Rosenthal, 1972). It would appear that the environment contributes more to the development of childhood schizophrenia than to autism (DeMyer, Hingtgen, & Jackson, 1981); however, the exact relationship between schizophrenia and environmental factors remains unclear.

Interventions that are generalizable, supported by research, and produce long-term behavioral change are few (Achenbach, 1982; Morgan & Jenson, 1988). Certain antipsychotic drugs are successful in individual cases (Mikkelsen, 1982). It may be that the promising studies of schizophrenia in adults will lead to a further understanding of the condition in children and adolescents.

Several topics are often associated with behavioral disorders without being synonymous. Juvenile delinquency, suicide, child abuse, and substance abuse are among them. The following discussion will define these topics and illustrate their relationships.

■ Juvenile Delinquency

Juvenile delinquent is a legal term to describe those under 21 who have been judged guilty of a crime. Not all antisocial behaviors are unlawful; however, many

**Box 6.3
About School**

The following poem was handed to a high school English teacher on a Friday.

He always wanted to explain things,
    but no one cared.
So he drew.

Sometimes he would just draw
    and it wasn't anything.
He wanted to carve it in stone
    or write it in the sky
    and the things inside him that needed saying.

And it was after that he drew the picture.
It was a beautiful picture.
He kept it under his pillow
    and would let no one see it.
And he would look at it every night
    and think about it.
And it was all of him and he loved it.

When he started school he brought it with him.
Not to show anyone, but just to have it with
    him
    like a friend.

It was funny about school.
He sat in a square brown desk
    like all the other square brown desks
    and he thought it would be red.

And his room was a square brown room
    like all the other rooms.
And it was tight and close. And stiff.

He hated to hold the pencil and chalk
    with his arm stiff and his feet flat on the
    floor,

authorities suggest that most adjudicated youngsters are likely to be emotionally disturbed or socially maladjusted (Murphy, 1986; Wolford, 1987). As we noted earlier, the federal definition of "seriously emotionally disturbed" specifically excludes the socially maladjusted. At present, unless juvenile delinquents have disabilities such as mental retardation, learning disabilities, physical impairment, or sensory impairment, they are excluded from the services available under PL 94-142. This denial of services lends support to the Council for Children with Behavioral Disorders' plea for including "socially maladjusted" in the federal definition. (See Chapter 5 for a discussion of the relationship between juvenile delinquency and learning disabilities.)

(Continued)

stiff,
with the teacher watching and watching.

The teacher came and spoke to him.
She told him to wear a tie like all the other
    boys.
He said he didn't like them
    and she said it didn't matter.
After that he drew. And he drew all yellow
    and it was the way he felt about morning.
And it was beautiful.

The teacher came and smiled at him.
"What's this?" she said.
"Why don't you draw something
    like Ken's drawing?

Isn't it beautiful?"
After that his mother bought him a tie
    and he always drew airplanes and rockets
    like everyone else.

And he threw the old picture away.
And when he lay out alone looking at the sky,
    it was big and blue, and all of everything,
    but he wasn't anymore.

He was square and brown inside
    and his hands were stiff.
And he was like everyone else.
All the things inside him that needed saying
    didn't need it anymore.

It had stopped pushing. It was crushed.
Stiff.
Like everything else.

Over the weekend, the student committed suicide.

■ Suicide

Suicide, the intentional ending of one's own life by any means, is associated with behavioral disorders—especially if the student is also depressed (Muse, 1990). In 1987 the National Center for Health Statistics reported that suicide was the second leading cause of death among persons aged 15 to 24. However, there is no agreement on the actual number of teenage suicides, because many deaths are not reported as such (Guetzloe, 1989; Muse, 1990). The reasons for underreporting include a lack of consensus about what constitutes a suicide (some medical examiners classify a death as suicide only if there is a signed note), inadequate information (in the absence of verbal or written intent, the cause is listed as "undetermined"), or certifier bias (family pressure or concern for the reputation of the neighborhood or community leads certifiers to classify the suicide as an accident). Medical examiners indicate that the number of reported suicides is less than half the actual number (Jobes, Berman, & Josselsen, 1986).

"A severe behavior disorder is by far the most significant handicapping condition associated with suicidal behavior" (Guetzloe, 1989, p. 37); depression and childhood schizophrenia are the leading diagnoses (Geller et al., 1985; Golumbek & Garfinkel, 1983; Pfeffer, 1986). The risk factors associated with suicide, according to Muse (1990), include the following.

- Emotional or behavioral problems, including the characteristics associated with those problems
- Depression, including feelings of worthlessness or helplessness
- Substance abuse, which decreases inhibitions
- Severe stress, such as a significant recent loss or a threat of or actual public humiliation
- Access to lethal means, such as prescription or street drugs or guns and ammunition
- Familiarity with suicide, such as previous attempts or threats, family members who have threatened or completed suicide, or a recently publicized suicide

Pfeffer (1986) noted that treatments for suicidal behavior are among the least understood and studied of all factors related to suicide. Because of the prevalence of teenage suicide, many schools are beginning to develop and implement suicide prevention programs; such programs are mandated in some states (Guetzloe, 1989). Teachers must take immediate action if they observe any overt or covert threats or statements. School policy regarding referral to appropriate personnel is to be carefully followed.

■ Substance Abuse

Substance abuse is the use of any substance to induce physiological or psychological effects that are nontherapeutic. Thus, prescription medications may be abused, as can legal substances such as tobacco and alcohol, seemingly innocuous substances such as paint, glue, and gasoline, as well as more commonly known illegal drugs such as cocaine, heroin, and marijuana. It is not the substance that is used that matters so much as the abuse of it. In 1985, the American Psychiatric Association indicated that as many as 80% of suicide attempts are made under the influence of alcohol, and high rates of depression were found in a study of habitual drug abusers (National Institute on Drug Abuse, 1985). Hawton suggested

■ Illegal behavior is not synonymous with behavior disorders. ■

that drug abuse may be a "suicide equivalent" when the individual uses potentially life-threatening substances and understands their dangers (1986, p. 2).

According to the National Institute on Drug Abuse (1982), substance abuse
usually proceeds through several stages.

1. *Experimentation:* infrequent use; few if any behavioral changes

2. *Social or situational:* used four to five times per week; used to facilitate
social interactions, to "come down" after stressful events, to stay awake, or to
sleep; behavioral changes, including decreased academic performance, loss of
interest in activities unrelated to substance abuse, and seeking friends who also
abuse substances

3. *Habitual:* used daily or almost daily; used alone; used to alleviate depression, guilt, personal problems, or stress; behavioral changes, including unkempt
appearance; erratic, impulsive behavior and mood swings

4. *Compulsive or dependent:* used several times daily; discomfort if drugs are not available; used to feel "normal"; behavioral changes, including major activities centering around acquiring and using; lying or stealing to get substances; aggression; paranoid and suicidal thoughts

This progression is not as clear as descriptions make it seem. Some who abuse substances may do so temporarily and then stop, or use them situationally and then stop. Others progress from experimentation to habitual use in a short span of time.

Teachers may not be aware of students' substance abuse until they notice behavioral changes in academic performance or usual activities. Figure 6.1 illustrates the type of checklist that may guide teachers in referring a student suspected of substance abuse. Figure 6.2 provides a list of behaviors that indicate substance abuse and overlapping ones that characterize behavioral disorders. Educational programs to prevent substance abuse are provided by most schools, though some are more effective than others (Miksic, 1987). Teachers must be aware of school policies regarding substance abuse and know how to recognize and manage suspected or real substance abuse or withdrawal episodes.

■ Child Abuse and Neglect

Child abuse and neglect can be defined as "any interaction or lack of interaction . . . which results in non-accidental harm to the individual's physical and/or developmental states" (Helfer, 1987, p. 61). The abuse of children with disabilities is not uncommon (*Child Abuse,* 1987); it is even more common among those with behavioral disorders (Wolfe, 1985; Zirpoli, 1990). Estimates of child abuse range from 1.25% to 1.50% of the population of youngsters under 18; however, this is regarded as an underestimate due to varied reporting procedures and unclear criteria for abuse and neglect (Helfer, 1987). Nutritionally or medically neglected children who are not provided with a safe environment or do not have a caring and supportive adult at hand are considered neglected, but such cases are rarely reported because of the difficulty of substantiating them.

Indicators of abuse and neglect that teachers should be aware of include the following.

- *Physical abuse:* bruises, burns, welts, bald spots indicative of hair being pulled out, unexplained marks
- *Sexual abuse:* itching, bleeding, or bruises around the genital area, fear of the opposite sex, unusual or bizarre sexual knowledge
- *Neglect:* being underweight or having an abnormal appetite, poor hygiene, inappropriate clothing (such as no shoes or coats in cold weather), difficulty in staying awake, lack of social contact, or depression

In addition, abused children often exhibit personality patterns similar to those of individuals with behavior disorders. They may be bullying or quarrelsome, reflecting a learned pattern of behavior. Feelings of inferiority or worthlessness may be masked by clowning or showing off. Defiant or hostile feelings toward authority figures may indicate these children's efforts to gain some control over their lives or may mirror parental attitudes. The child may be listless and a loner, unable to develop satisfying personal relationships because of the family's isolation and the lack of warmth, caring, and adequate social skills in the family.

Children who are abused and neglected often become depressed, abuse substances, or are suicidal (Guetzloe, 1989; Muse, 1990).

All states have legislation requiring teachers to report suspected child abuse,

The following behaviors have been found to predict substance abuse and other problems in children and adolescents. Please check all that you have observed directly.

Student _____ Grade _____

Person referring _____ Date _____

Subject or location _____ Time _____

Grades
___ Grades are dropping
___ Academic failure
___ Does not complete assignments
___ Apathetic, lacks motivation
___ Inconsistent daily work
___ Inconsistent test grades

School attendance
___ Truancy
___ Excessive absenteeism
___ Tardiness
___ Absent from class, but in building
___ Suspension
___ Frequent nurse or counselor visits

Classroom deportment
___ Change in class participation
___ Change in student-teacher rapport
___ Falls asleep in class
___ Disrupts classroom learning
___ Cheats on academic tasks
___ Defiance of teacher's rules
___ Projects blame onto others
___ Abusive language or behavior
___ Dramatic attention seeking
___ Obscene language or gestures
___ Sexually uninhibited
___ Fighting
___ Destructive

Please identify student's strengths:
___ creative   ___ enthusiastic
___ sense of humor   ___ good motivation
___ confidence   ___ physical strength
___ social skills   ___ good coordination
___ academic skills   ___ highly verbal
___ cooperative   ___ compassionate
___ artistic   ___ leadership skills
___ other:
_____
_____
_____

Other behavior
___ Hyperactivity
___ Appears sullen/depressed
___ Mood swings
___ Irritable
___ Extreme negativism
___ Easily distracted
___ Easily frustrated
___ Hostile
___ Jumpy if touched
___ Withdrawn
___ Disoriented to time
___ Defensive
___ Memory problems
___ Inappropriate responses
___ Takes excessive risks
___ Cigarette smoking
___ Talks freely about drug use
___ Change in friends
___ Loitering in parking lot

Physical appearance
___ Appears drowsy
___ Poor motor coordination
___ Unkempt clothing
___ Poor personal hygiene
___ Clothes advertising substance use
___ Drastic change in appearance
___ Weight fluctuations
___ Staggering or stumbling
___ Dilated pupils
___ Glassy or bloodshot eyes
___ Wears dark glasses
___ Speech garbled/slurred/incoherent
___ Difficulty breathing
___ Constant "cold" or stuffiness
___ Redness/irritation in nasal area
___ Increased heart rate
___ Vomiting
___ Physical injuries/bruises/cuts
___ Chronic cough
___ Chronic fatigue
___ Odor of alcohol
___ Odor of cigarettes
___ Odor of burning substance

___ Other behavior observed: _____
_____

Have you ever referred this student for similar behavior before? ___ yes ___ no
If yes, when? _____

Figure 6.1 At-risk behavioral checklist

SOURCE: *S. E. Forbing and C. L. Fox, Project STOP: How to set up a drug-free school/community program, San Diego State University, 1989. Used by permission.*

Overlapping characteristics	Symptoms of drug use	Possible drug used
Withdrawn	Sleeping in class	Barbiturates
	Lethargy	Tranquilizers
		Alcohol
		Many narcotics
Memory loss	Forgetfulness	Marijuana
	Long-term memory deficits	Barbiturates
	Blackouts	Alcohol
Concentration and attention deficit	Poor attention span	Marijuana
	Spacy/daydreaming	Alcohol
		Inhalants
Motor/physical extremes	Hyperactivity	Cocaine
	Nervousness	Codeine
	Quickened reactions	Speed
		Amphetamines
Poor coordination	Staggering	Alcohol
	Stumbling	Depressants
	Tremors	Narcotics
	Clumsiness	Inhalants
Mood swings	Yo-yo personality	Polydrug use
	Extreme highs and lows	Stimulants
Poor academic performance	Drop in grades	Marijuana
	Homework not done	Depressants
	Poor attendance	Inhalants
		Alcohol
Inappropriate social skills	Verbal abuse	Marijuana
	Physical abuse	Alcohol
	Obscene language	
Low self-esteem	Guilt and remorse	Any chemical dependency
	Denial of need	
	Self-loathing	
Poor appearance	Messy, dirty	Marijuana
	Unkempt	Alcohol
		Inhalants
Explosiveness	Irritability	Stimulants
	Restlessness	Hallucinogens
	Destructive/vandalism	Inhalants
	Uncontrolled violence	
Attention-getting behaviors	Cheating	Stimulants
	Stealing	Any chemical dependency
	Acting out	
Negative attitude	Blaming	Depressants
	Denial	Coming down from any drug-induced high
	Paranoia	Cocaine
Disregard for rules	Suspension from school	Dependency cycle for any drug
	Fighting	Marijuana
	Disrespect for others	Alcohol
	Irresponsible	
	Possession of drugs	
Delayed maturation	Amotivational	Dependency cycle for any drug
	No desires or direction	Marijuana
	Lack of participation	Alcohol
	Apathetic	

Figure 6.2 Overlapping characteristics, symptoms of drug use, and possible drugs used

SOURCE: *C. L. Fox and S. E. Forbing, Overlapping symptoms of substance abuse and learning handicaps: Implications for educators,* Journal of Learning Disabilities, 24, p. 25. Copyright 1991 by PRO-ED, Inc. Reprinted by permission.

■ Isolation—or is this child watching an interesting program? ■

and schools have policies and procedures for reporting suspected abuse or neglect. Teachers must assume the responsibility for reporting such cases. Treatment is multifaceted; because of its complexity, it requires resources beyond what the school and teachers can provide (Kempe, 1987). Treatment usually involves parents, siblings, and the child in marital and family therapy, group therapy, crisis facilities, hotlines, training in parenting, and stress reduction (Meier, 1985). Teachers can seek to establish trusting relationships in the context of supportive and stable environments to assist children who have been abused or neglected.

Issues

Throughout this chapter we've discussed a number of issues that remain perplexing for professionals, parents, and others; there are many more. Those that must be examined and acted on include these twelve.

People Who Make a Difference

CHI CHI RODRIGUEZ— EVERYTHING WITH HONOR

Juan Rodriguez, better known as Chi Chi Rodriguez, was born in Puerto Rico. His family was very poor: "There was no one poorer; maybe as poor but not poorer." He was hungry much of the time, often having only black coffee for breakfast. He doesn't drink coffee now, because it reminds him of being hungry. At age 6 he nearly died of rickets, a disease caused by vitamin deficiencies.

As a youngster he tried many jobs to earn money; one of them was picking up golf balls, but soon he realized that "the guys who carried the bags were making the money." So Chi Chi became a caddy. Later he began his golf career by hitting a tightly rolled tin can around with a guava stick.

When Chi Chi was 21 he worked in a psychiatric hospital, feeding and showering the patients. He said, "That was the best year of my life, because I was doing something for somebody. It gave me more satisfaction than any tournament I have ever won." But Chi Chi knew that he would need more money than that job paid if he were to support a family—so he continued to work at the hospital at night and practice golf during the day. His practice paid off. Today Chi Chi is a multimillionaire, winning regularly on the PGA Seniors Tour. But he doesn't take golf too seriously. He says, "I love making people laugh"—so he does the Mexican hat dance when he sinks the ball, or he pretends the hole is a bull and he is the matador. He slays the imaginary bull with his putter, elaborately wipes off the blood, and slips the imaginary sword into his imaginary scabbard. The crowd loves it—perhaps even more than seeing him win.

He is serious about helping others and often chooses no-fee charity fund-raisers over lucrative corporate-sponsored games or clinics. "My father would see a hungry kid and give him his own food. He always gave to others what he had. I want to be like that," said Chi Chi. He has established the Chi Chi Rodriguez Youth Foundation to provide counseling and educational services for emotionally disturbed children. He knows the students by name, and each time he is away from Clearwater, Florida, he calls 15 or 20 of them. He visits the foundation to talk with the students, to pitch pennies or play some golf, and to listen to them. "I see myself in them, so I want to give them what money can't buy—someone who cares about them."

His concern about others is not limited to the foundation. He sponsors an annual golf tournament in Puerto Rico whose proceeds go to a children's hospital, so that any child who needs surgery is able to get it regardless of financial status. He conducts golf clinics for disadvantaged children, and in 1986 received the Horatio Alger Award for his humanitarianism. It was the first time it was ever given to an athlete.

Chi Chi said, "I try to be a compassionate, good man who does everything with honor. When I see a kid suffer, I suffer, and I have to help any way I can."

1. Establishment of an acceptable definition
2. Clarification of terminology to be used and its implications
3. Inclusion of individuals who are socially maladjusted in the definition, to ensure an appropriate education for them
4. Assessment tools and practices that are educationally relevant
5. Underidentification of students who are behaviorally disordered—particularly those of preschool age
6. Coordination in planning and implementation of educational services for incarcerated youth
7. Students who, because of behavioral concerns, are encouraged to drop out of school and those who have dropped out for other reasons
8. Prevention of substance abuse and treatment for those abusing substances
9. Ensuring the least restrictive placement for students with behavioral disorders
10. Practices that relate to transition from school to work
11. Best employment practices
12. Child abuse and neglect

Summary

Behavioral disorders have been recognized for many years and have been labeled emotional disturbance and mental illness among other things. The federal definition as it relates to special education services specifies serious emotional disturbance; however, educators favor the term *behavior disorders*. Historically, the mentally ill (emotionally disturbed or behavior disordered) adult has been recognized for many years, but the similarly disabled child is a relatively recent discovery.

The prevalence of behavior disorders is uncertain; it depends heavily on which definition of behavioral disorders is accepted. Many characteristics are associated with behavior disorders, but whether an individual is considered behaviorally disordered depends on the degree to which a characteristic is exhibited, the length of time it is exhibited, and the context within which it occurs.

A number of therapeutic interventions are practiced, each one corresponding to a specific theory of causation. The biogenic or biophysical approach assumes chemical imbalance, genetic abnormalities, or brain dysfunction. The behavioral approach assumes that inappropriate behavior has been learned and reinforced. The psychoeducational approach relates behavior disorders to a negative self-image, anxiety, or stress. The psychodynamic approach assumes inner conflicts, childhood emotional trauma, or unsuccessful negotiation of psychological stages. The social-ecologic approach assumes negative interactions between the student and his or her various environments or between the student and societal norms. Finally, the humanistic approach relates unacceptable behavior to the depersonalization of the student, an irrelevant curriculum, or authoritarian teachers. Educational programming may vary widely according to the different approaches adopted.

Depression in children has only recently received attention as a phenomenon separate from depression in adults; it may be caused by several factors. Schizophrenia and autism are separate and serious types of behavior disorders. Juvenile delinquency, substance abuse, child abuse or neglect, and suicide are all related areas of concern.

Mrs. Kralick teaches kindergarten. During the course of the day she hears comments such as these:

"No drink milk."
"Me sit in big chair."
"I made my wabbit wed."
"I like pesghetti."
"You know Big Wheel?"
"I spill juice."
"It's a–a–a, you know."

Mr. Rodríguez teaches third-graders; most of them learned English as a second language. As he talks with his students he hears things such as these:

"Mary getting tired."
"He talk too fast."
"She go to Brownies tomor-row."
"No play that video game."
"I hurt elbow when I fell."
"The teacher pulling down blinds so sun not shine."
"I think test tomorrow or next."

Mr. Hammond teaches math to ninth-graders. As students talk before and after class, he overhears remarks such as the following:

"Gimme the comb, Dude."
"Hey man, you goin' tonight?"
"Some threads you got."
"McDonald's? I be there."
"Ain't you done yet?"
"She some lady. See them legs."
"I told her, like, I ain't goin' that place, like wha'd she expect."

How concerned should these teachers be about what they hear?

CHAPTER SEVEN

Communication Disorders

Speech and language disorders are among the most common of the disabling conditions served in school settings, yet when students preparing to go into teaching are asked to list disorders among schoolchildren, they often give them little notice or altogether overlook them. Explanations for this include the possibility that children with these disabilities are seen as having only "mild" problems.

Indeed, with the exception of the more obvious conditions such as stuttering or cleft palate, students who are communicatively disabled may not stand out in the classroom as do those with disorders of vision, hearing, cerebral palsy, or mental retardation. Perhaps an additional factor is that few of us have really stopped to think about the "miracle" of speech and language. Van Riper and Emerick, in an introduction to their text in speech pathology and audiology, make this point eloquently.

> We who have spoken so much so easily and for so long find it hard to comprehend the miraculous nature of speech—this peculiarly human tool. It comes as natural and as easy as breathing. But those of us who try to help those who have been deprived of normal communication soon come to know how utterly vital and necessary speech is to human existence. Not only do we use it in thinking and in the sending and receiving of messages, we also build our very sense of self out of word-stuff. Indeed language infiltrates every aspect of our lives; even the way in which we view the world is molded by the symbols we use. Further we need speech to command and restrain ourselves. Our words are our means of controlling others. Some religious sects isolate transgressors by refusing to talk to them. Department stores in large cities use a recording device that emits a subliminal message ("Honesty is the best policy") to reduce shop lifting. Verbally we express our loves and hates. It is the safety valve of our emotions, the medicine of psychotherapy. But speech is more than just a tool; it is basic to human life. We need it for its own sake. (1990, pp. 2–3)[1]

Lilyan Wilder (1986), a speech consultant to George Bush while he was running for president, sees speech and the communication process as a dynamic encounter between human beings that stimulates them, arouses their interest, and draws them into a personal connection with one another. If children are unable because of a communication disorder to receive those benefits and do not receive appropriate assistance, the impact may be great and long lasting in terms of their social acceptance and educational progress.

The impact of communication disorders on educational progress might best be viewed in light of popular educational reform movements' focus on "competencies." Certainly we are all aware by now of the need to be "computer literate." John Naisbitt, a popular "futurist," foresees the "emergence of a counterpoint to the new computer literacy that is just as important to making our way in the informational new world; the ability to communicate effectively in the oral language" (1982, p. 13).

The impact of **speech disorders** on social acceptance has been encapsulated by Van Riper and Emerick as PFAGH. This strange acronym is helpful in reminding us of the emotional costs of social rejection: Penalty, Fear, Anxiety, Guilt, and Hostility (1990, p. xx).

Historical Background

Speech disorders have received attention since ancient times. Perhaps the most notable of these accounts is the popular story of Demosthenes, perhaps the greatest of Greek orators. Afflicted with a congenitally weak voice, he would stroll the beaches of ancient Greece with a mouthful of pebbles, improving his speech by projecting above the sound of the waves. An example from ancient Rome was

[1] Van Riper/Emerick, *Speech Correction: An Introduction to Speech Pathology and Audiology,* © 1990, pp. 2, 34, 60, 105, 294. Reprinted by permission of Prentice-Hall, Inc.

Balbus Blaesus, a stutterer who would make speech attempts to amuse the crowd when they threw coins into his cage (Van Riper & Emerick, 1990). Some writers (Lundeen, 1972) point to evidence that disorders of speech such as stuttering and cleft palate were discussed in the ancient hieroglyphs of Egypt. Although these examples indicate that speech disorders have been recognized for thousands of years, it has only been in the last two centuries that any well-organized and systematic treatment programs have been established.

■ The Establishment of Early Programs

As is true of other special education interventions, our communication disorder programs had their origins in Europe. Paden (1970), in a report tracing the origins of the American Speech and Hearing Association, documented that a number of publications on speech disorders had already appeared in France, Ireland, England, Austria, and Germany by the 1850s. Most of those publications were written by physicians; as a result, the remediation of speech disorders was seen as a medical problem and not as an educational concern. Although charlatans and quacks promising quick and often expensive cures were abundant, by the early 1900s a number of ethical practitioners were providing treatment in the United States (Matthews, 1990). Those practitioners had gone to Europe (often to Germany or Austria) to train, as there were few formal training programs available in the United States at that time.

Although primarily remembered for his invention of the telephone, Alexander Graham Bell was among the first Americans to receive recognition for writing in the field of hearing and communication disorders (ibid.).

The first formal school programs in the United States began in 1910, when ten speech correction teachers were hired in both the Chicago and Detroit school systems (Paden, 1970). These pioneers were soon followed by Boston in 1913 and by New York City, San Francisco, and the state of Wisconsin in 1916. The shift to service delivery systems in schools from medical settings may be seen by a paper published in 1918 by Dr. Walter B. Swift, titled "How to Begin Speech Correction in the Public School" (ibid.).

■ Current Programs in the United States

Following the establishment of the public school programs in Chicago and Detroit, interest grew in the United States. In 1925 a small group of individuals beginning to practice this fledgling profession met in Iowa City to discuss their common interest in these disorders and their treatment (Matthews, 1990). This group became the nucleus of what would later be called the American Speech-Language-Hearing Association (ASHA). Certainly one of the most important early contributions of the association was the establishment and commitment to a code of ethics helping to protect those with communication disorders from the many abuses that had existed. Since then, the changes in titles used to describe the association's professionals (speech teacher, speech correctionist, speech clinician, speech pathologist, speech and language pathologist, and speech-language pathologist, to name some of the primary ones) have mirrored the changes affecting the field. Such changes in image were perhaps inevitable given the profession's progression in this country through medical, psychological, and educational disciplines. The more recent titles are evidence of the profound impact that language theory has had and is continuing to have upon the field.

The American Speech-Language-Hearing Association continues to play a dominant role in the profession and in the schools, with nearly 50% of its 60,249 members and certificate holders indicating schools as their primary place of employment (ASHA, 1990a).

Communication, Language, and Speech

In our experience it is not uncommon for teachers to confuse the terms *communication, language,* and *speech.* We are sure that many speech-language pathologists who have worked in the schools have been asked to assist a student with poor diction or one who speaks little or no English. While an individual pathologist may be of some assistance, the essential mismatch demonstrates the confusion about the three areas of specialization. In fact, it is possible for a speech-language pathologist to have specialized in an area such as children's language disorders and have relatively little experience in the areas of stuttering or disorders resulting from cleft palate. Though other pathologists may have a wide variety of skills and work in several areas, such misunderstandings prompt us to examine the interrelated areas of communication, language, and speech.

The broadest of the three areas is communication. We may communicate to others in a variety of ways. Facial expressions, posture, even the speed with which we move send messages that we have become accustomed to interpreting every day. Owens (1990) sees communication as primarily the process of exchanging information and ideas. He points out that the process depends on the encoding, transmission, and decoding of the intended message. Because there are many ways of communicating and different types of message systems, both sender and receiver have to be sensitive to each other if the message is to be conveyed and received appropriately. Think of the phrase "Sure, I like that idea." Said with a smile and enthusiasm it is a positive and reaffirming comment. Said without a smile and with a different intonation pattern, it can be a biting and sarcastic remark, meaning the opposite of what it says.

Language lies within the sphere of communication. Bernstein and Tiegerman see language as "a socially shared code," or conventional system that represents ideas through the use of arbitrary symbols and rules that govern combinations of these symbols" (1989, p. 4). These rules allow individuals to understand language and to use it to communicate ideas to others using the same system. Language is generally considered to have several components, including the following: (1) phonology, the way in which sounds are used to communicate; (2) syntax, the rules that govern how we use words to form meaningful utterances; (3) morphology, the way in which words themselves are structured to convey concepts such as plurals and present or past tense; (4) semantics, the special meaning that words convey to us as individuals; and (5) pragmatics, the ability to use language in a functional way.

Speech can be viewed as a form of communication that conveys meaning through an oral mode requiring precise coordination of the speech mechanism and neuromuscular control (Bernstein & Tiegerman, 1989). Van Riper, a respected pioneer in the field of speech disorders, and his associate Emerick provide the following description of how speech relates to communication language.

Language has two constituents: a supply of symbols (a code) and a set of procedures (rules) for combining them into coherent units of information. Words, the most

■ Communication requires interaction. These two children
are communicating. ■

common symbols, must be arranged in particular ways to fulfill the intent of the
person communicating. Although there are many ways in which we use language, the
sending and receiving of spoken messages is our most frequent and important way of
sharing our minds and relating to each other. By means of an incredibly swift and
complicated process . . . humans translate ideas into the magic of speech. The spoken
word is fundamental to civilization. (1990, p. 2)

Before we look at these areas and their disorders more closely, let's review
the physical process of speech.

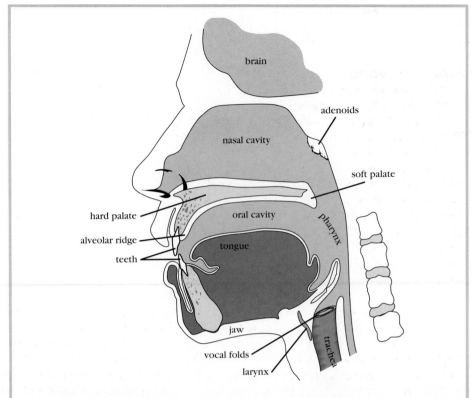

Figure 7.1 The speech mechanism. "Puffs" of air from the lungs pass through the larynx and are modified by the soft palate, tongue, lips, teeth, and jaw. These organs, through many variations in size and shape, produce sounds of various pitch, volume, and quality.

■ **Speech Development: The Mechanics of Speech**

To produce the sounds we use to formulate speech, the speaker must be able to maintain and alter a steady stream of breath. This modulation or alteration of the breath stream to create speech sounds can be thought of as occurring in four specific stages: the process resulting in an exhaled stream of air (respiration); controlling the vibration or nonvibration of the vocal folds (**phonation**); manipulating the sounds through movement of the organs in the vocal tract (**articulation** or resonance); and altering the sounds through movement from one sound to another, which Peterson and Marquardt (1990) explain as the effect that other sounds in the sequence have on the sound being produced (dynamic flow). This concept of dynamic flow also embraces such speech characteristics as duration, rhythm, rate, and fluency. The combination of these four factors—respiration, phonation, articulation or resonance, and dynamic flow—provides us with an oversimplified but helpful model of the events that must take place for speech to occur (see Figure 7.1).

1. As alveolar pressure increases, the lungs begin the exhalation of "puffs" of air flowing toward the vocal folds.

2. If the sounds to be produced are "voiced" sounds (such as /z/ or /a/), the pressurized "puffs" of air cause the vocal folds within the larynx to vibrate. The vibration rate of the folds controls the pitch of the sound. The faster the vibration rate, the higher the pitch.

3. If the sounds to be produced are "voiceless" (such as /p/ or /s/), the puffs of air flow through a more open larynx without causing the vocal folds to vibrate and produce phonation. Instead, they are directed to variously opening or constricting points within the vocal tract.

4. Above the larynx, these puffs of air are now modified by the various organs in the vocal tract, which include the soft palate, tongue, lips, teeth, and jaw. These organs, through a variety of complex movements, alter the oral cavity into remarkable variations of size and shape affecting articulation and resonance.

5. The combination of these four steps accounts for the modulations in the puff of air that transform it into a sound of a certain pitch, volume, and quality. However, those factors must now be combined with the other sounds that have been made or will be made. Timing in forming these sound sequences is necessary to form words and for words to flow into phrases and phrases into sentences to produce meaningful speech. This is the "dynamic flow" process that, as we have indicated, includes such characteristics as sequence, duration, rhythm, rate, and fluency. The dynamic flow of speech is both supplemented and constrained by a number of factors, including the complex muscular movements of the other parts of the vocal system, which McDonald (1968) first referred to as "rapid ballistic movements." Add to this complexity the more subtle influences of language—such as grammar, quality of vocabulary, and skill in functional use—or factors such as impaired hearing and we begin to appreciate the miracle that takes place every time we speak. We can now move on to consider the flow of thought that accompanies intelligible speech within the context of a language system.

■ Language Development

Language is one factor commonly used to set humans apart from most other animals. Although many animals can produce sounds of different pitch and volume, and indeed utilize them as meaningful signals, none appears able to use this tool with the complexity and purpose common to the human species. Certainly most children are able to learn to talk without difficulty. "By the time they get to kindergarten, children have amassed a vocabulary of perhaps 8000 words and almost all of the basic grammatical forms of the language. They can handle questions, negative statements, dependent clauses, compound sentences, and a great variety of other constructions. They have also learned much more than vocabulary and grammar: they have learned to use language in many different social situations" (Gleason, 1985, p. 5).

For most of us, then, acquiring language appears to be so automatic and so much an integral step in our maturity that the real complexity and depth of our competence with it pass unnoticed. Indeed, as McCormick and Schiefelbusch (1984) pointed out, whereas computers have been programmed to carry out some incredibly complex functions, we have yet to see them be very successful in simulating the generative nature of human language. Most of us do not spend much time thinking about language acquisition, perhaps because, as Chomsky (1972) proposed, we lose sight of the need to explain something that appears familiar and obvious to us.

But we are confronted with certain children who do not follow this normal developmental sequence. Failure to acquire language is a developmental disaster—a disaster that, if unremediated, can have far-reaching social and educational consequences for many aspects of a child's life. Such children and consequences lend weight to our study of language, its importance and complexity. How is language developed? What is wrong (dysfunctional, delayed, defective) when the normal developmental sequence does not occur within expected time limits? What is or can be done in such cases?

Keeping in mind McCormick and Schiefelbusch's comment that "the theoretical and applied literature related to language learning is almost as complex as language itself" (1984, p. 28), we will confine this introductory discussion to the shallow end of the deep complexities of language and its acquisition. It does appear essential, however, to provide some basic knowledge for a better understanding of speech and language disorders.

Theories of language acquisition have received a lot of attention in the past few decades. The two primary theories are based on the work of B. F. Skinner (1957) and Noam Chomsky (1957).

To greatly oversimplify, Skinner's work championed the viewpoint that language is strictly a learned behavior. An infant soon learns that vocalizations result in increased attention (hugs, smiles, cuddling, and so on) from the parent. The more the vocalizations resemble the sounds, words, and intonation patterns of the parents' native language, the more immediate the reinforcement. When babies imitate the words or sounds they hear ("num-num, milk") and receive food or drink along with friendly attention, the likelihood of that vocalization occurring is increased.

Chomsky, in contrast, views language as a basically innate behavior; that is, children arrive already "hard-wired" or programmed to learn language. Chomsky and his disciples feel that this inborn capacity is present in all humans as an outgrowth of general maturation keyed to the maturation of motor skills (Lenneberg, 1967). They argue that other theories don't account for children's rapid acquisition of language complexities nor for their ability to generate new words or phrases they've never heard before. They also maintain that there is a "readiness period" that is critical for proper environmental stimulation of language acquisition. Should that period be missed or hampered due to physical or psychological factors, adequate mental processes may also fail to develop.

Current work appears to be less dogmatic than either of those theories (Gleason, 1985), and a more broad-based approach called the interactionist perspective has been generated. This perspective hypothesizes that at birth infants are prepared to learn to talk but that the environment then teaches them how to do so (McCormick & Schiefelbusch, 1984). Van Riper and Emerick characteristically cut through much of the complex language theory in the following informative summary.

> Although the precise contribution of each is not yet known, both nature and nurture are involved in the process of language development. While a child does seem to be biologically programmed for acquiring symbols and the rules of early syntax, environmental stimulation may be very important for learning speech sounds and subtle nuances of more complex sentence structure. The variables of sex (females have a slight edge in rate of development), order of birth (firstborn and only children develop faster), and socioeconomic status (middle- and upper-class children seem to acquire language faster than do lower-class children) influence to some extent the rate of speech and language development.
>
> While the rate at which they move through the stages of speech and language development may vary from individual to individual, the sequence is similar for all

Table 7.1 The normal development of language

Age	Language Development Milestones
Early months (0–8 months)	Cries to signal pain or distress
	Smiles or vocalizes to initiate social contact
	Responds to the human voice
	Gazes at people's faces
	Uses vocal and nonvocal communication to express interest and influence environment
	Babbles, using all types of sounds
	Engages in private vocalizations when alone
	Combines babbles, understands names of familiar people and objects, laughs, listens when people are talking
Crawlers & walkers (8–18 months)	Understands many more words than can produce
	Looks in the direction of 20 or more objects when they are named
	Creates long, babbled sentences
	Shakes head side to side to say no
	Says two or three clear words
	Looks at various pictures with interest, pointing to some of the objects
	Uses vocal signals other than crying to gain help or attention
	Begins to use *me*, *you*, and *I*
Toddlers (18 months–3 years)	Combines words
	Will listen to stories for short periods
	Has speaking vocabulary of perhaps 200 words
	Begins to develop fantasy through language
	Begins to play "pretend" games
	Defines use of many household items
	Uses compound sentences
	Begins to use adjectives and adverbs and to describe day's events
	Uses *tomorrow* and *yesterday*

SOURCE: *Adapted from S. Bredekamp, "Developmentally Appropriate Practice in Early Childhood Programs Serving Children from Birth Through Age 8," NAEYC (National Association for the Education of Young Children), 1989, p. 31. Reprinted by permission.*

children. A child will not use inflected vocal play and then back up to begin babbling. Deviations in the sequence of development may signal a problem and should be thoroughly investigated.

At each stage of development, a child's manner of communication is an integrated whole, not an incomplete version of the form adults use. His performance is best described as a special type of language, "childese," if you will, complete with its own "rules." The acquisition of language is all one piece. All components, syntax, phonology, semantics, are acquired simultaneously; a child does not learn sentence structure and then phonology, for example. But the core of language development is the expression of meaning. The ability to express meaning depends on cognitive development. The way in which a person conceptualizes the process of language development will determine what he does to foster development in a normal child or help a language-impaired child. Theory, whether explicitly formulated by a speech pathologist or simply a parental intuition, dictates the form of therapy. (1990, p. 105)

Table 7.1 provides a broad look at the typical developmental milestones in language development.

By the time most children are 4 years old, they will have developed a vocabulary of over 1500 words and use sentences averaging 5 words in length. Although language continues to develop in a consistent pattern after age 4, its growth is less dramatic and tends to focus on grammatical forms. Most of the complex forms used by adults are absorbed by the time the child is 6, and most of the consonant and blend sounds are developed by 7 or 8 (Heward & Orlansky, 1988).

It is important to note that not all children who develop normal language follow the same pattern: just as environments, number of siblings, and individual abilities vary, so do patterns of development. Most authorities feel, however, that most children follow approximately the same sequence.

Definitions

In our discussion of the history of communication disorders we indicated that the professionals' numerous title changes have reflected the roots, emphasis in roles, and responsibilities of the discipline most directly responsible for treating speech and language disorders at any given time. Arguments continue over issues such as whether to use *speech-language pathologist* or *speech-language clinician,* but it is more important here to define or describe what those professionals do. Put simply, a speech-language pathologist is trained to diagnose disorders of speech and language and provide remediation for them. To be certified by their national organization, they must have completed a master's degree, served for a year under close clinical supervision, and passed a national test.

Another approach to understanding their function is to examine a bulletin prepared by the American Speech-Language-Hearing Association for use in school settings. A sample letter (see Box 7.1) is sent to the parents of kindergartners and first-graders to explain the school speech-language pathologist's role. It also draws a helpful and straightforward distinction between language disorders and speech disorders.

Language disorders have been defined by the American Speech-Language-Hearing Association (1982) to include the impairment or deviant development of comprehension or use of a spoken, written, or other symbol system. These disorders may involve (1) the form of language, (2) the content of language, or (3) the function of language in communication—in any combination. Although far less agreement might be found in the classification system of language, a reasonable argument can be made for viewing language disorders in those three broad categories.

All three types of disorders fit within the general term *communication disorders,* and indeed under the broad umbrella of *language disorders.* Specific interrelationships among speech and language disorders and other topics covered in this book—such as hearing impairment, cerebral palsy, and mental retardation—will not be discussed in this chapter. Rather than providing specific examples of the three categories, we will discuss them one by one later in the section titled "Types of Language Disorders."

A wealth of definitions is available for the term *speech disorder.* Though they vary in how specific or general they are (Perkins, 1977), most have recognizable commonalities. Gelfand, Jenson, and Drew (1982) found those commonalities to include the following.

1. Attracts attention by being sufficiently deviant from the norm
2. Interferes with communication
3. Adversely affects communication for speaker or listener

Van Riper and Emerick have included those three components in the following definition: "Speech is abnormal when it deviates so far from the speech of other people that it calls attention to itself, interferes with communication, or causes the speaker or his listeners to be distressed" (1990, p. 34). They go on to list three adjectives that are key to their definition of a speech disorder: conspicuous,

**Box 7.1
The Speech-Language Pathologist's Role in the Public Schools**

Dear Parents:

As the speech-language pathologist serving your child's school, I want to share some information with you about communication disorders. I also would like to tell you what we can do—together—if your child needs help with speech and language development.

The ability to communicate is perhaps the most important skill your child will acquire. Communication skills permit youngsters to make sense of their world, to express themselves, and to learn. Because these skills are central to success in school, early identification of a problem is crucial. Once a child with a communication disorder is identified, the appropriate treatment and the involvement of parents often make the difference between failure or frustration in school and a successful school experience.

Speech disorders include problems with making sounds correctly, voice quality, and stuttering.

Language disorders include difficulty in understanding or using language. For example, language disorders may include problems with understanding/identifying certain classes of words, understanding/giving directions, answering/asking questions, or understanding/using correct grammar. Language disorders also can be the inability to use appropriate social language or convey an idea to others.

By the age of 5, a child should be able to carry on a conversation, hear and understand most speech at home and school, answer simple questions about a story, say most sounds correctly, and speak in a way that sounds like other children.

Usually, children do not "outgrow" communication disorders. That's why early identification and treatment are so important. In fact, early treatment can help prevent communication disorders from turning into lifelong handicaps. My responsibilities include diagnosing a communication disorder and evaluating its nature and extent. In addition, I provide treatment as necessary.

If you have any concerns about your child's communication skills, please contact me at school. I look forward to meeting you and working with you to help your child develop better communication skills.

Sincerely,

SOURCE: ASHA, *Jan. 1989, 31, p. 50. Reprinted by permission of American Speech-Language-Hearing Association.*

■ The use of gestures such as this by very young children is normal. When older children overuse physical gestures for purposes of communication, delayed speech may be the cause. ■

unintelligible, and unpleasant. One of the key components, then, of a disorder is that it is perceived as deviating from the norm. A 3-year-old child who wants the "wittle wed" shoe does not attract the same attention as does a man of 30 using the same phrase. The degree to which speech is "conspicuous" also depends on the speech patterns of others in the same environment. There is evidence that some Native American tribes in which disfluent speech is almost the norm have no word for stuttering (ibid.). Ungrammatical or substandard English is much more noticeable in a college commencement address than on inner-city streets. Communities of German or Scandinavian descendants in the upper Midwest are able to use *dis* and *dat* for *this* and *that* without any significant social consequence.

Speech that is unintelligible or that interferes with the message the speaker is attempting to deliver strikes at the very heart of communication and is seen as disordered or defective. The head jerking, rapid repetitions, tongue clicking, and other secondary mannerisms of some stutterers often distract the listener from the message they are trying to deliver. The excessive nasality of the individual with a cleft palate or a very high-pitched falsetto voice can also distract the listener and detract from communication.

The third component—unpleasantness—has to do with the feelings of the speaker or listener. We once worked with a young college-age woman who despised her low-pitched voice. She felt that the combination of her athletic skills and low-pitched voice made her the victim of occasional but cruel remarks questioning her femininity. Her voice, though low, was not beyond the point that most would judge deviant; but her feelings about her voice were vital to our decision to accept her into therapy. An argument can be made that, given the increasing use of severity scales to determine when children with speech disorders should be seen for intervention, this third component is often overlooked. In that case, the cost in increased emotional distress could rise. Evaluators of speech disorders must recognize that some communicative handicaps are based more on emotional reactions to speech than to a specific, quantifiable disability.

Prevalence

Van Riper and Emerick (1990) have stated that communication disorders are the nation's largest disability. Based on their review of surveys, they estimate that approximately 20 million Americans, or 10% of the population, have a speech, language, or hearing impairment. While it is difficult to be precise about how many individuals have specific types of speech disorders—a point also made by Matthews (1990)—they conclude that clearly the number of people with communication disorders is growing at a faster rate than population growth, due to the increase in the average life span vis à vis the birthrate.

As might be deduced by the numbers just cited, there has also been continued growth in school programs serving persons with speech and language disorders. The U.S. Department of Education has estimated that in 1988 over 2 million school-age children with communication disorders were receiving services from over 45,000 speech-language pathologists, audiologists, and teachers of the hearing impaired.

The advent of PL 99-457, the Education of the Handicapped Act Amendments of 1986, with its focus on preschool programs, provided child count data suggesting that over 70% of disabled preschool children have a speech or language impairment as their primary disability.

As we saw in Table 2.5 in Chapter 2, the percentage served in public schools as "speech handicapped" is 1.72% in the United States as a whole. This ranges in the 50 states from a low of 0.62% to a high of 2.97%. The difference may reflect the fact that only those with severe problems are served in some states.

Reviewing a number of sample surveys and studies of specific categories in this area, Van Riper and Emerick (1990, p. 60) compiled the following estimates.

Articulation disorders	3–6%
Stuttering	2–7%
Voice disorders	1–3%
Language disorders	3–5%

Two difficulties in interpreting such estimates are that some individuals have more than one disorder and that estimates for each group may be affected by factors such as age and gender.

Types of Speech Disorders

■ Articulation Disorders

Articulation disorders are considered to comprise the majority of speech disorders: approximately 75% (Gearheart, 1980). They affect approximately 3% to 6% of the general population (Van Riper & Emerick, 1990) and are particularly prevalent among young children. Because many children outgrow their articulation errors by the time they are 10 or 11, there has been some debate about when and how much intervention is actually needed. As a result many states have adopted or are considering the adoption of severity scales designed to help the speech-language pathologist determine the educational significance of the articulation disorder. These scales must take into account the social context of the speech and whether or not it is consistent with the norm for the individual's group. In any case, articulation disorders are generally classified in three major categories: omissions, substitutions, and distortions.

Omission errors are among the most common of children's articulation problems and are usually corrected through maturation with little or no clinical intervention. Typically the speaker omits a sound that should be heard in the word: *ike* for *like, kool* for *school,* and *e it me* for *he hit me.* Often a child will consistently omit certain sounds, but inconsistencies are also common. If omissions occur in only one or two words of a phrase, the meaning is usually apparent. More omissions, however, can render the message unintelligible. Certainly, age-appropriate language needs to be considered, as well: what is "cute" for a 3-year-old loses its cuteness when uttered by a teenager.

In substitution errors, the speaker substitutes a different sound for the one that should be used. Some of the more common sound substitution errors include the following: *b* for *v,* as in *balentine* for *valentine; w* for *r,* as in *wed* for *red;* and *w* for *l,* as in *wittle* for *little.* The speech condition known as a frontal lisp also counts as a substitution. The protrusion of the tongue between the teeth results in a sound substitution of *th* (either voiced or unvoiced) for *s* or *z.* The resulting *thue* for *Sue, thoo* for *zoo,* and *bathket* for *basket* are examples. These are only a few of the more common substitutions, as any parent or baby-sitter can attest.

Sounds most commonly misarticulated:

s, z, voiceless *th* as in *bath, r, l, sh, j* as in *judge*

Distortions occur when the speaker produces a sound that is similar to but not quite the same as the one intended. Usually such distortions are the result of some misalignment of the articulators; that is, the teeth, jaw, lips, or tongue are not quite in the optimal position and produce a nonstandard rather than standard sound. "Slushy"-sounding *s* or *sh* sounds and nonstandard *r* sounds are common examples of distortions.

While these three classifications are the primary categories used to discuss articulation, some authorities also include errors of addition and those attributed to dialect or bilingualism. Additions are often characteristic of certain geographical regions. Speakers said to have a Boston accent may add an *r* sound to the words *idea* and *Cuba,* producing *idear* and *Cuber.* Bilingual speakers may omit a sound or substitute another because of the nature of their primary language.

Although articulation is among the most common of speech disorders and is often resolved developmentally, we must be careful not to ignore the effect of the more serious of these disorders. The unintelligible speech created by a presence of many and varied articulation errors is a serious barrier to communication. As Emerick and Haynes have pointed out, "An articulation disorder severe enough to interfere significantly with intelligibility is . . . as debilitating a communication problem as many other disorders. . . . Articulation disorders are not simple at all, and they are not necessarily easy to diagnose effectively" (1986, p. 53).

Articulation disorders can be caused by a variety of conditions; they may exist in isolation but many times coexist with several other disorders having different causes. The actual organic structure of the tongue and articulators plays an important role. If the articulators are damaged, teeth are missing or maloccluded, or the frenum unusually short, correct articulation may be difficult. Poor motor coordination—typical of muscular dystrophy, multiple sclerosis, or cerebral palsy—makes the rapid ballistic movements of speech difficult to produce. Sensory impairments such as hearing loss, poor auditory memory span, or poor sound discrimination make it difficult to hear, remember, or discriminate speech sounds. In addition a variety of developmental and environmental influences such as poor modeling and faulty family speech patterns can affect articulation quality. It is easy to see how difficult it is to determine the exact cause of many articulation disorders, given the interrelationship of so many contributing factors. This lack of a discrete causal factor will become a familiar pattern as we review other disorders of speech and language.

■ Voice Disorders

Voice disorders, or disorders of phonation, are frequently classified according to (1) pitch, (2) intensity or loudness, and (3) quality. The first two, pitch and intensity, are considered independent dimensions of vocal production. Vocal quality is much more complex and is considered a multidimensional composite of many other factors, including pitch and intensity. Quality disorders are the most common type of voice problem (Van Riper & Emerick, 1990), and can be further divided into difficulties with resonance and laryngeal tone.

Voices that are different from the norm (considering social, age, and gender factors) are said to be disordered. These disorders are noticed primarily when they offend the listener's esthetic judgment. Any particular voice may be judged to fall into one of three broad categories: (1) having a noticeably pleasant quality, (2) having a noticeably unpleasant quality, or (3) not particularly noticeable in regard to quality. Perkins (1977) has pointed out that though the esthetic standards of the culture and acoustical standards for comprehension must be considered by speech-language pathologists, their primary concern should be vocal hygiene. The contention is that when good vocal habits are promoted, the acoustical and esthetic components are also enhanced. Poor vocal hygiene in most instances means abuse. Such abuse in children results from yelling, imitating noises, or habitually talking under tension. This type of vocal behavior can irritate the vocal folds as well as produce benign and occasionally malignant growths. Thus, attending to voice characteristics such as hoarseness is particularly important.

Pitch disorders may take several different forms. The voice may be judged too high, too low, to have pitch breaks, or to be very restricted in tonal range—monopitched or monotone. Pitch disorders are often quite noticeable and can have significant negative social consequences. The male with a very high voice and the female with a very low voice may be subject to these consequences. Pitch breaks, which happen to many during adolescence, are a normal part of puberty and can occur in girls as well as boys (Hardman, Drew, & Egan, 1987). They normally cause only embarrassment to adolescents; however, concern is warranted if they persist after 6 to 12 months (Damste & Lehrman, 1975). Continuation much beyond adolescence could reflect laryngeal disorders that should be medically investigated (Brewer, 1975). Pitch disorders seldom interfere with communication, but the effectiveness of the communication may be hampered for affective reasons.

Pitch disorders can be caused by a variety of factors, physical as well as psychogenic. They range from a boy imitating the lower-pitched voice of his father or brother to organic conditions such as a hormone imbalance. Pitch disorders may often be reduced significantly with the assistance of a competent speech-language pathologist or through medical intervention.

Intensity disorders—frequently referred to as loudness disorders—result in a voice that is described as either too loud or too soft. These disorders are not likely to have the same degree of negative social consequences as are those of pitch—particularly for males. Like pitch disorders, they have a variety of causes ranging from imitation and poor monitoring to several organic problems. The term *aphonia* describes the total loss of voice; *dysphonia* refers to a partial or occasional loss of phonation. Persons who have had their larynx removed due to cancer are almost always left aphonic. Other individuals with a normal larynx may for organic or psychological reasons experience total or partial voice loss. Such disorders as hysterical aphonia and spastic aphonia are examples. Other organic conditions include laryngeal trauma due to accident or disease, partial paralysis of the vocal folds, and pulmonary diseases. These account for voices with little or no intensity, but excessively loud voices may also be caused by organic conditions such as hearing impairments and brain damage (Hutchinson, Hanson, & Mecham, 1979).

Quality disorders are often difficult to define, as they are more like a composite of many factors, including the ones we have already discussed. Included in this category are the voice disorders most frequently found among children of school age (Heward & Orlansky, 1988): hoarseness, breathiness, and nasality. Other descriptive words used for voices with quality disorders include *harsh, thin,* and *falsetto.*

As many of these quality disorders may have a concomitant medical condition (such as vocal nodules and tumors—which in a few cases are malignant), medical investigation, intervention, and treatment must be considered. Many authorities would not refer to the medical condition (vocal nodules or tumors) as the cause of the disorders but would instead single out as the culprit "vocal abuse." Excessive nasality or hypernasality is the result of too much resonance from the nasal cavity. This quality is often referred to as "talking through one's nose." People with hyponasality have too little resonance in the nasal cavity and sound like they have a cold or a stuffy nose. Like other disorders of quality, these conditions may have organic causes (such as a cleft palate or enlarged adenoids) as well as more functional causes such as emotional problems, imitation, or learned behavior patterns.

The effect of a **cleft lip or palate** on speech will vary greatly depending on the depth of the cleft and the success of the corrective surgical procedure. Most children born with cleft palates are treated surgically during the first few months of life. While cleft lip surgery seldom results in any residual problems, surgery on the palate is more complex, leaving residual speech impairments. The purpose of cleft palate surgery is to close off the oral cavity from the nasal cavity. The major speech goal will most frequently be to correct articulation errors and reduce nasality. Other, less common problems may include faulty dentition or abnormal laryngeal structure.

If excessive nasality is considered a problem, it may be remedied in one of three ways (Moller, Starr, & Johnson, 1990).

1. By working with a speech-language pathologist to see if the child can be coached into using less nasal speech
2. By surgery that reconstructs the closure mechanism
3. By inserting a prosthesis (and then establishing a prosthesis program to reduce nasality and eventually the need for the prosthesis)

Although creating acceptable speech in students with cleft palate can be time-consuming and difficult, it is usually successful (ibid.).

■ Disorders of Fluency (Speech-Flow Disorders)

In discussing the mechanics of speech we mentioned dynamic flow. Dynamic speech flow is composed of several characteristics such as sequence, rate, duration, and fluency (Perkins, 1980). Normal speech is perceived as being relatively fluent—a smooth-flowing process with occasional minor and natural interruptions. In reality, the line between normal and abnormal is often blurred by the perceptions of the evaluator and the reactions of the one being evaluated. Normal speech includes a number of disfluent moments in which the speaker may repeat, pause, hesitate, and display other speech behaviors that interrupt the flow of communication. Pointing out that we regularly accept many disfluencies such as *um* or *ah* or an excited speaker's repetitions of sounds and words, Shames made the point that "clearly, not all disfluencies are part of a disorder or a problem" (1986, p. 245). Shames went on to say, however, that most normal disfluencies are repetitions of whole words, pauses, or interjections. Speakers who repeat many words or the same word (or initial sound) over and over again in the same utterance may be considered to have abnormal disfluencies. When too much attention must be given to how the speaker is talking instead of what the speaker is saying, speech behavior is adversely interfering with communication and our definition is disordered. These **fluency disorders** are typically classified in two categories: stuttering and cluttering.

"Stuttering," according to Van Riper and Emerick, "occurs when the forward flow of speech is interrupted abnormally by repetitions or prolongations of a sound, syllable, or articulatory posture, or by avoidance and struggle behaviors" (1990, p. 294). It is this "abnormal" disruption of fluency that creates the primary communication problem of stuttering. But though the disruption of fluency is the initial difficulty, abnormal disorders, if persistent and prolonged, produce emotional reactions that add to the disorder and the anguish of the person with the disorder.

Stuttering is the primary subcategory of fluency disorders and affects approximately 1% of the population of children and adults in the United States (Shames, 1986). It comes as no surprise to any speech-language pathologist working with those who stutter to note that boys outnumber girls by a 4:1 ratio. Many authorities have accounted for this by pointing to the recognized difference between boys and girls in rate of language maturation.

Theories regarding the causes of stuttering are many and varied. Some believe stuttering to be a learned behavior; others see it as primarily psychological in nature, evidence of a maladjusted if not neurotic mental condition. Charles Van Riper (a self-described "controlled stutterer") was one of the first to view stuttering in a more eclectic fashion. He sees stuttering as a problem of many sources, and its cause as not nearly so important as the conditions that maintain the behavior (Van Riper & Emerick, 1990). Conture, in a similarly eclectic fashion, discusses stuttering as a complex, multidimensional problem that has defied a variety of simple, unidimensional explanations. He points out that although some explanations deal nicely with one part of the problem, they seem to overlook other aspects. Paraphrasing Sinclair Lewis, he summarizes this dilemma by concluding that "the reality of our clinical days has all too often failed to live up to the dreams of our theoretical nights" (1990, p. 1).

Box 7.2
Talking to Persons Who Stutter

Do you feel uncomfortable when you talk to a person who stutters? Many people do because they do not know how to react when the person who stutters is having trouble.

The National Stuttering Project, a nationwide network of support groups with 4000 members in 65 cities, has developed the following list of suggestions that will make it easier for you and the person who stutters to communicate more effectively:

- You will be tempted to finish sentences or fill in words. Please do not do this. No one likes words put in his or her mouth. Besides, if you guess wrong, difficulties can multiply.
- Stuttering may look like an easy problem that can be solved with suggestions such as "Slow down," "Take a breath," or "Relax." Such advice doesn't work and may be viewed as demeaning.
- Keep normal and natural eye contact. Try not to look embarrassed or alarmed. Just wait patiently and naturally until the person is finished.
- Be conscious of your own speech. Talk in a relaxed, slower than normal manner.
- Let the person know by your manner and actions that you are listening to what he or she is saying, not how he or she is saying it. Pause a little more than normally before you begin talking.
- People who stutter often have more trouble controlling their speech on the telephone. Please be extra patient in this situation. And, if you pick up the phone and hear nothing, before you hang up, be sure it is not a person who stutters trying to start the conversation.

If you give people who stutter a chance, you will find they have a lot to say.

SOURCE: *ASHA, Sept. 1989, 31, pp. 29–30. Reprinted by permission of American Speech-Language-Hearing Assocation.*

Communicative development	Communicative deviations	Communicative disorders
Development or preventive programs are carried out in class. Speech specialist is involved in total curriculum to emphasize the value of attention to speech and language development. Specialist serves as consultant and also provides some direct teacher training but essentially no *direct* service to students.	Mild to moderate problems (articulation, etc.) are evident. Specialist evaluates and provides instructions to regular class teacher, who implements major elements of program. Specialist monitors regularly and intervenes more directly as required.	Severe problems require more intensive one-to-one service by specialist. Regular class teacher's efforts are quite important here, but most direct service comes from the specialist.

Service is provided by regular class teacher.

Service is provided by speech specialist.

Figure 7.3 The comprehensive speech and language program continuum

SOURCE: *Reprinted with the permission of Merrill, an imprint of Macmillan Publishing Company, from* Exceptional Students in the Regular Classroom, *Fifth edition, by B. Gearheart, M. Weishahn, and C. Gearheart. Copyright © 1992 by Merrill Publishing Company.*

this trend to more classroom-based intervention as teachers and pathologists learn more about the powerful and complex relationships among language, reading, writing, and social interactions. Classroom-based interventions include a language specialist teaching in a self-contained room, a specialist team-teaching in the regular classroom, or a specialist providing one-on-one intervention in the regular classroom.

Along with—or perhaps because of—these new models for intervention, we are also seeing a strong movement toward curriculum-based assessment. In the language area, such assessment means using the actual classroom curricula contexts and content to measure a student's language intervention needs and progress (Nelson, 1989). Dublinske (1989) reported a growing emphasis on providing speech-language services in the regular classroom as part of the regular education initiative (REI) movement. While viewing this movement as a unique opportunity for innovative service delivery, he also cautioned that it should not be seen as the answer for all children with speech and language disorders. Clearly, current trends toward more classroom-based intervention will further emphasize the role of the teacher as an integral part of the delivery system.

Issues and Trends

Our discussion of the increase in classroom-based intervention and curriculum-based assessment provides an appropriate transition into some of the current issues and future trends in the field of speech and language disorders. Several current issues would seem to have considerable future importance.

The REI thrust toward serving most children with disabilities in the regular education classroom is already having a major impact (Dublinske, 1989). The fallout from this movement has increased the use of severity rating scales to help the pathologist determine which students' disorders will have a negative impact on their school performance. Closer ties to the academic work performed in the classroom are also gained through curriculum-based assessment.

Technology, with its unprecedented growth, should continue to have a profound impact on augmentative communication as well as on actual therapy, parent training, case management, and on other, more general facets of the field. Tools such as interactive videodisc, computer enhancements, and advancements in prosthetic devices can be expected to benefit the field in an almost logarithmic progression. As they will be for the general population, information management skills will be essential for those involved with communication disorders.

Our sensitivity to the multicultural aspects of our society and their relationship to speech and language disorders will increase as the size of minority groups increases. Public Law 94-457 has already deeply affected early education programs. Greater populations of preschoolers will also result in an increased emphasis on the family's role in intervention.

Continued medical advances will not only result in improved life-saving procedures and medical interventions but are also likely to increase the number of students whose severe disabilities must be addressed. The advent of "crack babies" and children infected with the HIV virus has increased our awareness of those with complex needs at all levels. These needs may be met by further emphasis on teamwork among professionals.

Finally, the increasing shortage of speech-language pathologists may lead to searches for a variety of supplements. Lenker and Michener (1989) have discussed a possible movement to utilize private speech and language practitioners in the public schools as a workable alternative to more traditional models.

Summary

Language, speech, and the communication that results from their use come so naturally to most children that their miraculous nature is often overlooked. Not all experts agree about how speech develops in young children, but all agree to its complexity, and most agree that though the rate of speech and language development varies from individual to individual, the sequence of development is similar for all children.

The three major types of speech disorders are articulation disorders, voice disorders, and fluency disorders. Language disorders may occur in relation to the form of language (phonology, morphology, and syntax), language content (semantics), or the functional use of language (pragmatics). Form, content, and function are interrelated, and the result of speech and language disorders alike is difficulty in communication.

Speech and language disorders may be caused by environmental deprivation, emotional deprivation, or structural abnormalities in the speech mechanism. They may also be related to cognitive ability, hearing disorders, or behavioral disorders. Often speech or language disorders have multiple causes.

Identification of speech- and language-disordered students means asking questions such as these: "Can they be understood?" "Is their communication appropriate to the setting?" "Are they embarrassed when attempting to communicate?" "Are they damaging their speaking mechanisms?" Any final decision about whether a student has a speech or language disorder should be made by a speech-language pathologist.

Educational interventions for students with speech disorders may be classroom based, the speech-language pathologist collaborating with the teacher in educational planning. In the case of more severe speech or language disorders, interventions may be provided on a one-to-one or small-group basis in a separate setting. Sensitivity to multicultural influences and recognition of the family's role are essential, both in the initial identification process and in ongoing therapy.

Parents of Children with Hearing Impairments Vary in Their Reactions

"The hearing aid is hard to get used to. It looks so ugly on her."

"I don't love him any less now that I know he's deaf."

"I resented having to learn sign language."

"Sending Anna Marie to an oral school was the best thing we did."

"My husband learned to sign right away, but I just couldn't get the hang of it. It made me feel so inadequate."

"It was helpful to have the tool of cued speech when we had to help Brian with the spelling words from his unit on China."

"When Judy took me to the refrigerator and signed 'milk' it was like a miracle. It was the first time I could respond to her when she made a request."

"Looking back, I'm not sure the day school program was best for Heather. She got a strong background in the academic areas but never did develop many social relationships. Probably, if I had it to do over, a residential school would have been better."

"The best thing we did was make sure Randy received all the help possible when he was younger. Now he goes to school with all the neighborhood kids and loves reading, soccer, and baseball. Randy has a good start and we'll continue to guide and love him, but what he becomes as an adult is up to him."

"We have two deaf children and two hearing children. All the worries we had about the older deaf children resenting the younger hearing ones just never materialized."

CHAPTER EIGHT

Hearing Impairments

"If I were to offer any advice, it would be to keep an open mind, trust your gut-level feelings—they are most likely right—and remember that no decision is forever, so it can be changed."

Each exceptionality has its own characteristics, but **hearing impairment** might be considered truly unique among the areas of exceptionality. It has, for example, the world's only separate, accredited university for students with a specific disability (Gallaudet University, in Washington, D.C.). It appears to have more national organizations serving as advocates for the rights of its population and for resources to meet its needs than any other exceptionality. Many educators and persons with severe hearing impairments recognize and speak of a "deaf community or culture"; that is, they recognize and support a degree of separateness at a time when advocates for other exceptionalities stress inclusion or integration into the mainstream of school and other aspects of life. Related to all these factors is the existence of a special language common among adults: American Sign Language. Perhaps no other exceptionality has had such a stormy beginning in the establishment of educational programs. Controversies that grew out of that beginning have shaped the development of educational practices for over 200 years.

Although there are fewer schoolchildren with a hearing loss than with, for example, a learning disability, mental retardation, or behavioral disorder, hearing disability is an area of concern. It is estimated that one out of ten persons in the United States has a hearing loss. Hearing loss affects more people than do blindness, cancer, kidney disease, multiple sclerosis, and tuberculosis combined (House Ear Institute, 1985).

Technological advances that assist individuals with a hearing loss continue, but the issue of communication remains central to this area of exceptionality. In one unusual situation, an entire tribe, isolated in the Philippine Islands, used signs to accommodate two tribal members who were deaf (Nance, 1975).

Historical Background

Ancient societies as long ago as 1550 B.C. recorded their concerns about the legal and religious rights of persons who were deaf. They weren't so concerned about their education, as the majority of people were illiterate then (Feldman, 1970). The Justinian Code, a legal system developed in the sixth century A.D., contains a section on deafness and shows that the Romans had given considerable thought to the condition. They recognized that complete deafness was not as common as hearing loss, and that there were differences between individuals who were born deaf and those who later became deaf. Under the Justinian Code, persons who were deaf and mute but literate, or deaf but not mute, or mute but not deaf, and those who became deaf after birth were all accorded full rights. Only those who could neither hear nor speak and who were illiterate were denied rights. The education of persons who were deaf was still not a concern (Peet, 1851). The treatment of individuals who were deaf during the early Christian era and most of the Middle Ages was similar to that of all persons who were viewed as handicapped. Usually they were denied the right to an inheritance, to marry, and to participate in religious services. They were often denied access to work, though they were allowed to fight in the army.

The first actual teacher of students who were deaf was Pablo Ponce de León (1520–1584), a Benedictine monk who established a school for the children of Spanish nobility who could not hear. His efforts were regarded as instruction rather than as the miracle that was usually inferred from an afflicted individual's learning to speak, read, or write. Unfortunately, we have no record of how he taught them. We do know that one of his first students, the son of a prominent Spanish nobleman, Don Francisco Velasco, regained his inheritance rights because of Ponce de León's teaching. A number of his other students, all sons of Spanish noblemen, also learned to speak, read, and write—and to do so in several languages.

A second individual of historical importance was Juan Martín Pablo Bonet (1579–1620), who is perhaps better known, because his work was recorded. He, too, worked in Spain, and much of his effort was directed toward teaching the grandson of a brother of the three Velasco brothers taught by Ponce de León. Bonet advocated a one-handed alphabet remarkably similar to the manual alphabet used today. He also recommended early intervention, a language-rich environment, that all family members learn the manual alphabet, early speech training, and reading as a means of developing speech (Deland, 1931).

■ The Establishment of Schools in Europe

Great Britain, France, and Germany all contributed to the fledgling attempts to educate individuals who were deaf. In Great Britain several people, including William Holder (1616–1698) and John Wallis (1618–1689), taught individuals who were deaf; both claimed to have invented the art of teaching them (Moores, 1987). Thomas Braidwood (1715–1806) established his own school in Edinburgh in 1767; he is often credited with initiating education for individuals with hearing impairments in Great Britain.

Others in France and Germany were developing similar educational programs. Abbé Charles Michel de l'Épée (1712–1789) established the first *public* school of its kind in France. In his school, de l'Épée first utilized an approach emphasizing oral language, but soon, because of high enrollment, developed a system of **manual communication,** or signs. This became the distinguishing characteristic of his approach. In Germany, Samuel Heinicke (1729–1790) became interested in deafness while in the military service and established a school for students with hearing impairments in 1778. Heinicke believed strongly in an oral approach and was opposed to de l'Épée's manual technique. The two men began a controversy—between oralism and manualism—that their counterparts have continued for over 200 years.

■ The Establishment of Schools in the United States

The first permanent school in the United States for students with impaired hearing was established in Hartford, Connecticut, in 1817; it was called the American Asylum for the Education and Instruction of the Deaf and Dumb. This school, now the American School for the Deaf, was established as a result of the determination of Dr. Mason Fitch Cogswell (whose daughter was deaf) and the interest of Thomas Hopkins Gallaudet (1787–1851). Gallaudet became interested in teaching Dr. Cogswell's daughter, was successful, and decided to study with the

Braidwoods in England to learn their oral methods. He also planned to study de l'Épée's manual methods in France, but the Braidwoods objected: they wanted to work only with people who would use their method exclusively, and they swore their trainees to secrecy. Gallaudet reluctantly gave up his idea of studying both methods and went instead to France.

When Gallaudet returned to the United States, he established what is now the American School for the Deaf. For many years this school was the center of education for students who were deaf, providing leadership to other states as they established their own schools. Thus, many of the early schools in the United States were influenced by the French manual method, in which little effort was directed toward the development of speech or articulation.

Horace Mann and Samuel Howe returned to the United States in 1844 after studying German schools for students who were deaf, convinced that the German (oral) method was superior to manual methods (Deland, 1931). They advocated oralism because it enabled those who were deaf to communicate with other members of society and thereby learn more readily (ibid.). After oralism was introduced in the United States, opposition to it arose, in the belief that signs were better suited to teaching morals and religion—two major components of education at the time (Moores, 1987). Persistent efforts by Gardiner Greene Hubbard, whose daughter was deaf, led to the opening of the Clarke School, a public school for the deaf using the oral approach, in Massachusetts in 1867.

In 1857 Edward Gallaudet, the son of Thomas Hopkins Gallaudet, had been appointed principal of the Columbia Institute for the Deaf and Dumb in Washington, D.C. In 1864 he was made president of a college division of that institution; it later became Gallaudet College. The college became a university in 1986, the only one in the world established for the education of individuals who are deaf.

After visiting schools in Europe, Edward Gallaudet called a meeting of the principals of all schools for the deaf in the United States, and advocated using *both* the oral and manual methods. As a result of this meeting, a resolution was passed enjoining administrators of those schools to provide instruction in lipreading (now called speechreading) and articulation to all pupils (ibid.). For his efforts, Gallaudet was strongly criticized by advocates of the manual method; yet, by the end of the century, oralism had gained so many advocates that, ironically, Gallaudet felt compelled to defend the value of manualism.

Another pioneer in the development of programs for students with impaired hearing was Alexander Graham Bell, whose father and grandfather had been speech teachers and whose mother was deaf. (Bell himself had a minor hearing impairment.) Bell played a major role in the continuing controversy between oralists and manualists. After working for a time with Edward Gallaudet, Bell became concerned about the continuing isolation of people with impaired hearing and the intermarriage of men and women who were deaf. He believed that the system of residential schools, the use of a special sign language, and the tendency of graduates to marry one another (which he believed propagated deafness) must be stopped. He therefore formally recommended educational integration, the elimination of sign language, and the discontinuation of employing teachers who were deaf in schools for children who were deaf.

In an effort to resolve the issue of oralism versus manualism, using a combined system or simultaneous method was advocated. These were not developed separately from oralism and manualism, but rather combined the existing methods of both (Scouten, 1983).

Today's discussions center around how best to teach both communication

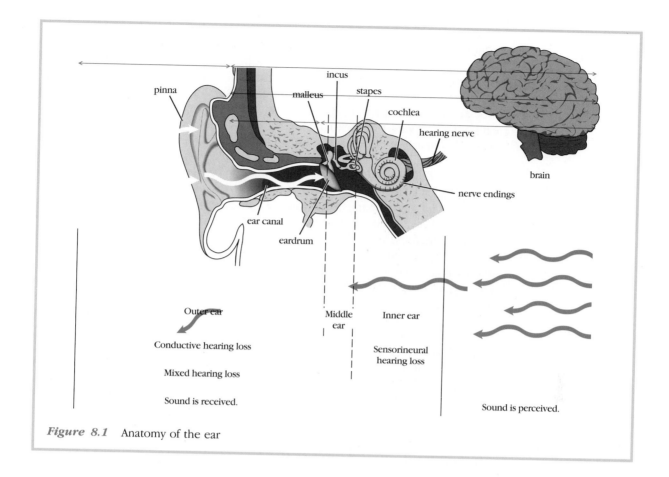

Figure 8.1 Anatomy of the ear

(manual or oral) and content areas (such as science or social studies). The most beneficial techniques for teaching receptive and expressive manual communication and English grammatical construction, speechreading, and oral language are likewise of great interest (Moores, 1987). This is a departure from the early controversy between oralism and manualism.

The Anatomy and Physiology of the Auditory System

The homely visible portion of the ear belies the complexity of functions conducted within it. The ability to hear the soft rustle of leaves as well as a jet plane on a runway—or to discriminate between the whispered sound of the *p* in *pan* and the *b* in *bam*—bespeaks the amazing capabilities of the human ear.

Sound traveling through the air in the form of waves of varying frequency and intensity are collected by the pinna, or auricle (the only portion of the ear that is external and visible) and are channeled into the ear canal to the tympanic membrane (eardrum). The ear canal is about .75 inch long in an adult and is lined with tiny hairs and glands that secrete cerumen, or wax. Their purpose is to keep the skin of the canal and tympanic membrane moist and to keep out dust and insects, which can damage the inner ear (see Figure 8.1).

The middle ear is lined with a mucous membrane similar to that in the mouth. It is ventilated by the Eustachian tube, which connects the middle ear cavity with the back of the nose and throat. In adults the Eustachian tube is about 1.5 inches long, but in children it is shorter and wider. Young children's propensity to middle ear infections may be due to the size and shape of their Eustachian tube and its proximity to their mouth. Another opening in the roof of the middle ear connects it with the mastoid bone, which is felt as a hard bulge just behind the pinna. The mastoid bone has a hard shell on the outside, but the inner portion is a honeycomb of air-filled cells. Its function is unknown.

The middle ear includes the tympanic membrane, which is tightly stretched across the ear canal, and three tiny bones (ossicles). The common names of these bones reflect their shapes: the malleus (hammer), the incus (anvil), and the stapes (stirrup). Their purpose is to conduct incoming sound vibrations from the tympanic membrane through the middle ear cavity to the oval window, a membrane-covered opening to the inner ear. The ossicles convert sound energy into mechanical energy, which amplifies the sound. This is essential to compensate for the loss of intensity of the sound as it travels from the air medium of the middle ear to the fluid medium of the inner ear. The ossicles are connected with each other by fluid-filled joints that, when subjected to a loud noise, are able to partially dislocate and reduce the amount of energy transmitted, preventing harmful levels of vibration from reaching the inner ear.

The process by which the inner ear transforms vibratory-type energy into a kind that can be transmitted by the nervous system is not fully understood. Sound vibrations are transmitted via the stapes to the oval window to the cochlea (a coiled, snail-shaped structure), which is filled with fluid and contains membranes and tiny hair cells. The sound then travels as waves of fluid to specific areas of the cochlea, depending on the frequency of the sound. The fluid movement causes vibrations of the hair cells, which creates an electrostatic current. The current is transmitted through the auditory nerve to the auditory center of the brain, where all the components of sound are coordinated and sent to higher centers of the brain for interpretation and the formulation of a response.

Sound may also be "felt" by vibrations transmitted directly through the bones of the skull. Such bone conduction may be used to determine whether a hearing loss has to do with how sound vibrations get to the inner ear (such as a malformation of the stapes) or with damage to the inner ear itself. Bone conduction is important for hearing normal speech, because the voice is partly monitored by vibrations carried directly to the inner ear via the skull. Normally a speaker hears both air-conducted and bone-conducted sounds—which makes it seem that our own voice is more powerful and impressive than it sounds to others, to whom it is only air conducted. It is possible to bypass the outer and middle ears by stimulating the inner ear directly. In this way sound is heard by bone conduction alone.

Hearing by air conduction depends on the proper functioning of the outer, middle, and inner ear and the neural pathways to the brain; hearing by bone conduction depends only on the functioning of the inner ear and the neural pathways to the brain.

The outer, middle, and inner ear are sometimes referred to as the peripheral system. They function together to *receive* sounds. The brain stem and the cortex of the central nervous system function to *perceive*—or to integrate, make sense of, or interpret—sounds sent to it by the peripheral system. Hearing aids and other amplification devices may improve the reception of sound, but cannot assist

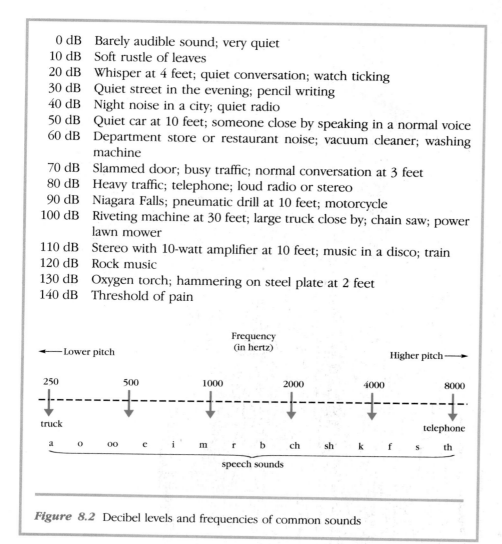

0 dB	Barely audible sound; very quiet
10 dB	Soft rustle of leaves
20 dB	Whisper at 4 feet; quiet conversation; watch ticking
30 dB	Quiet street in the evening; pencil writing
40 dB	Night noise in a city; quiet radio
50 dB	Quiet car at 10 feet; someone close by speaking in a normal voice
60 dB	Department store or restaurant noise; vacuum cleaner; washing machine
70 dB	Slammed door; busy traffic; normal conversation at 3 feet
80 dB	Heavy traffic; telephone; loud radio or stereo
90 dB	Niagara Falls; pneumatic drill at 10 feet; motorcycle
100 dB	Riveting machine at 30 feet; large truck close by; chain saw; power lawn mower
110 dB	Stereo with 10-watt amplifier at 10 feet; music in a disco; train
120 dB	Rock music
130 dB	Oxygen torch; hammering on steel plate at 2 feet
140 dB	Threshold of pain

Figure 8.2 Decibel levels and frequencies of common sounds

in its perception, which is a learned function. For example, when we hear a foreign language, the sounds and even individual words may be received but not perceived; that is, they are heard, but the brain cannot make sense of them until we learn the language.

The sensory cells in the cochlea are associated with our sense of balance and sensitivity to the pull of gravity and acceleration. These sensations are produced by the movement of sensory cells and resultant neural messages to the brain.

Sound waves moving through the air may be measured in either **decibels** (dB) or frequency. Decibels indicate the intensity—loudness or softness—of a sound. The higher the number of decibels, the louder the sound (see Figure 8.2). Frequencies are measurements of the number of cycles per second, called hertz (Hz), that a sound makes. A low sound, produced by fewer cycles per second, would have a lower frequency. The sound of a telephone may be measured by the decibel level—80 dB—*or* by the frequency—8000 Hz.

The term *hearing impairment* is broad in scope; it includes degrees of loss from minor hearing difficulty to no usable hearing. This broadness is clearly not useful for describing a hearing loss, nor for educational planning. The federal definition, stressing the impact on educational performance, differentiates between hearing impairment and deafness. Legislators modified language and terminology, added new categories of disability, and made additional modifications to PL 94-142 with the passage of PL 101-476 (see Chapter 2); however, they left intact the distinction between hearing impairment and deafness.

The federal definition covers

> [A] hearing impairment, whether permanent or fluctuating, which adversely affects a child's educational performance but which is not included under the definition of "deaf." . . . [Deafness is] a hearing impairment which is so severe that the child is impaired in processing linguistic information through hearing, with or without amplification, which adversely affects educational performance. (*Federal Register,* 1977, p. 42478)

Moores defines a person who is **hard of hearing** as "one whose hearing is disabled to an extent (usually 35–69 dB ISO) that makes difficult, but does not preclude, the understanding of speech through the ear alone, without or with a hearing aid." He defines a deaf person as "one whose hearing is disabled to an extent (usually 70 dB ISO or greater) that precludes the understanding of speech through the ear alone, with or without the use of a hearing aid" (1987, p. 9).

Educational definitions may include the level of hearing impairment and the ability to hear speech sounds as measured by intensity and frequency (see Box 8.1). However, such specific definitions must be viewed with caution because individuals with the same decibel loss may perform quite differently in academic and social environments, depending on a variety of factors: when the hearing loss occurred, when interventions were initiated, how successful they were, and similar variables.

■ Types of Hearing Loss

Hearing loss is caused by damage to or malfunction of the auditory system and may be classified on the basis of the location, cause, and level of speech and language development at the time of the damage or malfunction (Freeland, 1989; Northern, 1984; Schwartz, 1987).

A **conductive hearing loss** indicates that the damage or disease is located in the outer or middle ear. Many conductive-type losses can be corrected by medical or surgical treatment. If they are not corrected, a mild to moderate hearing loss may be experienced. Conductive hearing loss may be due to such conditions as fluid in the normally air-filled middle ear, an abnormally small ear canal, too much ear wax, or malfunctioning or malformed ossicles.

A sensorineural hearing loss results from an abnormality or disease in the inner ear, the cochlea, or the auditory nerve. Sensorineural hearing losses were generally considered uncorrectable until the advent of the cochlear implant (Clark, Tong, & Patrick, 1990; Owens & Kessler, 1989). Such conditions as a sudden blockage of circulation in or an infection of the inner ear, a leak in the inner ear fluid, a buildup of fluid in the inner ear, or tumors on the auditory nerve may be treated surgically or medically; hearing loss may be prevented or hearing improved if treatment is initiated before permanent damage occurs. Other causes of sensorineural hearing losses are complications from mumps, measles, or scarlet fever. A mixed-type hearing loss involves some component of both conductive and sensorineural hearing loss.

A **congenital** hearing loss occurs during fetal development or during birth. Most congenital hearing losses are sensorineural and due to either genetic defects or nongenetic factors such as rubella, diabetes, or an underactive thyroid in the mother during pregnancy. A hearing loss that develops shortly after birth and that is caused by factors such as fetal distress, lack of oxygen, or low birth weight is considered congenital (Schwartz, 1987). Congenital hearing losses may be accompanied by additional problems such as heart, kidney, or facial abnormalities. Acquired hearing losses develop some time after birth and are less common than congenital hearing loss. They may be due to a variety of factors, among which are trauma to the head or ear, excessive fluid in the middle ear, and **meningitis**.

Other terms also related to the point at which hearing loss occurs, but not as frequently used, are **prelingual** and **postlingual deafness** (Northern et al., 1986). *Prelingual* means prior to the development of speech and language, *postlingual* after the development of speech and language. The point at which speech and language can be considered "developed" is in question (Eisenburg, Kirk, Thielemeir, Luxford, & Cunningham, 1986; Mecklenburg, 1987; Northern, 1984). The problem is that young children spend several years developing language. For example, an 18-month-old child who uses 20 to 30 words, a 2-year-old who uses two-word sentences, and a 4-year-old who speaks intelligibly but has not yet mastered all aspects of syntax may be considered either prelingual or postlingual,

---

Box 8.1
Educational
Definitions
and Levels of
Hearing Loss

LEVEL 1 (35–54 dB LOSS) A stable hearing loss at this level requires little assistance, so educational services are provided in the regular classroom. It is considered a *mild hearing loss,* which means that soft sounds cannot be heard or that there may be difficulty in hearing over background noise.

LEVEL 2 (55–69 dB LOSS) A hearing loss at this level may delay speech and language development and may require speech, hearing, and language assistance. Services may be provided in the regular classroom or in a special class or school. This is considered a *moderate hearing loss,* which means that sounds must be fairly loud to be heard and that the speech of others may not be clear.

LEVEL 3 (70–89 dB LOSS) A hearing loss at this level indicates that without intervention, speech is not likely to develop. This level usually requires speech, hearing, language, and educational assistance; services may be provided in a special classroom or school. It is considered a *severe hearing loss,* which means that others' speech cannot be heard.

LEVEL 4 (90+ dB LOSS) Any hearing at this level is considered merely a complement to other communication modes; this degree of loss usually requires special speech, hearing, language, and educational assistance. Services are usually provided, at least to young children, in a special classroom or school. It is considered a *profound hearing loss,* which means that even shouted speech cannot be heard or that sounds may only be "heard" through vibrations in the body.

■ Environmental noise has led to a significant increase in the prevalence of hearing impairment. ■

depending on one's point of view. This ambiguity has led to the use of the term *perilingual,* which refers to young children between the prelingual and postlingual stages (Owens & Kessler, 1989).

Prevalence

The prevalence of hearing-impaired students, including the deaf, is estimated to be between 0.5% and 0.7% (see Table 2.4 in Chapter 2). But the number of such students served, reported to Congress by the 50 states (*Thirteenth Annual Report to Congress,* 1991) was only 0.10% of the national public school enrollment (Table 2.5 in Chapter 2). However, hearing impairments increase with age, so there is a much greater prevalence among the aging population than the student population. Moores (1987) has estimated that up to 15 million individuals of all ages in the United States have some degree of hearing loss.

There are a number of reasons why some states report such small prevalence figures. Because federal regulations allow states to report disabled children in only one category, children with hearing plus other disabilities may be included in another category. In addition, some states may report only those students with moderate to severe hearing impairments. Whatever the reasons for this apparent state-level underreporting, the estimated prevalence of from 0.5% to 0.7% may be conservative.

Characteristics of Hearing Impairments

The risk involved in describing any heterogeneous group of individuals with one label is clear. Numerous factors influence the development of every individual; however, some specifically affect the development of persons with hearing impairments. The type of hearing loss, the age at which the impairment occurred, whether the parents have a hearing impairment, the mode of communication used in the home during the acquisition of language (and that used in school) are all examples. The following characterizations, then, are merely generalizations; any or all of them may fail to describe a given individual with a hearing impairment.

■ Cognition and Intelligence

Research into the cognitive abilities and intelligence of persons with hearing impairments has provided some highly diverse conclusions.

1. Children who are deaf are less intelligent than those who hear (Pintner, Eisenson, & Stanton, 1941).
2. Children who are deaf are no less intelligent than their hearing peers but are qualitatively different in reasoning skills and conceptual formation and are more concrete thinkers (Myklebust & Brutton, 1953).
3. Children who are deaf do as well on cognitive tasks as children who hear (Vernon, 1967).
4. Children who are deaf reach the level of formal operative thinking but cannot progress further because of their lack of language (Furth, 1971).
5. Individuals who are deaf have normal cognitive abilities but have difficulty demonstrating them; any lags apparent in young children disappear as they grow older (Martin, 1985; Zweibel & Mertens, 1985).
6. There is no evidence to indicate that deafness limits cognitive capabilities, nor that persons who are deaf are more concrete thinkers than those who can hear. As a group, persons who have hearing impairments function in the normal range of intelligence and with the same variability as persons who hear (Quinsland & VanGinkel, 1990).

How are we to draw conclusions from such discrepant data? Moores (1987) has suggested that early research was not representative of the capabilities of persons with hearing impairments because tests were administered by individuals not fluent in alternative modes of communication. Therefore, they could not provide adequate instructions nor effectively understand students' responses, resulting in depressed scores. Further, many tests used were not normed on populations with hearing impairments (Luetke-Stahlman & Luckner, 1991; Salvia & Ysseldyke, 1988).

It would seem, then, that the intellectual and cognitive abilities of persons with hearing impairments are similar to those of persons who hear, and that the more recent research, indicating similar capabilities and a normal distribution of intelligence, is the more accurate. Future measurement tools may provide even more effective means of demonstrating their skills.

■ Academic Achievement

Reading   Students with hearing impairments gain information from print in the same manner as their peers who hear, but they are often learning to read at the same time as they are acquiring English (Leutke-Stahlman & Luckner, 1991). It is not surprising, then, to find that their achievement in reading is less than that of their peers and that they have difficulty with vocabulary, syntax, inferences, and narrative structures (Cole, 1987; Klecan-Aker & Bondeau, 1990; Meadow, 1980; Rogers, 1989).

Parents of children born with a hearing impairment often do not provide them with reading materials or read to them as much as to their hearing siblings. Therefore these children begin school having had fewer interactions with print materials and are at a disadvantage when learning to read (Rogers, 1989).

Others suggest that some of the reading difficulty these students experience may be related to the materials and techniques used. Phonetic approaches and syntactically simplified materials will tend to emphasize their deficits and make reading uninteresting (Quigley & King, 1980; Shulman & Decker, 1980). In addition, using measures other than standardized tests to determine reading ability may reveal less discrepancy than was previously reported (LaSasso, 1987). A comparison of the reading achievement scores of students with hearing impairments in 1974 with scores in 1983 indicated that for every age tested (8 to 18 years), scores were higher in 1983; however, they were still below those of students without hearing impairments (Allen, 1986).

Writing   Writing may be viewed as a more complex skill than reading, because readers can employ compensatory skills like word substitution or omit unknown words yet still grasp the essential meaning of the text. But compensatory skills are of little value in writing, in which difficulty with grammar, syntax, vocabulary, and sentence construction become apparent.

Comparisons between the written products of students with hearing impairments and those without indicate that the former make more errors in punctuation and grammatical construction, use fewer descriptive words, construct shorter sentences, and display less richness and spontaneity in their writing (Birch & Stuckless, 1963; Myklebust, 1964; Yoshinaga-Itano & Snyder, 1985).

More recently the process rather than only the products of writing has been examined, in line with other shifts in instructional methods. The emphasis is now on the writing process, which includes a final product but also addresses the various stages of writing. Indications are that substantial gains have been made by students with hearing impairments (Dahl, 1985; Ewoldt, 1985), though their skills associated with written expression are still less developed than those of their peers (Klecan-Aker & Bondeau, 1990).

Mathematics   Research related to the mathematical abilities of students with hearing impairments yields conclusions similar to those for reading. Their scores tend to be lower than those of their hearing age peers; however, there is less difference between the two groups than is seen for reading (Trybus, 1985). Obviously, the amount of language involved in an academic area affects these students' achievement scores. The computational aspects of math require less language usage, once the concepts are learned; this may lead to higher scores (Kaley & Reed, 1986). Fridriksson and Stewart (1988) suggest that lack of achievement in mathematics stems from a disproportionate instructional emphasis on the development of speech and language compared with the development of concepts through a variety of experiences. The latter approach would, they feel, increase both mathematical ability and language skills.

■ Communication

As we noted in Chapter 7, communication is a very broad term, encompassing any process of exchanging ideas and information. Language is a shared code that communicates ideas by means of arbitrary symbols and rules, and speech is the aspect of communication that conveys that code through oral expression. The way students with hearing impairments communicate varies greatly, depending on the time of onset of the hearing loss, the level of **residual hearing,** the hearing status of the parents, the mode of communication of the parents, and similar factors. Children with hearing impairments born to parents who are deaf develop effective communication systems through frequent parent/child interactions. The same children born to hearing parents typically have fewer interactions and thus more difficulty with communication as a whole (Moores, 1987).

Students with hearing impairments experience language delays or deficiencies but do have the capacity to develop language (Mendel & Vernon, 1987; Schlesinger, 1985). However, they are frequently deprived of language input (Meadow, 1980).

One characteristic of students with hearing impairments is related to English rather than to communication. They may be highly skilled in communication itself, using American Sign Language or another system (Luetke-Stahlman & Luckner, 1991; Moores, 1987). But many individuals in their environment may not know how to communicate with them manually (Bodner-Johnson, 1991). This suggests a need to master English, certain aspects of which present more difficulty than others. For example, idioms, figures of speech, and metaphors are a problem because they are not heard in a variety of contexts, as they will be by other children. They must therefore be specifically taught in the special instructional program (Arnold & Hornett, 1990; Webster & Wood, 1990).

As might be expected, students with little residual hearing have difficulty with speech, which requires control of rhythm, timing, pitch, and inflection. Problems in articulation are related to the production of vowels, omissions, and confusion of consonants (Moores, 1987).

All aspects of communication are central to an understanding of hearing impairments, and their effects will be addressed in later sections of this chapter.

■ Social and Emotional Development

The development of students with hearing impairments is similar to that of their peers who hear. Behavioral descriptors such as "withdrawn" or "acting out" may reflect their lack of communication skills rather than any emotional problems. Students with hearing impairments are often described as lacking in self-confidence, rigid, shy, stubborn, and lacking in self-awareness. But these labels may arise from test administrators not being fluent in communication systems other than English and from using tests not normed on populations of children with hearing impairments (Lane, 1988). Recent research conclusions concerning their social and emotional development are in conflict. The self-concept of students with hearing impairments is reported to be lower than that of their peers who hear (Loeb & Sargiani, 1986), but sociometric ratings of both groups indicate similar self-acceptance (Hagborg, 1987). Meadow (1980) has suggested that parental overprotectiveness inhibits the development of social maturity. The social skills of students with hearing impairments have been judged deficient in interactions with their hearing peers (Schwartz, 1990). But Cartledge, Paul, Jackson, & Cochran (1991) suggest that teachers' perceptions of those social skills may be biased, depending on how well teachers understand the disability. The more informed teacher may more clearly interpret the reluctance of a student to join a group when he or she must rely on an interpreter, sign language, or speech reading.

Of course, the added presence of other disabilities, such as mental retardation, cerebral palsy, visual impairments, or behavior disorders, will produce a different set of characteristics.

Causes of Hearing Impairments

Hearing impairments may be temporary or permanent, and what appears to be a temporary hearing loss may develop into a permanent loss or deafness. In nearly half the cases of hearing loss or deafness the cause is unknown (Moores, 1987; Trybus, 1985). As we've seen, disorders of the outer and middle ear result in conductive hearing losses, disorders of the inner ear in sensorineural hearing losses. And some conditions lead to a mixed loss—that is, both conductive and sensorineural. The following discussion will describe the known potential causes of these disorders by location of damage.

■ Outer Ear

• *Microtia* is a misshapen or extremely small pinna (external ear). This reduces the amount of sound channeled into the ear canal, resulting in a loss of hearing.

• *Atresia* is a blockage of the ear canal. It's often caused by a buildup of cerumen (wax), but may also indicate a growth in the ear canal. The blockage prevents sounds from reaching the middle or inner ear.

• *Otitis externa* is an infection of the outer ear, such as a boil or abscess, or a generalized infection that affects the lining of the ear canal. Generally, such infections can be treated with medication and result in only temporary hearing loss. However, if the infections are caused by bacteria or fungi and are not treated, they may spread to the middle and inner ear and cause permanent hearing loss or deafness.

• *Osteoma* is a growth of bone tissue in the ear canal that may block sound from entering the ear, thus inducing a hearing loss.

• *Otosclerosis* is an abnormal growth that immobilizes the base of the stapes, preventing sound waves from entering the inner ear. This results in either partial or complete hearing loss. Often both ears are affected, but not necessarily at the same time.

• *Barotrauma* is an imbalance of pressure in the middle and outer ear. This causes the eardrum to bow inward, usually because of a blocked Eustachian tube. A reduction in hearing is the result, unless the eardrum is ruptured.

• *Acute* **otitis media** is a bacterial or viral infection of the lining of the middle ear cavity. The infection may enter the middle ear through the Eustachian tube or a ruptured eardrum; in either case, it causes a buildup of fluid in the middle ear. This results in a hearing loss, which is usually temporary if the infection is treated.

• *Chronic otitis media* usually results from an acute infection that leaves organisms remaining in the ear or from a site that is left susceptible to continual infection. If fluid continues to develop, rupturing the eardrum and injuring the small bones in the inner ear, temporary or permanent hearing loss or deafness will result.

• *Cholesteatomas* develop when a blocked Eustachian tube isolates the air in the middle ear cavity. The air is gradually absorbed by cells lining the cavity, which causes a pocket to form. The pocket then collects the cells routinely shed by the eardrum, forming a ball—or cholesteatoma—that becomes infected. This erodes the bone that lines the cavity and damages the bones of the inner ear, resulting in a hearing loss.

• *Ruptured eardrums* result from an object inserted in the ear, an explosive sound, a middle ear infection, or a blow to the head. A torn or broken eardrum may heal with no resulting hearing loss, but if the inner ear is affected, there may be a hearing loss.

■ **Inner Ear**

• *Meniere's disease* is characterized by a marked increase in fluid in the portion of the inner ear associated with balance (the labyrinth), resulting in damage to the cochlea. Often both ears are affected, with partial or complete hearing loss.

• *Occupational or recreational damage* arises from prolonged exposure to noise at or above 90 decibels or from excessive high-frequency sounds, resulting in damage to the hair cells lining the cochlea. A partial or complete hearing loss may ensue, depending on the amount of damage.

• *Genetic abnormalities* are defects in genes that result in the abnormal development of the ear. Such abnormalities may lead to progressive hearing losses; that is, hearing that is progressively diminished, or in a stable loss. Several syndromes are associated with genetic abnormalities:

  • *Treacher Collins syndrome* is an abnormality of the jaw and face that also affects the ear.

  • *Crouzon's syndrome* includes head, eye, and facial abnormalities affecting the ear.

  • *Pendred's syndrome* is an enlarged thyroid affecting the development of the ear.

■ Without his binaural hearing aid, this boy would have little chance of normal learning. ■

- *Down syndrome,* a chromosomal abnormality resulting in mental retardation (see Chapter 4), sometimes may also include hearing disorders.
- *Maternal rubella* is a viral disease that—if contracted by the mother in the first 3 months of pregnancy—affects the development of the ear, resulting in hearing loss or deafness.

• *Meningitis* is a viral or bacterial inflammation of the coverings of the brain and circulating fluid, which invades and damages the ear with resultant hearing loss.

• *Maternal Rh-factor incompatibility* is an incompatibility in the blood type of mother and fetus that may affect the development of the ear (see Chapter 4).

• *Cytomegalic inclusion* is caused by a herpes virus that is transmitted to the fetus prior to birth, to the baby during birth, or after birth through breast milk. It may cause jaundice or mental retardation as well as severe hearing loss.

• *Congenital toxoplasmosis* is a central nervous system disorder resulting in seizures, hydrocephalus, and deafness.

• *Maternal ingestion of drugs*—whether prescribed or prohibited—may affect the fetus developing in a pregnant woman.

• *High-risk factors* for developing hearing impairments include several conditions in addition to those described earlier:

- Low birth weight (under 5 pounds)
- Fetal distress during birth
- Asphyxia or lack of oxygen during birth
- Poor ratings on vital signs at birth
- Insufficient functioning of the heart or lungs at birth
- Prolonged jaundice after birth, especially if transfusions were required

Hearing loss can occur at any time during life. A number of assessment procedures are conducted at birth, and additional procedures are available to detect hearing loss that occurs later.

Identification and Assessment

If there is reason to suspect a hearing loss—for example, a family history of deafness—infants should always be tested shortly after birth, and routine screening for hearing loss, as well as other conditions, is conducted in many hospitals.

A diagnostic test, the Auditory Brainstem Response (ABR), estimates the level of hearing in the middle and inner ear. Brain wave activity in the auditory center is recorded in response to a series of clicks sounded in each ear.

Very young children may be tested with loudspeakers or headphones. Sounds of different pitch and levels of loudness are emitted through the loudspeaker or headphone, and the children normally respond as soon as they hear them. Headphones allow for testing of each ear individually. Play activities are often incorporated with testing, to ensure the child's cooperation.

A hearing loss that is not identified or even suspected at birth may become obvious later, when parents or teachers observe physical or behavioral indicators (see Box 8.2). Toddlers, preschoolers, or school-age children undergo a variety of audiologic tests if a hearing loss is suspected. Tests may be administered by an audiologist (a person certified by the American Speech-Language-Hearing Association as skilled in **audiology**) or by medical personnel. A typical battery of such tests might include the following.

• A visual examination of the ear with a pneumatic otoscope, which provides lighted magnification and can test the mobility of the eardrum. Performed by an otologist (a physician specializing in diseases of the ear), this examination can reveal conditions such as otitis media or a ruptured eardrum.

• A pure-tone bone conduction test, performed by placing a bone oscillator (a headphonelike band with a round, flat disk at the end) directly on the bony area just behind the ear. The disk emits stimuli of different pitches and loudness, which are conducted to the inner ear. The results are plotted on an **audiogram** and help to determine where in the auditory system hearing occurs.

• A pure-tone air conduction test, in which sounds are sent through headphones and responses given as soon as the sound is heard. The tones generally vary in pitch (measured in frequencies) from 250 hertz to 8000 hertz, because that is the range of most of the speech sounds. Sounds of varying degrees of loudness (measured in decibels) are conveyed in a similar manner and results recorded on the audiogram (see Figure 8.3).

Box 8.2
Indicators of a Possible Hearing Loss in Children

PHYSICAL INDICATORS
Frequent colds
Frequent sore throats
Discharge from the ear
Infections in the outer ear
Severe allergies
Recurring tonsillitis
Breathing through the mouth
Earaches
Popping or buzzing in the ear

BEHAVIORAL INDICATORS
Speech that is limited in vocabulary or structure
Reluctance to participate in oral activities
Voice quality or tone that is different from normal
Difficulty in following oral directions
Unusual amounts of watching and following what other students do
Visual searching for location of sounds
Turning ear toward sounds
Asking for volume of TV or stereo to be turned up
More responsiveness in small than in large groups
Fatigue during and after tasks requiring listening
Daydreaming, inattention, short attention span
Omission of speech sounds, especially word endings
Confusion of similar-sounding words
Withdrawal
Acting out, especially during or after tasks requiring listening
Intense watching of the speaker's face
Frequent requests for repetition during verbal interactions
Quicker responses to visible than to verbal signals
Discrepancy between expected and actual achievement
Difficulty in verbal skills such as reading; sound blending and discrimination; spelling; and writing

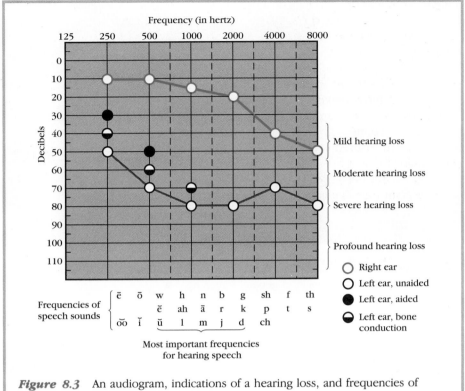

Figure 8.3 An audiogram, indications of a hearing loss, and frequencies of speech sounds

When no difference is found between the bone and air conduction tests the hearing loss is sensorineural, or due to an abnormality or malfunctioning of the inner ear. When bone conduction tests indicate near-normal functioning but the air conduction tests show abnormal results, the source of the hearing loss is likely to be in the outer or middle ear.

• Tympanometry, which measures the mobility of the tympanic membrane, or eardrum. A sound or puff of air is sent through the ear canal to the eardrum by means of a probe attached to a *tympanometer*. The sound or puff of air is bounced off the eardrum and measured, reflecting the movement of the eardrum. These measurements can reveal unequal pressure on either side of the eardrum, caused by conditions such as otitis media, a blocked Eustachian tube, or malformation of the middle ear, with resultant hearing loss.

• The Speech Awareness Threshold, Speech Reception Threshold, and Word Recognition Test. These all measure the frequency range and decibel level that a student requires to be aware of sound, to hear certain words, to discriminate between similar sounds, or to understand speech. Such tests, using words and speech sounds rather than pure tones, evaluate the student's ability to hear and understand conversation or classroom instruction, so have obvious implications for educational programming.

■ Audiologist giving hearing examination. More extensive hearing evaluation may be indicated as a result of general screening. ■

In addition to tests measuring the degree of hearing loss, academic achievement and cognitive ability tests are also administered. PL 94-142 regulations require that such tests be administered to determine the student's ability, not merely the effects of the disability. The Hiskey-Nebraska Test of Learning Aptitude (Hiskey, 1966), the Metropolitan Achievement Test (Prescott, Balow, Hogan, & Farr, 1984), and the Stanford Achievement Test—Hearing Impaired (Madden, Gardner, Rudman, Karlsen, & Merwin, 1972) are examples of tests normed on populations of students with hearing impairments and that allow for nonverbal instructions and responses.

When all the assessment information has been collected, the staffing team meets to determine eligibility for special education services according to state and federal guidelines (see Chapter 2 and the definitions section of this chapter). If the student meets the eligibility requirements, an IEP or an **individualized family service plan** (IFSP), depending on the age of the student, is developed to address her or his unique needs.

Placement in the least restrictive environment for the student is also decided at this meeting. Placement for students with severe hearing impairments raises an issue unique to this group of students. The Commission on the Education of the Deaf reported to Congress that special schools "with a sufficient number of children who are deaf on a particular age and grade level, are the least restrictive environment appropriate for many children who are deaf" (1988, p. 33). This reflects parental and professional concern that the needs of students with severe hearing impairments are not adequately met in the regular classroom or resource room. The social interactions of these students as well as their instructional opportunities may be restricted because peers or teachers may not be able to communicate effectively with them. Also, adequate support services such as note takers, interpreters, and tutors may not be provided to the degree that will maximize the student's educational progress. This is an issue not easily resolved.

How to assist persons with hearing impairments to develop language competence, which implies some mode of communication, may be among the most difficult decisions faced by parents and educators. Bochner and Albertini have commented that the development of language may be viewed either as "remediation to ameliorate the effects of a pathological condition" or as a means of providing "students from a subculture access to the academic and employment mainstream" (1988, p. 3). How language development is viewed by parents and educators has shaped the evolution of the methods advocated over time.

There have been four major shifts of theory within that evolution (Lou, 1988). The first theory, from 1817 to 1860, emphasized manual approaches; the next, from 1860 to 1900, was "characterized by growing interest in, and the ultimate domination of, oral methods" (ibid., p. 81). In the third period, from 1900 to 1960, oral methods predominated, with an active discouragement of manual methods unless the individual was old enough to make a choice. The most recent shift, from the 1960s to the present, has been toward the philosophy and instructional mode of **"total communication."**

This history of communication modes may be characterized as "almost exactly one and a half sweeps of the pendulum between American Sign Language and manual approaches at one end and oral English at the other end"; the pendulum is now at an approximate midpoint, with both oral and manual systems in use, frequently in combination (ibid., p. 75).

■ Manual Communication

Manual communication may be broadly defined as communication primarily using the hands. Fingerspelling means spelling words letter by letter, using the fingers. Each letter, number, and some punctuation has a specific finger/hand position that visually presents it. The Rochester Method of fingerspelling is among those most widely known; however, no school programs use fingerspelling exclusively (Luetke-Stahlman & Luckner, 1991).

Signing also uses the hands for communication, but rather than spelling individual words, a concept or idea is visually presented by means of "(1) the position of the hands, (2) the configuration of the hands, and (3) the movement of the hands to different positions" (Moores, 1987, p. 185). Signing as a means of communication may be considered either a language or a system. As a language, it is a means of communication that has evolved naturally; as a system, it is an invented means of communication.

American Sign Language (ASL), which does not correspond to English but does have a structure and vocabulary, is the one most widely used by adults (see Figure 8.4). Some educators of students who were deaf—and who in some cases were deaf themselves—became dissatisfied with ASL because it does not correspond to English. This means that when students begin to learn to read and write, they must also learn English. These educators developed alternative manual sign systems that more closely approximate English.

1. *Seeing Essential English (SEE-1)* signs both formal and colloquial English, using words, divisions of words, suffixes, prefixes, and different signs for multiple meanings of words.
2. *Signing Exact English (SEE-2)* signs almost everything that is said—even the

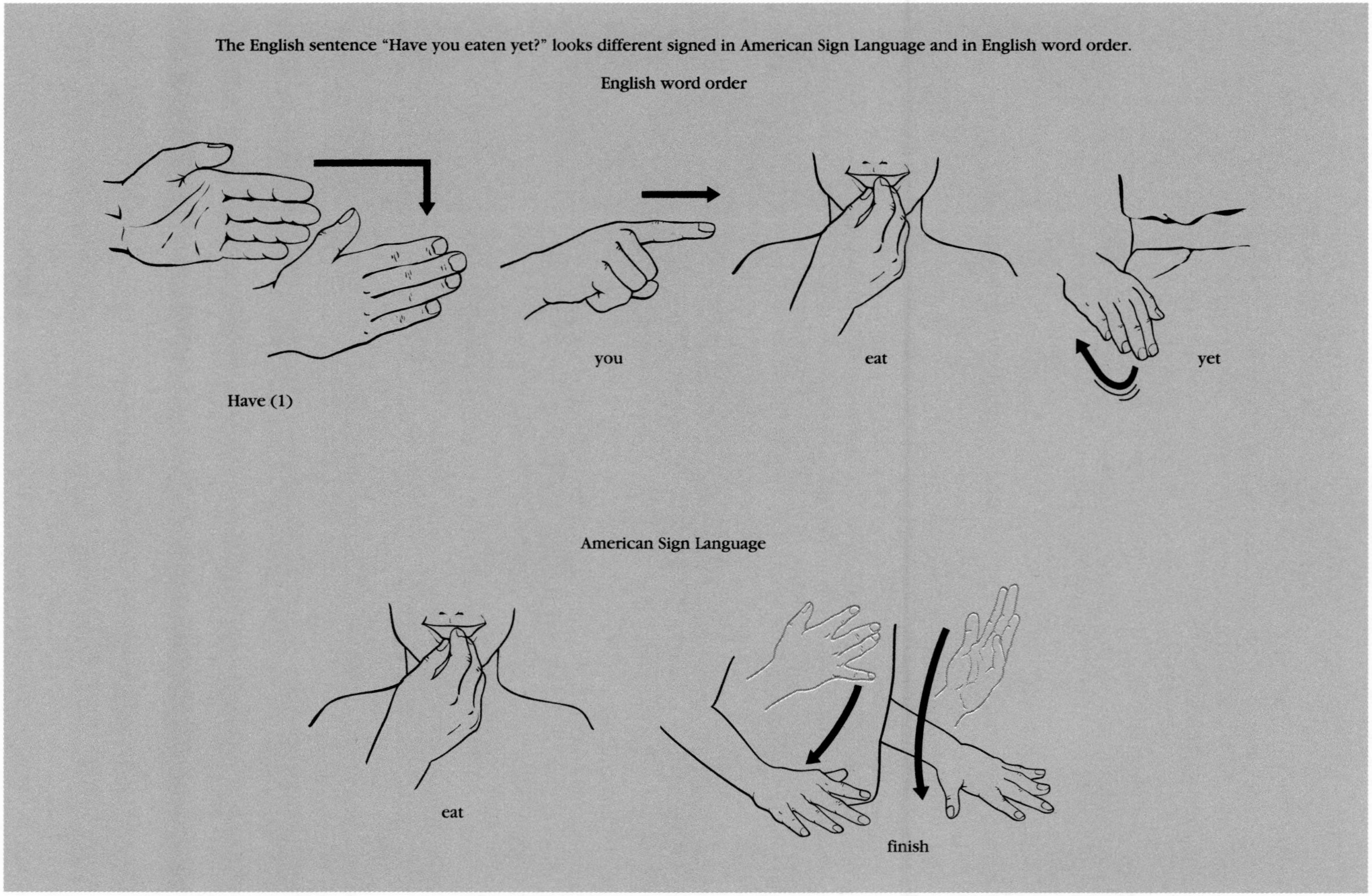

The English sentence "Have you eaten yet?" looks different signed in American Sign Language and in English word order.

English word order

Have (1)   you   eat   yet

American Sign Language

eat   finish

Figure 8.4 Differences between American Sign Language and English word order

SOURCE: *From "How Deaf People Communicate," Series 2. National Information Center on Deafness. Gallaudet University, Washington, D.C. Used with permission.*

■ Communicating through signing. ■

smallest meaningful unit in English. For example, the word *motorboat* has its own sign, because *motor* could be associated with *car, truck, lawn mower,* and so on.

3. *Signed English (SE)* follows English grammatical structure and borrows signs from ASL, SEE-1, and SEE-2.

4. *Pidgin Sign English (PSE),* like other pidgin languages, has developed out of a need to communicate. Sometimes ASL is modified to more closely resemble English; at other times signs are invented because signers do not know a sign for what they want to communicate. Gestures, facial expressions, and body language are also used freely.

Users of all four alternatives always use their voices with the signs. Using both voice and signs is called simultaneous communication. According to Luetke-Stahlman and Luckner (1991), none of these language systems is widely used throughout the United States; rather, one system may be emphasized in a particular geographic area.

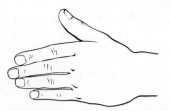

This cue signals the three different sounds /m/, /t/, and /f/.

This cue signals the three different sounds /b/, /n/, and /wh/.

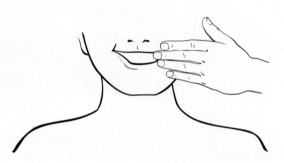

The hand shape made near the lips provides an additional cue.
This position indicates the sound /ee/, as in "*see.*"

Figure 8.5 Examples of cued speech

SOURCE: *From* "How Deaf People Communicate," *Series 2.* National Information Center on Deafness. *Gallaudet University, Washington, D.C. Used with permission.*

■ **Oral Communication**

Oral communication methods stress the use of residual hearing, speech, speaking, and **speechreading** (sometimes called lipreading). Students may be fitted with an auditory aid so they can hear at least minimal speech sounds. Often auditory training, in which the student is taught to listen and discriminate between sounds, is a part of oral communication. When auditory input is emphasized, the term *aural-oral* is used.

Students are taught to speak by means of a combination of visual, auditory, and tactile/kinesthetic modalities (Ling, 1988). Speechreading focuses on the visual aspect of communication. The speechreader watches the speaker's lips, face, and body language to gain meaning. Many sounds in English are not visible on the lips, and others look the same (such as *p* and *b*), so there may be confusion.

Cued speech was developed to avoid that confusion. Cued speech uses shapes and positions near the speaker's face to signal differences between sounds. A cue means nothing by itself, so it's not a sign, but it does tell the speechreader which of the sounds that look similar is being used—for example, the *m* in *me* or the *b* in *bee* (see Figure 8.5).

Hearing aids that amplify sound and vibrotactile aids are also used in the development of speech. A vibrotactile aid consists of a microphone that the speaker uses and a transmitter that "translates" the voice into a receiver that vibrates on the learner's skin. Receivers are worn on the arm, the hands, or near the face, as those areas are the most sensitive to vibrations. Feeling one's own face, voice box, or chest as well as those of the speaker is also helpful when learning to speak.

■ Total Communication

Total communication is both a philosophy and a communication mode (Moores, 1987). As a philosophy it supports the right of students with hearing impairments to use whatever means of communication is useful: writing, signing, finger-spelling, speech, gestures, or any combination of them. As an instructional mode, it is a combination of oral and manual modes, including reading and writing, that may be used alone or, at times, in conjunction with each other.

The communication mode to be taught should be chosen soon after diagnosis of a hearing impairment, so that language is developed and communication between parents and children as well as between teachers and children is established (Adams, 1988; Brown, Maxwell, & Browning, 1990; Schwartz, 1987). Factors influencing the choice include the mode of communication the entire family uses or will use, the age of onset of the hearing impairment, what seems easiest and most fluent, and the degree of hearing loss.

Assistive Devices

Hearing aids and tactile aids were at one time the only devices available to persons with hearing impairments. They are still available—but much improved. In addition, there is an array of other devices, some primarily for individuals with hearing impairments and others designed for other purposes but helpful to those persons.

■ Tactile Aids

Tactile aids were designed to provide persons with a severe hearing loss a tactile/kinesthetic manner of receiving or "feeling" sound. Early aids were meant to assist in developing speech. All use the same basic principle: they transduce acoustic signals into vibrating or electrical patterns that are felt on the skin, thereby supplementing or replacing the sound. Vibrotactile devices stimulate the skin using bone conduction. They are more efficient at conveying lower frequencies (Roeser, 1989). Electrotactile devices use electrical current for stimulation and are optimally efficient at higher frequencies. Wearers must be trained to attend to and interpret the tactile information provided. Research indicates that for profoundly deaf persons, who do not benefit from conventional amplification, tactile aids can improve sound awareness, gross and fine discrimination of certain speech sounds, and speech production (Hesketh & Osberger, 1990; Lynch, Eilers, Oller, & Cobo-Lewis, 1989).

■ Hearing Aids

The main function of a hearing aid is to amplify sound and deliver it to the ear. It may also block painfully loud sounds, reduce the range between louder and quieter sounds, adjust the balance between low- and high-pitched sounds, permit direct magnetic pickup of speech from the telephone, permit pickup from wireless microphones, and suppress some background noise. Digital hearing aids are similar to conventional analog aids, but because sound patterns do not exist as equivalent electrical patterns, the digital aid represents them as strings of electrically coded numbers. Special circuits convert the incoming sound into numbers, modify the numbers, and convert them back to sound. During the split second in which the sound exists as numbers, complex numerical calculations are performed to produce results not possible with analog aids. Certain sounds can be suppressed; specific speech sounds can be enhanced; acoustic feedback, which causes squealing in other aids, can be prevented; and reverberant echoes in a room can be canceled. Hearing aids may be beneficial for students having either

Box 8.3
A User-
Friendly
Assistive
Device

A dog that fetches its owner at the sound of the teakettle? Dogs have been trained to do this and more. They have been trained to recognize alarm clocks, doorbells, a knock on the door, smoke alarms, a baby crying, oven timers, and teakettles.

Hearing dogs—or, as they are also called, hearing ear dogs, signal dogs, or guide dogs for the deaf—are trained to identify a variety of sounds, get their owners' attention, and lead them to the source of the sound. When the dogs hear the sounds, they go to their owners and put their paws on a bed or chair; when the owners respond, they lead them to the sound source. Their response to smoke alarms is different, in that once they have their owners' attention, they drop down to the floor and lie still, as if to block the way. Thus they do not lead their owners to a potentially dangerous place, the fire.

Hearing dogs are often selected from humane societies and trained for 3 to 4 months. Owners and dogs are matched for compatibility. Then the owner spends about a week at the training center learning how to use the dog, and someone from the training center spends about a week in the owner's home to facilitate the adjustment. Many dogs are trained to work only part-time—for example, only when their owners remove their hearing aids for the night.

The same laws that apply to guide dogs apply to hearing dogs. They may accompany their owners to restaurants, fly in airplanes free of charge, and go to shopping malls and theaters. They wear an orange leash to indicate that they are working dogs.

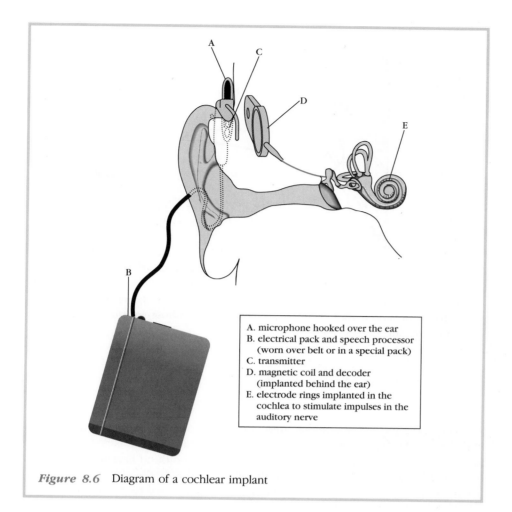

A. microphone hooked over the ear
B. electrical pack and speech processor
   (worn over belt or in a special pack)
C. transmitter
D. magnetic coil and decoder
   (implanted behind the ear)
E. electrode rings implanted in the
   cochlea to stimulate impulses in the
   auditory nerve

Figure 8.6   Diagram of a cochlear implant

a bilateral (loss in both ears) or unilateral hearing loss (Berg, 1987; Flexner, Wray, & Leavitt, 1990).

■ Cochlear Implants

A cochlear implant provides sound information through a small microphone connected to a speech processor (a tiny computer) and a transmitter, which send information to a receiver implanted in the ear. The receiver sends electrical signals to electrodes implanted in the cochlea, which stimulate nerve fibers. Those signals are recognized by the brain as sounds, thus simulating the normal hearing process (see Figure 8.6). Cochlear implants, unlike hearing aids, do not convert electrical signals back into acoustical sound.

Cochlear implants may allow individuals to interact with greater efficiency in the hearing world and are often used in conjunction with other forms of amplification such as hearing aids or frequency modulation systems (Roeser, 1989). Some recipients can hear normal speech that they would not have heard before, once they've completed the initial training (Clark et al., 1990; Ling, 1988).

Figure 8.7 An induction loop system. An audio loop wired to a television permits the viewer to adjust the volume on a hearing aid without interfering with the listening comfort of other viewers.

The Food and Drug Administration approved the use of cochlear implants in children over 2 years of age in 1991. In general, cochlear implants are designed to be used by persons of at least that age who have a profound hearing loss in both ears, receive little or no benefit from hearing or vibrotactile aids, and are motivated enough to persevere through the necessary **auditory training** (Clark et al., 1990).

■ Frequency Modulation (FM) Systems

Frequency modulation is a term applied to the radio transmission of sounds that, after being changed into electrical signals, are superimposed onto radio signals. These radio signals are picked up by a radio receiver and transmitted to listeners. An FM system comprises a microphone and transmitter that the teacher or other speaker wears and a radio receiver that the listener wears in an earphone or personal hearing aid.

In 1982 the Federal Communications Commission granted the use of the 72 to 76 megahertz segment of the radio band to the exclusive use of persons with hearing loss. The advantages of FM systems are that they compensate for distances (a problem with hearing aids), noise, and reverberation problems in classrooms and permit hearing even when the speaker turns away from the listener.

■ Induction Loop Systems

Most hearing aids have a telecoil "T" setting that, when activated, responds to magnetic coils. With the loop system, a string or loop of wire is placed (often permanently) just inside the periphery of a room or building such as a church, theater, classroom, or living room. The loop is connected to the amplifier of a microphone used by speakers or placed near the sound source, such as a TV (see Figure 8.7). The changing magnetic fields from the wire loop are received and converted back to sound by the induction coil in the hearing aid. The listener must sit inside the loop for the system to work. The system reduces the amplification of extraneous noises and allows the listener to hear the intended sounds more clearly. However, fluorescent lights sometimes interfere with this system.

■ **Infrared Systems**

An infrared system comprises a remote microphone placed near a sound source (speaker, actor, and so on) that sends a signal to a transmitter that in turn emits a signal consisting of infrared, or invisible, light waves that spread throughout the room. A stethoscopelike receiver worn in the listener's ears picks up the message carried on the light waves. Infrared systems must be used indoors within a single room. They provide a more direct sound and reduce the background noises and reverberation common in large rooms such as lecture halls, large classrooms, theaters, and auditoriums.

People Who Make a Difference

KENNY WALKER—GOOD VIBRATIONS Spinal meningitis at age 2 left Kenny Walker with a severe hearing loss (with a hearing aid he can just hear himself talk and very loud sounds). As a young boy, he was very interested in athletics, but was often chosen last for games. Soon, however, his peers recognized his extraordinary ability, and he was regularly chosen first. He said, "Athletics made them realize something about me; I wasn't just a deaf kid."

Kenny learned to sign and lipread while he was young. His mother recalls a picture he drew of his family in which all but himself had big smiles. He drew his own face without a mouth.

Although fond of all types of athletics, Kenny didn't begin to play football seriously until his sophomore year in high school. Then he made All-State in football *and* basketball. College coaches noticed.

He chose Nebraska University and, while playing football, maintained a 3.1 grade point average.

Then, even though he was a college All-American, he waited anxiously through most of the draft. Finally, the Denver Broncos drafted him as a linebacker. Kenny said, "Most teams are afraid of a deaf person"—but Wade Phillips, the Broncos' defensive coach, said, "We've got guys that don't hear as well. They don't listen. Kenny's attentive."

In the huddle Kenny reads the defensive captain's lips; if the alignment is changed, a teammate taps a signal on Kenny's back. At all times, he reacts to the ball rather than to the sound of the snap. Kenny has a full-time interpreter to convey instructions on the sidelines and during practice.

When 76,000 Bronco fans rock the stadium and his shoulder pads vibrate, even though he doesn't hear the noise of the crowd he feels the approval.

GOOD EVENING. I'M PETER JENNINGS.

■ Close-captioned television allows the hearing impaired to experience this medium. ■

■ Telecaption Decoders

A telecaption decoder is attached to a television set to make normally invisible captions (similar to film subtitles) visible across the bottom of the screen. The captions are print translations of the narration, dialogue, and sound effects of the TV program. The National Captioning Institute was established in 1979 by the U.S. Department of Education to make television viewing accessible to persons with a hearing loss. Captioning is provided free by the TV, cable, and video industries, but the decoder must be purchased. However, all TV sets made or sold in the United States after July 1, 1993, will have a built-in closed-caption decoder chip, so separate decoders will not be necessary. Many educational and recreational films are available with captions and do not require the use of a decoder.

■ Computer-Assisted Instruction (CAI)

Computers are available in most schools, and the smaller, portable, laptop types are useful in a variety of settings. CAI allows instruction to be tailored to the individual and self-paced. In addition to content areas such as reading, math, and science, useful courses in speech training and the development of listening, speechreading, and sign reading skills are available.

■ Video Laserdiscs

The video laserdisc is similar to the compact discs used for sound recordings with the added capacity of storing pictures. A 12-inch disk can store over 100,000 pages of print or of still or moving pictures that can be called up in a few seconds. The visual aspect of laserdiscs and the print allow for simultaneous presentation. Videodiscs integrated with computers offer almost unlimited possibilities for group and individual instruction.

■ Telecommunications

Telecommunications—communication at a distance—includes a variety of devices. Ironically, the telephone, though invented by a person with a hearing impairment, was for a long time inaccessible to those with hearing loss.

Amplifiers   Built into or portable and strapped onto the telephone handset, amplifiers permit individuals with a hearing loss to use telephones. Some amplifiers are hearing aid compatible. Speakerphones allow for more flexibility in movement while amplifying sound.

Hearing aids with a "T" setting   These also allow telephones to be used more easily. The coil in the hearing aid picks up signals from the magnetic field generated by most telephones and telephone amplifiers. When the "T" switch is on, the hearing aid's microphone is off, so background noise, feedback, and other noises are eliminated.

Telecommunication devices for persons who are deaf (TDDs)   TDDs are based on the concept of two typewriters talking by wire (TTYs). They are about the size of a laptop computer and have either a visual screen or a printer. Attached to a telephone, the TDD sends the typed message via ordinary telephone wires to another TDD. Thus a telephone "conversation" using TDDs is either displayed on a screen or printed by the printer. Some TDDs allow a person who is deaf to call someone without a TDD if the latter has a special touch-tone feature. When a message is typed into the TDD, an electronic voice speaks the message over the wires. The person without the TDD can respond by "dialing" a message with the touch-tone feature, and the message will be printed on the TDD. Other TDDs recently available do not require a telephone; they simply plug into the telephone jack on the wall. They can also function as a regular typewriter, computer terminal, calculator, answering machine, and alarm clock.

The 1982 Telecommunications for the Disabled Act specified that telephones for emergency use in elevators, along highways, in tunnels, and under bridges, plus all coin-operated phones, must be hearing aid compatible and have volume controls (many old telephones do not). The 1988 Hearing Aid Compatibility Act mandated that by 1991 all telephones—whether manufactured in the United

■ The scope of communication options is broadened through the use of the TDD. ■

States or imported, including cordless — must be compatible with hearing aid coils. Public telephones in hotels or motels, hospitals, and business offices that are hearing aid compatible are distinguishable by a blue connection cord (Kaplan, 1987; Skafte, 1990).

Facsimile (FAX) machines   FAX machines transmit any printed, handwritten, or drawn material over telephone wires within a few seconds. With a FAX machine an individual is not limited to keyboards, but is able to transmit maps, pages from books or magazines, and personal illustrations. Many businesses consider a FAX machine indispensible but may not install a TDD (Boothroyd, 1990).

The great variety of assistive devices, though not without their limitations, has enabled persons with a hearing loss to gain access to information and communication that was not available in the past. No doubt, as advances in technology continue, more avenues will open.

Educational Programming

Educational programming for students with hearing impairments varies depending on the degree of hearing loss. A student with a mild to moderate hearing loss may, with the use of an assistive device, require little modification of the ordinary school curriculum. The age of onset of the loss may also influence programming needs; for example, a student who is congenitally deaf requires a very different type of program from one who has lost some hearing through an illness at 8 years of age. The following generalizations indicate the types of factors that must be considered to provide an effective education to students with varying degrees of hearing impairment.

First, seating arrangements should allow the student to see both the teacher and other students so as to engage in the speechreading and attention to body language and facial expression that promote understanding.

People Who Make a Difference

MARLEE MATLIN, ACADEMY AWARD–WINNING ACTRESS

"I am an actress who happens to be deaf. I am not a deaf actress" the outspoken Marlee Matlin signs, trying to correct people's thinking.

The Oscar award–winning actress wants to be known for her acting abilities, not for being deaf. But she is a passionate advocate for the rights of people who are deaf. She refuses to be interviewed on programs or accept television roles that are not closed-captioned. She has testified before the Senate on the need for closed-captioning.

Marlee was criticized by some other individuals with hearing impairments for speaking part of her acceptance speech at the Academy Awards instead of signing only (they felt it suggested that signing was inferior to spoken communication). She replied, "It was a great accomplishment for me. I understand their opinions, but why don't they understand my values and qualities? It's what I wanted to do because people all over the world were able to see me for who I am. I wanted people to see that I could do both. I thought it would be good for my career. I have dealt with the outside world since I was 3. I was not shut out."

Marlee was born with normal hearing, but at 18 months of age she contracted roseola (a form of childhood measles sometimes referred to as baby measles), which affected her hearing. The hearing loss was not detected until she was 3 years old. She has some residual hearing and says that when she wears a hearing aid she can hear normal speaking voices and tell if they are low or high pitched, but she cannot clearly understand them. Her parents learned to sign and encouraged her interest in acting.

While in elementary school, Marlee spent much of her free time at the Center on Deafness near her hometown of Morton Grove, Illinois. Her first acting role, at age 7, was that of Dorothy in *The Wizard of Oz*. Later she hoped to go into police work, so she studied criminal justice in college. When it became clear to her that her career opportunities would be limited because of her hearing impairment, Marlee returned to acting. One of her roles was in the stage production of *Children of a Lesser God*. When the film was about to be made, a casting agent who had seen her act in the play sent a video of the stage production to the producers and she was immediately cast in the leading role, winning an Oscar for her performance.

Marlee is an excellent lip reader but uses an interpreter on movie sets, on television, and in business meetings, stating that "interpreters just make our lives easier." If Marlee had her way, everyone would learn to sign so they could communicate with people who have hearing impairments. Marlee smiles, "One of my dreams is to sing the national anthem at the beginning of a baseball, football, or hockey game (her favorite sports). Don't worry, I wouldn't sing. I wouldn't want everyone to leave."

When asked if the film industry is beginning to alter its views regarding the capabilities of the deaf, she responded, "I think times are changing. Some producers can deal with deafness, and I don't find their doors closed to me. Others can't deal with it." It would seem that if Marlee has anything to do with changing views, they will be changed.

■ Assistive devices such as hearing aids allow students to participate in class. Children with severe hearing impairments present a great challenge to educators. ■

Reverberation, or the echo effect, is the result of sound waves bouncing off hard surfaces, causing second or third sound waves to pass through the room. Amplifying devices pick up those repeated waves, causing distortion in what is heard (Blair, 1990). Reducing background noise by means of carpeting, drapes, and sound-absorbing ceilings provides an environment conducive to more efficient learning.

Supplementing auditory information with visual components such as drawing or writing on the chalkboard, the use of written outlines, summaries, and key words or phrases, the use of captioned films, and the use of an overhead projector when the room lighting is dimmed provides students with additional avenues to learning.

Some students may use an interpreter. The interpreter is usually located just outside of the direct line of sight from student to teacher so that the student is able to see both. The interpreter repeats what the teacher has said, using signs, fingerspelling, and nonvocalized speech. The interpreter is not a teacher but is skilled in communication; he or she may need to modify or paraphrase what the teacher has said or fingerspell certain technical terms for which there are no signs.

The primary concern in the education of students with hearing impairments is communication. Communication skills include reading, writing, and receiving and expressing ideas, either visually or by auditory means. Students usually enter school with some degree of proficiency in fingerspelling, American Sign Language, a manually coded English system, Pidgin Sign English, oral English, or combinations of those systems. As they learn to read and write, they must either begin to learn English or further develop their skills in using it without hearing it (DePietro, 1987). For some students this means becoming bimodal in their language use; that is, they develop an ability to communicate in two modalities such as manual and written or manual and oral. For other students it means becoming bilingual; that is, they develop the ability to communicate in two languages such as American Sign Language and Signing Exact English or English and American Sign Language.

The way they are taught such communication is at the core of educating students with severe hearing impairments. Luetke-Stahlman and Luckner (1991) have provided several principles to guide teachers in this process.

- Some students prefer one system or language over another and learn more efficiently using it; therefore, it should be used for instruction.
- Students must have competent and consistent models in the language or system used.
- The expectations of the teacher should challenge the students but not overwhelm them.
- The language or system should be learned in contextual situations.
- Optimal learning takes place in situations that are supportive and encouraging and in which the efforts of the students are recognized.
- Optimal learning takes place when the students have a positive attitude toward language acquisition. They are more likely to have such an attitude when they are interested in the topic or activity.
- Students must have sufficient exposure to the language or system.
- Optimal learning takes place through a conversational approach, which does not preclude specific instruction but rather focuses on how useful the language or system is. Then, as necessary, the teacher can refine the usage.

The Deaf Community

The deaf community may be thought of as "a group of people who simply share the same handicap" (Hafer & Richmond, 1988, p. 3) or, alternatively, as a culture (Wilcox, 1989). The former implies a common bond between deaf persons because they are deaf. The latter suggests a common bond based on a shared language (American Sign Language); cultural events; athletic competitions; and local, regional, and international organizations composed *of* deaf people as well as those *for* deaf people (Moores, 1987).

The deaf community may have had its beginnings in the early residential schools, in which strong friendships were established. Whatever the previous school experience, when deaf children grow up they "find the deaf community and become a part of it" (Prickett, 1989, pp. 6–7).

Efforts continue to instill a pride in their heritage in students who are deaf. Gallaudet University recently established a curriculum of courses in deaf history,

American Sign Language as the native language of deaf persons, deaf culture, and deaf role models (Johnstone, 1991). Articles such as "What Hearing Parents Should Know About Deaf Culture" (Hafer & Richmond, 1988) inform parents about how to ensure their child's appreciation for sign languages and deaf folklore and about the many church groups, social and sports clubs, and other organizations composed of persons with hearing impairments. Other authors have suggested organizing support groups for deaf persons who enter colleges in which they will be a minority (Flexner, Wray, & Black, 1990).

Some suggest that such efforts are needed because of the paternalistic attitudes of the hearing population (Lane, 1988). Others contend that these countermeasures exist because many educational decisions regarding the deaf are made by hearing persons who, no matter how well intentioned, "cannot possibly understand what it is to be deaf, any more than a white person can understand what it is like to be black or a man understand what it is like to be a woman. . . . You have to be deaf to understand" (Gentry, 1988, p. 13). Gannon (1981) criticized a variety of practices common in schools, such as emphasizing speech, which deaf adults use minimally; emphasizing auditory training, when deaf adults tend not to use hearing aids and do not depend on them to communicate with hearing persons; and failing to stress American Sign Language, which is among the most important elements in the life of a deaf person.

The phenomenon of a group of exceptional individuals organizing and speaking up on their own behalf is perhaps unique to this population. Prickett's text *Advocacy for Deaf Children* (1989) describes future actions that should be taken to make certain that the deaf community is heard in matters that affect it and, as Wilcox and Corwin (1990) urge, that hearing people "see the world through deaf eyes."

Issues and Trends

The issue of the least restrictive alternative for students with a severe or profound hearing loss will probably undergo further examination. When some students are deprived of many communication and social opportunities because of the "disabilities" of their teachers and peers in communicating with them, difficult questions must be asked.

The most effective way to teach communication skills when a hearing loss has occurred remains elusive. Emphasizing communication skills at the expense of teaching content areas remains controversial, as does the mode of communication used to teach content areas. The increasing emphasis on excellence in the schools will mandate additional decisions regarding these issues.

Medical and biological advances that restore hearing by regenerating dead nerves and recreating tissue will be likely to influence this field in the future. Surgical procedures such as cochlear implants may become as common as organ transplants, which 50 years ago were believed to be impossible.

Technological advances will provide more flexibility and opportunities for persons with impaired hearing. Voice recognition devices, greater capabilities of computers, universal access to captioned TV programs, and videos are just some examples.

The number of children with hearing plus additional disabilities is increasing as a result of improved medical procedures. That is, babies who would have died now live. The presence of an additional disability challenges educators, and the increasing numbers of these children will further challenge our society.

Summary

The first educational program for the deaf in the United States was established in 1817, and soon state residential schools for the deaf were established. The controversy between manual (signing) and oral methods that originated in Europe continued in these schools.

The anatomy of the ear and the way normal hearing functions is well established, as are the major causes of hearing impairment. Although deafness is considered an extreme degree of hearing impairment, it is often referred to as a separate condition, due to the different educational interventions required and to some extent to tradition and the influence of adults who are deaf. The major classifications of hearing loss (on the basis of location) are (1) conductive, with the damage or disease in the outer or middle ear, (2) sensorineural, in which the damage or disease is in the inner ear, and (3) mixed, a combination of the two. The prevalence of hearing-impaired students, including those who are deaf, is estimated to be between 0.5% and 0.7%. Characteristics of students with hearing impairments are primarily related to lower levels of academic achievement and to communication difficulties. Without specific assistance beginning at the early childhood stage and continuing through the preschool years, children with a hearing impairment may not develop normal language, often resulting in lower levels of achievement. Factors such as the type of hearing loss, the age of onset, and whether the parents are hearing impaired affect the ability to vocalize—in addition to the degree of hearing loss, of course.

Manual communication (chiefly American Sign Language, but also various alternative sign systems), pure oral communication (using any residual hearing, speechreading, speaking, and so on), and total communication (a combination of manual and oral communication, utilizing whatever means is most effective for each individual and learning taste) are the three major approaches to teaching language to children who are deaf. The concepts of the deaf community—that is, a separate community of the deaf—and of deaf culture are advocated by many deaf adults. These concepts, like the approaches to communication, are the topic of continuing controversy.

A variety of assistive devices has been developed for persons who are hearing impaired. Hearing aids amplify sound, tactile aids may be used to transduce sound into vibrating patterns on the skin, and cochlear implants may be effective with some individuals having profound hearing loss. Telecaption decoders can be used to produce captions across the bottom of a TV screen. The TDD, when attached to a telephone, sends and receives messages that can be displayed on a screen or printed by a printer. And hearing dogs can alert an individual at home to sounds such as the doorbell, telephone, or fire alarm.

Sheila grew up in a small town in the Midwest, where she went to grade school and belonged to the Girl Scouts. In high school, Sheila was the valedictorian of her graduating class. After college she taught school for five years and then returned to complete her master's degree; she eventually earned her doctorate.

Sheila is the mother of three college students and is active in her church, serving on several committees. She has composed over 20 pieces of music.

Sheila teaches at a university and has written three texts that are used by college students as they prepare to teach. She usually writes one or two articles per year that are published in leading journals. Sheila has become well known because of her expertise and has been asked to consult in every state in the nation. She has also been a consultant in England, France, Australia, and New Zealand.

Did we mention that Sheila has been blind since the age of 3?

CHAPTER NINE

Visual Impairments

The ability to see is so obviously precious that the general public mistakenly assumes that individuals with low or no vision must have a diminished quality of life. We also tend to be in awe of what individuals with impaired vision accomplish. This may be due to attitudes that have been with us for centuries. Throughout history humans have been concerned about vision impairments; some early philosophers suggested that the eye is related to the soul, which encouraged many superstitions about lack of vision. Treatment of individuals with impaired vision has ranged from destruction to veneration and worship—none of which addresses the role vision plays in individual development or the capabilities that exist concurrently with impaired vision. We hope to correct that imbalance in this chapter.

The history of how societies have treated individuals who are blind may be divided into several phases: separation, ward status or protectionism, self-emancipation, education, and assimilation (Lowenfeld, 1975; Tuttle, 1984).

■ Separation

In very early societies whose major concerns were acquiring food, clothing, and shelter, anyone who could not contribute was considered a liability. Such individuals were therefore ostracized, left to fend for themselves, or annihilated. Babies born blind were often abandoned in the wilderness, where they eventually starved or were killed by animals. Others were placed in clay baskets and left by the wayside or floating in rivers. This treatment was legal in ancient Athens, Rome, and Sparta. Persons who became blind later in life, however, were often venerated as sages and kept isolated from the corruptions of society.

■ Ward Status or Protectionism

In the pre-Christian Jewish communities and in the newly developing Christian church, orphans, the aged, and those who were blind were protected as special wards of the church or synagogue. From this type of thinking arose some asylums for persons who were blind, but it was more common for them to become beggars and to be provided for by the alms-giving public. Many considered blindness to be worse than death, so defeated armies or other foes were often intentionally blinded to ensure the worst possible punishment.

■ Self-Emancipation

Through the 17th and 18th centuries individuals who were blind distinguished themselves through their own efforts in various fields of endeavor, despite prevailing attitudes. Nicholas Saunderson and John Gough, professors of mathematics; John Metcalf, an engineer and bridge builder; Thomas Blacklock, a minister and poet; Nicholas Bacon, a lawyer; Huldreich Schonberger, a philosopher; François Huber, a naturalist; and Maria Theresia von Paradis, a vocalist and pianist, were among those who proved they could learn and make valuable contributions to society (Lowenfeld, 1973, 1975).

■ Education

Some took note of these accomplishments and established special schools or training programs for the visually impaired. Among them was Valentin Haüy (1745–1822) who, while being educated in Paris, became interested in Abbé de l'Épée's work educating persons who were deaf. After a personal encounter with a Parisian mob that was cruelly tormenting a group of men who were blind, Haüy vowed to play a role in providing education for individuals who were blind. Haüy became acquainted with Maria Theresia von Paradis and was impressed by her efforts to provide tactile reading for individuals who were blind. After observing a pupil without sight reading by recognizing the embossed negative of letters on the backs of pages, he developed a system of negative type that produced embossed positive letters. Those letters proved to be of great value and established that blind persons could effectively read "through their fingers."

Haüy established the first actual school for persons who were blind (The National Institution for Young Blind People) in Paris in 1784. He attempted to pattern its educational practices as nearly as possible on usual practices in schools for sighted persons, teaching the full range of subjects of his day. He also emphasized handicraft-related education (basketry, chair caning, sewing, spinning, and weaving), which established a pattern for years to come, though overemphasis on those skills later became a problem.

Before the turn of the century, schools had been established in Liverpool (1791), Bristol (1793), and Edinburgh (1793). By 1810, educational programs had been established in Vienna, Berlin, Milan, Amsterdam, Prague, Stockholm, Zurich, and Dublin (Napier, 1972). These schools, established by individuals or church groups, were primarily elementary-level schools, though they often included crafts-oriented vocational training.

The development of schools in the United States was motivated by reports of the success of the Haüy school in France. The New England Asylum for the Blind was incorporated in 1829, and in 1831 Dr. Samuel Gridley Howe, a wealthy Boston physician, was appointed director. Howe went to Europe to study its schools and to find teachers; he came back with the following principles, which he believed should guide education for blind persons in the United States.

1. All blind children should be educated in accordance with their personal needs and the expectation that they can apply such training in their community.
2. The curricula for schools for the blind should be similar to educational programs for all other children, but should include more music and crafts.
3. The major goal of education for the blind should be that they become contributing members of their home communities (Farrell, 1956).

Attempts to teach reading and writing in the schools varied in methodology. Tactual methods such as embossed letters, wood carvings, string glued to paper, writing on waxed tablets, letters pinpricked into felt, and any other method that could permit persons who were blind to "see" through their hands was tried. Howe developed embossed type (called Boston line type) that was used in the first American effort to provide printed materials for persons who were blind (Lowenfeld, 1973).

Meanwhile in Paris, Louis Braille (1809–1852), at age 10, entered the school that Haüy had established; later he stayed on as a teacher. While there, he developed the first version of the dot system of reading that bears his name.

At the school, Braille met Charles Barbier, a cavalry officer who had developed a system whereby messages could be read under battle conditions at night. This code utilized 12 raised dots, which Braille reduced to the 6-dot system in use today (see Figure 9.1). Braille's system enabled persons who were blind to read and also write. He devised a series of contractions, a system for mathematics, and one for musical notations. He had some difficulty convincing sighted teachers and administrators at the school that a viable reading or writing system could come from a person who was blind. They also seemed to prefer a system that resembled the alphabetic system with which they were already familiar (Napier, 1972). So Braille and others who believed in the merits of his system taught it secretly; in fact, it was not adopted until 1854, two years after his death. Thus began **braille,** the single most-used method of reading and writing by persons who are blind. Since its adoption in France, it has been recognized in and adapted to most other languages.

After the founding of the New England Asylum for the Blind (renamed the Perkins Institution and Massachusetts Asylum for the Blind), a number of other

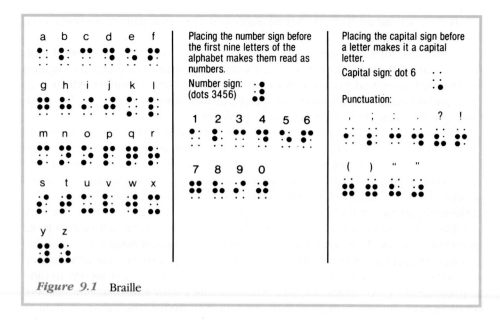

Figure 9.1 Braille

schools were established in other states. By 1870 there were 23 such schools in the United States, most of them state supported (Napier, 1972). Residential schools, following the pattern established by Howe, were the major vehicle for educating persons who were blind until the 1900s. In 1900 the first public school class for the blind was established in Chicago, and in 1913 classes for students who were partially sighted were begun in Boston and Cleveland. The latter discouraged students from using their residual vision. The thinking was that if residual vision were used it would more rapidly deteriorate. In 1914 the first large-print books were published for students with low vision.

◼ Assimilation

The practice of educating students who were blind in public schools increased during the early 1900s until approximately 15% of the total population of such school-age individuals was attending public schools. This percentage remained relatively stable until the 1950s, when there was a sharp increase to 60% by 1965. According to Lowenfeld (1981), this increase was accounted for by

1. The increasing integration of individuals who were blind into society
2. The increased interest in the education of all people
3. The recognition of the importance of the family in the life of the individual

The principle of the least restrictive environment established by the passage of PL 94-142 has also furthered the assimilation of persons who are blind into society. Lowenfeld (1981) and Tuttle (1984) cite (1) the development of mobility devices and training; (2) emphasis on daily living skills training, which enables adult persons who are blind to live in their own homes; (3) technologic developments that enable persons with low vision to more effectively use their residual vision; and (4) the leadership of individuals who are blind as contributing to the assimilation process.

This does not mean that assimilation has been accomplished. Physical integration does not necessarily result in social integration. There are still sighted individuals who would prefer segregated schools and protectionism, which is to deny an individual with low or no vision the fundamental right to be a full participating member of society.

The Anatomy and Function of the Eye

To understand how malfunctions or damage to the eye affect vision, it is necessary to have some knowledge of the functioning of the eye. The visual system in its entirety is complex but may be simplified to a few basic concepts.

The functioning of the eye is often compared with that of a camera—with a lens system, a variable aperture system, and a retina, which corresponds to film. Like the camera, we cannot see without light. But with sufficient illumination, light rays reflecting off an object travel through the **cornea** (the transparent outer cover of the eye), the aqueous humor (a watery substance), the pupil (the circular hole in the center of the colored iris), the lens (which has the ability to adjust, thereby more precisely focusing the light rays), and the vitreous humor (a substance with the consistency of egg whites). They are then projected onto the retina in such a way that the image is inverted and reversed with respect to the actual object (see Figure 9.2).

The **iris**—membranous tissue and muscles that adjust the size of the pupil to regulate the amount of light entering the eye—also provides what is perceived as the color of the eye.

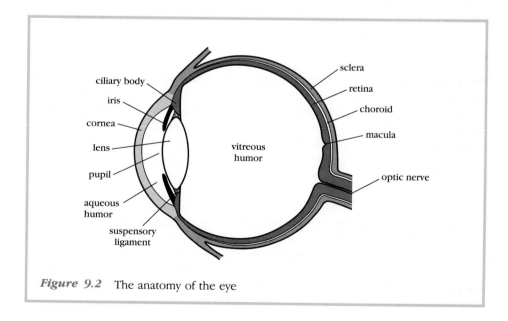

Figure 9.2   The anatomy of the eye

The retina is the light-sensitive portion of the eye at the back of the eyeball. It contains two types of light receptors, which change light into nerve impulses that are carried to the brain via the optic nerve. The first type of light receptor is the cones, which are concentrated in an oval area of the posterior part of the retina (the macula) but also scattered throughout the retina. They detect color. The other light receptors, the rods, are not present in the macula but are found throughout the periphery of the retina.

Normal vision may be divided into central, or macular—which has the highest visual acuity in highly illuminated situations—and peripheral, or extramacular—which is most efficient in low-illumination situations. Central vision is used to perceive fine detail, as in reading, writing, or seeing distant objects clearly; peripheral vision is more important for perceiving movement, as in traveling, and for night vision.

When an image falls on the retina, the light-sensitive receptors are activated and the image is carried to the brain for interpretation, which includes inverting the image to the upright and nonreversed position. For practical purposes the retina may be considered an expansion of the optic nerve endings in the eye; as various images fall on the retina, different parts of the optic nerve are stimulated to differing degrees, thus accounting for the almost infinite variety of messages that can be transmitted to the brain.

Accommodation (in which the ciliary muscles change the curvature of the lens) is a process by which the image is clearly focused on the retina. In normal vision the ciliary muscles do not need to adjust the lens unless the object is closer than about 20 feet. Then the ciliary muscles increase the curvature of the lens so the light rays are focused on the retina. This ability weakens with age. Children are most able to accommodate, and adults of 50 or 60 may have lost the ability entirely. Young children with poor distance acuity may be able to read fine print, but as their ability to accommodate lessens (which can happen as early as the teenage years) they find it more difficult to read that same fine print. Sometimes this is interpreted as failing vision instead of being recognized as a natural physiological phenomenon.

It is important to note that the brain's interpretation of the image falling on the retina depends on the normal, consistent operation of the total visual system, including the brain, and that visual messages received through this system are processed in conjunction with information received simultaneously through other sensory channels. Although we have treated the visual system as if it were separate, it is essential to remember that it is interrelated with other systems supplying information to the brain.

All functions of the visual system require the use of some of the many muscles that are also part of the system. Some of these—such as the six ocularmotor muscles that move the eyeball in the socket up, down, and sideways, and those used in focusing, tracking, and fixating—must be developed; if very little light reaches the retina, those muscles may not fully develop. The child with normal visual ability and environmental stimulation begins to develop the skills of fixation and tracking in the early stages of infancy in a primarily reflexive manner; once learned, the skills are exercised during most waking hours. In contrast, the child with impaired vision may have to be specifically taught those skills. Various muscles—for example, the ocularmotor muscle that brings the eyeballs into convergence (both eyes moving in the same direction or focusing in conjunction)—may be intact and have the potential for normal functioning, but without practice they are essentially useless. In cases of total blindness this is not of concern, but for students with low vision, an understanding of the physiology of the visual system and knowing how to maximize visual efficiency are of critical importance.

Definitions and Terminology

There has been and still is a great deal of variation in the vocabulary describing visual impairments. In general the terminology used reflects the divergent roles and attitudes of the various professions involved, such as psychologists, educators, and physicians. According to Barraga (1976), the following are just some of the terms used to describe visual impairments: *medically blind, vocationally blind, partially blind, visually defective, functionally blind, economically blind, braille blind,* and *adventitiously* or *congenitally blind.* The most useful terms are those that clarify the individual student's needs, that have no negative connotations, and that are not misleading or contradictory.

For purposes of clarification we will provide definitions from different points of view and define terms usually associated with vision.

The *Federal Register* definition of a visual disability reads "visual impairment which even with correction, adversely affects the child's educational performance. The term includes both partially seeing and blind children" (1977, p. 42479). This definition refers to the effects of limited vision on the education of the individual. Another educationally oriented definition is provided by Barraga: "A visually handicapped child is one whose visual impairment interferes with his optimal learning and achievement, unless adaptations are made in the methods of presenting learning experiences, the nature of the materials used, and/or in the learning environment" (1983, p. 25).

In addition to educational definitions there are legal definitions, which are used to determine eligibility for disability or Social Security payments, tax exemptions, and rehabilitation services. In 1934 the Section of Ophthalmology of the American Medical Society provided a definition of blindness that the government could use for those services and that, with a few modifications, remains workable today (Hatfield, 1975). The language is that of eye care specialists: a person is **legally blind** when the central visual acuity is 20/200 or less in the better eye after correction, or when the field of vision is no more than 20 degrees in diameter (American Federation for the Blind, 1987). This definition, then, emphasizes (1) visual **acuity** and (2) visual field.

Visual acuity is the ability to distinguish the details of an object at specified distances. The most common expression of visual acuity is the notation 20/20, indicating "normal" vision. Ratios such as 20/20, 20/50, 20/100, and 20/200 are used to express visual acuity at a distance. The first number is the distance, in feet, at which the test is made. The second number is the size of the letters or symbols on the Snellen chart (see photos), expressed in terms of the distance at which a person with normal vision can comfortably read them. If an individual can read the 20-foot-size symbol or letter while standing 20 feet away, the measured acuity is 20/20, or normal vision. However, if the individual can read only the symbol representing the 50- or 100-foot size on the chart, the measured visual acuity is indicated as 20/50 or 20/100. This test measures distance vision only, not the near-point vision necessary for close tasks such as reading or writing. Further, there may be wide variation in the functional vision of persons with the same measurement of acuity.

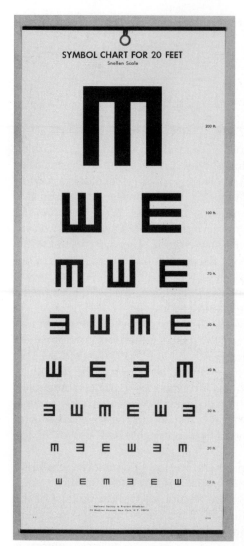

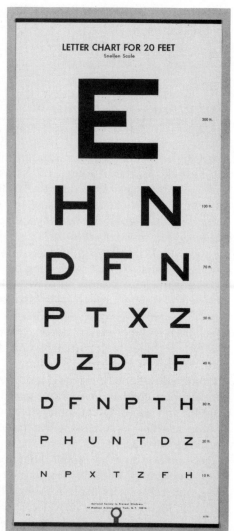

■ The Snellen Letter Chart and the Snellen Symbol Chart. Children who do not know the letters of the alphabet indicate with three fingers the orientation (up, down, and so on) of the symbols. ■

SOURCE: *Copyrighted by the National Society to Prevent Blindness. Reprinted by permission.*

The visual field, which is reported in degrees, is the entire area that can be seen while staring straight ahead. Individuals with a normal field of vision are able to see 180 degrees. A restricted visual field means some smaller number of degrees or angle within which the individual is able to see. It is expressed, for example, as 100 degrees, 80 degrees, or 50 degrees. For legal purposes, when the visual field is restricted to 20 degrees or less, the individual is considered blind (see Figure 9.3). Narrowed fields of vision are sometimes referred to as tunnel vision, tubular vision, or pinpoint vision, and may interfere with activities such as moving from place to place, playing some sports, and driving a car.

Barraga (1986) provided the following definitions of severity, which are related to levels of functional vision and the need for educational adaptations.

■ This boy's response to the Snellen Symbol Chart is the first step in a visual evaluation. ■

1. *Moderate visual disability:* comparable to normal vision after correcting with visual aids or special lighting
2. *Severe visual disability:* performance that is less accurate than normal even with the use of special aids and that may require more time and energy
3. *Profound visual disability:* no useful vision for detailed tasks, and great difficulty with gross visual tasks

The total population of individuals with visual impairments of any kind is described in many ways, most frequently and erroneously as **blind.** The American

Figure 9.3   Restricted field of vision

Federation for the Blind (1987) encourages the use of the terms *visually impaired, low vision,* or *partially sighted* to describe individuals with any usable sight. It reserves the term *blind* for those with no usable sight.

The variety of terminology used in popular and professional literature for individuals with vision impairments can lead to considerable confusion. To clarify the usage in this chapter and contribute to a more complete understanding of visual impairments, we'll define several of the more common terms here.

- *Blind* refers to individuals who have no vision or have only a perception of light versus darkness.
- *Functional vision* is a classification system or category based on how much assistance individuals require to learn effectively by using their vision—as in Barraga's (1986) classifications of moderate, severe, and profound.
- *Low vision* refers to limited visual ability that can be increased by means of optical aids and modifications of the environment.
- *Partially sighted* describes the same population as those regarded as having **low vision. Partially sighted** individuals are "persons with a visual acuity greater than 20/200 but not greater than 20/70 in the better eye after correction" (National Society for the Prevention of Blindness, 1966, p. 10).
- *Visual efficiency* means the ability to use available vision as determined by motivation, early training, intelligence, parental attitudes, and other relevant factors. **Visual efficiency** also reflects the degree of acuity and field of vision.

- *Visual impairment* is a generic term that refers to any disorder in the structure or function of the eye.
- *Visual perception* refers to the ability to interpret and understand information received through the visual sense; **visual perception** is primarily a function of the brain.
- *Visual functioning* refers to "how a person uses whatever vision he may have" (Barraga, 1976, p. 15). It includes the motivations, needs, and expectations of the individual who is using residual vision.
- *Visually limited* describes individuals who require additional aids, materials, or lighting, but who with such modifications are considered to be sighted.
- *Visually disabled* is a general term for the total population of individuals with impairments in the structure of functioning of the eye that limit them enough to be considered a disability.

Prevalence

Precise numbers of children who are blind or have visual impairments seem difficult to obtain. The U.S. Department of Education, the American Printing House for the Blind, and the American Foundation for the Blind all report different statistics. The disparity may be partially explained by the fact that governmental regulations allow a child to be counted only once even though he or she may receive services for several disabilities. Therefore, students who have visual impairments plus learning disabilities or visual impairments plus mental retardation may be reported in the statistics for the other disability. Children who are both deaf and blind are reported under a separate category, according to governmental regulations. Gates (1985), in a survey of 12 states in the Rocky Mountains area, reports that 30% of the individuals with visual impairments included in the study had additional disabilities such as mental retardation, learning disabilities, and hearing impairments. In a similar study in the eastern section of the United States, Harley, Garcia, and Williams (1989) found that 36% of the students receiving services for visual impairments had additional disabilities. Others suggest that many children with visual impairments are not identified and therefore are neither receiving services nor reported (Head, 1989).

It seems the one aspect on which there is general agreement is that the total number of children with visual impairments is relatively small compared with other disabilities.

The percentage of the school-age population who have been identified as having a visual impairment or being blind and who receive services is .04%, according to the U.S. Department of Education's *Thirteenth Annual Report to Congress*. But blindness and visual impairments occur increasingly with age. Approximately 75% of the persons who are blind are over 45 years of age (Hardman, Drew, Egan, & Wolf, 1990). As the population of the United States ages, that percentage is likely to increase.

Characteristics of Individuals with Visual Impairments

Individuals with visual impairments are, of course, individuals first; therefore, the array of their personality characteristics, intellectual abilities, educational aptitudes, and physical abilities is in general similar to that of the population as a whole. However, young children with limited vision may experience delays in certain areas of development. As adults, they may be uncertain of concepts such as mountains, vastness of land space, or clouds, because vision plays a vital role in the formation of such concepts. They may not, however, be any different in physical, social, or intellectual development.

Persons who either lose their vision or have severely restricted vision prior to age 5 have little remembered visual imagery on which to draw when learning, which affects the formation of certain concepts (Lowenfeld, 1980). In addition to the age of onset, the degree of the impairment and the presence of additional impairments affect the development of intellectual, physical, language, and social abilities. The degree of functional vision students have affects their use of visual information that can be used in conjunction with other sensory input in all areas of learning. The presence of such additional impairments as hearing loss, mental retardation, communication disorders, learning disabilities, or physical disorders further complicates the learning process for that individual. It has been suggested that more than one-half of all visually impaired children, including those not yet old enough to attend school, have additional developmental handicaps.

The total development of an individual depends on a complex interaction of various domains: motor, cognitive, communicative, and social. At different ages or developmental stages one domain may dominate the others, but all are continuously present. Because of this complex interaction, it is misleading to discuss separately the effects of impaired vision on the development of the various domains and their relationship to learning. However, for our purpose of conveying the impact low vision or blindness can have on learning, we will consider several of the domains and the manner in which they may be affected.

■ Motor

Very young infants use sight to become aware of and develop interest in their environment. They observe, look at, and reach toward objects, developing neck muscles and head control; they later learn to creep or walk toward those objects that arouse their curiosity. Infants without sight or with severely restricted vision depend more on audible or tactile cues to stimulate their curiosity or arouse their interest. If parents and teachers are aware of the increased need for such stimulation and provide it, they can help develop early motor abilities. Nonetheless, young children with visual impairments usually lag somewhat behind their sighted peers in motor development (Ferrell, 1986; Fraiburg, 1977). Young children with vision disorders are also less aware of their position in the environment and their relationship to it, which inhibits their development in creeping, standing, and walking. Unless specific stimulation activities are provided, they may not adequately develop body awareness and physical coordination and will tend to move hesitantly in their environment.

Eye/hand coordination and fine motor muscles may also be slower to develop, resulting in a delayed mastery of eating utensils, buttons and zippers, and—later—computers or braillewriters. Early planned experiences can ameliorate the effects of reduced vision on these skills.

Overprotectiveness on the part of parents or teachers may prevent the child from experimenting with movement in the environment, thus delaying development (Scholl, 1986). A balance between protection and encouraging exploration must be maintained.

Congenitally blind children seem to be more susceptible to poor muscle tone, obesity, poor awareness of the body's position in space, and general lack of physical fitness. Factors such as these can lead to developmental problems with posture, overall coordination, and walking patterns (Hill, Rosen, Correa, & Langley, 1984).

Perceptual-motor skills in relation to form identification, spatial relations, and perceptual-motor integration may also be compromised, especially in congenitally blind children. However, they may be as skilled as their sighted peers in areas more dependent on other senses—such as in discrimination of weight, texture, and sound—if sufficient experiences have been provided. Millar (1981) suggests that such abilities may be developed and enhanced until the child's mental images are similar to those of sighted children. The belief that persons with visual disorders develop a "sixth sense" or have extraordinary sensory compensation (being able to hear better or having a more acute tactile sense) has little validity. The skills that seem to be heightened or strengthened more likely reflect past training—for example, in listening or in paying more attention to cues that sighted persons regard as irrelevant (Telford & Sawrey, 1981).

Orientation—the establishment of one's position in space and position relative to other objects in the environment—and **mobility**—self-generated movement from one fixed position to another in the environment—are both delayed, but these skills can be learned by individuals with visual disorders. Orientation is a continuous process. For example, as we begin to move from one place to another, we visually scan the environment with little conscious awareness. We may note a table obstructing our path to the door, the width of the door relative to our body size, the steps down from the door, the width of the space between the porch railings near the steps, and similar factors. As each step is taken we reestablish our position in relation to those factors. Once they are passed, they are no longer of concern. In contrast, if we travel from the porch to the street, we may encounter moving objects such as neighborhood pets, automobiles, or other persons, and we must assess their position relative to us after each step. This is why we say that orientation to the environment is continuous.

Self-generated movement occurs simultaneously with orientation but requires additional skills. Proper heel-and-toe gait, control of the body's center of gravity, and upright posture are some of the skills exercised in locomotion or mobility. The combination of orientation and mobility allows an individual to move about independently; these skills must be learned by individuals with vision disorders. Aids for independent travel will be described in a later section of this chapter.

■ Cognitive

Cognitive development includes the formation of concepts, object permanence, cause and effect, spatial relationships, classification, and conservation. According to Tuttle (1984), blindness itself does not impair an individual's ability to intellectually manipulate sensory information and develop conceptual information, but rather is the result of impoverished interaction with the environment, which decreases the amount of sensory data received. Vision plays an important role in cognitive development that cannot be fully compensated for by hearing or touch. Concepts related to distance or height beyond arm's length are difficult to develop without sight. Imagine trying to develop the concept of mountains in the distance or the height of a 35-floor hotel without vision. Hearing may provide some clues to location such as the distance of an approaching car, but the various sizes and shapes of cars, trucks, and vans cannot be fully developed without sight. Vision allows for the perception of the whole: the total car, van, or truck, its various parts (sunroof, wheels, bumper, hood ornament), and the relationship of the parts to each other as well as to the whole.

■ Communicative

Communicative (language) development proceeds similarly in children with visual disorders and their sighted peers, though it is more important for the former to have a language-enriched environment (Bigelow, 1987). It is possible that their social communication is inhibited because they cannot observe nonverbal cues that lead to early language acquisition. Pointing, gesturing, and facial expressions are not clearly visible to these children and therefore cannot be used to direct their attention or to prolong and increase their involvement. This may result in less verbal interaction and delayed language acquisition.

Children with impaired vision must learn some concepts primarily through listening to another person's verbal descriptions or explanations rather than by direct experience. Their attempts to use words that have little experiential meaning for them and that are based on their memory of others' descriptions result in verbalisms (Parsons & Sabornie, 1987). Examples of verbalisms are phrases such as "fog as thick as smoke" or "a shirt as red as the sunset." Because of their lack of experience they often use such phrases inappropriately.

Although there may be differences in the language development of young children with visual impairments and their age peers, it appears that at later ages their abilities are very similar. The major differences are found in the richness of vocabulary and meaning as related to language usage (Warren, 1984). Reading, another form of language communication, may show the same problems we've noted regarding richness of vocabulary and concept formation.

Children with visual impairments may also tend to be more concerned about themselves, ask more questions about their own interests, and relate more frequently to adults in their verbal communications than to their sighted peers (Anderson, Dunlea, & Kekelis, 1984; Erin, 1990).

■ Social

Social development implies interaction and communication with other persons as well as the development of self-esteem. Early in development, social interaction is increased by the very young child's tendency to imitate. The child sees a smile, imitates it, and learns to associate it with pleasure. Later social skills are learned by observing approving looks or frowns, often in the absence of any verbal interaction. The meaning of spoken words may be altered by a facial expression: "What a nice shirt," accompanied by a rolling of the eyes and a grimace, conveys a meaning opposite to the actual words. Impaired vision may result in miscommunication in such interactions and cause embarrassment or confusion, which in turn inhibits further communication and increases the degree of isolation.

People can initiate and maintain social contact with a glance, sustained eye contact, a turn of the head, and other similar visual but nonverbal cues. Children with impaired vision are unable to participate in many such interactions. They may not know when someone has walked toward them, is speaking directly to them (especially in classrooms in which there is a high noise level), or has walked away. Having learned by experience that it is possible to do so, these children may initiate or try to maintain contact by touch. This can embarrass sighted children, who may not want to be touched, and may decrease the likelihood of additional social contacts (Kekelis & Sacks, 1988). Children who are blind or have low vision may also interact with peers less because of the importance of eye contact in sustaining social interactions; sighted children may interpret a lack of eye contact as apathy or disinterest.

Lack of participation in activities that are assumed (by sighted individuals) to be impossible for low-vision or blind children decreases social interaction. Unless efforts are made to include them and to increase the awareness of sighted persons, children with visual impairments will be left out of activities such as swimming, football, bicycle riding, and roller skating. To enhance interactions between sighted and low-vision children, styles of dressing, grooming, and current fads must also be taught to students with visual impairments.

The expectations of significant others in the child's environment play a role in the development of self-esteem and self-confidence. Tuttle (1984) suggests that a lack of self-esteem or self-confidence among persons who are visually impaired results from fewer interactions with others and from the negative attitudes of sighted persons. Children congenitally blind or with low vision do not think about their limitations; however, adults do. If adults' expectations are not limiting but still acknowledge the impact of visual impairments, the child's self-esteem and self-confidence should not be affected.

Causes of Visual Impairments

The most common types of visual impairments are caused by abnormal light refraction and are usually corrected with eyeglasses or contact lenses. If correction can be accomplished with glasses, no additional educational modifications are necessary. However, a variety of conditions result in impaired vision and require modifications in order to maximize learning. They include muscle disorders, inherited diseases that affect the structure or functioning of the eye, refractive disorders, injuries to the eye or to the head that affect the eye, and infectious diseases. We will briefly describe some of the more common causes of visual impairments.

■ Muscle Disorders

In general, muscle disorders result from muscle control problems leading to difficulty in maintaining eye focus, even for short periods of time. In some cases, muscle disorders result in loss of vision.

Nystagmus   A neurological disorder, **nystagmus** causes the eyes to roll or rotate involuntarily, resulting in difficulty in focusing on small print or objects or carrying out fine detail tasks. Often movement increases when the student is fatigued or under stress.

Strabismus   This is an imbalanced pull of the muscles surrounding the eye. When the muscles pull outward (external **strabismus**), it is difficult for the eyes to focus together. When the muscles pull inward (internal strabismus), it is likewise difficult for the eyes to focus. The imbalance may occur in only one eye, causing it to turn inward (cross-eye) or outward (sometimes referred to as walleye). Both conditions cause focusing problems as well as double vision or loss of depth perception. Surgery may correct these imbalances.

Amblyopia   When strabismus goes uncorrected and causes double vision, the brain, unable to process two images, attempts to suppress the image from one eye. The unused eye (lazy eye) may atrophy and lose the ability to see. Amblyopia may be corrected by wearing a patch over the working eye or by surgery.

■ Retinal or Optic Nerve Disorders

Optic nerve atrophy   Atrophy of the optic nerve results from damage to the nerve fibers connecting the retina to the brain. Electrical impulses are unable to travel through the damaged portions, so what is seen cannot reach the brain to be interpreted. The effects of atrophy on vision depend on the location and extent of the damage, but it often affects acuity, visual field, and visual color.

Retinal detachment   It is possible for the retina to separate from the choroid (the middle covering of the eyeball, which carries much of the blood supply) and the sclera (the tough, white coating over all of the eyeball except the cornea that we call the white of the eye). The retina "peels" away (as wallpaper might peel away from the wall), resulting in a loss of vision in the peeled-away portions. Vision is blurred, or portions of the image may be missing. Retinal detachment may result from glaucoma, retinal degeneration, extreme myopia, trauma to the eye, or a severe blow to the head. An untreated detached retina will lead to blindness; however, laser treatments can frequently seal tears, reattach the retina, and restore vision if damage is detected early.

Retinitis pigmentosa   A hereditary condition resulting from a break in the choroid, **retinitis pigmentosa** is characterized in its early stages by difficulty in seeing in dim light or at night. In later stages, a loss of peripheral vision progresses to a loss of central vision, eventually resulting in complete blindness.

Retinopathy of prematurity   Also called **retrolental fibroplasia,** this is the result of a potentially lifesaving administration of high concentrations of oxygen to premature infants. The amount of oxygen and the duration for which it is administered appear to cause changes in the retinal blood vessels and form scar tissue behind the lens of the eye, preventing light rays from reaching the retina. The severity of the visual impairment is from moderate myopia to total blindness. Individuals who, at a young age, appear to have moderate visual impairments may later experience retinal detachment as the scar tissue formed in the eye contracts and peels the retina away from the blood supply.

Diabetic retinopathy   This type may occur in individuals who have had **diabetes** for a number of years. Blood vessels in the retina coil up, causing retinal hemorrhaging that can damage the macula. If the macula is damaged, blindness results. The hemorrhage may break into the vitreous humor and later develop scar tissue that shrinks and detaches the retina.

■ Refractive Disorders

Myopia   Commonly referred to as nearsightedness, **myopia** is caused by an increased curvature of the cornea (a "too-long" eyeball) (see Figure 9.4). The incoming rays of light focus in front of rather than on the retina. Near vision is unaffected, but distance vision is distorted or blurred. If very young children have

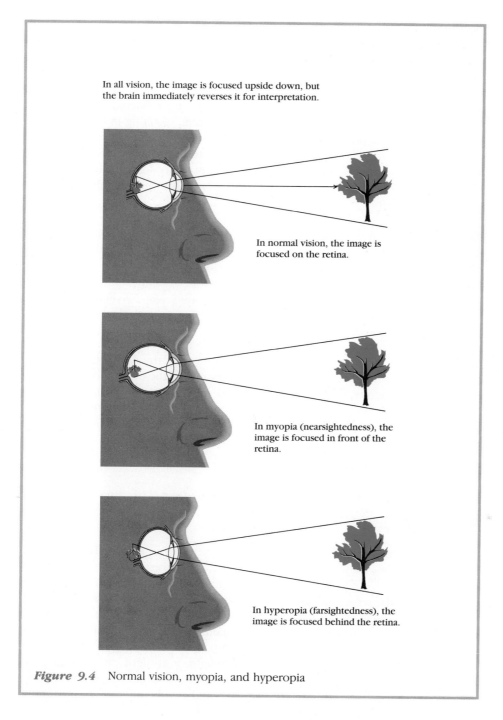

In all vision, the image is focused upside down, but the brain immediately reverses it for interpretation.

In normal vision, the image is focused on the retina.

In myopia (nearsightedness), the image is focused in front of the retina.

In hyperopia (farsightedness), the image is focused behind the retina.

Figure 9.4 Normal vision, myopia, and hyperopia

severe myopia, the concepts they form about objects they see in the distance may be distorted. Usually myopia can be corrected with eyeglasses or contact lenses.

Hyperopia Commonly referred to as farsightedness, **hyperopia** is the result of a flattened corneal surface (a "too-short" eyeball). The incoming rays of light focus beyond or behind the retina, resulting in a lack of clarity in close visual tasks. Distance vision is unaffected. Hyperopia in young children may go undetected until they enter school and are required to read, write, or complete other detailed visual tasks. Eyeglasses or contact lenses often correct this refractive error.

Astigmatism   This defect is the result of an elongated shape or an unevenness in the surface of the cornea. Incoming rays of light are refracted irregularly and therefore do not converge at one point on the retina, resulting in blurred vision. Young children may not be aware of blurred vision, assuming all people see the way they do, so the problem may not be detected until close visual tasks are required as they enter school. Eyeglasses or contact lenses usually correct the vision. Astigmatism may occur as a separate condition or in combination with myopia or hyperopia.

Presbyopia   When the ciliary muscles lose the ability to change the shape of the lens in the eye, it is impossible to clearly focus on objects at varying distances. The most notable impairment is in focusing on close work. Distance vision is not affected, because it does not require the contraction of the lens. Less common in younger persons, presbyopia is more common after age 40. Reading glasses, bifocals, or trifocals may ameliorate the condition.

Cataracts   The result of the soft, clear lens of the eye becoming hard, cloudy, or opaque, cataracts prevent the passage of light rays onto the retina. Cataracts may be present at birth (congenital) or a result of trauma to the eye (secondary). They cause decreased acuity, hazy or blurred images, and sensitivity to bright light. The degree to which vision is affected depends on the size, density, and location of the cataract. Treatment includes surgical removal of the cataract and corrective eyeglasses. When very young children's cataracts are removed, frequently the lens of the eye is also removed. This produces marked farsightedness, which is then corrected with eyeglasses or contact lenses.

■   **Other Disorders**

Glaucoma   This condition increases pressure in the eyeball because of a buildup of aqueous humor that does not drain away in the normal manner. Part of the pressure is exerted on the vitreous humor (the jellylike fluid) that fills the eyeball behind the lens; this causes the collapse of the blood vessels that nourish the retina and fibers of the optic nerve. Deprived of nourishment, they die; as they do, vision fades. **Glaucoma** may be congenital, inherited, or the result of eye trauma; it may be chronic or acute. Visual impairments resulting from glaucoma include blurred vision, difficulty seeing in dim light or at night, and a progressive loss of peripheral vision until blindness results. Medication or surgery is effective if the condition is detected prior to visual loss and may be effective in preventing further loss, but it cannot restore already reduced visual abilities.

Optic albinism   This disorder is genetically transmitted and results in reduced or absent eye pigmentation. In some cases, the reduced pigmentation may affect the entire body. The condition is characterized by decreased acuity, astigmatism, and nystagmus. The lack of pigment in the eye also causes increased sensitivity to bright light or glare. Wearing sunglasses outdoors and sitting in dim light in classrooms will reduce the discomfort that results from this sensitivity.

■ A street scene, as viewed by three individuals. ■

As viewed by an individual with normal vision.

As viewed by an individual with glaucoma.

As viewed by an individual with cataracts.

Retinoblastoma This malignant tumor of the retina can occur on one or both eyes and is usually found in children younger than 5 years of age. If the central vision of only one eye is affected, the child may be cross-eyed. When the condition is detected early radiation treatments, laser beam treatments, or freezing are effective correctives. If the tumor is well advanced before detection, surgical removal of the eye is necessary to prevent secondary tumors from spreading.

Neoplasms   These abnormal formations or growths of tissues or tumors may grow in the pituitary gland or in the brain, causing damage to the optic nerve or occipital lobe of the brain. The extent of visual impairment depends on size, location, and detection point.

Color vision problems   More commonly (but incorrectly) referred to as color blindness, color vision defects diminish the ability to distinguish between certain colors. All colors are made up of combinations of three colors—red, green, and blue—in the light rays that enter the eye. The cones in the retina contain light-sensitive substances that correspond to each of those colors. A partial or complete lack of one or more of these substances diminishes the ability to distinguish them. True color blindness (seeing everything in shades of gray) is very rare. Conditions affecting color vision are usually hereditary and present from birth.

Infectious diseases   German measles or rubella contracted by the mother during pregnancy can produce a variety of birth defects or visual impairments. Maternal rubella may result in the birth of children with mental retardation, hearing impairments, or cardiac abnormalities. It may also affect the structures of the eye as they are developing during the first trimester of pregnancy. Rubella was most common during the early 1960s but has been greatly reduced by the routine administration of vaccine. Outbreaks of rubella still occur in unvaccinated individuals, however.

Eye injuries   When one eye is damaged in an accident or trauma and the vision of the other eye remains in the normal range, the individual is not considered visually impaired. The degree of impairment depends on the type and degree of injury to the eye.

Identification and Assessment

When parents or teachers observe indicators of a visual problem, screening or more in-depth assessment procedures are initiated. Many visual difficulties are correctable with eyeglasses or contact lenses. When this is not possible, procedures for the comprehensive, individual assessment described in Chapter 2 are implemented. Its focus is on the degree of vision available (few children are actually blind), with four major aspects being assessed: visual acuity, visual field, color vision, and perception of light. In addition to testing the vision components, it should evaluate intelligence and cognitive development, psychomotor skills, academic achievement, unique academic needs, computer skills, listening skills, print-reading skills, quality of social interactions, orientation and mobility skills, functional and daily living skills, recreational and leisure skills, and community and vocational skills (Curry & Hatlin, 1988; Scholl, 1986). Consideration is also given to the age of onset of the visual impairment; the chronological age of the student; whether the condition is stable, deteriorating, fluctuating, or improving; the presence of additional impairments; the motivational level of the student;

reports from teachers on the social behavior and mobility of the student in the classroom; and the parents' concerns.

Examples of the types of information often included in a functional vision report are listed in Box 9.1.

Care must be exercised when administering any tests that rely primarily on vision, so that the student is not at a disadvantage because of the visual impairment. Standardized tests may have to be modified by allowing extra time or by having sections read to the student. If such modifications are made, they must be reported so that the validity of the test under such conditions may be estimated. Some tests widely used in the schools to assess sighted children are also available in large print or braille—for example, the Iowa Test of Basic Skills, the Stanford Reading Achievement Tests, and the KeyMath Diagnostic Test. The use of criterion-referenced tests, direct observation, teacher-developed tests, checklists, and interviews may provide additional information that helps determine the student's abilities.

Vision specialists who may be involved in the assessment of a child suspected of having a visual impairment include the following.

- *Ophthalmologists,* medical doctors who have continued their medical studies into the diagnosis and treatment of eye disorders. An ophthalmologist may perform surgery and prescribe medical treatment, medications, or lenses.
- *Optometrists,* nonmedical but licensed professionals who can measure refractive errors, eye muscle imbalances, and color vision problems, and who can prescribe corrective lenses. If medical conditions are suspected, an optometrist will refer the child to an ophthalmologist.
- *Opticians,* individuals who make lenses (grind them), fit the lenses into frames, and ensure their proper fit on the wearer. Opticians fill the prescriptions of optometrists or ophthalmologists for lenses.

Box 9.1 Functional Vision Report Measures

1. Nature of the eye condition and its educational implications; acuity (both near and far); color vision; preferred eye; preferred field of view; degree of light sensitivity
2. Ability to use distance vision in reading wall clocks; viewing overheads, films, slides, or flip charts; writing on the chalkboard; viewing television; using telescopes; distances required from materials for optimal vision
3. Ability to use near vision in reading; preferred print size; need for aids such as book stands, magnifiers, closed-circuit television, special lighting, or filters
4. Student's preferences for column width, spacing, and contrast in print materials; color of filters; reading speed; illumination; and seating in relation to light sources and ability to see (both far and near)
5. Student's need for special writing tools or paper or for extra time in writing tasks; ability to use braillewriter, computer, or typewriter
6. Degree of skills related to orientation and mobility such as balance, coordination, use of stairs, sound localization, use of left and right, outdoor and indoor play, reading street signs, riding a bicycle or roller skating, use of maps, use of school bus or public transportation, and location of rooms such as cafeteria, restrooms, and classrooms

- *Orthoptists,* nonmedical technicians who, under the supervision of ophthalmologists or optometrists, direct prescribed exercises or training to ameliorate the effects of muscle imbalances, to improve fusion, or to stimulate the use of central vision.
- *Vision specialists,* individuals who may have a variety of titles but who are likely to teach students with vision impairments or be the school's vision consultant.

The team members who develop the IEP include vision specialists, the classroom teacher, a teacher of the visually impaired, orientation and mobility experts, an administrator or special education supervisor, parents, and others, as described in Chapter 2. Additional information regarding options or services may be acquired through consultation with residential school personnel and low-vision clinics (Harley et al., 1989).

One or more of the vision specialists may be part of the assessment team for initial identification purposes and for periodic reevaluations as necessary or directed by law. Here are some of the tests that can form the screening process prior to referring children to an ophthalmologist or optometrist for further evaluation.

- The Snellen chart
- The Keystone Telebinocular, which measures both far and near distance vision, depth perception, color discrimination, the separate functioning of each eye, the functioning of both eyes together, and other visual abilities
- The Titmus Vision Tester, designed to assess acuity and the tendency of the muscles to pull the eyeball upward, downward, inward, or outward
- The Farnsworth Dichotomous Test for Color Blindness (Farnsworth, 1947); the Dvorine Pseudo-Isochromatic Plates (Dvorine, 1953); and the Ishihara Color Blind Test (Ishihara, 1970), all of which determine color vision (more commonly called color blindness)

Salvia and Ysseldyke (1988) suggested the use of at least two different tests to screen for color vision so that the likelihood of errors and consequent unnecessary referrals is reduced.

Routine screening procedures for detecting potential visual problems are in place in most schools. Alert teachers and parents, by noticing behaviors indicative of potential vision deficiencies, are perhaps the most important individuals in ensuring that appropriate referrals for further assessment are conducted for preschool and school-age children (see Box 9.2 for such behavioral indicators). Children are often unaware of their own visual deficiencies. Personnel in hospitals and clinics assess the visual abilities of newborns and infants, and local agencies as well as Child Find programs offer screening for visual impairments in young children.

The placement of students with visual impairments follows the principle of least restrictive placement described in Chapter 2. It may be in the regular classroom, with the services of an itinerant teacher of the visually impaired, or in any of several more restrictive placements depending on the student's educational programming needs as determined during the assessment process and discussions among the staffing team. The most common type of service delivery system is that of itinerant teacher (Harley et al., 1989).

Identification procedures are conducted to assess both the strengths and limitations of the visual impairment so that interventions may be developed and implemented to ensure an appropriate education for the student.

The educational needs of students with visual impairments may be divided into two categories: instruction in academic areas and instruction in disability-specific skills (Curry & Hatlin, 1988). Instruction in the traditional academic areas of reading, mathematics, science, social studies, and so on is the same as that for all other youngsters. The disability-specific skills include learning to be independent

Box 9.2
Behavioral and Observable Indicators of Vision Impairments

BEHAVIORAL INDICATORS

Rubbing the eyes, especially during close work

Sensitivity to light, indicated by shielding the eyes or turning away from the light

Complaints of burning, itching, or "sandiness" in the eyelids

Unusual facial expressions caused by squinting or blinking during near or far visual work

Difficulty in reading

- Reversal of letters: *n* for *u, p* for *d,* etc.
- Confusion of letters with similar shapes: *e* and *c, m* and *n,* etc.
- Reversal of words: *no* for *on, was* for *saw,* etc.
- Losing the place in a sentence or on the page

Closing or covering one eye during near or far visual tasks

Tilting or frequently moving the head during near or far visual work

Holding materials too close or too far away

Difficulty in writing

- Poor spacing between letters or words
- Reversals in writing letters: *q* for *p,* etc.
- Reversals in writing words: *pan* for *nap,* etc.
- Difficulty staying on the writing guide lines
- Severely slanted lines when writing on unlined paper

Complaints of discomfort while completing close visual tasks

Complaints of dizziness, headaches, or nausea during or after close visual work

Difficulty in seeing at a distance, indicated by a preference for close visual activities rather than playground or gym activities, etc.

OBSERVABLE INDICATORS

Red eyes

Red eyelids

Crustiness of eyelids or eyelashes

Swollen eyes

Watery eyes

Discharge from the eyes

Crossed eyes

Drooping eyelids

Pupils of uneven size

One eye physically lower than the other

Recurring sties

through **mobility training,** daily living skills, social skills, communication skills, recreational skills, the use of technological and nontechnological aids and devices that enable or enhance the acquisition of academic skills, and career and vocational skills.

A distinction may also be made between devices, skills, and aids used by students with low vision and by those who are blind. It will not be emphasized here but is of critical importance in the discussions of the staffing team and the development of the student's IEP. Here we simply discuss the wide range of skills that must be developed and the aids that are available to assist the student in learning and becoming an independent adult.

■ **The Development of Independence**

As we saw earlier, orientation and mobility are essential skills for all individuals but require specific training to develop in those whose sense of vision is impaired or unavailable. The ability to move about in the environment in a safe and efficient fashion directly contributes to the development of independence in the individual and, according to Tuttle (1984), fosters self-esteem.

Different techniques and aids for safe and efficient mobility are utilized depending on the personality, motivation, age, and other characteristics of the individual. Basic orientation skills are taught from a very early age and are essential prerequisites to the use of other techniques or aids in mobility.

Independent travel is accomplished through use of the auditory, tactual, **kinesthetic,** and olfactory senses plus any residual vision. Persons with low vision or who are blind cannot hear any better than others, but they may have learned to use their auditory powers more effectively than those who rely on vision to guide them. The five modes of travel commonly used by persons with visual disorders are (1) independent travel without the use of devices or other outside assistance, (2) reliance on a sighted guide, (3) the use of canes, (4) the use of a dog guide, and (5) the use of electronic devices.

Independent travel Without any assistance or device, this is probably the mode most commonly used among school-age children. Certain basic protective techniques are prerequisite to other modes of travel and are designed to ensure safe and efficient travel. These skills are taught at a very early age or immediately after the onset of the visual impairment. Some of the skills or techniques are as follows.

1. Using the hand and forearm in a raised position to protect the head and upper body from half-open doors, walls, and other potentially dangerous obstacles
2. Using the hand and forearm in a lowered position to protect the lower body from desks, tables, and other obstacles
3. **Trailing,** or lightly tracing straight surfaces with the backs of the fingertips to locate specific objects or to establish a parallel line of direction
4. Direction taking, or using an object or sound to establish a course of direction toward or away from an object

Patterns of familiarization, geographic directions, hearing acuteness for travel, sound localization, and the use of residual vision for detecting light or shadow are other necessary skills that are taught to foster independent travel.

Sighted guide technique   An efficient way to orient an individual to an unfamiliar area is to use a sighted guide. The person with the visual disorder grasps the sighted person's arm just above the elbow, placing the thumb on the outside and the fingers on the inside of the arm and walking about half a step behind the guide. In effect, the individual is "reading" the guide's arm or elbow, and any movement of the body or arm is communicated, so that appropriate adjustments can be made—such as stepping up or down or turning left or right.

Canes   The age at which an individual is trained to use a cane depends on his or her maturity and need for independent travel. In general, the use of canes was formerly not taught until the individual was about 16 years of age, but some now advocate teaching it to preschoolers. They argue that using a cane increases the child's mobility, making possible increased early exploration of the environment, increased self-confidence, and less dependence on others (K. L. Clark, 1988; Pogrund & Rosen, 1989).

Of the many types of canes, the most common are made of aluminum or fiberglass, are approximately half an inch in diameter, have a rubber grip for holding, a nylon or steel tip, and a crook for balance and easy placement. Users sweep the cane in an arc ahead of them to detect variations in the terrain or obstacles in the path. Efficient use of the cane allows the traveler to become aware of curbs, stairs, inclines, holes, and changes in the travel surface (such as grass to sidewalk) prior to encountering them. The cane provides information about the environment from ground level to about a foot above, but does not warn of higher hazards such as low-hanging wires or tree branches; nor can it reveal the total environment, especially in unfamiliar areas.

Dog guide   Seeing Eye dogs are not usually recommended for individuals under 16, because children may not have the maturity to direct the dog effectively—and they may have less need for independent travel. Contrary to the popular stereotype, only about 2% of individuals with vision impairments use dog guides. These dogs are taught to obey commands such as to walk forward, stop, turn right or left, walk faster or slower, locate a door, sit, lie down, and fetch dropped objects. They must also recognize when it is safe to cross a street and detect and lead their owners around obstacles. Persons using a dog guide must have well-developed orientation skills, because they must give the dog commands in order to arrive at the appropriate destination. The dog does not find locations alone; it follows directions. People seeking to use a dog guide are assessed for their maturity, ability to care for and command an animal, physical health, and orientation skills; they are then matched with a dog by factors such as size and personality. They then undergo intensive training together in safe and effective travel.

Electronic travel aids   These are used either as a primary mobility device or as a supplement to other devices such as canes. Here are some common electronic travel aids.

- The Mowat Sensor is a hand-held device that detects obstacles by means of a high-frequency sound. The sensor vibrates when it detects an obstacle, increasing the vibration rate as the obstacle is approached.
- The Sonicguide, built into glasses or worn on the head, detects obstacles and provides information about their distance, position, and surface features. It

DOROTHY HARRISON EUSTIS—"I'M FREE"

Dorothy Harrison was born in 1886 into a distinguished, wealthy Philadelphia family. As a young woman she owned a dog named Hans who was strong, courageous, intelligent, and faithful. Dorothy loved Hans and became interested in breeding German shepherds that would have the same characteristics. It was, to her way of thinking, a tribute to Hans.

She married George Eustis and moved to Switzerland but kept alive the dream of breeding shepherds. She began to work toward that goal by converting a chalet into a kennel known as Fortunate Fields. Her dogs distinguished themselves as highly trained working dogs. They were used as army messengers, where they were often the only reliable form of communication. Eventually they received a commendation from the Swiss army for their service.

Dorothy went to Germany in 1927; there she observed the precision with which dogs were trained to guide veterans of World War I who had been blinded. She saw the dogs assist their masters in making decisions. She saw men striding along sidewalks, walking up and down stairs, and crossing streets as easily as if they were sighted. Dorothy was astounded by the independence of these men who were blind. But she noticed one man who seemed insecure, walking with a hesitant, shuffling gait. Later she saw the same man with his dog and was amazed at the change in his demeanor. He strode along with confidence, just as the other men had. She knew then that she must begin a similar program. She was so moved that she wrote an article describing what she had seen for the *Saturday Evening Post* titled "The Seeing Eye." Dorothy chose that title from Proverbs 20:12—"the hearing ear and the seeing eye, the Lord has made both of them."

The article came to the attention of Morris Frank, a Nashville man who was blind. He wrote to Dorothy and asked how he could establish such a program in the United States. She told him to come to Switzerland to learn how to use a guide dog. People thought he was crazy for "going halfway round the world to learn how to be led around by a dog." One day in Switzerland, after he had achieved some skill in using his dog, Buddy, he decided he needed a haircut and asked to be taken for one. Dorothy told him that she would give him directions but that he should take Buddy and go. Later that evening he said, "Buddy and I did something by ourselves today, a simple little thing—but for the first time since I got here I know I'm going to be free—I'm free!"

When Morris and Buddy returned to America, Morris knew that he would have to convince Americans that their relationship was dignified and merited respect. He knew many would perceive it as a dumb animal leading a beggar around on a rope, because in 1928 most Americans viewed people who were blind as dependent and often as beggars.

Morris began to receive letters from individuals inquiring how they might get a Seeing Eye dog too. He wrote Dorothy to urge her to start something in America, and she agreed.

She arrived ready to establish a training program for dogs, but securing financial backing proved more formidable than she had expected. People were curious and marveled at what the dogs did, but they were not interested in contributing. In the meantime, Dorothy subsidized the program. Eventually she gained the support of wealthy New Yorkers and took her cause to other large cities. Dorothy spoke literally hundreds of times all over the country to gain this support.

The school began in Nashville in 1929, moved to the Morristown, New Jersey, area in 1931, and to its present location in 1965. The original house was demolished and a building built to Seeing Eye's specifications. They currently are in the final stage of an expansion program to accommodate 30% more blind people each year.

Seeing Eye, Inc., the training center Dorothy established, is now supported by an endowment of more than $60 million. Costs are nominal: $150 for the first dog and $50 for each replacement. Seeing Eye pays for the students' round-trip fare and room and board for the month of training. Nearly 230 people are matched with and trained to use a guide dog each year. Dorothy Eustis's tireless efforts and her love of Hans have provided independence for many people, enabling them as well to say "I'm free."

emits a high-frequency sound whose detection echoes are converted into stereophonic signals that are interpreted by the wearer.

- The Laser Cane converts infrared light into sound that warns the user of obstacles or drop-offs. The beams include upper, lower, and midrange signals to provide the user with full height protection.
- The Russell Pathsounder emits an ultrasonic signal when an obstacle is located. Chest-mounted and supported by a neck strap, it provides both auditory and tactile signals.

In a national survey to determine the use of electronic travel aids, researchers found the most frequently used to be the Laser Cane and the Mowat Sensor (Blasch, Long, & Griffin-Shirley, 1989).

■ Teaching Life Skills

Life skills include all activities that are part of the daily routine; they change according to the age of the individual. Such skills are often referred to as TDL (techniques of daily living) skills. Learning to play, eat, dress, and so forth characterizes the daily routine of a very young child. As the child grows older, personal grooming and hygiene, selecting appropriate clothing, and learning such simple household tasks as washing dishes, taking out the garbage, and cleaning are added. Still later come more complex household chores such as sewing or mowing the lawn; earning, saving, and spending money; care of clothing; and food purchasing and preparation. During development from childhood to adulthood, social and recreational opportunities also expand and require increasingly complex skills.

Sighted persons learn many of these skills by observation and imitation. Infants, using their vision, are aware of food that their parents and siblings select and lift from plate to mouth. Children who are unable to observe that procedure must be specifically taught. Similarly, simple tasks such as determining the front and back of a shirt or blouse or how to match the colors of a shirt and slacks must be taught. The more complex skills of managing money, grocery shopping, doing laundry, and housekeeping—which sighted children have observed long before they are expected to perform them—must be taught to individuals with vision disorders.

The skills required for daily living are almost limitless and continue to be learned and refined throughout life. Some educators question whether teaching such skills is the responsibility of the school. Tuttle (1984) responds that they are not optional "frills" but are an essential complement to success in academic areas. Many of these skills can be incorporated into school curricula. Some of the broad areas that can be addressed in school include purchasing and caring for clothing, managing a home, personal care, purchasing and preparing food, managing finances, and participating in such civic responsibilities as voting.

Social skills   The development of social skills depends on visual feedback; for sighted individuals they are frequently learned incidentally. Adequate social skills add a dimension of quality to life, and their absence leads to lonely, isolated lives. Seemingly minor aspects of social interaction such as maintaining erect body posture, establishing eye contact, knowing how to sit while wearing a dress, and identifying and articulating personal emotions or needs are powerful enhancements of social interaction. Broad skill areas that benefit from special instruction include (1) being aware of and discriminating between behavior that is appropriate when alone and when in public, (2) developing confidence in one's abilities, (3) establishing and maintaining close personal relationships, (4) recognizing alternatives and consequences, and (5) understanding the need for goals and how to achieve them.

Developing competence in these skills may be difficult for any person and is usually a lifelong task. The need to learn them is not unique to individuals with vision disorders, but because their visual input is diminished their awareness of and ability to imitate them may also be diminished.

No one is totally independent; we all require assistance from time to time. Skill in asking for help and refusing unnecessary assistance in a positive manner as well as in offering assistance to others must be learned by all. But individuals with impaired vision may require additional teaching. Risk-taking behaviors—defined as "those that are new, are a combination of previously learned behaviors applied to a new situation, and those for which the end result cannot be firmly determined until the deed is accomplished" (Swallow & Huebner, 1987, p. 30)—must also be fostered. Such encouragement broadens the experience of the individual, hastens the development of concepts, enhances coordination, and leads to feelings of accomplishment and self-worth. Problem-solving skills often learned by sighted children in an incidental manner are taught to persons with visual impairments, primarily through verbal input. Additional challenges to individuals with impaired sight include choosing appropriate styles of dress, encountering obstacles in familiar environments, obtaining class notes from a peer, and other activities that develop problem-solving skills (Swallow & Huebner, 1987).

Recreational and leisure skills   Students with visual impairments will need to learn adaptations of common recreations, in some cases. Audible balls, goal finders, braille game boards such as checkers and bingo, and large-type crossword puzzles are some of the materials available to encourage the development of recreational and leisure skills. The broad spectrum of recreational and leisure activities taught to persons with vision impairments includes, but is not limited to, water activities such as rafting, swimming, and snorkling; hobbies such as ham radio operation, sewing, and collecting buttons or rocks; dance activities such as popular dance, folk dancing, and ballet; drama activities; arts and crafts; and attendance at cultural offerings such as spectator sports, concerts, museums, and plays. Organized activities for youth such as Boy Scouts or Girl Scouts, children's theater, religious groups, and special-interest clubs provide age-appropriate opportunities for the productive use of leisure time and for social interaction; they also contribute to experiences that enhance academic learning. The preceding activities are representative of the innumerable skills and activities that are a part of daily living. At what point such skills are taught to persons who are blind or who have low vision depends on the age of the individual and his or her level of vision, previous experiences, and personal likes and dislikes. According to Swallow and Huebner (1987), the general sequence for teaching and developing such skills is as follows.

1. Learning a specific skill through small, structured, systematic steps—often being manually guided through the action by another person providing verbal information
2. Incorporating the skill into a daily routine
3. Applying the skill as appropriate occasions arise

Of the many types of transitions through which an individual progresses (see Chapter 13), that from school to employment and adulthood may be the most important. It is the combination of life skills, recreational and leisure skills, social skills, and academic skills that makes such transitions occur smoothly. These skills apply to all aspects of life and are synthesized, generalized, and continue to evolve so that the individual is enabled to live a full, satisfying, and productive life.

Academic and Specialized Curriculum Considerations

The academic curriculum of students with vision impairments is similar to that of their peers. However, as we previously noted, they may experience some delay in the motor, cognitive, communicative, and social domains as a result of their visual limitations. This section will cover the various adaptations, modifications, and devices that may assist them in the learning process.

The usual principles of effective teaching apply equally to teachers of students with vision impairments; however, certain additional principles should receive special emphasis (Lowenfeld, 1981).

■ Concreteness

Students with visual impairments use the tactile sense to gain knowledge of size, shape, texture, pliability, hardness or softness, and surface qualities. Verbal descriptions complement and help integrate the information. When actual objects are too large (mountains, ships) or too small (amoebas, parts of a flower, insects) to be investigated through the tactile sense, models that enlarge or contract them can provide the information required to construct the concept. When models are used the student must be told that the information is distorted. For example, models of mountain ranges provide some of the information required to develop the concept, but the vastness and height of the mountains are distorted.

■ Unified Instruction and Experiences

Vision serves as a unifying sense; it incorporates perception with auditory, tactile, and kinesthetic information, leading to a totality of experience. Unless specific efforts are made to assist vision-impaired students with concept unification, their impressions may be fragmented. A unit approach gives them a chance to organize and unify information. For example, a field trip to a farm provides an opportunity for experiencing component parts and the totality of a farm. This aids in the development of more complete concepts regarding animals, farm buildings, farm equipment or tools, and crops raised on a farm. Academic skills such as spelling, writing, mathematics, reading, and science may be integrated into the unit.

■ Independence

All students must learn to accomplish tasks independently, but when the ability to imitate is diminished because of impaired vision, additional assistance must be provided. The emphasis of such instruction is on learning the task but also on independent performance, which discourages an attitude of helplessness and

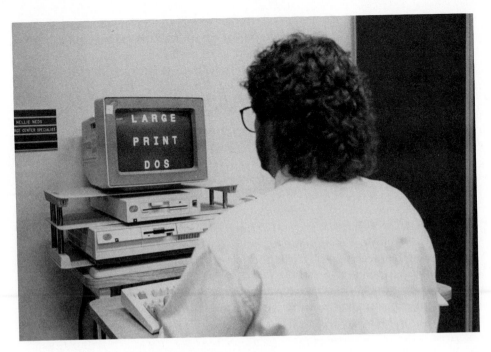

■ Large-print software for individuals with low vision. ■

fosters self-confidence and independence. This principle applies to all aspects of learning, whether it be using an optical aid, learning mobility, or in academic areas.

Educating students who are blind or who have low vision means providing additional opportunities for practice and a variety of experiences; teaching skills and concepts learned by sighted children through incidental observation; and teaching specific skills that are essential to individuals who have vision impairments. This may include developing and mastering additional listening skills, learning braille, or learning to use and care for such optical or communicative aids as the stylus or **optacon** (Hatlin & Curry, 1987).

■ Listening

Obtaining information through hearing is important to all students, but especially to students with vision impairments (Harley, Truan, & Sanford, 1987), because much of the information they receive may be through recorded books and technological devices that are primarily auditory. Listening skills such as discrimination and localization of sounds and sound patterns should be developed at a very early age, because they aid in mobility and stimulation. Later, such skills as following simple directions, auditory comprehension, and auditory memory are taught and developed. Finally, these skills are refined, so that an individual can organize and critically analyze auditory information. Specially trained teachers initiate a systematic, sequenced program designed to develop listening skills once the student is identified. These specialists continue as long as necessary, working in collaboration with other teachers during the school-age years. Such programs may be teacher developed or may follow specific listening skill curricula such as those produced by Alber (1974), Stocker (1973), and Swallow and Conner (1982). Additional training in listening is an example of expanding the curriculum to meet the unique needs of students.

Once listening skills are developed, speech synthesizers (a computer translation of print into speech) and recorded texts, magazines, and recreational books become efficient learning tools. Recorded materials are available from the American Printing House for the Blind, the Library of Congress, and Recordings for the Blind; additionally, each state has a library dedicated to recorded materials for the blind.

Visual Efficiency

Visual efficiency means making the best use of residual sight, no matter how limited the acuity or visual field. It may include training to develop control of eye movements, to attend to visual stimuli, and to process visual information (Barraga, 1983). Training may relate directly to the use of the eyes and of a variety of aids to assist the student to become actively involved in using vision.

Making the best use of vision implies the acceptance of visual aids on the part of the individual and, when appropriate, the ability to explain their function. The ability to effectively use low-vision aids is important but, according to Watson (1989), so is knowledge about how the devices actually work, their purpose, which ones are more suitable in various situations (classroom use or recreational use), how to clean and maintain them, and when and how to seek repairs or adjustments. It is also important to know how to employ relaxation techniques to avoid the fatigue associated with the use of certain devices; when to use vision with an aid, another sense, or another person; and how to plan in advance what optical or nonoptical devices may be required in particular situations. These attitudes and skills are not taught separately but rather as aspects of the total learning process.

Reading and Writing

Speaking, writing, listening, and reading comprise the communication skills used in academic study; they are all interrelated. For example, a speaking vocabulary is enhanced by reading, listening, and writing. In a similar manner writing ability is developed by listening, speaking, and reading. Reading in the broad sense includes reading directions for a math assignment or science experiment, reading literature, reading for information regarding a democratic form of government, and reading about science concepts.

Students with low vision may use a variety of aids to assist them in the reading process. Nonoptical aids (those not requiring a prescription) and adaptations used by the teacher include thicker chalk to make bolder lines, use of photocopied rather than dittoed materials, book stands designed to bring materials closer to the students' eyes or to angle it for improved lighting, and large-print materials that may be produced by typesetting or photoenlargement (see Figure 9.5). Other aids include yellow acetate sheets placed over print to increase contrast, dark-lined paper, felt-tip pens, a modified print style and extra spacing both between words on a line and between lines, lamps with adjustable intensities and flexible stands so they can be moved near the work area, off-white paper that

This is 8-point type.

This is 12-point type.

This is 16-point type.

This is 24-point type.

This is 30-point type.

Figure 9.5 Large print for students with low vision. Large print may be a curricular adaptation for students with low vision. Newspapers are usually 8- or 10-point type, adult books 10- or 12-point type. Large-type materials for students with low vision may be 18-point type or larger.

reduces glare, desktops that tilt, and dimmed light. Although these aids do not require prescriptions nor in general special training, they must be carefully selected to enhance the visual efficiency of the student. Low-vision specialists and teachers trained to teach students with vision impairments can provide guidance in the selection and use of such aids.

Optical aids, prescribed by ophthalmologists or optometrists who specialize in the assessment and treatment of low vision, include a variety of devices. Instruction in the care and use of these devices is provided by the vision specialist or teacher of students with vision impairments. Optical aids may be lent out for a trial period so that they can be used in the home as well as the school. Examples of optical aids are special glasses, telescopes that are hand-held or inserted into spectacles to see distant objects such as chalkboards or bulletin boards, and magnifiers that are hand-held, mounted on a stand, or clipped onto glasses. Closed-circuit TV systems in which the camera is used to scan ordinary-sized print materials permit the student to select the size of enlargement, degree of contrast, and a black-on-white or white-on-black image. Some closed-circuit televisions can be used with typewriters, computer terminals, and student-written materials.

Braille, a tactual form of reading, may be taught to students as the only method of reading or in conjunction with large print. Braille assigns a pattern of raised dots to each letter of the alphabet, another pattern for punctuation marks, and a different pattern for the numerals from 0 to 9. This form of braille produces bulky volumes of transcribed material, so another grade of braille is frequently used that substitutes a pattern of dots for common combinations of letters, such as *ing* (see Figure 9.6). This contracted form of braille requires less paper, but its materials are still larger than print materials. Students first learn grade 1 braille (letter by letter) and then progress to the grade 2 contracted form.

Braille is produced on a machine similar to a manual typewriter that has six keys corresponding to the six dots in the braille cell. When the keys are pressed, the braille characters are embossed on special heavy paper.

Braille may also be written by hand, using a stylus and slate. The stylus is a pointed instrument similar to a pencil or pen, and the slate is a metal frame with openings corresponding to the braille cells, through which the braille dots are

■ This reader provides magnification that permits the individual with low vision to utilize a variety of materials. ■

punched with the stylus. A slate and stylus require the individual to emboss the dots from right to left (in a mirror image) so that they can be read tactually on the reverse side.

Synthetic speech is a computerized transformation of phonemes into words. When information is entered into a computer, a voice output (synthetic speech) enables the user to hear that information. For example, a student composing a book report types it into the computer. A voice output will read aloud what has been written, allowing for revisions and modifications. Clocks, scales, and calculators that are referred to as "talking" also use synthetic speech.

The Xerox/Kurzweil Personal Reader is a computer-based reading machine that converts print material into synthetic speech. The speed and tone may be controlled, and the machine can also spell words letter by letter. Thus materials such as personal letters, books, or magazines may be read at speeds of up to 350 words per minute.

The optacon is an instrument that electronically scans print material and reproduces it in raised print so that it may be read tactually. It does not translate into braille; rather, it raises the actual print. As a miniature camera moves across

There will be many children out on the playground this afternoon to watch the soccer game.

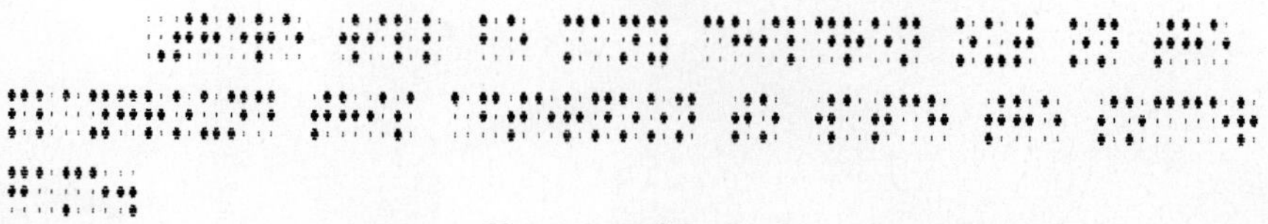

Uncontracted Braille

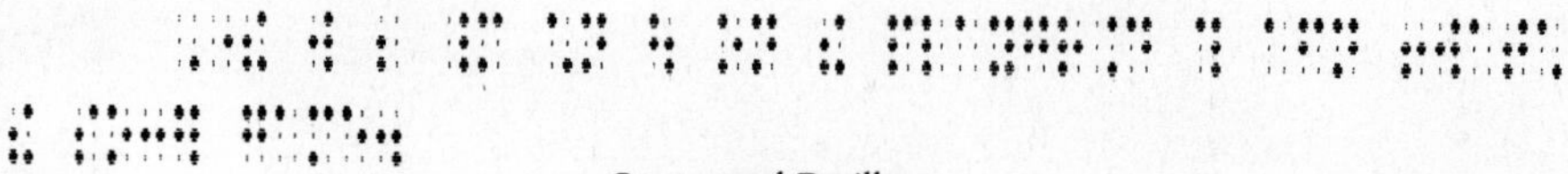

Contracted Braille

Figure 9.6 Samples of uncontracted (grade 1) and contracted (grade 2) braille

the line of print, the vibrating image of the letters is felt by the reader, whose index finger is laid on a special box that produces a tactual array. As the camera moves across the word *the,* the letters *t, h,* and *e* are felt as vibrations, with the *t* as a horizontal and vertical line. The optacon allows independent reading of a variety of print material.

A braille printer provides a braille printout of information stored in a computer's memory. The information is put into the computer in a conventional manner and may be printed using either a braille printer or a standard printer. Persons with low vision may use either one, and teachers can, for example, enter into the computer a chapter outline and print it in both standard print and braille.

Paperless braille stores braille on cassette tapes or disks. When placed in a playback unit, they generate the braille on a braille display strip. Braille 'n Speak, PocketBraille, VersaBraille II™, Eureka A4, and Note-a-Braille II are examples of paperless braille devices. The cassettes may be used in conjunction with a computer, printer, speech synthesizer, and braille printer to provide a wide variety of input and output alternatives. Braille input with print output, print input with speech output, or braille input with speech output are some of the possibilities. A 60-minute cassette can store nearly 400 pages of paper braille. VersaBraille II may be used as a portable note-taking device and also as a personal computer. VersaBraille II provides only braille output; Eureka A4, a similar note-taking device, functions as a personal computer but provides speech output.

The Cranmer Modified Perkins Brailler allows students to feed information directly into a computer and receive a braille printout. This is essentially a word-processing function in braille.

Ordinary tape recorders may be used for recording lectures or other spoken information and played back for later listening. Some tape recorders have a compressed speech option that allows for playback at speeds of up to 275 words per minute (compared with normal speech speed of 160 to 170 words per minute).

■ The Perkins Brailler. ■

■ Student using a brailler in class. ■

Typewriters are also used, and typing skills are usually taught to students with low vision or who are blind. The same typing skills are, of course, applicable to computer usage.

Handwriting as a means of communication may or may not be taught to a student with a visual impairment, depending on the degree of remaining vision. If the ability to develop the eye/hand coordination necessary for writing and the ability to visually monitor handwriting are restricted, only the ability to sign one's name is taught. This is essential because of all the legal applications, civic responsibilities, and banking activities that require signatures. Small templates or writing guides constructed of plastic, cardboard, or metal with a rectangular opening in the center provide boundaries for writing signatures. Checkbooks with a raised (embossed) signature line are also available.

The alternative methods of reading and writing are carefully selected and matched to the student's aptitude, age, developed and developing skills, long-

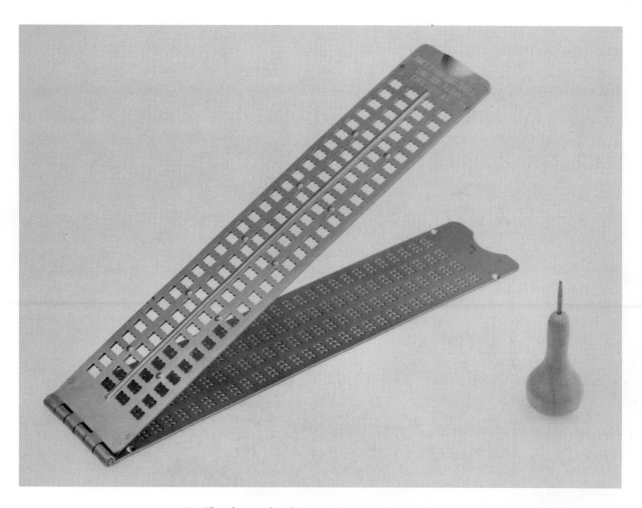

■ The slate and stylus permit note taking and are easy to carry. ■

term goals, and degree of visual impairment. It would be unlikely that any one student would be taught to use all of the various aids described or to use all methods of reading and writing. Teachers, parents, vision specialists, and, when appropriate, the student decide what aids will be used and what alternative reading or writing methods may be implemented; this information is incorporated into the IEP (Scholl, 1987). The special skills required (as in reading or writing braille) represent another facet of the additional curriculum.

■ Other Content Areas

Achievement in content areas such as science, mathematics, history, and geography assumes prerequisite skills in reading and writing. The communication alternatives and devices described in the previous section will be applied by the student in the content curricular areas. In addition, adapted materials and curric-

■ This model of the moon, in the exhibits room at the Johnson Space Center in Dallas, Texas, enables the student to develop a concept of the variations in the moon's surface. ■

ula are available to provide students with vision impairments the means to develop the concepts related to those areas. Examples include, but are not limited to, the following.

Mathematics aids
- Compasses, rulers, protractors, and slide rules with braille markings
- A braille code (Nemeth Code) that enables the student to perform more complex mathematical calculations
- A Cranmer abacus—used for counting, addition, and subtraction—that is pocket sized and has a special backing to prevent accidental movement of the beads
- Clock faces with either raised or braille numerals
- Models of geometric areas and of volume that are hand-held

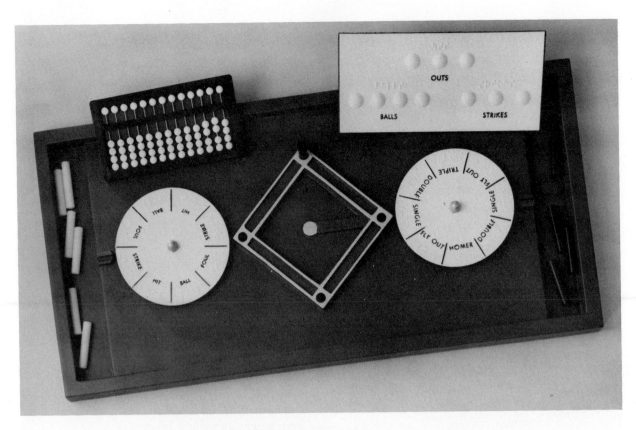

■ This baseball game for students with visual impairments is a valuable learning tool. ■

- Wire forms for matched planes and volume
- Calculators with voice output that report entries and results
- Form boards for manipulation of whole and fractional parts

Geography aids
- Braille atlases
- Embossed relief and landform maps
- Molded plastic dissected maps
- Enlarged or textured maps

Science aids
- Machine kits, including working models of pulleys and levers and of wheels and axles
- Spring-loaded scales
- Braille thermometers
- Insect identification kits
- An entire curriculum designed for teaching students with vision impairments includes all necessary adaptations. The Science Activities for the Visually Impaired curriculum teaches science concepts related to earth science, magnetism, electricity, biology, and others.

Social studies aids

* Materials Adaptation for Visually Impaired Students in Social Studies is a modi-fied curriculum that includes adaptations to enable students with vision impair-ments to participate in the same activities designed to promote learning as their sighted peers.

Physical education aids

* Audible balls
* Audible goal locators that may be used as a goal, base, or warning for other objects
* Raised drawings and models of various sports fields or courts

Issues and Trends

There are several issues related to the education of individuals with visual impair-ments. The concerns span all age ranges—from preschool through school-age and into adulthood—and some appear to question national trends.

The passage of PL 99-457 (see Chapter 12) and the modification of state laws to provide special education services to infants and preschoolers have led to new questions about appropriate curricular activities for these children. An example is the development of orientation and mobility skills programs for preschoolers that may include the use of a cane (Hill, 1988). It was previously assumed that young children should be taught "precane" skills but not the actual use of the cane until later, when their motor, cognitive, and social skills were ready. A variety of low-cost, readily available mobility devices, some of which were designed espe-cially for children with visual impairments, and other general-purpose devices such as suspended swings, toys propelled by pushing with the feet, wheeled push toys, and pedaled vehicles such as tricycles may be incorporated into the activities for infants and preschoolers. Proponents suggest that the planned use of these types of devices will increase body awareness and independent movement and will enable children to more effectively explore their environment (K. L. Clark, 1988; Pogrund & Rosen, 1989).

The shortage of teachers trained to teach unique curricular content to per-sons with visual impairments is a major worry (Head, 1989; Spungin, 1989). This is not a new phenomenon, but it is exacerbated by the increasing numbers of children with visual impairments and the recent extension of services to infants and preschoolers (Head, 1989; Kirchner, 1988). A related concern is the shortage of teachers with training to meet the needs of children with multiple impairments, including visual ones (Kirchner & Peterson, 1988). As this population continues to grow, the training of teachers may require crossing the traditional areas of exper-tise.

The provision of services to youngsters with visual impairments in age-appropriate, general education classrooms has steadily increased (American Print-ing House for the Blind, 1989; Kirchner, 1988). Whether or not that trend ensures adequate preparation for independent adult living and the full range of employ-ment opportunities is in question (Curry & Hatlin, 1988; Gallagher, 1988). There may not be sufficient time to adequately teach all aspects of the disability-specific skills in mainstream settings. Curry and Hatlin (1988) suggest that the "environment in which the student is educated is of less importance than the fact that the student is being thoroughly prepared for adult living" (p. 422). They add that if more restrictive placements are necessary for a time, the IEP must include specific alternative opportunities for work and recreation with sighted peers.

The most widely used delivery system of services to students with visual impairments is that of the itinerant teacher. However, because of the teacher shortage these teachers' caseloads often limit their visits to a student to once or twice weekly (Rex, 1989; Tuttle, 1986). Some worry that skills related to orientation, mobility, the use of specialized equipment such as the braillewriter or optacon, and similar disability-specific skills cannot be adequately taught without longer, more concentrated time. The problem is not the delivery system but rather the heavy caseloads, which, according to Rex (1989), may constitute a restrictive environment for students whose needs are not adequately met.

The technological advances that enhance the learning process and prepare students for a broader range of employment opportunities are costly; therefore, accessibility is often limited. Laser Canes, Sonicguides, and computers and word processors with braille-to-print and print-to-braille capabilities are examples of available equipment that remains costly. The relatively small numbers of students requiring such equipment lead schools to prefer other materials that will benefit a larger number of students when budgets are tight. Similarly, families and individuals often cannot afford such aids. While costs have decreased for many such items, they are still significant (Blasch et al., 1989).

The acceptance of persons with visual impairments in the workplace is an unresolved issue. The Americans with Disabilities Act and individuals with visual impairments' increased awareness of their rights provide new avenues for employment but do not ensure acceptance by sighted peers.

Summary

The treatment of individuals with visual impairments has passed through the stages of separation, ward status or protectionism, self-emancipation, education, and assimilation. The move toward assimilation with the sighted population came quickly once the public recognized that blind persons could learn effectively through tactual methods such as braille. Physical integration, however, does not necessarily result in social integration, and legal mandates for equal opportunity in employment are not always followed.

The anatomy and functioning of the eye and visual systems are well understood. Legal definitions of visual impairment emphasize visual acuity and visual field; an individual is legally blind when the central visual acuity is 20/200 or less in the better eye after correction or when the field of vision is no more than 20 degrees in diameter. Educational definitions and terminology emphasize the amount of useful vision in relation to educational settings. Although most students with visual impairments have otherwise normal learning abilities, approximately one-third have other disabilities, making educational planning more complex.

Educational programming may be approached with respect to two broad categories: instruction in academic areas and instruction in disability-specific skills. Instruction in academic areas involves the use of braille or other assistive devices that permit the individual to learn without vision or with low vision. Disability-specific skills include skills that permit safe, efficient movement about the environment, life skills, and social and recreational skills. A variety of special equipment to assist the individual to function more successfully is available and in use.

The development of adequate life skills remains one of the major areas of concern for individuals who are blind. This includes learning personal hygiene, how to select appropriate clothing, how to accomplish simple household tasks such as dish washing or more complex tasks such as food preparation, care of clothing, and earning, saving, and spending money. Both general and specific social skills also require direct instruction.

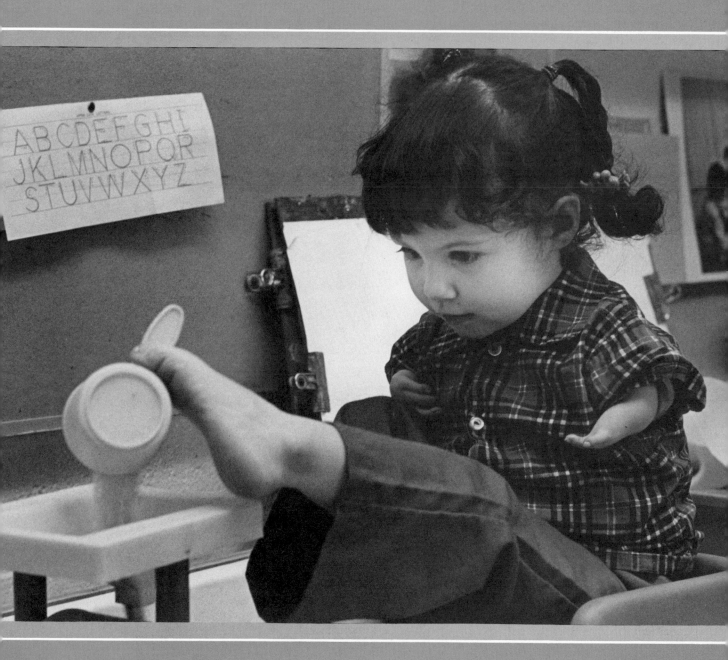

Angelica was born with spina bifida, which was surgically corrected shortly after birth. Now 17 years old, she has interests similar to those of other girls her age. She likes high school, belongs to the photography club, and has many girlfriends. She doesn't date, because although boys talk to her in school and seem friendly enough, they don't ask her out. She thinks it's because they aren't sure how to help her in and out of the car with her wheelchair.

Angelica and her friends enjoy going to the mall, but that, too, presents problems. Although the stores are supposedly wheelchair accessible, some of them have a step or two that is not noticeable to others. Such steps can be a major obstacle if you are in a wheelchair. The rest rooms indicate that they are accessible, but there really isn't enough room to maneuver a wheelchair around in them. None of the sinks is low enough, and some have a cabinet underneath so that it's impossible to get up to them in a wheelchair. The same is true of drinking fountains. The dressing rooms in the stores aren't large enough for a wheelchair, either.

Angelica has friends who live just a few blocks from her house, but the curbs are not ramped. She goes to visit them anyway, but wonders why ramps aren't more common rather than being the exception. But Angelica is not about to let all this get her down. She says, "Sooner or later people will realize that there are people like me." About the mall she says, "Sometimes I feel like marching into the manager's office and telling her that I spend money there, too, and if they want my money they better make it easy for me to be there."

Albert has juvenile rheumatoid arthritis. He has difficulty using his hands

CHAPTER TEN

Physical or Health Impairments

for writing and other activities that require gripping. This is particularly diffi-
cult for Albert, because two years ago he didn't have any problems.

Albert has to use large pencils in school, which he hates because "They're
like the little kids use." He is learning to use the computer, because that doesn't
require the same gripping that a pencil does and therefore is not as painful.

Albert misses playing ball, riding his bike, and going fishing more than
anything. The doctor told him that he has to balance his exercise and rest. This
is easier said than done. He experiences some pain in his finger joints when he
uses his hands a lot, but if he rests them too much they get stiff. Last week Albert
told his mother that he doesn't like going to bed at night because his hands hurt
so much when he uses them in the morning.

It's a lot for a 10-year-old boy to learn to deal with.

Students with mental retardation or learning disabilities require special education interventions because their disability directly affects the learning process. That is, the teaching/learning process must be different because of their unique learning characteristics. In contrast, unless students with physical or health impairments have other disabilities, they can learn successfully if (1) the school program is made accessible, (2) transportation and architectural barriers are removed, (3) adaptations are provided so they can do such things as turn pages, indicate answers in ways other than writing, and move into and out of learning environments. These and similar provisions can greatly offset the effects of their physical disabilities or health conditions.

Definitions and Classification of Physical Disorders and Health Impairments

Physical impairments or disorders may be defined and classified in a variety of ways, but we will follow the classification guidelines provided in Public Law 94-142.

It may be useful to first review how federal terminology for such impairments has changed over the years. When it first provided funds to encourage more effective education of the students who are the focus of this chapter, the government used the term *crippled and other health impaired,* so the acronym *COHI* became popular. Before long, however, federal officials and members of Congress realized the negative connotations of the word *crippled,* and the terminology became *orthopedic impairments* and *health impairments.* Today the term *crippled* is almost never used, but terms such as *physically handicapped, physically disabled,* and *physically impaired* are often heard. Some authors use these terms

■ This girl, an able hitter and runner, doesn't let her prosthesis slow her down. ■

to include both orthopedic and health impairments; others refer to a second category as *health impairments, special health conditions,* or perhaps *chronic health conditions.*

We will classify and discuss the various physical and health conditions under two general headings: (1) orthopedic and neurological disorders and (2) health impairments and special health care needs. In so doing, we follow a modified version of a classification system suggested by Umbreit (1983). This system expands **orthopedic impairments** to the term *orthopedic and neurological disorders.* Physical impairments or disorders are defined as those that involve primarily the joints, skeleton, and muscles and that interfere with an individual's mobility, motor coordination, general muscular ability, ability to maintain posture and balance, or communication skills to the extent that they inhibit learning or social development. Although vision and hearing impairments may be thought of as physical impairments or disorders, they are not included in this general classification but are considered separately.

Health impairments are conditions or diseases that disrupt and interfere with normal daily functioning—and thus possibly with the learning process—unless special interventions are implemented. Special health care needs grow out of or are related to health impairments. They may require educators to pay special attention to such areas as administering or monitoring medication; modifying participation in physical activities; providing for in-school rest; carefully observing and monitoring the physical condition; recognizing specific signs and symptoms of need for assistance; and initiating appropriate emergency procedures.

Other classification systems have been proposed, of course: for example, Bigge (1991) designates five major categories of students as having special health care needs. Bigge's categories, and a brief description of each, follow.

Students with chronic special health care needs Students with chronic health conditions make up the majority of the special health care needs population and ordinarily can participate in the regular class program with only minor modifications. Morrow suggests a differentiation between children who are chronically ill and those with more stable physical disabilities. She remarks that "chronic illnesses are often life-threatening or life-limiting," that "chronic illnesses are rarely cured," and that the chronically ill are different because of "the changeable course of an illness, the unpredictable future outcome, and, in many instances, the suffering of chronic pain" (1985, pp. 23, 24). Examples of such pain include the almost continual joint pain of juvenile rheumatoid arthritis and the possibility of excruciating pain during crisis periods of sickle cell anemia. Both Morrow and Bigge note that because many of the symptoms of such conditions are invisible, teachers and classmates may be nearly unaware of those special health problems. Bigge lists among chronic health conditions asthma, congenital heart disease, diabetes, leukemia, seizure disorders, spina bifida, sickle cell disease, juvenile rheumatoid arthritis, hemophilia, and cystic fibrosis.

Students with infectious diseases This group includes the common childhood diseases, hepatitis B, AIDS/HIV infection, and various others. Bigge notes that AIDS/HIV infection is receiving the most attention at present.

Students requiring medical technology Federal and state agencies tend to use the term *technology-dependent;* however, Bigge prefers *technology assisted.* Whatever the terminology, this may include technology to assist in breathing (some methods using room air, some oxygen), technology as an alternative to the usual bladder and bowel processes, and technology to deliver food directly to the stomach through a tube.

Neurological function disorders occurring after birth These are head injuries, many of them resulting from accidents but some from child abuse. Other students may have survived brain tumors, hematomas, brain aneurysms, or anoxia. In most cases of severe head trauma, there is a predictable path of recovery, which educators play a major role in facilitating.

Students who are medically fragile Bigge includes in this category students who are consistently fragile, those who are having a temporary medical crisis, and

Table 10.1 Orthopedic and neurological disorders

Cerebral palsy
Curvatures of the spine
Epilepsy
Hip disorders
Limb deficiencies
Muscular dystrophy
Musculoskeletal disorders
Spina bifida
Spinal cord injury
Traumatic head injury

Table 10.2 Health impairments and special health care needs

Allergies
Asthma
Blood diseases
Cancer
Cystic fibrosis
Diabetes
Heart disorders
Human immunodeficiency virus and AIDS
Juvenile rheumatoid arthritis
Maternal substance abuse–related conditions

those with progressive diseases who will predictably become medically fragile. For such students, improper placement or provision of special care may lead to death, so the choice of least restrictive educational placement requires particular care.

Bigge suggested the foregoing categorization of special health care needs be used as a partial basis for planning; that is, students in each category have predictable areas of special need that must be considered by educational planners. For example, some require the teacher to have very specific emergency plans and some do not. Some require understanding specific instructions regarding medication; others require a knowledge of equipment and technology, information about where to get emergency repairs, and so forth.

Tables 10.1 and 10.2 list the orthopedic and neurological disorders, health impairments, and special health care needs that will be discussed in this chapter.

Prevalence

Prevalence data on students with orthopedic and neurological disorders, health impairments, or special health care needs will vary considerably depending on a number of factors. As indicated in Table 2.5 in Chapter 2, the states report actually serving students with orthopedic and other health impairments in a range of .05% to .50%; however, it is likely that up to 1% of the school-age population may require assistance. The states' lower prevalence data do not reflect the students who are receiving some type of special assistance but whose conditions and the type of assistance provided do not qualify for inclusion in the reports made to the federal government.

If such data included (for example) young children at risk due to maternal substance abuse, and the geographic area were one in which there were a great deal of poverty, crime, and substance abuse, possibly ten times as many children would fall in this category compared with other geographic areas. In addition, there may be children with cancer or diabetes mellitus in some inner-city areas whose disease is not diagnosed until it becomes life threatening. Other geographic areas might give these conditions very early recognition and diagnosis. Thus considerable variation can result from this type of underidentification.

Causes of Physical or Health Impairments

The causes of physical disabilities and health impairments are many. In discussions of causation or etiology these disabilities are often broadly divided into congenital and acquired conditions, which simply reflects their time of origin. Regardless of cause—or presumed cause—a condition is congenital if it was present at birth. If it originated after birth, it is acquired.

A more useful classification might be one that specifies a prenatal (before birth), perinatal (during birth), or postnatal (after birth) cause. Prenatal factors might then be further divided into genetic (hereditary) factors and outside-the-fetus factors. Genetic factors are highly complex but are simply the result of genetic transmission from one or both parents to the child. Genetic counseling may reduce the incidence of these problems, but often they cannot be predicted in advance. Outside-the-fetus factors may or may not be preventable. Recently, much attention has been given to the effects of pregnant women's use of tobacco, alcohol, or drugs such as cocaine. Prescription drugs can also cause problems for the developing fetus. Inadequate diet, lack of health care, or illness of the mother-to-be can also contribute to the likelihood of physical disabilities in the newborn. It has long been recognized that an accident or physical trauma to the mother can injure the developing fetus.

During delivery (the perinatal period) there are two common risks. Anoxia, or lack of oxygen, can cause a variety of physical and mental disabilities. One cause of oxygen reduction is strangulation by the umbilical cord. A second cause is physical trauma caused by efforts to change the position of the child during the birth process to one appropriate for delivery.

Postnatal risks include damage caused directly by diseases—especially those that attack the central nervous system—by accidents, or by less direct factors such as anoxia resulting from a high fever. Some of the diseases that can cause problems can be forestalled with proper vaccination. Some accidents and diseases may result only in temporary disabilities. The quality of medical management immediately after an accident may make a great deal of difference in the degree of severity of any resulting disability. In a similar manner, timely, appropriate medical treatment of certain diseases may reduce the degree of disability or in some cases prevent disabilities.

■ Contributing Factors

As with other disabilities, a number of factors can modify the overall impact of orthopedic and neurological disorders, health impairments, and special health care needs. Lewandowski and Cruickshank (1980) outlined six of them: (1) age of onset, (2) degree of disability, (3) visibility of condition, (4) family and social support, (5) attitudes toward the individual, and (6) peer acceptance, or social status. As you might expect, each of these influences the others. The age of onset, degree of disability, and visibility of the condition are not subject to a great deal of outside control. The last three, however, can be modified. In fact, a major role of educators must be to encourage more family and social support, promote more positive attitudes and realistic expectations among peers and others who interact with the student, and structure the school setting for meaningful, continuing contact between able-bodied students and those with physical or health disorders.

A great deal of effort has been expended on attempts to prepare teachers to facilitate positive interactions between students with disabilities and their nondisabled peers. Various studies have indicated that the quality of such interactions can be enhanced (Gearheart, Weishahn, & Gearheart, 1992), and one study by Armstrong, Rosenbaum, and King (1987) has provided interesting evidence of "spin-off" effects. This study paired able-bodied students with schoolmates having physical impairments in weekly social activities. There was a significant, positive attitude change on the part of 43% of the able-bodied students after three months. The spin-off effect was a corresponding positive change in the attitudes of parents of the able-bodied "buddies." This effect is likely to have a continuing, circular influence: parents reinforcing more positive attitudes in their children, children reinforcing parents, and so forth.

Gearheart, Weishahn, and Gearheart (1992) suggest that the following factors have a considerable influence in planning programs for students with more severe physical impairments: (1) potential modes of communication, (2) stamina level, (3) present level of academic achievement, (4) intellectual ability, (5) independence in mobility and ambulation, and (6) personal motivation. These factors influence the manner in which interactions with other students may be most effectively implemented.

Most programs designed to promote more positive interactions and better peer acceptance of students with disabilities emphasize educating nondisabled students, and this certainly is essential. Others, however, include an emphasis on early awareness and self-knowledge on the part of children with disabilities. It is suggested that if children know more about their disability, accepting and understanding their own abilities and limitations, they can be involved in more meaningful interactions with nondisabled peers. Research on the self-esteem of 4- to 8-year-old students with normal IQs and cerebral palsy indicated that over half of them denied having any difficulty in running (Teplin, Howard, & O'Connor, 1981). The researchers believed that this denial resulted from a combination of defensiveness and lack of knowledge. They suggested that though it is important to encourage students with physical impairments or chronic health conditions not to discount their own ability, it is also important to give them accurate information about their physical condition and realistic goals. In another study of children aged 3 to nearly 7 with orthopedic impairments, Dunn, McCartan, and Fuqua (1988) concluded that preschool children both with and without orthopedic impairment may be ready for and able to profit from basic instruction in the conditions that lead to disabilities. However, they found home discussions to be of more value for preschoolers.

This discussion of the many factors influencing the impact of physical disorders and health impairments should illustrate the complexity of planning the most appropriate educational programs for students with such conditions. The number of possible conditions and their educational implications, discussed in the next two sections, will make that challenge even more apparent.

Orthopedic and Neurological Disorders

■ Cerebral Palsy

Nature of the disorder   "Cerebral palsy is the most common motor disorder of infants and children" (Shapiro, Palmer, & Capute, 1987, p. 23). Most definitions of **cerebral palsy** are variations of one that describes it as "a disorder of movement and posture due to a defect or lesion of the immature brain" (Bax, 1964). Cerebral palsy (CP) may also be described as a group of conditions characterized by motor disorders due to abnormalities of brain function. Bigge (1991) refers to disorders of movement and posture due to damage of areas of the brain that control motor function, and estimates an incidence of 3 per 1000 live births. Jones (1983) reports incidence estimates ranging from less than 1 to nearly 6 per 1000 live births.

Cerebral palsy is most often discovered at or immediately following birth, but it may be acquired later as the result of a head injury or infectious disease. Jones (1983) indicates that CP may result from prenatal, perinatal, or postnatal factors, and that although it was once assumed that perinatal factors predominated, recent information suggests that it is more often prenatal in origin. It may be described as mild, moderate, or severe—depending on the severity of motor involvement and the degree to which related impairments interfere with perceptual or sensory-integrative abilities—or as minimal, mild, moderate, or severe/profound—depending on the rate of early motor development, severity of motor involvement, extent of neurological findings, and severity of associated dysfunctions such as communication disorders and mental retardation (Shapiro et al., 1987). Some studies have shown that a large percentage of children diagnosed as having neurological symptoms substantiating a diagnosis of CP at age 1 no longer have such symptoms by school age (Nelson & Ellenberg, 1982). Jones stresses that "a prognosis determined at birth or during the first weeks of life is often unreliable. Even when there is definite clinical central nervous system damage, some young infants will make tremendous spontaneous improvements" (1983, p. 56). However, this improvement in motor abilities is not often seen once children reach school age.

Described according to limb involvement, CP may result in (1) **hemiplegia,** damage to one arm and leg on the same side; (2) **paraplegia,** damage to both legs; (3) **quadriplegia,** damage to all four extremities; (4) double hemiplegia, more damage to the arms than the legs and to one side more than the other; and (5) **monoplegia,** damage to only one extremity (Jones, 1983).

Clinical types of cerebral palsy are described on the basis of posture and movement patterns. The two most common are spasticity and **athetosis** (Gearheart, Weishahn, & Gearheart, 1992); however, athetosis is technically a subtype of a more inclusive classification called dyskinesia. Clinical types outlined by Jones include (1) spasticity, (2) dyskinesia (including athetosis, dystonia, rigidity, hypotonia, and tremor), (3) ataxia, and (4) mixed types. Often a mixture of types of posture and movement patterns is displayed, but if there is *primarily* one clinical type, that is ordinarily the diagnosis. If more than one type is fairly evident, then the mixed types diagnosis may be made. Spasticity and athetosis will be given

■ A keyguard makes the computer accessible to this student. ■

further consideration, as they best illustrate the problems that may be typical in students with cerebral palsy.

In the child diagnosed as spastic, some muscles are normal, some weak, and the others "spastic." The problem shows up in voluntary movements— movements that the neurological system directs and that most persons take for granted. Spastic movements may be characterized as "jerky" and out of control. As the child's bones grow longer, the uneven muscle pull is usually increased, so the range of motion of the affected joints decreases. Problems of the back may include various types of curvature—or, in some cases, twisting—of the spine.

Athetosis is a specific type of dyskinesia resulting in involuntary and uncoordinated movements. The movements are sometimes described as "writhing." Even more than with spasticity, there is difficulty moving in the desired direction. The student with athetosis may also have a great deal of difficulty with head control, which makes attention to a task (for example, attending to class discussion or lectures) even more challenging. In all types of CP, as severity increases difficulties in normal life activities intensify. In general, if both sides of the body are affected it is far more problematic than if only one side is affected.

Because the origin of the problem is neurological, there are likely to be other associated disabilities. Visual problems, hearing problems, tactile-kinesthetic sensory loss, problems in eating and speaking, and convulsions are among the more common (Jones, 1983). Mental retardation may be associated with CP; however, many students with cerebral palsy have normal mental ability, and some are mentally gifted.

Educational implications   Many of the educational needs of students with cerebral palsy may be inferred from the preceding description. Depending on the nature and degree of the disorder, assistance from physical therapists, occupational therapists, and speech or language pathologists is often required. Gearheart, Weishahn, and Gearheart (1992) suggest the need for pencil holders to adjust for fine motor coordination difficulties, adapted typewriters and hand-held calculators, alternative communication systems, body supports to attain and maintain proper positioning, page turners, weights to reduce random or uncontrolled movements, book holders, modified desks, paper holders, talking books, cassette recorders, stand-up work tables, and other similar adaptations. These all attempt to compensate for, correct, or partially control the effects of nonstandard motor activity. In addition, the general school environment may need to be adapted so that the student can get into the building, move from floor to floor, class to class, and into areas such as the rest rooms and cafeteria. If the student with CP has an associated problem, such as a visual impairment or mental retardation, that disability must also be taken into account in developing an appropriate IEP.

■ Curvatures of the Spine

Nature of the disorder   Curvatures of the spine are of three types: **scoliosis, lordosis,** and **kyphosis.** Scoliosis is a side-to-side curvature when viewed from the back; lordosis is an anterior (forward) curvature when viewed from the side; and kyphosis is a posterior (backward) curvature when viewed from the side (Rangaswamy, 1983). Scoliosis is the most common type, and with early detection can be treated with relative success. In the past, untreated cases led to death in 30% to 40% of severe cases, due primarily to related cardiopulmonary difficulties (ibid.).

The most common type of scoliosis is idiopathic (of unknown causes); the next most common is neuromuscular (associated with neuromuscular diseases such as muscular dystrophy and cerebral palsy). Treatment with orthotics (braces or other orthopedic appliances) and surgery to stabilize the spine is effective in most cases. Kyphosis and lordosis require similar treatment.

Educational implications   The teacher's role is to be alert for possible spinal disorders and refer them to the school nurse. The nurse will then contact the parents and establish appropriate follow-up procedures. Many students will require no special modifications; others—for example, those with braces or in wheelchairs—may require monitoring and certain physical adaptations. The teacher may play an additional role with respect to psychological support, as needed.

■ **Epilepsy (Seizure Disorders)**

Nature of the disorder   Nealis notes that **epilepsy** is one of the most common disorders of humanity; also, though there are many definitions of it, none is completely satisfactory. He defines it as "an episodic and recurrent disease of the

*Box 10.1
Helping
Hands*

Dr. Mary Joan Willard was a postdoctoral fellow in psychology when she became obsessed with finding a way to bring more independence to a young person with paraplegia with whom she was working. She had been a research assistant to B. F. Skinner and decided to use his behavior modification techniques to train chimpanzees as "helping hands." Skinner suggested that she use capuchin monkeys, which are smaller and more manageable. They weigh only about 5 pounds, stand 18 inches tall, and live to be about 30 years of age. They also tend to form long-lasting bonds with humans. Willard called her program Helping Hands, and though it was nearly shut down due to lack of funding, a major grant from the Paralyzed Veterans of America kept it alive.

Capuchins are specially bred to be trained as helpers for persons with physical disabilities. After weaning, they are placed in foster homes where the only agenda is to promote sociability and affection for humans. At maturity (between 30 and 36 months), they are returned to Helping Hands for a 6-month training program. In this program, if they do a new task properly, they receive a reward; if not, they don't. A critical point in the program is finding a successful "match" between monkeys and masters. The human masters learn that they must remain in control, and that although monkeys can be friends of sorts, they will take advantage of friendship very quickly if improperly handled.

Counselors from Helping Hands screen candidates before placing a monkey, and the new master receives specific training. For example, due to simian instincts that cannot be trained away, new masters learn not to smile at the monkey until a relationship is firmly established. To a monkey, bared teeth are a sign of aggression.

Monkeys function as helping hands by turning on and off lights, bringing their master a prepared meal or glass of water, opening and closing doors, turning on and off the TV, putting a tape cassette in the player and turning it on, or bringing a magazine for their master to read. Commands are usually given orally, but in cases of quadriplegia, monkeys are directed to the object of the command by a laser pointer controlled by the master's chin. Details of this arrangement are individually planned for each person to match his or her physical abilities.

Many individuals are able to live more independently as a result of Mary Joan Willard's efforts and the assistance of Helping Hands.

nervous system evidenced by an electrical dysfunction of neuronal circuitry that, at least temporarily, disrupts the function of the central nervous system'' (1983, p. 74). Other physicians avoid definitions of epilepsy and speak instead of seizure disorders (Golden, 1987a). (There is also disagreement about whether epilepsy should be called a disease or a disorder.)

Though epilepsy is a seizure disorder, the fact that a seizure has occurred does not mean an individual has epilepsy. In general, epilepsy is not diagnosed until several seizures occur in a relatively short span of time, unaccompanied by fever or illness (Jones-Saete, 1988). Seizures resulting from alcohol and drug withdrawal, severe allergic reactions, an imbalance of body fluids or chemicals, or a lack of oxygen to the brain are not indications of epilepsy.

The majority of children with diagnosed epilepsy are said to have idiopathic epilepsy (Nealis, 1983). Known causes would include any physical abnormality of the brain such as brain damage (as from an accident), brain tumors, and the existence of other disorders that indicate neurological abnormalities.

Seizures related to epilepsy have been traditionally classified as grand mal, petit mal, and psychomotor; however, an alternative classification substitutes the terms *generalized tonic-clonic* for *grand mal, absence* for *petit mal,* and *complex partial* for *psychomotor.*

Generalized tonic-clonic seizures usually produce a loss of consciousness, general convulsive movements, and at times frothy saliva from the mouth. Vomiting may occur, and the lips and fingers may turn a bluish color. The individual may also lose control of the bowel or bladder. After such a seizure (which may last for several minutes) the individual will probably be sleepy and want to rest for a time. He or she will have little or no memory of the episode.

Absence seizures generally last no more than 5 to 30 seconds, but may occur 100 to 200 times per day if untreated. Short absence seizures may lead to a student being labeled a daydreamer. The student may miss short segments of what is happening in class, then appear to be a slow learner or inattentive.

Complex partial seizures are characterized by behaviors that may last from a few minutes to an hour. The range of possible behaviors includes chewing and smacking the lips, wandering about aimlessly, taking off clothing, or other apparently unmotivated activity. As with the generalized tonic-clonic seizure, afterward the individual will probably be quite tired and have little or no memory of what happened during the episode.

The most common diagnostic tool other than a composite report of observed behavior is the electroencephalograph (EEG). Proper diagnosis of the type of seizure is important, because different medications may be prescribed for different types. With proper medication, seizures can usually be controlled.

Educational implications Any type of seizure can have serious educational implications. Absence seizures can mean that the student misses a great deal of what takes place in the classroom, and because class content is missed intermittently, the information and events of an entire day may be lost. Also, because they are not easily observed, absence seizures may not be discovered for months or years. The teacher may be the first to become aware of the symptoms of absence seizures; when they are suspected, prompt referral must be made.

Generalized tonic-clonic and complex partial seizures are more easily recognized. When they are, the teacher should determine, through the school nurse, whether the student is receiving proper medical care. School records, including information about medication and management after seizures, must be kept up to date; at times, the physician may ask for specific information, because the effects of medication are monitored.

In most cases, the student can participate in the usual school activities, but verification from a physician is essential. If a seizure occurs, teachers may turn it into a learning experience for the class, which will increase students' understanding and help to relieve any fears they may have. This must be handled differently depending on the severity of the seizure and the age of the student's peers. The Epilepsy Foundation of America offers a variety of information and suggestions to educators. Also, many larger school districts have developed their own information packets and aids for the classroom teacher.

■ Hip Disorders

Nature of the disorder Various disorders affect the hips of school-age children, but the most frequent are Legg-Perthes disease and congenital dislocation (Katz, 1983). Legg-Perthes disease results from an interruption of the blood supply to the femoral head (the "ball" that fits into the "socket" at the hip joint), which in turn leads to degeneration and eventually fragmentation of the femoral head. As this disease progresses the student feels pain, begins to limp, and attempts to avoid physical activity. Treatment ordinarily involves an orthosis (an orthopedic device that supports and adds stability to a joint or limb), which reduces pressure on the joint. In many cases the defective bone will regenerate as new, live bone, and the joint will become normal again. In some cases, surgery to reshape the femoral head or the hip socket is required.

If discovered early, congenital hip dislocation can be treated through manipulation or use of a brace or cast and may require no special treatment by school age. If the disorder is not discovered until school age, treatment may require surgery and, in some cases, an extended stay in the hospital or at home. Symptoms of congenital hip dislocation are similar to those of Legg-Perthes disease.

Educational implications Depending on the severity of the condition, whether surgery is required, and whether an orthosis is needed, hospital and home tutoring may be necessary during the months lost from school. If the condition is less severe, the student may remain in school with some physical modifications. In either case modifications in activities may be required, as directed by the physician. Hip disorders exemplify the type of orthopedic problems that require some modification and monitoring of physical activities but essentially no modifications in instructional methods.

■ Limb Deficiencies

Nature of the disorder **Limb deficiencies** are defined as a partial loss or absence of one or more limbs (Bigge, 1991). They may be either congenital or acquired. Among congenital deficiencies, some type of growth arrest, probably occurring during the fourth to sixth week of gestation, accounts for most cases (Brooks, 1983). This may result in the complete absence of a limb or, for example, an arm that extends below the elbow but ends above the wrist. Acquired limb deficiencies (amputations) may be caused by accidents, surgery, or disease. Acquired deficiencies may be categorized as either traumatic (the result of an accident) or surgical (a result of surgery for uncontrolled infection, loss of blood supply, or other medical conditions). At times, surgery will be used to revise a

Prostheses (artificial replacements for missing body parts)

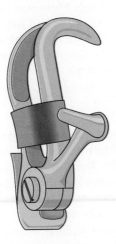

a. Below-the-elbow prosthesis

Permits the individual to successfully carry out most functions of the arm and hand.

b. Split hook prosthesis

c. Artificial hand

Either b or c will permit the user to successfully grasp and manipulate a wide variety of objects. In c, the myoelectric hand, electrical signals from small muscle contractions in the residual limb control the hand. The myoelectric hand can be made to be very cosmetically pleasing.

Orthoses (splints or braces for support or control)

d. Ankle-foot orthosis

e. Knee-ankle-foot orthosis

f. Hand-splint orthosis

d and e function to support body weight, prevent or correct deformities, or control involuntary movements.

f is designed to permit greater control of fine hand movements.

Figure 10.1 Prostheses and orthoses

congenital limb deficiency in preparation for a **prosthesis,** or artificial limb (see Figure 10.1).

Educational implications   Like hip disorders, limb deficiencies have a limited effect on classroom performance. Until students learn to use their prostheses with maximum effectiveness, they may require assistance from an occupational or physical therapist, and teachers may need to be sensitive to any social rejection because of the missing limb. If a child loses a limb while enrolled in school, the teacher will have to play a greater role than if the loss was congenital or occurred before enrollment. The teacher may need to encourage the student to use the prosthesis, because students sometimes prefer to use the existing limb or to compensate with other body parts rather than learn to use a prosthesis (Bigge, 1991).

Most educational modifications required have to do with such matters as seating arrangements, holding a pencil, and turning pages. Once the prosthesis is mastered, normal classroom activities should be the rule. Ordinarily, limitations on physical activities would be only those related to other, general health factors.

■ Muscular Dystrophy

Nature of the disorder   "Muscular dystrophy refers to a group of disorders that share several common features: (1) primarily involving muscle, (2) progressive disability, and (3) hereditary pattern" (Golden, 1987b, p. 29). Some less common forms of **muscular dystrophy** may not occur until the late teens, and though they reduce life expectancy, the individual may live to middle age (Lyle, 1983). In contrast, the most serious type—and the type most commonly seen in the schools—is Duchenne, or progressive muscular dystrophy, which is often recognized before age 2. Children with **Duchenne muscular dystrophy** have a life expectancy of approximately 18 years.

Duchenne muscular dystrophy is genetically linked: in the vast majority of cases it is carried by the mother and passed on only to sons. A few girls may have muscular dystrophy due to non-sex-linked genetic causes, but they are the exception (ibid.).

Early indications of the disease include clumsiness in walking and difficulty in running or climbing stairs. The progression of Duchenne muscular dystrophy is from the calf muscles upward. The child will eventually need crutches, then a wheelchair to move about. Physical therapy may reduce the speed of progress of the disease, but it cannot arrest it. Eventually there will be a loss of respiratory function due to the weakness of abdominal and thoracic muscles, and pneumonia may result. Death is usually caused by heart failure or respiratory failure related to weakened muscles.

Educational implications   In the early stages no adaptations may be required, but as the condition progresses special equipment such as a standing table (so students may stand as they work) may be essential. This is useful after leg braces are fitted and before walking ceases. In addition, adaptive physical education programs may be helpful: adaptive swimming programs are particularly valuable because the water supports the body. The primary role of the teacher is to work along with the parents and therapists to stimulate the student academically and to provide maximal social interaction.

Kleinberg notes that "with degenerative conditions such as muscular dystrophy, educational orientation needs to be redirected, away from planning for

■ Athletic participation is important to individuals with physical and health impairments. It builds confidence, self-esteem, and social skills. ■

future career goals and more toward the enhancement of the quality of life each day. The child's interests and genuine abilities should form the core of the curriculum, with emphasis on short-term goals, leisure pursuits such as literature, art, music, hand work (when possible), and practical, functional skills'' (1982, p. 192). She also notes that degenerative diseases present an unusual situation compared with others with which educators work. In degenerative diseases, "the normal developmental progression from dependency to independence is reversed, creating increasing psychological conflicts. A lack of motivation to continue school, job training, or therapy often occurs as the disease progresses" (ibid., p. 191). This suggests a different frame of reference in developing the IEP and more frequent reevaluation and reconsideration of educational plans in the light of physical abilities and available medical information.

■ Musculoskeletal Disorders

Nature of the disorder Two diseases manifested by skeletal deformities in children will be considered under the general category of musculoskeletal disorders. Arthrogryposis multiplex congenita and osteogenesis imperfecta are otherwise unrelated, do not share an etiology, and follow dissimilar courses (Molnar, 1983). In arthrogryposis multiplex congenita, there is stiffness and deformity in the limbs and joints prior to birth. Limb muscles are grossly underdeveloped, sometimes almost absent. Treatment may include physical therapy, surgery, and plaster casts or braces. Arthrogryposis is a nonprogressive condition.

In osteogenesis imperfecta, often called brittle bone disease, improperly formed bone results in frequent fractures. Related difficulties are disorders of the teeth and skin and, in some cases, hearing impairments by the early 20s (Bigge, 1991). Bone fragility is the major characteristic; osteogenesis imperfecta is progressive.

Educational implications Both of these disorders demand careful physical management. Each may require safe, alternative forms of transportation and the use of braces or wheelchairs. **Control braces** may be needed to reduce purposeless movement or **corrective braces** to correct or prevent deformities. Surgical corrections for the student with arthrogryposis multiplex congenita will ordinarily have been completed before school entrance, so the main need is for an environment in which normal learning can take place. Physical activities may require modification, but there is only a limited chance of additional physical damage. Osteogenesis imperfecta presents a more serious problem, in that additional fractures must be avoided. Adaptations may include standing devices, equipment to increase the speed of writing (such as an electronic typewriter or word processor), and a generally protected environment. Because of these students' fragility and difficulties in mobility, special attention should be given to planning for occupational options. In the case of students with osteogenesis imperfecta, attention should also be given to the possibility of slowly progressive hearing impairment.

■ Spina Bifida

Nature of the disorder **Spina bifida** is a condition in which the bones of the spine fail to close properly during fetal development. If the contents of the spinal column—nerves, nerve covering, and fluid—then protrude from the spine, covered only by a thin membrane, the diagnosis is **myelomeningocele,** popularly called spina bifida ("split in two"). Given the level of awareness of this condition in hospitals, this protrusion is generally surgically treated during the first 24 to 48 hours after birth; however, physical disabilities often result. One of the more common associated conditions is hydrocephalus, in which excess spinal fluid accumulates. The head may become enlarged, and brain abnormalities, seizures, and mental retardation often result (Bigge, 1991). Other symptoms or results include muscle weakness (almost always of the lower limbs), sensory loss, **incontinence,** and orthopedic deformities (Kleinberg, 1982). The degree to which these symptoms occur varies considerably; thus, the degree of disability also varies.

Educational implications In the more serious cases, special management procedures are necessary. Because of the loss of feeling in the lower trunk and limbs, the student may not be aware, for example, that the wheelchair or brace is causing pressure sores; he or she could sustain a severe cut and not be aware of bleeding. An artificial device may be used to collect urine, and after some experience these students can take care of their own toileting needs. But until that time, the teacher or classroom aide must provide assistance.

Although students with spina bifida may have average or above-average learning ability, some will have learning disabilities (Bigge, 1991). Most will also have difficulties with ambulation, but an equally serious problem is the potential for social rejection based on the odor from accidental urination. Teachers can help to minimize this situation by being aware of factors that may cause such an accident and permitting the student to leave the classroom suddenly.

Because of the variety of medically related problems, successful educational programming for students with spina bifida requires ongoing contact with parents, the physician, and in many cases a physical therapist. Adaptations related to mobility may be necessary, but students may require very few educational modifications.

■ Spinal Cord Injury

Nature of the impairment   Spinal cord injury is most often a result of fractures of the spine and is most common among risk-taking adolescents (Kleinberg, 1982). Although the spine is seldom completely severed, the damage that can result from fractures—bruising, pinching, and twisting—will be permanent; that is, the nerve cells regenerate very little if at all. Motor vehicle accidents remain the major cause of spinal cord injuries among children; falls are the second most common cause (Gilgoff, 1983).

Immediately after the paralysis that results from serious spinal cord injury, medical treatment is directed toward the prevention of further damage. Surgery may be employed to stabilize dislocated or fractured vertebrae, but there is presently no available surgical procedure to reconnect the split or severed neural tissue of the spinal cord. Some normal functioning may return as the swelling in the cord lessens; this may be interpreted as a recovery from shock (Kleinberg, 1982). The extent of the resultant disability depends primarily on the point on the spinal cord at which the injury occurs. The higher up the cord, the greater the paralysis. Related factors are whether the damage cuts across the entire cord and the cause of the injury (Gilgoff, 1983).

Educational implications   Immediately following spinal cord injury, individuals should receive treatment at an acute care medical facility, and treatment should continue at a rehabilitation center. A multidisciplinary approach is essential, with emphasis on reducing the psychological shock of going from normal functioning to the loss of independent mobility and self-reliance in a matter of minutes. Kleinberg suggests that the services of physical therapists, occupational therapists, neurologists, orthopedic specialists, urologists, and vocational counselors will be essential.

Many of the same types of adaptation used for cases of spina bifida are suitable for spinal cord injury, including wheelchairs and various other mobility modifications. One major difference is the emotional trauma suffered, due to the overnight nature of the change from independence to complete helplessness (as the individual may view it). It is essential that educators work closely with rehabilitation personnel and counselors who specialize in working with this condition, if they are to be of maximum support as the student returns to school. In many cases, problems with ambulation and related restrictions in what had been normal activity are the major hurdle.

If the injury results in paraplegia, many school tasks may be resumed in a fairly normal manner, due to the student's ability to use the arms. When it results in quadriplegia, students may need to learn such basic self-help skills as eating. They will require much more training and rehabilitative effort, including the use of highly specialized assistive devices. Here, educators must rely on the advice and assistance of specialists.

Given recent technological advances and the wide variety of assistive devices available, most students with spinal injuries should be able to complete their educational programs in the regular classroom. The types of modifications and adaptations required will depend on the degree of their disability and the extent to which they can be motivated to regain as much of their independence as possible.

People Who Make a Difference

RICK HANSEN, MAN IN MOTION Rick Hansen was a promising young athlete living in the interior of British Columbia and looking forward to graduating from high school. He was riding in the back of a pickup truck on the way home from a fishing trip when the truck was involved in an accident, resulting in a spinal cord injury and Rick's permanent disability. After months of inaction, Rick entered rehabilitation with total commitment and concentration. Following rehabilitation, he became an outstanding wheelchair athlete, winning three world championships in wheelchair marathons and sharing the Lou Marsh Trophy for athletic excellence in Canada with Wayne Gretsky in 1983.

In 1985 Rick implemented a project to raise international awareness of the needs and accomplishment potential of persons with disabilities. Starting from Vancouver, the Rick Hansen Man in Motion World Tour wheeled 40,000 kilometers around the world in two years and two months. Rick visited 34 countries and raised $23 million for a legacy trust fund to support spinal cord research, rehabilitation, wheelchair sports, and awareness. The interest from this fund, $10 million to date, is distributed annually throughout Canada.

As a result of Rick's efforts, many cities he visited reviewed their accessibility for people with disabilities and committed themselves to removing long-standing barriers. One example of the warm receptions Rick received was that accorded him in China: there he was greeted by tens of thousands of people, celebrated as a hero—"the wheelchair man"—and allowed to travel through closed cities in which no other foreigner had been permitted for more than 50 years.

Rick Hansen is a hero to Canadians and is recognized worldwide for his efforts on the Man in Motion World Tour. He has been awarded the Order of Canada and the Order of British Columbia. Upon Rick's completion of the tour in 1987, the prime minister of Canada made a commitment to him that the last week in each May will be National Access Awareness Week across Canada. That week is designed to evaluate the progress made on behalf of persons with disabilities, to recognize important and innovative initiatives, and to plan objectives for the coming year. Rick Hansen has created ongoing social change internationally and promoted athletic competitions for athletes who have a disability.

Rick is currently the National Fellow—Disabilities at the University of British Columbia. The Rick Hansen National Fellow Programme was established in 1989 to ensure continuance of the ideals and values that were perpetuated by Rick Hansen and the Man in Motion World Tour. Its principal mandate is to support national and international advocacy for persons with disabilities; the program focuses on all areas of society and is a positive influence for social change on a broad basis in Canada and throughout the world.

■ **Traumatic Head Injury**

Nature of the condition   Traumatic head injury is defined by the National Head Injury Foundation as an insult to the brain caused by an external physical force. Traumatic head injury in children may be the result of an automobile accident or a fall from a bike, on skates, or in another recreational activity. There is also increasing evidence of traumatic head injury as a result of child abuse. According to Bigge (1991), severe head trauma occurs in the 1-month-old to 15-year-old population at the rate of 23 cases per 10,000 persons.

Box 10.2
Thoughts
from a
Rehabilitation
Engineer

I am a rehabilitation engineer. Sometimes I am asked what I do; and when I tell them, it is apparent that this answer is inadequate. I further explain that I work with extremely physically limited people and devise methods and equipment so that they are able to function more independently. This brings a glimmer of understanding. Rather frequently their reply is that this must be "very rewarding work." I assent and the conversation immediately moves in some other direction.

I've had a real problem in how to describe the reward. It certainly isn't monetary. There aren't a lot of other people around who appreciate technically what I do. The description of the struggle with details and subtleties escapes most. I know that people squirm and feel faint when they must face individuals with the kinds of disabilities that I consider daily. There are seldom appreciative peers around.

What I do is look for signals from people who produce few signals. (According to the dictionary, a signal is a gesture, act, indication, token, etc., serving to warn, direct, command, communicate, or the like.) Then, I look for ways to use those signals so that people who can't do, can do.

Recently, a quadriplegic friend and associate died. He was helping me on a project. He was very eager to see the next day because it held the prospect of his becoming more functional. There were a lot of things he expected to be able to do. He was looking forward . . . .

The poem that follows is written as an imagined view from inside someone with many physical complications. I'm not sure that some aspects of the poem's structure are original. I seem to remember hearing a poem premised on "can't." But I know that my sense of reward comes, in part, from helping someone come to the place where he thinks or says, "I can't wait!"

Can't/Can
Can't walk, can't handle, can't touch, can't hold.
Can't talk, but see, can feel, can know.
Can think, can dream, can want, can cry . . .
Can cry! Can signal! Can wait . . . can hope.
Can signal, can do, can make, can be.
Can't wait!

D. M. Bayer, 21 APR 88

SOURCE: *D. M. Bayer, "Approaching the Control Problem," 1988. Reprinted by permission of DU-IT Control Systems Group.*

■ A range of learning opportunities, including music, should be available to children with disabilities. ■

One major indication of severe head trauma is coma, a loss of consciousness after the injury. Continuing coma requires supportive, multidisciplinary therapy and, in many cases, neurosurgery (ibid.). When the child emerges from a coma, he or she may be left with disabilities that may or may not be temporary: speech deficits, physical disabilities, and cognitive and behavioral deficits. Given physical, behavioral, and speech therapy, the child may eventually return to normal or near-normal status. The major determinant (other than the prompt provision of appropriate treatment and therapy) is the degree of residual neurologic damage.

Educational implications After initial treatment at a medical facility and recovery from coma, the individual must receive a comprehensive evaluation to determine the extent and type of disabilities. For example, visual, auditory, and tactile-kinesthetic perception plus gross and fine motor skills should be evaluated. In many cases, the rehabilitation process will begin within the medical setting. There may be a continuing state of confusion, and memory, attention, and speech or language skills may be impaired. Therapies and remedial efforts should address the areas of need determined by this evaluation. At times there will be rapid improvement following brain trauma, so plans for long-term educational interventions should be flexible; the situation may change rapidly.

Rosen and Gerring (1986) note that in addition to the direct results of head injury, extended absence from school imposes its own difficulties. Mira and Tyler (1991) described the special transition needs of a 16-year-old girl as an example of how professionals can work together to facilitate a more successful return to school. A summary of their description is presented in Chapter 13 (Box 13.1).

Placement alternatives for students with traumatic head injuries include the full continuum from full-time attendance in the regular class to a special class setting. Bigge notes that "the major unresolved issue in the education of these students relates to the timing of a student's return to an educational system" (1991, p. 70). As for all students with disabilities, a comprehensive individual evaluation must be the basis for development of the IEP and educational programming.

Although many students have received special education services over the years as a result of disabilities related to traumatic head injury, it was not specifically mentioned in the original PL 94-142. However, the 1990 amendments (PL 101-476) specifically list traumatic brain injury in the definition of "children with disabilities," thus formally recognizing the special needs of this population.

Health Impairments and Special Health Care Needs

■ Allergies

Nature of the condition   Allergies are experienced by a large proportion of the population, but because many cases are relatively mild, the potential for severe allergic reactions may be overlooked. Silkworth (1988) notes that allergies can emerge at any time and can be life threatening in some cases. An allergy is an adverse response or reaction to a substance that may cause no problem to most others. This response may take the form of sneezing, a runny nose, watering eyes, itching, or other skin reactions. Mild allergic reactions can ordinarily be controlled through medication prescribed by a physician and are therefore of minor consequence. Severe allergic reactions (also known as anaphylactic reactions) to foreign protein from food, medication, pollen, or insect stings may cause death if improperly handled (ibid.). Symptoms of anaphylactic reactions include itching or flushed skin, skin rash, breathing difficulty, tightness of chest and throat, and weak pulse. If not promptly and properly managed, they may progress to seizures and unconsciousness.

Educational implications   Mild allergies require little or no adaptation of the educational program; however, both teacher and student need accurate information to understand how to deal with problems that may occur. Students with the potential for severe allergic reactions can participate in most school activities, but if they experience a severe allergic reaction, teachers must take immediate steps. Some students may miss school due to allergies and may become fatigued more easily—but the key to success in dealing with severe problems is having accurate information, including specific instructions from the managing physician. Teachers should also urge students with potentially severe allergic reactions to wear "alert bracelets" or other identification.

■ Asthma

Nature of the condition   Asthma is "a complex disease in which inflammation of the airways is both the cause and effect of the problem" (Kraemer & Bierman, 1983, p. 160). When an asthma episode occurs, the airways narrow and the individual has difficulty breathing. This may be caused by colds or viral infections, by allergens, overexertion, irritation from air pollution, or—in some unusual cases—emotional problems (Silkworth & Jones, 1988). Use of appropriate medications can relieve the muscle spasm that is the major characteristic of acute asthma, but damage to the cells that line the airway and the related inflammation may last for days. When there are repeated episodes, those cells never completely recover. According to Silkworth and Jones, childhood asthma affects about 6% of children in the United States and "causes more hospital admissions, visits to emergency rooms and more school absences than any other chronic disease of childhood" (1988, p. 75).

Educational implications   The educational implications of asthma are in many ways similar to those of severe allergies. It is important that teachers understand the condition and how to treat it. Students with asthma should be treated in as normal a manner as possible, but teachers should be aware of factors that may trigger an attack in a specific student. If exercise is one precipitating factor, modifications should be planned and implemented with care. Although timed-release medications have reduced the need to administer medication at school, this may be necessary. Any medication that might be required should be readily available, along with specific administration instructions from the physician.

The school can play a major role in monitoring and controlling environmental variables and can assist with medication as required. Awareness and accurate information are two essential ingredients in educators' efforts to assist students with asthma to have a more normal educational experience.

■ Blood Diseases

Nature of the condition   In this section, we will discuss two common disorders of the blood, hemophilia and sickle cell anemia. **Hemophilia** is a failure of blood to coagulate and is among the most common hereditary diseases in the United States (Corrigan & Damiano, 1983). Females carry the hemophilic gene and pass it to their male children as hemophilia (Bigge, 1991). Most persons with hemophilia have few problems with minor cuts and scratches, but may bleed excessively from tooth extraction. More dangerous, however, is bleeding into joints and muscles, especially the knee joint (because of its weight-bearing function).

Students with hemophilia may feel a tingling or bubbling sensation in the affected joint when bleeding begins; if they are properly treated at that time, no permanent damage will occur (Corrigan & Damiano, 1983). If they go untreated, pain and swelling will follow, and permanent restriction of joint movement may result. It is often difficult to determine what triggers the bleeding; however, too much physical exercise seems to be one cause. The most effective treatment appears to be to administer a concentrated blood-clotting factor. Both parents and children may be taught to administer this missing coagulation factor (Kleinberg, 1982).

In sickle cell anemia (also called sickle cell disease), red blood cells contain sickle hemoglobin. Because of the way the body reacts to these more fragile, elongated cells (shaped somewhat like a sickle), they are destroyed at a fairly rapid rate. As a result, persons with sickle cell anemia have one-third to one-half as many red blood cells as persons with normal blood (ibid.). Sickle cell anemia is much more prevalent among African Americans, though it may also affect persons from areas of the Mediterranean and Middle East. It is estimated that 1 in 10 African Americans carries the sickle cell trait, but that only 1 in 400 actually has sickle cell anemia (Corrigan & Damiano, 1983).

There is no cure for sickle cell anemia, but anything that reduces oxygen in the blood—such as climbing to high altitudes or flying in airplanes that do not have pressurized cabins—may precipitate a crisis. Complications of sickle cell anemia include dysfunctions of the spleen, heart, and liver. Treatment during crisis periods includes bed rest, nonaspirin pain relievers, antibiotics to reduce the chance of infection, and plenty of fluids. In some cases, blood transfusions may be indicated.

Educational implications   Students with either hemophilia or sickle cell anemia require modifications in their physical activity. Each condition has specific signs or indicators for which teachers should watch. Students may have reduced levels of stamina yet try to "keep going" when they shouldn't. Teachers must know how to proceed in cases of impending crisis and must maintain close contact with parents with regard to physical symptoms. Sickle cell anemia may cause more frequent urination; this must be considered and appropriate class routines established. With both hemophilia and sickle cell anemia, efforts to normalize social contacts are important.

■ Cancer

Nature of the disease   Cancer is a term applied to a group of diseases whose main characteristic is an excessive growth of abnormal body cells that can spread to other parts of the body. These different types of malignant disorders have different initial manifestations and varied patterns of spreading. Different forms or types of cancer likewise require different medical treatments (Hutter & Farrell, 1983).

Leukemia, a cancer of the blood cells that leads to anemia, is the most common cancer in children (Hutter & Farrell, 1983; Kleinberg, 1982). Children with leukemia often lack appetite, are listless, or have severe pain in their bones and joints. They are also more susceptible to other diseases and infections. Cancerous brain and bone tumors may also occur in children. Any of these forms of cancer is potentially life threatening.

A change in the perception of children with cancer is described as follows by Bartholome.

> The child with cancer prior to about 1940 played the role of a dying child. Cure, even prolonged survival, was exceedingly rare. There were no children who wore the label child-with-cancer for longer than several months. That situation has changed dramatically. What was once an almost universally fatal disease is now almost always a chronic disease. By our efforts we have created a new social role; there are now relatively large numbers of children who wear a new label. And although for some their label is relatively invisible from a social perspective, for most there are the combined scars of

disease and treatment. Many, if not most, are handicapped in one way or another. (1982, p. 23)

Depending on the type of cancer and the extent of its spread throughout the body, treatment may be radiation, chemotherapy, surgery, or some combination of the three. Some treatments require hospitalization, but many permit the student to remain in school and maintain normal activities.

Educational implications   Students may be absent from school and experience difficulty in learning as a result of their treatment. They may change in physical appearance or develop obvious abnormal growths, and there may be a general loss of energy. Some children may withdraw. The teacher must be aware of the effects of the type of cancer and the nature of the treatment. Modifications in the amount of work expected or provisions for work to be made up after absences may be appropriate. Cancer often creates an atmosphere of fear and anxiety, so discussing it with the other students may be necessary. Discussion should provide both factual information and an opportunity to express feelings. Specific efforts to include the student who withdraws because of the illness may be necessary. Ongoing communication between student, parents, health care team, and teacher will provide solutions to the problems that the child will encounter during the stages of this chronic illness (Hutter & Farrell, 1983).

■ Cystic Fibrosis

Nature of the condition   **Cystic fibrosis** is a hereditary disease in which the pancreas fails to produce the enzymes needed to break down food. As a result, food does not provide its normal nutritional benefits, and the individual is undernourished. In addition, the glands in the lining of the bronchial tubes of the lungs malfunction. Instead of the thin, clear, slippery mucus they normally produce, there is thick, sticky mucus that tends to stay in the tubes. Bacteria multiply in this mucus and lead to many respiratory infections (Kleinberg, 1982; Mangos, 1983).

Treatment of cystic fibrosis includes administering extracts of animal pancreas, which may replace some of the missing enzymes and permit more normal digestion of food; antibiotics to suppress bacterial growth; and respiratory physical therapy. The physical therapy can be done by parents or others who can learn to pound and vibrate the individual's chest to dislodge the infected secretions. Coughing up the offending mucus is the best defense against the obstruction and infection of the airways typical in cystic fibrosis. Any measure that encourages coughing is viable; however, because of the possible reactions of other students and their parents, it is important to stress that cystic fibrosis is not contagious.

Educational implications   Most of the educational implications are obvious in light of the preceding description. The teacher's role is to educate class members about cystic fibrosis, establish an environment in which it is perfectly acceptable to cough frequently, and, when necessary, administer medication. In some instances there will be need for a special diet, and students with cystic fibrosis may need to go to the rest room more often than is regularly scheduled. Arrangements to meet those needs should draw the least amount of attention possible.

In some cases, certain physical activities will be restricted. Instructions and guidelines should be established in writing, and continuing communication with

■ Talent should be encouraged in all students. Painting is an activity this wheelchair-bound girl can learn and enjoy. ■

parents is essential. As with other health conditions, maintaining the most normal classroom situation in light of the student's special needs is the ultimate goal.

■ Diabetes Mellitus

Nature of the condition   Diabetes mellitus is a chronic condition in which the pancreas produces little or no insulin. There are two major forms of diabetes mellitus: type I (insulin-dependent) and type II (insulin-independent). **Juvenile diabetes mellitus** is almost always type I, so we'll confine our discussion to insulin-dependent diabetes.

Diabetes affects 1 out of 600 school-age children and is therefore of concern to educators (Balik & Haig, 1988; Winter, 1983). Students with diabetes must take a daily injection of insulin to continue their normal growth and development. Without this injection their bodies cannot properly use and store glucose and will instead use protein and fat as energy sources. If this continues, the body produces acids called ketones, and an excess of ketone bodies in the blood can lead to a diabetic coma. In extreme cases, it can lead to death (Balik & Haig, 1988).

Treatment for diabetes includes a comprehensive plan including several elements: insulin (which is essential for survival), diet, exercise, and continuing education and monitoring (Winter, 1983). The goal is to maintain acceptable levels of insulin in the blood throughout the day. Older children eventually learn to give themselves the injections and do their own blood glucose testing.

Although injections and testing are troublesome, a more annoying problem for many children may be the dietary aspects of management. The amount of insulin required is based on the child's usual levels of exercise and diet. Changes in either one may result in an insulin imbalance. Improper balance of insulin, food intake, and exercise results in either hypoglycemia (low blood sugar) or hyperglycemia (high blood sugar). Hypoglycemia, often called an insulin reaction, is more common, resulting from too much insulin, too little food, or too much strenuous exercise. Symptoms include a rapid heart rate, sweatiness, weakness, drowsiness, confusion, and hunger (Balik & Haig, 1988). If untreated, this may lead to a hypoglycemic coma. Fortunately, most children soon learn to interpret the signals and symptoms of hypoglycemia and can ask for help or help themselves. Treatment alternatives will be recommended by the physician, but usually include eating raisins and other dried fruit, hard candies, or perhaps glucose tablets.

Hyperglycemia (high blood sugar) is less common; it may be indicated by abdominal pain, rapid breathing, severe nausea, and blurred vision (ibid.). Severe hyperglycemia leading to ketoacidosis develops relatively slowly; these symptoms tend to occur after the blood sugar level has been elevated for some time. If proper monitoring procedures are followed, severe hyperglycemia is unlikely. If it should occur, it should be treated as life threatening: medical help should be obtained immediately.

A number of potential long-term problems with diabetes seem to be related to improper early management and to continuing, long-standing hyperglycemia. These long-term problems include possible blindness, kidney failure, heart attacks, and gangrene that leads to amputations of one or both feet.

Educational implications   For most students with diabetes, school days are routine. The specifics of diabetes management for any one student—such as what to do in emergencies, when to call, and whom to call—should be available in writing for the immediate reference of each teacher who regularly contacts the student and kept in the emergency files in the school nurse's office. The timing for testing blood glucose levels can often be arranged so that no testing need be done at school. At most one test should be needed during the school day. The diet can normally be followed with little effort. Students with well-controlled diabetes should have no need to deviate from the school program.

■   **Heart Disorders**

Nature of the condition   Heart disorders are much less common in children than in adults. Congenital heart disease may affect as many as 1% of newborns but may not be readily apparent at birth. If untreated, about one-third of these children would die before reaching school age (Bricker & McNamara, 1983). "Of the 35 types of heart malformations, most can be corrected or alleviated by surgery" (Kleinberg, 1982, p. 121). In addition to congenital heart disorders are a number of conditions causing acquired disorders, including rheumatic fever.

Heart disorders may also be associated with other syndromes—for example, Down syndrome.

Educational implications   Most children with heart disorders can function in an entirely normal manner at school. Given close communication with parents, teachers will know what problems might arise and how to proceed if they do. The most likely special needs or adaptations are reduced (or no) participation in competitive athletics, special rest periods, and medication. Written instructions from the physician are essential.

■ Human Immunodeficiency Virus (HIV) and AIDS

Nature of the disorder   The terms *human immunodeficiency virus (HIV)* and *acquired immune deficiency syndrome (AIDS)* are often erroneously used interchangeably. The HIV virus is one that, when introduced into the body, attaches to the helper T cells that coordinate the body's immune system. More and more viruses are then produced, and the body's immune system is deprived of its ability to fight off disease. As various diseases successfully invade the body, the individual becomes more and more ill. Persons infected with HIV are diagnosed as having AIDS only if they develop one of the serious diseases associated with a deficient immune system. According to the Centers for Disease Control, as many as 1.5 million persons in the United States may be infected with HIV, and that number is growing. However, most have not developed AIDS (Frazer, 1989).

Educational implications   Modifications or adaptations required by students with HIV vary from none to many, depending on the stage of development. When the student is infected with HIV but has no symptoms, no modifications are necessary. When various associated symptoms such as lack of energy or a need for additional food and fluids appear, modifications related to those specific needs may be made. When the student has symptoms such as pneumonia, hospitalization is likely. Other symptoms may also require treatment, and frequent absences from school necessitate adjustments in academic expectations. As the disease progresses, both student and peers may need counseling or other psychological assistance.

Many school districts have developed specific guidelines for monitoring the body fluids of persons with HIV and other infectious diseases. Most authorities appear to count proper hand washing among the essential additional procedures. School districts that have no policies with respect to students who have HIV can find specific recommendations and guidelines in the publication *Someone at School Has AIDS* (ibid.) or in similar publications developed by state-level education agencies. The policy statement on managing communicable and contagious diseases provided later in this chapter may also be pertinent.

■ Juvenile Rheumatoid Arthritis

Nature of the condition   Juvenile **rheumatoid arthritis** (JRA) is a form of chronic arthritis (inflammation of the joints) that affects children. The first symptoms are usually "(a) pain and swelling in one or more joints, (b) stiffness with pain on motion when arising in the morning, and (c) in about 25 percent of the children, fever (greater than 100 degrees F)" (Hanson, 1983, p. 243). There are three major subtypes of juvenile rheumatoid arthritis: (1) pauciarticular onset, (2) polyarticular onset, and (3) systemic onset.

Pauciarticular onset JRA affects fewer than five joints in the early stages of the disease and tends to occur in children under the age of 7. Additional joints may be affected later, making it more similar to polyarticular JRA. It may include an inflammation of the eye that, if untreated, can lead to blindness. Polyarticular onset JRA affects five or more joints, and its onset is usually less sudden than that of the other two types. Systemic onset JRA is accompanied by unusually high temperatures (often over 103°F) and a skin rash. It may also include inflammation of the pericardium, or outside cover of the heart; if untreated, it may damage the heart permanently. Both pauciarticular and systemic subtypes tend to appear and require treatment for several months, disappear for months or years, then reappear. Treatment for the pain, swelling, fever, and contractures of the joints is

People Who Make a Difference

RYAN WHITE—HE ACCOMPLISHED A LOT When Ryan White and his mother were told that he was infected with HIV, the doctor said he would probably live three to six months. Five years later, when the doctor was asked about Ryan's continued longevity, he responded, "Because he's Ryan White. He's got a great attitude and he's no quitter."

Ryan was infected with HIV through a blood transfusion. At that time neither he nor his family could envision what that would mean for them. They had no idea of the hate and fear that would be engendered nor of the love and support they would receive.

Ryan became an unwilling celebrity because he wanted to attend school. Out of fear, the parents of Ryan's fellow students in Indiana prevailed upon the school board to prevent his attendance. Ryan and his mother decided to challenge that decision.

Because the issue of whether or not students with HIV or AIDS should or could attend school had not yet been faced by most schools, there was a great deal of publicity regarding the case. It seemed that everyone had an opinion. Ryan was deluged with requests for interviews, and his every attempt to attend school was televised—as were the demonstrations for and against his attendance. The court decisions were headline news.

Throughout the legal battles and publicity, Ryan was fighting a relentless disease. He remained cheerful and optimistic, trying not to return hate with hate. He just wanted to be able to go to school for as long as possible.

Ryan won the right to attend school, but bitterness had divided his school and community. Ryan and his family moved to Illinois, thinking that he might be better accepted in a different school. The publicity over Ryan's challenge was a major factor in the nationwide development of school policies that were more sensitive to the needs and rights of students with AIDS. There were information campaigns to enlighten the general public, parents, and students themselves regarding AIDS. It seemed that no one wanted another student to have to go through the rejection Ryan had faced.

Ryan attended school as long as he was able, until his death on April 8, 1990. Since his death Ryan's mother, Jeanne, has traveled extensively, speaking to parent and school groups and testifying before Congress. She also speaks at benefits for those who have AIDS and to support AIDS-related research. She keeps in touch with celebrities such as Elton John, Phil Donahue, Michael Jackson, and Greg Louganis who supported Ryan's cause. She says "I want my son to be remembered as someone who accomplished a lot."

similar regardless of subtype, but the diagnosis of subtype is helpful as a guide for monitoring other potential problems (such as eye or heart problems).

With any of the JRA subtypes, students may experience stiff joints that are difficult to move, especially on awakening in the morning or after any long period of inactivity. They will also experience considerable pain. If this pain leads to immobility, muscle function will be affected. In severe cases, joints become frozen, usually in a flexed position. Treatment includes medication to reduce the pain and swelling, **physical** and **occupational therapy,** and in some cases orthopedic surgery.

Educational implications   As is so often the case, the role of educators will vary depending on the severity of the symptoms. Adjustments must be made to accommodate the need for continued exercise (to maintain strength and maximum range of motion), the pain that may accompany JRA, and the fatigue that may result. Though exercise is essential, the regular program of physical education may be too strenuous for many of these students, so adaptations should be developed by physical and occupational therapists. If casts, braces, or splints are necessary, appropriate modifications of mobility and seating may be required. Adaptations such as page turners or modified writing tools may also be necessary if the hands are affected. With adaptations, most students with juvenile rheumatoid arthritis will be able to participate in the regular school curriculum.

■ Maternal Substance Abuse–Related Conditions

Nature of the conditions   Children born to mothers who have ingested substances that affect the development of the fetus exhibit a variety of symptoms, depending on the substance involved and the degree of use during pregnancy. Symptoms may include unusual sensitivity to touch or sound, an inability to relate normally to the mother or other adults (which may lead to parental rejection and additional problems), and a variety of neurological problems that can lead to learning disabilities or mental retardation. Though a wide variety of such disabilities has been documented in young children, there have not been sufficient longitudinal studies to determine how these students will fare as they reach their teens and adulthood (VanDyke & Fox, 1990).

Babies with fetal alcohol syndrome, due to their mothers' ingestion of excessive amounts of alcohol, may have certain facial characteristics: low nasal bridges; short, upturned noses; and narrow eyelids. They may also have heart defects and joint and limb abnormalities (Leerhsen & Schaefer, 1989; Schiamberg, 1988) or be hyperactive, have short attention spans, or mental retardation (Behrman, Vaughan, & Nelson, 1987; Creasy & Resnick, 1989).

VanDyke and Fox (1990) point out that in addition to alcohol abuse, the use of cocaine, "crack" cocaine, PCP, heroin, and similar drugs is on the increase. Health officials in New York City estimate that cocaine abuse among pregnant women increased 3000% in the 1980s (Rist, 1990). Babies born to mothers addicted to cocaine or crack cocaine may already have experienced neurologic insult or the equivalent of a stroke (Revkin, 1989).

Educational implications   Early intervention may have ameliorated some of the difficulties the child has experienced or will experience (see Chapter 12). The specific symptoms exhibited by school-age students will determine the educa-

■ School is a happy place for these children. Despite physical impairments, they are eager learners. ■

tional interventions required. Modifications and adaptations may include reducing the amount of stimulation in the classroom and providing a structured, stable routine on which the child can depend. Modifications related to learning basic skills such as reading or math may be similar to those used with students with learning disabilities or mental retardation, and specific instruction in social skills may be required. Ultimately, educational efforts directed toward influencing pregnant women to stop substance abuse may be the most effective educational intervention.

The Management of Health Impairments in the School

Some educators may have misgivings about working with students with health impairments because they have limited training in how to proceed—or their school district may lack comprehensive policy guidelines. Information that teachers and other school personnel may need includes how to feed through a gastrostomy tube; how to manage encopresis; how to deal with colostomies, ileostomies, and urostomies; how to do catheterizations and handle body fluids in school; how to deal with a tracheostomy tube; and how to use various orthopedic devices.

Management techniques for these and other topics are outlined in detail (with appropriate diagrams and illustrations) in published sources such as the manual *Managing the School-Age Child with a Chronic Health Condition: A Practical Guide for Schools, Families, and Organizations* (G. Larson, 1988). State departments of education and larger school districts have similar manuals.

**Box 10.3
The Council
for
Exceptional
Children's
Policy
Statement on
Managing
Communicable
and
Contagious
Diseases**

Controlling the spread of communicable and contagious diseases within the schools has always been a problem faced by educators, the medical profession, and the public. Effective policies and procedures for managing such diseases in the schools have historically been developed by health agencies and implemented by the schools. These policies and procedures were primarily designed to manage acute, temporary conditions rather than chronic conditions which require continuous monitoring and remove children from interaction with other children while the condition is contagious or communicable.

The increased prevalence of chronic communicable diseases such as hepatitis B, cytomegalovirus, herpes simplex virus, and acquired immune deficiency syndrome has raised public and professional concern, necessitating the reassessment of existing school policies and procedures. The Council believes that having a communicable/contagious disease does not in itself result in a need for special education. Further, the Council believes that in developing appropriate policies for managing communicable diseases, schools and public health agencies should assure that any such policies and procedures:

a. Do not exclude the affected child from the receipt of an appropriate education even when circumstances require the temporary removal of the child from contact with other children.

b. Provide that determination of a nontemporary alteration of a child's educational placement should be done on an individual basis, utilizing an interdisciplinary/interagency approach including the child's physician, public health personnel, the child's parents, and appropriate educational personnel.

c. Provide that decisions involving exceptional children's nontemporary alterations of educational placements or services constitute a change in the child's Individualized Education Program and should thus follow the procedures and protections required.

d. Recognize that children vary in the degree and manner in which they come into contact with other children and school staff.

e. Provide education staff with the necessary information, training, and hygienic resources to provide for a safe environment for students and educational staff.

f. Provide students with appropriate education about communicable diseases and hygienic measures to prevent the spread of such diseases.

School districts often have established policies regarding the management of communicable and contagious diseases and the administration of medication in the schools. The Council for Exceptional Children has developed a policy statement on managing communicable and contagious diseases (Council for Exceptional Children, 1989) that can be used as a model for developing local school district policy (see Box 10.3).

The American Academy of Pediatrics committee on school health has published guidelines on administering medication in the schools (1984) that may also help formulate local school district policy. Those guidelines may be summarized as follows.

Box 10.3
Continued

g. Provide, where appropriate, carrier children with education about the additional control measures that they can practice to prevent the transmission of the disease.

h. Enable educational personnel who are medically at high risk in regard to certain diseases to work in environments which minimize such risk.

i. Provide educational personnel with adequate protections for such personnel and their families if they are exposed to such diseases through their employment.

The Council believes that special education personnel preparation programs should:

a. Educate students about communicable and contagious diseases and appropriate methods for their management.

b. Counsel students as to how to determine their level of medical risk in relation to certain diseases and the implications of such risk to career choice.

The Council believes that the manner in which policies for managing communicable and contagious diseases are developed and disseminated is critically important to their effective implementation. Therefore, the following must be considered integral to any such process:

a. That they be developed through the collaborative efforts of health and education agencies at the state, provincial, and local levels, reflecting state, provincial, and local educational, health, and legal requirements.

b. That provision is made for frequent review and revision to reflect the ever-increasing knowledge being produced through research, case data reports, and experience.

c. That policies developed be based on reliable identified sources of information and principles endorsed by the medical and educational professions.

d. That such policies be written in content and format to be understandable to a variety of consumers including students, professionals, and the public.

e. That policy development and dissemination be a continual process and disassociated from pressure associated with precipitating events.

SOURCE: *Council for Exceptional Children, 1989, Policies Manual (Reston, VA: Council for Exceptional Children).*

1. The parents must request, in writing, that school staff administer the medication according to the physician's instructions.
2. The medication must be provided in a container labeled by the pharmacist.
3. Written instructions must be provided by the physician, including the name of the medication, the dosage, how often it is taken, why it is needed, and an approximate termination date.
4. When the student is able to self-administer medication, written permission for self-medication should be signed by both parents and physician and kept on file.
5. Any medications administered by school personnel should be stored in a locked space and a record maintained indicating the date and time of day of medication and the individual who administered it.

Issues and Trends

Certain issues and concerns are of critical importance—particularly those involving the coordination of efforts by the various community agencies servicing students with multiple special health care needs. At issue are the definition of roles, the limits of legal responsibilities, and finally how specific personnel, programs, and services will be funded.

Several definite trends in this arena can be pinpointed, as well. The most notable and far-reaching trend is the increasing inclusion in the public schools of students with more complex health care needs. Lehr (1990) attributes this to technological advances in medicine, acceptance of the principle of **normalization,** an increase in programs for very young students, an increase in services to students with severe handicaps, and an increase in school acceptance of responsibility for children with communicable diseases. Other related trends include (1) greater attention to students who have been variously described as medically fragile, technologically dependent, or having specialized health needs by professional groups such as the Council for Exceptional Children; (2) more attention to the needs (other than purely medical) of such children by individual medical professionals and medical associations such as the American Academy of Pediatrics; and (3) efforts to provide more useful technology (such as apnea monitors, colostomy bags, urinary catheters, and mechanical respiratory support) for technology dependent children, encouraged by the U.S. Department of Health and Human Services.

Summary

A wide variety of orthopedic and neurological disorders and health impairments may affect the education of students. If students with these disorders have no additional disabilities, they can learn successfully when the school program is made accessible and adaptations are provided to compensate for the effects of their disabilities. Accessibility implies providing transportation and removing architectural barriers. It means enabling all students to reach different areas and levels of the school building, laboratories, and any equipment that is an essential part of the learning process. Adaptations include those that permit the student to turn pages and to write (such as an electronic typewriter or word processor), braces, special desks, and similar equipment. In addition, special health care needs may grow out of or be related to health impairments that require special attention, such as administering or monitoring medication, modifying participation in physical activities, and watching for and providing emergency assistance when indicated.

A policy statement on managing communicable and contagious diseases provided by the Council for Exceptional Children may be of value in guiding school officials' development of local policies. The American Academy of Pediatrics has also provided helpful guidelines. But despite increased awareness and information and the many advances made in appropriate provision for students with physical or health problems in the schools, additional, cooperative efforts with members of the medical profession must be pursued, and coordination of efforts with various public agencies must be improved.

Anthony, Lizabeth, Stacy, and Jon are all in tenth grade and well liked by their friends. However, each has a school-related complaint.

Anthony excels at gymnastics. He practices daily, has won local and regional awards, and wants to compete nationally. He works hard to keep up his grades because he knows that unless he does, he won't be able to compete. But the school only provides programs for students with outstanding athletic ability in football, basketball, and baseball. Anthony would like to have a coach to help him meet his goals.

Lizabeth enjoys writing and has published a short story in the local newspaper and a poem in a national children's magazine. She always gets A's in English; her other grades are above average. Lizabeth's dream is to write a best-selling novel. Her English teacher critiques her writing, but Lizabeth wishes she had additional help.

Stacy and Jon are bored with school and feel totally unchallenged. When they were in grade school they explored most of the material now being taught. Stacy talks to her friends about dropping out of school because she doesn't think it is worth her time. Jon has a friend in another city who can take some college classes even though he has not yet graduated from high school. Jon wonders why his school does not provide such opportunities.

CHAPTER ELEVEN

Giftedness, Talent, and Creativity

Most of the chapters in this text concern students with disabilities. In some cases their disabilities are visible, in other cases not—but they do have one thing in common. Due to their disability, most will require modifications in the learning environment or adapted learning strategies. Without appropriate educational intervention, most would slip further and further behind their age peers.

In this chapter we will be concerned with a quite different population of students. They, too, are "exceptional" students—that is, they are significantly different from the norm—but many are not immediately or visibly identifiable as exceptional. An experienced teacher may be able to tell rather quickly that certain students have exceptional ability or talent, but others' talents may be hidden, for a variety of reasons. Some might be potentially gifted, talented, or creative yet never have those abilities or characteristics fully developed.

These students are often considered fortunate, but that very perception has led others to doubt that they should receive differentiated educational programs—particularly if such programs cost more than the regular school program. After all, if they are already doing better than other kids, why give them any special help? A recurring concern with "elitism" plays a role here, as well.

We believe that such students deserve the opportunity to develop their unusual potential simply because that is the inherent right of all students. Over the years, many have given lip service to this philosophy but have not always followed through with significant action. Public schools may have provided special educational opportunities for students when it seemed to be important to the nation to do so, or when students demonstrated talent in certain performance areas (such as sports or music)—but schools may not have been consistently concerned about their students' needs on the basis of educational rights. We will begin our discussion of these students by reviewing the historical development of programs for the gifted or talented since the time of Plato.

Historical Background

One of the earliest documented references to special programs for the gifted was in a proposal by Plato in the third century B.C. In it, he recommended that talented youth be sought out and trained as future leaders.[1] In a similar manner, various Roman emperors sought out young men to train for responsibilities in law, politics, and military strategy. These logical recommendations were for the good of societies or empires, however, not for some inherent right to self-development.

The New World saw parallel efforts long before the American Revolution. During that time "two separate educations existed in the colonies: one for the gifted, another for the masses" (Sisk, 1987, p. 6). For example, the Boston Latin Grammar School was established in 1635 and Harvard College in 1636. These private programs were for talented students, but they also reflected wealth and in many ways served to perpetuate class distinctions. Thomas Jefferson proposed, in a formal educational plan developed for the state of Virginia, that able students be provided special educational programming, and that bright students be sent to William and Mary College at public expense. It was clear, however, that such education was for the good of the state of Virginia. These early examples were for the most part copies of similar educational proposals in Europe; however, some educational programs for the gifted and talented were unique to the United States.

---

[1] Historical events noted in this summary were drawn from a variety of sources but primarily from Greenlaw and McIntosh (1988) and Rice (1985).

Greenlaw and McIntosh (1988) believe that modern interest in the gifted child grew out of the publication of Sir Francis Galton's book *Hereditary Genius* in 1869. Whatever the origin of interest and motivation, a number of milestones in the establishment of public school programs for the gifted were reached in the United States in the following four decades.

* *1868:* St. Louis, Missouri, initiated a variable promotion plan that provided additional opportunity to gifted students. Fixed, rigid, grade-level promotion was the national pattern at that time.
* *1886:* Elizabeth, New Jersey, initiated a type of homogeneous grouping based on academic achievement. Academically talented students were encouraged to move more rapidly through the established content of the school curriculum.
* *1898:* Santa Barbara, California, started a type of ability grouping as a substitute for acceleration, thereby broadening the experiences of gifted and talented students without moving them through the total school program more rapidly.
* *1900:* New York City public schools established what are sometimes considered the first "special classes" for gifted students. These classes, in contrast to the Santa Barbara program's, were designed to facilitate acceleration.

Since about 1920 scientific studies by high-visibility authorities, formal reports of ongoing programs, and efforts by federal and state governments, private foundations, and parent groups have led to spurts of high-level interest. The following sample of such efforts demonstrates their influence on program development.

* *1921:* Lewis Terman initiated his investigations of giftedness, which eventually led to the *Genetic Studies of Genius* publications and our best-known longitudinal study of gifted children and adults (Terman, 1925; Terman & Oden, 1947, 1959). Though his criteria for inclusion in the study and some of his methodology have been questioned, he established several facts of significance. One of the most important is that children of considerably above-average mental ability (an IQ of more than 140) and related academic achievement grow up to contribute to art, science, journalism, politics, and essentially all other arenas of life far beyond what may be expected of average students. The publication of his first volume stimulated interest at a critical time in the development of new programs, and subsequent volumes led to the discarding of many myths about gifted individuals.
* *1928:* The Cleveland, Ohio, schools published a lengthy report on their Major Work Program, thus providing a written model for other school districts. After its wide dissemination among school administrators, similar programs were initiated by many other districts. However, the Great Depression occurred at about the same time, so severe economic problems inhibited the development of most programs that would increase costs. As a result, many school districts emphasized acceleration programs, which saved money, and "many inaccurate generalizations that prejudice us against acceleration stem from this period" (Rice, 1985, p. 9).
* *1942:* The Westinghouse Corporation initiated a Science Talent Search in an attempt to discover high school students with unusual promise to become creative scientists. Their program emphasized the importance of gifted individuals to the war effort and heightened attention to the potential of gifted students in our schools.
* *1947:* The American Association for Gifted Children was established, and *The Gifted Child* (Witty, 1951) was published as an outgrowth of that association's

work. Development of this text brought together many of the recognized authorities in the field and gave additional impetus to educational efforts on behalf of gifted students.

• *1953:* An organization was formed that is today known as the National Association for Gifted Children (NAGC). It has promoted interest in designing more effective programs for gifted children; its publication, *The Gifted Child Quarterly,* provided an early forum for debate and dissemination of information to both parents and professionals. The NAGC has also played a role in establishing professional standards to guide teacher education programs for instructing the gifted.

• *1958:* A federal law, the National Defense Education Act (NDEA), was enacted following the USSR's 1957 launching of the first man-made satellite. There was still little talk about students' rights to an appropriate education; instead, the concern was that no other nation surpass the United States in the space race. Like Plato, the Roman emperors, and others throughout history, the U.S. government backed education of the gifted out of concern for the state, not for the individual. The NDEA targeted, and primarily provided money for, improved programs in science, mathematics, foreign languages, and guidance and counseling. It was the forerunner of many other federal efforts that have led to the improvement of educational programs for all exceptional children.

Since the early 1960s, federal legislation has reflected continuing interest in promoting better educational programs for gifted and talented students; a number of its enactments were outlined in the summary of legislation in Chapter 1. It has not been, however, as extensive and influential as legislation to aid students with disabilities. Special educational provisions for gifted, talented, or creative students have depended primarily on the extent of state-level interest.

Definitions

Throughout this text we refer to students who are gifted and talented—or perhaps gifted, talented, and creative. Students may be all three; however, depending on the definition utilized, they may have only one or two of these characteristics. In program planning, if all three are recognized and the appropriate educational provisions made, school districts may accurately speak of programs for the gifted, talented, and creative; more often, they are called programs for the gifted and talented. In such school districts, planning for students who are gifted, talented, or creative is linked administratively, and there may be considerable overlap in actual program provision. However, identification of a talented student may be quite different from identification of a gifted one. *Gifted and talented* was the terminology used in most of the federal reports relating to this broad area of concern, as reflected in Public Law 91-230 (1970):

> The Commissioner of Education shall: (A) determine the extent to which special educational assistance programs are necessary or useful to meet the needs of gifted and talented children, (B) show which existing Federal educational assistance programs are being used to meet the needs of gifted and talented children, (C) evaluate how existing Federal educational assistance programs can be more effectively used to meet these needs, and (D) recommend which new programs, if any, are needed to meet these needs. (Section 806c)

■ Artistic talent should be recognized and stimulated. ■

In 1972 Commissioner of Education Sidney Marland completed a comprehensive study of education of the gifted and talented and presented his report. Included in it was the following definition, popularly called the Marland definition.

Gifted and talented are those identified by professionally qualified persons who by virtue of outstanding abilities, are capable of high performance. These are children who require differentiated educational programs and/or services beyond those normally provided by the regular school program in order to realize their contribution to self and society.

Children capable of high performance include those with demonstrated achievement and/or potential ability in any of the following areas, singly or in combination:

1. general intellectual ability
2. specific academic aptitude
3. creative or productive thinking

4. leadership ability
5. visual and performing arts
6. psychomotor ability (p. 2)

A second federal definition grew out of the 1976 Public Law 93-380, which essentially matched the Marland definition except for deleting psychomotor ability. Both definitions refer to potential abilities and to children and youth who require differentiated services. The 1976 federal definition follows.

> "Gifted and talented" means children and, where applicable, youth, who are identified at the preschool, elementary, or secondary level as (1) possessing demonstrated or potential abilities that give evidence of high performance capability in areas such as intellectual, creative, specific academic, or leadership ability or in the performing and visual arts; and (2) needing differentiated education or services (beyond those being provided by the regular school system to the average student) in order to realize these potentialities. (*Federal Register,* May 6, 1976, p. 18666)

In addition to federal definitions are others that have gained national or international recognition. One developed by Renzulli, the creator of the Enrichment Triad Model, describes the interaction of three clusters of human traits. According to Greenlaw and McIntosh (1988), it is both broader and narrower than many previous definitions. It is broad because it includes so many general performance areas and even more specific performance areas. It is narrow in that it requires the presence of all three traits that Renzulli believes to characterize giftedness. His definition might be more accurately described as a conceptualization of giftedness. It includes the following generalizations.

1. There are three traits common to all truly gifted individuals: above-average intellectual ability, task commitment, and creativity.
2. Giftedness should be recognized in all socially useful areas of performance.
3. It is essential that we increase our efforts to measure or assess a broad range of abilities in addition to general intellectual ability (Renzulli, Reis, & Smith, 1981; Renzulli & Smith, 1980).

Renzulli's three-ring, interactive definition has been of interest to professional educators of the gifted and talented, but reveals considerable shortcomings when applied in the practical, school-based setting (Borland, 1989).

Yet another definition has been proposed by Barbara Clark. This one is based on her belief that the gifted have advanced or accelerated brain function development. Here is her definition.

> Giftedness is a biologically rooted concept, a label for a high level of intelligence that results from the advanced and accelerated integration of functions within the brain, including physical sensing, emotions, cognition, and intuition. Such advanced and accelerated function may be expressed through abilities such as those involved in cognition, creativity, academic aptitude, leadership, or the visual and performing arts. Therefore, with this definition of intelligence, gifted individuals are those who are performing, or who show promise of performing, at high levels of intelligence. Because of such advanced or accelerated development, these individuals require services or activities not ordinarily provided by the schools in order to develop their capability more fully. (1988, p. 7)

Finally, Borland provides a definition reflecting the special education rationale—that is, reflecting the perceived need to provide special educational opportunities in the schools.

For the purposes of education, gifted children are those students in a given school or school district who are exceptional by virtue of a markedly greater than average potential or ability in some area of human activity generally considered to be the province of the educational system and whose exceptionality engenders special-educational needs that are not being met adequately by the regular core curriculum. (1989, pp. 32–33)

This definition leaves many specifics unstated but is consistent with how the various states tend to establish their own guidelines, cutoff points, and program eligibility requirements. This type of definition, along with the federal definitions, underpins the way most state and local educational agencies actually identify and plan programs for gifted and talented students.

Each of the definitions described here has problems in application. No matter how giftedness is defined it will mirror biases in terms of the cultural values of those who establish the guidelines. In addition, these definitions often reflect political priorities. An apparent trend today toward broader definitions of gifted-ness and talent offers no assurance that any set of parameters will long endure. Whenever it is said that a given individual is gifted, or that a given school program is for students who are gifted, we must ascertain what the term *gifted* means in that context, and particularly how identification procedures are handled within it.

Prevalence

Estimates of the prevalence of gifted, talented, or creative students mirror the definition employed. When gifted is defined as the top 2% academically or intellectually, estimating is simple. At the other extreme, the Enrichment Triad/Revolving Door Model (Renzulli, 1977; Renzulli & Reis, 1986) utilizes a plan and concept in which up to 20% of the total school population is identified for a "talent pool" after meeting certain prescribed criteria. Students then engage in various special projects and activities reflecting their ability, task commitment, and creativity. Renzulli believes that individuals should be given special program-ming based on the presence of certain behaviors, but that individuals are not necessarily intrinsically gifted. Other complications to estimating the prevalence of gifted, talented, or creative students are the degree to which talent—for example, in dance or music—is to be recognized and included.

The Marland report to Congress (1972) indicated that if the criteria of that report were applied, a minimum of 3% to 5% of the school population would be identified as gifted and talented. In Chapter 2, Table 2.4 indicates a prevalence of 2% to 3%, which is a generally accepted, conservative estimate. The question of prevalence remains unanswered, except that it is subject to considerable variation according to the definition in use.

Talent versus Giftedness

Not all authorities include talent, as they define it, within the giftedness construct. In some states, programs for the gifted do not target any students who do not possess high-level cognitive ability, even when they demonstrate unusual talent in some specific area.

Greenlaw and McIntosh distinguish giftedness as follows: "The gifted child possesses cognitive ability that is noticeably superior to that of age-mates. This cognitive superiority is coupled with a propensity for creative action in any of a multitude of areas." They add that "the term gifted will not be used interchangeably with the term talented. The latter refers to those students who are indistinguishable from average individuals of the same chronological age except for a single outstanding ability, such as sculpting or miming. Talent, unlike intelligence, is expressive rather than analytic" (1988, p. 33).

Rice (1985) speaks of "varieties" of talent and comments that the word *talent* may be used in two ways: to indicate general mental superiority and to indicate specific gifts or skills. He then proposes the term *mental giftedness* to refer to persons with unusually high intelligence as determined by a measure of general mental ability. Such giftedness, then, might be considered one kind of talent.

To understand what a specific author includes in the parameters of giftedness, then, we must first identify the definition of giftedness to which the author subscribes. A similar caution applies to the interpretation of various public school programs for students who are gifted. In fact, with respect to these programs, it would be best to know how that particular school district identifies students who are gifted. (Identification should be related to the accepted definition of giftedness, but does not always seem to be.)

Creativity

Creativity is often viewed as an element of giftedness; however, not all gifted children are creative in the same manner. B. Clark claims that "creativity is a very special condition, attitude, or state of being that nearly defies definition" (1988,

Box 11.1
Who Is Gifted?

John Torres was a strong, energetic, 12-year-old sixth-grader who had never learned to read. He was known as the school vandal. Although no one could ever prove that he and the boys he led made a shambles of the school each weekend, he had been a problem for teachers almost from the first day of his schooling. No one thought he could learn.

[But] his sixth-grade teacher thought he was gifted. He was a veritable mechanical genius and could repair any kind of audio-visual equipment or anything else mechanical. He was also a genius in leadership. He could attract other boys, organize them, and lead them in doing almost anything. His artwork was also superior.

John's sixth-grade teacher influenced the student council to appoint John the chairperson of the lunchroom committee, which was responsible for the arrangement and functioning of the school cafeteria. John recruited several of his friends to help in this effort, and became involved in other school leadership activities. Almost magically, school vandalism ceased, and John made rapid improvement in reading, soon catching up with many other sixth-graders in reading ability. He decided he liked going to school (Torrance, 1985, pp. 2–3).

Is John gifted?

p. 46). Guilford, in a much-cited discussion of the traits of creativity (1959b), speaks of four dimensions of creative behavior: (1) fluency, (2) flexibility, (3) originality, and (4) elaboration. Many have since analyzed creativity in relation to those four dimensions.

In a review of writing and research on creativity, Tannenbaum concluded that "[creativity] consists of a not yet known combination of general and specific abilities and personality traits associated with high potential that can be realized in a stimulating environment with the help of good fortune" (1983, p. 328).

Torrance (1962, 1965) has provided considerable leadership in attempts to describe creativity and to assist teachers to promote and guide it. He has also developed recognized tests of creativity; however, all such tests have been criticized for lack of reliability and validity. The following overview of two creativity tests (Guilford, 1971; Torrance, 1981) illustrates how we attempt to assess this trait. To some extent, it may also provide insight into the type of thinking and behaviors that typify creativity.

Thinking Creatively in Action and Movement (TCAM) was developed by Torrance for use with children from 3 through 8. It has four subparts (called activities), as follows.

1. *How Many Ways?* is scored for fluency and originality with respect to the ways "invented" by the child to move across the floor. The child's originality score is the total of the points assigned to particular responses, which are rated from 0 to 3. For example, simple crawling is rated 0, jogging is rated 1, duck-walking is rated 2, and goose-stepping is rated 3. The fluency score is the total of the number of ways and combination of ways.

2. *Can You Move Like?* is scored for imagination. For example, one question asks "Can you move like a tree in the wind? Imagine you are a tree and the wind is blowing very hard." Children are asked to show how many ways a tree in the wind can move. Responses on the six questions in this part of the TCAM are rated from 1 to 5.

3. *What Other Ways?* is scored for fluency and originality. In this part of the TCAM, the child is encouraged to put a paper cup into a wastebasket in a variety of ways.

4. *What Might It Be?* is scored for fluency and originality. The child is asked to think of different ways in which she or he can play with paper cups. Many cups are provided, with the suggestion that the child try to imagine that they are something else.

Guilford's Creativity Tests for Children (CTC) may be used with fourth-grade or older students to measure various aspects of their production. Here are the ten subtests of the CTC.

1. *Names for Stories:* A series of stories is presented, and the student must think of names for each.
2. *What to Do with It:* The names of objects are given, along with the objects' common use. The student must think of unusual uses for each one.
3. *Similar Meanings:* Words are given, and the student must think of other words that mean about the same thing.
4. *Writing Sentences:* Five words are listed. Students must write as many sentences as they can, using two or more of those words in each sentence. They are encouraged to develop as many sentences as possible in which all five words are used.

5. *Kinds of People:* A series of "signs" is presented (for example, a picture of a book in a circle). Students must name a kind of person or activity that might be related to each sign.
6. *Make Something Out of It:* A group of figures is presented; students are to visualize what they might "make out of" those figures, naming what they visualize.
7. *Different Letter Groups:* Groups of letters are given to students, who must name ways in which letters within each group are similar.
8. *Making Objects:* A number of geometric shapes and "pieces" are given to students, who put them together to make real objects.
9. *Hidden Letters:* A figure with many intersecting lines contained within an outer perimeter is presented. Students are directed to find all the possible letters "hidden" within the figure.
10. *Adding Decorations:* Students are given very plain, outlined pictures of real objects. They are encouraged to use lines to "decorate" them.

Tests of creativity are more subjective than many of the other assessment tools used to identify exceptional students. Of course, test developers have attempted to standardize them, to produce clear instructions for administering and scoring them, and to reduce ambiguities, but the very nature of creativity makes it quite difficult to assess other than through product creativity, as evaluated by expert judges.

Clark (1988) notes that although there are many aspects to creativity, the two most commonly recognized are rational thinking and talent. According to her, rational thinking may be measured by existing tests of creativity. It reflects potential for creative thinking or performance; that is, it is primarily predictive in nature. Talent is manifested by creativity in products, such as sculpture, painting, or performance in dance or vocal music. Creativity in talent is generally judged by a jury of experts in the field of endeavor.

One traditional concept of creativity is bringing something new into existence. This might be called the product or the inventiveness concept; Clark would classify it with the talent aspect of creativity. If we subscribe only to this concept, it is relatively easy to agree on which students are creative. However, this does not permit us to predict which students are potentially creative. It is almost useless in identifying those who are creative in their thought processes, which is often a prerequisite for solving environmental problems, finding a cure for medical disorders, or leading a nation.

Guilford (1959a) developed a three-dimensional conceptual model called the structure of intellect, in which he predicted 120 distinct types of intellectual ability. His concept led to a great deal of discussion and research into the nature of "convergent" and "divergent" thinking: divergent thinking quickly became related to, if not synonymous with, creativity.

Clark (1988) views creativity as "the highest expression of giftedness." She advocates an integrated concept of creativity in which we recognize the following four states or functions.

1. A thinking state: rational, measurable, subject to development through practice
2. A state of talent: creating new products and often requiring high levels of skill
3. A feeling state: requiring self-awareness and self-actualization—often eliciting an emotional response
4. A state of higher consciousness: an intuitive state

Clark's holistic concept of creativity suggests that schools might do far more to promote creativity than they do at present, because even those schools that make the most efforts focus solely on her first two categories.

Research with students identified as creative has led to some interesting results. For example, Halpin, Payne, and Ellett (1973), in a study of creative adolescents, found significant differences between males and females. In their study, the females generally liked school, especially courses in science, art, and music; the males disliked school. Females liked their teachers; males thought their teachers uninteresting and disliked them. Females completed a great deal of nonrequired reading and special reports; males did little homework. These results might be interpreted in a variety of ways; however, they demonstrate the difficulty of relating characteristics to creativity.

Identifying and promoting the development of creativity in students appears to be more difficult than doing the same for intellectual giftedness. This is true for many reasons.

1. People disagree on the concept of creativity.
2. Except for the creative talent exhibited through products, it is difficult to identify creative potential.
3. Many educators who reward academic achievement do not reward, nor recognize the value of, divergent thinking (which often leads to nonconformity or "breaking the rules").
4. Some educators apparently do not fully recognize the potential value of mental activities such as daydreaming, fantasizing, or even brainstorming.
5. The characteristics of creative or potentially creative students can vary widely.
6. There is limited research on creativity, and much of it is difficult to interpret.

Characteristics of Giftedness and Creativity

We have already discussed many of the characteristics of giftedness and creativity; however, a "profile," organized to be relatively comprehensive, may be useful. The primary value of such a profile is in helping parents and teachers identify children as gifted, talented, or creative and thus requiring more specialized educational attention. With that in mind, we will present characteristics in two different formats. The first is a discussion from a chapter in Education Commissioner Marland's report to Congress, titled "Profile of the Gifted and Talented Population." Because the writers of this report directed it to Congress, they provided a profile representing the middle ground in thinking about education of the gifted and talented rather than one with a specific theoretical or programmatic bias.

> Probably the area in which the gifted and talented are recognized most frequently is achievement. Large-scale studies over the past 50 years have uniformly agreed that these individuals function at levels far in advance of their age-mates. Beginning at the early primary grades and even at the time of school entry, the gifted and talented present challenging educational problems because of their deviation from the norm.
>
> Typically, half of the gifted have taught themselves to read before school entry. Some of them learn to read as early as 2 years and appreciable numbers are reading at 4. In comparison with their classmates, these children depart increasingly from the average as they progress through the grades, *if their educational program permits.*

■ Unusual intensity is one characteristic of gifted students. ■

In one statewide study of more than 1000 gifted children at all grade levels, the kindergarten group on the average performed at a level comparable to that of second-grade children in reading and mathematics; the average for fourth- and fifth-grade gifted children in all curriculum areas was beyond that of seventh-grade pupils. In another study a representative sample of gifted high school seniors took the Graduate Record Examinations in social sciences, humanities, and natural sciences—examinations normally used for admission to graduate study.

In all of the tests, the high school seniors made an average group score which surpassed the average for college seniors; in the social sciences, they surpassed the average of college seniors with majors in that field. These findings on the attainments of gifted students are typical. . . .

In general, gifted children have been found to be better adjusted and more popular than the general population, although there are definite relationships between educational opportunities and adjustment.

Exceptional capacities create problems for most people, even at the earliest ages. Young gifted children encounter difficulties in attempting to manage and direct activities. Since their ideas differ, they lose the participation of others and find themselves marginal and isolated. Of all children in a large gifted population, those at kindergarten level were reported by teachers to have the highest incidence of poor peer relationships. This was ascribed to the lack of experience at this age in adapting to requirements, in coping with frustrations, or in having available a repertoire of suitable substitute activities, as older pupils would.

When conditions are changed and the gifted and talented are given opportunities to satisfy their desires for knowledge and performance, their own sense of adequacy and well-being improves. Those who can function within an appropriate learning milieu also improve in their attitudes toward themselves and others. If education and life experiences for the gifted are what they should be, the likelihood that the gifted and talented will relate to the total society and work within it actually is enhanced.

The gifted explore ideas and issues earlier than their peers. While they enjoy social associations as others do, they tend early to relate to older companions and to games which involve individual skills or some intellectual pursuits. The gifted child is not necessarily a "grind" or a "loner," despite the fact that he develops special interests early. Biographical data from studies of large populations reveal that these individuals characteristically perform in outstanding fashion — in widely varied organizations, in community groups, in student government, and in athletics. The total impression is of people who perform superbly in many fields and do so with ease.

While the academic advancement of the gifted has generally been recognized even though it has not been served, the early social and psychological development of the gifted has been less frequently noted.

Gifted pupils, even when very young, depart from self-centered concerns and values far earlier than their chronological peers. Problems of morality, religion, and world peace may be troublesome at a very early age. Interest in problems besetting society is common even in elementary-age gifted children.

The composite impression from studies ranging from childhood to adults is of a population which values independence, which is more task- and contribution-oriented than recognition-oriented, which prizes integrity and independent judgment in decision making, which rejects conformity for its own sake and which possesses unusually high social ideals and values.

Of all human groups, the gifted and talented are the least likely to form stereotypes. Their traits, interests, capacities, and alternatives present limitless possibilities for expression; the chief impression one draws from studying this group, at either the child or adult level, is of almost unlimited versatility, multiple talents, and countless ways of effective expression. Because gifted people have many options, they often also encounter problems of choice. When you do well in science but also love music, where does the energy go in a career? Again, there are numerous examples in Terman's longitudinal study of men and women who have been as productive in an avocation as in their chosen careers. (1972, pp. 15–17)

A more common way to indicate the characteristics of any group of exceptional students is to list attributes or characteristics that appear with relative frequency in students identified as part of that group. Such an attempt, titled "Characteristics of Intellectually Gifted Children," has been provided by the Association for the Gifted, a division of The Council for Exceptional Children. Though its title speaks of "intellectually gifted" children, this list also includes a subsection on creative characteristics (see Table 11.1).

To it we would add a few additional behavioral characteristics from pertinent literature.

1. Gifted students have difficulty conversing with age-mates.
2. They can become obnoxious or rebellious when asked to do repetitive tasks.
3. They recognize and are uncomfortable with unresolved ambiguity.

Table 11.1 Characteristics of intellectually gifted children

Few gifted children will display all of the characteristics in a given list; however, they do serve as fairly reliable indicators. These characteristics are signals to indicate that a particular child might warrant closer observation and could require specialized educational attention, pending a more comprehensive assessment.

General Behavioral Characteristics

- Many typically learn to read earlier with a better comprehension of the nuances of the language. As many as half of the gifted and talented population have learned to read before entering school. They often read widely, quickly, and intensely and have large vocabularies.
- They commonly learn basic skills better, more quickly, and with less practice.
- They are better able to construct and handle abstractions than their age mates.
- They are frequently able to pick up and interpret nonverbal cues and can draw inferences which other children have to have spelled out for them.
- They take less for granted, seeking the "hows" and "whys."
- They display a better ability to work independently at an earlier age and for longer periods of time than other children.
- They can sustain longer periods of concentration and attention.
- Their interests are often both wildly eclectic and intensely focused.
- They frequently have seemingly boundless energy, which sometimes leads to a misdiagnosis of "hyperactive."
- They are usually able to respond and relate well to parents, teachers, and other adults. They may prefer the company of older children and adults to that of their peers.
- They are willing to examine the unusual and are highly inquisitive.
- Their behavior is often well organized, goal directed, and efficient with respect to tasks and problems.
- They exhibit an intrinsic motivation to learn, find out, or explore and are often very persistent. "I'd rather do it myself" is a common attitude.
- They enjoy learning new things and new ways of doing things.
- They have a longer attention and concentration span than their peers.

Learning Characteristics

- They may show keen powers of observation, exhibit a sense of the significant, and have an eye for important details.
- They may read a great deal on their own, preferring books and magazines written for youngsters older than themselves.
- They often take great pleasure in intellectual activity.

- They have well developed powers of abstraction, conceptualization, and synthesizing abilities.
- They generally have rapid insight into cause-effect relationships.
- They often display a questioning attitude and seek information for the sake of having it as much as for its instrumental value.
- They are often skeptical, critical, and evaluative. They are quick to spot inconsistencies.
- They often have a large storehouse of information regarding a variety of topics which they can recall quickly.
- They show a ready grasp of underlying principles and can often make valid generalizations about events, people, or objects.
- They readily perceive similarities, differences, and anomalies.
- They often attack complicated material by separating it into its components and analyzing it systematically.

Creative Characteristics

- They are *fluent* thinkers, able to produce a large quantity of possibilities, consequences, or related ideas.
- They are *flexible* thinkers, able to use many different alternatives and approaches to problem solving.
- They are *original* thinkers, seeking new, unusual, or unconventional associations and combinations among items of information. They also have an ability to see relationships among seemingly unrelated objects, ideas, or facts.
- They are *elaborative* thinkers, producing new steps, ideas, responses, or other embellishments to a basic idea, situation, or problem.
- They show a willingness to entertain complexity and seem to thrive in problem situations.
- They are good guessers and can construct hypotheses or "what if" questions readily.
- They often are aware of their own impulsiveness and the irrationality within themselves and show emotional sensitivity.
- They have a high level of curiosity about objects, ideas, situations, or events.
- They often display intellectual playfulness, fantasize, and imagine readily.
- They can be less intellectually inhibited than their peers in expressing opinions and ideas and often exhibit spirited disagreement.
- They have a sensitivity to beauty and are attracted to aesthetic dimensions.

SOURCE: Reprinted from Whitmore, J. R. (1985) ERIC Digest No. 344, pp. 1–2. Reston, VA: The Council for Exceptional Children.

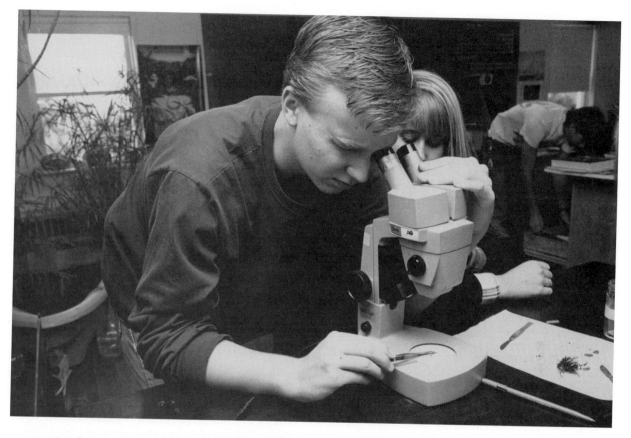

■ Our future scientists are in today's classrooms among the gifted students. ■

4. They can be deliberate underachievers under certain conditions.
5. They dislike group projects (with normal peers).

These five characteristics are less positive than those listed earlier; however, they are very likely to be seen in some gifted or creative students. In part they may reflect the inappropriate programs that are often provided students with unusual intellectual ability or high-level creativity. But they also reflect the fact that students who are gifted, talented, or creative are, first of all, students.

A final way to view the characteristics of the gifted is provided by Terman's follow-up studies. In his study, 1528 subjects who had been identified as intellectually gifted 35 years earlier were studied again at midlife (Terman & Oden, 1959). The following results were reported.

1. Their mortality rate was lower than that of the general population.
2. Their incidence of crime and delinquency was very low compared with the general population's.
3. The gifted men were far more likely to hold professional and higher-level business positions than were a group of randomly selected men of the same age.

4. The income of the gifted group was nearly double the average income of others in the same vocational categories.
5. The divorce rate among individuals in the gifted group was significantly lower than that of the general population of the same ages.
6. The children of these gifted individuals had a mean score on the Stanford-Binet Individual Test of Intelligence (an IQ) of 132.7 (theoretical average of the general population is 100). Of the total of 2452 children, only .5% tested as having mental retardation, whereas 33% had an IQ of 140 or above.

In this follow-up, data for men and women were analyzed separately because the majority of the women did not work outside the home. Nevertheless, seven women were listed in *American Men of Science* and two in *Who's Who in America.*

Among the men, 70 were listed in *American Men of Science,* 31 in *Who's Who in America.* Together they had produced 60 books and monographs, 2000 scientific and technical papers and articles, 33 novels, and 375 short stories. At least 230 patents had been granted to members of the group. The characteristics of these adults earlier identified as intellectually gifted appeared to include good personal adjustment, success, and meaningful contributions to society.

Identification and Assessment

All comprehensive texts on the education of the gifted include a major section or chapter on identifying these students, and all agree that it should be accomplished using multiple criteria. Borland (1989), however, suggests that the process of selecting students and placing them in appropriate programs is the most difficult, controversial, and thankless of all the tasks in developing and implementing programs for the gifted. He believes that the process is the source of much anxiety—even hostility—for several reasons.

From the parents' point of view, selection may become a matter of personal ego or family honor. They may also believe that their child's involvement in a program for the gifted will improve her or his odds of entering a first-rate university with a scholarship. Some teachers, too, may be upset when one or several of their nominations for such a program are not eventually identified as gifted. And students may have their own feelings about the identification process or joining the existing program. Some do not want to leave their friends; others may feel that placement will lead to a negative label; still others may not want to have to work harder to be at the top of some new peer group. Some will be delighted with their identification.

The identification process usually recommended by authorities is quite similar to that outlined in Chapter 2, which grew out of mandated programs for students with disabilities. Major differences are that prereferral intervention is not usually a factor and that there are no federally mandated requirements for parental permission and involvement. Also, if either a parent or student does not want to be involved in special programming, there is not the same potential for litigation against the school. In the following sections we will describe a representative, comprehensive identification plan, but the definition of giftedness used may lead to variations in any generic plan.

Step 1 Multidimensional screening is the first step in identification. This normally includes nomination procedures (by teachers, administrators, counselors, parents, the student's peers, or the student), and such procedures require structure. Several commercial scales or checklists to guide teacher nominations—and some that appear to be useful for parents—are available, but many local educational agencies have developed their own versions. Lists of characteristics such as we show in Table 11.1—with expanded explanations of "what to look for"—may be provided, and usually staff will receive in-service training to clarify their use. Teachers need assistance to make meaningful nominations, and good programs provide such assistance.

Other information included in the initial screening process may be the results of group tests and any other existing records, such as cumulative files and anecdotal records. Teachers may be asked to complete a standardized behavioral checklist in addition to the nomination form (though some nomination forms are miniversions of the more popular standardized checklists). If the program targets students with specific talents in addition to those intellectually gifted, samples of products or performance may be gathered.

Step 2 After the screening information is collected and assembled into a usable format, either a small committee or a designated coordinator will review the information and decide whether to refer the case to a larger identification and placement committee. If referral seems appropriate, the parents will be contacted for approval and additional information. A case study will be completed, ordinarily including individual assessment of cognitive ability (individual IQ tests), creativity, and perhaps more intensive testing in academic subject areas. Unlike planning for students with disabilities, in which theoretically the local educational agency must provide a full continuum of services, planning for students who are gifted may include only a limited number of program options. The type of individual testing chosen will ordinarily be dictated by the available program options.

Step 3 The identification and placement committee and parents meet to consider the information compiled in step 2, and a decision is made based on the student's needs and the school's ability to meet them. If the options available in the existing program for the gifted seem to be appropriate, and if the parents agree to the placement (option) recommended, the process continues.

Step 4 When the program implementation choice appears to be quite obvious after step 3, step 4 may be bypassed and the IEP developed in step 3. In other instances, before the actual placement, additional functional assessment may be done—particularly if new questions surfaced in the committee meeting. After such assessment, an IEP may be developed (see Chapter 2).

Step 5 The program is implemented. Procedures are established so that program results may be reviewed on a regular basis.

These identification procedures may not be followed, because not all states offer the same degree of monitoring—and in some states there is no state-level monitoring. However, a few states now require IEPs and due process procedures for students who are served by programs for the gifted (Zerkel & Stevens, 1986).

One final word about identification is essential. There are unique problems in identifying gifted or potentially gifted students who are members of culturally diverse populations, or who have, for example, learning disabilities. More will be said about this topic later in this chapter.

■ Creativity and talent may be highly developed at a young age. ■

Educational Interventions

The only justifiable reason to consider special programming for students who are gifted, talented, or creative is to assist them to develop their abilities to the fullest. To provide an educational program that will accomplish this goal, individualized planning is essential. This does not mean that each student is taught individually, but rather that each one's school experience is planned so that individual goals may be met.

The educational approaches used with gifted students have been reported in various studies (Cox, Daniel, & Boston, 1985; Greenlaw & McIntosh, 1988). Such studies provide information just as states and local districts have always reported program options, but theirs is typically a mixture of information about administrative structure or organization and about the type and objectives of instruction. For example, "part-time special class," "resource rooms," "special schools," and "cluster grouping" refer primarily to how students are scheduled and the settings in which they receive instruction. "Acceleration," "enrichment," and "mentorships or internships" also refer to organization and setting but tell us more about how instruction should take place and its objectives. Each type of information is important, but we must also recognize the differences.

Another way to categorize educational services for gifted, talented, or creative students is to call them direct or indirect. Direct services offer the student direct contact with the service providers. For gifted students these will most often be educators, but some might be community resource personnel who are not professional educators. Indirect services would encompass the expertise of consultants who work with the student's teachers, unique materials provided for some special instructional purpose, and other, similar assistance.

One further complication is the number of recognized instructional models: the Autonomous Learner Model, the Enrichment Triad Model, the Structure of Intellect Model, Futuristics, and many more. These models may be based on a philosophy of education or on a theory of the nature of intelligence, but their end product is a specific instructional approach. In fact, the education of gifted students may have spawned more recognized, potentially applicable learning interventions than any other exceptionality.

Regardless of the administrative structure or instructional model utilized, most instruction of these students can be characterized as acceleration, enrichment, or some mixture of the two. Those two terms indicate something about how the student is taught, but the primary focus is the goal of such instruction. We will now examine both approaches, as well as mentorships and internships.

■ Acceleration

Acceleration is any means whereby a student meets educational goals more quickly than is planned in the typical curriculum sequence, and then moves on to the next step. "Pure acceleration" might be interpreted to mean learning exactly the same material as other students without modifying content, sequence, or mode of presentation. In practice, pure acceleration seldom occurs, because many students who can comfortably move at a more rapid pace also mentally modify the content and skip steps in the normal sequence, no matter how educators attempt to present learning materials and opportunities to them.

Acceleration may include early entrance to school, grade skipping, compacted courses, credit by exam, advanced placement classes, and other strategies. Acceleration has been maligned over the years, but curiously there is no research basis for such criticism. Various researchers have, in fact, found that there are no significant negative effects from acceleration (Gallagher, 1985; Pollins, 1983; Stanley, 1981; VanTassel-Baska, 1988). In fact, it appears to improve the motivation, confidence, and scholarship of gifted students and may prevent them from developing habits of mental laziness (VanTassel-Baska, 1988). As is true of any strategy, of course, if acceleration is improperly or inappropriately applied, it may have negative effects.

B. Clark (1988) summarized the advantages of, rationales for, and caveats concerning acceleration as follows.

1. Gifted students appear in any case to naturally select older companions due to their similar maturity level.
2. Acceleration is applicable in any school.
3. Acceleration permits students to enter careers at an earlier age and hence be more productive.
4. Because they spend less time in school, educational costs may be lowered.
5. Acceleration engenders less boredom and dissatisfaction in school.

6. The social and emotional adjustment of accelerated students is generally above average.
7. Acceleration must be continual and coordinated to be successful.
8. Teachers and school administrators tend to oppose acceleration; parents and students who have experienced acceleration tend to favor it.

An expanded version of acceleration advocated by Cox and her colleagues is called flexible pacing. According to them, "the conviction that students should move ahead on the basis of mastery may be the single most important concept for educators designing programs for able learners" (1985, p. 135).

> [Flexible pacing is] any provision that places students at an appropriate instructional level, creating the best possible match between students' achievement and instruction, and allows them to move forward in the curriculum as they achieve mastery of content and skills. For able learners, flexible pacing will generally result in some form of acceleration, accomplished either by moving students up to advanced content or by moving advanced content down to the students. In practice, flexible pacing can be achieved by a variety of methods. (Daniel & Cox, 1988, pp. 1–2)

Daniel and Cox include under the flexible pacing "umbrella" (1) early entrance, (2) concurrent or dual enrollment, (3) continual progress (which they call the "purest form of flexible pacing"), (4) compacted courses, (5) grade skipping, (6) credit by examination, and (7) advanced-level courses.

Flexible pacing then is both a concept and a series of techniques or educational options that allow a student to move ahead on the basis of mastery. It might also be called acceleration at its best.

Enrichment

Enrichment and acceleration are the two most often utilized programs or techniques through which special education is provided for gifted students (Cox et al., 1985; Greenlaw & McIntosh, 1988). Regarding enrichment, B. Clark (1988) notes the following.

1. It is usually implemented in the regular classroom, without utilizing any type of pullout program.
2. It is used at both elementary and secondary levels.
3. It usually adds areas of learning not found in the regular classroom.

In addition, she suggests that

1. It may appeal to administrators because it is the least expensive of the major options for educating gifted students.
2. If it is the total program, growth in content and process needs may be overlooked.
3. It often means just a greater quantity of work for the student.

Clark notes that research indicates that enrichment has "seldom been carefully implemented, and it causes the least change in the opportunities provided for the gifted learner" (1988, p. 202). As for the extent to which enrichment activities are pursued, in the well-known Richardson study (Cox et al., 1985) it was found that of the school districts that reported using enrichment, 58% indicated that students were occupied in enrichment activities for fewer than three hours a week. We would echo the authors' conclusion that "this hardly constitutes a 'program' of enrichment" (p. 37).

Enrichment may be defined by some school district officials as anything extra—that is, anything provided in addition to the regular school program. There are carefully planned enrichment programs such as those that have grown out of Renzulli's Enrichment Triad Model (Renzulli, 1977), but all too often enrichment means too little, too haphazardly planned or coordinated with other components of the student's educational program.

The general category of enrichment often overlaps other categories of planning for gifted students—such as advanced placement. Enrichment activities might include such things as summer programs, mentorships, guest instructors, guided work with community resource persons, field trips, writing for special publications, hobby clubs, or education in some alternative environment. It has proven value, but unless it is part of a well-planned program of services, is based on identified needs of the student, and is coordinated with a consultant who can assist the teacher with ideas and materials, its value may be severely limited. We concur with Clark that "enrichment is most effective when combined with other provisions and modifications" (1988, p. 202).

■ Mentorships and Internships

Mentorships and internships can provide valuable enrichment via after-school, Saturday, or summer programs. When provisions for flexible scheduling during the school day permit, they may also be a part of the student's regular schedule. Mentors are individuals who are willing to share their knowledge and expertise with gifted learners who have a special interest in their field. It is important that the students' interest and level of knowledge in the field be developed sufficiently to benefit from such mentoring. Teachers and program coordinators must therefore exercise judgment in selecting students for such programs.

Mentors may be retired persons who have an unusual record of achievement plus continuing interest in a given field or, in some cases, persons still actively involved in the targeted business or profession. Older students may sometimes serve as mentors for younger students.

Mentorship programs require careful organization and monitoring by educators so that enrichment goals are reached. Mentors must understand the program goals, and parents must approve such programming. Without organization and monitoring, the program can evolve into little more than socialization.

Internships enable the student to work with a professional, learning through observing while providing assistance in some preplanned manner. One common type of internship is with elected government officials. Like mentorships, internships require careful planning and monitoring. In either case, an appropriate match between student and mentor or other individual responsible for the learning experience is essential.

Placement and Program Options

Greenlaw and McIntosh reported the results of a request sent to all state departments of education, asking what programs for the gifted and talented they offered. Specific programs named in responses were (1) acceleration, (2) advanced placement, (3) honors, (4) pullout, (5) IEP, (6) mentorships or internships, (7) special programs, (8) enrichment (independent projects, field trips, seminars, and so on), (9) cluster grouping, (10) resource centers, and (11) self-contained classrooms (1988, p. 439). A student might be served by a combination of these programs (such as pullout and acceleration, resource centers and acceleration, or pullout and IEP). The information presented in Table 11.2 was derived from this report.

Forty-two states had state-level curriculum guides for the education of the gifted and talented, but only six had state-level identification guidelines. The latter fact is particularly interesting because all 50 states have guidelines for identifying students with disabilities.

A second study of national trends and practices in programming for gifted and talented students focused on local school districts. It was conducted by June Cox for the Sid W. Richardson Foundation (Cox et al., 1985), and divided programming categories into 16 types:

Enrichment in the regular classroom
Part-time special classes

People Who Make a Difference

KARI WARING SCHAERRER, FACILITATOR AND ORGANIZER Public school personnel in Salt Lake City, Utah, and staff at the University of Utah had expressed interest in and discussed the need for a viable program for gifted junior high students for years, but it never materialized. Then Kari Schaerrer entered the picture. She says that her motivation was the obvious, urgent need for such a program: there were programs for gifted students in the elementary and high schools, but a glaring gap at the junior high level. Unlike many advocates for these programs, Kari was not trying to help someone in her own family. She was the coordinator of youth education programs for the University of Utah and believed in the potential for such a program.

After analyzing what it would take to initiate the program, Kari structured a setting in which public school personnel and university staff could work together and was successful in counteracting the negative input of those she calls non-believers. Then she got a grant that provided the funds to begin. After considerable persuasion, persistence, facilitation, and organizational effort,

Kari saw the culmination of her efforts. She also accepted an additional responsibility, that of director of the Youth Academy of Excellence.

The Youth Academy of Excellence (YAE) in Salt Lake City is a summer program for highly motivated junior high school students with advanced academic skills. YAE, held on the University of Utah campus, includes a variety of advanced academic experiences, workshops, field trips, and special projects, led by outstanding secondary teachers and university faculty. This interdisciplinary program focuses on creative thinking, problem-solving and decision-making skills, and personal development. In addition to advanced work in more traditional academic areas, YAE has explored such topics as ethical choices in caring for the terminally ill—led by College of Nursing personnel—and substance abuse—assisted by Western Institute of Neuropsychiatry staff. It also includes field trips to the university's Artificial Heart Research Center and the Animal Research Center. The success of the Youth Academy of Excellence is a tribute to the efforts of Kari Waring Schaerrer, recognized by the Utah State Association for Gifted and Talented with their annual Award of Excellence.

Table 11.2 Programs for the gifted in effect in the 50 states (1988)

Program	Number of States Reporting Use
Acceleration	31
Enrichment (individual projects, seminars, etc.)	31
Special programs	28
Cluster grouping	23
Mentorships or internships	20
Resource centers	15
Advanced placement	9
Self-contained classrooms	9
Pullout	8
Honors	6
IEP	5

SOURCE: Derived from data from state departments of education (Greenlaw & McIntosh, 1988).

Full-time special classes
Independent study
Itinerant teacher
Mentorships
Resource rooms
Special schools
Early entrance
Continuous progress
Nongraded schools
Moderate acceleration
Radical acceleration
College Board and Advanced Placement
Fast-paced courses
Concurrent or dual enrollment

With respect to these options, the study uncovered myriad facts.

• The most commonly offered program was the part-time special class or pullout option (72% of the reporting districts).
• Enrichment (63%), independent study (52%), and resource rooms (44%) were the next most frequently offered options.
• The least common options were nongraded schools (3%), special schools (4%), and fast-paced courses (7%).
• There were 15 different configurations or combinations of programs offered in all. The most common combination was enrichment with a part-time special class (25%). That was followed by enrichment, a part-time special class, and a full-time special class (10.3%)—then enrichment, a part-time special class, and an itinerant teacher (9.5%).
• Affluence of the school district had little if any influence on the type of programs offered.
• 63% of the districts had regular evaluation procedures.
• 75% of the districts had an advisory group.
• Special budgeting for these programs was provided in 73% of the districts. Sources for such funds were state education agencies (64%), local funds (49%),

■ Library research, often boring to other students, can be highly stimulating to gifted students. ■

federal funds (15%), and private funds or specific grants (8%). There was no significant correlation between fund source and type of program, except that "private funds" correlated positively with mentorship and continuous progress programs.

Program Models

Several established program models may be followed in planning programs for gifted students. In some instances, two or more models may be used, and in all cases consideration should be given to the need for local adaptations.

■ The Autonomous Learner Model

The Autonomous Learner Model (ALM) for the gifted and talented, developed by Betts (1985), is designed for use in a special class setting. Figure 11.1 graphically portrays the model; Figure 11.2 details one of its dimensions. In a three-year sequence, students move through the five major dimensions: orientation, individual development, enrichment activities, seminars, and in-depth study. The ALM was developed for use at the secondary level; however, Betts reports that it is also used at the elementary level. Like all other models, it is sometimes adapted, used with different timelines, or used with a variety of modifications. Its five dimensions are described as follows.

The Orientation Dimension of the model provides students, teachers, administrators and parents the opportunity to develop a foundation of information concerning the program. Emphasis is placed on understanding the concepts of giftedness, creativity and the development of potential. Students learn more about themselves, their abilities and what the program has to offer. Activities are presented to give students an opportunity to work together as a group, to learn about group process and interaction, and to learn more about the other people in the program.

During the Orientation Dimension of the program, a series of inservices are presented for teachers, administrators, parents and involved community resource people. Again, emphasis is placed on the opportunities possible for students, the

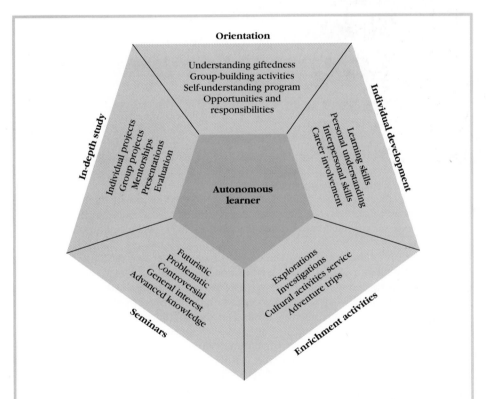

Figure 11.1 The Autonomous Learner Model. All five dimensions of the Autonomous Learner Model are essential for the development of an individual as an autonomous learner. If we look at the environment, either in or out of school, we see all five dimensions being experienced by the individual who has become an Autonomous Learner.

SOURCE: *The figures and description of the ALM model are from the* Autonomous Learner Model for the Gifted and Talented *by G. T. Betts, 1985. Greeley, CO. Autonomous Learning Publications & Specialists (ALPS) copyright 1985 by ALPS. Reprinted by permission.*

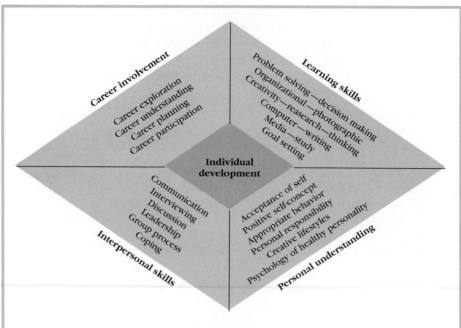

Figure 11.2 Individual Development Dimension

SOURCE: *The figures and description of the ALM model are from the* Autonomous Learner Model for the Gifted and Talented *by G. T. Betts, 1985. Greeley, CO. Autonomous Learning Publications & Specialists (ALPS) copyright 1985 by ALPS. Reprinted by permission.*

responsibilities for students and involved personnel, and information given regarding the overall format of the program.

The Individual Development Dimension of the model provides students with the opportunity to develop the cognitive, emotional and social skills, concepts and attitudes necessary for life-long learning; in other words, to become autonomous in their learning.

The Enrichment Activities Dimension of the model was developed to provide students with opportunities to explore content which is usually not part of the everyday curriculum. Most content in the schools is prescribed. Someone beyond the student is deciding what is to be learned, when it is to be learned, and how it is to be learned. Within the Enrichment Activities Dimension students are able to begin explorations into their major area(s) of emphasis, related areas of interest, and new and unique areas. Students decide what they want to pursue, how it is going to be arranged, and where and when the learning will take place. Gifted and talented students need responsibility in selecting what they are going to study and how they are going to learn.

The Seminar Dimension of the model is designed to give students, in small groups of three to five, the opportunity to research a topic, present it as a seminar to the rest of the group and other interested people, and to evaluate it by criteria selected and developed by the students. A seminar is essential because it allows students the opportunity to move from the role of a *student* to the role of a *learner*. If students are to become learners, they must have an opportunity for independent individual and group learning, which means having a structure which allows and promotes the development of knowledge by the individuals.

The In-Depth Study Dimension of the model allows learners to pursue areas of interest through the development of a long-term small group or individual in-depth study. The learners determine what will be learned, how it will be presented, what help will be necessary, what the final product will be and how the entire learning process will be evaluated. In-Depth Studies are usually continued for a long period of time. Plans are developed by learners, in cooperation with the teacher/facilitator, content specialists, and mentors. The plans are then implemented and completed by the learners, with presentations being made at appropriate times until the completion of the project. A final presentation and evaluation is given to all who are involved and interested. (Betts, 1985, pp. 2–3)

■ Bloom's Taxonomy of Educational Objectives Model

Unlike the other models reviewed in this section, Bloom's taxonomy (1956) was not intended to apply to the education of gifted students when it was developed. Rather it was just what its name implies: a **taxonomy** of educational objectives. Its purpose was to provide a comprehensive hierarchy for classifying learning objectives in relation to assessment. Those objectives could then be used to develop activities that would systematically include all six levels of the taxonomy: (1) knowledge, (2) comprehension, (3) application, (4) analysis, (5) synthesis, and (6) evaluation.

Bloom's taxonomy is used in a variety of ways in programs for students who are gifted. One of its values is that it reminds teachers and program developers that children should learn far beyond the knowledge level, and it provides a systematic way to regularly check whether the program is, in fact, encouraging the higher-level skills of analysis, synthesis, and evaluation. Bloom's taxonomy might not be considered by some as a "program" in the same way that others mentioned here are; however, it has been used as the basis for a wide variety of programs for students who are gifted or talented.

■ The Enrichment Triad Model

Renzulli's Enrichment Triad Model (1977) is a guide for program planning for gifted students that involves three types or levels of enrichment and is recommended for use with a "revolving door" concept. In this concept, 15% to 20% of the school population is identified as a talent pool (for which specific identification procedures are provided). This population is "revolved" into a resource room setting in which all are likely to participate in level 1 and level 2 activities, but only a limited number who show readiness move into level 3 activities.

Type 1 (level 1) activities are called exploratory activities. At this level, students survey a wide variety of topics, seeking to determine which interests them enough for further study. Type 2 activities are called group training activities. At this level, students learn how to develop skills that permit more in-depth study. This is, in many respects, a preparation for type 3 activities.

Type 3 activities are the culmination of this program and might be thought of as preparation to do serious research. Type 3 activities are individual or small-group investigations of real problems. Unless students show an intense interest at level 2 in moving into this third level, they do not do so. As Clark (1988) notes, a strength of the Enrichment Triad Model is that its procedures are clearly outlined and a step-by-step decision-making format is provided. Also, this model can be adapted to fit many different settings.

The Enrichment Triad Model is based on a unique set of assumptions that differentiate it from most other models. Renzulli assumes that giftedness is the result of the interaction of above-average ability, a high level of task commitment, and a high level of creativity. He also assumes that gifted behaviors can be taught, but that if they are not exhibited after exposure and opportunity, service should be discontinued.

Special Programs, Program Elements, or Emphases

In addition to models intended to provide the basis of programs for the gifted, there are various special purpose programs, special program elements, or emphases.

■ Advanced Placement Programs

The Advanced Placement Program offers college-level courses and related examinations sponsored by the New York City–based College Examination Board. Advanced Placement Programs are available in about one-fourth of the secondary schools in the United States and offer advanced courses, honors classes, or independent study projects or tutorials. Courses are usually a full year in length, and credit is determined on the basis of exams. Participating colleges and universities give credit toward graduation, sometimes permitting a full year of credit to be taken.

■ Futuristics and the Future Problem Solving Program

Futuristics is the study of the future. The Future Problem Solving Program, inspired by Paul Torrance (Torrance & Torrance, 1981), involves a yearlong project; local, state, and national competition (both individual and team); and a variety of opportunities for gifted students to learn more about future options for our civilization and to utilize higher-level thinking skills to evaluate them. Nationwide, this program enrolls some 80,000 gifted students in grades 4 through 12. One of the more important premises of futuristics is that the future can be changed.

In addition to the formal Future Problem Solving Program, which permits networking of students and faculty sponsors, there are many games, exercises, and the like that encourage futuristic thinking (Epley, 1985). These resources can be used whether or not a school is part of the Future Problem Solving Program.

■ Special Schools for the Gifted and Talented

Cox and her colleagues (1985) have described a number of successful special schools for gifted or talented students, including those that follow.

1. Project Pegasus, a program for gifted and talented preschoolers sponsored by the education department at Iowa State University
2. The Oaks Academy, a private school for gifted 3-year-olds through sixth-graders in Houston, Texas
3. Windsor Park Elementary School, a public school in Corpus Christi, Texas
4. Walnut Hills High School in Cincinnati, Ohio, a school for the academically talented in which 40% of the students at the 11th- and 12th-grade level enroll in advanced placement classes
5. Bronx High School of Science in the Bronx, New York

■ This gifted child is completing a complex, detailed project. These solar panels should keep occupants of this dollhouse warm through the winter. ■

6. North Carolina School of Science and Math, a state-sponsored school that provides free dormitory space, meals, and tuition to eligible students throughout the state
7. North Carolina School of the Arts, a state-sponsored residential high school and college combined

As you can see, these special school programs are primarily in larger cities and are state sponsored or affiliated with universities. According to Borland, "Some of the soundest programs for gifted students are found in special schools for the gifted. However, it is unlikely that this program format will be seen as a viable option for most schools or school districts" (1989, p. 128).

■ Summer Programs for the Gifted and Talented

Summer programs for gifted and talented students are in many ways quite similar to the special school programs. They serve similar populations, often are joint university–public school programs, residential in nature, and supported—at least in part—by foundation grants. They are different in one significant way: they serve as enrichment for students who remain with their peer group for the majority of their educational experience.

■ Community-Based Resources

A number of authors point out the considerable potential of community resources, the way some school districts utilize them with positive results, and the fact that they are too often overlooked in planning programs for gifted and talented students (B. Clark, 1988; Haring & McCormick, 1990; Sisk, 1987). The following are some of the ways in which community resources are being utilized.

1. Mentorship programs utilize businesspersons, performing artists, engineers, scientists, teachers, professors, college students, and others as appropriate to encourage the interests of gifted or talented students.

2. Facilities such as hospitals, pharmacies, stock exchanges, real estate or insurance company offices, and scientific laboratories provide more information for students who have specific interests. This arrangement might benefit individuals but is usually organized for small-group involvement.

3. Local or nearby "experts" can conduct special purpose seminars at the school.

4. The telephone company, electric power company, electronic companies, construction companies, hardware stores, meat packers, nurseries, park departments, and branch offices of major national corporations are a potential source of free materials.

Corporate officials may be happy to support a local program for students who are gifted or talented, keeping in mind both positive public relations and tax write-offs for donations of materials and supplies. School personnel must be gifted, talented, and especially creative in planning programs for the gifted, talented, and creative.

Special Populations

A significant number of gifted and talented (or potentially gifted and talented) students are never identified, never given special learning opportunities, and thus never achieve the level of personal satisfaction that might have been possible had educators been more successful in their identification efforts. This is unfortunate for these individuals, their families, and all those around them. From a societal benefit point of view, it is an appalling waste of human potential. Some of these students are unidentified due to the lack of programs in their school districts. Some are excluded by very narrow definitions of giftedness or by narrow, limited program provisions. But many fall into special subpopulations that are overlooked or underserved.

Sisk (1987) considers the following populations in her discussion of gifted students who may be underidentified or overlooked: (1) the culturally diverse, (2) the disadvantaged, (3) the highly creative, (4) the gifted with disabilities, (5) gifted females, and (6) the highly gifted. Clark (1988), in a similar discussion, includes (1) the underachieving gifted, (2) the disadvantaged gifted, (3) the culturally diverse gifted, (4) gifted learners with disabilities, and (5) gifted females.

Many issues deserve consideration with respect to these special populations, but the first is that of identification. If students are not identified, special programming cannot be implemented. The problems in identification are simple to pinpoint but difficult to solve. Different language or cultural backgrounds, different early education opportunities, different neighborhood values, and so forth make existing assessment instruments and procedures inappropriate or inapplicable for many.

Whitmore and Maker (1985), in their discussion of educating gifted students with disabilities, provide ideas and suggestions that are applicable to many of these other special populations as well. They single out four major obstacles to identification: (1) the assessor's stereotypic expectations, (2) the child's developmental delays, (3) the assessor's incomplete information, and (4) the child's lack of opportunity to demonstrate his or her superior abilities. They believe that if we are to improve our ability to identify giftedness, professionals "must be trained to stimulate productive and creative thought and to observe the manifestation of those traits in atypical forms" (ibid., p. 21). Cummins (1984) suggests that to meaningfully assess students from bilingual or culturally diverse populations, we must be fully aware of what giftedness means in that subculture. Cummins also believes that observations other than traditional assessment may be of particular value, and that three requirements must be met if such observation is to be meaningful. He believes that assessment personnel must (1) have access to the child's linguistic and cultural world outside of the school, (2) be knowledge-

People Who Make a Difference

RAY KURZWEIL AND THE MAGIC OF COMPUTERS Raymond Kurzweil became interested in magic at an early age and was soon an accomplished magician. Magic was his passion until he discovered computers. By the time Ray was 12 he had written a statistical analysis program that saved so much time that IBM distributed it throughout the country.

Once Ray learned that people recognize things by patterns, he began to dream of a unique and challenging concept. He wanted to develop a computer program that could "read" the letters of the alphabet, no matter what style of print was used. By 1976, Ray Kurzweil had succeeded in making a computer read printed material and reproduce it through a voice synthesizer. When media representatives heard his machine "read" and publicized his invention, he became an instant celebrity.

Ray Kurzweil's first print reader weighed about 350 pounds and cost $50,000. Today's Personal Reader weighs about 20 pounds and costs about $8000. He still aims for a reader that will weigh considerably less, be about the size of a book, and cost less than many personal computers.

While dreaming of improvements to his personal reader, Ray is not idle, and he continues his interest in pattern recognition. He has developed a voice-recognition device (the Kurzweil Voice Report) that allows a dictated report to be produced as printed copy in a matter of minutes. The same voice-recognition technology is being further developed to translate the indistinct speech of persons with cerebral palsy into print, thus increasing their ability to communicate.

Ray Kurzweil has many dreams. For example, he envisions a small screen that will enable people who are deaf to read what others are saying to them. The device may be incorporated in eyeglasses or hand-held and will provide print much like that in closed-caption television or the subtitles in foreign films. Just as Ray once enjoyed the looks of wonderment among his magic show audience, he now dreams of the enjoyment in the faces of those who use inventions that utilize another form of magic: the computer.

able about research findings on bilingualism and second language learning, and (3) ensure that curricular and extracurricular activities encourage the display and development of a diverse range of talents (ibid., p. 219).

One special population that has received limited attention and yet comprises at least half of the talent pool is gifted females. Smutny and Blocksom (1990) speak of them as a "population at risk," and Clark (1988) believes there are barriers to equity for females at home, at school, and in society. Many of these barriers reflect stereotypic expectations that are only slowly changing. Because career motivation and educational goals related to career planning may help develop certain aspects of giftedness, this arena must be explored. Clark cites the lack of encouragement for females to enter the field of mathematics as one example. Grau (1985) outlines a number of psychosocial barriers to career achievement in gifted girls, including (1) a construct of femininity that is inconsistent with achievement; (2) the motherhood, home, and hearth mandates; (3) male-or-female labeling of occupations and professions; and (4) the lack of nontraditional female role models. Girls are more likely to be taught to be passive and accepting, reducing their likelihood of taking risks and developing a spirit of competitiveness. Smutny and Blocksom note that, in addition to the various factors that have led to underrepresentation of females in programs for the gifted, "those women who do enter high status professions tend to achieve less, as measured by both product (for instance, published work) and recognition (awards, *Who's Who* listings) than their male colleagues" (1990, p. 41). Whatever the factors are that have inhibited the development and identification of giftedness in females, they must be targeted and corrected. "The underachievement of gifted girls and women is a loss for both the individuals involved and for society in general. By addressing those factors that contribute to underachievement, educators can nurture the talents of gifted girls and help them make contributions to society that are commensurate with their abilities" (ibid., p. 44).

Another special population may be identified yet provided with inappropriate programming: the highly gifted. This terminology is more often applied to students with unusually high scores on IQ tests. Some larger cities that have provided separate programs for these students use an IQ of 150 as the dividing line between gifted and highly gifted. Whatever the criterion, students with unusually high levels of cognitive ability may require more specialized and separate programming than gifted students who have lower levels of cognitive ability. On the basis of experience with such highly gifted students, it appears that educational programming must be even more individualized for such students to realize their true potential.

For most special populations, identification is the problem that must be solved first; however, once identified, different populations will require different program elements. One element, however, is applicable and important to all. Supplee speaks to this element with respect to her instructional program for gifted underachievers.

> Self-concept and academic achievement appear to be very closely related, particularly in gifted students who underachieve. It is important to include both if we are to be successful. But both goals are not stressed equally at all times. It is essential that the children first learn that *this* classroom is a safe place, *this* classroom is a supportive arena where it is okay to practice new things because nobody is allowed to make another person feel badly. (1990, p. 32)

Supplee's point—that the affective element must be addressed before the cognitive can be successfully developed—is a fitting closing thought.

Issues and Trends

Issues in the education of students who are gifted, talented, or creative are as follows.

- What is an acceptable definition? (Who are the gifted?)
- How can we improve identification procedures, especially for students from culturally diverse and other special populations?
- Should special programs be provided for students who are gifted, talented, and creative?
- Who should fund the excess costs of program provision?
- How, and in what settings, should programs be provided?

Major trends in this area include the broadening of identification procedures, increasing efforts to identify students from special populations, and a move toward more individualized planning through the use of an IEP or similar planning tool.

Summary

Some gifted, talented, and creative students have been given special educational attention throughout history, but almost always to serve the nation, not to benefit the individual. Gifted females were seldom even recognized. There is a growing recognition of the special needs of students who are gifted, talented, or creative, but only a limited effort to provide for their needs on a national basis.

There are varying, divergent conceptualizations of giftedness, talent, and creativity. The most common characteristics associated with these exceptionalities are demonstrated high levels of learning ability and academic achievement. Other definitions have included an unusual ability in leadership or in the performing or visual arts. Potential (as opposed to demonstrated) abilities in each of these areas is also emphasized. The federal definition states that students must need differentiated education or services in order to be identified as gifted or talented.

Characteristics of gifted children may include reading earlier than their peers, expanded vocabularies (for their age), an unusual ability to construct and handle abstractions, wide interests, an above-average ability to work independently, and unusual curiosity, motivation, and attention span. Also, they are often exceptionally well organized and goal directed.

Programs designed for gifted and talented students include acceleration, enrichment, and mentorships or internships. Often a combination of programs may be required, and individual planning is essential.

Three useful program models are the Autonomous Learner Model, Bloom's taxonomy model, and the Enrichment Triad Model. In addition to these more comprehensive models are a number of potentially useful program elements, several of which can be used in conjunction with each other or with other curriculum efforts.

Special populations that may be overlooked include the culturally diverse, the disadvantaged, the highly creative, the disabled, females, and the highly gifted. Each of these populations deserves separate consideration with respect to both initial identification and program interventions following that identification.

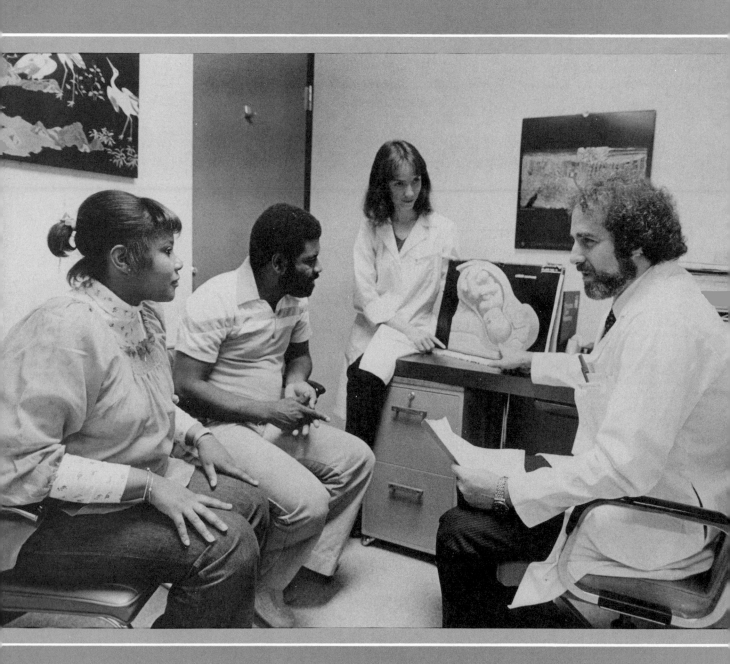

Bethany is 4 years old and has a hearing impairment. She attends a preschool program in which she receives instruction in signing and speech reading. She is learning the names of the colors, listening to stories, playing games, and learning to count. Bethany's parents meet frequently with her teacher to discuss her progress and how they can complement the instruction she receives in preschool. The three of them are beginning to plan for her entrance into kindergarten. Some of the children in her preschool class will attend the same kindergarten class. Bethany is looking forward to kindergarten, which she thinks is more "grown-up."

Allison is 18 months old, and her parents have been told that she has many of the characteristics of autism. She has very little interaction with her parents and 3-year-old brother. She engages in a variety of repetitive behaviors and sometimes has severe temper tantrums. A psychiatric social worker comes to her home weekly to discuss her needs as well as the family's. She has also provided the family with information about autism, helped them make appropriate baby-sitting arrangements, and discussed how they can help Allison's brother adjust to his sister's difficulties. Her parents appreciate the assistance but also have serious concerns about Allison's future.

CHAPTER TWELVE

Early Intervention

For almost all parents[1] the birth of a child is a doorway to the future, a future they imagine as holding almost unlimited possibilities for their new son or daughter. For some parents, however, the experience is tragically different. In researching

[1] Throughout this text, the term *parents* should be interpreted as any individuals responsible for the care and well-being of the child.

her *After the Tears,* Robbin Simons talked with parents raising a child with disabilities; she has these comments.

> For some parents it begins the day their child is born. For others there are weeks, months, even years of foreboding—knowing but not knowing that something is wrong. At some point it is confirmed by a doctor: your child is not the perfect baby you expected. Then the struggle to cope begins.
>
> As soon as a woman becomes pregnant, both parents begin to fantasize about the child they will have. The child will be perfect—beautiful, successful, all the things the parents would like to be themselves. Sometimes they talk about the dreams together. Sometimes they don't even realize they have them . . . until their child is born. Then suddenly they hit. In the case of a child with a disability, parents spend much of the child's early life learning to accept that the child they have is not the child that they wanted.
>
> The initial reaction is usually shock and panic. "I can't handle this! What will I do?!" They are terrified—afraid that they will not be able to cope with the situation; afraid of the future—both theirs and the child's—which they assume will be terrible. (1987, p. 5)

The courage of parents caring for children who have special needs was and is a powerful force in instigating and supporting efforts to produce legislation and services for them. As we have mentioned, parental and professional partnerships were instrumental in the passage of PL 94-142. These ongoing efforts can also be credited with the popularity of early education and intervention programs. Indeed, the passage in 1986 of PL 99-457, Amendments to the Education of the Handicapped Act, was the catalyst for an "explosion" of programs and services for children with special needs from birth through preschool.

Analyzing the popularity of early childhood education, Morrison (1991) has pointed out several factors that have contributed. Among them is the increasing recognition among parents and the public of the importance of early education to later learning and development. This realization is perhaps epitomized by the upwardly mobile parents who believe they have only a few years in which to set the course of their children's futures. Many of these parents exhibit the same goal-oriented drive toward their children as they do toward their careers. The focus on early childhood and infant programs has also been spurred by such serious problems as addicted babies and infants born with AIDS, in addition to the ever-present problem of children living in abject poverty. The media spotlight on these topics has both reflected the popularity of the subject and been a source of public information and provoker of further interest. Morrison points to magazines like *First, Working Mother,* and *Parenting* as proof of an expanding interest. These publications have combined with a multitude of professional journals and newsletters to provide a forum for information, theory, and debate over early childhood issues.

The Importance of Early Intervention

Early intervention with children who are disabled or at risk seems to have its own intrinsic logic. Theoretical arguments, the needs of society, and research evidence have further strengthened the rationale for such intervention. Hanson and Lynch (1989) have formulated four bases of this rationale.

1. The importance of early intervention interactions
2. A desire to prevent or lessen secondary disabilities and effects
3. A concern for the needs of the families of children who are disabled or at risk
4. The benefits of early intervention to all of society

We will briefly discuss some key points contained within each of these areas.

The importance of early intervention interactions for later developmental stages was clearly outlined by Jean Piaget (1952). His theory of cognitive develop-

---

**Box 12.1
What
Research Says
about Early
Childhood
Education**

Both the Council of Chief State School Officers and the National Association of State Boards of Education have called for a new pedagogy for the elementary school: one that's based on what experts know about how young children develop and learn.

But what does good practice look like? Many of the ideas innovative educators are working with today aren't really new: John Dewey, Jean Piaget, and others described good practice years ago. For starters, though, consider the following:

• *Good early childhood education recognizes that young children learn best by doing.* Young children are active learners who construct an understanding of themselves and their surroundings through direct experience, not rote knowledge. Effective early childhood education encourages children to become actively involved in their own learning and takes full advantage of all their senses. Young children learn by playing.

• *Good early childhood education is developmentally appropriate.* Psychologists and educators have a good idea of how youngsters develop. Good classroom practice matches classroom activities with each child's interests and abilities—and recognizes that all youngsters progress at different rates.

• *Good early childhood education is multicultural and community-based.* Developing a strong, positive sense of identity and the social skills to interact well with others are important tasks in the early years. Culture, ethnicity, race, language, and neighborhood are part of what defines each child's identity. Early childhood educators nurture every aspect of a child's identity and help children become aware of both their unique and common characteristics.

• *Good early childhood education is a teacher-dependent enterprise.* No cookbook curriculum exists for early childhood education. Instead, teachers must create personal learning experiences for each child, taking what they know about the normal process of child development and adapting it to the child's situation. Effective elementary school teachers are constantly reinventing the curriculum.

• *Good early childhood programs recognize that learning is an integrated process.* Young children don't recognize the distinction between math and science, reading and physical education. And they don't learn just in school. Effective programs don't draw lines around elements of the curriculum, and they don't lock kids inside the schoolhouse. They also recognize that children's physical and social well-being are as important as their cognitive skills.

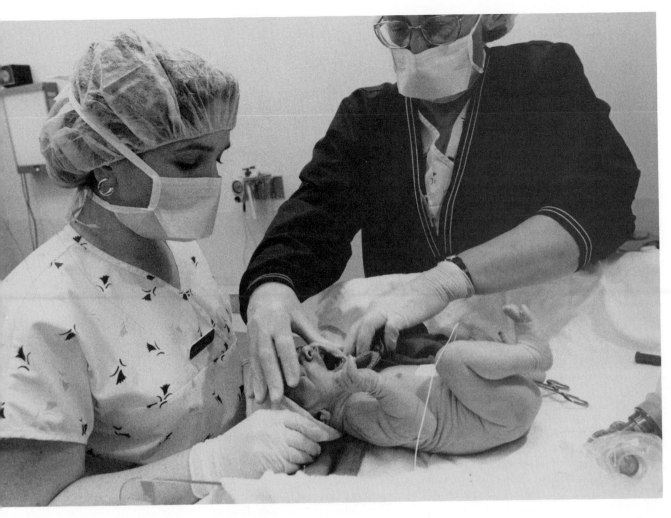

■ Newborns should be thoroughly evaluated by a physician, including the use of appropriate screening scales. ■

ment had a profound effect on many fields, including education. Its central concept is that cognitive and affective development results from a series of adaptations in response to interactions with the environment. This process occurs in several stages somewhat sequentially, each stage being built on the cognitive advances of the preceding one (Wadsworth, 1989). Other research in the 1950s and 1960s (Hunt, 1961; Skeels, 1966; Stone, Smith, & Murphy, 1973) caused professionals to begin to see the infant as capable and active in adapting to the environment and emphasized the importance of providing an optimal environment for intellectual development. The combination of these and many other theoretical constructs and research studies helped to establish the early years as crucial to the child's later development. Though some later studies found that the early years are not the only crucial periods of development (Clarke & Clarke, 1976), failure to address early interactions in the life of the child may result in significant developmental lags or wasted time for the child who is disabled or at risk (Hanson & Lynch, 1989).

The desire to reduce or prevent secondary disabilities or effects is another strong motivation for early intervention. As the theories and research findings imply, an optimal environment can be important in preventing or reducing further negative effects on disabled or at-risk children. Young children and infants who are hard of hearing, deaf, or visually impaired can benefit from alternative ways of exploring their environment and expanding intellectual growth. Some conditions, if not treated early, can result in further negative effects. The infant who is physically disabled can suffer from increased problems—such as contracture of the muscles or tendons that further restricts movement and range of motion—if preventive therapeutic steps are not taken. Assisting the family to deal with an infant or child who is disabled and providing supportive counseling can reduce the powerful emotional impact of disability on the family and the child. Such help might prevent or lessen the likelihood of emotional or behavioral problems.

When a child has disabilities or is at risk the family is presented with major new challenges, including working with a variety of professionals at a time when emotional, financial, and informational needs are greatest. While lengthy and sometimes complex assessment may be taking place with the child, the family, too, needs attention. The concept of family assessment is discussed by authorities such as Bailey and Simeonsson, who list five reasons for supporting it.

1. To meet legal mandates
2. To understand the child as a part of the family system
3. To identify the family's need for services
4. To identify the family's strengths that promote adaptation
5. To expand the base for evaluating services (1988, p. 2)

Family assessment procedures afford a more focused view of the family's needs. Needs as general as emotional support and as specific as information about feeding or positioning the child must be met and fulfilled early, so that positive and nurturing interactions can be maximized between child and family.

A number of studies have evaluated the cost effectiveness of early intervention. Most of them have concentrated on the elementary years and provided data indicating the savings realized when students were able to reduce or eliminate the need for special education services. A project that has received a great deal of attention and analysis in regard to both efficacy and cost effectiveness is the long-term follow-up of the Ypsilanti Perry Preschool Project in Ypsilanti, Michigan. Schweinhart and Weikart (1980) reported data demonstrating that the financial investment for the preschool project produced a cost savings for society. The cost benefits were summarized as follows.

1. A major portion of the cost savings was in fewer and less costly special and compensatory education services for participating children following the project.
2. Preschool participants would have higher projected lifetime earnings.
3. Fewer parental hours would be lost from work while the child attended preschool.

Further study, conducted when the students had reached age 19 and had completed school (Schweinhart & Weikart, 1986), indicated that the return on the initial investment was equal to three and one-half times the cost of two years of

Table 12.1 Cost effectiveness of early intervention

Age at Which Services Begin	Projected Educational Costs
Birth	$50,000
2 years	$50,000
6 years, with attrition and entrance into regular education	$56,250
6 years, remaining in special education	$67,625

preschool and seven times the cost of one year of preschool. The major benefits were the reduced cost of later education and the actual increase in earnings that had been predicted. In addition, the study cited other decreased costs related to welfare assistance, crime, and delinquency.

Another study conducted by Garland, Stone, Swanson, and Woodruff (1981) compared cost benefits of early intervention for children who are disabled beginning at birth, at age 2, at age 6 with attrition and entrance into regular education, and at age 6 remaining in special educational services. Adjusted to 1991 rates, these costs make a convincing argument for cost effectiveness (see Table 12.1).

Bricker (1986) also reviewed a number of studies demonstrating the cost effectiveness of early intervention. After comparing cost data from a variety of studies she summarized, "At the very least, significant savings can be realized if early intervention only prevents the need for residential or institutional care" (p. 55). Bricker goes on to state that even more savings are realized if early intervention increases the likelihood of regular education placement. Additional benefits, such as enabling the parents to become more self-sufficient or reducing the level of services for children needing long-term placement, were also reported.

Taken as a whole, these reviews support the conclusion that the economic benefits to society are greater, or at least justify, the cost of such programs.

■ The Effectiveness of Early Intervention

Peterson (1987) has pointed out that the most powerful argument for early intervention stems from data that document the positive, long-term effects on children. Research in this area has been expanding rapidly, and though it is generally positive about the long-term efficacy of early intervention, methodological problems have become an important concern in any review of such research. Odom (1988) suggests that the problem is that early childhood special education is an applied discipline, and by its nature research in the area is designed to answer pragmatic questions. This engenders a "good news, bad news" scenario. The good news is that the research usually occurs in real settings such as homes, preschool classrooms, and neonatal intensive care units. These natural settings may be presumed to have greater "ecological validity" (Bronfenbrenner, 1976; Brooks & Baumeister, 1977) than do laboratory settings. Ecological validity, according to Odom, is the degree to which results accurately reflect events or happenings in the natural environment. The bad news is that the researcher may have only limited control over a large number of variables of interest to the research. Hanson and Lynch (1989) point out that much of the research in the last several decades has been short-term studies, limited in resources, and conducted by the specific intervention program. Some of its more serious methodological flaws have been difficulties in including a control group, limited documentation of

NORMA CLAYPOOL—"HOW GHASTLY IT WOULD BE!" Norma Claypool, an itinerant teacher of students with visual impairments, used to service a home for children who were considered unadoptable. One little girl, Elaine, seemed to have more problems than the others. Elaine was blind and appeared to be mentally retarded. At age 2 she couldn't feed herself, speak, or understand more than a few words. Attempts to stimulate Elaine did not arouse her interest, and she showed no sign of pleasure in response to attention.

As part of her professional responsibility, Norma completed several types of assessment and questioned whether Elaine was in fact mentally retarded. Further assessment was completed, and as a result of Norma's continued interest, she was permitted to take Elaine home for weekends and later for longer visits.

Norma literally bombarded Elaine with experiences. She told her stories, read to her, arranged to have her play with neighborhood children, and encouraged her to explore her environment. She provided Elaine with a variety of motor experiences such as swinging in swings, climbing jungle gyms and slides, and rolling balls around. Elaine learned to "help" around the house, and all the while Norma talked to her about her experiences, thus developing language skills.

Norma knew through her interactions with Elaine and the additional assessments that she was a bright child. After weekends, when it was time to take Elaine back to the home, she cried and so did Norma. "I thought, 'This is ridiculous! This baby needs a home,'" says Norma, "so I decided to adopt her."

Norma was allowed to take Elaine home as a foster child, but the social worker told her, "You can't adopt her. You are 37—too old to adopt and you are single. It won't happen." Norma hired an attorney and took the case to court. "When the judge said, 'This court now recognizes this child as Elaine Claypool' and she turned to me and said,

'Mommy, my Mommy,' everyone in that courtroom was moved," recalls Norma.

Norma has since adopted five other children. Her family includes Gayle, who was born with only part of her brain and is fed through a tube in her stomach; Dawna, who was born with Down syndrome; Tommy, who was so severely beaten by his mother that he has permanent brain damage; Danny, who is seriously emotionally disturbed; and Richard, who was born with a disfigured face and has no sight in one eye. Elaine, now in her 20s, plays the piano, cornet, and violin and is finishing college. "I like being the oldest," says Elaine. "I get to mother the other kids, and that's fun."

When Norma began her program of intervention with Elaine, it was based on both professional and personal experience. The youngest of six children, Norma had become blind at 2 as the result of retinoblastoma. When she could no longer see she refused to walk, and with older siblings and parents available, she was carried wherever she wanted to go. Her ophthalmologist, warning the family that their aid was more harmful than helpful, advised them to get a puppy, put Norma down, and let her go. Norma says, "It worked. Mother brought home a 6-week-old puppy who wasn't as well trained as my family. She'd hop off the couch and when I'd yell for her to come back, she wouldn't. After crawling after her a few times, it just seemed natural for me to walk."

Norma graduated from a school for the blind and wanted to attend college. Money was a big problem, but she had a plan. She would attend business school for a year, get a guide dog, and take any job she could find to earn money. She graduated from college, became a teacher of students with visual impairments, and later earned her doctorate.

Norma is now retired from college teaching and is surrounded by her young family. She says, "I've thought about what it would have been like to have a life different from this. I could have just taught, saved my money, and traveled. But then I always wind up thinking how ghastly it would be!"

■ How do we best help this teenager prepare for the responsibilities of parenthood? ■

the type or degree of treatment, failure to control for effects of related services, small sample sizes, and lack of measurement instruments or their inappropriateness to the populations examined. In spite of these limitations, some positive conclusions regarding the effectiveness of early intervention can be drawn.

In a meta-analysis study conducted by the Early Intervention Research Institute at Utah State University, White, Bush, and Castro (1986) studied 52 previous reviews of early intervention efficacy studies. They found that 94% of those reviews concluded that early intervention provided significant immediate benefits for children who are disabled, at risk, or disadvantaged. In further study at the Institute, researchers concluded that early intervention does result in significant positive program effects and that the more intensive and structured the program, the greater its effects (Castro & Mastropieri, 1985; White & Castro, 1985; White, Mastropieri, & Castro, 1984). Within the last decade other researchers have borne out both the educational and economic benefits of early intervention for children and infants who are disabled or at risk (Fewell & Oelwein, 1991; Meisels, 1985). In a summary of the House report that accompanied PL 99-457, Smith (1988) highlighted the following accomplishments of early intervention.

1. The enhancement of intelligence in some children
2. Substantial gains in all developmental areas
3. The prevention or reduction of secondary disabling conditions
4. Reduction in family stress
5. Reduction in institutionalization and dependency
6. Reduction in the need for and intensity of school-age special educational services
7. Substantial reduction of health care and educational costs

Although there is no doubt about the need for more and "cleaner" empirical research into early intervention for children and infants who are at risk or disabled, the preponderance of evidence seems to bear out the intuitive logic of conducting early intervention with these children and their families.

Historical Background

Several authors (Morrison, 1991; Peterson, 1987) have traced the historical roots of early childhood education. As can be seen from the contribution of early theorists and educators (Table 12.2), many currently popular concepts in the field have been long established by early theory and practice. The work of these theorists and educators provided concepts and paved the way for current programs for children who are disabled or at risk. The migration of nursery schools and kindergarten programs to the United States from Great Britain and continental Europe brought a new focus to early education in the United States.

Compensatory programs have also played a major role in the creation of early intervention programs for these children; primarily illustrated by the Head Start program, they were designed to *compensate* for deficits in children's living environments. The goal was to assist disadvantaged children by providing educational and environmental experiences that might better prepare them for the school experience. An outgrowth of the War on Poverty movement of the 1960s, Head Start was a community-centered approach. It stressed parent involvement and attempted a comprehensive approach through the use of a wide variety of health, social service, and educational professionals. Harnessing the idealism and energy of the socially conscious sixties, these programs were often colorful, dynamic, and hotly debated throughout the country.

The effectiveness of the Head Start movement as a whole has been difficult to judge, for the name itself tends to be a generic rather than a specific identifying term for a particular instructional program. Whereas some programs apparently achieved few lasting academic gains (McKey et al., 1985), the social and medical

Table 12.2 Historical influences on early education

Martin Luther (1483–1546)	Emphasized individuals interpreting scriptures for themselves, thereby pressuring schools to teach children to read. Argued for public support for education.
John Amos Comenius (1592–1670)	Advocated lifelong education beginning at an early age. Argued that education should follow the order of nature: a timetable for growth and learning should not be forced.
John Locke (1632–1704)	Popularized the "blank tablet" view of children: experience and environment form the mind and nature of the child. Sensory training is an important key to learning.
Jean Jacques Rousseau (1712–1778)	Advocated naturalism, a return to nature, and a natural approach to educating children. We should observe a child's unfolding and provide experiences at appropriate times.
Johann Henrick Pestalozzi (1746–1827)	Promoted the integration of home life, vocational education, and education in reading and writing. Felt the best route to learning was to teach children, not subjects. Promoted multi-age grouping and parent programs.
Robert Owen (1771–1858)	Believed good traits were instilled at an early age, and that behavior was primarily influenced by the environment. Opened an infant school for children of mill workers and gave night classes to the workers themselves. Linked social change with education. Infant schools became the forerunner of kindergartens.
Friedrich Wilhelm Froebel (1782–1852)	Considered by many to be the "father" of kindergarten. Devoted his life to a system of educating young children and teachers. Said the role of an educator is like that of a gardener who watches the plant unfold and provides nourishment at proper times. His "gardens of children" or, in German, *Kindergärten*, stressed the importance of play to learning.
Maria Montessori (1870–1952)	Developed a system of educating young children that had profound effects on almost all preschool programs. The first woman in Italy to earn a medical degree, she began her work educating children with mental retardation and later applied her theories to nursery schools. Montessori emphasized learning in graded sequences, self-pacing, and self-correcting instructional materials. She, too, felt there were "sensitive periods" for children's learning and emphasized active sensory involvement with the environment.
John Dewey (1859–1952)	Championed the importance of active learning through social and child-initiated interactions. His theory of progressivism stressed child-centered schools and curricula. His concepts encouraged correlating subjects with problem-solving activities.
Jean Piaget (1896–1980)	After working with Theodore Simon and Alfred Binet, went on to devote his life to the study of the development of the intellect. Popularized the stages-of-development approach to cognitive growth, which led to the development of educational curricula and programs for young children. His concepts included the active role of play in cognitive development and cognitive development through interaction with and adaptation to the environment.

goals included in the program may have diffused an overall positive effect. In a review of some of the Head Start research, Stein, Leinhardt, and Bickel stated that "it is important to note that individual programs under Head Start have been successful even if the total collection of initiatives demonstrated mixed results"(1989, p. 149).

One of the benefits of the Head Start initiative was that it served as a forerunner of other compensatory programs such as Follow Through and the Title I program, later to become the Chapter I program for disadvantaged and low-achieving children. All of these programs have sharpened the increasing focus on the need for early intervention.

Along with early education and compensatory education, special education played a crucial part in the development of early intervention programs for the disabled. The thrust of special education was toward the needs and problems of individual children as opposed to the economic and social needs addressed by compensatory education. As we saw in Chapter 1, the societal and legal precedents established by special education litigation and law established the rights for all children with disabilities. As Peterson (1987) points out, each of these three movements—early childhood education, compensatory education, and special education—have acted as "parent fields," contributing greatly to the field of early childhood special education. They have engendered a rich set of theories, practice, and insight that can be used as this new field prepares for the 21st century.

■ Recent Legislation

Public policies regarding early intervention and the legislation that gave birth to them are relatively recent. Among the early legislative milestones in the 1960s were the expansion of the maternal and child health programs in 1963 (PL 88-156); educational assistance to state-operated schools and institutions for the handicapped (PL 89-313), which was used as a frequent revenue source for early intervention initiatives (Allen, 1984); and the creation and funding of the Head Start program in 1965. In 1967 the passage of PL 90-248 added a component to Medicaid by establishing the Early and Periodic Screening, Diagnosis, and Treatment (EPSDT) program. This program provided a much-needed emphasis on the early treatment and identification of developmental and medical problems.

Landmark legislation was passed in 1968 when PL 90-538 created the Handicapped Children's Early Education Program (HCEEP), whose purpose was to expand the knowledge base regarding the potential impact of early intervention. Model Demonstration programs, also known as First Chance programs, were developed and funded through this legislation. Since its inception in 1968, over 500 projects have been funded to study programming and effective methods for early intervention and to support research, technical assistance, and planning (Garland, Black, & Jesien, 1986).

The early 1970s saw other significant steps in early education for the disabled when requirements for Head Start programs were modified to include 10% disabled children and services and programs to meet their needs (Allen, 1984). The consequences of these federal requirements were to make Head Start the largest provider of "mainstreamed" services for preschool children with disabilities in the nation (Smith, 1988).

The impact of PL 94-142 on these services has been discussed, but note that along with its basic provisions for special education and Child Find (a program to discover disabled or at-risk children early) it included a Preschool Incentive Grant program. This program encouraged states to voluntarily provide special education services and offered funding for those services for eligible children 3 through 5 years old. It also mandated that if funds were received for those children, all the requirements of PL 94-142 must be met.

Just as PL 94-142 was the cornerstone of special education services in the public schools, the 1986 Education of the Handicapped Act Amendments (PL 99-457) was the framework for extending those services, procedural safeguards, and rights to younger children with disabilities. This act authorized two new programs, one designed to assist the birth-through-age-2 population (Title I, Part H) and the other the 3-through-5 population (Title II, Part B). Though incorporating much of PL 94-142, its specific goal of providing services to infants and toddlers and their families resulted in a focus on the following three key areas.

1. Preventive services were highlighted and described as follows.

Family training, counseling, and home visits; special instruction; speech pathology and audiology; occupational therapy; physical therapy; psychological services; case man-

■ Support and assistance in the home setting. With guidance, parents are the best source of assistance for infants at risk. ■

agement services; medical services for diagnostic or evaluation purposes; early identification, screening, and assessment services; health services necessary to enable the infant or toddler to benefit from other early intervention services. (PL 99-457, Sec. 672)

2. Eligibility requirements focused on developmental delays rather than on categorical disabilities. The requirements included the following.

Individuals from birth to age two, inclusive, who need early intervention services because they (1) are experiencing developmental delays in cognitive development, physical development, language and speech development, psychosocial development, or self-help skills or (2) have a diagnosed physical or mental condition which has a high probability of resulting in developmental delay. (PL 99-457, Sec. 672)

3. PL 99-457 brings a special focus to the family. Though PL 94-142 required parental involvement, it was primarily in the areas of decision making and due process. PL 99-457 sought more integral parent participation in the identification, planning, and delivery of services. It emphasized identifying both the

child's and the family's needs and called for service plans that would speak to both.

Like the IEP, the individual family service plan (IFSP) was designed around goals and objectives; it does not guarantee individual or family success in the program. Krauss (1990) has discussed the IFSP from two perspectives: (1) as a bold radical step taken by the federal government and (2) as a logical extension of existing service practices that focus on the child but involve parents in planning and implementation. He points out that in spite of congressional intent, the real success of the integration of family and child services will depend on subtle and overt ways in which local service providers and programs "negotiate" the IFSP into reality. Future events will determine whether professionals will champion the intent of the IFSP or just minimally comply with its mandates.

Prevalence and Funding

The explosive increase in preschool and infant programs brought about by PL 94-142 and PL 99-457 are evidenced by the following.

- The attendance rate for 3- and 4-year-olds in school-related programs rose from 16% in 1969 to 39% in 1989 (National Center for Education Statistics, 1991).
- The number of 3- to 5-year-olds with disabilities receiving services nationwide increased from 260,000 in 1985 to an estimated 360,000 in 1992. By March 1991 only six states had failed to mandate services for this age group (Viadero, 1991).
- The U.S. Department of Education estimated that the number of disabled toddlers and infants served grew from 36,000 in the 1984/1985 school year to 247,000 in the 1990/1991 school year (ibid.).

This growth brought with it concerns regarding funding, particularly of the mandated services to disabled 3- to 5-year-olds. Changing fiscal realities from the inception of PL 99-457 in 1986 to the fear of a national recession by late 1990 placed preschool and early education initiatives in competition with other demands for rapidly decreasing resources.

The initial funding of PL 99-457, which was designed to provide incentives for programs for 3- to 5-year-olds, followed two separate tracks (see Figure 12.1). Track A represents the money received by the states for the actual number of children served. Track B illustrates the bonus grant money allotted on an estimate of children expected to receive services during the following school year. Adjustments were made each year when actual numbers were compared with the estimates. A single district could serve more children than it had in the year before but receive less money, either because the state overestimated the number of children served and thus received less federal money or because all the states served more than the estimated number, reducing the total money to be distributed. The total amount of federal funding was dependent on the number of children served in each state as well as in all the states combined. Such an uncertain and confusing funding basis made implementation of these services a true administrative challenge for district programs, and the growth of services in the face of such challenges a significant act of courage and commitment.

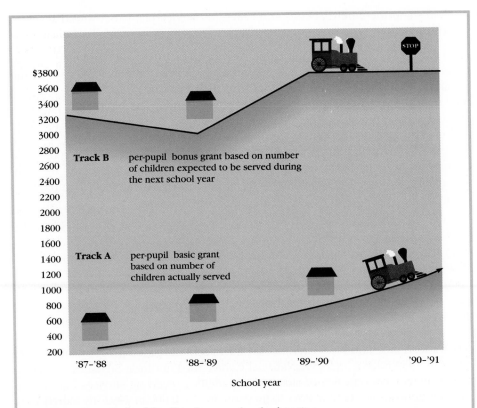

Figure 12.1 Federal funding for preschool education

The Focus on Infants and Toddlers

Rapid growth in services brought with it an increasing awareness of the specialized needs within each of the two highlighted populations. Although services to 3- to 5-year-olds are similar in many ways to those needed by and supplied to newborns and infants, there are also some distinguishing differences. We will therefore consider each of these age groups discretely.

■ **Newborns and Infants**

Thorp and McCollum (1988) discuss three significant themes that differentiate programs for infants from those for preschoolers.

1. The role of the family in the life of the infant
2. The unique nature of the infant as a learner and its implications for instruction
3. The significance of specific medical issues in infancy

The role of the family is crucial during infancy, as the child is most dependent at this time. Family environment is thought to be critical to the future development of the child due to the early formation of attachment relationships. Such relationships must be supported by infant specialists, particularly when infants are ill or disabled. To enhance the outcomes desired for the infant, specialists must be aware that infancy is a period of reorganization for the family. For parents to gain confidence in and knowledge of parenting skills, their needs must also be assessed and integrated into the service plan (Winton, 1986).

The way in which infants learn significantly affects the nature of service delivery. Because social interaction plays a key role in future development, a primary goal of infant intervention is to foster social and communicative competence. Given that group interventions are less useful with infants, service is much more centered on the individual. As infants are thought to learn best through active exploration of the environment, direct instructional strategies are emphasized less than structuring the environment for optimal learning. Any intervention implemented with infants must be sensitive to their level and inherently flexible.

Medical needs during infancy can play a significant role in any plan of service delivery. Infants who are at risk or have specific disabilities often receive intervention in a neonatal intensive care unit (NICU) or other program within a hospital setting. Infant specialists must therefore be comfortable with such settings and with medical approaches and vocabulary. This same level of comfort and familiarity is essential for caregivers who must use medical technology and procedures that allow medically fragile infants to be discharged to the home setting. These situations increase the need for a knowledge of community resources to assist and support the family. In such situations as well as when ongoing diagnosis is needed, infant special educators must be equipped with specific knowledge to assist the family in navigating the complex medical world.

Not only has the combination of these three themes resulted in establishing a base for a new specialty, but the complexities of service provision within it have tended to require going beyond the multidisciplinary team approach and toward transdisciplinary team relationships (Widerstrom, Mowder, & Sandall, 1991). In the transdisciplinary approach team members, including parents, must work as a close-knit unit toward common goals. Its distinguishing characteristic is the sharing of roles and responsibilities in assessment and program implementation. Such teamwork is a response to the ever-growing complexities of service delivery to infants and an aid to the screening, assessment, and intervention process.

■ **Screening, Developmental Milestones, and Risk Factors**

Screening has been defined as the application of simple, accurate measures to determine which children in the population need special intervention to develop optimally (Dumars, Duran-Flores, Foster, & Stills, 1987). To be effective, screening measures should be of short duration and identify two groups of children: those who appear to be at risk and those who do not. Such measures should not be used to provide assessment information (Hutinger, 1988), concentrating instead on their simple sorting task. Effective screening relies on a knowledge of normal development and risk factors. Although this chapter will not attempt to provide an in-depth discussion of these two important areas, some discussion is warranted.

In Chapter 7 we discussed the vital role language plays in learning and the development of the child, and outlined the milestones in speech and language development. Table 12.3 presents additional milestones in other important areas of development. Certainly the significant delay of a developmental milestone may lead to parental or caregiver concern and possible referral for screening. However, other significant risk factors pertain to the infant and the family, according to Hanson and Lynch (1989).

Factors pertaining to the infant
Admitted to NICU following birth
Required 1:1 or 1:2 nurse-patient ratio for longer than 24 hours
Under 32 weeks gestation
Under 1500 grams
Small for gestational age
Severe respiratory distress requiring assisted ventilation for over 48 hours during the first 4 weeks of life
Asphyxia with a 5-minute APGAR of 5 or less
Sustained hypoxemia, acidemia, hypoglycemia, or frequent apnea
Hyperbilirubinemia requiring an exchange transfusion
Severe, persistent metabolic abnormality
Neonatal seizures or nonfebrile seizures during the first 3 years of life
Seizure activity during the first week of life
Evidence of intracranial hemorrhage
Central nervous system lesion or abnormality

Table 12.3 Developmental milestones of children from birth to age 3

	Interest in Others	Self-Awareness	Motor Milestones and Eye/Hand Skills
The Early Months (Birth through 8 Months)	Newborns prefer the human face and human sound. Within the first two weeks, they recognize and prefer the sight, smell, and sound of the principal caregiver. Social smile and mutual gazing is evidence of early social interaction. The infant can initiate and terminate these interactions. Anticipates being lifted or fed and moves body to participate. Sees adults as objects of interest and novelty. Seeks out adults for play. Stretches arms to be taken.	Sucks fingers or hands fortuitously. Observes own hands. Places hand up as an object comes close to the face as if to protect self. Looks to the place on body where being touched. Reaches for and grasps toys. Clasps hands together and fingers them. Tries to cause things to happen. Begins to distinguish friends from strangers. Shows preference for being held by familiar people.	The young infant uses many complex reflexes: searches for something to suck; holds on when falling; turns head to avoid obstruction of breathing; avoids brightness, strong smells, and pain. Puts hand or object in mouth. Begins reaching toward interesting objects. Grasps, releases, regrasps, and releases object again. Lifts head. Holds head up. Sits up without support. Rolls over. Transfers and manipulates objects with hands. Crawls.
Crawlers and Walkers (8 to 18 Months)	Exhibits anxious behavior around unfamiliar adults. Enjoys exploring objects with another as the basis for establishing relationships.	Knows own name. Smiles or plays with self in mirror. Uses large and small muscles to explore confidently when a sense of security is offered by presence of caregiver.	Sits well in chairs. Pulls self up, stands holding furniture. Walks when led. Walks alone. Throws objects. Climbs stairs.

THE MANY FACETS OF EARLY INTERVENTION

The term *early intervention* is appropriately descriptive. In any developing sequence of events, early intervention can change probable later outcomes. Parents, supplied with information and adequate health care, may prevent or reduce the likelihood of giving birth to a child with a disability. When children do not have the best possible chance for normal development and realization of their full potential, early intervention is not only desirable, it is a must.

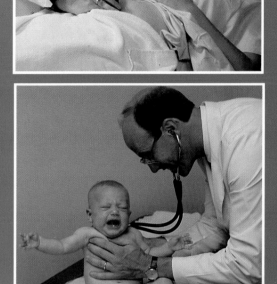

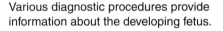

Various diagnostic procedures provide information about the developing fetus.

Regular physical examinations facilitate early intervention.

Prenatal care may minimize some disabilities and eliminate other potential disabilities.

Group activities are essential for all young children, particularly for those at risk, and those with known disabilities. It is also important for young children with disabilities and nondisabled peers to be together for such activities.

Early intervention means reducing the effects of existing disabilities and preventing or reducing the effects of secondary disabilities. It can provide assistance to parents and other family members as they nurture the child with disabilities. It may help reduce feelings of guilt or inadequacy, prevent emotional problems in both parents and siblings of the child with a disability, and help hold marriages together. These benefits to the family mean direct benefits to the child with a disability.

Early intervention aids cognitive, social, physical, and language development. Such planned interventions may be carried out in home-based, center-based, or a combination of home-based and center-based locations. Parents or specially trained professionals provide the needed assistance.

One-on-one (or one-to-one) interaction is an important element of early intervention.

A special teacher-friend can help a child through a difficult time.

Direct early intervention efforts have targeted two major groups of infants and children, those with identifiable disabilities and those considered to be at risk. These infants and children are served through organized, center-based programs, through home-based programs, and through combinations of these two service delivery modes. In all instances, parent education and continuing parent involvement are essential.

Children with disabilities often benefit from assistance from nondisabled peers. Although the teacher may not appear to be directly involved, such peer assistance must be carefully monitored.

Playing as part of a group, with caring supervision, has direct benefits for children with disabilities.

"Working" at motor-skill development can be great fun.

Positive experiences with books pay big dividends later in school.

Playing together expands social skills.

The report accompanying the federal legislation that gave strong impetus to early intervention programs pointed out that early intervention (1) has led to documented, long-term, positive effects for children; (2) can reduce family stress; (3) can reduce institutionalization and dependency; and (4) can reduce the need for and intensity of special education services for school-age children. These known effects mean that early intervention can reduce costs for both health care and education. It is, in short, a "win/win" situation.

This child is involved in one of a variety of household tasks, which are part of preschool programs. Similar tasks are planned to provide opportunities in play and to expand language experience.

Central nervous system infection
Congenital anomalies that may affect developmental outcome
Serious biomedical insult that may affect developmental outcome
Positive neonatal toxicology screen, symptomatic neonatal drug withdrawal,
    or known prenatal drug exposure
Prenatal exposure to known teratogens
Persistent muscle tone abnormality
Failure to thrive

Factors pertaining to the family

Infant born to a developmentally disabled parent
Infant born to a mother under the age of 18 or over 35 years of age
Born to a mother with an educational level of less than 10th grade
Poor maternal attachment
Home environment lacks stimulation
Developmental delay as a consequence of biomedical and/or environmental
    factors[2]

[2] From *Early Intervention: Implementing Child and Family Services for Infants and Toddlers Who Are At-risk or Disabled,* by M.J. Hanson & E.W. Lynch (1989), p. 93. Reprinted by permission of Pro-Ed Inc.

Physical, Spatial, and Temporal Awareness	Purposeful Action and Use of Tools	Expression of Feelings
Comforts self by sucking thumb or finding pacifier. Follows a slowly moving object with eyes. Reaches and grasps toys. Looks for dropped toy. Identifies objects from various viewpoints. Finds a toy hidden under a blanket when placed there while watching.	Observes own hands. Grasps rattle when hand and rattle are both in view. Hits or kicks an object to make a pleasing sight or sound continue. Tries to resume a knee ride by bouncing to get adult started again.	Expresses discomfort and comfort/pleasure unambiguously. Responds with more animation and pleasure to primary caregiver than to others. Can usually be comforted by familiar adult when distressed. Smiles and activates the obvious pleasure in response to social stimulation. Very interested in people. Shows displeasure at loss of social contact. Laughs aloud (belly laugh). Shows displeasure or disappointment at loss of toy. Expresses several clearly differentiated emotions: pleasure, anger, anxiety or fear, sadness, joy, excitement, disappointment, exuberance. Reacts to strangers with soberness or anxiety.
Tries to build with blocks. If toy is hidden under one of three cloths while child watches, looks under the right cloth for the toy. Persists in a search for a desired toy even when toy is hidden under distracting objects such as pillows.	When a toy winds down, continues the activity manually. Uses a stick as a tool to obtain a toy. When a music box winds down, searches for the key to wind it up again. Brings a stool to use for reaching for something.	Actively shows affection for familiar person: hugs, smiles at, runs toward, leans against, and so forth. Shows anxiety at separation from primary caregiver. Shows anger focused on people or objects.

(continued)

Persaud (1990) has elaborated on some of these risk factors, focusing on environmental causes of human birth defects. He names eight specific causes:

1. Intrauterine infections
2. Radiation
3. Drugs
4. Substance abuse
5. Industrial and occupational hazards
6. Alcohol
7. Cigarette smoking
8. Caffeine

Though various screening measures have been designed to assist in the process, no nationally sponsored screening program currently exists in the United States. The Early and Periodic Screening, Diagnosis, and Treatment (EPSDT) program, a provision of the Social Security Amendments of 1967, has serviced a number of children but only those eligible for Medicaid—a small portion of the nation's infants and preschoolers (Thurman & Widerstrom, 1985).

Table 12.3 (continued)

	Interest in Others	Self-Awareness	Motor Milestones and Eye/Hand Skills
Crawlers and Walkers (8 to 18 months)	Gets others to do things for child's pleasure (wind up toys, read books, get dolls). Shows considerable interest in peers. Demonstrates intense attention to adult language.	Frequently checks for caregiver's presence. Has heightened awareness of opportunities to make things happen, yet limited awareness of responsibility for own actions. Indicates strong sense of self through assertiveness. Directs actions of others (e.g., "Sit there!") Identifies one or more body parts. Begins to use *me, you, I.*	Uses marker on paper. Stoops, trots, can walk backward a few steps.
Toddlers and 2-Year-Olds (18 Months to 3 Years)	Shows increased awareness of being seen and evaluated by others. Sees others as a barrier to immediate gratification. Begins to realize others have rights and privileges. Gains greater enjoyment from peer play and joint exploration. Begins to see benefits of cooperation. Identifies self with children of same age or sex. Is more aware of the feelings of others. Exhibits more impulse control and self-regulation in relation to others. Enjoys small group activities.	Shows strong sense of self as an individual, as evidenced by "NO" to adult requests. Experiences self as a powerful, potent, creative doer. Explores everything. Becomes capable of self-evaluation and has beginning notions of self (good, bad, attractive, ugly). Makes attempts at self-regulation. Uses names of self and others. Identifies six or more body parts.	Scribbles with markers or crayon. Walks up and down stairs. Can jump off one step. Kicks a ball. Stands on one foot. Threads beads. Draws a circle. Stands and walks on tiptoes. Walks up stairs one foot on each step. Handles scissors. Imitates a horizontal crayon stroke

Lacking a nationally sponsored screening program, we have relied on a variety of allied health fields and their professionals to provide initial information regarding atypical development (Hanson & Lynch, 1989). These professionals are often the first to observe the infant's early development and to initiate some of the first screening assessment measures we will discuss.

For screening programs to achieve optimal results, mass screenings are necessary. Such screenings require community coordination as a primary prerequisite. In addition, interagency cooperation is required to ensure a variety of screening settings, thereby reaching as many people as possible. Such settings include mobile vans, schools, churches, community centers, health fairs, and other places where people who may not seek regular medical care gather. Information exchange, publicity, and continued close working relationships are essential to successful screening.

The need for cooperation and coordination is further implied by the components of Peterson's suggested comprehensive screening program.

* Pediatric examination.

Physical, Spatial, and Temporal Awareness	Purposeful Action and Use of Tools	Expression of Feelings
When chasing a ball that rolled under sofa and out the other side, will make a detour around sofa to get ball. Pushes foot into shoe, arm into sleeve.	Pushes away someone or something not wanted. Feeds self finger food (bits of fruit, crackers). Creeps or walks to get something or avoid unpleasantness. Pushes foot into shoe, arm into sleeve. Partially feeds self with fingers or spoon. Handles cup well with minimal spilling. Handles spoon well for self-feeding.	Expresses negative feelings. Shows pride and pleasure in new accomplishments. Shows intense feelings for parents. Continues to show pleasure in mastery. Asserts self, indicating strong sense of self.
Identifies a familiar object by touch when placed in a bag with two other objects. Uses "tomorrow," "yesterday." Figures out which child is missing by looking at children who are present. Asserts independence: "Me do it." Puts on simple garments such as cap or slippers.	When playing with a ring-stacking toy, ignores any forms that have no hole. Stacks only rings or other objects with holes. Classifies, labels, and sorts objects by group (hard versus soft, large versus small). Helps dress and undress self.	Frequently displays aggressive feelings and behaviors. Exhibits contrasting states and mood shifts (stubborn versus compliant). Shows increased fearfulness (dark, monsters, etc.). Expresses emotions with increasing control. Aware of own feelings and those of others. Shows pride in creation and production. Verbalizes feelings more often. Expresses feelings in symbolic play. Shows empathic concern for others.

Note: This list is not intended to be exhaustive. Many of the behaviors indicated here will happen earlier or later for individual infants. The chart suggests an approximate time when a behavior might appear, but it should not be rigidly interpreted. Often, but not always, the behaviors appear in the order in which they emerge. Particularly for younger infants, the behaviors listed in one domain overlap considerably with several other developmental domains. Some behaviors are placed under more than one category to emphasize this interrelationship.
SOURCE: *Adapted from S. Bredekamp (Ed.),* Developmentally Appropriate Practice in Early Childhood Programs Serving Children from Birth through Age 8, *1989, pp. 30–31. Reprinted with permission of the National Association for the Education of Young Children.*

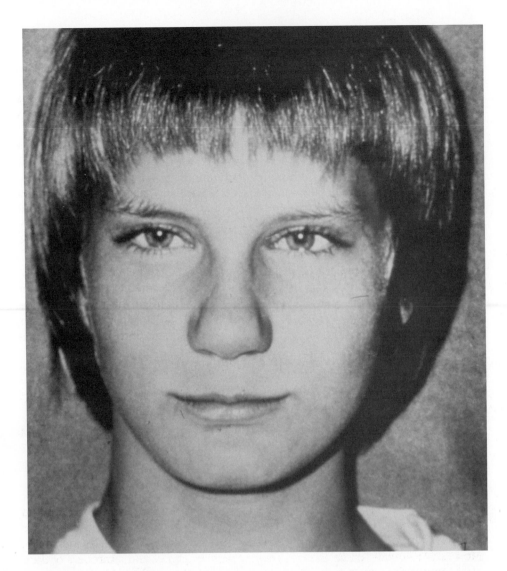

■ Fetal Alcohol Syndrome (FAS) may result when alcohol is consumed during pregnancy. FAS children are usually identifiable by facial characteristics. They may experience a variety of learning problems. ■

• Developmental history obtained through interview of the parent(s) or primary caregiver and possible use of a checklist or questionnaire to gather specific facts about the developmental history.

• Parental or primary caregiver input regarding special problems or concerns about the child.

• Evaluation of child's general developmental status using a screening instrument.

• Specialized developmental reviews (as determined by the services available, the child population, and the individual subject) in four domains: (a) physical status, (b) psychological/developmental status, (c) family status, and (d) environmental, social/cultural status. The psychological-developmental domain may include a review of cognitive development, emotional development, speech and language development, auditory perception, visual perception, self-help and adaptive skills, and motor development. (1987, p. 291)

One of the most common screening procedures in use is the APGAR Scale. Developed by Dr. Virginia Apgar in 1952, this scale was designed to measure a newborn's physical responsiveness, development, and overall health (Apgar, 1953). The measure is administered by a member of the delivery team in the hospital at 60 seconds, 5 minutes, and 10 minutes following birth. The infant is judged on five characteristics and given from 0 to 2 points on each one—2 points reflecting the best possible condition. The five measures include muscle tone, heart rate, reflex to stimulation, color, and respiration effort. The APGAR Scale is widely used in Western countries and administered to virtually 100% of the babies born in American hospitals (Heward & Orlansky, 1988). There appears to be a relationship between the APGAR score and variables such as maternal health and emotional status, perinatal conditions, and infant mortality during the neonatal period. Although it is currently the only widely used screening test to identify high-risk infants, relating its scores to later development is questionable (Self & Horowitz, 1979).

Another widely used screening test for infants detects phenylketonuria (PKU). If undetected, this enzyme defect can result in severe mental retardation, but given early diagnosis and treatment mental retardation can be prevented. The screening entails studying a drop of blood taken from the infant's heel. Other newborn tests are available for conditions such as cystic fibrosis, galactosemia, and congenital hypothyroidism.

The Neonatal Behavioral Assessment Scale (NBAS), also referred to as the Brazelton, was designed to measure the infant's response to the environment (Brazelton, 1984). Administered by a skilled observer, the test is appropriate for 1-day-old to 1-month-old infants. The NBAS consists of 28 behavioral and 18 reflex measures. They record the infant's responses to a variety of sensory stimuli and activity levels and also measure reflexes such as sucking, rooting, and plantar grasp. The examiner assesses the infant's ability to modify its own systems in response to external manipulation.

An interesting utilization of the NBAS has been as a clinical teaching tool for parents. The parents are present during the administration of the measure and are able to observe the infant's skills and capabilities as well as the way the examiner holds, positions, and in general interacts with the infant (Widerstrom, Mowder, & Sandall, 1991). Observation of these strategies and awareness of their child's particular signals may increase their knowledge of child development and foster positive parenting skills (Szajnberg, Ward, Krauss, & Kessler, 1987).

The Assessment of Preterm Infants' Behavior (APIB) focuses on the preterm and high-risk infant (Als et al., 1986). It was designed to be an extension of the NBAS, and though it uses variations of some of the same items, particular attention is given to the infant's communicative signals (such as color changes, movement, alertness, or startle responses). Skilled examiners may use the APIB to determine the amount of support the infant needs for optimal development and to identify intervention goals (ibid.). Box 12.2 is an example of how the APIB can be used.

The Denver Developmental Screening Test (DDST) is also widely used to screen infants (Frankenburg, Dodds, & Fandal, 1975). It evaluates four developmental areas: language, gross motor, fine motor–adaptive, and personal social. Each test item is scored to provide a comparison with normally developing children. A bar on the scoring form indicates at what ages 25%, 50%, 75%, and 90% of normally developing children achieve success on the item. A child's performance would be considered delayed if two of the four developmental areas contained two or more delayed items.

Three approaches have been developed to assess visual acuity (Widerstrom, Mowder, & Sandall, 1991).

1. Optokinetic response: Response to visual movement in the form of a black-and-white striped cylinder is measured (London, 1982).
2. Visually evoked response: Electrodes measure the brain's response to visual stimuli (Harley, 1983).
3. Forced preferential looking: Infant must choose between a blank or patterned target; the assumption is that those of more normal acuity will select the patterned (Teller, McDonald, Preston, Sebris, & Dobson, 1986).

These methods are supplemented by others through which an infant's functional vision is evaluated.

Methods to monitor an infant's behavior can also screen for possible hearing problems. Chief among these have been the blink and startle response to a variety of auditory stimuli, including a bell, whistle, buzzer, or human voice. These methods can provide a gross indication of auditory function, but the need for more controlled and dependable measures has led to new procedures. Among these are the Crib-O-Gram, a device that measures an infant's movements in response to auditory stimuli (Simmons, 1977); automatic brain response (ABR) procedures, which utilize electrodes to measure brain stem response to noise (Cox, 1988); and, for older infants (6 months or more), Visual Reinforced Audiometry (Thompson & Wilson, 1984), which utilizes a conditioning response to a lighted display when a sound is presented.

As Peterson (1987) has reminded us, no matter how ideal and comprehensive the screening process is, it serves no functional purpose if follow-up assessment and intervention services are not available.

Box 12.2
A Use of
the APIB

Michelle is a 3-month-old infant in the NICU. She was born after 27 weeks' gestation and weighed 895 grams. She has bronchopulmonary dysplasia and is on a ventilator. Using the APIB, Michelle was observed during rest, taking of vital signs, diaper change, and return to rest. Based on these observations, the following recommendations were made:

- Side-lying is a good position for Michelle. Make sure she is in total flexion and that her airways are not occluded. Use a rolled sandbag or blanket behind her head and neck. It will help her maintain this position.
- Michelle likes to suck on her fingers. When she is lying on her side, make sure that her arms are positioned forward so that she can easily find her fingers. When holding her, position her shoulders and arms forward so that she can easily reach her fingers.
- When caring for Michelle, uncover her slowly. Watch her for signs of stress (color, change, arching, grimace). Use your hands to contain her limbs and maintain her flexion. Michelle should have something to suck on during and after handling.

■ Painting is an important means of self-expression and can aid in determining coordination and developmental level. ■

Assessment

■ Assessment of the Child

Although assessment procedures vary, McLoughlin and Lewis (1990) have suggested three primary purposes for them.

1. Detection: determination of a developmental disability
2. Diagnosis: description of the nature of the developmental problem
3. Prescriptive study: determination of programmatic needs

At the detection level, infants screened and thought to differ from the norm are further tested. If a disability is suspected, children receive more in-depth study to determine the specific nature of the disability. This may result in a specific physical diagnosis such as visual impairment, hearing impairment, and cerebral palsy or in educational diagnoses stated in terms of levels of performance or degrees of developmental delay. It is at this stage in the process that eligibility is determined. Such eligibility, to be consistent with PL 99-457, must be based on evaluations that are both multidisciplinary and multidimensional. The multidimensional requirement of assessment assists greatly in fulfilling the third, or prescriptive, stage. Having determined an infant's eligibility for services, a thorough look is given to strengths and weaknesses so that programmatic needs can be identified. To provide a more in-depth look at this process, we will further examine the key components of interdisciplinary teams and multidimensional assessment.

Earlier we commented on the trend, promoted by both PL 94-142 and PL 99-457, to move from multidisciplinary through interdisciplinary to transdisciplinary intervention teams. As the following descriptions imply, the primary difference in these three models is the amount of overlap between the various disciplines.

1. A *multidisciplinary team* is a group of professionals who independently perform tasks related to the same purpose. They are considered a team only because they share a common goal. The medical field takes this approach: many disciplines may make separate diagnoses; however, there is no collaboration among members. They have a patient in common and one member may be responsible for informing the patient of all the results.

2. An *interdisciplinary team* is a group of professionals who independently perform tasks related to a common goal and who coordinate their efforts. They are a team because they share a common goal as well as information throughout the time in which they function as a team. The various disciplines support and complement each other by means of that shared information.

3. A *transdisciplinary team* is a group of professionals who perform related tasks, share information, and share roles. They are a team because they coordinate all of their efforts and, when appropriate, assume the role of one another. This role-sharing is what makes the transdisciplinary team distinctive.

Regardless of the model used, it's obvious that they have much in common.

The intervention team should be composed of the parents or other appropriate family members or caregivers plus appropriate professionals from a variety of fields. While a team's composition will vary depending on the needs of the family and child, certain professional fields are frequently included (see Table 12.4). One of the initial tasks of the team is to decide what information will be collected and how. Information related to the following areas should be included.

* Language development
* Cognitive development
* Fine and gross motor skills
* Social and emotional development
* Health and medical concerns
* Hearing, vision, and social interaction

Sensitivity to the family's situation is essential so that the family is not overwhelmed by people seeking to obtain information. Various professionals can

Table 12.4 Professionals frequently included on intervention teams

Early Childhood Special Education Teacher	Conducts screening and administers evaluative measures focused on individualized programming needs of children with disabilities.
Nurse	Conducts assessments and gathers information in health-related areas, including health history. Coordinates medical screening and assessments by physicians and helps relay diagnosis and treatment plan from medical specialists to the intervention team.
Occupational Therapist	Conducts an evaluation of motor development, focusing on self-help skills—skills needed to become more independent. Suggests activities to assist in developing fine motor skills and adaptations necessary for such special functions as feeding.
Physical Therapist	Assesses needs in the area of gross motor development, including range of motion, muscle strength, posture, and muscle tone. Provides special assistance with areas of development that use large muscle groups: walking, crawling, sitting, and so on. Often assists with special needs in these areas, such as wheelchairs, crutches, or walkers.
Psychologist	Conducts screening and other evaluative measures primarily focused on cognitive and emotional areas. Provides programming assistance in areas such as social and behavioral problems.
Social Worker	Works closely with the family and provides "intake" counseling, helping the family understand the procedures and intervention process. Provides coordination and facilitates communication among all members of the team, including parents. Provides important family and infant history.
Speech-Language Pathologist	Conducts assessments regarding communication needs and assists in the development of speech and language.

be assigned more than one information-gathering task and the use of videotape can be of assistance in shared observation. Throughout the process care should be taken to obtain all the required information in the least intrusive manner.

The assessment procedures must also be multidimensional. They should view the child through several modes, including direct testing, observation in the child's natural environment, interviews with the parents or other caregivers, and comprehensive review of pertinent records (Widerstrom, Mowder, & Sandall, 1991).

In summary, after studying assessment within the framework of the IFSP, a national task force of early intervention professionals (Johnson, McGonigel, & Kaufmann, 1989) suggested the following.

- Assessment is a continually evolving process.
- Informed consent must be obtained from the family for all assessments.
- Family priorities and needs, child characteristics, and diagnostic concerns should all be considered in planning assessment.
- Identifying family needs must be based on the individual family's decision about which aspects of family life are relevant.
- Assessment must reflect respect and sensitivity for the specific family's values and styles of decision making.

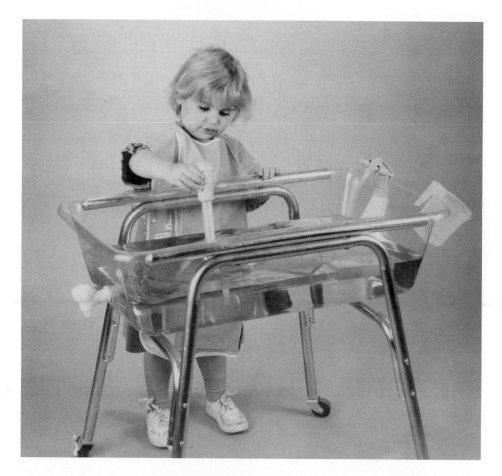

■ A water table provides opportunities for experimentation and demonstrates a child's fine motor skills. ■

- Information should be shared by the team, with opportunities for "give and take" among all members; family members should be allowed to be present for all discussion.
- Language associated with the assessment should be sensitive to the family's preference as much as possible.

■ Assessment of the Family

We have pointed out what some have felt to be the "radical" change in the role of the family with the enactment of PL 99-457. Certainly families were included in the provisions of PL 94-142, but their involvement primarily had to do with established rights and due process procedures, a role Krauss (1990) has referred to as "passive review and approval." When goals and objectives concerning the family were included, they may have reflected—primarily or exclusively—staff members' perceptions of family needs.

PL 99-457, through the IFSP, mandated a much different relationship between parents and the assessment and intervention team. Its philosophy has challenged

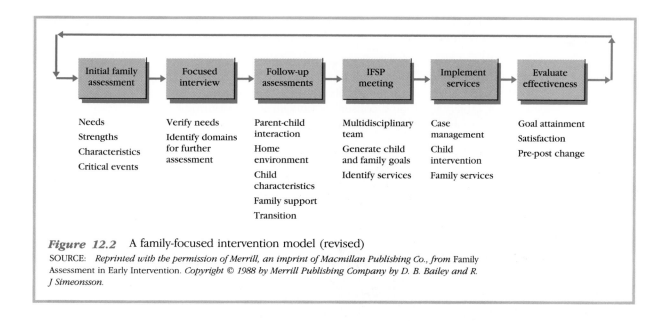

Figure 12.2 A family-focused intervention model (revised)

SOURCE: *Reprinted with the permission of Merrill, an imprint of Macmillan Publishing Co., from* Family Assessment in Early Intervention. *Copyright © 1988 by Merrill Publishing Company by D. B. Bailey and R. J Simeonsson.*

intervention teams to develop new procedures and assessments that encourage parents to play an active part in assessing their family's needs as well as their child's. The goal is true collaboration in the treatment plan.

Bailey and Simeonsson (1988) have argued for an effective family assessment model that would be (1) comprehensive—considering all important domains; (2) based on multiple sources and measures; (3) sensitive to various families' values and traditions; (4) able to utilize family priorities as it sets goals and determines services; (5) flexible, to adapt to program needs; and (6) able to periodically evaluate family outcomes. To further assist in promoting such a system they created a functional model (see Figure 12.2) as a guide.

For such models to be successful, assessment instruments are needed that can assist family members and professionals alike in the family planning process. McGonigel and Garland (1988) report on several scales developed by the Family, Infant, and Preschool Program (FIPP) in Morganton, North Carolina. The FIPP provides both home-based and center-based early intervention services to over 300 families. Among the assessments it uses are the Family Support Scale, the Family Resource Scale, the Support Functions Scale, and the Family Needs Scale. The scales are designed to provide assistance and information to families, enabling them to be active partners in establishing their needs and services and enhancing the likelihood of reaching the desired outcomes.

A number of measures useful in establishing family needs have been reviewed by Bailey and Simeonsson (1988), including their own Family Needs Survey. Through a rating scale format, this survey helps parents examine their need for assistance in six areas: (1) information, (2) support, (3) explaining to others, (4) gaining access to community services, (5) financial needs, and (6) family functioning. Other scales assist in measuring parent responsiveness, stress, child/parent interaction, maternal behavior, and parent involvement.

These measures and others are designed to enable the family and the professional intervention team members to collaborate on the integrated goals mandated by the IFSP. For this new relationship to be successful, says Bailey (1987), early intervention staff must develop five skills.

1. Viewing the family from a systems perspective
2. Systematic assessment of relevant family needs
3. Effective listening and interviewing techniques
4. Ability to reach a consensus on values and priorities
5. Ability to fulfill a "case manager" role, matching needs with resources

Note that the second skill, systematic assessment of relevant family needs, recognizes that a family may have many problems beyond the scope of a team's skills and resources. Some of these might include marital problems, limited cognitive abilities of the parents, unemployment, and chronic personality problems (Bailey, 1987).

The Individual Family Service Plan (IFSP)

According to PL 99-457, the IFSP must include the following.

1. A statement of the child's current level of development in the areas of language and speech, cognition, psychosocial and physical development, and self-help skills.
2. A statement of the family's strengths and needs as they pertain to enhancing the infant's or child's development.
3. A list of the major outcomes to be achieved, along with the criteria, deadlines, and procedures for doing so, so that progress and needed modifications may be evaluated.
4. A list of the specific intervention services necessary to meet the infant's or toddler's and the family's needs. It must state the frequency of, intensity of, and methods for delivering intervention services.
5. The dates of service implementation and duration of those services.
6. The name of the case manager who will be responsible for seeing that the plan is implemented and who will coordinate services. The case manager will be chosen from the profession providing the bulk of services to the family and child or infant.
7. Specific steps to assist in transferring the toddler to services under PL 94-142, if need continues.

Most IFSPs are more informal and focus more on the family than does the individualized education plan (IEP). Figure 12.3 illustrates the child and family goals and objectives one might find in an IFSP. In this case the team has agreed that Melissa, an infant with multiple physical disabilities, needs physical therapy. It has also determined that the family needs good baby-sitting and respite care options. (To emphasize their more informal nature, many IFSPs are purposely written by hand, but this sample is printed for the ease of the reader.)

Although the IFSP must be reviewed every six months, the rapid changes inherent in the child's stage of development and changing needs within the family may necessitate more frequent review. In addition, the timelines embedded within the goals and criteria will also impose periodic review at stated intervals. Each review meeting should be part of an overall evaluation of the success of the

I. DESIRED OUTCOME:

Melissa will receive physical therapy to help prevent loss of motor skills and to build body strength and mobility.

STRATEGIES:

1. Peggy Griffin, the physical therapist, will visit Melissa and Julie at home once a week to monitor Melissa's motor development for any signs of loss of attained skills.
2. Peggy will work with Melissa on her balance. She will share with Dave and Julie ways to play with Melissa that will help her balance.
3. Peggy will show Dave and Julie how to move Melissa's arms and legs to help her grow stronger.
4. When Julie plays with Melissa, she will use the methods she has learned from Peggy.

CRITERIA/TIMELINE:

Melissa's therapy will begin next week. Peggy will use clinical observation to judge Melissa's progress in motor skills and strength as well as to monitor the maintenance of those skills.

II. DESIRED OUTCOME:

Julie would like to have someone who could care for Melissa so that she can go to her appointments and get some occasional respite.

STRATEGIES:

1. Barbara Simon will check with the Horizon Development Center to see what options they have identified for respite care and report back to Julie next week.
2. Jan will check with the day-care center to see if it has a list of parents or neighbors that could help. She will bring it with her to our conference on Friday.
3. Julie, Jan, and Barbara will meet to go over the list for possible choices and arrange for Julie and Dave to visit the three most promising.
4. Dave and Julie will make their choice and use their anniversary dinner to try out the placement.

CRITERIA/TIMELINE:

Julie and Dave will have a list of at least three good baby-sitting and respite care options for Melissa by April 1.

Figure 12.3   Child and family goals

intervention plan and should allow for any needed revisions. Dunst, Leet, and Trivette (1988) have suggested the following rating scale for IFSP outcomes, which can assist in this evaluation.

Rating scale for outcomes

1. Situation has changed or worsened; no need, goal, or project exists.
2. Situation is unchanged; need, goal, or project is still lacking.
3. Implementation has begun; goal or project is still necessary.
4. Outcome has been partially attained or accomplished.
5. Outcome is mostly accomplished, but not to extent sought by family.
6. Outcome is mostly accomplished or attained to extent sought by family.
7. Outcome is completely accomplished or attained to family's satisfaction.

There is no doubt that a new partnership between professionals and the families of disabled infants and toddlers is being forged on the anvil of PL 99-457 and its mandated IFSP. It will be up to all those involved at the local level to work together so that its metal will stand the test of time.

■   Constructive play is essential to early development.   ■

Prevention and Intervention Strategies

Early intervention programs and services have been expanding rapidly since the passage of PL 99-457. They tend to be very eclectic in their approach to the delivery of service, but may be classified generally as home- or center-based programs and parent- or child-oriented curricula. Programs may also vary with regard to other characteristics such as intervention age, program intensity, number of children seen, primary target for intervention (child, one or both parents), educational activities, and site of intervention (Ramey & Bryant, 1988).

For the purposes of this chapter, we will review the programs using the three general categories noted by Odom, Yoder, and Hill (1988).

1. Preventive intervention
2. Infant-focused
3. Parent/infant-focused

■   Preventive Intervention Programs

The goal of preventive programs is to avert possible problems; therefore, as Widerstrom, Mowder, and Sandall (1991) have stated, such programs are often difficult to describe and justify to the general public. These authors divide such programs according to three groups of women and infants who are at risk: mothers with biological difficulties, mothers with low socioeconomic status, and pregnant adolescent women.

In general, the goals of such programs include (1) a reduction in the number of disorder cases, (2) early intervention for children showing signs of a possible disability that is not yet established, and (3) a reduction in the effects of a disability along with rehabilitation and eventual adjustment to community life.

Mothers with biological difficulties   These programs aid women who have had chronic health problems, problems with pregnancies, or known genetic backgrounds that might cause difficulty. They provide information to the mothers and take steps to lessen any possible problems with their children. Direct medical intervention may be utilized if appropriate, as well as instructional programs, nutritional guidance, and prepregnancy counseling.

Mothers of low socioeconomic status   Mothers in this category often present a variety of risk factors, including frequent pregnancies with short intervals in between; inadequate medical care and support systems; greater exposure to hazardous materials or experiences; and a greater likelihood of bearing low birth weight or premature infants. Programs such as the Special Supplemental Food Program for Women, Infants, and Children (WIC) and Maternal and Infant Care programs (MIC) provide nutritional food, dietary education, and pre- and post-pregnancy medical care for mothers and children.

Pregnant adolescent women   Many of these mothers come from low socio-economic settings and share the problems of the last group. In any case, adolescent mothers can have many birth-related difficulties, including a higher infant mortality rate, more premature deliveries, and low birth weight babies. Preventive programs focus on child development, health, parenting skills, and childbirth education. Strong social support systems are helpful, as is an understanding of the mother's own developmental level and an awareness of its changing nature.

Programs serving these populations are found in a variety of settings, including hospitals, schools, clinics, and other agency or community settings. Lourie (1988) has pointed out that the most significant issue in preventive programs may be how to reach women and families who presently cannot or will not use them. Preventive programs offer opportunities for effective intervention at a time in which the expectant parent is usually most interested in the subject. An increase in parenting knowledge and skills can provide significant gains to both mother and infant. To be effective, however, these programs must view the women's position in the light of complex social and ecological factors, such as long-term cultural or institutionalized sex roles and relationships between parents and their children (Brody, 1988).

■   **Infant-Focused Programs**

Having the longest and most diverse history of all three types of programs, infant-focused programs grew out of medical settings and have long been identified with the neonatal intensive care unit (NICU). Such programs understandably were focused on the medical needs of the child and frequently may have overlooked the mother's and child's many other needs (Widerstrom, Mowder, & Sandall, 1991). Due to the recent rapid increase in intervention programs, there is now a great choice of settings and administering agencies for such programs. Indeed, hospital settings, though still an important part of the intervention picture, appear to be a minority (Karnes & Stayton, 1988). With so many settings, it is perhaps not surprising that program focus is equally varied. We will discuss a few examples of infant-focused intervention programs.

Center-based programs   Karnes and Stayton (1988) have reported that in a survey of 144 HCEEP or First Chance projects the majority of children were served in center-based programs. These programs are carried out in settings outside the home, such as schools, special day-care centers, hospital complexes, or preschools. The study showed that a wide range of professionals is frequently utilized by center-based programs: administrators, infant interventionists, physical and occupational therapists, speech-language pathologists, psychologists, paraprofessionals, and volunteers. The majority of these programs reported efforts at teaming, with meetings held on a weekly basis.

Advantages of center-based programs are focused, multidisciplinary assistance with opportunities to work as a team and social support—either formal or informal—for parents of the disabled.

Tuesday's Child is an example of an ongoing center-based program. Developed by Children's Memorial Hospital in Chicago in 1980, this center serves children from 18 months to 5 years of age who display a variety of behavioral disabilities. A major focus is assistance to parents in managing conflicts with their children. Children are placed in social and educational environments designed to improve their developmental functioning, improve parent/child relationships, and offset future conflict. Center staff work with the public schools to ease the transition into programs offered by the schools (ibid.).

Home-based programs   As the name indicates, these services are delivered in the home setting. Professionals and often their aides or paraprofessionals work closely with the child as the parents observe (and often assist). Home-based programs are often the preferred service delivery option for infants who are medically fragile or biologically at risk (Sandall, 1991). Due to concern over increased risk for respiratory or other illness, these children may be restricted in their interactions or difficult to transport to center-based programs because of their supportive devices or specialized treatments. This approach also offers convenience and ease to busy parents. Home-based programs may provide some ethical challenges to the visiting professionals (Bryant, Lyons, & Wasaik, 1991), including working in multicultural settings having different values, customs, and beliefs. Indeed, while home-based approaches show evidence of effectiveness, it may depend on the cultural sensitivity of the professionals and paraprofessionals paying such visits (Wayman, Lynch, & Hanson, 1991).

Home- plus center-based programs   More and more programs are offering a home- plus center-based option (Karnes & Stayton, 1988). These can range from primarily home-based (with special sessions at center locations for parent education and intervention modeling) to primarily center-based (with outreach and a gradual shift to home intervention and follow-up).

The San Francisco Infant Program (Hanson & Krentz, 1986) is an example of this combination approach. It provides both a home educational component and center-based intervention. The focus is on cognitive development, communica-

■ The best early intervention programs for children with disabilities include nondisabled peers. ■

tion skills, self-help, social development, and fine and gross motor development. The program, based at San Francisco State University, serves infants and toddlers who are at risk and offers a parent training and support component.

In addition to these program models, Widerstrom, Mowder, and Sandall (1991) discuss other specific infant-focused programs that have been developed. Some of them have utilized technology in which infants have been taught to interact with microcomputers designed to foster their cognitive, language, and motor development. Programmed instruction models have been developed to work with infants who are blind and multidisabled, with special focus on infant orientation and mobility. Systems such as the Iowa Regional Child Health Centers and the High Risk Registry established by the Tennessee Department of Health and Environment are designed to network resources and assist in follow-up.

■ Parent/Infant-Focused Programs

Although all intervention programs will have components that deal with infants with disabilities and their parents, some are specifically designed to integrate those components into their service delivery. These integrated programs grew out of carry-over activities from center-based programs. As the literature and research focused more and more on the importance of the family, more programs began to consider the whole family in intervention planning.

Growing awareness of the family's role in infant intervention is now reflected by medical intervention settings. Neonatal Intensive Care Units and their medically related staff and therapists are incorporating parent education and parent/child adaptation into their goals and objectives. Guides for therapists to assess parents' needs and ensure sensitivity to families and their environments have been suggested (Semmler & Hunter, 1990).

Shifting from concentration on the newborn to intervention with older infants, many other intervention programs are continuing this parent/infant focus. Widerstrom, Mowder, and Sandall (1991) discuss program models that help build parents' skills in approaching their infant and responding to his or her achievement (called parent/infant reciprocity). Successful interactions are built upon each other, enhancing the infant's autonomy and the parents' confidence.

The transactional intervention models also focus on parents' interactions with their infants. Through such approaches, parents learn skills such as "turn-taking" that are designed to increase successful interaction and build parents' responsiveness and sensitivity to their child. These models can assist parents in analyzing how they normally interact and adjust to their infant.

In general, program models adopting this integrated approach have certain common goals.

- To help parents gain needed information and skills
- To promote the infant's social and physical adaptation
- To provide supportive intervention that will reduce stress and enhance the family environment
- To provide ongoing assessment and evaluation of the infant's and related family needs and of the intervention program itself

Preschool Programs

We have discussed the important ground-breaking precedents established by Title I, Part H of PL 99-457, covering infants and toddlers with disabilities from birth to age 3. Title II, Part B of the amendments also has had an important impact on service delivery for children aged 3 through 5 who have disabilities. The change from permitted to mandated services for this population led school districts and their special education units to explore how best to meet those demands. Under the legislation, states were to designate "lead agencies" that would be responsible for service provision through school districts or other contracted service agencies.

Those agencies were responsible for providing direct or indirect services. Although these services could be given in traditional school settings, they might also be offered by other community-based agencies such as day-care centers or programs for developmentally disabled children. Home- or family-centered programs might be an additional or alternative way to provide direct or indirect services.

As Weber and Binkelman (1990) pointed out, school districts' obligations do not begin when a child reaches 3 but extend back to birth for identification and evaluation, whether services are provided or not. Timelines and federal "child find" requirements mandate that districts have programs for individual children who are disabled in place when they turn 3. Such child find requirements state that it is the school district's responsibility to identify all infants, toddlers, and children who might be disabled. Failure to do so incurs a variety of legal penalties already in place. Such requirements have underscored both the child find process and associated procedures and methods for screening, identification, and assessment.

■ Screening

Screening is the initial step in the intervention process, and its goal is to establish a potential disability. Preschool children and infants who have already been diagnosed with disabling conditions through medical or other child find procedures are referred directly to the school or agency responsible for further evaluation.

Preschool screening programs vary greatly from state to state and community to community (Peterson, 1987). Some states and communities call for heavy involvement by medical personnel; others primarily depend on school-related special services personnel and teachers. Comprehensive child find programs are more likely to involve a variety of medical and school special services personnel who consider the child from many different perspectives. These comprehensive screening programs are more likely to use a variety of screening tools, including formal standardized screening tests. It is important to remember that such tests, while providing useful information for the screening process, should not be relied on for purposes of diagnosis or as a basis for programmatic decisions (Meisels, 1985).

A number of screening tests for preschoolers exist in the current market, and Cook, Tessier, and Armbruster (1987) have suggested some specific factors to weigh when selecting them.

1. Qualifications of the individual administering the test
2. Reliability of the test (Is it consistent?)
3. Validity of the test (Does it test what it says it is testing?)
4. Coverage of the major functioning areas, including language, cognitive skills, fine and gross motor skills, and social and emotional adjustment
5. Similarity of the children to be screened to the group used to establish the test norms
6. Degree of bias in the instrument against specific disabling conditions or minority groups
7. Factors of time and cost

Hanson and Lynch (1989) indicate that such screening tests should be simple, accurate, comprehensive, cost-effective, and used in partnership with parents. Regardless of the specific tests utilized, it should be remembered that they are only one part of the multifaceted approach necessary for comprehensive screening.

Preschool "roundups" have been in use for many years. These often involve both provision of information to parents and a degree of screening potential kindergarten enrollees. Such events are typically preceded by a variety of public awareness activities to inform the parents of the events and encourage as much participation as possible. A variety of school, community, and medical personnel as well as volunteers often participates and assists in this screening process. Properly designed, implemented, and followed through, these events can be of great value. They afford opportunities to build effective communication with all segments of the community and can be utilized to the benefit of children with disabilities.

Regardless of the care given to the selection of tests and other measures to be used in such events, special care must go into planning who will administer them. Although preschool teachers may be able to bring special expertise to some measures of general language competency and development, they may not have the training to detect other language or articulation disorders. Even individuals qualified to administer appropriate sections of the screening program need to be sure they have practiced the necessary skills. Coordination in any large-scale enterprise is also crucial. Appropriate rooms for the various stations must be designated and a plan for traffic flow carefully worked out.

Sensitivity to parents' feelings and concerns is a primary requirement for test administrators. As Cook, Tessier, and Armbruster (1987) point out, whereas most of the screening activities are designed to be fun for the children, this is a time of anxiety for most parents. Care should be taken that they are well informed about the results of the screening and assured that the procedure is an initial stage in a routine process and not a final diagnosis of a disabling condition. Time spent in a brief exit or "debriefing" conference can prove beneficial for all parents attending such screening.

■ Assessment

As with infants, the assessment of preschool children comprises the three stages of determining the presence of a disability, establishing the child's needs, and selecting appropriate interventions. Neisworth and Bagnato (1988) have discussed measures to facilitate the assessment of preschool children. These can be organized into three major categories.

1. *Norm-based instruments* that compare a child's developmental skills and abilities with those of a group of children comparable in age and demographic characteristics
2. *Curriculum-based assessment* that traces a child's achievement as it follows a developmentally sequenced curriculum
3. *Judgment-based assessment,* through checklists, rating scales, and other measures that collect and structure the impressions of parents, professionals, and caregivers regarding the child's environment

In general, appropriate assessment procedures will incorporate all of these measures to provide the information needed to develop the IEP required for each child.

Perhaps the primary differences between infant and preschool assessment are the emphasis on instructional evaluation and—due to the rapid growth of school-administered programs—the role of preschool teachers in the assessment and intervention programs.

The teacher's role in assessment   To the extent that assessment identifies the child's skills, learning characteristics, and needs, it allows the teacher to know where in a prescribed curriculum a child should be placed and what behaviors should be taught. Through this process the child's IEP denotes specific goals and objectives and provides for the measurement of progress toward the objectives as well as evaluation of the overall plan. For this to take place implies ongoing assessment. Whereas initial assessment by the teacher and team may use many of the measures discussed, ongoing assessment is directly tied to teaching and may incorporate additional measures. The importance of the role of the teacher as an observer has been discussed by Cook, Tessier, and Armbruster (1987), who stress the importance of observation in initial assessment and in the later, ongoing stages. In initial assessment teacher observation may be used to corroborate or question formal test results and add to the overall information base. As part of ongoing assessment, such observations can identify special needs not initially addressed, continually monitor progress, and determine modifications necessary to help ensure the child's success in the program. Some of the observational techniques suggested include photographs; videotape and audiotape recordings; collections of children's work; lists of children's activities; anecdotal records, diaries, and logs; checklists and rating scales; and time sampling and event recording. These techniques can also provide extra bonuses for all involved. For example, photographs and samples of each child's work can be collected during the year and compiled into a scrapbook for each parent. Such collections serve three valuable purposes: as part of the curriculum, as an observational technique, and as a cherished gift to appreciative parents!

The teacher's role as an observer and indeed the role of observation in assessment is indicative of the overall movement toward more curriculum-based assessment (Heward & Orlansky, 1988; Stafford, 1989). These measures are directly related to the teaching curriculum of the program. Gickling and Thompson have pointed out the dual focus of curriculum-based assessment. It involves both assessment and instruction, in that it concentrates "on how to collect, interpret, and use data in order to impact directly upon instruction" (1985, p. 217). Such criterion-referenced methods, then, focus on a specific goal, outcome, or "criterion" to be met. They then provide ways to determine whether the child can accomplish that criterion.

Other considerations in preschool assessment   Other considerations are also important to assessment. They include a sensitivity to such factors as establishing rapport with the child; providing ample time for assessment (students with disabilities may need more time or a series of testing sessions); selecting an appropriate time (removing a child from a favorite activity can cause problems); selecting an appropriate setting (removing distractions, utilizing appropriate furniture, and persuading or dissuading parents from observing can all help); and taking care that instructions are clear and appropriate (Cook, Tessier, & Armbruster, 1987).

■ Intervention Strategies

Curricula   A curriculum can be defined as an organized set of activities and experiences designed to achieve specific developmental or educational goals (Hanson & Lynch, 1989). Many programs are still quite eclectic in their choice of a curriculum and attempt to match the child's needs as determined by the assessment process with their curriculum offerings. Often preschool teachers find themselves faced with the task of designing the curriculum, the reporting and evaluation systems, and daily plans (Cook, Tessier, & Armbruster, 1987). It is not unusual, however, to have components of a program structured around particular theoretical perspectives. Heward and Orlansky (1988) report the popularity of the developmental approach in early childhood special education programs and outline their five basic purposes of intervention.

1. To remediate delays or gaps in a child's development, whether in language, motor skills, self-help, or other areas
2. To help the child develop the basic elements of attention, perception, sensorimotor skills, language, social skills, and memory
3. To teach developmental tasks in areas such as language, motor, self-help, and social skills in sequences that most closely match those of normal children
4. To teach psychological constructs such as self-esteem, creativity, motivation, and thinking skills, assuming that this training will enhance later learning
5. To teach preacademic skills in a variety of areas such as reading, math concepts, nature studies, and art

Discussing the variety of theoretical perspectives used in preschool programs, Hanson and Lynch (1989) focused on four major approaches: cognitive, behavioral, functional/ecological, and developmental.

The *cognitive approach* has also been referred to as the cognitive-developmental approach; it is usually closely associated with the theories of Jean Piaget. It views the child as an active learner who is internally motivated to develop through adaptation and through interactions with the environment. Sensorimotor skills are among those singled out for specific cognitive improvement by promoting and guiding a child's interactions in a planned, enriched environment.

Behavioral approaches are typically associated with the work of B. F. Skinner; they view the environment as the principal factor determining a child's behavior. The child is seen primarily as reacting to environmental factors, so instruction consists of a prescribed series of structured activities. Target behaviors are chosen; then strategies to increase desired behaviors and decrease less desirable ones are implemented. This approach emphasizes the method of instruction rather than the content or curriculum offerings.

The *developmental approach* views a child's development as genetically determined and as following a specific sequence. Following theories such as those of Arnold Gesell, curricula based on this approach are typically fitted to an ordered list of developmental milestones and aimed to provide environments in which the child is encouraged to engage in self-directed play and learning activities. Many of these milestones are selected from developmental assessment tools and take a diagnostic-prescriptive approach to education.

The *functional or ecological approach* emphasizes the development of functional skills for daily living. As these skills are needed to interact with the environment in a normal fashion, they are geared more to daily living experiences than to developmental or academic sequences. Hanson and Lynch (1989) see this approach less as a theory and more as a practical perspective to guide assessment and goals selection. This approach can be particularly helpful to children with more severe disabilities.

■ Developmentally Appropriate Practice in Early Childhood Special Education

Increasing debate in the field of early special education is heard over the value of developmentally appropriate practice (DAP) compared with the more direct early intervention practices found in many early childhood special education programs. The National Association for the Education of Young Children (NAEYC) has led other professional early childhood organizations in taking a strong position for "developmentally appropriate practice" and has provided guidelines for designing and evaluating early childhood programs (Bredekamp, 1987). Its guidelines list both appropriate and inappropriate practices, according to the developmental approach. Carta, Schwartz, Atwater, and McConnell (1991) have discussed this popular approach and listed areas of overlap and areas of concern in regard to other early childhood special education practices. They point out that while age appropriateness and individual appropriateness are primary concerns in DAP, it also conveys the message that children should not be pushed to achieve when very young (Elkind, 1986). DAP's philosophy is that children learn differently than adults; it proposes that preschool education be child centered and child directed, allowing children to make choices about what they will learn. Feeling that such a philosophy is logical for normally developing children, Carta and her colleagues (1991) caution that it falls short of meeting the more direct needs of preschoolers with disabilities. Norris (1991) also cautions against applying developmental approaches that may be too advanced for some preschoolers with disabilities.

■ Promoting Quality Learning Environments

The importance of the learning environment has gained attention in early education research with a shift in focus from skill development to the fit between child and environment (Sainato, 1985). This search for an appropriate environmental fit can be viewed from the point of view of programmatic characteristics as well as physical design. We will take a brief look at both of these areas.

Programmatic characteristics A number of factors can assist children by enhancing the learning environment and lessening the occurrence of emotional and behavioral problems. Among those discussed by Cook, Tessier, and Armbruster (1987) are the following:

• *Consistency:* Predictability helps children feel safe. It is helpful for children to know what is expected of them and what they can expect from the teacher. Consistency in instruction helps children learn the rules necessary for social acceptance.

• *Routines:* Set schedules help children identify consistency and enable them to make better transitions between activities. Though they must be flexible enough to take advantage of "teachable moments," routines provide the predictability necessary for children to prepare for necessary changes throughout the instructional day.

• *Limits:* Rules also help the child by establishing consistency and providing security regarding the presence of control in the environment. But only rules that are absolutely necessary should be established. (An old rule states, "Never offer a choice if the child doesn't really have one!" Be careful not to ask questions such as "Do you want to put the blocks away?" if you do not want to accept a "no" answer.) Rules should be definable, reasonable, and enforceable.

Box 12.3
Jamie: A Rose in Bloom

When Jamie, the youngest of five children, was 4, his mother was worried about him. "He isn't interested in things we do around the house; he doesn't even like the stories we try to read to him. If things go wrong, he screams or throws himself on the floor. He won't talk, he won't listen, he doesn't ask questions like his brothers did at his age. I'm afraid he's going to have problems in school, too."

That was a year ago. Then Jamie's mother heard about a preschool for children who have trouble communicating. She decided to take Jamie and talk to the teachers.

Jamie began school in January. He liked it from the start. Nobody else in his family had done this. He didn't have to go with his brothers or sister but could do it all by himself. After just a few weeks he began to come home saying, "Mom, guess what I learned today."

On a special visiting day, Jamie's grandmother came to visit the school. She remembers how excited Jamie was. "He took me by the hand and showed me every toy and activity area in the room. He told me how everything worked, and what he liked to play with most." "The blocks are my favoritest thing, 'cause you can really build things," Jamie told her. He was really proud of his school.

In spring, the entire class and the parents went to the zoo. After the trip, the children were asked to draw their favorite animal; Jamie drew an elephant. His mother told the teacher, "Before school he only made scribbles; I didn't know he could draw so well."

Jamie's mom worked as a volunteer at the school, helping with extra projects. When she was there she saw children busy building with blocks, sharing, and talking with each other about the stories they had heard. She saw how the teacher encouraged cooperation among the children, and soon realized that she was doing some of the same things at home with her family.

Jamie's relationships with his brothers began to change. He went from crying and whining to knowing how to talk to and cooperate with them. They still fought at times, but settled many of their differences without their mom's intervention.

"The way he talks is so different," his mother and teacher both said. "Before preschool he would point at something and say, 'See that thing there?' Now he will say, " 'See that red car with the white stripes and big tires? I want it.' "

"I used to call him my little headache," says Mom. "Now I call him my little rose, because he's really blooming. And what's also nice is that I feel like I'm blooming, too. I may go back to school myself, because there's a lot more I'd like to learn. I'll never be able to thank those teachers enough."

SOURCE: Colorado Preschool Project: Progress Report, *1989, a report to the Colorado General Assembly.*

• *Constructive consequences:* Emphasis on natural and logical consequences can assist young children in developing social responsibility. Within an educational context, natural consequences are those that occur when an adult does not interfere and the child learns from experience. If a child does not eat a snack when it is prepared and offered at snack time, he may get hungry and remember to eat it the next time it is offered. If a child does not take turns when playing with other children, she may learn that others will not want to play with her. Logical consequences are those developed by adults if they feel that the natural consequences are unavailable or harmful. Children who throw sand at other children will be removed from the sandbox. These consequences need to be logical and to occur as soon as possible so that the relationship between cause and effect is obvious to the child.

• *Variety:* Changing the pace of instructional activity is important to the learning process. Group and individual activity, quiet and active times must all be incorporated into the day. Preschoolers have short attention spans, and novelty, humor, and fun are all important aids in learning.

• *Avoiding frustration:* Establishing a therapeutic environment depends on recognizing stress and frustration. Building in an appropriate success ratio by breaking activities into manageable tasks can be helpful. An awareness of illness, fatigue, or hunger is important. Reduction of noise and confusion through management and planning will also help reduce the frustration level.

• *Encouraging the appropriate expression of feelings:* Opportunities to help children accept and express their feelings appropriately should be sought out and capitalized on. Children can't assimilate long lectures explaining such feelings, but short statements and a gentle touch can be utilized. Simple acknowledgment of their feelings and brief comments or questions on coping behaviors can be helpful. A teacher might say, "Mary, it is all right to be mad at Susan for ripping up your paper, but I can't let you hit her. How else can you show her that you are really angry?"

• *Facilitating positive behavior:* Group children of similar developmental levels for play, but when you wish to foster imitation, mix children with slightly higher levels of skills into the group. Group socially compatible children for more positive interactions. Sufficient materials foster imitation and promote cooperation; the materials must be appropriate for the skills and interactions desired. Plan activities that encourage active cooperation. Study and identify what to use as reinforcers for specific children and be sure to reinforce specific desired behaviors.

Physical and design characteristics A variety of physical environmental and design characteristics is necessary for preschool environments. We will make a few suggestions related to health and safety, equipment, and utilization of space.

Basic safety and health concerns for preschool programs should be considered in planning, including awareness of the potential hazards in the physical environment. To assist in this process, ask yourself several questions: Are electrical outlets, plugs, and cords covered, and is access to water faucets controlled and safe? Are furniture pieces, shelving, and other items stable? Are children protected from the sharp edges of toys, materials, scissors, and furniture? Are potentially harmful materials such as medical and cleaning supplies appropriately stored and locked? Are small items, blocks, and removable parts used only under close supervision to avoid children swallowing and choking on them? Is the paint used in the building and room and on furniture and toys lead-free?

■ The loft concept makes excellent use of space (see Figure 12.4). ■

Early childhood special education programs will serve children with a variety of health and developmental problems. With these children hygiene is especially important. Caregivers must wash their hands with warm, soapy water before and after such tasks as feeding and changing diapers. Disposable gloves and bags are used in most programs to ensure adequate care regarding contact with body fluids. Toys and materials handled by children should be washed. Food preparation areas should receive special attention to maintain hygienic conditions.

Adequate space, bathroom facilities, playground, and storage are essential for any preschool program. A preschool for children with disabilities, however, has some additional requirements. These include space for diapering and cleanup; facilities for preparing small meals or snacks; and a large, flexible classroom space with different types of partitions to create various classroom centers. Hanson and Lynch (1989) point out that care should also be given to locating programs in public facilities or in those with access to public resources.

The physical arrangement of the classroom itself needs to be designed to meet instructional and programmatic goals. Of course, a great variety of plans may be used; Figure 12.4 shows only one possibility. Lund and Boss (1981) offer a number of general suggestions for room arrangements: Arrange areas so that those for individual or quiet activities are separated from more active ones. Consider the ease of traffic flow from one area to another, and place equipment and group areas accordingly. Activity areas, storage and individual lockers, or boxed areas can be color coded or identified by pictures to assist students and staff. Materials most often used together should be kept together. Materials used in the various centers should be kept near those centers. A large, open, central area with a rug or table is helpful, as it can be used for a variety of group activities.

■ Intervention Settings

Preschool services are supplied in a variety of intervention settings. Those settings include the same primary divisions of home-based, center-based, and combination home- and center-based programs. We will consider some traditional and some emerging models demonstrating those settings.

The Portage-Project (Shearer & Shearer, 1972) began as a cooperative approach encompassing 23 school districts in south-central Wisconsin. The project produced its own screening and assessment materials along with associated teaching activities for parents. Typically a project teacher visited the parents and trained them to assist their child in the primary areas of motor skills, language, social and emotional development, self-help, and cognition. The training included a review of the past activities and accomplishments of the child; a summary of the new activities for the coming week, modeling the week's activities for the parents; guiding the parents as they practiced the activities; and summarizing the records and information to be kept for the next visit. This project has served as a model for hundreds of similar ones, and its results evidence some benefit, particularly for more mildly delayed children (Shearer & Snider, 1981; Sturmey & Crisp, 1986).

The Educational Television Intervention Programs Project was designed to meet the early intervention needs of parents and service providers in rural areas, where access to center-based programs is limited. The project utilizes 30 15-minute videos designed to help parents and others understand child development. It also models skills and intervention strategies that can be used with infants and preschoolers with disabilities. The video series titled "Stepping Stones: Pathways to Early Development" comes with a *User's Guide* and a *Leader's Guide* to assist parents and professionals, respectively. The project offers a videotape presentation as well as broadcasting over public television stations. Parental home visitors assist in the effective use of the videos and in record keeping and communication activities.

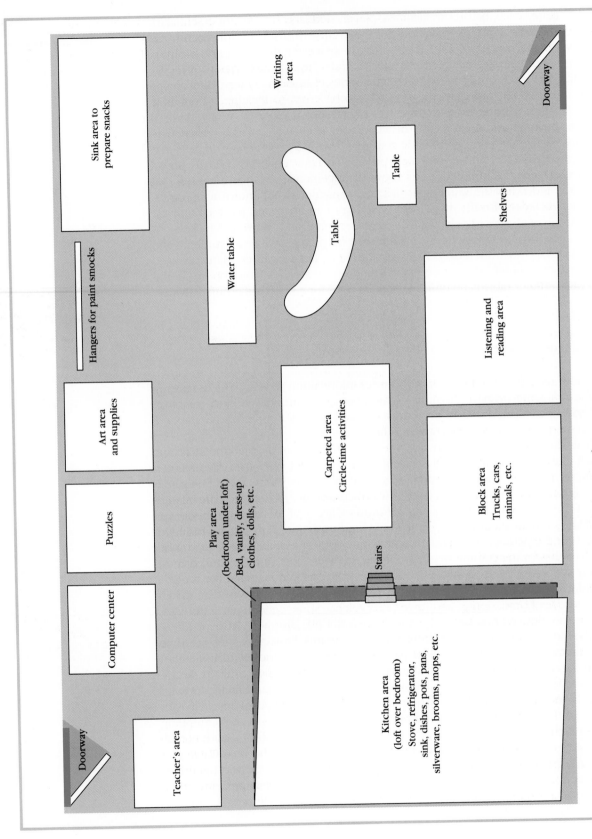

Figure 12.4 Sample floor plan for early childhood education classroom

Morrison (1991) reports on a unique community-based model utilized in Alberta, Canada. The Alberta Children's Hospital Mobile Team approach utilizes four mobile teams, each staffed with a speech-language pathologist, a physical therapist, and an occupational therapist. These teams travel daily from their hospital base to provide assistance to the families of children with disabilities in their homes, day-care centers, preschools and schools, and other community settings. Though some direct services are provided, there is an emphasis on collaborative efforts in which primary caregivers, including parents, are involved in the planning, implementation, and evaluation of intervention efforts.

These models are just a sample of the approaches being used to provide preschool services. Traditional settings such as hospitals, day-care centers, pre-schools, and schools are continually developing and expanding their programs under new federal and state guidelines.

Transition

The rapid expansion of infant and preschool services has engendered increasing concern over the transition from one service delivery model to the next (Wolery, 1989). Noonan and Kilgo have defined transition for young children as "(a) a longitudinal plan, (b) a goal of smooth/efficient movement from one program to the next, (c) a process including preparation, implementation, and follow-up, and (d) a philosophy that movement to the next program implies movement to a program less restrictive than the previous program" (1987, p. 26).

Wolery (1989) has commented on some of the transitions faced by parents of infants and children with disabilities. He remarks that one of the first transitions faced by these parents is from the hospital NICU to the home and to infant-focused programs. Planning for this transition, as for all others, should be part of the basic program. In this case, parents should be encouraged to visit the infant in the NICU frequently and at different times of the day. Constant communication regarding the infant's status, progress, and prognosis is important. Discharge plans need to take into account the medical and developmental status of the child; an assessment of the family's needs; the home environment; and community resources that can be utilized to support the family's and the infant's needs. Much of the transition plan should consider the family's ability to care for the child in the home setting and assist the family in linking up with necessary resources—both formal and informal—in the community.

Other transitions, such as from infant program to preschool program, can also utilize several dimensions to increase success. Such dimensions include (1) the assessment of and sensitivity to the needs of the infant or child and the family; (2) fostering open communication and information exchange between parents and staff members of the sending and receiving programs; and (3) family participation and involvement in the decision-making process.

Active parent involvement is necessary for successful transition, and a number of roles for parents have been suggested. Those roles are listed in Table 12.5. Perhaps the most powerful force in the transition process is of true open communication. If the flow of information regarding needs, expectations, limitations, progress, and roles can be maximized, it will increase the likelihood of successful collaboration and smooth transition.

Table 12.5 Parents' Roles in Transitions

Role	Responsibilities
Teachers	Help instruct infant or child in skills, with assistance of staff, and promote generalization. Home-based models more often emphasize role for parents.
Information providers	Supply information regarding child's skills, needs, effective strategies, and family needs pertaining to transition.
Decision makers	Become an active part of the team in deciding placements best suited to their child, skills and behaviors to be taught, transition services needed by the family, and when transition should occur.
Advocates	Understand their child's and their own rights. Ensure that due process is followed and that child's and family's needs are being met; initiate appropriate action if service is not adequate. Assist and support other parents in need of services by lobbying for appropriate governmental assistance.
Transition coordinators	Assume responsibilities for transition planning, implementation, and provision of follow-up information regarding the transition process. Such active involvement can assist in reducing the stress of transition by establishing some control and building skills that will be helpful in future transitions.

Issues and Trends

A number of contemporary issues and trends provide thought-provoking possibilities for the future of early childhood special education services.

Financial resources Will services mandated by PL 99-457 be associated with an increase in financial resources, or will such services compete for the shrinking educational dollar? A decline in resources may well foster more community-based and integrated programs if the interest and popularity of early education programs continues. Will there be a trend toward corporate funding for such programs?

Curriculum wars The continuing popularity of developmentally appropriate programs may promote additional debate among special education providers about modifications necessary for students who are more disabled. Modifications of both main approaches may be likely, with DAP approaches moving to more outcome-based methods through strategies designed to structure child choices. Special education programs may move toward modifying traditional direct intervention by employing a more structured environment and Piagetian strategies.

Demographics Increasing numbers of children from ethnic minorities and nontraditional homes will impose changes on all of education. These factors will cause early educators to consider the multicultural appropriateness of all intervention services.

Social and health concerns As the impact of drugs, AIDS, child abuse, and chronic poverty and homelessness becomes more obvious, profound changes in service delivery and in the need for services may occur. Such changes may be a catalyst for new and increasingly effective models of intervention.

Technology   The prevention of medically related disabling and at-risk conditions through new advances in medical technology seems certain. Computerized and roboticized intervention techniques may antiquate many of our current procedures. Educational technology, as we illustrated in Chapter 3, can be expected to make continual advances by providing new interactive and interconnected tools and procedures for more effective intervention.

Summary

The value of early intervention programs for infants and young children is supported by both theory and research. The rationale for such programs seems even clearer with respect to infants and children with disabilities, to reduce the effects of existing disabilities and to reduce or prevent secondary ones. Federal legislation has encouraged, and in some cases mandated, programs for children with disabilities that begin at birth. Such programs also cover children who are at risk.

Assessment techniques include several that offer a comparison with normal developmental milestones and screening tests designed for certain special purposes. Family assessment is also a part of the total planning process, recognizing the family's influence on any effective intervention plan. A number of prevention and intervention strategies have been found effective; all involve some type of multidisciplinary intervention team. The individual family service plan (IFSP) for infants or toddlers and their families, which parallels the IEP for school-age children, is an essential part of what is often called a family-focused intervention model.

Infant-focused programs include center-based programs carried out in schools, preschools, special day-care centers, or hospital settings; home-based programs, which emphasize professional assistance to parents to enrich the home environment and improve management in the home; and combination home-plus center-based programs. Each approach has its advantages and disadvantages and has shown evidence of success. Parent involvement and parent education are essential elements in all of these.

Preschool programs for children aged 3 to 5 who have disabilities have a longer history than do programs of infant intervention. They typically include goals related to development in language, motor skills, social skills, and self-esteem. They also offer preacademic skills training in reading, math concepts, and areas such as nature studies and art. Parent education and parent involvement are important but are not emphasized as much as in infant-focused programs.

The facilitation of transition from one program to the next has received increasing attention. Financial resources—specifically, which agency is responsible for providing them—remains an unsettled issue.

Jimmy was born prematurely, weighing only 3 pounds at birth, and was considered to be at risk. He has been in small, special programs designed to increase his chances for normal development since he was 2 years old. Jimmy's language and motor development are below average for his age, and he is socially immature. Next year Jimmy will be 6, and enrollment in kindergarten has been recommended by his preschool teachers.

Todd has had problems in reading and language development. His parents have moved a great deal and thought he would do better if he could stay in one school and attend it regularly. Todd's father therefore managed to get a stable job. Now in third grade, Todd has been found to have a moderate hearing loss in both ears. He was beginning to establish friendships in his class, but his parents and school officials agree that he should have at least part time special assistance in a program for students with hearing impairments.

Denise is 15 years old, is believed to have an IQ of 40 to 50, and has been in a residential school since age 2. Her adaptive behavior is about what might be predicted by her measured intellectual ability. She has had limited contact with the world outside of the residential facility, but this spring she will be moved to a community residential setting under the guardianship of a foster mother and father. Denise will also enter the public school program in the fall.

Sue Ann, now 17 years old, was found to have learning disabilities at age 11. She has received special assistance since that time and now achieves within the normal range in many academic areas. However, though she has excellent understanding of material that is read to her or is on tape, her independent reading ability is very poor. She can answer questions verbally and can dictate

CHAPTER THIRTEEN

Transitions

meaningful papers, but she has difficulty putting her thoughts into writing. Sue Ann hopes to go on to the local community college next year, after she graduates from high school.

These students all have a common need that is often overlooked.

The progress of an individual through life may be viewed in many ways. If we are concerned with physical growth and development, we can readily measure and record increases in weight and height, muscular strength, physical dexterity, agility, and similar physical abilities. If we are concerned with mental growth, we measure growth in basic information, academic skills, ability to generalize and conceptualize, and related abilities. Other types of growth include more difficult-to-quantify areas such as responsibility, ethics, morality, and social conscience. All of these areas are of concern in planning for individuals with disabilities.

Life may also be viewed as a series of major and minor transitions. Growth and development will likely continue without special attention to these transition points, but it will proceed more efficiently if they can be navigated smoothly, with a minimum of confusion and trauma. The first major transition is birth. When the developed fetus leaves the womb, the individual is experiencing an incomparable transition. Through our attention to possible special medical needs, our provision of warmth, food, and physical protection, and the various ways in which we encourage early bonding with the mother, we attempt to help all newborns through this first, traumatic transition.

Transitions that follow will vary, but most, like birth, involve a change of environment. The more radical the change, the greater the need to prepare for it. The transition to care by persons other than parents, the transition between levels in school (elementary, middle school, secondary schools, and so on), and the transition from school to employment and adult responsibilities are just some examples. Many students with disabilities will also face transitions between regular classes and special programs. Birth and the transition to employment and adult responsibilities are probably the two most difficult and potentially traumatic.

Students with disabilities may become the responsibility of educators as infants or at the preschool or kindergarten level; they remain their responsibility until they complete their formal education. In this chapter, we will consider various ways in which we may meet their transition needs.

Historical Background

The emphasis on transition planning for all students with disabilities that began to receive popular attention in the 1980s had its origins in a variety of earlier efforts. Berkell and Brown (1989), in their consideration of the historical roots of transition planning, relate transition to vocational education, to the integration concept in special education, to work experience programs, and to the efforts of vocational rehabilitation agencies. We will consider these areas later in this chapter, but will list here certain other factors that have influenced the development of transition programs.

A number of deinstitutionalization efforts have targeted persons with mental retardation housed in residential facilities. These efforts reflected an acceptance of the principle of normalization, which had its beginnings in the Scandinavian countries in the early 1960s. Wolfensberger (1972) promoted this principle in the United States and Canada, and it was quickly supported by the National Association for Retarded Citizens. This principle does not deny the existence of a disability, but encourages maximum efforts to provide a total setting—including both residential variables and daily activities—that is as normal as possible. Beginning in the 1970s and directly related to the normalization movement, a considerable number of higher-functioning individuals were released from residential facilities, after varying degrees of preparation for their new, community-based environment. However, Patton, Beirne-Smith, and Payne (1990) have noted many readmissions of these individuals, who could not cope with life in the mainstream. A parallel deinstitutionalization movement took place with respect to individuals with mental illness. Many of these persons, who functioned relatively well in a controlled environment while taking medication regularly, were unable to cope outside of the institution. Because of their visibility, the popular press gave considerable attention to the number of "street people" who were former inmates of institutions for the mentally ill.

In most cases, the individuals involved were adults who received limited preparation for the radical changes in environment they faced. Bad experiences with these mainstreaming programs highlighted the need for better preparation for this transition and for considerable follow-up support at the community level.

A second factor that provided part of the basis for transition planning was the evolving field of **career education.** As career education evolved from a vocationally oriented effort focused primarily on high school students into a concept of career development beginning at the elementary level, it became clear that students with disabilities had as great or greater need for such programs as did other students. Career education came to include concerns about employment, social adjustment, and residential setting and living conditions. Learning from those adults who had been deinstitutionalized, specialists now recognized that, in addition to preparing individuals for the transition to new settings, it was essential to do advance planning and to make specific provisions for follow-up after students graduated from public school programs. They also recognized that transition planning was essential for all students with disabilities; hence, a written transition plan was specifically required by the 1990 provisions of PL 101-476.

Finally, though the origins of transition planning were related primarily to the movement from school to adult life in the community, the importance of many other transitions—starting with the home-to-school transition—was soon recognized. Therefore, though the major emphasis is still on planning and preparation for the transition that follows formal schooling, other transitions are now the focus of additional planning efforts.

The Transition to Care by Persons Other Than Parents

A first, major transition for infants, very young children with disabilities, and those considered to be at risk is from the home to whatever program of intervention is determined most appropriate. In our consideration of early intervention in Chapter 12, we described various ways to facilitate that transition. For the infant or young child who is serviced by a home-based program, little transition is involved. If he or she then joins a center-based program, the transition is a major one. In a properly structured center-based program, information will be shared and cooperative efforts between parents and center staff will be an integral part of the intervention program. Similarly, a great deal of information should be obtained if the child leaves home for the first time to enter a preschool intervention program at age 3 or 4. Parents must be involved through regular conferences, formal parent education, and cooperative efforts between home and school to reach established objectives. If, for example, the child moves from an organized program for at-risk infants to a preschool program, staff members in both programs must cooperate to ensure a smooth transition.

There is value to sharing information about specific children between any early childhood program and a kindergarten program in the public schools, as well as to preparing *any* child for entrance to the kindergarten program, but our concern is with children considered at risk or those with an identified disability. In 1986, PL 99-457 led to expanded programs for children from birth to age 5 (see Chapter 12). As part of these programs, a variety of assessment data is gathered,

People Who Make a Difference

RUTH LEFF—"YOU JUST TAKE ONE STEP AT A TIME" Ten years ago Ruth Leff's doctor told her that her arthritis would only get worse unless she started to exercise. Now Ruth Leff is the fastest female race walker over 60 in the United States. She says "You just take one step at a time."

Ruth is a speech-language pathologist and president of the Crestwood Company, a firm that develops augmentative communication aids for children and adults. The company is the outgrowth of Ruth's efforts to help her sister, who had multiple sclerosis and could not communicate. Ruth developed a series of flash card pictures that permitted her sister to communicate with a glance or other facial expression. She soon began to work with other techniques that base communication on what a person *can* do. For example, her Opticommunicator system enables people to "talk with their eyes."

Ruth has developed a number of alternative communication systems, including communication boards and head pointers. One of the more innovative is a series of Passport cards that affords individuals with limited communication a considerable degree of independence. This card system includes kits related to fast-food outlets, supermarket shopping, casual dining, personal needs (clothing), shopping centers, drugstores, recreation, and school. For example, the Supermarket Kit includes 315 cards picturing items that an individual might want to purchase. The items needed are selected, then placed in a Porta Book, which is taken to the store. This helps communicatively limited individuals remember their "shopping list" and provides a way for them to "tell" (show) store employees what they want, if they can't find it. A similar procedure applies with the fast-food passport, personal needs passport, and all the rest.

Ruth Leff continues to develop new products based on the needs of individuals with disabilities. Her motto is "I can," represented by a sign on her desk.

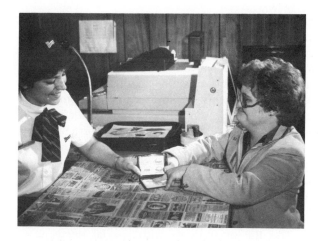

The Fast Food Passport™ can be used to order a meal in any fast food restaurant.

The new Casual Dining Passport™ enables a person to order a meal in a full-service restaurant.

Using the Personal Needs Passport™, a person can now select and purchase clothing in a department store.

The Supermarket Shopping Passport™ allows the user to be completely independent when buying groceries.

■ Use of Passport cards, developed by Ruth Leff (see People Who Make a Difference, p. 428), promotes independence. ■

and, if the program is properly implemented, information is recorded with respect to social abilities, health status, probable learning strengths and weaknesses, interests, motivational factors, and related information. The results of any assessments completed in the preschool program can be of great value to kindergarten or first-grade teachers. Such information should be reviewed in a planned conference with designated personnel from the receiving school, to facilitate the transition. The teachers involved may all be employees of the public schools, but often a variety of outside agencies may have provided services through contractual arrangements; therefore, planned, scheduled efforts are essential. Parents are usually involved in conferences with both sending and receiving schools and teachers, and the student and parents should have made orientation visits to the receiving facility. Given advance planning, information sharing, and the active involvement of parents, teachers, and child, this transition can be accomplished with a minimum of difficulty.

The Transition to Another School Level

Moving from grade to grade within a school requires that information be forwarded to the receiving teacher; if the sending teacher is in the same building, this is often a simple matter. The IEP of students with special needs is of considerable value in providing continuity; and often the same special education specialist will continue to work with the student through several grades. It is a different matter when the student moves from elementary to middle school, middle school to junior high, or junior high to high school. Attending school in a new building, with new rules for behavior, older and more numerous students in the halls, and all that goes with this change can be intimidating to any student. It is therefore essential that a procedure be established through which all records are forwarded and a conference is held between the former and new special educators and the teachers in the new setting. The special educator responsible in the new setting must have the records in time to review them and ask for clarification and interpretation as needed. Depending on the nature and severity of the disability, considerable effort may be required in such areas as physical orientation to a new, often larger school, the use of lockers, and moving from class to class. These needs must be anticipated by the sending teacher and clearly communicated to the receiving teachers or counselors. Without careful attention, this transition can "lose ground" for the total program.

The Transition between Special and Regular Class Programs

Transitions between regular and special classes must be consistent with the regulations of PL 94-142 and state regulations. A move into a program of special intervention must be thoroughly planned. Likewise, a move out of more intensive services—or, in some cases, discontinuance of all special services—must be made on the basis of objective data and professional judgment. This applies to moves out of self-contained special classes, discontinuance of resource room service, or any similar program change. Parents must be a part of this procedure, just as they were in the placement into a program of special education services. There may, however, be less information on how a return to the regular program should be accomplished.

Wood and Miederhoff (1988) suggest using a transition checklist. Theirs provides a systematic means whereby the special educator can first observe and evaluate or rate the mainstream setting into which the student may be returned. They recommend rating three categories: classroom, interpersonal and social relations, and related environments. Classroom characteristics to be observed include the type of grouping for instruction, evaluation techniques (including the types of classroom tests utilized, how they are given, and related factors), the extent and type of homework assigned, and teaching techniques. Interpersonal and social relations include the types of student interaction (cooperative, competitive, and so on), the dress code and other standards for student appearance, and other significant characteristics of class interactions. Related environments to be observed are areas such as physical education facilities, assembly rooms, the school cafeteria, and the behavioral requirements in all such areas.

For each category the evaluator determines the skills, abilities, and understanding required for success. This information should be a major factor in determining whether such a transition is appropriate at the time or whether to look for another reintegration setting. It will also provide direction for additional instruction. Such information is of special importance in the case of students who have been previously enrolled full-time in special classes.

George and Lewis believe that "specific steps that special education teachers can initiate to implement a smooth transition from special to regular education have been lacking in the literature" (1991, p. 34). They propose a more detailed, four-phase process designed to help educators and parents make more meaningful, "data-based decisions about a student's readiness to move to a less restrictive setting and [provide] for a positive, fluid transition" (ibid.). They call their system EASE: Exit Assistance for Special Educators.

Phase 1   The first phase of EASE is long-range planning. George and Lewis recommend that when the initial IEP is developed consideration be given to the types of academic, behavioral, and social skills the student will need to function successfully in the regular class. This is often, but not always, a part of the IEP. A general indication of these skills may be inferred by reviewing applicable curriculum guides (for the general education classes), statements of behavioral or student discipline standards, and the student handbook. Input from the regular class teacher (in the IEP meeting) and observations of the regular class will provide further information.

Obvious academic and behavioral competency requirements should become major, long-range goals. Yearly IEP meetings provide a means for evaluating progress toward those goals and will permit compiling a record of progress toward the ultimate goal of reintegration into the regular program.

Phase 2   The second phase begins when it appears that the student is approaching the targeted IEP goals. Step 1 in phase 2 is to make a closer examination of the classroom into which the student may be placed. The Classroom Inventory Checklist (CIC) developed by George and Lewis (1991) is shown in Figure 13.1. Though the long-range goals established in the original IEP should have listed the competencies required for the student to function successfully in a regular class environment, they would have been based on past conditions that need reevaluation.

Step 2 in phase 2 is an attempt to approximate the conditions in the anticipated future class placement while the student is still in the special class setting. The CIC provides a basis for this simulation of what the student may expect when reintegrated in the regular class. George and Lewis also note that it is important "to begin during this phase . . . the fading of any reinforcement systems used in the special education classroom to those occurring in the new placement" (1991, p. 36).

Step 3 in phase 2 is a final assessment of student readiness for the new setting. The exact nature of this assessment will vary considerably depending on the student but will be related to the information collected through the CIC.

Teacher: _____ Grade: _____ Date: _____

Subject/Activity: _____

Observer: _____

Directions: Several observations should be made at different times and over different days and activities. It may be useful to develop a summary observation listing occurrences throughout the school day and situation-specific activities based on all the observations that have been made. In addition, the observer may wish to interview the teacher briefly to complete the inventory when all the information cannot be gained through observation. For questions 1 through 7, check all that apply or estimate percentage of time.

1. How is the room arranged?
   ☐ desks ☐ study carrels ☐ tables
   Notes:

2. What materials are used in the classroom?
   ☐ blackboard ☐ textbooks ☐ audiovisuals ☐ workbooks
   ☐ worksheets ☐ activity centers ☐ games
   Notes:

3. What instructional format is used in the classroom?
   ☐ team teaching ☐ independent activities ☐ peer tutoring
   ☐ lecture/whole group ☐ individualized instruction ☐ small group
   Notes:

4. At what grade levels (or series/texts) are the students working?
   ☐ mathematics ☐ reading ☐ language arts
   Notes:

5. What other personnel are there in the classroom?
   ☐ teaching assistants ☐ peer tutors ☐ volunteers ☐ no other personnel
   Notes:

6. How is student progress assessed?
   ☐ tests/quizzes ☐ attendance ☐ assignments ☐ class participation
   Notes:

7. How does the classroom teacher manage student behavior?
   ☐ reinforcement (tangible/verbal)
   ☐ response cost (loss of recess, free time, etc.)
   ☐ use of school discipline procedures (List those procedures the teacher feels are important.)
   Notes:

8. What personal responsibilities does the student have? (E.g., assignments due by certain time, in seat before bell rings, assignments can be taken home vs. assignments must be completed in class.)

9. What are the daily routines in the classroom? (E.g., lunch at 11:20, PE on Thursdays only.)

10. What behaviors does the teacher like? (List behaviors the teacher emphasizes as important.)

11. What are the behaviors the teacher dislikes? (List behaviors the teacher disapproves or punishes.)

Figure 13.1 Classroom inventory checklist

SOURCE: *"EASE: Exit Assistance for Special Educators" by N.L. George and T.J. Lewis,* Teaching Exceptional Children, 23 *(Winter 1991), p. 36. Copyright 1991 by The Council for Exceptional Children. Reprinted by permission.*

Phase 3 This is the actual transition to the regular classroom. As was the original placement into a special program, this should be decided by a multidisciplinary team including the parents, the special education teacher, and the regular classroom teacher. The student's perceptions about any such move should be carefully considered, and the student should be directly involved in certain aspects of the final decision making. In many cases, more than one option may be available; if so, both parents and student should have input into the choice.

Phase 4 The last phase is the follow-up and evaluation phase. Definitive arrangements (time, dates, and so forth) should be made for future consultation between the regular class teacher and a designated special educator. The regular class teacher should also be encouraged to contact special educators at other times, as immediate need dictates. Procedures should be established for the collection of data that will permit evaluation of the success of this new placement, and dates should be established for review of those data.

One final consideration with respect to transitions between special and regular class programs is their timing. Clark and Kolstoe discuss a variety of issues that must be considered in transition planning for special needs students. One relates to the question of elementary school versus secondary school mainstreaming. They pose the following question: "Given the continued priority on least restrictive environment and progressive inclusion, are regular high school classes as well suited to assimilating students with disabilities as the elementary school is for its students with disabilities?" (1990, p. 376). In their related discussion they note that elementary and secondary schools differ in basic goals. Elementary schools tend to teach and emphasize basic tools or skills; secondary schools focus on the use of those skills to learn new information and develop new skills. Further, as students progress through the grades, "the discrepancy between handicapped and nonhandicapped students in intellectual functioning, academic achievement, learning skills, social experience, and personal maturity becomes greater rather than less" (ibid., p. 377). They remark that despite the teachers' best efforts to include special needs students, nondisabled students "are capable of more rigorous assignments and, consequently, of more sophisticated class participation" (ibid.). As a result, many students with disabilities may be left in a state of confusion.

These authors also believe that "IEP planners at the high school level must make more difficult decisions about content priorities and placement in integrated settings than at the elementary level" (ibid.). This may be particularly true if curriculum provisions to enhance the student's success in transition from school to adult life are available only (or primarily) as part of a separate, segregated program.

The Transition from School to Community Integration

The Office of Special Education and Rehabilitative Services (OSERS) in 1984 initiated a national effort to promote more successful transitions from school to working life for persons with disabilities. Though Will stated at the time that its "concern with employment does not indicate lack of interest in other aspects of adult living," and that "success in social, personal, leisure, and other adult roles enhances opportunities both to obtain employment and to enjoy its benefits" (1984, p. 1), in fact, the OSERS model placed little emphasis on any other transition goal. Halpern has pointed this out, indicating that "the authors of this policy seem to be suggesting . . . that the nonvocational dimensions of adult adjustment are significant and important only insofar as they contribute to the ultimate goal of employment" (1985, p. 480). Halpern suggested a revised model emphasizing community adjustment and named three pillars of equal importance in supporting community adjustment: employment, social and interpersonal networks, and residential environment. Halpern suggested that success in employment is *not* necessarily accompanied by success in other areas. Rather, it appears that "success along only one or even two dimensions is not likely to be sufficient to support the desired goal of community adjustment. Programs will need to be directed specifically toward each dimension, with client needs determining the selection of specific services" (ibid., p. 482). It should be noted that Halpern's research was done with persons with mental retardation, and that research relating to one disability may not be applicable to others. Perhaps modified transition models are needed for different disabilities.

■ Secondary-Level Transition Programs

Though the concept of transition is applicable at all levels, the major emphasis has been at the secondary school level. Transition planning for students with disabilities aged 16 and older became a specific requirement of the IEP with the passage of PL 101-476 in 1990. As we noted earlier, Berkell and Brown (1989) related the concept of transition planning to historical efforts in three different fields: vocational education, vocational rehabilitation, and special education. They traced vocational education back to the Morrill Act of 1856 and the Land Grant College Act of 1862, which established the principle of college-level vocational training. Vocational rehabilitation services were initiated on the federal level through passage of the Vocational Rehabilitation Act of 1920, directed primarily toward assisting disabled veterans of World War I but also applying to others who were disabled. Special education programs for students with disabilities at first stressed basic skills—the three R's. However, by the 1950s, many programs for students classified as educable mentally retarded began to include an emphasis on practical daily living skills and on work study or work experience programs. This emphasis was stimulated by the research and program recommendations of Kolstoe (1961), Kolstoe and Frey (1965), and others in the field of mental retardation. In combination, these efforts were of considerable value in preparing students for family, citizenship, and career responsibilities.

A fourth factor in the development of secondary-level transition programs was the concept of career education. This is perhaps not a "field" in the sense that vocational education, vocational rehabilitation, and special education are fields, but it has had a significant, continuing influence on the development of transition programs. Biller notes that developmental career theory views career formation as "an unfolding of behaviors within a framework of career life stages over the life span" (1987, p. 7).

Super played a major role in initiating the concept of career education in 1957 through his book *The Psychology of Careers.* Almost 30 years later, in a chapter titled "The Application of Career Development Theory to the Handicapped," Super had this to say:

■ Preparation for transition begins early. Being able to use a computer is a useful skill that this student can use throughout life. ■

Because the core of the career development problems of the handicapped is their limited communication capacity, whether the limitations are visual, auditory, spoken, or motoric, the implications for helping them with these problems are implications for finding better ways of communication with and for them. These must include exposing handicapped individuals to opportunities for learning about the world of work and to ways in which they might fit into it for the maximum realization of their potential. (1985, p. 34)

Super further indicated that individuals with disabilities need both shelter and exposure. Exposure to the real world is essential, but they must also be sheltered from demands that outstrip their (present) capacity to respond successfully.

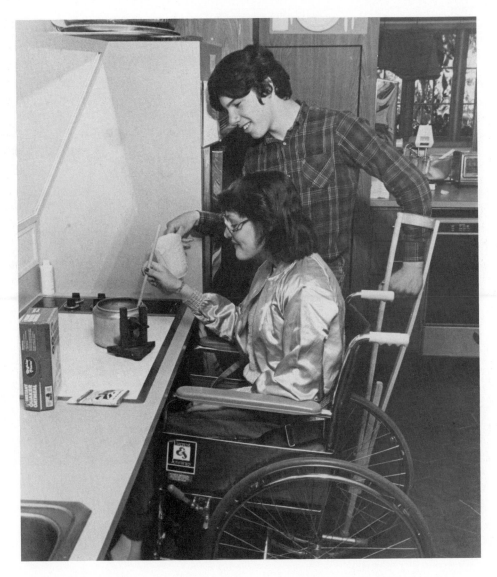

■ With adaptations in living arrangements, independent living can become a reality. ■

Clark and Kolstoe refer to career education as "a concept parallel to vocational special needs education" (1990, p. 18) and recommend it as an alternative to the more narrow, job-preparation approach of vocational education. They credit Dr. Sidney Marland with beginning a practical emphasis on career education in the public schools, as a result of his address to a secondary school principals' national convention in 1971. In this address, Marland described career education as follows:

> I do not speak of career education solely in the sense of job training, as important as it is. I prefer to use career in a much broader connotation—as a stream of continued growth and progress. Career in that sense strongly implies that education can be made

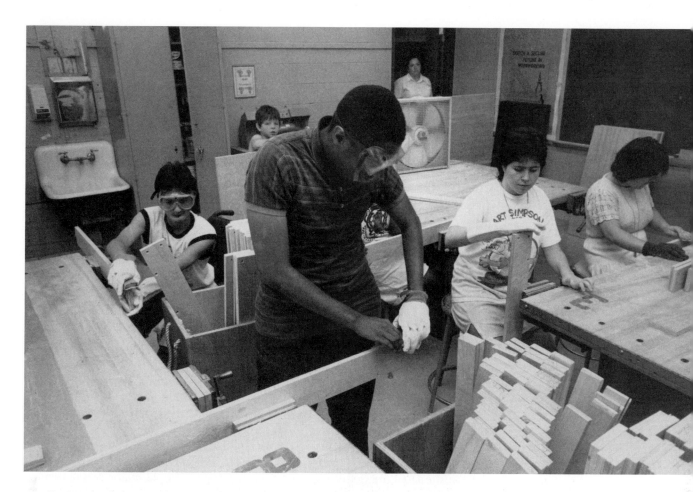

■ In-school vocational training provides opportunities to experience a variety of work-related skills. ■

to serve *all* the needs of an American — teaching, to begin with, the skills and refinements of the workaday world, for if we cannot at the minimum prepare a man or woman to earn a living, our efforts are without worth. But career education must go beyond occupational skills — the interpersonal and organizational understanding without which one simply cannot exist in a modern nation-state, addressing effectively the matter of living itself, touching on all its pragmatic, theoretical, and moral aspects. That is what I mean in the broadest sense by career education — and that is the way in which I envision the learning process being carried forward in the schools of this Nation, in its homes and businesses, and government offices, and perhaps its streets, since for some, much of what is really educational occurs there. (1971, p. 1)

Secondary-level transition programs can take many directions. They may target further education followed by employment and independent living; employment and independent living immediately following the secondary school program; or, for a few individuals with more severe disabilities, independent or semi-independent living. Transition programs should ideally start prior to the secondary level, but it appears that most of them are presently carried out in the secondary schools or at secondary school-age levels. A definition of transition provided by Wehman, Kregel, Barcus, and Schalock reflects this secondary school emphasis. According to these researchers, transition is

> a carefully planned process, which may be initiated either by school personnel or adult service providers, to establish and implement a plan for either employment or additional vocational training of a handicapped student who will graduate or leave school in 3–5 years; such a process must involve special educators, vocational educators, parents and/or the student, an adult service system representative, and possibly an employer. (1986, p. 114)

This definition emphasizes the need for interdisciplinary cooperation, shared responsibility, multiple goals or outcomes, and the role of parents. It relegates the transition process to a period of 3 to 5 years before students graduate or leave school, thus indicating that it is primarily a secondary school function.

In addition to the three outcome areas usually associated with transition programs — further education, employment, and independent living — many additional variables must be considered, because planning must meet the needs of students with many different disabilities. And, within each kind of disability, planning will vary for students with different levels of severity of disability.

■ Career Education and Transition Planning

Although many models can provide a basis for planning effective career education, it appears that Brolin and his co-workers have described "one of the most comprehensive career education models developed to date" (Patton, Beirne-Smith, & Payne, 1990). Brolin's contributions include the strategies recommended in *Life-Centered Career Education: A Competency Based Approach* (Brolin, 1978, 1983, 1988) and the Life-Centered Career Education (LCCE) Transitional Model based on that approach (Brolin & Schatzman, 1989).

In the LCCE model, Brolin and Schatzman describe 22 major competencies, clustered within the following three curriculum areas.

1. Daily living skills–nine skills (such as managing personal finances and buying, preparing, and consuming food)
2. Personal-social skills — seven skills (such as acquiring self-confidence and maintaining good interpersonal relations)
3. Occupational guidance and preparation — six skills (such as knowing about and exploring occupational possibilities and exhibiting appropriate work habits and behavior)

The LCCE model conceptualizes four career education stages: (1) career awareness, (2) career exploration, (3) career preparation, and (4) placement and follow-up. It includes a kindergarten-to-adult services scope and sequence that recommends beginning career education and transition efforts during the elementary grades and continuing indefinitely into postsecondary and adult years.

The LCCE competency-based curriculum and the LCCE Transitional Model originated in efforts directed primarily toward individuals with mild or moderate mental retardation; they have since been expanded and modified in an attempt to apply them to all students with disabilities. Implementation of the model will be somewhat different for, say, a student with moderate mental retardation who needs considerable postsecondary and adult assistance to function successfully in the community and a student with learning disabilities who, with transition

■ A degree of independent living is achieved through group homes. This one is
for individuals with mental retardation. ■

assistance, may complete a four-year college program, perhaps a master's degree
program, and then function with considerable success as an adult. The model is of
value in both cases, but given the unique needs of students with different disabilities and the different degrees of disability, individual planning remains the basic
requirement.

Four elements must be considered in career education: (1) values, attitudes,
and habits; (2) human relationships; (3) occupational information; and (4) the
acquisition of job and daily living skills (Clark, 1979). Clark places emphasis on the
early implementation of career education, advocating that career awareness begin
in kindergarten and continue throughout the school years. He views junior high
school as a time for career exploration, with actual career preparation beginning
in high school and continuing through postsecondary programs. He also provides
a model of school-based career education that illustrates how such education for

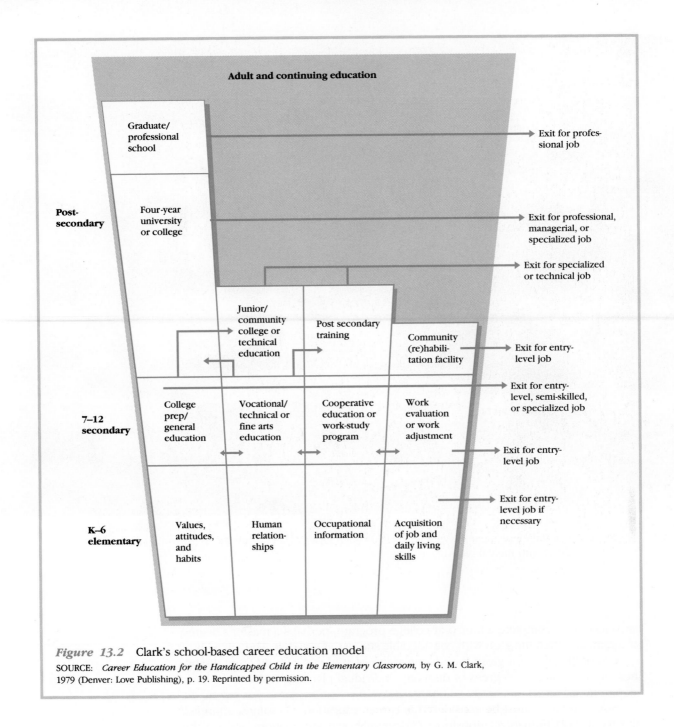

Adult and continuing education

Post-secondary
- Graduate/professional school → Exit for professional job
- Four-year university or college → Exit for professional, managerial, or specialized job
- → Exit for specialized or technical job

- Junior/community college or technical education
- Post secondary training
- Community (re)habilitation facility → Exit for entry-level job

7–12 secondary
- College prep/general education
- Vocational/technical or fine arts education
- Cooperative education or work-study program
- Work evaluation or work adjustment

→ Exit for entry-level, semi-skilled, or specialized job

→ Exit for entry-level job

K–6 elementary
- Values, attitudes, and habits
- Human relationships
- Occupational information
- Acquisition of job and daily living skills

→ Exit for entry-level job if necessary

Figure 13.2 Clark's school-based career education model

SOURCE: *Career Education for the Handicapped Child in the Elementary Classroom,* by G. M. Clark, 1979 (Denver: Love Publishing), p. 19. Reprinted by permission.

students with disabilities relates to that for nondisabled students, including those who proceed through a four-year university program and graduate or professional school. This model (see Figure 13.2) shows how career education should permeate all of education. It can increase our understanding of the elements necessary in a career education program for students with special needs.

■ Sharing a meal enhances the quality of life in this group home. ■

Before concluding this overview we should list certain assumptions that are basic to career education.

1. Career development begins shortly after birth, in the form of a developing work personality. Parents and educators alike have a role in the maturation of this work personality.
2. A *career* includes productive activities engaged in at home, leisure activities, avocational pursuits, and any other productive activity. Employment is only one part of an individual's career.
3. Predictable stages of career development and certain instructional domains required for successful career development must be recognized and become a part of systematic curriculum planning.

4. Career education instruction should not be considered as separate from regular instruction. In most instances it can be integrated with regular courses and taught concurrently.
5. Career development programs and related transition planning require a partnership of parents, educators, business and industry, and community agencies equipped to work with individuals with disabilities.
6. With regard to the involvement of agencies other than the schools, specific interagency agreements should be drawn up that specify responsibilities, allocation of funds, and use of facilities.
7. Transitional resource coordinators should be designated. Their responsibilities should include both carrying out and monitoring all aspects of programs (Brolin & Schatzman, 1989).

■ Transition Planning for Students with Severe Disabilities

Planning for a successful transition from the school setting to adult life requires an unusual degree of interagency cooperation when students have severe disabilities. Peters, Templeman, and Brostrom comment on that cooperation as follows.

> Schools must go a step beyond an individual teacher, or even a school district, to look unilaterally at needed skills in future environments and to involve community-based service providers and support personnel in the longitudinal planning and program development process. The need for interagency cooperation is critical when one examines the myriad of complex training needs presented by individuals with severe handicaps. In order for the teacher to develop truly meaningful and functional programming objectives for these students, there needs to exist a system whereby the schools bring together educational, social, and rehabilitation service agencies for collaboration in the coordination and integration of planning efforts leading to postschool transition to community services for the student. (1987, p. 532)

A number of models have been proposed that would appear to ensure more successful transition of students with severe disabilities. All seem to contain at least the following attributes.

1. A formal, written transition plan, including goals and objectives, timelines, and designations of responsible persons and agencies
2. Concrete outcomes (including job placements)
3. A school curriculum that is functional in nature and that includes community-based vocational instruction (Moon, Diambra, & Hill, 1990)

In a program described by Moon and her colleagues, the initial step was the formation of a local interagency core team to establish guidelines for all activities to be included in the project. In the team's transition plan, goals were specified for each student in at least four areas: (1) vocational placement or postsecondary education, (2) residential or other living arrangements, (3) leisure and recreation skills, and (4) personal management skills. Goals were established for five additional areas as possible or as necessary according to the individual's needs: (1) personal and family relationships, (2) medical services, (3) financial arrangements, (4) transportation, and (5) advocacy or legal services.

Supported employment was established as the goal for a majority of the graduating students. Supported employment includes placement, job instruction, and follow-along services for individuals with severe disabilities—in integrated job sites and at competitive wages. In this program, the employment specialist and job instructor found jobs, provided instruction at the job site, and gave initial follow-along support after job performance became stable. Successful employment roles for these former students included hospital housekeeper, grocery bagger, laundry worker, dishwasher, and fast-food host. Not all students were placed prior to graduation, but for those not placed, the individual transition plan specified the types of jobs that might be appropriate and which of the various adult service providers should make the placement and provide continued training. This is an example of the comprehensive nature of some transition programs.

**Box 13.1
*Barbara's
Very Special
Transition
Needs***

There are many very special transition situations. The following case of a 16-year-old girl exemplifies them and the planning they may require.

Barbara was injured in an auto accident, resulting in traumatic brain injury (TBI). After the accident, she was hospitalized for 10 weeks; during the first several weeks she was in a coma. Her family reacted to her TBI with stability, supported her rehabilitation program, investigated her school's potential for assistance, and advocated for her with the school. Physical and occupational therapy were provided and daily speech and language therapy was begun during the fifth week. In the seventh week Barbara began attending the hospital school. School district personnel recognized her potential need, consulted with hospital staff, and were ready to support her return to school. When Barbara was discharged from the hospital it was near the end of the school year; due to the short time left and to her physical and endurance limitations, she did not return to school that spring. She was given a 10-week program of homebound instruction during the summer that focused on regaining her academic skills plus physical, occupational, and speech therapy.

Planning for the transition to school began while Barbara was still hospitalized. The rehabilitation team, the staff from her school, and her family met to review her status, her probable future needs, and the services that would be required for her reentry to school. Just before the start of the next school year, a reentry planning meeting was held, attended by the 15 school staff members who would be making contact with Barbara, representatives from the hospital program, Barbara, and her parents. Taking into account the information provided by the hospital staff and by the teacher of the summer homebound program, an IEP was developed. The plan called for a reduced course load, special scheduling (Barbara was more alert early in the day), resource room assistance, rest breaks, adaptive physical education, a student aide (one of her friends, to help her get from class to class), an extra set of books to keep at home, and a number of other special provisions such as assistance with note taking, a tape recorder to tape lectures, and a computer to complete assignments. In addition, a schedule was established for monthly IEP reviews.

Barbara had some difficulties after reentering school. Most were recognized during the monthly IEP meetings, and corrective actions were taken. Psychosocial problems occurred as she began to realize the extent of her disabilities and as friends became less supportive with the passage of time. She was helped through counseling. Barbara completed her junior and senior years with passing grades and graduated with her class. She entered college the following fall.

SOURCE: *Based on "Students with Traumatic Brain Injury: Making the Transition from Hospital to School," by M. Mira and J. Tyler,* Focus on Exceptional Children, 23 *(5), 1991, pp. 1–12 (Denver: Love Publishing).*

Transition, then, is an essential concept in programs for students with disabilities. In a discussion of the future of transition planning, Taylor and Knoll comment as follows.

> "Transition" has become a buzz word used to characterize the need that many special education graduates have for supportive services as they move from a school system to adulthood. There is now a generation of students, graduating from special education, who challenge the existing adult service system. They have had an education that prepared them to be active participants in their communities. Many of these students, including those with very severe disabilities, have been educated in integrated settings, alongside nondisabled peers. Many of them have received a functional, community-based education that has prepared them to continue, as adults, to work with nondisabled people. And, it is just this type of employment that their teachers and parents expect the vocational service sector to aid them in finding. (1989, pp. 321–322)

Their comments aptly summarize the challenge for transition planners, particularly when working with individuals with severe disabilities.

The Transition to College and Other Postsecondary Programs

Students with learning disabilities are entering postsecondary education programs in increasing numbers (McGuire, Norlander, & Shaw, 1990; Rose, 1991). A much larger *percentage* of students identified as visually impaired will attend college (Fairweather & Shaver, 1991), but the *total* number in college programs is smaller. Students with other disabilities are also entering postsecondary education programs in increasing numbers.

A great deal of effort was expended during the 1980s on studying the problems associated with providing students with disabilities a more effective transition from secondary school to college or some other type of postsecondary

People Who Make a Difference

1000+ PERSONNEL DIRECTORS—TRANSITION OPPORTUNITIES This "Person Who Makes a Difference" is really many thousands of persons in businesses large and small throughout the 50 states. We have pictured the familiar "golden arches" of McDonald's because the symbol is familiar to all and because McDonald's employs many persons with disabilities. But it is only one of many. Throughout the nation, in increasing numbers, business owners are providing valuable training sites for individuals with disabilities, employing them, and finding that many become highly valued employees. These are indeed people who make a difference.

educational program. Though much of that effort targeted students with learning disabilities, a great deal of what it taught us can be applied to planning for students with any disability.

McGuire, Norlander, and Shaw (1990) point to two major issues affecting students with disabilities that may originate at the secondary level.

1. There is a potential for "underpreparedness" for college admission due to limited flexibility in course selection—sometimes as a result of curricular decisions made early in the high school program.

2. Controversies over definitions may lead to confusion at the college level (this affects primarily students with learning disabilities). For example, college officials may require prior identification to corroborate the existence of learning disabilities before granting eligibility for special accommodations and academic adjustments.

At the postsecondary level they indicate the following issues.

1. Admissions requirements related to college entrance examinations may be influenced by Section 504 of the Rehabilitation Act of 1973, which requires consideration of "otherwise qualified individuals."

2. Asking preadmission questions regarding a disability is prohibited, yet test scores are often "flagged" when reported if they are obtained (for example) on an untimed basis, with a large-print test book, or with a tape cassette.

3. The need for academic adjustments for students with disabilities may be negatively affected by national concerns about "lowered standards" in higher education and the recent move to more stringent requirements for graduation.

4. College-level adaptations and services may have little or no grounding in theory or support by research.

5. Requirements for economic "belt tightening" may reduce programs of higher cost or of less appeal in terms of usual college goals and purposes.

A number of negative factors affecting transition should be considered at the secondary school level when choosing among postsecondary options. Getzel cites three such factors: "(a) the lack of interagency collaboration between secondary and postsecondary programs; (b) the difficulty of sharing written educational records among various programs; and (c) the reluctance on the part of educators in postsecondary classrooms to adapt or modify their materials or teaching methods to meet the needs of students with handicaps" (1990, p. 52). She suggests that secondary school transition teams explore the areas of admission policies, assistance with registration, financial assistance, academic support, and availability of other support services. Information about those areas can be of great assistance in preparing the student for the transition.

Fairweather and Shaver (1991) drew a number of conclusions from a study of youth with disabilities who recently graduated from high school. Of that group, 15.1% went on to some type of postsecondary program. The percentage of participation in such programs ranged from a high of 42.6% of students with visual impairments to a low of 4.8% of students with multiple disabilities. The authors found that (1) there was more movement into postsecondary vocational education programs than into either two-year or four-year college programs, and (2) though a much smaller percentage of youth with disabilities (as compared with nondisabled youth) continued on to postsecondary programs, those who did so shared demographic characteristics (such as parental education, income, and high school graduation status) with the nondisabled.

■ Training in a bakery may contribute to success in permanent, competitive employment for this person with mental retardation. ■

Two main questions grew out of their study.

1. Is postsecondary vocational training and direct participation in employment programs or participation in community or four-year college programs more strongly related to long-term success in employment?
2. Why is there such limited participation in two-year institutions (community colleges) that have a vocational focus and that cost considerably less than proprietary vocational institutions?

Finally, a survey of regular and special education high school teachers and college faculty (Seidenberg & Koenigsberg, 1990) suggested that knowledge acquired in the high school special education setting often was not generalized and reinforced in regular class settings. Thus, even though students attend secondary mainstream classes that are to some extent college preparatory, unless they learn to meet many of the performance demands of college classes, their transition will remain difficult. This suggests that far more cooperation between regular and special class teachers is required if transition to postsecondary settings is to be more successful.

Many published studies of transition to postsecondary education programs emphasize problems and the need for change. This is unfortunate; however, the problems have existed for some time, and it is encouraging that there is an increasing awareness of the need for further study and that problem areas are now being addressed.

Issues and Trends

As has been illustrated throughout this chapter, transition may have different meanings to persons from different disciplines—and even to individuals within any given discipline. One issue, then, is finding an acceptable definition and description of transition, including a clarification of its basic goals, the essential elements of a successful transition plan, when specific individual planning should be initiated, and who is primarily responsible for the management and monitoring of individual progress. Knowlton and Clark address this issue in their discussion of important transition issues for the 1990s when they ask "Who identifies with the transition movement?" (1987, p. 562). The roots of the transition movement were in programs for persons with moderate to severe mental retardation, yet a great deal of the present emphasis is on individuals with milder levels of disability. Knowlton and Clark suggest that "if the transition movement in special education is to have a positive impact on the quality of adult living for all persons with handicapping conditions, then the literature needs to broaden its focus and parameters so that a wider audience may identify with its findings and benefit from its implications" (ibid.).

A second issue mentioned by Knowlton and Clark (1987), Clark and Kolstoe (1990), and others is that of the potential influence of the "excellence in education" movement—that is, the movement to upgrade educational standards in secondary education in general. How that movement fares will influence the type of curriculum variance that may be permitted in high school programs for students with disabilities. A subissue here is that of "common versus differentiated exit documents" (Clark & Kolstoe, 1990). This in turn relates to minimum competency tests, the meaning of a high school diploma, and the many debates that have taken place about maintaining higher standards in secondary education.

A third issue is what is most important and should get most emphasis in transition planning: employment, social and interpersonal networking, or independent living? This may be answered by finding a more generally accepted definition of transition, but at present it is an important issue in establishing outcomes and in planning transition programs for individual students.

Fourth is the need for more successful collaboration between public school personnel and personnel from agencies such as vocational rehabilitation, state

■ This woman, with Seeing Eye dog and baby, has made a successful transition to independent living. ■

agencies that serve persons with developmental disabilities, and the various institutions of higher learning. Publicly supported agencies operate with a specific budget, stated goals, guidelines for service provision, requirements for reporting, and so forth. If transition planning is to be time- and cost-efficient, specified goals and guidelines for schools and these other agencies must "mesh" with respect to the ways individuals in need of transition assistance are served and how service dollars are allocated and accounted for. Finally, information is needed about transition in relation to economic and social contexts. Chadsey-Rusch, Rusch, and Phelps stress that it is essential to learn more about "the importance of work to human development; the nature, causes and consequences of youth unemployment; and the interaction of disability and youth unemployment" (1989, p. 228). They further point out that not enough is known about labor markets, the forces of supply and demand, and such things as potential trade-offs between income from Social Security programs and income earned by persons with disabilities in the labor market. All of these forces and factors will determine the availability and success of supported employment.

There is one major trend with respect to planning for more successful transitions for students with disabilities. That trend is toward more interest, more emphasis, and more effective transition programs.

Summary

There are predictable times when an infant, child, or youth will move into a significantly different phase of life. Such moves often mean a different physical setting, different peers, different authority figures, and different expectations and behavioral requirements. This can mean tension and perhaps trauma for any child, and a child with special needs may be affected even more.

Children with disabilities may require extra preparation for the transition from home to school. Transitions between special education programs and the regular classroom are unique to children with special needs. Such transitions may elicit damaging negative comments and attention from other students, so they must be carefully planned and implemented. Effective career education programs can have a very positive impact on secondary school transition planning and are an important element at that level. Recognition of the importance of transition planning led to a specific requirement for a transition plan in the IEPs of students 16 and older who are part of special education programs.

A great deal of interagency planning is essential if the transition from a school setting to community integration is to be successful for students with severe disabilities. Such planning requires specific consideration of financial arrangements, medical services, transportation, and personal or family roles, relationships, and responsibilities. It is also important that future advocacy and legal service responsibility be established.

Studies of transition needs and planning seem to emphasize problems that remain unresolved. One such issue is the division of responsibility between the public schools and the agencies that assist adults with disabilities. Another, closely related issue is fiscal support for such collaborative program efforts. Unless transition planning is given continuing, thoughtful consideration, the positive results of earlier special education interventions may be undermined.

Angelo often touches his friends and teachers when he speaks to them. He puts his arm around his friends and lays his hand on his teacher's arm. He is puzzled when they move away.

Ho feels insulted when his sixth-grade friends slap him on the back after he hits a home run. But they don't act as if they are insulting him.

Sam bows his head and does not look at his teacher when she speaks. His teacher thinks that he is not paying attention.

When she is asked if she is guilty of some infraction of the rules, Ashley does not respond. The teacher therefore assumes she is guilty.

Every time the teacher asks Charmaine when she will finish her project, Charmaine feels as though she should hurry and get finished, so she does. Then the teacher points out that her work is carelessly completed.

Robert cannot understand why his teacher and friends get upset because he speaks louder and faster when he notices that they want to speak. He thinks they should just start talking.

John and Mary have three children, the oldest of which is beginning kindergarten. They do not understand why they must provide information about their family to the school. They can't see why they would be asked whether or not Grandmother lives with them, where they work, how many children are at home and how old they are, and the dates of their own births.

Do these children have a problem? Do the parents? Or do the teachers?

CHAPTER FOURTEEN

Cultural and Language Diversity

Culture may be defined as the way of life of a given society, including its customs, ideas, attitudes, concepts, habits, skills, art, and music. Culture is transmitted primarily through language and personal experiences, and is maintained through human institutions: economic, social, political, and religious. Some version of this concept of culture is basic to the work of both anthropologists and sociologists.

Historical Background

In the early 20th century, the "melting pot" theory was advocated in the United States, emphasizing cultural assimilation and the development of a common American culture. A basic part of this concept was encouraging all Americans to speak English and discouraging them from speaking any other language. This effort was reflected in all aspects of society. In a review of how English attained its privileged position in the United States, Hakuta said that "its dominance has been ensured by pressures applied at the institutional level, primarily in the public schools, and by the psychological needs of immigrants to learn English so that they might fully achieve membership in American society" (1986, p. 165). This effort to build a nation of one language and one culture continued throughout the first half of the century; it received a strong additional impetus from the anti-German sentiments during World War I. During and following that period, the German language was barred from use in many private and public schools, and in some cases from telephone communications and public meetings. Similar actions were taken during World War II , against schools in which Japanese was spoken; later, Mexican-American children were sometimes punished for speaking Spanish in school (Hakuta, 1986).

Earlier—and for an extended period of time—Native American children were whipped in schools administered by the federal government for using their native language. In this case, the punishment was felt to be a justifiable attempt to strip away their language as well as a supposedly inferior Indian culture and identity (Giago, 1978).

This attitude began to change during the 1960s and 1970s. The first federal action was the passage of the Bilingual Education Act of 1968 (Title VII, an amendment to the Elementary and Secondary Education Act of 1965). This act in part funded experimental programs designed to meet the needs of children with limited English-speaking ability. A number of influential individuals and groups began to support the concept of cultural pluralism and multicultural education, and in 1973 the American Association of Colleges for Teacher Education (AACTE) issued a statement titled "No One Model American." That statement included the following.

**Box 14.1
Another Use
for Closed-
Captions**

Millions of recent immigrants are struggling to learn English. Closed-captioned television, developed for persons with hearing impairments, may help many of them. The National Captioning Institute reports that half of all caption decoders are sold to Hispanics and Asian Americans who find it easier to learn idioms and other unfamiliar English expressions when they can both hear and see the words.

Multicultural education is education which values cultural pluralism. Multicultural education rejects the view that schools should seek to melt away cultural differences or the view that schools should merely tolerate cultural pluralism. Instead, multicultural education affirms that schools should be oriented toward the cultural enrichment of all children and youth through programs rooted to the preservation and extension of cultural diversity as a fact of life in American society, and it affirms that this cultural diversity is a valuable resource that should be preserved and extended. It affirms that major education institutions should strive to preserve and enhance cultural pluralism. (1973, p. 4)

This statement was intended to encourage and support a positive attitude and philosophical orientation toward multicultural education and was effectively incorporated in the curricula of some teacher training institutions. It was less effective in others, however. As a result, in 1980 the National Council for the Accreditation of Teacher Educators (NCATE) established a special standard requiring teacher training institutions to demonstrate that they included training in multicultural education for all prospective teachers.

The Special Education–Bilingual Education Interface

Title VI of the Civil Rights Act of 1964 bans discrimination based on race, color, or national origin in any program or activity receiving federal financial assistance. In litigation related to the educational needs of students with little or no English-language facility (*Lau* v. *Nichols,* 1974), the U.S. Supreme Court ruled that "there is no equality of treatment merely by providing students with the same facilities, textbooks, teachers, and curriculum; for students who do not understand English are effectively foreclosed from any meaningful education" (quoted in Teitelbaum & Hiller, 1977, p. 7). In a **consent decree,** the San Francisco School District provided a bilingual-bicultural program for the Chinese, Filipino, and Hispanic students in the district. Subsequent cases in various parts of the nation reaffirmed students' rights to a bilingual education.

Bilingual special education has been addressed by several court decisions in New York; for example, in *Dyrcia, S., et al.* v. *Board of Education of the City of New York* (1979), the court directed that students be evaluated by school-based teams using bilingual evaluation procedures, in the students' own environment. It also required a Spanish-version booklet of parents' rights and hiring neighborhood workers to facilitate parental involvement in both evaluation and development of the IEP. Finally, it ordered appropriate bilingual programs, available in a full continuum of placement options, for children with limited English proficiency and disabilities.

Court decisions have been consistent: bilingual students with disabilities must receive assistance from both bilingual and special education programs. Details are not prescribed, except as they relate to specific court cases, and "there is still considerable debate concerning how and where the bilingual exceptional child should be served" (Collier, 1989, p. 262). Some advocate special class placement for students who are bilingual and eligible for special education; others believe that all but the most severely disabled and those with almost no proficiency in English should be mainstreamed. Such decisions are complicated by the fact that few bilingual teachers have the training to serve exceptional students, just as few special education teachers are competent to work in bilingual education. However, it is clear that students who are bilingual and have a disability must be provided the benefits of both bilingual and special education programming.

■ Happiness has no cultural boundaries. ■

Although Black English is not generally recognized as needing a formal bilingual program, it, too, has been the subject of litigation. For example, in 1979 the parents of 11 African-American students in Ann Arbor, Michigan, filed a federal suit accusing school officials of insensitivity to the language used by their children. These parents demanded that the school recognize Black English as a formal and distinct dialect with its own grammatical structure and cultural-historical basis. The judge ruled that the school district must "recognize Black English, the language the students speak at home, and develop a program for helping teachers to recognize this language and take it into account when teaching Standard American English to speakers whose indigenous language is Black English" (Nuru, 1983, pp. 307–308). The judge noted that the Black English dialect is not acceptable for communication in the educational world, in the commercial community, in the community of arts and sciences, or among professionals, but that it must be taken into account in educational planning (Nuru, 1983).

Terminology

A variety of terms will be found in the literature about individuals from diverse cultures. Terms used synonymously by some will be considered distinctly different by others. Various departments of the federal government use different terminology, and federal legislation has not always been terminologically consistent.

• *Culturally diverse populations* refers to individuals from populations other than the majority, white, English-speaking population of the United States. Wood (1989) indicates that culturally diverse populations include but are not limited to at least the following four broad categories: (1) Asians or Pacific Islanders (origins in the Far East or Southeast Asia), (2) Black Americans (origins in black racial groups of Africa), (3) Hispanics (origins in Mexico, Puerto Rico, Cuba, and Central or South America), and (4) Native Americans (origins in original North America or Alaskan peoples). Some recommend using the term *African American* rather than *black* or *black American;* others suggest using *Latino* rather than *Hispanic,* arguing that *Latino* is a more inclusive term.

• *Culturally different* is sometimes used synonymously with the term *culturally diverse,* though some feel it is less acceptable.

• *Cultural pluralism* describes a concept that reflects the belief that the contributions of many diverse cultural groups strengthen and enrich our society.

• *Ethnic minority* has traditionally been used by the Office of Civil Rights of the U.S. government. This term has ordinarily designated any one or all four of the groups comprising culturally diverse populations.

• *Bilingual* has a range of meanings: for instance, it can mean nativelike fluency in two languages or simply some ability to use two languages. Hakuta (1986) suggests a broader definition that indicates the ability to produce meaningful utterances in two languages.

• *Bilingual education* is, according to Baca and Cervantes (1989), the use of two languages as media of instruction.

• *Limited English proficiency (LEP)* refers to students for whom English is a second language and who are to some degree unable to benefit from English-language instruction. LEP is widely used in texts and journal articles about bilingual education, but some authors now seem to feel that PEP (potential English proficiency) is a more positive, acceptable term (Hamayan & Damico, 1991).

The Target Population

The annual reports to Congress required by Public Law 94-142 have not included data on the number of students from culturally diverse backgrounds served in special education programs, but we can infer it from other data. For example, an Office of Civil Rights survey (1986) reported that the percentage of ethnic minority children in U.S. public schools increased from one-fourth to over one-third in the 6-year period between 1978 and 1984. It also indicated a disproportionately large number of children from ethnic minority backgrounds in special education classes, the greatest overrepresentation being that of African Americans in classes for students labeled educable mentally retarded, trainable mentally retarded, or behaviorally disordered. This overrepresentation continues despite litigation directed specifically at it. White students and those from the Asian and Pacific Islanders category were reported to be overrepresented in classes for the gifted and talented.

Yates (1988) notes that the U.S. population is becoming older and less white, and that by the year 2000 one of every three Americans will be an African American, Hispanic, or Asian American. Given the nation's present makeup and age distribution, the percentage of white students in public schools will drop

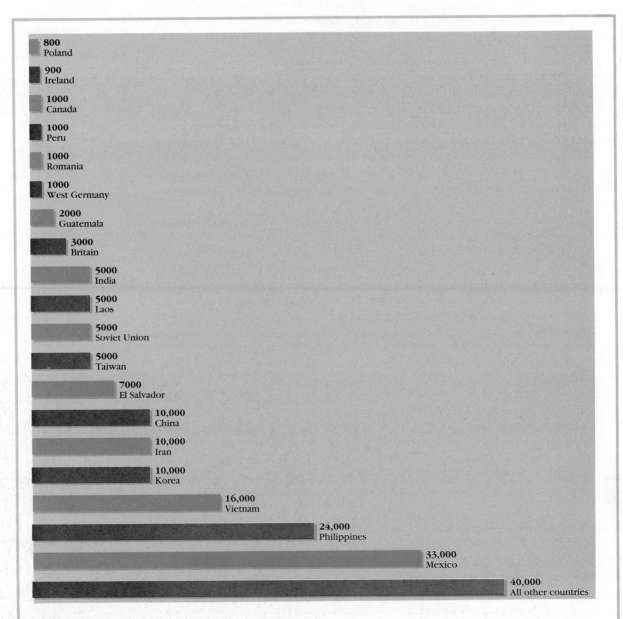

Figure 14.1 The United States: A cultural tapestry. Immigration is transforming the United States into a cultural tapestry. For example, according to the California Department of Finance, 180,700 legal immigrants entered the state in 1989; estimates of illegal immigrants reached 90,000 to 100,000. The graph illustrates the diverse origins of the legal immigrants who became residents of California in 1989.

below 50% by the year 2000 (see Figure 14.1). This has already occurred in the elementary schools of California and is about to occur in Texas (Wood, 1989). It is clear that more consideration and attention must be given to the needs of exceptional students who come from culturally diverse populations.

An additional consideration is the variance in the educational needs of students from the different cultural and linguistic groups included in this population.

CULTURAL DIVERSITY
VALUES AND PROBLEMS

Cultural diversity is a fact of life in the United States. After decades of acceptance of the "melting pot" concept, the many values of an opposite concept, cultural diversity and cultural pluralism, have been recognized. Multicultural education, which recognizes and utilizes the strengths of cultural pluralism, has become widely accepted. An orientation toward cultural enrichment of the lives of all children and youth, through the preservation of cultural diversity, is affirmed by most educators. But this approach is not without problems. With respect to students with disabilities, cultural diversity relates both to identification and planning of appropriate, effective educational interventions.

Unfortunately, a disproportionately high number of students from diverse cultural groups live in conditions of poverty and sometimes of neglect. Some of the effects of these conditions may be mistaken for disabilities.

Celebrations, parades, special holidays, and concerts contribute to a better understanding of the native dress, music, food, and customs of individuals from diverse cultures. An understanding of the richness of various cultures is important to both students and teachers.

One major problem in identification of students from diverse cultural and linguistic backgrounds has been the lack of appropriate diagnostic tools. This is further complicated by the fact that a disproportionately high number of students from diverse cultural groups live in poverty. The combination of language differences, assessment tools developed for middle-class Anglo populations, the effects of poverty, and teachers who often do not understand the culture and values of all their students has led to misidentification and misclassification.

All students benefit from exposure to the culture of other students.

Negative environmental conditions can lead to underdeveloped learning abilities.

Even when teachers are able to accurately identify students, they may not be able to provide the most appropriate, effective programs because of lack of experience with the students' background. Teachers may therefore be unable to use methods and materials that are of maximum motivational value to the students.

This girl is sharing aspects of her cultural background.

Different habits of dress ordinarily signal different cultural orientation.

Many students and teachers from middle-class backgrounds have no understanding of the conditions under which some other students live.

Perhaps the first and most important step to correct this situation is for educators to develop a more complete understanding of the history and values of the cultures represented in the school. This should provide educators with additional information about the students' cultural, linguistic, and experiential background, and such factors as differences among cognitive learning styles. This in turn will permit more meaningful interpretation of the students' present educational status and needs, and a more meaningful basis for individual educational planning. Anything less than this type of effort means that we are deliberately overlooking the needs of a significant segment of the student population.

Working and playing together is an important part of learning about others.

This mother is working with school personnel, in order to be better able to help her daughter at home.

Peer tutoring can take many forms.

For example, much of the research and available literature about culturally diverse populations is about bilingual programs, which in turn usually implies Hispanic students. However, this population's needs may not be met through a single pattern of educational programming. The Hispanic population may be further subdivided (following federal guidelines) into Mexican Americans, Puerto Ricans, Cubans, Central or South Americans, and "other" Hispanics. The Mexican-American population—clustered primarily in the West and Southwest—is by far the largest subgroup, but in Connecticut, Massachusetts, New Jersey, New York, and Pennsylvania, the Puerto Rican subgroup is largest. In Florida, the Cuban subgroup is largest. There may be wide variations in the cultural patterns and educational needs of these Hispanic subgroups.

Another bilingual group is made up of Indo-Chinese refugees, a subgroup of the Asian and Pacific Islanders category. Students from this background have a different set of cultural values and language proficiencies than do students from other subgroups within the larger category. Native Americans comprise another important group of bilingual, bicultural children who require different educational provisions.

In addition to these varied groups of students who require educational programs that ensure appreciation of their cultural identity, who often require bilingual programs, and who may require special programs based on giftedness or disability is another major group, for whom bilingual programs are usually not considered. These students, African Americans, make up a majority of the student body in many schools. They should have the same opportunities with respect to special education programming as, for example, students of Hispanic descent. They may or may not have significant language differences, but many have cultural differences that require consideration. Given the more recent broad consideration of the needs of culturally diverse students who are bilingual, the needs of African-American students may have been underemphasized.

We agree with Wood that "given the size and diversity of our minority population, it is not possible to generalize across ethnic groups in order to describe the educational characteristics of the culturally diverse child with special educational needs" (1989, p. 108). However, it is obvious that there are special needs and that educators must attend to those needs.

■ **Characteristics**

As we've just noted, it is not possible to generalize across ethnic groups to describe educational characteristics. Further, a great deal of the literature that attempts to summarize learning characteristics of specific cultural groups lacks empirical research support. But it is at least generally accepted that there is a relationship between cultural values experienced at home and students' approaches to learning, their achievement at school, and their perceptions of school personnel (Wood, 1989). Despite the lack of empirical research support, certain characteristics have been regularly attributed to specific cultural groups, and are worthy of mention as *possible* contributors to school attitudes and learning styles and to the relevance of instructional approaches.

Nazzaro (1981) attempted to generalize about certain culture-related characteristics of Asian-American, African-American, Hispanic, and Native American students, relating those characteristics to exceptional students who were members of those groups. The following examples of these presumably culture-related characteristics permit some conceptualization of the kinds of difficulties that may result and the adjustments and modifications that must be made as assessment and educational interventions are implemented.

An Asian cultural background may encourage traditional cultural traits leading to more inhibited behavior, including an unusual degree of subservience to authority in the school. A passive learning style may have been absorbed at home, and students may tend to wait for authority figures to direct their behavior. Students of Asian descent may excel in rote learning and written language yet be less verbal than their majority-group peers. They may have greater-than-normal skills in observing and imitating. Depending on when they were first broadly exposed to English, they may have difficulty with sounds not present in their native language. The family may place a high value on industriousness and academic achievement and feel that a child's lack of success in school brings shame to the entire family.

An African-American cultural background may produce more interactive and independent students, who may tend to be quite verbal. They may have less of an internalized need to please school authority figures or to conform to the standards of the school, and less motivation to complete school. Disagreements may be settled by fighting or other aggressive behavior that is perceived by the majority as antisocial. To the extent that nonstandard English has been spoken in their home and neighborhood, African-American students may have difficult-to-detect language problems when interpreting written material. Excellence in athletics may receive the highest priority of school activities.

A Hispanic cultural background may foster a set of role expectations of males and females significantly different from those of the Anglo culture. It may also encourage a greater degree of family loyalty. Less value may be attached to the completion of school. Some students of Hispanic origin will not hear all English sounds, because some do not exist in the Spanish language. In addition, a number of different English words may sound exactly alike to a Spanish speaker.

A Native American cultural background may lead to a passive learning style and to a desire for anonymity rather than personal recognition. Therefore, academic competitiveness is less often seen. A great deal of communication may be

Box 14.2 The Implications of Microcultures in the United States

The current macroculture in the United States has deep roots in the traditions of Western Europe. This national culture has been characterized by highly valuing industriousness, ambition, competitiveness, individualism, and independence, and by the conviction that humans are superior to and separate from nature (Gollnick & Chinn, 1986). Most Americans share these values and beliefs to some extent, but not equally. A number of microcultures or subsocieties in the United States embrace other values and beliefs that are not common to all members of the macroculture. "The most common microcultures in the United States are based in ethnicity or national origin, religion, gender, age, socioeconomic status, language group, geographical region, and exceptionality" (Plata & Chinn, 1989, p. 150).

Such differences are important in any classroom, but particularly in classes containing students who have special learning needs. Teachers are faced with a considerable challenge when choosing, developing, or adapting teaching materials for culturally diverse and exceptional children. "Materials must promote both academic and cognitive growth and a sense of unity with cultural diversity, as well as include humanizing teaching strategies" (ibid., p. 158).

■ Alienation may influence academic achievement. ■

conducted at the nonverbal level, and children may be expected to be quiet and observant. This is often incorrectly interpreted to mean that they are not listening or participating. The use of eyeglasses, hearing aids, or prostheses may be ridiculed in this culture.

To the extent that these or other culture-related behaviors are present in any student, modifications in carrying out assessment and interpreting its results will be essential. Cultural factors may also require adjustments in how placement alternatives, the nature of educational interventions, and general modifications of the curriculum are explained to parents. The presence or suspected presence of disabilities or of giftedness or unusual talent will have different ramifications from culture to culture. For example, a passive learning style will have different implications with respect to identification of behavior disorders, as compared to identification of mental retardation or giftedness.

This consideration of unique characteristics that may be present in individuals who are members of various cultural groups is intended to introduce the concept of culturally related characteristics, not to provide an authoritative or comprehensive listing of them. An appreciation of cultural diversity should lead educators to incorporate various aspects of the richness of these cultures into teaching strategies. The discussion that follows shows how a knowledge of cultural patterns can aid in the education of students with disabilities.

In her description of ways in which children of Hispanic descent from low socioeconomic backgrounds and with moderate to severe intellectual handicaps can learn more effectively, Duran (1988) provides a number of practical teaching suggestions. Because the Hispanic culture often emphasizes learning by doing, touching, seeing, manipulating, and experiencing as opposed to discussing or reading about ideas, students should be shown concrete objects or pictures of objects to help them learn new vocabulary and master related concepts. For example, if students who have no experience with a modern kitchen are to learn about an electric mixer or an automatic dishwasher, they should be shown the mixer or dishwasher, encouraged to touch it, manipulate its moving parts, and turn it on and off. In this manner, the function of this equipment and related vocabulary take on meaning.

One cultural implication noted by Duran reflects the greater belief in the supernatural common to students of Hispanic origin along the Mexican border. Duran suggested that teachers and aides take time to ask parents and grandparents about some of the stories common to their cultural group. Folklore stories can then become a part of the reading or other language development activities in the program. In a similar manner, teachers or aides may ask families about songs commonly sung in the home and community and use them, as appropriate, in school.

Another suggestion is to take an ecological survey or inventory. As part of this inventory, educators determine, for example, which foods are common in the students' homes and neighborhoods. This might be accomplished by asking the parents which foods they most often buy at the grocery store and at fast-food restaurants. Information about those foods can then be made a part of the curriculum, along with information about typical Anglo foods. Duran provides specific suggestions for teaching this food-related language, including some that maximize parental involvement.

An understanding of the characteristics of students from diverse cultural backgrounds is important for many reasons. It is essential to the completion of meaningful assessment, for planning educational interventions, and to assist teachers to better understand behaviors that may not mean the same thing as when they are exhibited by white students from the majority culture. Without this deeper level of understanding of their students, teachers' effectiveness is severely limited.

■ Assessment

It appears that more has been written on the assessment and potential misidentification of students from diverse cultural populations with disabilities than has been written about how they may be more appropriately educated. In part, this is a result of the litigation that has focused attention on this topic. As Table 1.1 in Chapter 1 shows, three of the first four cases summarized addressed assessment practices that led to inappropriate, inaccurate labeling of and decision making about minority students. This in turn led to educational program planning and placements that were disadvantageous if not actually harmful to the students involved. In general, the concern was that the tests used were not appropriate to the culture or experience of these students, and that classification based on such assessment was unjustifiable.

There have been many attempts to reduce the potential bias inherent in many standardized test instruments. The problem is real and is widely recognized, but opinions vary about its exact nature and what should or can be done about it. For example, several so-called culture-fair tests have been developed that attempt to eliminate, or at least reduce, factors that seem to depress the performance of many students who belong to a minority group. These factors include high verbal demands, stressful timed tasks, and emphasis on school-based learning. Some of these newer tests are completely nonverbal, but even they require some degree of verbal mediation as the individual thinks through the question and determines how to respond (McLoughlin & Lewis, 1990). Gonzales (1982) cites studies indicating that these tests may be as discriminatory as the verbal tests they were designed to replace. Culture-specific measures such as the Black Intelligence Test of Cultural Homogeneity (Williams, 1972) are yet another avenue taken by those concerned about bias, but these may be better described as tests of sensitivity to a given culture—in this case, Black culture.

Another approach to reducing test bias is pluralistic assessment, such as the System of Multicultural Pluralistic Assessment (SOMPA) (Mercer & Lewis, 1977). The SOMPA includes traditional assessment procedures plus sociocultural data that in effect modify the predictions of the traditional assessment. Use of the SOMPA has reduced the number of students classified as mildly mentally retarded (Gonzales, 1982), but there is as yet insufficient information about its ability to predict academic success in various school settings.

Witt, Elliott, Gresham, and Kramer (1988) indicate six types of test bias: (1) mean differences bias—the average scores for various cultural or economic groups are significantly different; (2) item (content) bias—test items are biased so

*Box 14.3
Children
at Risk*

A 1989 Denver Public Schools study indicated that, on the average, second-grade students in Denver who had changed schools at least twice since kindergarten scored 20% lower on math and reading tests than those who had not moved. Other studies have reported a higher high school graduation rate among students who do little or no moving from school to school. A victim of transience is Sarah, a fourth-grade student who has already been enrolled in five schools. (She had been enrolled in one school three times since first grade.) In addition to academic problems, students like Sarah may give other indications of stress at school such as unusual defensiveness, belligerence, or withdrawal.

According to Herrick, "the pattern of stops and starts deprives poor youngsters of what may be their most solid social foundation: a school they can call home. The academic results can be devastating" (1991, p. 8). Officials of the Piton Foundation, an organization that studies poverty, believe that as poverty increases, more students move from school to school (Herrick, 1991). Often these are students who are already at risk academically. At present there are few organized efforts that attempt to offset the results of this significant factor in lower academic achievement. Given their unusual need for long-range, closely monitored educational planning and programming, it seems likely that the negative effect of transiency may be a compounding factor for many students with disabilities.

that they differentially affect the performance of various groups (African American, Hispanic, and Caucasian, women and men, and so on); (3) factor analysis bias—factors measured (such as attention or verbal abilities) are different for various cultural, racial, or economic groups; (4) predictive validity bias—scores predict with different levels of confidence for different groups; (5) social consequences bias—test results are misused to justify restrictive social policies; and (6) selection ratios—the use of test results leads to over- or underrepresentation in various classification categories (such as mental retardation or behavioral disorders). Theoretically, each of these types of bias can be remedied, but at present there is no set of assessment tools that is clearly acceptable for use with students from culturally diverse populations.

The discussion thus far has related to *test* bias. But it appears that bias also exists in the way tests are administered. For example, Fuchs and Fuchs (1990) assert that certain students with disabilities obtain higher scores when tested by examiners known to them, whether the examiners are experienced or relatively inexperienced. McLoughlin and Lewis (1990) suggest modifying test administration procedures to reduce bias in assessing students from diverse cultural backgrounds. They note, however, that standardized tests then become informal test instruments. McLoughlin and Lewis also suggest that training students in test-taking skills may be another method of reducing test bias. This does not mean practice with the questions or tasks to be included on the test, or even with similar questions or tasks. Rather it means, for example, practice in recording answers on sheets similar to those used in the test, practice in responding verbally to an examiner, and similar basic skills.

The emotional intensity that surrounds the issue of bias in the assessment of cognitive ability derives from three major factors.

1. American majority society has a long record of discriminating against African Americans through a variety of mechanisms. Slavery, restrictive voting laws, segregated educational systems, and other more covert measures are a part of this history. Despite improvements and official governmental commitment to equal opportunity for all, discrimination remains.

2. As a group, African Americans have consistently obtained lower average scores than whites on tests of cognitive ability. Disagreement continues about the reasons for this discrepancy.

3. All of the widely used tests of cognitive ability "have been developed by whites, published by whites, made money for whites, and are used to estimate and predict performance in a society that is dominated by the white culture" (Witt et al., 1988, p. 163).

Though these factors can be most dramatically documented with respect to African Americans, they apply to a considerable degree to all other culturally diverse populations except Asians. Asians tend to score as high as or higher than whites in many instances.

Witt and his colleagues believe that technical evidence indicates that most items on tests such as the WISC-R and the Binet (individually administered tests of "cognitive ability") tend to measure the same factors and predict academic success equally well for all racial groups. That is, they provide a useful measure of probable success in the existing academic programs of the public schools. They are *not* tests of intelligence, though they do result in an IQ score. If they are not used properly and are considered to measure intelligence, they have limited meaning when used with many students from diverse cultural backgrounds.

Ortiz and Yates (1988) have derived the following specific policy and practice implications from PL 94-142 and various judicial decisions related to assessing and educating students from culturally diverse populations.

1. Assessment of language competence in both English and the student's native language must be completed prior to any other assessment.

2. To be identified as eligible for special education services, the student must exhibit a disability when evaluated in his or her dominant language.

3. Due to the shortage of standardized measures available for students speaking languages other than English, it will often be necessary to adapt existing assessment instruments.[1]

4. It must be recognized that English-language test scores of students who speak a language other than standard English often reflect a *minimal* measure of their abilities. This fact should be reflected in the written assessment summaries that are provided to decision-making committees.

5. Students should be assessed by personnel fluent in their dominant language.

6. The traditional 1- and 3-year follow-up assessment may be insufficient for some students. Because there may be quite rapid improvement in both English and native language skills after an appropriate intervention program is implemented, more frequent assessment—and the information such assessment will provide—may be essential to redirect the program.

Identification of Gifted and Talented Students

Much of the preceding discussion of assessment alternatives applies equally to efforts designed to discover gifted and talented students. The policy and practice implications listed by Ortiz and Yates (1988) were intended to apply to students with disabilities, but their ideas about adapting existing assessment measures and considering scores to reflect minimum levels of ability are also applicable to the gifted and talented. Their recommendation that students be assessed by personnel fluent in the student's dominant language also applies.

Perrone and Aleman (1983) have described their efforts to identify gifted students from diverse cultural backgrounds in a program developed at the Guidance Institute for Talented Students at the University of Wisconsin. They suggested broadening the definition of giftedness after conferring with educational leaders, spiritual leaders, family members, and students representing the populations under consideration. They believe developing specific definitions of giftedness based on the culturally diverse populations in a given geographical area to be essential. Identification procedures derived from those definitions would necessitate different assessment procedures for different populations.

Barbara Clark (1988) notes that many suggestions for identifying cognitively gifted persons in culturally diverse populations depend heavily on identifying

[1] Adapting existing assessment instruments may be essential, but it is nearly impossible in some cases. This is illustrated in a discussion by Harris (1986) of the possibility of a "Native American Assessment Battery." Harris notes that "over 200 different Indian languages are spoken in the United States, with dialectal variations within each" (1986, p. 226). This may be an extreme example, but similar difficulties are found in other languages and cultural subgroups.

■ Poverty and linguistic differences may mask intellectual giftedness. ■

noncognitive skills. Her concern is that we may identify creative talent but then confuse creativity and cognitive talent as we provide programs. She suggests using the SOMPA mentioned earlier in this chapter and bilingual proficiency scales that could provide indications of advanced growth in language, thus indicating high-level intelligence.

Gregory, Starnes, and Blaylock described a program designed to discover and nurture potential giftedness in young African-American and Hispanic students. Called the Program of Assessment, Diagnosis, and Instruction (PADI), it is "a program to identify and foster potential which also enables 'hidden' gifted students to emerge and refine their skills sufficiently to move into programs for the gifted" (1988, p. 77). The PADI includes three components: assessment, long-term nurturing of abilities, and a special program of teacher training and support. The diagnostic battery used in identification includes seven assessment tools to tap a broad range of potential abilities, but the teacher training and support and the nurturing of student abilities may be the most important components. Of the first 400 PADI students, over 125 were later identified as gifted or talented.

Sociocultural Factors, or Learning and Behavior Problems?

Perhaps the single major problem in determining whether students from culturally diverse populations are truly exhibiting learning and behavior problems is the possible influence of a variety of sociocultural factors. These factors must be

Table 14.1 The influence of cultural factors on educational planning

Cultural Factor	*Educational Considerations*
Language	If students are non-English-speaking or bilingual, written communications in the native language and translators for conferences may be required.
Family role orientation	Educators should determine which family members take major leadership roles and respect that preference in school-family communications and conferences.
Family attitudes about children	The "value" of children in the culture will influence how planning with the family should proceed.
Role of the extended family	The extent of involvement of extended-family members should be considered in long-range planning, how much information to supply to them, and so on.
Achievement expectations	Expectations may influence family attitudes toward students' achievement at school and how school personnel should approach discussions about achievement.
Attitudes toward professionals	If professionals are regarded with too much or too little respect, or are perhaps feared, it will reduce the potential for a meaningful parent/professional partnership.
Attitudes toward accepting assistance	Negative attitudes may restrict family members' willingness to share information and will restrict their willingness to involve persons from other, outside agencies.
Attitudes toward disabilities	If disabilities are viewed as shameful or disgraceful, it will influence the family's willingness to talk about them, their willingness to accept help, and ultimately their acceptance of the disability.

carefully considered when collecting and evaluating the data necessary to make meaningful educational decisions (see Table 14.1). Collier believes that considering such factors will help assessment personnel determine "whether the learning and behavior problems exhibited by the minority student are due to either sociocultural factors, some other problem or disability, or a combination of these" (1988, p. 9). Collier describes five major sociocultural factors that must be considered.

Cultural and linguistic background   This is the first and probably the most significant factor. Most educational programs are predicated on culturally based assumptions about what should be learned, where and how it should be learned, and why it is important. Students from culturally diverse populations bring to school different experiences and different clusters of knowledge that may have been learned in a manner inconsistent with the assumptions on which the educational program is based. This will influence how the students learn in school and how they react to assessment procedures.

Experiential background   This factor overlaps yet differs from cultural background. Children from immigrant and migrant families are likely to have very different experiential backgrounds than children from the middle-class Anglo population. Poor, inner-city Native Americans from families having limited experience with the educational system have another type of experiential background. Because discovery (versus rote) learning, inquiry techniques, emphasis on establishing cause-and-effect associations, and similar instructional strategies in common use in the schools are so different from what may have been previously experienced, confusion and below-average achievement may result. If these skills are required for the successful completion of tasks required in assessment, and assessment personnel are not alert to the problem, underestimation of both achievement and ability may result.

Acculturation   Different students adapt to a new cultural environment at different rates. Some are faced with a two-part cultural adjustment: to the general American culture and to the cultural expectations of the school. For some students it is a slow, steady process; others may show no apparent change for a considerable length of time, then very rapidly become acculturated. Some suggest that too much acculturation is not desirable because it deemphasizes original cultural values; however, the degree of acculturation will influence both academic achievement and formal assessment results.

Sociolinguistic development   If students' general development in knowledge and use of language is slow, they will probably have difficulty using language to communicate within the social context. Some are concerned that we often cannot or do not adequately assess sociolinguistic development.

Cognitive learning styles   Individuals learn in different ways. Assessment of their learning styles might reveal (1) an impulsive versus a reflective approach to learning, (2) an internal versus an external locus of control, (3) a global versus an analytic frame of reference, (4) narrow versus broad generalizations, and (5) greater or lesser degrees of tolerance for ambiguous stimuli. This information, plus indications of how students approach the learning task and organize environmental cues and data can be of great value in assessment. It may have greater value for planning a meaningful educational program than for determining the existence of disabilities, however.

Collier suggests that information about sociocultural factors may be derived from a wide variety of assessment techniques such as observation, interviews, work sampling, analytic teaching, and other types of informal evaluation. Sources for such information would include the parents, social workers, others in the student's neighborhood, and school personnel (teachers, aides, counselors, and others) who are members of the same cultural group as the student. This type of assessment adds meaning to results obtained through other assessment procedures and might be considered the "filter" through which other information should be passed (Collier, 1988). Collier's focus in the discussion of these sociocultural factors was on their potential influence on assessment results. These factors will have an even greater influence on the planning and implementation of an appropriate educational program, so an awareness of their continuing influence is essential.

Educational Interventions

Educational interventions for students from diverse cultural backgrounds are in many ways no different from those for other students. If students have visual or hearing impairments, they need the same types of assistance as middle-class Anglo students need. If they have learning disabilities, mental retardation, or behavior disorders, similar strategies apply. However, there are some additional factors, concerns, and program options.

The major concern is one that has been addressed in some detail in this chapter. Assessment to determine the nature of the disability—or whether a disability exists—requires very special care.

A potential program option is adapting existing program elements to take full advantage of any unusual cultural interests or strengths of the student. Inclusion of unique, culture-related interests will increase student motivation; enabling students to use their culturally related strengths will increase their motivation and lead to more efficient learning. In addition, exploring culturally related interests increases the likelihood of the active involvement of parents, an advantage in any program. However, to be able to use this potential, teachers must develop a greater understanding of different cultures and a sensitivity to culture-related values and beliefs. Therefore, the effective use of this program option often requires additional teacher education.

Another program option, one particularly applicable when the class contains several students from one specific ethnic population, is to use teacher aides from that same population. This has proved very effective in bilingual programs for nondisabled students and could be equally effective for students with disabilities.

**Box 14.4
You and I
Are the Same**

You and I are the same
but we don't let our hearts see

Black, White and Asian
Africa, China, United States and all
other
countries around the world

Peel off their skin
like you peel an orange

See their flesh
like you see my heart

Peel off their meat
And peel my wickedness with it too

Until there's nothing left
but bones

Then you will see that you and I
are the same

Kein Po

SOURCE: *"You and I Are the Same," by Nina A. Mullen and Laurie Olsen, 1990,* California Tomorrow, *5, (1), p. 34. Reprinted by permission.*

The obvious program option for bilingual students with disabilities is some type of bilingual special education program. The majority of the efforts presently under way reflect this orientation. These two programs may be linked in several ways; so far there is little evidence about which types of linkage are most effective. Baca and Cervantes (1989) view bilingual special education as an emerging effort, not yet fully defined. Their view seems to be supported by others. We will outline some of the present efforts to better define it and provide a structure for future development.

People Who Make a Difference

JAIME ESCALANTE—"YOU ARE THE BEST" Jaime Escalante and his family came to the United States from Bolivia. He spoke no English, and, although he had taught calculus in La Paz, his credentials were useless in the United States. Within 10 years, while supporting his family through a variety of jobs, Jaime learned English, earned a B.S. in mathematics from Cal State, and landed a job teaching math at Garfield High School in East Los Angeles. Garfield was then noted for gang violence, the availability and widespread use of drugs, and lack of academic achievement.

When Jaime arrived at Garfield and began teaching he quickly learned that his students were in trouble academically. He began preparing them to take the Advanced Placement Calculus test— nearly 80% of his students passed this difficult math test. Of all the high school seniors in the United States, only about 2% attempt it.

He prepared his students for this test by using strong discipline practices, traditional teaching practices, and unwavering faith in his students. Underlying these methods was the strong conviction that the current conventional wisdom of the psychological approach to teaching weakens students' certainty that they can overcome barriers in school and later education. Jaime does not believe that students need to "adjust" (that is, accept their "limitations"), but instead he believes that one must give them unflagging admiration and encouragement. Then even the most "impossible" child can outperform the expectations that have been laid for that child.

His most trying time, he says, was the year he had a minor heart attack ("which I could handle") and 14 of his 18 students who took the advanced placement test were accused of cheating ("I knew they couldn't have, and that the accusations were unfair."). The examiners thought the errors the students made were too similar to be attributed to chance, and therefore assumed cheating. The students were required to take another, more difficult test or be disqualified. Many people believed that if the students had been from another high school or if they had not had Hispanic surnames the issue would not have surfaced.

But Jaime's students knew that they knew the material and were determined. They remembered "You are the best" and *wanted* to retake the test. All of them took the more difficult test, and all passed!

The changes at Garfield High School and in the students were noticed by Hollywood, and the movie *Stand and Deliver* was made based on the situation. When producers came to Garfield to see Jaime and begin writing the script, his response was "Go ahead and write; I don't have much time for that." Later he realized the potential for Garfield and for his students to be known as "the best" and did try to find time to cooperate with the producers.

After Jaime Escalante's students graduate they often come back to see him: "Other teachers teach us, but Mr. Escalante cares about us, too." "Mr. Escalante makes us feel powerful, so we succeed." "After being in Mr. Escalante's class, I know I can do anything I decide to." "I come back to see him because I miss him."

■ Computers are helpful in bilingual programs for students with
learning disabilities. ■

One way to plan for bilingual students who have a disability is to develop a
program that provides special educational interventions (specific to the student's
special needs) to facilitate the established goals of the bilingual program. The
California Office of Bilingual and Bicultural Education (1992) has developed a
theoretical framework for educating students whose primary language is not
English; it specifies major objectives, program principles, and implementation
standards. The four major objectives are (1) high levels of English-language
proficiency, (2) appropriate levels of cognitive and academic achievement,
(3) sufficient levels of primary-language development, and (4) adequate psychosocial and cultural adjustment. Implementation standards that provide guidelines

to local educational agencies recommend that students whose primary language is other than English should

1. Receive instruction in and through their primary language on a consistent basis from kindergarten through sixth grade
2. Receive formal reading instruction in their primary language
3. Have a variety of reading materials in their primary language in all subject areas and at all grade levels
4. Acquire the ability to use English within meaningful contextual situations
5. Receive second-language instruction that emphasizes the communication of content rather than memorization of language forms
6. Be permitted, without disapproval, to respond in either their primary or secondary language during the initial stages of second-language instruction.

If, in developing the special education IEP, interventions and adaptations related to the disability were planned within the framework of the preceding four major objectives and consistent with the six implementation standards, it would comprise an individualized bilingual special education program.

An unusual program utilizes the expertise of speech-language pathologists in programs for nondisabled bilingual students in the Language Services Department of the Cleveland Heights–University Heights City School District in Ohio. In recognition of the unusually large number of mother languages represented within the system over the years, the district decided to expand the Language/Speech/Hearing Department to include programs for non-English-speaking and nonstandard-English-speaking students, in addition to more traditional special education services. The department was renamed the Language Services Department in recognition of its expanded function. In this K-through-12 program, a core team of speech-language pathologists coordinate programs in Bilingual Education, English as a Second Language (ESL), and English as a Standard Dialect, in addition to the more traditional speech-language program. The bilingual and ESL programs serve foreign-born limited English proficient (LEP) students whose first language is not English. The bilingual program, extending from kindergarten through sixth grade, targets seven language groups: Spanish, Korean, Hebrew, Arabic, Russian, Japanese, and Yiddish. Bilingual aides and community liaison aides travel to program sites and are supervised by the speech-language pathologist assigned to those sites. They conduct assessment procedures and interpret the school program to non-English-speaking parents.

The ESL program is provided by ESL aides supervised by the speech-language pathologist assigned to the building. A support resource teacher provides additional consultative assistance. This program extends through high school.

The English as a Standard Dialect program is a K-through-12 program created for American-born students who do not speak standard English, but it is also open to students born in an English-speaking country where nonstandard English is the norm (such as Jamaica). Language aides provide direct instruction, individually or in small groups, from two to five times a week. The intent is to teach standard English, emphasizing its essential role in school, business, and the professions, but to show continuing respect for the nonstandard English dialect of the home.

Much of this total program is carried out by language aides who, in addition to being directly supervised by speech-language pathologists, are involved in a great deal of ongoing instruction through seminars and in-service training programs. A major theme is respect for and continuing pride in the student's cultural background. Though not a special education program (these students are not

■ Together at lunch. The children in this class represent a number of ethnic backgrounds. ■

considered to have language disabilities), this program may serve a preventive function for at least some students.

Many exceptional students from culturally diverse populations will not need a formal bilingual program but will need special program planning related to their disability or giftedness and to their cultural background. Their academic needs may be for the development of additional linguistic competence in English, broadened exposure to and experience with cultures other than their own, and continued recognition of and emphasis on values unique to their ethnic and cultural heritage. A general emphasis within the classroom on multicultural values will benefit all students and will enhance the program of the special needs student.

Consultation and collaboration with parents and other family members is particularly important when planning for students from diverse cultural populations. A more detailed discussion of this topic, including how such parent and family collaboration can be encouraged, will be found in Chapter 15. Home/school collaboration based on a better understanding of the school's goals and expectations can help strengthen parental support of the school program. Information and understanding gained from interactions with parents can assist school personnel to better understand the student and to more consistently relate the school program to cultural experiences and expectations.

Toliver-Weddington and Meyerson (1983) point out that trained paraprofessionals can translate, interpret stimuli and responses between student and teacher, and in some instances administer certain assessments in the native language. In addition, they can provide direct intervention by implementing the program planned by the staffing team, serve as translator and interpreter for the student's family, be a liaison with other community agencies, and perform other related tasks.

A model for a special education multilingual and multiethnic instructional team, including a team resource specialist and several paraprofessionals representing different languages and cultures, has been developed by Miramontes (1991). She outlines the elements necessary to develop a well-prepared, effective itinerant instructional team utilizing the talents of paraprofessionals and special educators. Miramontes views the paraprofessional duties as threefold: instruction, home contacts, and assessment.

> In their instructional role, paraprofessionals are positive ethnic and linguistic role models whose intervention can promote students' positive self-concept in relation to school. They can also provide students access to previous knowledge (through the primary language) to support new learning. Instruction is the paraprofessional's primary responsibility. It cannot be assumed, however, that paraprofessionals are to accomplish these responsibilities without support, guidance, and training. The collaboration, guidance, and instructional leadership of the team resource specialist should be focused precisely on facilitating these tasks. (1991, pp. 32–33)

Heward and Orlansky indicate that "it would not be possible to offer a comprehensive list of teaching approaches that would apply to all children of diverse cultural backgrounds" (1988, p. 469). Yet, they add, "effective instructional procedures apply to children of all cultural backgrounds" (ibid.). We want to reaffirm their point of view, adding that knowledge of the culture from which children come, understanding of the values and motivations that are part of that culture, and continual sensitivity to how children may be affected by the teaching techniques and expectations of the majority culture will permit teachers to more effectively teach students from culturally diverse populations.

Issues and Trends

Major unresolved issues in this field include the following.

1. The effectiveness of bilingual education as it is currently structured and implemented
2. Whether bilingual education is truly in the best interests of minority populations
3. The value of cultural pluralism
4. How best to promote cultural pluralism and a better understanding of multicultural values
5. How to more appropriately assess the intellectual abilities, academic achievement, and basic skill development of students from diverse cultural and language backgrounds
6. How to effectively plan and implement educational programs for exceptional students (both gifted and with disabilities) from culturally diverse populations

A number of general trends seem apparent with respect to the culturally diverse populations in the United States. One is an increased awareness by the general population of their presence. People have different opinions about how American society should respond to these populations, but they are at least aware of them. A similar heightened awareness is evident within the nation's various educational communities. National teacher associations have supported—and teacher accreditation associations have required teacher training programs to provide additional emphasis on—multicultural understanding and values. These trends have influenced the planning and implementation of special education programs for students from culturally diverse populations. There has likewise been an increase in interest in implementing bilingual special education programs.

Conversely, the United States has grown increasingly monolingual (Hakuta, 1986). Since World War I there has been a rapid drop in language diversity and at least some support for an amendment to the U.S. Constitution that would make English the "official language" of the United States. Some states have already passed such a law.

Summary

In terms of cultural diversity, the United States has evolved from advocacy of the "melting pot" theory, which emphasized cultural assimilation and a common American culture, to a philosophy of cultural pluralism. Influential groups such as the American Association of Colleges for Teacher Education have supported this philosophy by calling for multicultural education, which rejects the mere toleration of cultural pluralism and strives instead for cultural enrichment and the preservation of cultural diversity.

The use of one language—English—was a central element of the melting pot concept. With recognition of the value of cultural diversity came a recognition of the value of languages other than English. These changes have had a considerable impact on special education. Court decisions have supported the need to communicate with parents in their native language, assess children in their native language, and provide bilingual special education programs.

Greater understanding and appreciation of a variety of cultures and cultural characteristics is essential when assessing and identifying students with disabilities, because some culture-related characteristics might be mistaken for characteristics of a disability. Similarly, a greater understanding of cultural values, traditions, and basic beliefs is important when choosing, developing, or adapting instructional materials.

The major controversy in this field has been over biased or inappropriate assessment of minority students. Landmark court cases have verified that biased assessment has often led to misidentifying children from culturally diverse backgrounds as having disabilities. Although the obverse has not received a great deal of attention, gifted and talented students from culturally diverse populations may be underidentified due to biased assessment and therefore denied the benefits of existing programs.

More effective intervention programs have been receiving increased emphasis: program options that make full use of unusual cultural interests or strengths of the student appear to hold the greatest promise. This generalization applies to both students with disabilities and those who are gifted or talented.

"What are my main concerns? I worry about Michael having to go back to the hospital for another heart surgery. I worry about whether the drugs he's taking are causing side effects. I worry about whether he's going to be terrified by the lab technician next week when he goes in for X rays and they won't let me stay in the room with him. I worry about how he's going to feel in preschool next year when younger children can do things he can't. These are very pressing concerns for me and I just don't share them with my friends who have normal children. They worry about when their kids fall off their bikes and don't get A's in school. I don't have much in common with them anymore."[1]

"I know that Jason needs to get out and do things—go to the zoo, go to the park, see other children. I try to take him out as much as I can. But it's such a hassle. Getting in and out of the car. Getting the wheelchair in and out of the car. Making sure the other kids have what they need, plus diapers for the baby. Getting everyone organized to go. And then you get there and you find out the place isn't accessible. Or people stare at the wheelchair and the other kids get uncomfortable. . . . I know it's wrong—but it's a lot easier to just stay home."

"I worry about Melissa twenty or thirty years from now. Who will care for her when I'm too old or am not here anymore? Will she be shunted from place to place with no one really loving her?"

"Rex is twenty-eight years old. Most kids are on their own by this time. When we had our family, we thought they would grow up and get out on their own

CHAPTER FIFTEEN

Parents and Families

---

[1] From *After the Tears: Parents Talk about Raising a Child with a Disability,* by Robin Simons, copyright © 1987 by The Children's Museum of Denver, Inc., reprinted by permission of Harcourt Brace Jovanovich, Inc. Quote from pp. 19–20.

and we could enjoy traveling and retirement. Now we know that won't happen.
I think we have adjusted to it, but at times I look at our friends who are our age
and I envy their freedom."

Everyone agrees that the nature of the home environment and the attitudes and involvement of parents are critically important in the social and educational development of any child. According to Gough, "Effective parent involvement programs acknowledge the fact that parents are a child's earliest and most influential teachers. Trying to educate the young without help and support from the home is akin to trying to rake leaves in a high wind" (1991, p. 339). Gough also observes that, due to social and demographic changes, the connection between the home and the school has become increasingly fragile.

Davies (1991), documenting a new trend for schools to reach out to the home, suggests the following broadened definitions of parent involvement.

1. The term *family* should be substituted for *parents*. Today the most significant adults in a child's life may be grandparents, aunts and uncles, brothers and sisters, or even a neighbor who is the primary caregiver.
2. "Family involvement" should deliberately include representatives from community agencies, as such agencies' efforts are essential to the unique needs of the student.
3. Activities and services should be extended into the home and neighborhood setting. Having family members come to the school is not sufficient.
4. School initiatives should seek beyond those parents who readily respond to scheduled meetings and the normal invitations to participate in school activities. Particular attention should be given to families having problems with English-language proficiency, those who may fear school officials, and those who have never participated.
5. Parent participation should include attention to family priorities, not just the academic expectations of the school.

Davies's comments and observations are directed toward school, family, and community relationships in general, not specifically those of exceptional students and their parents. They are, however, on target with respect to an essential element in planning and implementing effective educational programs for exceptional students. Recognition of parents' importance is reflected in the degree of parental involvement mandated by PL 94-142, PL 99-457, and related amendments. It is also reflected in the variety of additional provisions for parental involvement that have become common practice in many local educational agencies. The unique features of parental and family roles and relationships as they relate to exceptional students will be explored in this chapter.

The Family

The word *family* can have many meanings. In the idealized version of the "good old days," it meant mother and father and several children, living together until the children left home to find their own place in the world. It included the extended family of aunts and uncles, grandparents, and a few assorted cousins. There were family conflicts, but for the most part all worked together for the good of the whole.

It's not that way anymore! "America now has the highest family dissolution rate in the world, with the possible exception of Sweden. About 50% of today's children will spend a significant proportion of childhood in one-parent homes" (Blankenhorn, 1991). Simpson (1990) notes that single parents' economic and time restraints may be greater than those of two-parent families, and that both parents and children are likely to experience increased strain following separation, divorce, and family reconstitution. Each of these potential sources of conflict makes it more difficult for parents to focus on school-related problems. As a result, it may require unusual skill on the part of educators to find ways to involve parents actively in school planning and the total school experience.

Turnbull and Turnbull have "synthesized the sociology literature on family systems theory with the special education literature on the impact of children and youth with exceptionalities on their families" (1990, p. 17). As a result of that research they propose a family systems framework composed of four major components as the basis for considerations of family/professional relationships in special education settings in the schools. Here are the four components of this framework.

Family characteristics   This includes characteristics such as family size and form, cultural background, socioeconomic status, and geographic location. It includes personal characteristics such as health and coping styles and special problems such as abuse. This component also includes the nature and severity of the disability.

Family interactions   This comprises interactions between all of the family subsystems: the parental subsystem (parent and child), the marital subsystem (husband and wife), the sibling subsystem (child and other children), and the extended family subsystem (child and extended family, parents and extended family members, and all combinations of relationships).

Family functions   The third component is the various ways in which the family meets its needs, including economic needs, daily care (cooking, cleaning, transportation, health care), recreation, social activities, self-identity needs, need for affection, and educational or vocational needs.

Family life cycle   Each of the changes that occur with the passage of time alters to some extent the family characteristics, interactions, and functions. For example, a new child is born, and siblings must adjust; a child leaves home for college, graduates from college and accepts employment, or is married. The child with a disability grows up, maybe or maybe not becoming independent. Parents grow older, become grandparents, retire. All these changes have a major impact on the family system. The key concept of the family life cycle is change and the way relationships evolve.

The family plays a particularly essential role in the development of individuals with disabilities. In this role, the family complements the function of the school, and the school becomes a significant part of family interactions, affecting not only the student with a disability but to varying degrees the entire family. It is therefore

■ Parental interaction with children influences both social and intellectual development. ■

essential that educators understand the nature of family systems and gain sufficient information about the families of students with disabilities to permit beneficial family/school interactions.

Educators must also understand and appreciate the various roles that parents and families can play in the lives of the child with a disability. Turnbull and Turnbull indicate that "parents have assumed or have been expected by professionals to assume eight major roles: parents as (a) the source of their child's problems, (b) organization members, (c) service developers, (d) recipients of professionals' decisions, (e) learners and teachers, (f) political advocates, (g) educational decision makers, and (h) family members" (1990, p. 2). In the next section we will consider parent and family reactions to a child with a disability, the beginning point for the assumption of any of these roles.

■ Parent and Family Reactions to a Disability

There is little doubt that parents and families will react strongly to the information that a child is, or may be, disabled. Many writers suggest that parents must pass through a series of stages before actually accepting that their child has a disability. Some have commented that this process is similar to that through which one must go before accepting the death of a loved one (Turnbull & Turnbull, 1990).

Typical descriptions of these sequential stages include shock, denial, guilt, shame, anger or sadness, adaptation, and finally acceptance. There are many versions of this "stages" theory, supported by studies of parents of children with disabilities; Gargiulo (1985) has developed a composite model featuring three major stages.

1. A primary phase of initial shock followed by denial, then grief and depression
2. A secondary phase of ambivalence, followed by guilt, then anger, shame, and embarrassment
3. A tertiary phase of bargaining, adaptation, and reorganization, culminating in acceptance and adjustment

Some version of these phases, and the feelings they involve, may be experienced by all parents on first hearing that their child has a disability, but the feelings may be most acute when the child is a newborn. Opinions differ about

> ### Box 15.1
> ### *Why Communications with Parents Can Be Difficult*
>
> - Some parents feel guilty about their exceptional children. They ask themselves "What did I do wrong?"
> - Some are generally disappointed with the services being provided to their youngsters.
> - Some are bitter, believing this tragedy should not have happened to them.
> - Some parents are as disabled as their youngsters; they, too, have problems with reading, for example.
> - Some have received only negative reports about their children when they have visited schools in the past.
> - Some may have experienced considerable disappointment in the past because overzealous teachers, in their desire to help, promised that their child could attain academic or social goals that were unrealistic.
> - Some parents have given up on themselves, on schools in general, and on their children. They have been through so much that they've simply quit.
>
> SOURCE: Introduction to Learning Disabilities *by Thomas Lovitt, 1989, pp. 131–132.*

how such an initial diagnosis should be communicated; Heddell (1988) recommends the following guidelines.

- Parents should be told as soon as possible, preferably by a doctor. This information should be communicated in an appropriate place, such as an interview room or office.
- There should be no casual observers—this is a private matter.
- Both parents should be told at the same time. It should not be left to one parent to inform the other.
- The newborn should also be in the room, if possible.
- Parents should be given time and opportunity to ask questions, even though they may be confused and at a loss for words.
- Another interview should be scheduled, not more than a day or two later. Parents should be encouraged to bring questions that will inevitably come up in the interim, and should be told that another person having experience with the specific type of disability will be at the next meeting to help answer questions and suggest sources of help.

Although early diagnosis and relation of information is generally considered important, Patton, Beirne-Smith, and Payne (1990) caution that immediately after the birth parents may be exhausted and under stress, and total rejection of the newborn is possible. They note, however, that honest disclosure is essential in maintaining and building a relationship of trust, and that providing written materials that can be read by the parents in their own home may be the way to communicate needed information in a private setting. They further suggest that, as soon as the new parents are ready, the kind of support provided through, for example, the Association for Retarded Citizens' Parent-to-Parent program can be of great help. It must be recognized, however, that some parents will require considerable time before they will accept this or any other type of outside help. If the disability is not obvious, they may deny its existence for some time.

Parents' acceptance of their child's disability and their active involvement in early intervention programs such as those described in Chapter 12 are essential to prepare the child for entrance into educational programs offered by the public schools.

Parental Involvement in the Education of Exceptional Students

Exceptional students can realize their maximum potential only if their parents become actively involved in all aspects of their education. This involvement may take many possible paths: for example, participation in the assessment process, the program-planning and decision-making process, the program evaluation and reevaluation process, and home support of both educational and behavioral interventions. Acting as an advocate through individual efforts and through parent groups provides valuable support for future programs, just as it has been important in establishing the present level of programming for exceptional students. Supporting other parents of exceptional students and participating in parent education efforts are also important, though some parents are more comfortable than others in these roles.

Recently there has been increased interest in organized national efforts to promote a closer working partnership between parents and the schools. Joyce

■   Winning is a family affair.   ■

Epstein has been a leader in efforts directed at all parents and all school programs; Table 15.1 summarizes some of her ideas about practices that will promote better educational outcomes. She emphasizes parenting skills, communication practices, volunteering, supporting learning at home, and representing other parents through participation in parent groups (Epstein, 1989). This chapter will consider parental involvement in the education of exceptional students through a similar set of six areas of involvement:

1. Assessment and initial program planning
2. Program monitoring and ongoing program planning
3. Improving parenting skills
4. Supporting learning at home
5. Parent education and parent support efforts
6. Advocacy for better educational programs

Table 15.1 Examples of practices to promote, and outcomes from, the five types of parent involvement

Type 1 Parenting	Type 2 Communicating	Type 3 Volunteering	Type 4 Learning at Home	Type 5 Representing Other Parents
Help all families establish home environments to support learning	Design more effective forms of communication to reach parents	Recruit and organize parent help and support	Provide ideas to parents on how to help child at home	Recruit and train parent leaders

A Few Examples of Practices of Each Type

Type 1 Parenting	Type 2 Communicating	Type 3 Volunteering	Type 4 Learning at Home	Type 5 Representing Other Parents
School provides suggestions for home conditions that support learning at each grade level. Workshops, videotapes, computerized phone messages on parenting and child-rearing issues at each grade level	Teachers conduct conferences with every parent at least once a year, with follow-up as needed. Translators for language-minority families. Weekly or monthly folders of student work are sent home and reviewed and comments returned	School volunteer program or class parent and committee of volunteers for each room. Parent Room or Parent Club for volunteers and resources for parents. Annual postcard survey to identify all available talents, times, and locations of volunteers	Information to parents on skills in each subject at each grade. Regular homework schedule (once a week or twice a month) that requires students to discuss schoolwork at home. Calendars with daily topics for discussion by parents and students	Participation and leadership in PTA/PTO or other parent organizations, including advisory councils or committees such as curriculum, safety, and personnel. Independent advocacy groups

A Few Examples of Outcomes Linked to Each Type

Parent outcomes

Type 1 Parenting	Type 2 Communicating	Type 3 Volunteering	Type 4 Learning at Home	Type 5 Representing Other Parents
Self-confidence in parenting. Knowledge of child development. Understanding of home as environment for student learning	Understanding school programs. Interaction with teachers. Monitoring child's progress	Understanding teacher's job and school programs. Familiarity with teachers. Comfort in interactions at school	Interaction with child as student at home. Support and encouragement of schoolwork. Participation in child's education	Input to policies that affect child's education. Feeling in control of environment

Student outcomes

Type 1 Parenting	Type 2 Communicating	Type 3 Volunteering	Type 4 Learning at Home	Type 5 Representing Other Parents
Security. Respect for parent. Improved attendance. Awareness of importance of school	Student participation in parent-teacher conferences, or in preparation for conferences. Better decisions about courses, programs	Increased learning skills receiving individual attention. Ease of communication with adults	Homework completion. Self-concept of ability as learner. Achievement in skills practiced	Rights protected. Specific benefits linked to specific policies

Teacher outcomes

Type 1 Parenting	Type 2 Communicating	Type 3 Volunteering	Type 4 Learning at Home	Type 5 Representing Other Parents
Understanding of family cultures, goals, talents, needs	Knowledge that family has common base of information for discussion of student problems, progress. Use of parent network for communications	Awareness of parent interest, in school and children, and willingness to help. Readiness to try programs that involve parents in many ways	Respect and appreciation of parents' time, ability to follow through and reinforce learning. Better design of homework assignments	Equal status interaction with parents to improve school programs. Awareness of parent perspectives for policy development

SOURCE: "Five Types of Parent Involvement; Linking Practices and Outcomes" by Joyce L. Epstein, in *School and Family Connections: Preparing Educators to Involve Families*, forthcoming. Reprinted by permission.

Epstein's examples of practices that can promote a closer working relationship between parents and schools illustrate the simplicity of the concept. Such cooperative efforts will require educators to be more open and accepting of parental input, recognizing the potential long-term benefits to all involved—but particularly to students.

■ Assessment and Initial Program Planning

The clear intent of those who developed PL 94-142 was to provide a meaningful role for parents in evaluating students for possible eligibility for special educational services and in planning the nature of the program. The extent of actual parent involvement has been investigated, but so far the conclusions are mixed. For example, Strickland and Turnbull (1990) indicated that in some school districts less than 50% of the parents had attended their child's last IEP meeting, whereas in others as many as 95% had. Singer and Butler (1987) reported higher levels of participation in districts in which special efforts were expended to promote attendance. They also indicated that, in general, there appeared to be higher levels of attendance in more affluent districts.

**Box 15.2
Parents and
the Special
Education
"Maze"**

In their book *Negotiating the Special Education Maze: A Guide for Parents and Teachers* Anderson, Chitwood, and Hayden provide suggestions and guidance to parents of students with disabilities. In their introductory chapter they suggest that parents approaching the school system may, based on previous experiences, feel inadequate, fearful, tentative, anxious, angry, hopeful, intimidated, challenged, overwhelmed, frustrated, exhausted, confused, worried, or troubled. They also offer the following insight into why parents might have such feelings.

> As parents going into school meetings, you are moving into a situation where the people you meet use a language and a body of knowledge you may not understand completely. They are familiar with routines and regulations you know little or nothing about. Then, too, everyone carries some remnants of their own school experience—good and not so good—into school buildings. Your perceptions of school professionals and your own school experiences may cause you to question your ability to say the right thing at the right time and to convey your cares, hopes and opinions about your child's best interests and needs. (1990, p. 2)

Negotiating the Special Education Maze and similar guides are of value in many ways to parents of students with disabilities. For one thing, they help them better understand their own feelings. As more knowledgeable advocates, they can play a more meaningful role in partnership with educators in charting the most advantageous educational course for their child. Some larger school districts provide comprehensive guidebooks for parents, outlining their role and including their rights and responsibilities. Various major parent advocacy groups have also developed such guidebooks.

The factors that influence parent involvement are diverse and often difficult to document. Strickland and Turnbull (1990) suggest that some parents simply do not choose to play an active role in the education of their children, whether or not they have a child with a disability. These parents must be targeted for special efforts to encourage their participation. Other parents might choose to participate and truly want to provide further support for their child, but have had negative experiences with the schools. Such experiences might be related to language or cultural differences, to feelings about their inability to express themselves, or to any of a variety of factors leading to low self-esteem. Some may lack transportation or have no one to care for other children who must stay at home during school conferences. It is the responsibility of school personnel to anticipate such problems and to do everything possible to circumvent them. The problem is great, but with more effort on the part of educators, improvement is possible.

Professional attitudes toward parent participation also influence that participation, according to studies such as those by Gerber, Banbury, Miller, and Griffen (1986). Their study revealed that 71% of 145 special education teachers surveyed believed that parents should be permitted to waive the parent participation requirement and leave decision making entirely to professionals. Such attitudes toward parent participation may contribute to the other discouraging factors we've mentioned. If school personnel are not willing to encourage parent participation, to sincerely solicit and listen to their input, they will not benefit from potentially valuable information and insights about the student who is the focus of educational intervention. The potential scope of such information is very broad: it may include information about early growth and development, traumatic experiences (for example, abuse, abandonment, or witnessing any of a variety of disturbing events), relations with siblings and extended family members, health problems not recorded with physicians, unusual living conditions, experiences in other schools, and a variety of anecdotal information. In relation to program planning, parents may know that certain management techniques are likely to be ineffective and can explain why. They will be likely to know what kinds of activities are particularly motivating to their child. They can describe home instruction that may have been attempted and report on its relative success or failure. While exchanging information, school personnel may be able to clarify issues that might later have proved deterrents to progress because of misunderstandings. The potential for information exchange is almost limitless, but it will require additional efforts on the part of school personnel.

■ Program Monitoring and Ongoing Program Planning

Some parents are involved in the evaluation process, developing the IEP, and making certain that the original interventions are implemented as planned—and then assume all is well unless they hear otherwise from their child or the teacher. This approach may not lead to problems, but the PL 94-142 guidelines require that the program be reevaluated annually.

This provision reflects the need to systematically monitor progress toward stated objectives and recognizes that unless such monitoring is scheduled in advance, it may be overlooked. It provides for the more formal, annual evaluation in addition to frequent evaluations throughout the year. Parents are participants in this annual evaluation, because, as Strickland and Turnbull (1990) suggest, such revision, based on documented evaluation, may result in a redefinition of objec-

■ A supportive home environment enhances educational opportunities. ■

tives and goals, a modification of time lines, changes in the amount of special education service provided, or modification of teaching strategies.

Parents are also a valuable source of information about how skills targeted and apparently learned in school are carrying over into the home setting. Such information will assist the teacher to modify teaching strategies to meet stated objectives. Particularly important may be information about how children approach problem situations, how they interact with siblings and neighborhood peers, and, in some cases, how they apply such academic skills as basic mathematics in the home and community at large.

But there is also another reason to involve parents (Anderson et al., 1990). Although educators can ordinarily be trusted to carry out the IEP, such variables as lack of funds to hire specialized personnel, sudden enrollment increases that reduce the time spent with a special needs student, or the illness of a teacher may lead to nonimplementation of the student's IEP. In such cases, parents should pressure the school to provide alternative means to achieve the instructional goals. If these alternatives mean significant changes, parents must approve them.

■ Improving Parenting Skills

There may be considerable overlap between improving parenting skills, supporting learning at home, and parent education and parent support efforts. We will, however, consider them separately to emphasize the importance of each.

Improving parenting skills will benefit any child, but is particularly helpful to children with disabilities. Unlike some other types of potential parental involvement, parenting automatically takes place: parents are involved in some level of parenting if they and their children continue to live together. But are they well-informed, skilled parents? Are they confident about their parenting skills? Do they understand normal child development and their role in promoting it? Do they know what to look for and how to monitor ongoing progress toward normal development? Do they understand how their child's disability may influence his or her need for modified parenting practices?

The schools and related community support agencies are making worthwhile efforts to assist parents of children with disabilities at the preschool level, as we discussed in Chapter 12. The structure of the Individualized Family Service Plan (IFSP) for young children is such that parenting skills may be one target of the plan. A number of parent organizations have also developed handbooks for parents that can be of great value in improving parenting skills. One example is The National Association for Retarded Citizens (NARC), which has provided handbooks, workshops, and a variety of parent-training opportunities. Another example is information provided the parents of hearing-impaired children through the National Information Center on Deafness and the Center for Curriculum Development, Training, and Outreach at Gallaudet University. State and local parent associations organized in relation to other disabilities have also provided information and assistance to parents for the development of better parenting skills. Parents receive some assistance at the various conferences with school personnel, and individual teachers may take it upon themselves to work with parents, but systematic assistance in parenting skills is not a part of the normal scope of special education intervention with school-age children.

Fewell suggests that there are similarities in the experiences of all parents of children with special needs, and that assistance in parenting skills is important to the future development of the child with a disability. She believes, however, that "although most experiences of domestic life are shared by all families, there are certain experiences that are felt more strongly by parents whose children have one impairment as opposed to another" (1991, p. 214). She recommends that, as much as possible, parenting be approached on the basis of the specific disability or impairment. This is the approach taken by national parent groups, and it appears to be effective.

Parents can be trained to be agents of change with respect to a number of specific parenting practices (Simpson, 1990). One is the use of behavior management techniques. Simpson suggests that an additional benefit to training parents in the use of behavioral approaches is their wide applicability. A related benefit is that behavioral techniques require parents to learn to identify and observe their child's behavior.

An unusual application of training in parenting skills that involves the extended families of children with disabilities is described by Fewell (1991). The Extending Family Resources project (EFR) at the Children's Clinic and Preschool in Seattle, Washington, established contracts with teams of persons to provide care and training for a group of children with disabilities. These teams were composed of a child's parents, aunts, uncles, other relatives, friends, and neighbors. Team members agreed to participate in specific ways for specific time periods each week. For example, someone might agree to take a child to the park for 3 hours each week to work on the development of motor skills. Funds are provided for transportation, equipment, and respite. Results of this program indicated that a family support network can be established and trained to provide many of the experiences that might normally be viewed as parental responsibilities. The child receives the benefit, and, because all members of the team are made aware of total team efforts and the purposes of those efforts, all learn more about good parenting.

■ Supporting Learning at Home

"All parents must understand that they are indeed 'teaching' their children things that they need to know. As parents, we are teachers whether we acknowledge it or not, and can provide much worthwhile learning" (Stainback, Stainback, & Forest, 1989). This concept of teaching refers more to skills such as learning to be

***Box 15.3
The Parents
As Teachers
National
Center***

"In 1984 Missouri became the first state in the nation to mandate parent education and family support services, beginning at the child's birth, in every school district" (Ehlers & Ruffin, 1990, p. 1). As an outgrowth of this legislation, the Parents As Teachers (PAT) program has developed within the state; in addition, PAT provides special training programs outside the state as part of a national dissemination program. The PAT program is delivered by the schools but has been a public and private partnership program from the start. Representatives from various agencies are members of the school district PAT Advisory Committee. All related community agencies cooperate and serve as sources of referral. Several national foundations provide continuing support, supplementing state funds.

Each school district provides staff members to be trained to serve as parent educators. These individuals must have a background in social work or nursing young children or in early childhood education and development. After completion of additional training at the PAT National Center and final approval of the local school district plan, they are certified by the state. PAT also provides ongoing in-service training and on-site consultation.

The PAT program is designed to help parents cope more effectively with the unique needs of their family. The program assumptions are as follows.

- Information on child development assists parents in their parenting role.
- Parental support in the first years of a child's life serves a preventive function.
- The availability of social networks, mutual aid, and peer groups is essential to the family's ability to enhance the child's development.
- The family is part of the community; therefore, support is provided through links with community resources.
- Support enables parents to build the confidence required to manage their lives.
- Families will be involved if the support makes sense to them.
- Families will be involved if they participate in decision making and get good feedback.
- Families will feel best when the support is specific and they can see a direct application (ibid., pp. 10–11).

The PAT program is intended to assist parents but not lead to dependence on outside agencies. It is based on the belief that children learn more during their early years and that parents are their most important teachers. It is an example of what can be accomplished through the existing framework of public schools when a state undertakes to support the role of parents as teachers and the schools and other community agencies truly cooperate.

■   Children learn about social interaction through observation.   ■

responsible, interacting with peers, and the like than to academic skills, and children with disabilities require at least as much home teaching of these skills as do other children. There are, however, other ways in which parents may support learning at home. These will vary depending on the age of the child and the type and degree of disability. In all cases, if the child is in a formal school program, home learning is more effective if developed cooperatively with the school. Some examples of home teaching and home learning follow.

A major goal for most students with developmental disabilities is to prepare for independent living. This includes many aspects: attitudes, self-care skills, physical abilities, and certain types of basic information. A number of authors have developed parent guides for teaching children in the home—many of which use token systems for both building the initial skill and maintaining it. Baker and Brightman (1989), in their skills-training guidebook, provide detailed programs for teaching four basic information skills: reading simple sight words, using a telephone, telling time, and using money. They note that such teaching requires structured daily instruction; they tell both what to do and how to do it. It is essential that home instruction be coordinated with school instruction so as not to cause confusion. It is quite possible to arrange such coordination, and it's one of the better ways in which parents can support learning at home.

Another example is arrangements through which the parent makes regular contact with the teacher (perhaps at a set time each week) to determine what specific activities in the home will support instruction in the classroom. In the area of math skills, this might mean involving the student in counting, keeping a record of an allowance received and spent, grocery costs, and the like. In the area of science, this might mean parent and child watching certain educational television programs together. Such collaboration between parent and teacher directly benefits the curricular areas targeted and indirectly benefits other issues that inevitably are discussed when parent and teacher plan together.

In addition, learning at home is generally enhanced when parents provide a home environment in which education is valued, a variety of good books is present, and regular discussions take place about school activities.

■ Parent Education and Parent Support Efforts

Parent education and support efforts include (1) education about the nature of their child's disability, (2) education about the role of special education interventions, (3) active support of the school program, including volunteer work in the classroom, (4) educational efforts with other parents, and, when possible, (5) assistance as a part-time, special project aide in the classroom.

We have already discussed the improvement of parenting skills and support for home learning efforts, which may involve parent education. But it is also of great value for parents to become better informed about their child's disability and about potential special educational interventions and to share this information with other parents. Armed with such information, parents can more effectively participate in educational planning for their child. They are also better able to contribute to meaningful advocacy efforts.

Parents can become better informed about their child's disability through reading (most parent organizations will provide reading lists, and a variety of material is available at public libraries), through discussions with other parents of children with disabilities, through college courses, and through attendance at local, state, and national meetings. They can become informed about educational provisions in their school by participating as volunteers. Such efforts will also lead to greater self-confidence and ease in whatever discussions may be necessary at school. Efforts to share their knowledge with other parents can further the cause of education of all students with special needs.

The provision of disability-related information was one major topic of concern at the international Cross-Cultural Conference on Supports for Families with a Child with a Disability held in 1988 (Gartner, Lipsky, & Turnbull, 1990). The nine participating countries agreed that such information is essential to family support and ultimately to effective educational programming. More comprehensive, accurate, readily available information can become a reality given expanded support for parent education.

■ Advocacy

The influence of parents as advocates for the special needs of their children was reviewed in Chapter 1 in a section titled "Catalysts, Initiators, Agitators, and Organizers." Early parent efforts were essential to the improved treatment of more severely disabled individuals in state residential facilities. Parents pressured local school officials to provide programs for their children and later, through litigation, established the right to education for all students with disabilities. If school districts did not comply with judicial stipulations, parents took actions that forced them to do so.

When it appeared that money was the major impediment to better programs, parents lobbied at the state legislative level for more state support. When it appeared that the best way to accomplish a national revolution was via federally mandated services and federal financial support, parents initiated efforts that ultimately led to the passage of PL 94-142.

Parent groups have contributed to programs and services for individuals of all ages with disabilities. Though many of their original goals appear to be met, parents are still needed to monitor the activities of the various public agencies. Because not all states have reached the same level of programs and services, national parent organizations can assist state-level groups in their fight for parity.

Advocacy by individual parents remains critically important. Although parent groups are the most effective vehicle for national advocacy, individual efforts can mean more in the local community. The old dictum that "It's not what you know

**Box 15.4
Parent
Insights**

Raising a child with a disability often strengthens parents by unlocking previously undiscovered potential.

Kathy Taylor had had no intentions of developing a career before she gave birth to Bonnie. But when Bonnie was six months old, economics required that Kathy work. She reflects on what she's learned over the last three years. "I have capabilities I didn't know I had. I've been able to be a full-time mom *and* hold down a job. I think, 'what if she hadn't been handicapped? Where would I be now?' I probably wouldn't be at this job or this committed to doing both things so well."

Deborah Stein found other strengths: "I've learned that I'm not afraid to take a stand. I just argued with Michele's school about a program they're cutting and I won. I can't believe it! I never thought I'd do that. If it weren't for Michele I wouldn't have."

Linda Chavez concurs. Although she had never been a joiner or an activist, dissatisfaction with programs at her daughter's school prompted her to speak out and work with the school to implement changes. When she met with success she was encouraged to continue. Now she's a "resource mother" for the school district whom they call for advice in structuring new programs. "It's helped me as much as it's helped the kids. It's helped me meet people. I've done things I never thought I could do (like talk in front of the City Council!). It's given me opportunities I never would have had otherwise. It's also relieved a lot of the anger and frustration I felt about the system. I feel like I'm helping it be better for someone else."

Lois Lanier also finds inner satisfaction in helping other people. "I remember the first person I talked to who also had a Down child. She came to visit me shortly after I brought Carrie home from the hospital. She was so helpful to me—just to see that you didn't die or fall apart because your child has Down syndrome. She still enjoyed life. I wanted to do that for other people so I started visiting other new parents of Down children. I've seen a lot of them. I don't remember most of them, but I'll tell you, they remember you. One day a woman came up to me at school and said, 'I know you.' I said, 'No you don't. I don't know you.' She said, 'Yes, I do. You came to talk to me when I was in the hospital with Timmy. The things you said and the books you gave me to read were so helpful to me then; I've always wanted to thank you.'"

SOURCE: From *After the Tears: Parents Talk about Raising a Child with a Disability,* by Robin Simons, pp. 78–79, copyright © 1987 by The Children's Museum of Denver Inc., reprinted by permission of Harcourt Brace Jovanovich, Inc.

but who you know" is applicable at all levels of government, and successful parent advocates pursue their goals with that in mind.

Relationships with Siblings and the Extended Family

According to Seligman and Darling, "until recently, professionals have either neglected or consigned to secondary importance the effect a disabled child in the family context has on siblings" (1989, p. 111). They note that children who share in the anticipation of a new brother or sister can also share in the pain that results when that new brother or sister has a disability. They consider the study of the effects of a disabled brother or sister on nondisabled siblings to be a significant, emerging area of concern.

Research on whether these nondisabled siblings should be considered children at risk has met with conflicting findings. Some studies conclude that they are definitely at risk, whereas others seem to indicate that they are as well adjusted as the control subjects. Factors such as age, gender, and parental attitudes toward both the child with disabilities and the nondisabled sibling may influence the findings of any such study (Seligman & Darling, 1989).

The issues faced by siblings share some degree of commonality regardless of the nature of the disability (Powell & Ogle, 1985). Powell and Ogle outline six issues of concern to nondisabled siblings: (1) the sibling with a disability, (2) their parents, (3) themselves, (4) their friends, (5) the community (especially the school), and (6) their adult responsibilities and the effect that their exceptional adult brother or sister may have on their family and adult friends.

Concerns about their sibling include questions about the cause of the disability, the feelings of their brother or sister, and whether they will improve or be cured. They also wonder about their own role, their responsibility to shelter or protect, and what will happen to their brother or sister in the future.

Concerns about their parents are related to parental expectations of them: why their parents expect so much yet expect so little of their brother or sister. They also wonder how openly they can talk with their parents about their brother or sister, why their parents fight so much about them and don't spend more time with them (the nondisabled children), why they always have to baby-sit, why the sibling with a disability is given so much special parental consideration, and related questions that suggest feelings of rejection.

Concerns about themselves include their own feelings about their brother or sister (such as jealousy), why they often feel angry, and whether they really love their sibling. They also wonder about whether the disability is "catching" and how they can improve their relationship.

Concerns about their friends are how to tell them about their sibling and whether their friends will think they have a disability, too. They are concerned about their role in protecting their sibling from teasing and how they should react when others make fun of persons with disabilities. They have misgivings about inviting friends to their home and how to include, or not include, their sibling with a disability. When they begin dating, they worry about what their date will think of their sibling, how much and when to tell their date about the disability, and what to do if their sibling causes a scene when the date is present.

Concerns about school and community acceptance generally parallel the foregoing. Two unique, school-related questions are whether they must associate

■ The extended family can provide a variety of experiences for the child and respite for the parent. ■

with their sibling at school and why teachers always call them when the sibling has a problem.

In addition to these "here-and-now" concerns, siblings of exceptional children apparently think a great deal about the future. Powell and Ogle (1985) note their concerns about possible future financial or other guardianship responsibilities, and the sibling's acceptance by a potential spouse and the spouse's family. They also report concerns about whether the disability might be a genetic defect, how they will balance responsibility to their sibling with responsibility to their spouse and children, and other, similar issues.

Siblings of children with disabilities may have unique needs that should be recognized and dealt with as early as possible. This is important not only for the sake of the nondisabled brother or sister, but also because an emotionally healthy sibling is important in the life of the student with the disability. Baker and Brightman note that "siblings in families with a handicapped member are variously seen by the professional community as at risk for psychiatric disorder, and as resources for the handicapped child's development" (1989, p. 170). They believe that the potential for both is real but that effective programs for these children can reduce the risk of psychiatric disorder and increase their potential as a resource in the life of their sibling.

There is little question that parents and siblings of children with disabilities are those most affected by the child's presence in the family—and most likely to be facilitators and contributors to their social and educational progress as well. They are, then, the key family members. But it has also been established that grandparents may be another important part of the family constellation (Seligman & Darling, 1989). How much they influence the situation depends on the closeness of their relationship to the parents and on their initial, and continuing, reactions to the news that their grandchild has a disability.

Grandparents may mourn just as the parents do and be of little value as a source of support. Seligman and Darling report that one common pattern is expression of resentment toward the daughter-in-law by the paternal grandmother. This seriously exacerbates the feelings the new mother is already experiencing and places the father in an awkward situation when he is already under stress. Grandparents may also worry about the financial implications of the infant, and are even more likely to do so if they have been significant financial contributors to the family unit in the past. They may also feel, for example, that the new baby will never grow up to be the grandson or granddaughter that they had hoped for. On the other hand, grandparents can sometimes be the glue that holds the family constellation together. They may be knowledgeable about available community resources, may help the parents tap those resources, and may share strategies that they have used in the past to cope with difficulties in their own lives. Perhaps the most important help they can give is emotional support.

As parents are helped through individual or family counseling or through support groups, it is becoming increasingly common to involve the grandparents, especially if they are very close members of the family constellation. They are an important source of strength and stability in many cases; in others, they need support similar to that needed by the parents. Their potential influence, positive or negative, certainly cannot be ignored.

Depending on the individual circumstances, the extended family and close friends are also important contributors to the parents' ability to adjust to their new responsibilities. An aunt or uncle who is particularly close may provide unexpected strength and counsel. Close friends at work, neighbors who are particularly close, members of a social group to which the parents belong, or friends from the church or synagogue may prove to be invaluable sources of strength. Many persons are potential sources of assistance, but unfortunately, these same individuals may prove to have a negative effect. Parents must be assisted in determining when and from whom they wish to receive support, must learn that it is all right to accept such support, and must develop strategies to filter out and attempt to ignore negative input. Educators, parent groups, and community agencies must work with parents and siblings to discover and develop their own personal support system.

Culturally and Linguistically Diverse Families

Cultural and linguistic differences can greatly affect parent/school communication about the child and, as we saw in Chapter 14, many differences exist between various ethnic or cultural groups (Lynch & Stein, 1987). Based on one study, it appears that Hispanic parents are likely to give higher ratings to special education professionals than are African-American parents. Hispanic (in this instance, Mexican-American) parents tended to be more satisfied than either African-American or Anglo parents with their child's program of special education. However, they were less knowledgeable about and less involved in the program than either the African-American or Anglo parents. They seemed more likely to believe that "the school knows best" (ibid.).

School personnel often complain that parents of minority children do not take an interest in their children and are not helpful to education professionals. The problem may be a conflict in values, especially in the case of minority parents in lower socioeconomic classes. The parents' priorities may be finding shelter and clothing for the family and providing adequate nutrition. They may want to participate in school conferences but lack the flexibility or control over their environment to do so. According to Ortiz and Yates, "conferences may be a luxury parents can ill afford" (1988, p. 187).

Some parents, especially Hispanics, may believe that educational decision making is the school's responsibility (Lynch & Stein, 1987; Ortiz & Yates, 1988). They may have profound respect for school authorities, but their respect and faith lead them to believe that there is little reason for them to be involved in joint decision making. When they do attend planning meetings, they may provide very

---

People Who Make a Difference

DONNALEE VELVICK AND HOPE HOUSE Donnalee Velvick spent much of her childhood in a foster home; it's only appropriate, therefore, that she's now "mother" to 50 to 60 children. She is executive director of Hope House, a facility she founded to provide a safe home for developmentally disabled children and youth. These are primarily children who were battered, mentally retarded, emotionally disturbed, or simply unwanted. They are also ineligible for help through state agencies, local organizations, or private homes. Because of her own experiences as a child, Donnalee wanted a home in which children could stay until they finished school and were ready to be on their own. They live in a modified formerly abandoned schoolhouse on a budget of approximately $400,000 per year. Most of this money comes from bartering, donations, wages (the teenagers hold jobs during the summer and at other times when possible), Social Security for individuals with disabilities, a thrift shop, and from other special fund-raising projects. The "family" has a quarter-acre garden from which it preserves vegetables and fruit for its own

use all year. The children also raise livestock.

Velvick moved into the abandoned schoolhouse in 1976 with children of her own and three foster children. From very small beginnings, Hope House has expanded to its present staff of a dozen or more volunteers, all who live at Hope House. Three teachers and a cook draw wages. Donnalee has seen over 250 children come and go, and notes that over 150 have graduated from high school. There have been "failures"—those she could not reach—but only a few.

Things were difficult at first, but now a number of organizations such as Rotary, Kiwanis, Lions, and Civitans donate generously. Other local businesses and individuals donate time and materials for special needs. Donnalee also tells of a "grandma lady" from a small town in Oregon who has been sending $3 a month since 1979; she says this kind of donation is especially precious to her. Hope House, only a dream in 1976, is truly a home filled with hope for children with disabilities, those who have been abused, those who have no place to go. Donnalee Velvick has received local and national awards, but she feels her most satisfying reward is providing a permanent home for kids who really need one.

■ Parents learn the benefits of water therapy for their children with cerebral palsy. ■

limited input. Thus the result of their respect for and faith in the school is an attitude that conflicts with the parental involvement thrust of PL 94-142.

Ortiz and Yates (1988) recommend that schools establish training programs to help parents understand their potential role in planning processes and to furnish them the skills to participate. To be successful, such programs must be consistent with the parents' culture, language, and related characteristics. If school officials believe that parent input is of value and want to increase the involvement of parents from culturally diverse backgrounds, they must make additional efforts to prepare the parents to contribute.

In a discussion of recommendations for enhancing the involvement of African-American parents of adolescents with handicaps, Olion (1988) provided a number of insights into the unique traits of those families. Although some African-American families are no different in basic characteristics than Anglo families, Olion notes that many more African-American children are living in a family headed by a single female and that more are living below the poverty level. They may have lowered expectations for academic achievement and for future economic success. They are likely to have inferior medical services and may have experienced a variety of social and economic discrimination. Although some African-American parents will require the same approach to encourage participation as would any other parent, some will require modified strategies. Olion believes that greater parental participation can be achieved, but cautions that a major problem may be that many educators do not really want parents present— especially parents of significantly different educational or income backgrounds or from racial minority groups.

Although educators may attempt to modify the beliefs, attitudes, and actions of parents, they may be unsuccessful if they do not have a knowledge of other cultures. The first and most essential element for success, then, may be changing their own beliefs, attitudes, and actions. Correa (1989) suggests a number of professional development activities that can broaden teachers' knowledge bases and sensitivity toward individuals from other cultures. She suggests the following examples of actions and activities to help achieve this enhanced level of understanding and sensitivity.

* Attend and participate in social events and meetings held within the culturally diverse community.
* Invite community members from culturally diverse groups to work in the school as volunteers.
* Learn more about local community newspapers, radio stations, and meeting places.
* Make home visits.

In addition, more positive relationships with culturally diverse families may be promoted by assisting in the training of local individuals as translators, by arranging for transportation and child care to facilitate parent attendance at school conferences, and by summarizing all decisions made in school conferences through written or telephone follow-up contacts in both English and the primary language (ibid.).

Obtaining useful, continuing participation by parents from culturally diverse ethnic groups clearly may require considerable additional effort on the part of school personnel. Factors that inhibit participation must be locally analyzed, and strategies must be designed to circumvent or overcome them. Only then will the school be able to benefit from information unique to the student and family unit and from a variety of essential parental input.

Parent and Family Roles and Giftedness

Parental roles of parents of gifted children are in many ways similar to those of parents of children with disabilities. Improvement of parenting skills, supporting learning at home, parent education, and advocacy for better educational programs also apply to parents of students who are gifted. There are some differences, partly related to the fact that in most states it is not compulsory for school districts to provide comprehensive programs for gifted students. Neither is there legislation for the gifted comparable to PL 94-142. In other words, there are few if any guarantees of appropriate educational programs. There are also few protections of the rights of these parents and students other than the implied guarantee of a publicly supported educational program that is supposed to apply to all children. Thus the basis for these parents' advocacy efforts is quite different.

In spite of this weaker advocacy base, advocacy for more appropriate programs for gifted students is an essential parental role. It must, however, be based on student need, the right to an appropriate education, and the student's potential contribution to society rather than on federal and state legislation and the threat of litigation. Advocacy on behalf of programs for students who are gifted is, then, much more difficult than advocacy on behalf of students with disabilities.

Most of the books written for parents of students who are gifted are designed to further explain the nature of giftedness and to encourage parents to provide a great deal of home support and home-based learning opportunities. There is some degree of concurrence among authors that parents and families must be highly involved in the development of their gifted child from a very young age, or the potential giftedness will be seriously underdeveloped. For example, Alvino discusses what he considers a difficult-to-dispel belief that gifted toddlers can make it on their own: "This is truly a myth—it just isn't so. Far too often, insufficient parenting or teaching techniques contribute to unhappiness, behavioral problems, underachievement, and sometimes even suicide among these children once they grow older" (1989, p. 17). Others are not as vehement in predicting serious future effects as a result of poor parenting practices and inappropriate teaching techniques, but all agree that parental involvement and good parenting practices are important (B. Clark, 1988; Gallagher, 1985; Rice, 1985; Sisk, 1987).

Parents are, however, cautioned against various types of thoughtless or unproductive behavior. For example, there is a tendency for parents to brag about their gifted child (Periono & Perino, 1981). Children who are gifted—who are, after all, children first—will undoubtedly model their parents' behavior at some later date, to their own social disadvantage. Parents may also tend to try to push their child toward some lofty goal they have determined to be appropriate to their child's great intellectual ability. If the principle of self-determination is accepted for other children, it should apply equally to children who are gifted.

In a discussion of the role of significant others in the life of the young child who is gifted, Alvino (1989) suggests that parents of students later identified as gifted tend to exhibit certain distinctive parenting styles. For example, they may spend more time reading to their children and be specifically involved in language development–related activities. They spend minimal time watching TV at home themselves and may prohibit the child from watching violent programs. In their use of community cultural resources, they are more likely to visit a broad range of resources—those established primarily for children as well as those more oriented to adults (adult sections of the natural history museum, art museums, and so on). Parents of students who are gifted also tend to be quite involved in their child's schooling. It is generally believed that such parenting styles enhance the development of giftedness, but this has not been established through research.

Alvino also notes the considerable potential of grandparents as listeners, storytellers, mentors, reinforcers of values and standards, guides to social living, and as sources of love, comfort, and security. Brothers and sisters may also influence the development of a gifted sibling, but much will depend on how the parent handles this sibling relationship. Periono and Perino remind parents that "favoring one child because he or she is gifted or talented is destructive to that child's future development" (1981, p. 177). Favoritism also has a negative effect on sibling relationships and may promote hostility toward the gifted child.

B. Clark (1988) suggests that parents who have nurtured their child's development through the preschool years may begin to feel powerless when he or she moves into the school system. She believes, however, that they can accomplish a great deal through cooperative, organized, knowledgeable efforts.

■ Parental involvement with children's education at the local level affects the quality of that education. ■

Step one, according to Clark, is to organize with other parents of gifted children in the school. She believes that through such organization they may find "understanding, and even relief, in their sharing of common concerns and experiences" (p. 567). She adds a note of caution, however, because gifted children may have gifted parents who, like their children, are of independent, divergent natures. As a result, parental organization may present some real challenges.

A second step is to compare experiences and establish some vehicle for parent in-service related to giftedness and to decide how parents can collaborate with the school to nourish and develop giftedness. The successful completion of the first step makes accomplishing the second much easier.

Once organized and recognized as parents sincerely interested in their children's education and willing to cooperate with the school, various activities and undertakings may be considered. One is volunteering to serve as resources in the classroom in a variety of ways. This will depend on local needs but might include providing materials, preparing special interest centers, or even some direct instruction. Requests for such assistance should come from teachers once they understand the potential and availability of the parent group.

One final possibility is attempting to have an impact on state legislation that would encourage better educational provisions for students who are gifted. This is one task that parents can often tackle more effectively than educators. They have the advantage of sheer numbers, if they become organized. And they have a strong belief and vested interest that motivates them to continue far beyond the point at which professionals might concede defeat.

Issues and Trends

One issue in the area of parent involvement is convincing all teachers that parent participation is of value. Another is convincing all parents of students with disabilities that they are an important part of the planning process and that their participation can be of value to their child. A third issue, closely related to the first two, is whether it is the school's responsibility to provide parent training to

People Who Make a Difference

SYLVIA PIPER—MOTHER, ACTIVIST, ADVOCATE Sylvia Piper is a mother with a cause, one who gets things done. She and her son, Dan, who has moderate mental retardation, have testified before a Joint Subcommittee of the U.S. House of Representatives and Senate in support of the Americans with Disabilities Act. From her own experience, Sylvia speaks to various groups on integrating students with mental retardation into regular education facilities while ensuring quality programming. She has served as a member of the Integration Team for the Iowa Department of Education, providing statewide leadership. For five years she was a governor-appointed member of the Board of Directors of Iowa Protection and Advocacy Ser-

vices, Inc. Sylvia also formed a Religious Education Committee for persons with disabilities, to give them access to religious services and appropriate instruction.

As resource development director for the Iowa Association for Retarded Citizens (ARC/Iowa) from 1984 to 1991, Sylvia coordinated the efforts of 85 county ARC chapters to raise awareness of the potential and ability of 87,000 Iowans with mental retardation. Currently the advocacy consultant for Iowa Protection and Advocacy Services, Inc., she specializes in educational advocacy for children who have developmental disabilities. She also coordinates Iowa's Partners in Policymaking leadership training program for persons who have disabilities and their families.

develop the parents' role in the educational process. If it is determined to be the school's responsibility, how should such training be provided and should it also include training in parenting skills? One final issue is that of the division of responsibility between the school and other community agencies in providing the full spectrum of services required by families of students with disabilities. A subissue is the source of funding for such services.

Trends relating to parent and family roles in the care and education of children with disabilities are relatively clear and predominantly positive. Recognition and appreciation of the potential value of parent involvement in educational planning for their exceptional child is on the increase. In most instances, parents' legal right to such involvement is established by law. There has been increased study of this relationship and of related efforts by educators to encourage parent participation. These trends have been reinforced by a similar movement outside of the field of special education to promote a more meaningful parent/school partnership for the benefit of all children. International conferences on the support of families with exceptional children have reflected parallel trends in many other nations. A subtrend within the general trend of increased parent involvement is an increase in efforts to attract low-socioeconomic and minority parents.

Trends with respect to parents and families of children who are gifted are less clear. There may be a trend toward greater parent advocacy on behalf of special educational provisions for gifted students. Several issues remain unresolved with respect to the education of gifted students, but they are not closely related to parent and family relationships.

Summary

There is no doubt about the importance of parents to the social and educational development of their children; other members of the family, including extended family members, can also be of importance in planning and improving educational programs for exceptional students. Parents of children with disabilities, on becoming aware of the disability, go through predictable stages of shock, denial, grief, depression, ambivalence, guilt, anger, shame, and embarrassment. The final phase for most parents includes adaptation, acceptance, and adjustment. Educators must understand and be sensitive to these feelings as they work with parents on behalf of the child.

Parents must be actively involved in assessment and initial planning, program monitoring, and ongoing program planning. They must be encouraged and assisted to support learning at home. They can be effective advocates for their children and for others with similar needs and can assist in parent education efforts targeting other parents. Educators must do everything possible to encourage and ensure such parent participation.

Educators have too often focused only on the child with a disability and his or her parents. They have also too often considered only the school environment, overlooking community acceptance and the potential of the community to contribute to or detract from educational progress. There are a number of ways in which the concerns of siblings, grandparents, aunts and uncles, or close family friends may influence the effectiveness of educational interventions. These must be considered, for the sake of both the student and the other family members.

Effective working relationships with members of culturally diverse families may pose special problems related to language differences, culturally related beliefs, or patterns of behavior. In such cases, special efforts are required to obtain input from parents.

Parent and family roles regarding children who are gifted are generally similar to those regarding children with disabilities. Some schools encourage organizing the parents of gifted students to establish parent education programs and a framework within which parents can serve as classroom resource persons. However, because there is no national, legislation-based guarantee of special educational provisions, parents of gifted children must be stronger, more active advocates if their children are to have varied, appropriate, effective educational programs.

APPENDIX A

Sources of Additional Information

ADMINISTRATION ON DEVELOPMENTAL DISABILITIES
200 Independence Avenue, S.W.
Washington, DC 20201
ALEXANDER GRAHAM BELL ASSOCIATION FOR THE DEAF, INC.
3417 Volta Place, N.W.
Washington, DC 20007
AMERICAN ACADEMY FOR CEREBRAL PALSY AND DEVELOPMENTAL
   MEDICINE
2405 Westwood Avenue
P.O. Box 11083
Richmond, VA 23230
AMERICAN ASSOCIATION OF THE DEAF-BLIND, INC.
814 Thayer Avenue
Silver Springs, MD 20910
AMERICAN ASSOCIATION FOR GIFTED CHILDREN
15 Gramercy Park
New York, NY 10003
AMERICAN ASSOCIATION ON MENTAL RETARDATION
1719 Kalorama Road, N.W.
Washington, DC 20009
AMERICAN ASSOCIATION OF PSYCHIATRIC SERVICES FOR
   CHILDREN
1133 Fifteenth Street, N.W., Suite 1000
Washington, DC 20005

AMERICAN ASSOCIATION OF SCHOOL ADMINISTRATORS
1801 North Moore Street
Arlington, VA 22209
AMERICAN BAR ASSOCIATION CHILD ADVOCACY CENTER
1800 M Street, N.W., Suite 200
Washington, DC 20036
AMERICAN CANCER SOCIETY
777 Third Avenue
New York, NY 10017
AMERICAN COALITION OF CITIZENS WITH DISABILITIES
1012 14th Street, N.W., Suite 901
Washington, DC 20005
AMERICAN COUNCIL FOR THE BLIND
1010 Vermont Avenue, N.W., Suite 1100
Washington, DC 20005
AMERICAN DIABETES ASSOCIATION
1819 H Street, N.W., Suite 1200
Washington, DC 20006
AMERICAN EPILEPSY SOCIETY
179 Allyn Street, Suite 304
Hartford, CT 06103
AMERICAN FOUNDATION FOR THE BLIND
15 West 16th Street
New York, NY 10011

AMERICAN JUVENILE ARTHRITIS ORGANIZATION
1314 Spring Street, N.W.
Atlanta, GA 30309

AMERICAN OCCUPATIONAL THERAPY ASSOCIATION
1383 Piccard Drive, P.O. Box 1725
Rockville, MD 20850

AMERICAN PHYSICAL THERAPY ASSOCIATION
1111 N. Fairfax Street
Alexandria, VA 22314

AMERICAN PRINTING HOUSE FOR THE BLIND
1839 Frankfort Avenue
Louisville, KY 40206

AMERICAN PSYCHIATRIC ASSOCIATION
1400 K Street, N.W.
Washington, DC 20005

AMERICAN PSYCHOLOGICAL ASSOCIATION
1200 Seventeenth Street, N.W.
Washington, DC 20036

AMERICAN SOCIETY FOR DEAF CHILDREN
814 Thayer Avenue
Silver Springs, MD 20910

AMERICAN SPEECH–LANGUAGE–HEARING ASSOCIATION
10801 Rockville Pike
Rockville, MD 20852

APPLE COMPUTER'S OFFICE OF SPECIAL EDUCATION PROGRAMS
20525 Mariani Avenue
Cupertino, CA 95014

ASSOCIATION FOR THE EDUCATION AND REHABILITATION OF THE
    BLIND AND VISUALLY IMPAIRED
206 North Washington Street, Suite 320
Alexandria, VA 22314

ATTENTION DEFICIT DISORDER ASSOCIATION
8091 South Ireland Way
Aurora, CO 80016

ATTENTION DEFICIT DISORDER ADVOCACY GROUP
8091 South Ireland Way
Aurora, CO 80016

AUTISM SOCIETY OF AMERICA
1234 Massachusetts Avenue, N.W., Suite 1017
Washington, DC 20005

BRAILLE CIRCULATING LIBRARY
2700 Stuart Avenue
Richmond, VA 23220

CHILDREN WITH ATTENTION DEFICIT DISORDERS
499 N.W. 70th Avenue, Suite 308
Plantation, FL 33317

CLEARINGHOUSE ON THE HANDICAPPED, OFFICE OF SPECIAL
    EDUCATION AND REHABILITATION SERVICES
330 C Street, S.W., Switzer Building
Washington, DC 20202

CLEARINGHOUSE AND RESEARCH IN CHILD ABUSE AND NEGLECT
P.O. Box 1182
Washington, DC 20013

COALITION ON SEXUALITY AND DISABILITY, INC.
853 Broadway, Suite 611
New York, NY 10003

COMMITTEE FOR PROMOTION OF CAMPING FOR THE HANDICAPPED
2056 South Bluff Road
Travers City, MI 49684

COUNCIL FOR DISABILITY RIGHTS
343 South Dearborn, Suite 318
Chicago, IL 60604

COUNCIL FOR EXCEPTIONAL CHILDREN
1920 Association Drive
Reston, VA 22091

CYSTIC FIBROSIS FOUNDATION
6931 Arlington Road
Bethesda, MD 20814

DISABILITY LAW CENTER, INC.
11 Beacon Street, Suite 925
Boston, MA 02108

DISABILITY RIGHTS CENTER, INC.
1616 P Street, N.W., Suite 435
Washington, DC 20036

EPILEPSY FOUNDATION OF AMERICA
4351 Garden City Drive, Suite 406
Landover, MD 20785

GALLAUDET UNIVERSITY PRESS
800 Florida Avenue, N.E.
Washington, DC 20002

GIFTED CHILD SOCIETY, INC.
190 Rock Road
Glenrock, NJ 07452

IBM NATIONAL SUPPORT CENTER FOR PERSONS WITH
    DISABILITIES
P.O. Box 2150
Atlanta, GA 30055

JUVENILE DIABETES FOUNDATION INTERNATIONAL
60 Madison Avenue
New York, NY 10010

KURZWEIL COMPUTER PRODUCTS
33 Cambridge Parkway
Cambridge, MA 02142

LEARNING DISABILITIES ASSOCIATION OF AMERICA
4156 Library Road
Pittsburgh, PA 15234

LEUKEMIA SOCIETY OF AMERICA
733 Third Avenue, 14th Floor
New York, NY 10017

MUSCULAR DYSTROPHY ASSOCIATION
810 Seventh Avenue
New York, NY 10019

NATIONAL AID TO THE VISUALLY HANDICAPPED
3201 Balboa Street
San Francisco, CA 94121

NATIONAL ASSOCIATION OF THE DEAF
814 Thayer Avenue
Silver Springs, MD 20910

NATIONAL ASSOCIATION FOR THE DEAF-BLIND
12573 S.E. 53rd Street
Bellevue, WA 98006

NATIONAL ASSOCIATION FOR DOWN SYNDROME
P.O. Box 4542
Oak Brook, IL 60521

NATIONAL ASSOCIATION FOR GIFTED CHILDREN
5100 N. Edgewood Drive
St. Paul, MN 55112

NATIONAL ASSOCIATION OF PARENTS OF THE DEAF
814 Thayer Avenue
Silver Springs, MD 20910
NATIONAL ASSOCIATION FOR PARENTS OF THE VISUALLY IMPAIRED
P.O. Box 180806
Austin, TX 78718
NATIONAL ASSOCIATION FOR RETARDED CITIZENS
2501 Avenue J
Arlington, TX 76006
NATIONAL ASSOCIATION OF SCHOOL PSYCHOLOGISTS
1511 K Street, N.W., Suite 716
Washington, DC 20005
NATIONAL ASSOCIATION FOR SICKLE CELL DISEASE
3460 Wilshire Boulevard, Suite 1012
Los Angeles, CA 90010
NATIONAL ASSOCIATION OF STATE DIRECTORS OF SPECIAL
    EDUCATION
2021 K Street, N.W., Suite 315
Washington, DC 20006
NATIONAL ASSOCIATION FOR THE VISUALLY HANDICAPPED
305 East 24th Street
New York, NY 10010
NATIONAL BRAILLE PRESS
86 St. Stephen Street
Boston, MA 02115
NATIONAL CENTER FOR STUTTERING
200 East 33rd Street
New York, NY 10016
NATIONAL COUNCIL FOR THE HANDICAPPED
800 Independence Avenue, S.W.
Washington, DC 20008
NATIONAL CUED SPEECH ASSOCIATION
P.O. Box 31345
Raleigh, NC 27622
NATIONAL DOWN SYNDROME CONGRESS
1800 Dempster Street
Park Ridge, IL 60068
NATIONAL EASTER SEAL SOCIETY FOR CRIPPLED CHILDREN AND
    ADULTS
2023 West Ogden Avenue
Chicago, IL 60612
THE NATIONAL FOUNDATION FOR ILEITIS AND COLITIS
444 Park Avenue South
New York, NY 10016
NATIONAL HANDICAPPED SPORTS AND RECREATION ASSOCIATION
1341 G Street, N.W., Suite 815
Washington, DC 20005
NATIONAL HEAD INJURY ASSOCIATION
18A Vernon Street
Framingham, VA 01701
THE NATIONAL HEMOPHILIA ASSOCIATION
The Soho Building
110 Greene Street, Room 406
New York, NY 10012
NATIONAL INFORMATION CENTER FOR HANDICAPPED CHILDREN AND
    YOUTH
P.O. Box 1492
Washington, DC 20013

NATIONAL KIDNEY FOUNDATION
2 Park Avenue, Suite 908
New York, NY 10016
NATIONAL LIBRARY SERVICES FOR THE BLIND AND PHYSICALLY
    HANDICAPPED
Library of Congress
1291 Taylor Street, N.W.
Washington, DC 20542
NATIONAL MULTIPLE SCLEROSIS SOCIETY
205 East 42nd Street
New York, NY 10017
NATIONAL REHABILITATION INFORMATION CENTER
4407 Eighth Street, N.E.
Washington, DC 22990
NATIONAL RETINITIS PIGMENTOSA (RP) FOUNDATION, INC.
1401 Mount Royal Avenue
Baltimore, MD 21217
NATIONAL/STATE LEADERSHIP TRAINING INSTITUTE ON GIFTED AND
    TALENTED (NS/LTI/GT)
Ventura County Superintendent of Schools
535 East Main Street
Ventura, CA 93009
NATIONAL TAY-SACHS AND ALLIED DISEASES ASSOCIATION
92 Washington Avenue
Cedarhurst, NY 11516

THE ORTON DYSLEXIA SOCIETY
724 York Road
Baltimore, MD 21204

PRESIDENT'S COMMITTEE ON EMPLOYMENT OF THE HANDICAPPED
1111 20th Street, N.W., Room 600
Washington, DC 20036
PRESIDENT'S COMMITTEE ON MENTAL RETARDATION
Regional Office Building, #3
7th and D Streets, S.W., Room 2614
Washington, DC 20201

RECORDING FOR THE BLIND, INC.
215 East 58th Street
New York, NY 10022

SCOLIOSIS RESEARCH SOCIETY
444 North Michigan Avenue
Chicago, IL 60611
SPECIAL OLYMPICS, INC.
1350 New York Avenue, N.W., Suite 500
Washington, DC 20005
SPINA BIFIDA ASSOCIATION OF AMERICA
1700 Rockville Pike, Suite 540
Rockville, MD 20852

TELECOMMUNICATIONS FOR THE DEAF, INC.
814 Thayer Avenue
Silver Springs, MD 20910

UNITED CEREBRAL PALSY ASSOCIATION, INC.
66 East 34th Street
New York, NY 10016

Speech and Language Communication Checklist

Student _____ Parent(s) _____ Grade _____ Date _____

Please fill out this checklist based on your personal observations. Check the appropriate box for each behavior. Feel free to add your comments on the back of this paper. Thanks!!!

☐ Educational performance is not affected.
☐ Educational performance may be affected and may require classroom modification.
☐ Educational performance is usually affected.
☐ Educational performance is significantly affected.

Receptive language

Not a problem area	Problem area	
		Is able to follow oral directions.
		Says *Huh* or *What* frequently.
		Has a short attention span.
		Is able to ask for clarification/repetition of a direction(s).
		Sometimes appears not to be listening.
		Repeats what has been said rather than responding to the meaning.
		Appears not to remember or understand what has been said.
		Is easily distracted by sounds or noises.
		Has difficulty remembering family routines and following directions.

Expressive language

		Participates in discussions.
		Uses complete thoughts when speaking.
		Uses correct sentence structure and grammar.
		Uses logical sequence of ideas to tell a story or relate events.
		Appears to grope or struggle for words.
		Uses a limited speaking vocabulary.
		Below age 7: poor articulation makes speech difficult to understand.
		Age 8 or above: articulation errors seem to interfere with academic or social functioning.
		Uses appropriate volume, pitch, and intonation.
		Voice often sounds hoarse or harsh.
		Uses rhythmical, fluent speech.

Pragmatic (social communication) language

		Can carry on a meaningful conversation with adults.
		Can carry on a meaningful conversation with peers.
		Introduces a topic appropriately.
		Makes relevant comments on the topic.
		Can take turns in conversations.
		Attends to speaker—maintains eye contact, etc.
		Can end a conversation appropriately.
		Does not seem to understand jokes or abstract remarks.

Please return to: _____ Speech/Language Specialist
By: _____ Date

This checklist is for teachers, but can be used by parents with minimal modifications: delete the educational performance box at the top and modify or delete some statements under Expressive Language, for instance.

GLOSSARY

ABSENCE SEIZURES Epileptic seizures of short duration (5 to 20 seconds) that may occur many (100 or more) times a day. The individual may stare into space, become pale, or make jerky movements.

ACCELERATION An educational process leading to accelerated progress through school. It may mean early entrance to school, skipping grades, or advanced college placement.

ACUITY Acuteness or keenness of the senses (such as hearing or vision).

ADAPTIVE BEHAVIOR Skills and competencies utilized by individuals to meet the challenges of their environment. Included are aspects of motivation, social behavior, intellectual functions, and physical abilities. Standards of adaptive behavior are generally age related.

ADVOCATE One who pleads the cause of others or takes actions that attempt to improve the life or opportunities of others.

AMNIOCENTESIS A procedure that analyzes the amniotic fluid of the uterus to aid in identification of various congenital defects. A hollow needle is inserted through the abdomen into the uterus of the pregnant woman to draw the sample.

ANOXIA A lack of oxygen in the blood severe enough to cause damage to brain tissue. Anoxia may result in mental retardation or other disabilities.

ARTICULATION Movement of the vocal tract, including the stream of breath that produces voiced and unvoiced sounds; the enunciation of words or vocal sounds; and the movements of the jaws, lips, and tongue. The desired end result of articulation is the production of distinct language.

AT RISK (INFANTS OR CHILDREN) Infants or children who are not currently identified as having a disability but who—for identifiable socioeconomic, environmental, physiological, or genetic reasons—have a greater-than-usual chance of developing a disability. The term *at risk* may be more specifically defined in legislation.

ATHETOSIS (OR ATHETOID CEREBRAL PALSY) A type of cerebral palsy characterized by twisting or writhing movements and facial grimaces.

AUDIOGRAM A graphic representation of a person's ability to hear each of several frequencies throughout the range of normal speech. It includes information for each ear.

AUDIOLOGY The science of diagnosing hearing impairments and assisting in remedial planning.

AUDITORY TRAINING A systematic program to train the hearing impaired to utilize all of their residual hearing.

AUTISM A severe behavior disorder with a wide variety of possible characteristics. Many children diagnosed as autistic are noncommunicative and withdrawn. Others may exhibit self-stimulation or aggressive behavior. The description "exhibits autisticlike behavior" is often used as an alternative for a specific diagnosis of autism.

BEHAVIORISM A school of psychology that explains causes of emotional disturbance or behavioral disorders in terms of learned behavior. Treatment is then based on behavioral principles and methods.

BEHAVIOR MODIFICATION The systematic arrangement of environmental events and variables to produce specific changes in observed behavior. It may include positive or negative reinforcement, time out, modeling, and shaping.

509

BIOPHYSICAL THEORY A theory that attempts to explain emotional disturbance or behavior disorders on the basis of biological factors.

BLIND A general term that can refer to no vision or to limited vision (see also *legally blind*).

BRAILLE A system of raised dots used by persons who are blind to read and write. The system was named after Louis Braille, its developer.

CAREER EDUCATION The totality of experiences through which an individual acquires attitudes, knowledge, and the skills required for success in the community and in employment. Career education is much broader than vocational or professional training.

CEREBRAL PALSY A group of conditions that limit motor coordination, primarily influencing voluntary movement. Cerebral palsy is caused by brain damage, and though it is more often present at birth, it may be acquired thereafter.

CLASS-ACTION LITIGATION Litigation initiated on behalf of a specific individual or group of individuals but structured to include all others in a similar situation (a "class" of individuals).

CLASSIFICATION A written specification that a committee of professionals has determined that a certain type of disability exists in an individual. Classification categories were established by PL 94-142 and were to some degree expanded in later, related legislation.

CLEFT LIP OR PALATE A congenital fissure of the palate or lip that results in articulation errors and problems with voice quality (typically, nasality). In most instances, a cleft lip or palate may be corrected through surgery.

COMPLEX PARTIAL SEIZURES Seizures that affect both motor systems and mental functioning and are manifested by behavior such as chewing or licking of lips or a variety of purposeless activities. This activity may last for a few minutes or several hours.

CONDUCTIVE HEARING LOSS A loss caused by obstructions or malformations in the outer or middle ear that interfere with sound conduction to the inner ear.

CONGENITAL Present in an individual at birth.

CONSENT DECREE Formal court approval of an out-of-court agreement reached by the plaintiff and the defendants. This procedure is often followed in litigation related to educational issues because it saves both time and cost.

CONTINUUM OF EDUCATIONAL SERVICES (OR PLACEMENTS) PL 94-142 requires that school districts provide a student with disabilities a full spectrum (a continuum) of alternative placements and educational services, ranging from least restrictive (most nearly normal) to most restrictive.

CONTROL BRACES Braces that reduce or prevent purposeless movement by allowing movement in only one or two directions.

CORNEA The transparent outer covering of the eyeball, in front of the iris and pupil, that admits light to the interior of the eye.

CORRECTIVE BRACES Braces designed to prevent or correct a deformity during the child's period of rapid growth.

CYSTIC FIBROSIS An inherited disorder in which there is generalized dysfunction of the pancreas, resulting in severe respiratory difficulties.

DECIBEL (dB) The unit of measurement of intensity or loudness of sound. Hearing evaluations, specifically audiograms, are presented in terms of decibels.

DELAYED SPEECH OR LANGUAGE Failure to develop speech or language at the time expected according to established developmental guidelines. Delayed speech refers to a delay in talking, delayed language to a delay in the ability to understand as well as to speak a language.

DIABETES A metabolic disorder in which the body is unable to utilize and store sugar in the normal manner. It results from failure of the pancreas to produce the correct amount of the hormone called insulin. Juvenile diabetes mellitus is the type of diabetes experienced by children; it can lead to coma and even to death if it's not properly and promptly treated. Visual impairment, including blindness, and limb amputation can also result in severe cases.

DOWN SYNDROME A clinical type of mental retardation related to a chromosomal disorder. Moderate to severe mental retardation, poor muscle tone, flat facial features, and other congenital defects are often associated with Down syndrome.

DUCHENNE MUSCULAR DYSTROPHY A hereditary disease, usually fatal, that typically attacks children between 1 and 6 years of age. It is characterized by slow deterioration of the voluntary muscles and results in a state of complete helplessness.

DUE PROCESS In general, the right of citizens to formally protest any action that may result in a deprivation of their constitutional rights. With respect to students with disabilities (and their parents or guardians), it means a set of legal procedures and policies established to ensure appropriate educational opportunities.

DYSLEXIA A severe reading disability usually having certain specific characteristics and considered in most states to be a type of learning disability.

ECOLOGICAL APPROACH A number of related views of causation and treatment procedures for behavior disorders that assume a high degree of interrelatedness between the organism (the child) and the environment.

EDUCABLE MENTALLY RETARDED (EMR) The term used by some special educators to refer to students who would be classified as having mild mental retardation according to the American Association on Mental Retardation classification. Measured IQ limits considered to indicate educable mental retardation may vary considerably from state to state.

ENRICHMENT An educational approach that emphasizes the provision of extra, broadened educational experiences, above and beyond those of the standard curriculum. Enrichment is advocated by some educators of students who are gifted.

EPILEPSY A disorder in the nervous system that may be manifested in a variety of symptoms, including convulsions or seizures. Most epileptic seizures can be controlled by medication; however, these drugs may have undesirable side effects.

ETIOLOGY The origins or causes of a disease or condition, or the study thereof.

FETAL ALCOHOL SYNDROME A cluster of characteristics often found in the infants of mothers who are alcoholics, or those who ingested large amounts of alcohol during pregnancy. It may include low birth weight; a variety of physical defects, including cardiac problems; and, in some cases, mental retardation.

FLUENCY DISORDERS Inappropriate pauses, hesitations, or repetitions that interrupt the natural, fluent flow of speech.

GENETIC COUNSELING Information provided to parents or prospective parents about the chances of their baby inheriting a disability. Such counseling is based on probability statistics related to the parents' genetic backgrounds.

GLAUCOMA A condition of unknown cause resulting in excessive pressure inside the eyeball. If detected early, most cases can be successfully treated; if left untreated, glaucoma may result in total blindness.

GENERALIZED TONIC-CLONIC SEIZURES Major seizures, usually resulting in loss of consciousness and general, often violent, convulsive movements.

HANDICAP The difficulties or reduced functional ability that may result from various disabilities. In general, the term *disability* is now preferred to handicap or handicapping condition.

HARD OF HEARING A general term used to describe a hearing loss that makes it difficult to understand normal speech without other cues (such as speechreading) or a hearing aid. Many degrees of hearing loss may be included under this nonspecific terminology.

HEARING IMPAIRMENT Sufficient hearing loss to require special assistance in educational programming.

HEMIPLEGIA Paralysis of one side of the body.

HEMOPHILIA A hereditary blood disorder in which the blood's clotting ability is significantly reduced.

HERTZ (Hz) The unit of measurement of frequency of sound.

HYDROCEPHALUS A condition in which cerebrospinal fluid accumulates in the cranial cavity. It may cause brain damage or severe mental retardation, but it can often be successfully treated with a shunt.

HYPERACTIVITY A condition characterized by excessive motor activity, inattention, or impulsivity.

HYPEROPIA Farsightedness, or poor close vision due to a shortened eyeball. Can often be corrected by a convex lens.

HYPOGLYCEMIA A condition in which there is a very low level of circulating glucose in the blood. This may lead to lethargy and may inhibit learning, apparently due to an insufficient blood supply to the brain.

INCONTINENCE Lack of bladder or bowel control.

IMPAIRMENT In general use, a synonym for disability. Both terms imply reduced functioning, injury, or deficiency.

INDIVIDUALIZED EDUCATION PROGRAM (IEP) A written plan describing short-term educational objectives, long-term educational goals, how they will be accomplished, and who will carry them out. It is a planning tool required by PL 94-142 to help ensure appropriate educational programming for students with disabilities. It must be signed by both parents and educators.

INDIVIDUALIZED FAMILY SERVICE PLAN (IFSP) A plan parallel to the IEP, required by PL 99-457, and designed to ensure effective coordination of early intervention services for infants or toddlers with disabilities. The IFSP includes much more direct involvement of family members than the IEP.

INTEGRATION The inclusion of students with disabilities in the regular classroom. Successful integration requires cooperation and coordination between regular and special educators.

INTOXICATION With reference to mental retardation, poisoning by toxins such as arsenic, mercury, alcohol, and narcotics.

IRIS The colored portion of the eye that functions somewhat like a camera shutter, opening or closing depending on the amount of light.

ITINERANT TEACHER A teacher who travels from school to school, or between schools, homes, hospitals, and so on, providing needed services.

JUVENILE DIABETES MELLITUS See *diabetes.*

KINESTHETIC SENSE The sense through which an individual perceives movement, weight, and position in space. For example, efficiency in both writing and running requires adequate kinesthetic perception.

KYPHOSIS A posterior curvature or bowing out of the spine.

LABELING The assignment of a general name or term that is intended to describe a specific condition. With respect to students with disabilities, such labeling or classification may be required to qualify students for special educational services. Labeling is currently considered by many special educators to have negative connotations.

LANGUAGE A system of symbols that permits one individual to communicate with others. Language may be verbal, written, gestural, or some combination of those modes.

LEARNING DISABILITIES A general term used to describe a demonstrated, significant discrepancy between the actual level of achievement in academic areas and the expected level of achievement based on ability (intelligence, sensory acuity, and related factors), and experience (past opportunity to learn). Learning disabilities are more evident in relation to the acquisition and use of language or mathematical skills and are presumed to be the result of central nervous system dysfunctions.

LEAST RESTRICTIVE ENVIRONMENT The educational setting that is most like the regular classroom yet in which the student with a disability can achieve success.

LEGALLY BLIND Central visual acuity of 20/200 or less in the better eye after the most effective possible correction, or visual acuity of more than 20/200 if there is a defect in which the widest diameter of the visual field subtends an angle no greater than 20 degrees. The concept of legal blindness (as opposed to effectiveness of vision for purposes of reading, independent travel, and the like) is important primarily with respect to the availability of certain specialized services or benefits or matters such as income tax deductions.

LIMB DEFICIENCY The absence of one or more limbs, regardless of causation.

LORDOSIS An anterior curvature of the spine when viewed from the side.

LOW VISION Vision that permits recognition of objects only at very close distances and that in many cases permits reading of large print or reading with magnification but that requires special educational services for the development of other skills and abilities.

MAINSTREAMING The maximum integration of students with disabilities into regular classrooms that is consistent with providing the most appropriate educational program. Mainstreaming requires close collaboration between regular and special educators.

MANUAL COMMUNICATION A communication system used by individuals with more severe hearing impairments, in which fingerspelling or sign language is used in place of spoken language.

MENINGITIS A bacterial or viral inflammation of the membranes encasing the brain and spinal cord. Meningitis can cause problems with hearing and vision or mental retardation.

MENTAL RETARDATION Significantly subaverage general intellectual functioning existing concurrently with deficits in adaptive behavior and manifested during the developmental period. Mental retardation has many possible causes.

MINIMAL BRAIN DYSFUNCTION A general term referring to a suspected malfunction of the central nervous system; it's usually used with children classified as having learning disabilities.

MOBILITY The ability to move safely from one place to another.

MOBILITY TRAINING Training of persons with visual impairments that enables them to detect obstacles in their environment and to move safely from place to place.

MODELING Demonstrating some particular behavior.

MONOPLEGIA Paralysis or dysfunction affecting only one limb.

MUSCULAR DYSTROPHY A muscular disease characterized by weakness and deterioration of the skeletal muscles, resulting in increasing disability.

MYELOMENINGOCELE A characteristic of one type of spina bifida, in which a sac containing part of a malformed spinal cord bulges through a cleft in the spine.

MYOPIA Poor distance vision resulting from an overly long eyeball; it is usually corrected by means of a concave lens.

NEUROLOGIC IMPAIRMENT A general term for a number of conditions that result from injury to or dysfunction of the central nervous system.

NORMALIZATION A principle quite similar to that of mainstreaming, but emphasizing, in addition to education, normal surroundings for place of residence, work, and recreational activities.

NYSTAGMUS Continuous, involuntary movements of the eyeball.

OCCUPATIONAL THERAPY Therapy focused on the upper extremities, with an emphasis on daily living–related activities.

OPTACON A device that converts printed material into either tactile or auditory stimuli, thus permitting persons who are blind to "read" the material.

ORIENTATION The ability to establish one's position in space relative to other objects in the environment without visual clues. Orientation is an essential element in the education of individuals who are blind.

ORTHOPEDIC IMPAIRMENTS Impairments related to disorders of the muscles, joints, or skeleton.

OTITIS MEDIA Inflammation of the middle ear that, without treatment, can cause a permanent conductive hearing loss.

PARAPLEGIA Paralysis or dysfunction of the lower part of the body, including both legs.

PARTIALLY SIGHTED A classification of individuals who have better than 20/200 vision but still have significant visual impairment.

PERCEPTUAL DISORDERS Disorders involving visual, auditory, tactile, or kinesthetic perception that lead to a faulty interpretation of incoming sensory information.

PERSEVERATION Persistent repetition without apparent purpose or the inability to change from one activity to another in a normal manner.

PHENYLKETONURIA (PKU) A metabolic condition that can result in severe mental retardation. PKU can be detected at birth and can be controlled through dietary restrictions.

PHONATION The production of sounds by the larynx.

PHYSICAL THERAPY Therapy focused on the lower body extremities, emphasizing posture, gait, movement, and the prevention of contractures.

POSTLINGUAL HEARING IMPAIRMENT OR DEAFNESS Hearing impairment occurring after speech and language have been developed (also called adventitious hearing impairment).

PRELINGUAL HEARING IMPAIRMENT OR DEAFNESS Hearing impairment occurring before the development of speech and language.

PREREFERRAL INTERVENTION An effort to adjust or remediate educational problems through consultative assistance prior to formal referral for comprehensive assessment and possible classification as disabled.

PROSTHESIS An artificial device designed to replace a missing or impaired body part.

QUADRIPLEGIA Paralysis affecting all four limbs.

REFERRAL The procedure whereby a request for assistance in educational planning is implemented. Referral may result in consultative or collaborative efforts, or it may lead to considerable additional data gathering, including both formal and informal assessment.

REINFORCEMENT A technique that strengthens an existing behavior or teaches a new one.

RESOURCE ROOM A room in which students with special needs receive individual or small-group assistance on a part-time basis.

RESIDUAL HEARING An individual's remaining hearing after a hearing loss.

Rh INCOMPATIBILITY A reaction to opposite Rh factors in a mother and fetus that causes the destruction of red blood cells in the fetus and the release of bilirubin in the blood. Untreated, this will cause brain damage to the fetus.

RETINITIS PIGMENTOSA A hereditary disease of the eye in which the retina gradually deteriorates, causing the field of vision to narrow progressively.

RETROLENTAL FIBROPLASIA A condition in which scar tissue covers the retina. It is usually caused by excessive levels of oxygen administered to premature infants. In most cases the result is retinal detachment and blindness.

RHEUMATOID ARTHRITIS A systemic disease in which inflammation of the joints and related manifestations usually lead to deformity and destruction of the joints.

RUBELLA German measles. When rubella is contracted by a pregnant woman, especially during the first trimester of pregnancy, it can result in such disabilities as hearing or visual impairments, heart defects, or mental retardation.

SCOLIOSIS An abnormal sideways curvature of the spine.

SCREENING Broad-scale testing procedures, usually of groups of children, to determine those who may require more intensive, individual assessment. Vision and hearing screening are the most common kind.

SELF-CONTAINED SPECIAL CLASS A classroom, usually in a regular public school building, that enrolls and serves only children with identified disabilities.

SHELTERED WORKSHOP A structured work facility in which specific work and tasks are provided for individuals who are not yet capable of competitive employment. For some employees this may be terminal employment; for others, it will provide training for future competitive employment.

SPEECH DISORDER Speech that interferes with communication, causes the speaker to be maladjusted, or calls undue attention to the speech as opposed to what the speaker is attempting to communicate.

SPEECHREADING A method used by persons with hearing impairments to decode lip movements and facial expressions in order to understand spoken language.

SPINA BIFIDA A birth defect in which the bones of the spine fail to close during fetal development, often resulting in paralysis in the lower body extremities.

STRABISMUS A condition characterized by the failure of both eyes to focus on an object simultaneously. It is usually caused by weak or unbalanced muscles.

SUPPORTED EMPLOYMENT Employment in meaningful, productive work in an integrated setting with wages for work performed, with long-term, possibly lifelong, support from employment training specialists.

TALENTED A term used to characterize individuals with highly developed skills in some specific arena (such as music, art, or drama) who don't necessarily have an unusually high degree of general intelligence.

TAXONOMY A classification system.

TECHNIQUES OF DAILY LIVING (TDL) Skills such as those required to live independently, perform on the job, manage personal affairs, and travel independently. These skills must be specifically taught to some individuals with visual impairments.

TOTAL COMMUNICATION The total-language approach for individuals with hearing impairments. In this approach there is a balanced emphasis on speech, auditory training, and some system of visual communication.

TRAILING The technique whereby persons with visual impairments lightly touch a surface with the back of the fingertips to locate specific objects or to establish a parallel line of direction.

TRANSITION PROGRAMS Programs that help prepare students with disabilities for a successful transition to adult life, employment, and independent or semi-independent living. Such programs require careful planning and cooperation on the part of school personnel, parents, and the various agencies who may be of assistance during the postschool period. More recently they include transitions from home to school, preschool to school, special class to regular class, and any other move facilitated by advance planning and cooperation.

TRAUMA An injury that is violently produced, or

the condition—physical or mental—that results from shock.

VISUAL ACUITY The measured ability to see; the ability to distinguish images at some established distance.

VISUAL EFFICIENCY The overall effectiveness of one's eyesight. It includes such factors as control of eye movements and speed of visual processing in addition to acuity.

VISUAL PERCEPTION The ability to interpret and organize the information provided by sight.

VOICE DISORDERS (OR VOICE PROBLEMS) Impairments in spoken language such as in pitch, intensity, quality, or flexibility.

REFERENCES

ABROMS, K. K., & BENNETT, J. W. (1980). Current genetic and demographic findings in Down's Syndrome: How are they presented in college textbooks on exceptionality? *Mental Retardation, 18,* 101–107.

ACHENBACH, T. M. (1982). *Developmental psychopathology* (2nd ed.). New York: Wiley.

ACHENBACH, T. M., & EDELBROCK, C. S. (1981). Behavioral problems and competencies reported by parents of normal and disturbed children aged 4 through 16. *Monographs of the Society for Research in Child Development, 46*(Serial No. 188).

ADAMS, J. (1988). You and your hearing impaired child. Washington, DC: Clerc Books/Gallaudet University Press.

ADDIS, G., & LOVITT, T. C. (1987). *Recommendations in the field of learning disabilities.* Unpublished manuscript, University of Washington, Seattle.

ALBER, M. B. (1974). *Listening: A curriculum guide for teachers of visually impaired students.* Springfield: Illinois Office of Education.

ALBERTO, P. A., & TROUTMAN, A. C. (1990). *Applied behavior analysis for teachers.* Columbus, OH: Merrill.

ALGOZZINE, B., MAHEADY, L., SACCA, K. C., O'SHEA, L., & O'SHEA, D. (1990). Sometimes patent medicine works: A reply to Braaten, Kauffman, Braaten, Polsgrove, and Nelson. *Exceptional Children, 56,* 552–557.

ALGOZZINE, R. (1981). Introduction and perspective. In R. Algozzine, R. Schmid, & C. D. Mercer (Eds.), *Childhood behavior disorders: Applied research and educational practice.* Rockville, MD: Aspen.

ALLEN, H. (1986). A study of the achievement patterns of hearing-impaired students: 1974–1983. In A. Schildroth & M. Karchmer (Eds.), *Deaf children in America.* San Diego, CA: College Hill.

ALLEN, K. E. (1984). Federal legislation and young handicapped children. *Topics in Early Childhood Special Education, 5,* 9–18.

ALS, H., LAWHORN, G., BROWN, E., GIBES, R., DUFFY, F. H., McANULTY, G., & BLICKMAN, J. (1986). Individualized behavioral and environmental care for the very low birth weight preterm infant at high risk for bronchopulmonary dysplasia: Neonatal intensive care unit and developmental outcome. *Pediatrics, 78,* 1123–1132.

ALVINO, J. (1989). *Parents' guide to raising a gifted toddler.* Boston: Little, Brown.

AMERICAN ACADEMY OF PEDIATRICS. (1984). Administration of medication in school. *Pediatrics, 74,* 433.

AMERICAN ASSOCIATION OF COLLEGES FOR TEACHER EDUCATION: COMMISSION ON MULTICULTURAL EDUCATION. (1973). No one model American. *Journal of Teacher Education, 4,* 264.

AMERICAN FEDERATION FOR THE BLIND. (1987). *Low vision questions and answers.* New York: Author.

AMERICAN PRINTING HOUSE FOR THE BLIND. (1989). *Distribution of federal quota based on the registration of eligible students.* Louisville, KY: Author.

AMERICAN PSYCHIATRIC ASSOCIATION. (1985). *Facts about teen suicide.* Washington, DC: Author.

AMERICAN PSYCHIATRIC ASSOCIATION. (1987). *Diagnostic and Statistical Manual of Mental Disorders* (3rd ed., rev.). Washington, DC: Author.

AMERICAN SPEECH-LANGUAGE-HEARING AS-SOCIATION. (1982). Definitions: Communicative disorders and variations. *ASHA, 24,* 949–950.

AMERICAN SPEECH-LANGUAGE-HEARING AS-SOCIATION. (1989). Let's talk. *ASHA, 31,* 29–30.

AMERICAN SPEECH-LANGUAGE-HEARING AS-SOCIATION. (1990a). A report to members. *ASHA, 32*(3), 9–11.

AMERICAN SPEECH-LANGUAGE-HEARING AS-SOCIATION. (1990b). Standards for the certificate of clinical competence. *ASHA, 32,* 111–112.

ANDERSON, E., DUNLEA, A., & KEKELIS, L. (1984). Blind children's language: Resolving some differences. *Journal of Child Language, 11,* 645–664.

ANDERSON, W., CHITWOOD, S., & HAYDEN, D. (1990). *Negotiating the special education maze: A guide for parents and teachers.* Rockville, MD: Woodbine House.

ANDREWS, J. F., & MASON, J. M. (1991). Strategy usage among deaf and hearing readers. *Exceptional Children, 56,* 535–545.

ANDREWS, M., & SUMMERS, A. (1988). *Voice therapy for adolescents.* Boston: Little, Brown.

APGAR, V. (1953). APGAR rating scale: A proposal for a new method of resolution of the newborn infant. *Current Research in Anesthesia & Analgesia, 32,* 260–267.

ARAM, C., EKELMAN, B., & NATION, J. (1984). Preschoolers with language disorders: Ten years later. *Journal of Speech and Hearing Research, 27,* 232–244.

ARMSTRONG, R. W., ROSENBAUM, P., AND KING, S. (1987). A randomized controlled trial of a "buddy" programme to improve children's attitudes toward the disabled. *Developmental Medicine & Child Neurology, 29,* 327–336.

ARNOLD, K. M., & HORNETT, D. (1990). Teaching idioms to children who are deaf. *Teaching Exceptional Children, 22*(4), 14–17.

ASHBY, J. E. (1967). Machines, understandings, and learnings: Reflections on technology in education. *The Graduate Journal, 7*(2). Austin: University of Texas Press.

BACA, L. M., & CERVANTES, H. T. (1989). Bilingual special education: A juridicial perspective. In L. M. Baca & H. T. Cervantes, *The bilingual–special education interface.* Columbus, OH: Merrill.

BAILEY, D. B. (1987). Collaborative goal setting with families: Resolving differences in values and priorities for services. *Topics in Early Childhood Special Education, 7*(2), 59–71.

BAILEY, D. B., & SIMEONSSON, R. J. (1988). *Family assessment in early intervention.* Columbus, OH: Merrill.

BAKER, B. L., & BRIGHTMAN, A. J. (1989). *Steps to independence: A skills training guide for parents and teachers of children with special needs* (2nd ed.). Baltimore: Paul H. Brookes.

BAKER, E. M., & STULKEN, E. H. (1938). American research studies concerning the "behavior" type of exceptional child. *Journal of Exceptional Children, 4,* 36–45.

BALIK, B., & HAIG, B. (1988). The student with diabetes. In G. Larson (Ed.), *Managing the school age child with a chronic health condition.* Minneapolis: DCI.

BANDURA, A. (1973). *Aggression: A social learning analysis.* Englewood, Cliffs, NJ: Prentice-Hall.

BARR, M. W. (1913). *Mental defectives: Their history, treatment and training.* Philadelphia: Blakiston.

BARRAGA, N. (1976). *Visual handicaps and learning.* Belmont, CA: Wadsworth.

BARRAGA, N. (1983). *Visual handicaps and learning* (rev. ed.). Austin, TX: Exceptional Resources.

BARRAGA, N. (1986). Sensory perceptual development. In G. Scholl (Ed.), *Foundations of education for blind and visually handicapped children and youth.* New York: American Foundation for the Blind.

BARTHOLOME, W. G. (1982). Good intentions become imperfect in an imperfect world. In J. van Eys (Ed.), *Children with Cancer: Mainstreaming and reintegration.* New York: Spectrum.

BAX, M. C. (1964). Terminology and classification of cerebral palsy. *Developmental Medicine & Child Neurology, 6*(3), 295–297.

BEHRMAN, R. E., VAUGHAN, V. C., & NELSON, W. E. (1987). *Nelson textbook of pediatrics* (13th ed.). Philadelphia: Saunders.

BELL, A. G. (1898). *National education association minutes.*

BERG, F. S. (1987). *Facilitating classroom listening.* Boston: College Hill/Little, Brown.

BERKELL, D. E., & BROWN, J. (1989). *Transitions from school to work for persons with disabilities.* New York: Longman.

BERNSTEIN, D. K., & TIEGERMAN, E. (1989). *Language and communication disorders in children* (2nd ed.). Columbus, OH: Merrill.

BETTLEHEIM, B. (1950). *Love is not enough.* New York: Macmillan.

BETTS, G. (1985). *Autonomous Learner Model: For the gifted and talented.* Greeley, CO: ALPS.

BIGELOW, A. (1987). Early words of blind children. *Journal of Child Language, 14,* 47–56.

BIGGE, J. L. (1991). *Teaching individuals with physical and multiple disabilities* (3rd ed.). Columbus, OH: Merrill.

BILLER, E. F. (1987). *Career decision making for adolescents and young adults with learning disabilities.* Springfield, IL: Charles C Thomas.

BIRCH, J., & STUCKLESS, E. (1963). *Programmed instruction as a device for the correction of written language in deaf adolescents.* Pittsburgh: University of Pittsburgh Press.

BLAIR, J. C. (1990). Front-row seating is not enough for classroom listening. In C. Flexner, D. Wray, & R. Leavitt (Eds.), *How the student with hearing loss can succeed in college: A handbook for students, families and professionals.* Washington, DC: Alexander Graham Bell Association for the Deaf.

BLAKE, A. (1989). Real rainmen: The mystery of

the savant. *Autism Research Review International, 3,* 1–7.

BLALOCH, J. (1984). Persistent auditory language deficits in adults with learning disabilities. *Journal of Learning Disabilities, 15,* 604–609.

BLANKENHORN, D. (1991). The American family is in big trouble. *Bottom Line: Personal, 12*(13), 7.

BLASCH, B. B., LONG, R. G., & GRIFFIN-SHIRLEY, N. (1989). Results of a national survey of electronic travel and use. *Journal of Visual Impairment and Blindness, 83*(9), 449–453.

BLOOM, B. (Ed.). (1956). *Taxonomy of educational objectives. Handbook I: Cognitive Domain.* New York: David McKay.

BOCHNER, J., & ALBERTINI, J. (1988). Language varieties in the deaf population and their acquisition by children and adults. In M. Strong (Ed.), *Language learning and deafness.* Cambridge: Cambridge University Press.

BODNER-JOHNSON, B. (1991). Family conversation style: Its effects on the deaf child's participation. *Exceptional Children, 57,* 502–509.

BOOTHROYD, A. (1990). The impact of technology on the management of deafness. *Volta Review, 92*(4), 72–82.

BORKOWSKI, J. G., PECK, V. A., & DAMBERG, P. R. (1983). Attention, memory, and cognition. In J. L. Matson & J. A. Mulich (Eds.), *Handbook of mental retardation.* New York: Pergamon Press.

BORLAND, J. H. (1989). *Planning and implementing programs for the gifted.* New York: Teachers College Press.

BOWER, E. (1960). *Early identification of emotionally handicapped children in school.* Springfield, IL: Charles C Thomas.

BOWER, E. (1981). *Early identification of emotionally handicapped children in school* (3rd ed.). Springfield, IL: Charles C Thomas.

BOWER, E. (1982). Defining emotional disturbance: Public policy and research. *Psychology in the Schools, 19,* 55–60.

BRAATEN, S., KAUFFMAN, J., BRAATEN, B., POLSGROVE, L., & NELSON, C. M. (1988). The regular education initiative: Patent medicine for behavioral disorders. *Exceptional Children, 5,* 21–28.

BRANDWEIN, H. (1973). The battered child: A definite and significant factor in mental retardation. *Mental Retardation, 11*(5), 50–51.

BRAZELTON, T. B. (1984). *Neonatal behavior assessment scale.* Philadelphia: Lippincott.

BREDEKAMP, S. (Ed.). (1989). *Developmentally appropriate practice in early childhood programs serving children from birth through age 8* (rev. ed.). Washington, DC: NAEYC.

BREWER, D. W. (1975). Early diagnostic signs and symptoms of laryngeal disease. *Laryngoscope, 85,* 499–515.

BRICKER, D. D. (1986). *Early education of at-risk and handicapped infants, toddlers, and preschool children.* Glenview, IL: Scott, Foresman.

BRICKER, J. T., & McNAMARA, D. G. (1983). Heart disorders. In J. Umbreit (Ed.), *Physical disabilities and health impairments: An introduction.* Columbus, OH: Merrill.

BRODY, E. B. (1988). Advocacy for healthy infancy-prenatal intervention. In E. D. Hibbs (Ed.), *Children and families: Studies in prevention and intervention.* Madison, WI: International Universities Press.

BROLIN, D. (Ed.). (1978, 1983, 1988). *Life-centered career education: A competency based approach* (1st, 2nd, 3rd eds.). Reston, VA: Council for Exceptional Children.

BROLIN, D., & SCHATZMAN, B. (1989). Lifelong career development. In D. Berkel & J. Brown, *Transitions from school to work for persons with disabilities.* New York: Longman.

BRONFENBRENNER, U. (1976). The experimental ecology of education. *Educational Researcher, 5,* 5–15.

BROOKS, M. B. (1983). Limb deficiencies. In J. Umbreit (Ed.), *Physical disabilities and health impairments: An introduction.* Columbus, OH: Merrill.

BROOKS, P. H., & BAUMEISTER, A. A. (1977). A plea for consideration of ecological validity in the experimental psychology of mental retardation: A guest editorial. *American Journal of Mental Deficiency, 81,* 407–416.

BROWN, L., SHIRAGA, B., YORK, J., KESSLER, K., STROM, B., ROGAN, P., SWEET, M., ZANELLA, K., VANDEVENTER, P., & LOOMIS, R. (1984). Integrated work opportunities for adults with severe handicaps: The extended training option. *Journal of the Association for Persons with Severe Handicaps, 9,* 262–269.

BROWN, S., MAXWELL, M., & BROWNING, L. (1990). Relations in public: Hearing parents and hearing impaired children. *Journal of Childhood Communication Disorders, 13*(1), 43–61.

BRYANT, D., LYONS, C., & WASAIK, B. H. (1991). Ethical issues involved in home visiting. *Topics in Early Childhood Special Education, 10*(4), 92–107.

BUCHANAN, M., & WOLF, J. S. (1986). A comprehensive study of learning disabled adults. *Journal of Learning Disabilities, 19,* 34–38.

BUTTRILL, J., NIIZAWA, C. B., BIEMER, C., TAKA-HASHI, C., & HEARN, S. (1989). Serving the language learning disabled adolescent: A strategies based model. *Language, Speech & Hearing Services in Schools, 20,* 185–204.

CAIN, L. (1976). Parent Groups: Their role in a better life for the handicapped. *Exceptional Children, 42,* 432–437.

CALIFORNIA OFFICE OF BILINGUAL AND BICULTURAL EDUCATION. (1992). *Suggested standards for bilingual, bicultural programs.* Sacramento: Author.

CARLSON, E. (1984). *Human genetics.* Lexington, MA: Heath.

CARTA, J., SCHWARTZ, H., ATWATER, J., & Mc-CONNELL, S. (1991). Developmentally appropriate practice: Appraising its usefulness for young children. *Topics in Early Childhood Special Education, 11*(1), 1–20.

CARTER, D. J. (1990). Message from the president: What have educators learned about using microcomputers? *ASCD: Update, 32*(9), 2.

CARTER, J., & SUGAI, G. (1989). Survey on pre-referral practices: Responses from state departments of education. *Exceptional Children, 55,* 298–302.

CARTLEDGE, G., PAUL, P., JACKSON, D., & COCHRAN, L. (1991). Teachers' perceptions of the social skills of adolescents with hearing impairments in residential and public school settings. *Remedial and Special Education, 12*(2), 34–39.

CARTWRIGHT, G. P., CARTWRIGHT, C. A., AND WARD, M. E. (1984). *Educating special learners.* Belmont, CA: Wadsworth.

CASTRO, G., & MASTROPIERI, M. (1985). *The efficacy of early intervention programs for handicapped children: A meta analysis.* Unpublished manuscript, Early Intervention Research Institute, Utah State University.

CHACE, M. (1958). Dance in growth or treatment settings. *Music Therapy, 1,* 119–121.

CHADSEY-RUSCH, J., RUSCH, F. R., & PHELPS, L. A. (1989). Analysis and synthesis of transition issues. In D. Berkell & J. Brown (Eds.), *Transition from school to work for persons with disabilities.* New York: Longman.

CHALFANT, J. (1985). Identifying learning disabled students: A summary of the national task force report. *Learning Disabilities Focus, 1,* 9–20.

CHALFANT, J., & SCHEFFLIN, M. (1969). *Central processing dysfunctions in children.* NINDS Monograph No. 9. Bethesda, MD: U.S. Department of Health, Education and Welfare.

CHANEY, C., AND FRODYMA, D. A. (1982). A noncategorical program for preschool language development. *Teaching Exceptional Children, 14,* 152–155.

CHENEY, C., & MORSE, W. C. (1972). Psychodynamic interventions in emotional disturbance. In W. C. Rhodes & M. L. Tracy (Eds.), *A study of child variance: Vol. 2. Interventions.* Ann Arbor: University of Michigan Press.

CHILD ABUSE AND THE HANDICAPPED CHILD. (1987). (ERIC Digest No. 446). Reston, VA: Author. ERIC Clearinghouse on Handicapped and Gifted Children.

CHOMSKY, N. (1957). *Language and the mind.* New York: Harcourt, Brace, Jovanovich.

CHOMSKY, N. (1972). *Syntactic structures.* The Hague: Mouton.

CLARIZIO, H. F., & McCOY, B. (1976). *Behavior disorders in children.* New York: Thomas Y. Crowell.

CLARK, B. (1988). *Growing up gifted* (3rd ed.). Columbus, OH: Merrill.

CLARK, G., TONG, Y. C., & PATRICK, J. F. (Eds.). (1990). *Cochlear prosthesis.* New York: Churchill Livingstone.

CLARK, G. M. (1979). *Career education for the handicapped child in the elementary classroom.* Denver: Love Publishing.

CLARK, G. M., & KOLSTOE, O. P. (1990). *Career development and transition: Education for adolescents with disabilities.* Boston: Allyn & Bacon.

CLARK, K. L. (1988). Barriers or Enablers? Mobility devices for visually impaired and multi-handicapped infants & preschoolers. *Education of the visually handicapped, 20*(3), 115–132.

CLARKE, A. D., & CLARKE, A. M. (1976). *Early experience: Myth and evidence.* New York: Free Press.

CLARKE, C. A., & McCONNELL, R. B. (1972). *Prevention of Rh-hemolytic Disease.* Springfield, IL: Charles C Thomas.

CLEMENTS, S. D. (1966). *Minimal brain dysfunction in children* (PHS Publication No. 1415). Washington, DC: U.S. Department of Health, Education and Welfare.

COLE, P. R. (1987). Recognizing language disorders. In F. N. Martin (Ed.), *Hearing disorders in children.* Austin, TX: Pro-Ed.

COLEMAN, J. C. (1972). *Abnormal psychology and modern life* (4th ed.). Glenview, IL: Scott, Foresman.

COLLIER, C. (1988). *Assessing minority students with learning and behavior problems.* Lindale, TX: Hamilton Publications.

COLLIER, C. (1989). Mainstreaming and bilingual exceptional children. In L. Baca & H. Cervantes (Eds.), *The bilingual–special education interface.* Columbus, OH: Merrill.

COMMISSION ON THE EDUCATION OF THE DEAF. (1988). *Toward equality: Education of the deaf.* Washington, DC: U.S. Government Printing Office.

COMMISSION ON INSTRUCTIONAL TECHNOLOGY. (1970). *To improve learning: An evaluation of instructional technology: Vol. 1.* New York: Bowker.

CONTURE, E. G. (1990). *Stuttering.* Englewood Cliffs, NJ: Prentice-Hall.

COOK, R. E., TESSIER, A., & ARMBRUSTER, V. B. (1987). *Adapting early childhood curricula for children with special needs.* Columbus, OH: Merrill.

CORREA, V. I. (1989). Involving culturally diverse families in the educational process. In S. H. Fradd & M. J. Weismantel (Eds.), *Meeting the needs of culturally and linguistically different students: A handbook for educators.* Boston: College Hill.

CORRIGAN, J. J., & DAMIANO, M. L. (1983). Blood diseases. In J. Umbreit (Ed.), *Physical disabilities and health impairments: An introduction.* Columbus, OH: Merrill.

COSTELLO, C. G. (1981). Childhood depression. In E. J. Mash & L. G. Terdal (Eds.), *Behavioral assessment of childhood disorders.* New York: Guilford.

COTT, A. (1985). *Dr. Cott's help for your learning disabled child.* New York: Times Books.

COUNCIL FOR EXCEPTIONAL CHILDREN POLICIES MANUAL. (1989). Reston, VA: Council for Exceptional Children.

COX, J., DANIEL, N., & BOSTON, J. B. (1985). *Educating able learners: Programs and promising practices.* Austin: University of Texas Press.

COX, L. C. (1988). Screening the high-risk newborn for hearing loss: The crib-o-gram *v.* the auditory brain stem response. *Infants and Young Children, 1*(1), 71–81.

CREASY, R. K., & RESNIK, R. (1989). *Maternal-fetal medicine: Principles and practices* (2nd ed.). Philadelphia: Saunders.

CROOK, W. (1974). *The allergic tension-fatigue syndrome*. New York: Insight Books.

CROOK, W. (1980). Can what a child eats make him dull, stupid, or hyperactive? *Journal of Learning Disabilities, 13*, 281–286.

CRUICKSHANK, W., BENTZEN, F., RATZBERG, F., & TANNHAUSER, M. (1961). *A teaching method for brain-injured and hyperactive children*. Syracuse, NY: Syracuse University Press.

CRYSTAL, J. D. (1985). *A dictionary of linguistics and phonetics*. Oxford: Basil Blackwell.

CULATTA, R., & CULATTA, B. K. (1985). Communication disorders. In W. H. Berdine & A. E. Blackhurst (Eds.), *Exceptional children and youth* (4th ed.). Boston; Little, Brown.

CULLINAN, D., & EPSTEIN, M. H. (1986). Behavior disorders. In N. Haring (Ed.), *Exceptional children and youth* (4th ed.). Columbus, OH: Merrill.

CUMMINS, J. (1984). *Bilingualism and special education: Issues in assessment and pedagogy*. San Diego, CA: College Hill.

CURRY, S. A., & HATLIN, P. H. (1988). Meeting the unique educational needs of visually impaired pupils through appropriate placement. *Journal of Visual Impairment and Blindness, 82*(10), 417–424.

DAHL, K. (1985). Research on writing development. *Volta Review, 87,* 35–46.

DALY, D. (1986). The clutterer. In K. St. Louis (Ed.), *The atypical stutterer*. Orlando, FL: Academic Press.

DAMSTE, P. H., & LEHRMAN, J. W. (1975). *An introduction to voice pathology*. Springfield, IL: Charles C Thomas.

DANIEL, N., & COX, J. (1988). *Flexible pacing for able learners*. Reston, VA: Council for Exceptional Children.

DAVIDSON, J. (1989). *Children and computers together in the early classroom*. Albany, NY: Delmar.

DAVIES, D. (1991). Schools reaching out: Family, school and community partnerships for student success. *Phi Delta Kappan, 72*(5), 376–382.

DeAVILLA, E. A., & HAVASSY, B. E. (1975). Piagetian alternatives to I.Q.: Mexican-American study. In N. Hobbs (Ed.), *Issues in the classification of exceptional children*. San Francisco: Jossey-Bass.

DECKER, S. N., & DeFRIES, J. C. (1981). Cognitive ability profiles in families of reading disabled children. *Developmental Medicine & Child Neurology, 23*(2), 217–227.

DEDE, C. J. (1990). Educators, take hold of the future: How educators can anticipate and shape emerging developments in instructional technology. *Electronic Learning, 9*(1), 8–9.

deHIRSCH, K. (1952). Specific dyslexia or strephosymbolia? *Folia Phoniatrica, 4,* 231–248.

DE LA CRUZ, F. (1985). Fragile x syndrome. *American Journal of Mental Deficiency, 90,* 119–123.

DELAND, F. (1931). *The story of lipreading*. Washington, DC: Volta Bureau.

DeMYER, M. K., HINGTGEN, J. M., & JACKSON, R. K. (1981). Infantile autism reviewed: A decade of research. *Schizophrenia Bulletin, 7,* 388–451.

DENNETT, D. C. (1990). Can machines think? In R. Kurzweil (Ed.), *The age of intelligent machines*. Cambridge: MIT Press.

DePIETRO, L. (Ed.). (1987). *Educating deaf children: An introduction*. Washington, DC: National Information Center on Deafness, Gallaudet University.

DESJARLAIS, D. C. (1972). Mental illness of social deviance. In W. C. Rhodes and M. L. Tracy (Eds.), *A study of child variance* (Vol. 1). Ann Arbor: University of Michigan Press.

D'IGNAZIO, F. (1990). Integrating the work environment of the 1990's into today's classroom. *T-H-E, Technological Horizons in Education Journal, 18*(2), 95–96.

DLM. (1988). *Apple computer resources in special education and rehabilitation*. Allen, TX: Author.

DUBLINSKE, S. (1989). Action: School services. *Language, Speech and Hearing Services in the Schools, 20*(2), 222–224.

DUMARS, K. W., DURAN-FLORES, D., FOSTER, C., & STILLS, S. (1987). Screening and diagnosing handicapped infants. *Topics in Early Childhood Special Education, 3*(1), 14–28.

DUNN, N. L., McCARTAN, K. W., & FUQUA, R. W. (1988). Young children with orthopedic handicaps: Self-knowledge about their disability. *Exceptional Children, 55,* 249–252.

DUNST, C. J., LEET, H., & TRIVETTE, C. M. (1988). Family resources, personal well-being, and early intervention. *Journal of Special Education, 22,* 108–116.

DURAN, E. (1988). The culturally and linguistically different student. In E. Duran (Ed.), *Teaching the moderately and severely handicapped student and autistic adolescent*. Springfield, IL: Charles C Thomas.

DURKHEIM, E. (1951). *Suicide*. New York: Free Press.

DVORINE, I. (1953). *Dvorine pseudo-isochromatic plates* (2nd ed.). Baltimore: Waverly Press.

DYRCIA, S., ET AL. *v.* BOARD OF EDUCATION OF THE CITY OF NEW YORK. (1979). 79c. 2562 (E.D.NY).

EARLY YEARS. (1991, April 17). *Education Week*, p. 8.

EHLERS, V. L., & RUFFIN, M. (1990). The Missouri Project—Parents as teachers. *Focus on Exceptional Children, 23*(2), 1–14.

EISELE, J. E., & EISELE, M. E. (1990). *Educational technology: A planning and resource guide supporting curriculum*. New York: Garland.

EISENBURG, L. S., KIRK, K. I., THIELEMEIR, M. A., LUXFORD, W. M., & CUNNINGHAM, J. K. (1986). Cochlear implants in children: Speech production and auditory discrimination. *Otolaryngologic Clinics of North America, 19,* 409–421.

ELKIND, D. (1986). Formal education and early childhood education: An essential difference. *Phi Delta Kappan, 67,* 636.

ELLIS, E. S., & SABORNIE, E. J. (1986). Effective instruction with microcomputers: Promises, practices and preliminary findings. *Focus on Exceptional Children, 19*(4), 1–16.

ELLIS, N. R. (1970). Memory processes in retardates and normals. *International Review of Research in Mental Retardation, 4*(1), 4.

EMERICK, L. L., & HAYNES, W. O. (1986). *Diagnosis and evaluation in speech pathology* (3rd ed.). Englewood Cliffs, NJ: Prentice-Hall.

EPLEY, T. M. (1985). *Futuristics: A handbook for teachers of the gifted/talented.* Ventura, CA: National/State Leadership Training Institute on the Gifted and Talented.

EPSTEIN, C. J. (1988). New approaches to the study of Down syndrome. In F. Menolascino & J. Stark (Eds.), *Preventive and curative intervention in mental retardation.* Baltimore: Paul H. Brookes.

EPSTEIN, J. (1989). On parents and schools: A conversation with Joyce Epstein. *Educational Leadership, 47*(2), 26.

EPSTEIN, J. L. (forthcoming). Five types of parent involvement; linking practices and outcomes. In *School and family connections: Preparing educators to involve families.*

EPSTEIN, M. H., KINDER, D., & BURSUCK, B. (1989). The academic status of adolescents with behavioral disorders. *Behavioral Disorders, 14*(3), 157–165.

EPSTEIN, S. (1987). A medical approach to hearing loss. In S. Schwartz (Ed.), *Choices in deafness: A parent's guide.* Kensington, MD: Woodbine House.

ERICKSON, M. T. (1987). *Behavior disorders of children and adolescents.* Englewood Cliffs, NJ: Prentice-Hall.

ERIN, J. N. (1990). Language samples from visually impaired four- and five-year olds. *Journal of Childhood Communication Disorders, 13*(2), 181–191.

ESPOSITO, L., & CAMPBELL, P. (1987). Computers and severely and physically handicapped individuals. In J. D. Lindsey (Ed.), *Computers and exceptional individuals.* Columbus, OH: Merrill.

EWOLDT, C. (1985). A descriptive study of the developing literacy of young hearing impaired children. *Volta Review, 87,* 109–126.

EXECUTIVE COMMITTEE OF THE COUNCIL FOR CHILDREN WITH BEHAVIORAL DISORDERS. (1987). Position paper on definition and identification of students with behavioral disorders. *Behavior Disorders, 13*(1), 9–19.

FAIRWEATHER, J. S., & SHAVER, D. M. (1991). Making the transition to postsecondary education and training. *Exceptional Children, 57,* 264–270.

FARNSWORTH, D. (1947). *The Farnsworth Dichotomous Test for Color Blindness.* San Antonio, TX: Psychological Corporation.

FARRELL, G. (1956). *The story of blindness.* Cambridge: Harvard University Press.

FEDERAL REGISTER. (1977). Definition and criteria for defining students as learning disabled (Vol. 42, No. 250, p. 65083). Washington, DC: U.S. Government Printing Office.

FEINGOLD, B. (1975). *Why your child is hyperactive.* New York: Random House.

FEINGOLD, B. (1976). Hyperkinesis and learning disabilities linked to the ingestion of artificial food colors and flavors. *Journal of Learning Disabilities, 9,* 554.

FELDMAN, H. (1970). *A history of audiology.* New York: Columbia University Press.

FENICHEL, C. (1966). Psychoeducational approaches for seriously disturbed children in the classroom. In P. Knoblock (Ed.), *Intervention approaches in educating emotionally disturbed children.* Syracuse, NY: Syracuse University Press.

FENICHEL, C., FREEDMAN, A. M., & KLAPPER, L. (1960). A day school for schizophrenic children. *American Journal of Orthopsychiatry, 30,* 130–143.

FERNALD, G. (1943). *Remedial techniques in basic school subjects.* New York: McGraw-Hill.

FERRELL, K. A. (1986). Infancy and early childhood. In G. T. Scholl (Ed.), *Foundations of education for blind and visually handicapped children and youth.* New York: American Foundation for the Blind.

FERSTER, J. (1973). A functional analysis of depression. *American Psychologist, 28,* 857–869.

FEWELL, R. R. (1991). Parenting moderately handicapped persons. In M. Seligman (Ed.), *The family with a handicapped child* (2nd ed.). Boston: Allyn & Bacon.

FEWELL, R. R., & OELWEIN, P. L. (1991). Effective early intervention: Results from the model preschool program for children with Down syndrome and other developmental delays. *Topics in Early Childhood Special Education, 11*(1), 56–58.

FLEXNER, C., WRAY, D., & BLACK, T. (1990). We're all in this together: The support group for college students with hearing loss. In C. Flexner, D. Wray, and R. Leavitt (Eds.), *How the student with a hearing loss can succeed in college.* Washington, DC: Alexander Graham Bell Association for the Deaf.

FLEXNER, C., WRAY, D., & LEAVITT, R. (1990). *How the student with a hearing loss can succeed in college.* Washington, DC: Alexander Graham Bell Association for the Deaf.

FOLSTEIN, S., & RUTTER, M. (1977). Infantile autism: A study of 21 pairs. *Journal of Child Psychology and Psychiatry, 18,* 297–321.

FOREHAND, R., McCOMBS, A., & BRODY, G. H. (1987). The relationship between parental depressive mood states and child functioning. *Advances in Behavior Research & Therapy, 9,* 1–20.

FORNESS, S. R. (1988). School characteristics of children and adolescents with depression. In R. B. Rutherford, C. M. Nelson, & S. R. Forness (Eds.), *Bases of severe behavioral disorders of children and youth.* Boston: Little, Brown.

FOXX, R. M., & AZRIN, N. H. (1973). *Toilet training and the retarded: A rapid program for day and nighttime independent toileting.* Champaign, IL: Research Press.

FRAIBURG, S. (1977). *Insights from the blind: Comparative studies of blind and sighted infants.* New York: Basic Books.

FRANKENBURG, W. K., DODDS, J., & FANDAL, A. (1975). *Denver developmental screening test.* Denver: LADOCA Project.

FRAZER, K. (1989). *Someone at school has AIDS: A guide to developing policies for students and school staff members who are infected with HIV.* Alexandria, VA: National Association of State Boards of Education.

FREELAND, A. (1989). *Deafness: The facts.* New York: Oxford University Press.

FREUND, H. (1966). *Psychopathology and problems of stuttering.* Springfield, IL: Charles C Thomas.

FRIDRIKSSON, T., & STEWART, D. A. (1988). From the concrete to the abstract: Mathematics for deaf children. *American Annals of the Deaf, 133*(1), 51–55.

FUCHS, L. S., & FUCHS, D. (1990). Traditional academic assessment: An overview. In R. Gable & J. Hendrickson (Eds.), *Assessing students with special needs.* New York: Longman.

FURST, M. (1990). Self respect: Programs that give learning-disabled students a sense of pride in learning. *Electronic Learning, 9*(2), 42–46.

FURTH, H. (1971). Education for thinking. *Journal of Rehabilitation of the Deaf, 5*(1), 7–71.

GADOW, K. (1986). *Children on medication: Vol. 1. Hyperactivity, learning disabilities, and mental retardation.* Boston: College Hill.

GADOW, K., & POLING, A. (1988). *Pharmacotherapy and mental retardation.* Boston: College Hill.

GAGNÉ, R. M. (1987). Introduction to Instructional Technology. In R. M. Gagné (Ed.), *Instructional technology: Foundations.* Hillsdale, NJ: Erlbaum.

GALLAGHER, J. (1985). *Teaching the gifted child* (3rd ed.). Boston: Allyn & Bacon.

GALLAGHER, W. F. (1988). Categorical services in the age of integration: Paradox or contradiction? *Journal of Visual Impairment and Blindness, 82,* 221–228.

GANNON, J. R. (1981). *Deaf heritage: A narrative history of deaf America.* Silver Springs, MD: National Association for the Deaf.

GARGIULO, R. M. (1985). *Working with parents of exceptional children: A guide for professionals.* Boston: Houghton Mifflin.

GARLAND, C., BLACK, T., & JESIEN, G. (1986). *The future of outreach: A DEC position paper.* Unpublished manuscript, the Division for Early Childhood, Council for Exceptional Children.

GARLAND, C., STONE, N. W., SWANSON, J., & WOODRUFF, G. (Eds.). (1981). Early intervention for children with special needs and their families: Findings and recommendations. INTERACT. Seattle: University of Washington, Western States Technical Assistance Resource (WESTAR).

GARTNER, A., LIPSKY, D. K., & TURNBULL, A. (1990). *Supporting families with a child with a disability: An international outlook.* Baltimore: Paul H. Brookes.

GATES, C. (1985). Survey of multiply handicapped visually impaired children of the Rocky Mountain/Great Plains region. *Journal of Visual Impairment and Blindness, 79,* 385–391.

GEARHEART, B. (1980). *Special education for the 80's.* St. Louis, MO: C. V. Mosby.

GEARHEART, B., & LITTON, F. (1979). *The trainable retarded: A foundations approach.* St. Louis, MO: C. V. Mosby.

GEARHEART, B., WEISHAHN, M., & GEARHEART, C. (1992). *Exceptional students in the regular classroom* (5th ed.). Columbus, OH: Merrill.

GEARHEART, B. R., & GEARHEART, C. J. (1985). *Learning disabilities: Educational strategies* (4th ed.). Columbus, OH: Merrill.

GEARHEART, B. R., & GEARHEART, C. J. (1989). *Learning disabilities: Educational strategies* (5th ed.). Columbus, OH: Merrill.

GEARHEART, C. J., & GEARHEART, B. R. (1990). *Introduction to special education assessment.* Denver, CO: Love Publishing.

GEIGER, K. (1991, March 27). A remarkable teaching tool: Improving learning through technology. *Education Week,* p. 4.

GELFAND, D. M., JENSON, W. R., & DREW, C. J. (1982). *Understanding children's behavior disorders.* New York: Holt, Rinehart & Winston.

GELLER, B., CHESTNUT, E. C., MILLER, M., PRICE, J., & YATES, E. (1985). Preliminary data on DSM III associated features of major depressive disorders in children and adolescents. *American Journal of Psychiatry 142,* 643–644.

GENTRY, R. G. (1988, May/June). Why we won at Gallaudet. *Gallaudet Today,* pp. 12–13.

GEORGE, N. L., & LEWIS, T. J. (1991). EASE: Exit assistance for special educators. *Teaching Exceptional Children, 23*(2), 34–39.

GERBER, P. J. (1986). Learning disabled adult nexus: Emerging American issues and European perspectives. *Journal of Learning Disabilities, 19,* 2–4.

GERBER, P. J., BANBURY, M. M., MILLER, J. H., & GRIFFEN, H. D. (1986). Special educator's perceptions of parental participation in the individual education plan process. *Psychology in the Schools, 23,* 158–163.

GERDTZ, J., & BERGMAN, J. (1990). *Autism: A practical guide for those who help others.* New York: Continuum.

GETZEL, E. E. (1990). Entering postsecondary programs: Early individualized planning. *Teaching Exceptional Children, 23*(1), 51–53.

GIAGO, J. T. (1978). *The aboriginal sin.* San Francisco: The Indian Historian Press.

GICKLING, E. E., & THOMPSON, V. P. (1985). A personal view of curriculum-based assessment. *Exceptional Children, 52,* 205–218.

GILGOFF, I. S. (1983). Spinal cord injury. In J. Umbreit (Ed.), *Physical disabilities and impairments: An introduction.* Columbus, OH: Merrill.

GLEASON, J. B. (1985). *The development of language.* Columbus, OH: Merrill.

GLIDEWELL, J. C., & SWALLOW, C. S. (1968). *The prevalence of maladjustment in elementary schools.* Chicago: University of Chicago Press.

GOLDEN, G. S. (1987a). Common seizure disorders. In M. Gottlieb & J. Williams (Eds.), *Textbook of developmental pediatrics.* New York: Plenum.

GOLDEN, G. S. (1987b). Common neuromotor disorders. In M. Gottlieb & J. Williams (Eds.), *Textbook of developmental pediatrics.* New York: Plenum.

GOLLNICK, D., & CHINN, P. (1986). *Multicultural education in a pluralistic society* (2nd ed.). Columbus, OH: Merrill.

GOLUMBEK, H., & GARFINKEL, B. (1983). *The adolescent and mood disturbance.* New York: International Universities Press.

GONZALES, E. (1982). Issues in assessment of minorities. In H. L. Swanson & B. L. Watson (Eds.), *Educational and psychological assessment of exceptional children.* St. Louis, MO: C. V. Mosby.

GOUGH, P. B. (1991). Tapping parent power. *Phi Delta Kappan, 72*(5), 339.

GRADEN, J., CASEY, A., & CHRISTENSON, S. (1985). Implementing a prereferral system: Part I. The model. *Exceptional Children, 51,* 377–384.

GRADEN, J. L. (1989). Redefining "prereferral" intervention as intervention assistance: Collaboration between general and special education. *Exceptional Children, 56,* 227–231.

GRANT, R. (1991). The special needs of homeless children: Early intervention at a welfare hotel. *Topics in Early Childhood Special Education, 10*(4), 76–91.

GRAU, P. N. (1985). Counseling the gifted girl. *Gifted Child Today, 38,* 8–11.

GREENLAW, M. J., & McINTOSH, M. E. (1988). *Educating the gifted: A sourcebook.* Chicago: American Library Association.

GREGORY, D. A., STARNES, W. T., & BLAYLOCK, A. W. (1988). Finding and nurturing potential giftedness among Black and Hispanic students. In A. A. Ortiz & B. A. Ramiriz (Eds.), *Schools and the culturally diverse student.* Reston, VA: Council for Exceptional Children.

GRESHAM, F. M. (1985). Behavior disorder assessment: Conceptual, definitional and practical considerations. *School Psychology Review, 14,* 495–509.

GROSSMAN, H. J. (1983). *Classification in mental retardation.* Washington, DC: The American Association on Mental Retardation.

GUETZLOE, E. C. (1989). *Youth suicide: What the educator should know.* Reston, VA: Council for Exceptional Children.

GUILFORD, J. P. (1959a). Three faces of intellect. *American Psychologist, 14,* 469–479.

GUILFORD, J. P. (1959b). Traits of creativity. In H. H. Anderson (Ed.), *Creativity and its cultivation.* New York: Harper.

GUILFORD, J. P. (1971). *Creativity tests for children.* Beverly Hills, CA: Sheridan Psychological Services.

HAFER, J. C., & RICHMOND, E. (1988). What hearing parents should know about deaf culture. *Perspectives, 7*(1), 2–4.

HAGBORG, W. (1987). Hearing impaired students and sociometric ratings: An exploratory study. *Volta Review, 89,* 221–223.

HAKUTA, K. (1986). *Mirror of language: The debate on bilingualism.* New York: Basic Books.

HALLAHAN, D. P., & CRUICKSHANK, W. (1973). *Psychoeducational foundations of learning disabilities.* Englewood Cliffs, NJ: Prentice-Hall.

HALLAHAN, D. P., HALL, R. J., IANNA, S. O., KNEEDLER, R. D., LLOYD, J. W., LOPER, A. B., & REEVE, R. E. (1983). Summary of research findings at the University of Virginia Learning Disabilities Research Institute. *Exceptional Education Quarterly, 4*(1), 95–114.

HALLAHAN, D. P., & KAUFFMAN, J. M. (1988). *Exceptional children: Introduction to special education* (4th ed.). Englewood Cliffs, NJ: Prentice-Hall.

HALPERIN, J. M., GITTELMAN, R., KLEIN, D., & RUDEL, R. (1984). Reading disabled hyperactive children: A distinct subgroup of attention deficit disorder with hyperactivity. *Journal of Abnormal Child Psychology, 12,* 1–14.

HALPERIN, M. (1979). *Helping maltreated children: School and community involvement.* St. Louis, MO: C. V. Mosby.

HALPERN, A. (1985). Transition: A look at the foundations. *Exceptional Children, 51,* 479–486.

HALPIN, G., PAYNE, G., & ELLETT, C. (1973). Biographical correlates of the creative personality: Gifted adolescents. *Exceptional Children, 39,* 652–653.

HAM, R. (1986). *Techniques of stuttering therapy.* Englewood Cliffs, NJ: Prentice-Hall.

HAMAYAN, E. V., & DAMICO, J. S. (Eds.). (1991). *Limiting bias in the assessment of bilingual students.* Austin, TX: Pro-Ed.

HAMMILL, D., LEIGH, J., McNUTT, J. G., & LARSEN, S. (1991). A new definition of learning disabilities. *Learning Disability Quarterly, 4*(4), 336–342.

HANNAFORD, A. E. (1987). Computers and exceptional individuals. In J. D. Lindsey (Ed.), *Computers and exceptional individuals.* Columbus, OH: Merrill.

HANSON, M. J., & KRENTZ, M. K. (1986). *Teaching the young child with motor delays: A guide for early intervention program personnel.* San Francisco: Department of Special Education, San Francisco State University.

HANSON, M. J., & LYNCH, E. W. (1989). *Early intervention: Implementing child and family services for infants and toddlers who are at-risk or disabled.* Austin, TX: Pro-Ed.

HANSON, V. (1983). Juvenile rheumatoid arthritis. In J. Umbreit (Ed.), *Physical disabilities and health impairments: An introduction.* Columbus, OH: Merrill.

HARDMAN, M. L., DREW, C. J., & EGAN, M. W. (1984). *Human exceptionality: Society, school and family.* Boston: Allyn & Bacon.

HARDMAN, M. L., DREW, C. J., & EGAN, M. W.

(1987). *Human exceptionality: Society, school and family* (2nd ed.). Boston: Allyn & Bacon.

HARDMAN, M. L., DREW, C. J., EGAN, M. W., & WOLF, B. (1990). *Exceptionality: Society, school & family.* Boston: Allyn & Bacon.

HARING, N., & McCORMICK, L. (Eds.). (1990). *Exceptional children and youth* (5th ed.). Columbus, OH: Merrill.

HARING, T. G., BREEN, C., PITTS-CONWAY, V., LEE, M., & GAYLORD-ROSS, R. (1987). Adolescent peer tutoring and special friend experiences. *Journal of the Association for Persons with Severe Handicaps, 12,* 280–286.

HARLEY, R. D. (Ed.). (1983). *Pediatric ophthalmology* (2nd ed.). Philadelphia: Saunders.

HARLEY, R. K., GARCIA, M., & WILLIAMS, M. F. (1989). Educational placement of visually impaired children. *Journal of Visual Impairment and Blindness, 83*(10), 512–517.

HARLEY, R. K., TRUAN, B. B., & SANFORD, L. D. (1987). *Communication skills for visually impaired learners.* Springfield, IL: Charles C Thomas.

HARNISCH, D. L., & FISHER, A. T. (1989). *Transition — literature review: Vol 3. Educational, employment and independent living outcomes.* Urbana-Champaign, IL: University of Illinois Press.

HARRINGTON, R., & GIBSON, E. (1986). Preassessment procedures for learning disabled children: Are they effective? *Journal of Learning Disabilities, 19,* 548–551.

HARRIS, D. B. (1963). *Children's drawings as measures of intellectual maturity: A revision and extension of the Goodenough Draw-a-Man Test.* New York: Harcourt Brace Jovanovich.

HARRIS, F. C., & AMMERMAN, R. T. (1987). Depression and suicide in children and adolescents. *Education and Treatment of Children, 9,* 334–343.

HARRIS, G. A. (1986). Barriers to the delivery of speech, language, and hearing services to Native Americans. In O. L. Taylor (Ed.), *Nature of communication disorders in culturally and linguistically diverse populations.* Boston: College Hill.

HATFIELD, E. M. (1975). Why are they blind? *Sight Saving Review, 45,* 3–22.

HATLIN, P., & CURRY, S. (1987). In support of specialized programs for blind and visually impaired children: The impact of vision loss on learning. *Journal of Visual Impairments & Blindness, 81,* 7–13.

HAWLEY, A. (1950). *Human ecology: A theory of community structure.* New York: Ronald Press.

HAWTON, K. (1986). *Suicide and attempted suicide among children and adolescents.* Newbury Park, CA: Sage.

HAYES-ROTH, F., WATERMAN, D., & LENAT, D. (1983). *Building expert systems.* Reading, MA: Addison-Wesley.

HEAD, D. N. (1989). The future of low incidence training programs: A national problem. *In RE:View, 21*(3), 145–151.

HECHT, J. B., BADARAK, G., & MITCHELL, D. E. (1990). *School staff and parent evaluations of California's resource specialist programs: Executive summary.* Sacramento, CA: California Department of Education.

HEDDELL, F. (1988). *Children with mental handicaps.* Ramsbury, Marlborough, England: Crowood Press.

HELFER, R. E. (1987). The developmental basis of child abuse and neglect: An epidemiological approach. In R. E. Helfer & R. S. Kempe (Eds.), *The battered child* (4th ed.). Chicago: University of Chicago Press.

HELLER, H. W., & SCHILIT, J. (1987). The regular education initiative: A concerned response. *Focus on Exceptional Children, 20*(3), 1–7.

HENTOFF, W. (1977). *Does anyone give a damn?* Westminster, NC: Namar Productions.

HERRICK, T. (1991, October 20). Transience imperiling pupils. Denver: *Rocky Mountain News,* pp. 8, 94.

HESKETH, L., & OSBERGER, M. J. (1990). Training strategies for profoundly hearing-impaired children using the Tactaid II. *Volta Review, 92*(6), 265–273.

HEWARD, W. L., & ORLANSKY, M. D. (1988). *Exceptional children* (3rd ed.). Columbus, OH: Merrill.

HEWETT, F. M. (1967). Educational engineering with E.D. children. *Exceptional Children, 33,* 459–467.

HEWETT, F. M. (1968). *The emotionally disturbed child in the classroom.* Boston: Allyn & Bacon.

HIBBEN, J., & SCHEER, R. (1982). Music and movement for special needs children. *Teaching Exceptional Children, 14*(5), 171–176.

HILL, E., ROSEN, S., CORREA, V., & LANGLEY, B. (1984). Preschool orientation and mobility: An expanded definition. *Education of the Visually Handicapped, 16*(2), 58–72.

HILL, E. W. (1988). *Preschool orientation and mobility for visually impaired children: Final report* (Project No. 24AH40132). Nashville, TN: Vanderbilt University, Peabody College.

HISKEY, M. S. (1966). *Manual for the Hiskey-Nebraska Test of Learning Aptitude.* Lincoln, NE: Union College Press.

HOBBS, N. (1966). Helping disturbed children: Psychological and ecological strategies. *American Psychologist, 21,* 1105–1115.

HOBBS, N. (1969). A brief history of project Re-ED. *Mind Over Matter, 13,* 9–14.

HOFFMAN, E. (1974). Treatment of deviance by the educational system. In W. C. Rhoads and S. Head (Eds.), *A study of child variance* (Vol 3). Ann Arbor: University of Michigan Press.

HOFFMAN, J. J., SHELDON, K., MONSKOFF, E., SAUTTER, S., STEIDLE, E., BAKER, D., BARLEY, M., & ECHOLS, L. (1987). Needs of learning disabled adults. *Journal of Learning Disabilities, 20*(1), 43–52.

HOLCOMB, R. (1985). *Silence is golden: Sometimes.* Berkeley, CA: Down Sign Press.

HOLDEN, C. (1989). Computers make slow progress in class. *Science, 244,* 906–909.

HOLT, J. (1972). *Freedom and beyond.* New York: Dutton.

HOUSE EAR INSTITUTE. (1985). *So all may hear.* Los Angeles: Author.

HOWE, S. G. (1866). Address delivered in 1866 at Batavia, New York. Republished in *Blindness.* (1965). Washington, DC: American Association of Workers for the Blind, pp. 165–188.

HUBBARD, G. (1868). *The first annual report of the Clarke Institution for Deaf Mutes.* Boston: Wright & Potter.

HUNT, J. M. (1961). *Intelligence and experience.* New York: Ronald Press.

HUNTZE, S. (1985). A position paper of the Council for Children with Behavioral Disorders. *Behavioral Disorders, 10*(3), 167–174.

HUTCHINSON, B. B., HANSON, M. L., & MECHAM, M. J. (1979). *Diagnostic handbook of speech pathology.* Baltimore: Williams & Wilkins.

HUTINGER, P. L. (1988). Linking screening, identification and assessment with curriculum. In J. Jordan, J. J. Gallagher, P. L. Hutinger, & M. B. Karnes, (Eds.), *Early childhood special education: Birth to three.* Reston, VA: Council for Exceptional Children.

HUTTER, J. J., & FARRELL, F. Z. (1983). Cancer in children. In J. Umbreit (Ed.), *Physical disabilities and health impairments: An introduction.* Columbus, OH: Merrill.

ISHIHARA, S. (1970). *The Ishihara color blind test book (children): 12 plates.* Tokyo: Kanehara Shuppan.

JACOBS, L. M. (1989). *A deaf adult speaks out* (3rd ed.). Washington, DC: Gallaudet University Press.

JANDA, K. (1990). Videopaths to learning American government. *T.H.E. Journal,* Special Issue, 42–47.

JENKINS, J. R., PIOUS, C. G., & JEWELL, M. (1990). Special education and the regular education initiative: Basic assumptions. *Exceptional Children, 56,* 479–491.

JOBES, D. A., BERMAN, A. L., & JOSSELSEN, D. (1986). The impact of psychological autopsies on medical examiners' determination of manner of death. *Journal of Forensic Science, 31*(1), 177–189.

JOHNSON, B., McGONIGEL, M., & KAUFMANN, R. (Eds.). (1989). *Guidelines for recommended practices for the individualized family service plan.* Chapel Hill, NC: NECTAS.

JOHNSTONE, N. (1991). Deaf studies: Opening worlds . . . *Preview Spring,* 5–8. Washington, DC: Gallaudet College.

JONES, M. H. (1983). Cerebral palsy. In J. Umbreit (Ed.), *Physical disabilities and health impairments: An introduction.* Columbus, OH: Merrill.

JONES-SAETE, J. C. (1988). The student with epilepsy. In G. Larson (Ed.), *Managing a school age child with a chronic health condition.* Wayzata, MN: DCI.

KALEY, R., & REED, V. (1986). Language and hearing-impaired children. In V. Reed (Ed.), *An introduction to children with language disorders.* New York: Macmillan.

KANNER, L. (1943). Autistic disturbances of affective contact. *Nervous Child, 2,* 217–250.

KANNER, L. (1957). *Child Psychiatry.* Springfield, IL: Charles C Thomas.

KANNER, L. (1964). *A history of the care and study of the mentally retarded.* Springfield, IL: Charles C Thomas.

KAPLAN, H. (1987). Assistive devices for the hearing impaired. *The Hearing Journal, 40* (5), 13–18.

KARNES, M. B., & STAYTON, V. D. (1988). Model programs for infants and toddlers with handicaps. In J. B. Jordan, J. J. Gallagher, P. L. Hutinger, & M. B. Karnes (Eds.), *Early childhood special education: Birth to three.* Reston, VA: Council for Exceptional Children.

KASLOW, N. J., & REHM, L. P. (1985). Conceptualization, assessment and treatment of depression in children. In P. H. Barnstein & A. E. Kazdin (Eds.), *Handbook of behavior therapy with children.* Pacific Grove, CA: Brooks/Cole.

KATZ, J. A. (1983). Hip conditions. In J. Umbreit (Ed.), *Physical disabilities and health impairments: An introduction.* Columbus, OH: Merrill.

KAUFFMAN, J. M. (1977). *Characteristics of children's behavior.* Columbus, OH: Merrill.

KAUFFMAN, J. M. (1982). Social policy issues in special education and related services for emotionally disturbed children and youth. In M. M. Noel & N. G. Haring (Eds.), *Progress or change: Issues in educating the emotionally disturbed: Vol. 1. Identification and program planning.* Seattle: University of Washington Press.

KAUFFMAN, J. M. (1989). *Characteristics of behavior disorders of children and youth* (4th ed.). Columbus, OH: Merrill.

KAVALE, K. (1982). The efficacy of stimulant drug treatment for hyperactivity: A meta-analysis. *Journal of Learning Disabilities, 15,* 280–289.

KAVALE, K. A., FORNESS, S. R., & ALPER, A. E. (1986). Research in behavioral disorders/emotional disturbance: A survey of subject identification criteria. *Behavioral Disorders, 11,* 159–167.

KEILITZ, I., & DUNIVANT, N. (1986). The relationship between learning disability and juvenile delinquency: Current state of knowledge. *Remedial and Special Education, 3,* 18–26.

KEKELIS, L., & SACKS, S. (1988). *Mainstreaming visually impaired children into regular education programs: The effects of visual impairment on children's interactions with peers.* San Francisco: San Francisco State University.

KELLY, R. R. (1987). Computers and sensory impaired individuals. In J. D. Lindsey (Ed.), *Computers and exceptional individuals.* Columbus, OH: Merrill.

KEMPE, R. S. (1987). A developmental approach to treatment of the abused child. In R. E. Helfer & R. S. Kempe (Eds.), *The battered child* (4th ed.). Chicago: University of Chicago Press.

KINSBOURNE, M. (1987). Specific learning disabilities and attention-deficit disorder with hyperactivity. In M. Gottlieb & J. Williams (Eds.),

Textbook of developmental pediatrics. New York: Plenum.

KIRCHNER, C. (1988). *Data on blindness and visual impairment in the U.S.* New York: American Foundation for the Blind.

KIRCHNER, C., & PETERSON, R. (1988). Multiple impairments among institutionalized blind and visually impaired persons. In *Data on blindness and visual impairment in the U.S.* New York: American Foundation for the Blind.

KIRK, S. (1963). *Proceedings of the Annual Meeting of the Conference on Exploration into the Problems of the Perceptually Handicapped Child* (Vol. 1). Chicago: Association for Children with Learning Disabilities.

KLECAN-AKER, J., & BONDEAU, R. (1990). An examination of the written stories of hearing impaired school age children. *Volta Review, 92*(6), 275–282.

KLEINBERG, B. (1982). *Educating the chronically ill child.* Rockville, MD: Aspen.

KNOWLTON, H. E., & CLARK, G. M. (1987). Transition issues for the 1990's. *Exceptional Children, 53,* 562–563.

KOCH, R., FRIEDMAN, E., AZEN, C., WENZ, E., PARTON, R., LEDUC, X., & FISHLER, K. (1988). Inborn errors of metabolism and the prevention of mental retardation. In F. Menolascino & J. Stark (Eds.), *Preventive and curative intervention in mental retardation.* Baltimore: Paul H. Brookes.

KOLSTOE, O. P. (1961). An examination of some characteristics which discriminate between employed and not-employed mentally retarded males. *American Journal of Mental Deficiency, 66,* 472–482.

KOLSTOE, O. P., & FREY, R. M. (1965). *A high school work study program for mentally subnormal students.* Carbondale: Southern Illinois University Press.

KOTT, M. G. (1971). The history of mental retardation. In J. H. Rothstein (Ed.), *Mental retardation: Readings and resources.* New York: Holt, Rinehart & Winston.

KRAEMER, M. J., & BIERMAN, C. W. (1983). Asthma. In J. Umbreit (Ed.), *Physical disabilities and health impairments: An introduction.* Columbus, OH: Merrill.

KRAUSS, M. W. (1990). New precedent in family policy: Individualized family service plan. *Exceptional Children, 56*(5), 388–395.

KREGEL, J. (1989). Career and vocational education. In J. Wood (Ed.), *Mainstreaming: A practical approach for educators.* Columbus, OH: Merrill.

KRETSCHMER, R. (1985). Learning to write and writing to learn. *Volta Review, 87,* 5.

KURZWEIL, R. (1990). *The age of intelligent machines.* Cambridge: MIT Press.

LAMBERT, N., & BOWER, E. (1976). In-school screening of children with emotional handicaps. In N. J. Long, W. C. Morse, & R. G. Newman (Eds.), *Conflict in the classroom: The education of emotionally disturbed children.* Belmont, CA: Wadsworth.

LAMBERT, N. M., WINDMILLER, M., THARINGER, D., & COLE, L. (1981). *AAMD Adaptive Behavior Scale — School Edition.* Monterey, CA: CTB/McGraw-Hill.

LANE, H. (1988). Is there "a psychology of the deaf"? *Exceptional Children, 55,* 7–19.

LARSON, G. (Ed.). (1988). *Managing the school-age child with a chronic health condition: A practical guide for schools, families, and organizations.* Minneapolis, MN: DCI.

LARSON, K. (1988). A research review and alternative hypotheses explaining the link between learning disability and delinquency. *Journal of Learning Disabilities, 21,* 357–363.

LaSASSO, C. (1987). What parents of hearing impaired students need to know about student reading levels. *American Annals of the Deaf, 132*(3), 218–220.

LAU *v.* NICHOLS (1974). 414 U.S. 563.

LeBLANC, J. M., HOKO, J. A., AANGEENBURG, M. H., & ETZEL, B. C. (1985). Microcomputers and stimulus control: From the laboratory to the classroom. *Journal of Educational Technology, 7*(1), 23–30.

LEERHSEN, C., & SCHAEFER, E. (1989, July 31). Pregnancy + alcohol = problems. *Newsweek,* p. 57.

LEHR, D. H. (1990). Providing education to students with special health care needs. *Focus on Exceptional Children, 22*(7), 1–12.

LENKER, M. A., & MICHENER, M. C. (1989). Private practitioners in public schools. *ASHA, 31,* 59–60.

LENNEBERG, L. (1967). *Biological foundations of language.* New York: Wiley.

LERNER, J. (1989). *Learning disabilities: Theories, diagnosis and teaching strategies* (5th ed.). Boston: Houghton Mifflin.

LESSEN, E., DUDZINSKI, M., KARSH, K., & VAN ACKER, R. (1989). A survey of ten years of academic intervention research with learning disabled students: Implications for research and practice. *Learning Disabilities Focus, 4*(2), 106–122.

LEWANDOWSKI, L. J., & CRUICKSHANK, W. M. (1980). Psychological development of crippled children and youth. In W. M. Cruickshank (Ed.), *Psychology of exceptional children and youth.* Englewood Cliffs, NJ: Prentice-Hall.

LEWIS, R. B., & DOORLAG, D. H. (1991). *Teaching special students in the mainstream.* Columbus, OH: Merrill.

LIEBERMAN, L. (1990). REI: Revisited . . . again. *Exceptional Children, 56,* 561–562.

LIEBERSON, S., DALTO, G., & JOHNSTON, M. E. (1975). The course of mother-tongue diversity in nations. *American Journal of Sociology, 81,* 34–61.

LILLY, M. S. (1988). The regular education initiative: A force for change in general and special education. *Education and Training in Mental Retardation, 23,* 253–260.

LINDMAN, F. T., & McINTYRE, K. M. (1961). *The mentally disabled and the law.* Chicago: University of Chicago Press.

LING, D. (1988). *Foundations of spoken language for hearing impaired children.* Washington, DC: Alexander Graham Bell Association for the Deaf.

LOEB, R., & SARGIANI, P. (1986). The impact of hearing impairment on self perceptions of children. *Volta Review, 88,* 89–91.

LONDON, R. (1982). Optokinetic nystagmus: A review of pathways, techniques, and selected diagnostic applications. *Journal of American Optometric Association, 53,* 791–798.

LONG, N. J., MORSE, W. C., & NEWMAN, R. G. (1976). *Conflict in the classroom* (3rd ed.). Belmont, CA: Wadsworth.

LOU, M. W. (1988). The history of language use in the education of deaf in the United States. In M. Strong (Ed.), *Language learning and deafness.* Cambridge: Cambridge University Press.

LOURIE, R. S. (1988). Implications for intervention and service delivery: Cross-cultural considerations. In E. D. Hibbs (Ed.), *Children and families: Studies in prevention and intervention.* Madison, WI: International Universities Press.

LOVITT, T. (1989). *Introduction to learning disabilities.* Needham Heights, MA: Allyn & Bacon.

LOWENBRAUN, S., & THOMPSON, M. D. (1990). Hearing impairments. In N. Haring & L. McCormick (Eds.), *Exceptional children and youth* (5th ed.). Columbus, OH: Merrill.

LOWENFELD, B. (1975). *The changing status of the blind from separation to integration.* Springfield, IL: Charles C Thomas.

LOWENFELD, B. (1980). Psychological problems of children with severely impaired vision. In W. M. Cruickshank (Ed.), *Psychology of exceptional children and youth* (4th ed.). Englewood Cliffs, NJ: Prentice-Hall.

LOWENFELD, B. (1981). The child who is blind. In B. Lowenfeld (Ed.), *Berthold Lowenfeld on blindness and blind people.* New York: American Foundation for the Blind.

LOWENFELD, B. (Ed.). (1973). *The visually handicapped child in school.* New York: John Day.

LUCKNER, J. L., & ISAACSON, S. L. (1990). Teaching expressive writing to hearing impaired students. *Journal of Childhood Communication Disorders, 13*(2), 135–152.

LUETKE-STAHLMAN, B., & LUCKNER, J. (1991). *Effectively educating students with hearing impairments.* New York: Longman.

LUND, K. A., & BOSS, C. S. (1981). Orchestrating the preschool classroom: The daily schedule. *Teaching Exceptional Children, 14,* 120–125.

LUNDEEN, D. J. (1972). Speech disorders. In B. R. Gearheart (Ed.), *Education of the exceptional child.* Scranton, PA: Intext.

LYLE, R. R. (1983). Muscular dystrophy. In J. Umbreit (Ed.), *Physical disabilities and health impairments: An introduction.* Columbus, OH: Merrill.

LYNCH, E. W., & STEIN, R. C. (1987). Parent participation—by ethnicity: A comparison of Hispanic, Black and Anglo families. *Exceptional Children, 54*(2), 105–111.

LYNCH, M., EILERS, R., OLLER, D. K., & COBO-LEWIS, A. (1989). Multisensory speech perception by profoundly hearing-impaired children. *Journal of Speech and Hearing Research, 54,* 57–67.

MacMILLAN, D., & BORTHWICK, S. (1980). The new educable mentally retarded population: Can they be mainstreamed? *Mental Retardation, 18*(4), 155–158.

MADDEN, R., GARDNER, E. F., RUDMAN, H. C., KARLSEN, B., & MERWIN, J. (1972). *Stanford achievement test: Special edition for hearing impaired students.* Washington, DC: Gallaudet Office of Demographic Studies.

MAGEAU, T. (1990). Software's new frontier: Laser-disc technology. *Electronic Learning, 9*(6), 22–28.

MAGEAU, T. (1991a). Redefining the textbook. *Electronic Learning, 10*(5), 14–18.

MAGEAU, T. (1991b). Introduction: How to buy an ILS. *Electronic Learning,* (Special Suppl., Winter 1991), 5.

MANFREDINI, D. (1988). *Down syndrome.* Reston, VA: The Council for Exceptional Children. (ERIC Digest No. 457)

MANGOS, J. A. (1983). Cystic fibrosis. In J. Umbreit (Ed.), *Physical disabilities and health impairments: An introduction.* Columbus, OH: Merrill.

MANGRUM, C. T., II, & STRICHART, S. S. (Eds.). (1988). *Peterson's colleges with programs for learning disabled students.* Princeton, NJ: Peterson's Guides.

MARLAND, S. P. (1971). *Career education now.* Speech presented January 23, 1971, to the National Association of Secondary School Principals, Houston, TX.

MARLAND, S. P. (1972). *Education of the gifted and talented: Report to the Congress of the United States by the U.S. Commissioner of Education.* Washington, DC: U.S. Government Printing Office.

MARSH, M. (1991). ACOT findings: Allowing time for change. *Electronic Learning, 10*(5), 10–11.

MARTIN, D. (Ed.). (1985). *Cognition, education and deafness: Implications for research and instruction.* Washington, DC: Gallaudet College Press.

MARTIN, D. S. (1987). Reducing ethnocentrism. *Teaching Exceptional Children, 20*(1), 5–8.

MARTINEZ, M. E., & MEAD, N. A. (1988). *Computer competence: The first national assessment.* Princeton, NJ: Educational Testing Service.

MASTERSON, J., SWIRBUL, T., & NOBLE, D. (1990). Computer generated information packets for parents. *Language, Speech, and Hearing Services in Schools, 21,* 114–115.

MATHENY, A. P., DOLAN, A. B., & WILSON, R. S. (1976). Twins with academic and learning problems: Antecedent characteristics. *American Journal of Orthopsychiatry, 46*(3), 464–469.

MATTES, J. (1983). The Feingold diet: A current reappraisal. *Journal of Learning Disabilities, 16,* 319–323.

MATTHEWS, J. (1990). The professions of speech-language pathology and audiology. In G. Shames & E. H. Wiig (Eds.), *Human communication disorders.* Columbus, OH: Merrill.

McCARTHY, J. (1969). Learning disabilities: Where have we been? Where are we going? *CEC selected convention papers, 1969.* Arlington, VA: Council for Exceptional Children.

McCARTHY, J. M. (1987). A response to the regular education/special education initiative. *Learning Disabilities Focus, 2*(2), 75–77.

McCLUSKEY, K. W., & WALKER, K. D. (1986). *The doubtful gift.* Kingston, Canada: Ronald P. Frye.

McCORMICK, L., & SCHIEFELBUSCH, R. L. (1984). An introduction to language intervention. In L. McCormick & R. L. Schiefelbusch (Eds.), *Early language intervention.* Columbus, OH: Merrill.

McDONALD, E. (1968). *Screening deep test of articulation.* Pittsburgh: Stanwix House.

McDOWELL, R. (1975). *Program designs for teachers of the behaviorally disordered.* Santa Fe, NM: State Department of Education, Division of Special Education.

McDOWELL, R. L., ADAMSON, G. W., & WOOD, F. H. (1982). *Teaching emotionally disturbed children.* Boston: Little, Brown.

McGONIGEL, M., & GARLAND, C. (1988). The individualized family service plan and the early intervention team: Team and family issues and recommended practices. *Infants and Young Children: An Interdisciplinary Journal of Special Care Practices, 1*(1), 10–21.

McGUIRE, J. M., NORLANDER, K. A., & SHAW, S. F. (1990). Postsecondary education for students with learning disabilities: Forecasting challenges for the future. *Learning Disabilities Focus, 5*(2), 69–74.

McKENZIE, R. G., & HOUCK, C. S. (1986). The paraprofessional in special education. *Teaching Exceptional Children, 18,* 246–252.

McKEY, R. H., CONDELLI, L., GANSON, H., BARRETT, B., McCONKEY, C., & PLANTZ, M. (1985). The impact of Head Start on children, families and communities (A final report of the Head Start Evaluation, Synthesis and Utilization Project). Washington, DC: CSR.

McLAREN, J., & BRYSON, S. E. (1987). Review of recent epidemiological studies of mental retardation: Prevalence, associated disorders, and etiology. *American Journal on Mental Retardation, 92,* 243–254.

McLOUGHLIN, J. A., & LEWIS, R. B. (1990). *Assessing special students.* New York: Macmillan.

MEADOW, K. P. (1980). *Deafness and child development.* Berkeley: University of California Press.

MECKLENBURG, D. J. (1987). The nucleus children's program. *American Journal of Otology, 8,* 436–442.

MEICHENBAUM, D. (1977). *Cognitive-behavior modification: An integrative approach.* New York: Plenum.

MEICHENBAUM, D. (1979). Teaching children self-control. In B. B. Lahey & A. E. Kazdin (Eds.), *Advances in clinical psychology* (Vol. 2). New York: Plenum.

MEICHENBAUM, D. (1983). Teaching thinking: A cognitive-behavioral approach. In *Interdisciplinary voices in learning disabilities and remedial education.* Austin, TX: ProEd.

MEIER, J. H. (1985). *Assault against children.* San Diego, CA: College Hill.

MEISELS, S. J. (1985). Prediction, prevention and developmental screening in the EPSDT program. In H. Stevenson & A. Siegel (Eds.), *Child development and social policy* (Vol. 1). Chicago: University of Chicago Press.

MELLARD, D. F. (1990). The eligibility process: Identifying students with learning disabilities in California's community colleges. *Learning Disabilities Focus, 5*(2), 75–90.

MELTON, D. (1975). *Burn the schools—save the children.* New York: Thomas Y. Crowell.

MENDEL, E. D., & VERNON, M. (1987). *They grow in silence: Understanding deaf children and adults.* Boston: College Hill.

MENOLASCINO, F. J., & STARK, J. A. (1988). *Preventive and curative intervention in mental retardation.* Baltimore: Paul H. Brookes.

MERCER, C. D. (1987). *Students with learning disabilities* (3rd ed.). Columbus, OH: Merrill.

MERCER, C. D. (1990). Learning disabilities. In N. G. Haring & L. McCormick, *Exceptional children and youth* (5th ed.). Columbus, OH: Merrill.

MERCER, C. D., HUGHES, C., & MERCER, A. R. (1985). Learning disability definitions used by state education departments. *Learning Disability Quarterly, 8*(1), 45–55.

MERCER, C. D., & MERCER, A. R. (1989). *Teaching students with learning problems* (3rd ed.). Columbus, OH: Merrill.

MERCER, J. R., & LEWIS, J. F. (1977). *System of multicultural pluralistic assessment.* San Antonio, TX: Psychological Corporation.

MIKKELSEN, E. J. (1982). Efficacy of neuroleptic medication in pervasive developmental disorders of childhood. *Schizophrenia Bulletin, 8,* 320–332.

MIKSIC, S. (1987). Drug abuse management in adolescent special education. In M. M. Kerr, C. M. Nelson, & D. L. Lambert, *Helping adolescents with learning and behavior problems.* Columbus, OH: Merrill.

MILLAR, S. (1981). Crossmodal and intersensory perception and the blind. In R. Walk & H. Pick, Jr. (Eds.), *Intersensory perception and sensory integration.* New York: Plenum.

MILLER, L. (1989). Classroom-based language intervention. *Language, Speech & Hearing Services in Schools, 20,* 149–152.

MINSKY, M. (1990). Thoughts about artificial intelligence. In R. Kurzweil (Ed.), *The age of intelligent machines.* Cambridge: MIT Press.

MIRA, M., & TYLER, J. (1991). Students with traumatic brain injury: Making the transition from hospital to school. *Focus on Exceptional Children, 23*(5), 1–12.

MIRAMONTES, O. B. (1991). Organizing for effective paraprofessional services in special education: A multilingual/multiethnic instructional service team model. *RASE, 12*(1), 29–36.

MITCHELL, A. W. (1990). Schools that work for young children. *The American School Board Journal, 177*(11), 27.

MITCHELL, D. C. (1983). Spina bifida. In J. Umbreit (Ed.), *Physical disabilities and health impairments: An introduction.* Columbus, OH: Merrill.

MOLLER, K. T., STARR, C. D., & JOHNSON, S. A. (1990). *A parent's guide to cleft lip and palate.* Minneapolis: University of Minnesota Press.

MOLNAR, A. R. (1990). Computers in education:

A historical perspective of the unfinished task. *T.H.E. Journal, 18*(4), 80–83.

MOLNAR, G. E. (1983). Musculoskeletal disorders. In J. Umbreit (Ed.), *Physical disabilities and health impairments: An introduction.* Columbus, OH: Merrill.

MOON, M. S., DIAMBRA, T., & HILL, M. (1990). An outcome-oriented vocational process. *Teaching Exceptional Children, 23*(1), 47–50.

MOORES, D. F. (1987). *Educating the deaf: Psychology, principles and practices.* Boston: Houghton Mifflin.

MORGAN, D. P., & JENSON, W. R. (1988). *Teaching behaviorally disordered students.* Columbus, OH: Merrill.

MORRISON, G. S. (1990). *The world of child development: Conception to adolescence.* Albany, NY: Delmar.

MORRISON, G. S. (1991). *Early childhood education today* (5th ed.). Columbus, OH: Merrill.

MORROW, G. (1985). *Helping chronically ill children in school.* West Nyack, NY: Parker Publishing.

MULLEN, E. A. (1990). Decreased braille literacy: A symptom of a system in need of reassessment. *In RE:view, 22*(3), 164–169.

MULLEN, N. A., & OLSEN, L. (1990). You and I are the same. *California Tomorrow 5*(1), 26–34.

MURPHY, D. M. (Ed.). (1986). Handicapped juvenile offenders [Special issue]. *Remedial and Special Education, 7*(3).

MUSE, N. J. (1990). *Depression and suicide in children and adolescents.* Austin, TX: Pro-Ed.

MYERS, P., & HAMMILL, D. D. (1990). *Learning disabilities: Basic concepts, assessment practices and instructional strategies* (4th ed.). Austin, TX: Pro-Ed.

MYKLEBUST, H. (1964). *The psychology of deafness.* New York: Grune & Stratton.

MYKLEBUST, H., & BRUTTON, M. (1953). A study of visual perception in deaf children. *Acta Oto-Laryngologica,* Supplementum, 105.

NAISBITT, J. (1982). *Megatrends.* New York: Morrow.

NANCE, J. (1975). *The gentle tasaday.* New York: Harcourt Brace Jovanovich.

NAPIER, G. (1972). The visually disabled. In B. Gearheart (Ed.), *Education of the exceptional child: History, present practices and trends.* Scranton, PA: Intext Educational Publishers.

NATIONAL CENTER FOR EDUCATIONAL STATISTICS. (1991). In *Digest of Educational Statistics: 1990.* Washington, DC: U.S. Government Printing Office.

NATIONAL CENTER FOR HEALTH STATISTICS. (1987, August 28). *Advance report of final mortality statistics, 1985* (Monthly vital statistics report, 36[5], Supplementary DHHS Publication No. PHS 87-1120). Hyattsville, MD: U.S. Public Health Service.

NATIONAL INSTITUTE ON DRUG ABUSE. (1982). *Marijuana and youth* (DHHS Publication No. ADM 82-1186). Washington, DC: Department of Health and Human Services.

NATIONAL INSTITUTE ON DRUG ABUSE. (1985). *Indicators of suicide and depression among drug abusers* (DHHS Publication No. ADM 85-1411). Washington, DC: U.S. Government Printing Office.

NATIONAL JOINT COMMITTEE ON LEARNING DISABILITIES. (1986). Adults with learning disabilities: A call to action. *Learning Disabilities Quarterly, 9,* 3–4.

NATIONAL SOCIETY FOR THE PREVENTION OF BLINDNESS. (1966). *Estimated statistics on blindness and vision problems.* New York: Author.

NAZZARO, J. N. (1981). Special problems of exceptional minority children. In J. N. Nazzaro (Ed.), *Culturally diverse exceptional children in school.* Washington, DC: National Institute of Education. (ERIC document services No. 199993)

NEALIS, J. C. (1983). Epilepsy. In J. Umbreit (Ed.), *Physical disabilities and health impairments: An introduction.* Columbus, OH: Merrill.

NEISWORTH, J. T., & BAGNATO, S. J. (1988). Assessment in early childhood special education: A typology of dependent measures. In S. L. Odom & M. B. Karnes (Eds.), *Early intervention for infants and children with handicaps: An empirical base.* Baltimore: Paul H. Brookes.

NELSON, C. M., RUTHERFORD, R. B., & WOLFORD, B. I. (Eds.). (1987). *Special education in the criminal justice system.* Columbus, OH: Merrill.

NELSON, K. B., & ELLENBERG, J. H. (1982). Children who outgrew cerebral palsy. *Pediatrics, 69*(5), 529–535.

NELSON, N. W. (1989). Curriculum-based language assessment and intervention. *Language, Speech & Hearing Services in Schools, 20,* 170–184.

NICOL, S. E., & ERLENMEYER-KIMLING, L. (1986). Genetic factors and psychopathology: Implications for prevention. In B. A. Edelstein & L. Michelson (Eds.), *Handbook of prevention.* New York: Plenum.

NOONAN, M. J., & KILGO, J. L. (1987). Transition services for early age individuals with severe mental retardation. In R. N. Ianacone & R. A. Stodden (Eds.), *Transition issues and directions.* Reston, VA: Council for Exceptional Children.

NORRIS, J. A. (1991). Providing developmentally appropriate intervention to infants and young children with handicaps. *Topics in Early Childhood Special Education, 11*(1), 21–35.

NORRIS, J. A., & HOFFMAN, P. R. (1990). Language intervention within naturalistic environments. *Language, Speech, and Hearing in the Schools, 21,* 72–84.

NORTHERN, J. L. (Ed.). (1984). *Hearing Disorders* (2nd ed.). Boston: Little, Brown.

NORTHERN, J. L., BLACK, F. O., BRIMACOMBE, J. A., COHEN, N. L., EISENBERG, L. S., KUPRENAS, S. V., MARTINEZ, S. A., & MISCHKE, R. E. (1986). Selection of children for cochlear implantation. *Seminars in Hearing, 7,* 341–347.

NURU, N. (1983). Educational issues, ideology and the role of national organizations. In D. R. Omerk & J. G. Erickson (Eds.), *The bilingual exceptional child.* San Diego, CA: College Hill.

ODOM, S. L. (1988). Research in early childhood special education: Methodologies and paradigms. In S. L. Odom, & M. B. Karnes, (Eds.), *Early intervention for infants and children with handicaps: An empirical base.* Baltimore: Paul H. Brookes.

ODOM, S. L., YODER, P., & HILL, G. (1988). Developmental intervention for infants with handicaps: Purposes and programs. *Journal of Special Education, 22*(1), 11–24.

OFFICE OF CIVIL RIGHTS. (1986). *The 1984 elementary and secondary schools civil rights survey.* Washington, DC: U.S. Department of Education.

OLION, L. (1988). Enhancing the involvement of black parents of adolescents with handicaps. In A. A. Ortiz & B. A. Ramirez (Eds.), *Schools and the culturally diverse exceptional student: Promising practices and future directions.* Reston, VA: Council for Exceptional Children.

O'NEIL, J. (1990). Computer "revolution" on hold. *Update, 32*(9), 1, 4–5.

ORTIZ, A. A., & YATES, J. R. (1988). Characteristics of learning disabled, mentally retarded and speech-language handicapped Hispanic students at initial evaluation and reevaluation. In A. A. Ortiz & B. A. Ramirez (Eds.), *Schools and the culturally diverse exceptional student: Promising practices and future directions.* Reston, VA: Council for Exceptional Children.

OSKA, R. S. (1987). When computers talk with videodiscs. In M. Abrams (Ed.), *Your computerized classroom: Using computers with hearing impaired students.* Washington, DC: Gallaudet University Press.

OWENS, E., & KESSLER, D. K. (Eds.). (1989). *Cochlear implants in young deaf children.* Boston: College Hill/Little, Brown.

OWENS, R. E., JR. (1990). Development of communication, language & speech. In G. H. Shames & E. H. Wiig, *Human communication disorders* (3rd ed.). Columbus, OH: Merrill.

PADEN, E. P. (1970). *A history of the American Speech and Hearing Association, 1925–1958.* Washington, DC: American Speech and Hearing Association.

PARETTE, H. P., JR. (1991). The importance of technology in the education and training of persons with mental retardation. *Education and Training in Mental Retardation, 26*(2), 142–150.

PARSONS, A. S., & SABORNIE, E. J. (1987). Language skills of young low-vision children: Performance on the preschool language scale. *Journal of the Division for Early Childhood, 11,* 217–225.

PATTON, J. R., BEIRNE-SMITH, M., & PAYNE, J. S. (1990). *Mental retardation* (3rd ed.). Columbus, OH: Merrill.

PATTON, J. R., PAYNE, J. S., KAUFFMAN, J. M., BROWN, G. B., & PAYNE, R. A. (1987). *Exceptional children in focus.* Columbus, OH: Merrill.

PEET, H. (1851). Memoir on origin and early history of the art of instructing the deaf and dumb. *American Annals of the Deaf, 3,* 129–161.

PEET, H. (1855). Notions of the deaf and dumb before instruction. *American Annals of the Deaf, 8,* 1–44.

PERCIVAL, F., & ELLINGTON, H. (1988). *A handbook of educational technology* (2nd ed.). London: Korgan Page.

PERIONO, S. C., & PERINO, J. (1981). *Parenting the gifted.* New York: Bowker.

PERKINS, W. (1977). *Speech pathology: An applied behavioral science* (2nd ed.). St. Louis, MO: C. V. Mosby.

PERKINS, W. H. (1980). Disorders of speech flow. In T. J. Hixon, L. D. Shriberg, & J. H. Saxman (Eds.), *Introduction to communication disorders.* Englewood Cliffs, NJ: Prentice-Hall.

PERRONE, P. A., & ALEMAN, N. (1983). Educating talented children in a pluralistic society. In D. R. Omark & J. G. Erickson (Eds.), *The bilingual exceptional child.* San Diego, CA: College Hill.

PERSAUD, T. V. N. (1990). *Environmental causes of human birth defects.* Springfield, IL: Charles C Thomas.

PETERS, J. M., TEMPLEMAN, T. P., & BROSTROM, G. (1987). The school and community partnership: Planning transition for students with severe handicaps. *Exceptional Children, 53,* 531–536.

PETERSON, H. A., & MARQUARDT, T. P. (1990). *Appraisal and diagnosis of speech and language disorders.* Englewood Cliffs, NJ: Prentice-Hall.

PETERSON, N. L. (1987). *Early intervention for handicapped and at-risk children: An introduction to early childhood special education.* Denver, CO: Love Publishing.

PETRUSO, S. (1990). Designing schools for technology from the ground up. *T.H.E. Journal* (Special Issue, Macintosh), 55–58.

PFEFFER, C. R. (1986). *The suicidal child.* New York: Guilford.

PIAGET, J. (1952). *The origins of intelligence in children* (M. Cook, Trans.). New York: International Universities Press.

PINTNER, R., EISENSON, J., & STANTON, M. (1941). *The psychology of the physically handicapped.* New York: Crofts.

PLATA, M., & CHINN, P. (1989). Students with handicaps who have cultural or language differences. In R. Gaylord-Ross (Ed.), *Integration strategies for students with handicaps.* Baltimore: Paul H. Brookes.

POGRUND, R. L., & ROSEN, S. J. (1989). The preschool blind child can be a cane user. *Journal of Visual Impairments and Blindness, 83,* 431–439.

POLLINS, L. D. (1983). The effects of acceleration on the social and emotional development of gifted students. In C. Benbon & J. C. Stanley (Eds.), *Academic precocity.* Baltimore: Johns Hopkins University Press.

POLLOWAY, E. A., PAYNE, J. S., PATTON, J. R., & PAYNE, R. A. (1985). *Strategies for teaching retarded and special needs learners.* Columbus, OH: Merrill.

POWELL, T. H., & OGLE, P. A. (1985). *Brothers and sisters—A special part of exceptional families.* Baltimore: Paul H. Brookes.

POWERS, H. J. (1974). Dietary measures to improve behavior and achievement. *Academic Therapy, 9,* 203–214.

PRESCOTT, G. A., BALOW, I. H., HOGAN, T. R., & FARR, R. C. (1984). *Metropolitan Achievement Tests 6: Survey battery.* San Antonio, TX: Psychological Corporation.

PRICKETT, H. T. (1989). *Advocacy for deaf children.* Springfield, IL: Charles C Thomas.

QUAY, H. C. (1979). Classification. In H. C. Quay & J. S. Werry (Eds.), *Psychopathological disorders of childhood* (2nd ed.). New York: Wiley.

QUIGLEY, S., & KING, C. (1980). *Reading milestones.* Beaverton, OR: Dormac.

QUINSLAND, L. K., & VANGINKEL, A. (1990). Cognitive processing and the development of concepts by deaf students. *American Annals of the Deaf, 135,* 280–284.

RAGOW, S. M. (1988). *Helping the visually impaired child with developmental problems.* New York: Teachers College Press.

RAITI, S., & NEVINS, G. H. (1971). Cretinism: Early diagnosis and its relation to mental prognosis. *Archives of Diseases in Children, 46,* 692–694.

RAMEY, C. T., & BRYANT, D. M. (1988). Prevention-oriented infant education programs. In E. D. Hibbs (Ed.), *Children and families: Studies in prevention and intervention.* Madison, WI: International Universities Press.

RANGASWAMY, L. (1983). Curvature of the spine. In J. Umbreit (Ed.), *Physical disabilities and health impairments: An introduction.* Columbus, OH: Merrill.

RAVEN, J. C. (1977). *Raven progressive matrices.* San Antonio, TX: Psychological Corporation.

RAY, S. (1979). *Manual for the adaptation of the WISC-R for the deaf.* Natchitoches, LA: Steven Ray Publishing.

REDL, F. (1959). The concept of life space interview. *American Journal of Orthopsychiatry, 29,* 1–18.

REDL, F., & WINEMAN, D. (1952). *Controls from within.* New York: Free Press.

REDL, F., & WINEMAN, D. (1954). *The aggressive child.* New York: Free Press.

REED, V. A. (1986). *An introduction to children with language disorders.* New York: Macmillan.

REINERT, H. R., & HUANG, A. (1987). *Children in conflict.* Columbus, OH: Merrill.

RENZULLI, J. S. (1977). *The enrichment triad model: A guide for developing defensible programs for the gifted and talented.* Mansfield Center, CT: Creative Learning Press.

RENZULLI, J. S., & REIS, S. (1986). The enrichment triad/revolving door model: A schoolwide plan for the development of creative productivity. In J. Renzulli (Ed.), *Systems and models for developing programs for the gifted*

and talented. Mansfield Center, CT: Creative Learning Press.

RENZULLI, J. S., REIS, M., & SMITH, L. H. (1981). The revolving door model: A new way of identifying the gifted. *Phi Delta Kappan, 62,* 648–649.

RENZULLI, J. S., & SMITH, L. H. (1980). An alternative approach to identifying and programming for gifted and talented students. *G/C/T, 15,* 3–11.

REVKIN, A. C. (1989). Crack in the cradle. *Discover, 10,* 62–69.

REX, E. J. (1989). Issues related to literacy of legally blind learners. *Journal of Visual Impairment and Blindness, 83,* 306–307, 310–313.

RHODES, W. C., & HEAD, S. (Eds.). (1974). *A study of child variance: Vol. 3. Service delivery systems.* Ann Arbor: University of Michigan Press.

RHODES, W. C., & TRACY, M. L. (Eds.). (1972a). *A study of child variance: Vol 1. Theories.* Ann Arbor: University of Michigan Press.

RHODES, W. C., & TRACY, M. L. (Eds.). (1972b). *A study of child variance: Vol 2. Interventions.* Ann Arbor: University of Michigan Press.

RICE, J. P. (1985). *The gifted: Developing total talent* (2nd ed.). Springfield, IL: Charles C Thomas.

RICHMOND, G. (1983). Shaping bowel and bladder continence in developmentally retarded preschool children. *Journal of Autism and Developmental Disorders, 13,* 197–205.

RIMLAND, B. (1964). *Infantile autism.* New York: Century-Crofts/Prentice-Hall.

RIST, M. C. (1990, July). The shadow children: Preparing for the arrival of crack babies in school. *Phi Delta Kappan Research Bulletin,* No. 9.

RITTENHOUSE, R., MORREAU, K., & IRAN-NEJAD, A. (1981). Metaphor and conservation in deaf and hard-of-hearing children. *American Annals of the Deaf, 126,* 450–453.

RIZZO, J. V., & ZABEL, R. H. (1988). *Educating children and adolescents with behavioral disorders: An integrative approach.* Boston: Allyn & Bacon.

ROESER, R. J. (1989). Tactile aids: Development issues and current status. In E. Owens & D. Kessler (Eds.), *Cochlear implants in young children.* Boston: College Hill/Little, Brown.

ROGERS, D. (1989). "Show-Me Bedtime Reading": An unusual study of the benefits of reading to deaf children. *Perspectives for Teachers of the Hearing Impaired, 8,* 2–5.

ROSE, E. (1991). Project TAPE: A model of technical assistance for service providers of college students with learning disabilities. *Learning Disabilities Research and Practice, 6,* 25–30.

ROSEN, C. C., & GERRING, J. P. (1986). *Head trauma: Educational reintegration.* San Diego, CA: College Hill.

ROSENSTEIN, J. (1961). Perception, cognition, and language in deaf children. *Exceptional Children, 27,* 276–284.

ROSENTHAL, D. (1972). Three adoption studies of heredity in schizophrenic disorders. *In-*

ternational Journal of Mental Health, 1, 63–75.

ROSS, D., & ROSS, S. (1982). *Hyperactivity, research, theory, and action* (2nd ed.). New York: Wiley.

ROTHMAN, D. (1971). *The discovery of the asylum: Social order and disorder in the new republic.* Boston: Little, Brown.

RUBIN, R. A., & BALOW, B. (1978). Prevalence of teacher identified behavior problems: A longitudinal study. *Exceptional Children, 45,* 102–111.

RUSCH, F. (Ed.). (1986). *Competitive employment issues and strategies.* Baltimore: Paul H. Brookes.

SACCO, P. R. (1986). The elephant revisited. *Hearsay: Journal of the Ohio Speech and Hearing Association, 1,* 80–83.

SAFER, D., & KRAGER, J. (1984). Trends in medication therapy for hyperactivity: National and international perspectives. In K. Gadow (Ed.), *Advances in learning and behavioral disabilities.* Greenwich, CT: JAI Press.

SAFER, D. J. (1982). *School programs for disruptive adolescents.* Baltimore: University Park Press.

SAFFORD, P. L. (1989). *Integrated teaching in early childhood: Starting in the mainstream.* White Plains, NY: Longman.

SAINATO, D. M. (1985). The behavioral ecology of preschool classrooms. *DEC Communicator, 12,* 2.

SALVIA, J., & YSSELDYKE, J. (1988). *Assessment in special and remedial education* (4th ed.). Boston: Houghton Mifflin.

SANDALL, S. R. (1991). Developmental interventions for biologically at-risk infants at home. *Topics in Early Childhood Special Education, 10,* 1–14.

SARGENT, L. (1991). *Social skills for school and community: Systematic instruction for children and youth with cognitive delays.* Reston, VA: Division of Mental Retardation of the Council for Exceptional Children.

SCHEERENBERGER, R. C. (1987). *A history of mental retardation: A quarter century of promise.* Baltimore: Paul H. Brookes.

SCHIAMBERG, L. R. (1988). *Child and adolescent development.* New York: Macmillan.

SCHLESINGER, H. S. (1985). Deafness, mental health, and language. In F. Powell, T. Finitzo-Hieber, S. Friel-Patti, & D. Henderson (Eds.), *Educating the hearing impaired child.* San Diego, CA: College Hill.

SCHOLL, G. (1986). Visual impairment and other exceptionalities. In G. Scholl (Ed.), *Foundations for blind and visually handicapped children and youth.* New York: American Foundation for the Blind.

SCHOLL, G. T. (1987). Appropriate education for visually handicapped students. *Teaching Exceptional Students, 19,* 33–36.

SCHWARTZ, S. (1990). Psycho-social aspects of mainstreaming. In M. Ross (Ed.), *Hearing-impaired children in the mainstream.* Parkton, MD: York Press.

SCHWARTZ, S. (Ed.). (1987). *Choices in deafness: A parent's guide.* Kensington, MD: Woodbine House.

SCHWEINHART, L. J., & WEIKART, D. P. (1980). Young children grow up: The effects of the Perry preschool program on youths through age 15. *Monographs of the High/Scope Education Research Foundation.* Ypsilanti, MI: High/Scope Press.

SCHWEINHART, L. J., & WEIKART, D. P. (1986). What do we know so far? A review of the Head Start synthesis project. *Young Children, 41,* 49–55.

SCOUTEN, E. L. (1983). *Turning points in the education of deaf people.* Danville, IL: Interstate.

SEIDENBERG, P. L., & KOENIGSBERG, E. (1990). A survey of regular and special education high school teachers and college faculty: Implications for program development for secondary learning disabled students. *Learning Disabilities Research, 5,* 110–117.

SELF, P. A., & HOROWITZ, F. D. (1979). The behavioral assessment of the neonate: An overview. In J. D. Osofsky (Ed.), *Handbook of infant development.* New York: Wiley.

SELIGMAN, M., & DARLING, R. B. (1989). *Ordinary families, special children.* New York: Guilford.

SELLING, L. S. (1943). *Men against madness.* New York: Garden City Books.

SEMMEL, M. I., & LIEBER, J. A. (1986). Computer application in instruction. *Focus on Exceptional Children, 18,* 1–12.

SEMMLER, C. J., & HUNTER, J. G. (1990). *Early occupational therapy intervention: Neonates to three years.* Gaithersburg, MD: Aspen.

SENF, G. M. (1987). Learning disabilities as sociologic sponge: Wiping up life's spills. In S. Vaughn & C. Bos (Eds.), *Research in learning disabilities: Insights and future directions.* Boston: College Hill.

SHAMES, G. H. (1986). Disorders of fluency. In G. H. Shames & E. H. Wiig (Eds.), *Human communication disorders* (2nd ed.). Columbus, OH: Merrill.

SHAMES, G. H., & WIIG, E. H. (1990). *Human communication disorders* (3rd ed.). Columbus, OH: Merrill.

SHAPIRO, B. K., PALMER, F. B., & CAPUTE, A. J. (1987). Cerebral palsy, history and state of the art. In M. Gottlieb & J. E. Williams (Eds.), *Textbook of developmental pediatrics.* New York: Plenum.

SHEARER, D. E., & SNIDER, R. S. (1981). On providing a practical approach to the early education of children. *Child Behavior Therapy, 3,* 78–80.

SHEARER, M. S., & SHEARER, D. E. (1972). The portage project: A model for early childhood education. *Exceptional Children, 39,* 210–217.

SHELL, D. F., HORN, S., & SEVERS, M. K. (1989). Computer-based compensatory augmentative communication technology for physically disabled, visually impaired, and speech impaired students. *Journal of Special Education Technology, 10,* 29–42.

SHULMAN, J., & DECKER, N. (1980). *Readable*

English for hearing impaired students. Boston: Line Services.

SIGELMAN, C. K., & SHAFFER, D. R. (1991). *Life-span human development.* Pacific Grove, CA: Brooks/Cole.

SILKWORTH, C. S. (1988). Dealing with allergic reactions. In G. Larson (Ed.), *Managing the school age child with a chronic health condition.* Minneapolis, MN: DCI.

SILKWORTH, C. S., & JONES, D. (1988). Helping the student with asthma. In G. Larson (Ed.), *Managing the school age child with a chronic health condition.* Minneapolis, MN: DCI.

SILVER, L. B. (1990). Attention deficit-hyperactivity disorder: Is it a learning disability or a related disorder? *Journal of Learning Disabilities, 23,* 394–397.

SIMMONS, F. B. (1977). Automated screening test for newborns: The crib-o-gram. In B. F. Jaffe (Ed.), *Hearing loss in children.* Baltimore: University Park Press.

SIMON, B. A. (1991). *A relationship between at-risk preschoolers' language achievement before and after developmentally appropriate programming.* Unpublished manuscript, Division of Graduate Studies, Adams State College, Alamosa, CO.

SIMONS, R. (1987). *After the tears: Parents talk about raising a child with a disability.* San Diego, CA: Harcourt Brace Jovanovich.

SIMPSON, R. L. (1990). *Conferencing parents of exceptional children.* Austin, TX: Pro-Ed.

SINGER, J. D., & BUTLER, J. A. (1987). The education of all handicapped children act: Schools as agents of social reform. *Harvard Educational Review, 57,* 125–152.

SISK, D. (1987). *Creative teaching of the gifted.* New York: McGraw-Hill.

SKAFTE, M. D. (1990). Fifty years of hearing health care. *Hearing Instruments Commemorative, 41,* 94–117.

SKEELS, H. M. (1966). Adult status of children with contrasting early life experiences. *Monographs of the Society for Research in Child Development, 31* (Serial No. 105).

SKINNER, B. F. (1953). *Science and human behavior.* New York: Macmillan.

SKINNER, B. F. (1957). *Verbal behavior.* New York: Appleton-Century-Crofts.

SMITH, B. J. (1988). Early intervention public policy: Past, present, and future. In J. B. Jordon, J. J. Gallagher, P. L. Hutinger, & M. B. Karnes (Eds.), *Early childhood special education: Birth to three.* Reston, VA: Council for Exceptional Children.

SMITH, S. D. (Ed.). (1986). *Genetics and learning disabilities.* San Diego, CA: College Hill.

SMITH, S. W., & SIMPSON, R. L. (1989). An analysis of individualized education programs (IEP's) for students with behavior disorders. *Behavioral Disorders, 14,* 107–116.

SMUTNY, J. F., & BLOCKSOM, R. H. (1990). *Education of the gifted: Programs and perspectives.* Bloomington, IN: Phi Delta Kappan.

SOLTESZ, M. J., & BROCKWAY, M. F. (1989). The high risk infant. In J. S. Tecklin (Ed.), *Pediatric physical therapy.* Philadelphia: Lippincott.

SPENCER, K. (1988). *The psychology of educational technology and instructional media.* London: Routledge.

SPIVAK, M. P. (1986). Advocacy and legislative action for head-injured children and their families. *Journal of Head Trauma Rehabilitation, 1,* 41–47.

SPUNGIN, S. J. (1989). Trends and issues in international education programs for visually handicapped children. *Journal of Visual Impairment and Blindness, 83,* 41–43.

STAFFORD, P. L. (1989). *Integrated teaching in early childhood: Starting in the mainstream.* White Plains, NY: Longman.

STAINBACK, S., & STAINBACK, W. (1987). Integration versus cooperation: A commentary on "Educating children with learning problems: A shared responsibility." *Exceptional Children, 54,* 66–68.

STAINBACK, S., STAINBACK, W., & FOREST, M. (1989). *Educating all students in the mainstream of regular education.* Baltimore, MD: Paul H. Brookes.

STANLEY, J. (1981). Rationale of the study of mathematically precocious youth during its first five years of promoting educational acceleration. In W. Barbe & J. Renzulli (Eds.), *Psychology and education of the gifted.* New York: Irvington.

STARK, J. A., MENOLASCINO, F. J., & GOLDSBURY, T. L. (1988). An updated search for the prevention of mental retardation. In A. F. Menolascino & J. A. Stark (Eds.), *Preventative and curative intervention in mental retardation.* Baltimore: Paul H. Brookes.

STEFIK, M., AIKENS, J., BALZER, R., BENOIT, J., BIRNBAUM, L., HAYES-ROTH, F., & SACERDOTI, E. (1983). The architecture of expert systems. In F. Hayes-Roth, D. A. Waterman, & D. B. Lenat (Eds.), *Building expert systems.* Reading, MA: Addison-Wesley.

STEIN, M. K., LEINHARDT, G., & BICKEL, W. (1989). Instructional issues for teaching students at risk. In R. E. Slavin, N. L. Karweit, & N. A. Madden (Eds.), *Effective programs for students at risk.* Needham Heights, MA: Allyn & Bacon.

STEPHENS, O. (1989). Braille—implications for living. *Journal of Visual Impairment and Blindness, 83,* 288–289.

ST. LOUIS, K., & HINZMAN, A. (1986). Studies of cluttering: Perceptions of cluttering by speech-language pathologists and educators. *Journal of Fluency Disorders, 11,* 131–149.

STOCKER, C. (1973). *Listening for the visually impaired: A teaching manual.* Springfield, IL: Charles C Thomas.

STONE, J. L., SMITH, H. T., & MURPHY, L. B. (Eds.). (1973). *The competent infant.* New York: Basic Books.

STRAUSS, A. A., & KEPHART, N. C. (1955). *Psychopathology and education of the brain-injured child* (Vol. II). New York: Grune & Stratton.

STRAUSS, A. A., & LEHTINEN, L. E. (1947). *Psychopathology and education of the brain-injured child.* New York: Grune & Stratton.

STRICKLAND, B. B., & TURNBULL, A. P. (1990). *Developing and implementing individualized education programs* (3rd ed.). Columbus, OH: Merrill.

STROBER, M. (1983). Clinical and biological perspectives on depressive disorders in adolescence. In D. Cantwell & G. Carlson (Eds.), *Affective disorders in childhood and adolescence.* New York: Spectrum.

STURMEY, P., & CRISP, A. G. (1986). Portage guide to early education: A review of research. *Education Psychology, 6,* 139–157.

SUPER, D. E. (1951). Vocational adjustment: Implementing a self-concept. *Occupations, 30,* 88–92.

SUPER, D. E. (1957). *The psychology of careers.* New York: Harper.

SUPER, D. E. (1985). The application of career development theory to the handicapped. In M. Bender, L. J. Richmond, & N. Pinson-Millburg (Eds.), *Careers, computers and the handicapped.* Austin, TX: Pro-Ed.

SUPPLEE, P. L. (1990). *Reaching the gifted underachiever: Program strategy and design.* New York: Teachers College Press.

SWALLOW, R. M., & CONNER, A. (1982). Aural reading. In S. S. Mangold (Ed.), *A teacher's guide to special education needs of blind and visually handicapped children.* New York: American Foundation for the Blind.

SWALLOW, R. M., & HUEBNER, K. M. (1987). *How to thrive, not just survive.* New York: American Foundation for the Blind.

SWAP, S. M., PRIETO, A. G., & HARTH, R. (1982). Ecological perspective of the emotionally disturbed child. In R. L. McDowell, G. W. Adamson, & F. H. Wood (Eds.), *Teaching emotionally disturbed children.* Boston: Little, Brown.

SZAJNBERG, N., WARD, M. J., KRAUSS, A., & KESSLER, D. B. (1987). Low birth weight prematures: Preventative intervention and maternal attitude. *Child Psychiatry and Human Development, 17,* 152–165.

TANNENBAUM, A. J. (1983). *Gifted children: Psychological and educational perspectives.* New York: Macmillan.

TAYLOR, R. L. (1985). Measuring adaptive behavior: Issues and instruments. *Focus on Exceptional Children, 18,* 1–8.

TAYLOR, R. L., & STERNBERG, L. (1989). *Exceptional children: Integrating research and teaching.* New York: Springer.

TAYLOR, S. J., & KNOLL, J. A. (1989). Community living and the education of students with severe disabilities. In R. Gaylord-Ross (Ed.), *Integration strategies for students with handicaps.* Baltimore: Paul H. Brookes.

TEITELBAUM, H., & HILLER, R. J. (1977). *The legal perspective in bilingual education: Current perspectives* (Vol. 3). Arlington, VA: Center for Applied Linguistics.

TELFORD, C. W., & SAWREY, J. M. (1981). *The exceptional individual* (4th ed.). Englewood Cliffs, NJ: Prentice-Hall.

TELLER, D. Y., McDONALD, M., PRESTON, K., SEBRIS, S. L., & DOBSON, V. (1986). Assessment of visual acuity in infants and children: The acuity card procedure. *Developmental Medicine and Child Neurology, 28,* 779–789.

TEPLIN, S. W., HOWARD, J. A., & O'CONNOR, M. J. (1981). Self concept among young children with cerebral palsy. *Developmental Medicine and Child Neurology, 23,* 730–738.

TERMAN, L. (1925). Mental and physical traits of a thousand gifted children. In L. Terman (Ed.), *Genetic studies of genius* (Vol. 1). Stanford, CA: Stanford University Press.

TERMAN, L., & ODEN, M. (1947). The gifted child grows up. In L. Terman (Ed.), *Genetic studies of genius* (Vol. 4). Stanford, CA: Stanford University Press.

TERMAN, L., & ODEN, M. (1959). The gifted group at mid-life: Thirty-five years' follow-up of the superior child. In L. Terman (Ed.), *Genetic studies of genius* (Vol. 5). Stanford, CA: Stanford University Press.

TERRYBERRY, E., & POLK, A. (1987). Hearing dogs: Another alternative for the hearing impaired. *The Hearing Journal, 40,* 21–24.

THOMAS, R. M. (1987). Part I: Computer technology, an example of decision-making in technology transfer. In R. M. Thomas & V. N. Kobayashi (Eds.), *Education technology—Its creation, development and cross-cultural transfer* (Vol. 4). Oxford: Pergamon Press.

THOMPSON, G., & WILSON, W. (1984). Clinical application of visual reinforcement audiometry. In J. Northern & W. Perkins (Eds.), *Seminar in hearing: Early identification of hearing loss in infants* (Vol. 5). New York: Thieme-Stratton.

THORNDIKE, R. L., HAGEN, E. P., & SATTLER, J. M. (1986). *Stanford-Binet intelligence scale* (4th ed.). Chicago: Riverside.

THORP, E. K., & McCOLLUM, J. A. (1988). Defining the infancy specialization in early special education. In J. B. Jordan, J. J. Gallagher, P. L. Hutinger, & M. B. Karnes (Eds.), *Early childhood education: Birth to three.* Reston, VA: Council for Exceptional Children.

THRASHER, M. (1991). Technology aided teaching spreads to schools nationwide. *Research: Report on Educational Research, 23,* 7–8.

THURMAN, S. K., & WIDERSTROM, A. H. (1985). *Young children with special needs.* Boston: Allyn & Bacon.

THURMAN, S. K., & WIDERSTROM, A. H. (1990). *Infants and young children with special needs: A developmental and ecological approach* (2nd ed.). Baltimore: Paul H. Brookes.

TIGER, R., IRVINE, T., & REIS, R. (1980). Cluttering as a complex of learning disabilities. *Language, Speech & Hearing Services in Schools, 11,* 25–33.

TOLIVER-WEDDINGTON, G., & MEYERSON, M. D. (1983). Training paraprofessionals for identification and intervention with communicatively disordered bilinguals. In D. Omark & J. G. Erickson (Eds.), *The bilingual exceptional child.* San Diego, CA: College Hill.

TORGESEN, J. K. (1986). Computer assisted instruction with learning disabled children. In J. K. Torgesen & B. Wong (Eds.), *Psychologi-*

cal and educational perspectives on learning disabilities. Orlando, FL: Academic Press.

TORRANCE, E. P. (1962). *Guiding creative talent.* Englewood Cliffs, NJ: Prentice-Hall.

TORRANCE, E. P. (1964). The Minnesota studies of creative thinking, 1959–1962. In C. W. Taylor (Ed.), *Widening horizons in creativity.* New York: Wiley.

TORRANCE, E. P. (1965). *Rewarding creative behavior.* Englewood Cliffs, NJ: Prentice-Hall.

TORRANCE, E. P. (1981). *Thinking creatively in action and movement.* Bensonville, IL: Scholastic Testing Services.

TORRANCE, E. P. (1985). "Who is gifted?" *Illinois Council for the Gifted Journal, 4,* 1–3.

TORRANCE, E. P., & TORRANCE, J. P. (1981). Educating gifted, talented, and creative students for the future. *American Middle School Education, 4,* 39–46.

TRAPANI, C. (1990). *Transition goals for adolescents with learning disabilities.* Boston: College Hill.

TRIPP, E. D. (1988). Perivolaki: A model therapeutic nursery school. In E. D. Hibbs (Ed.), *Children with families: Studies in prevention and intervention.* Madison, WI: International Universities Press.

TROTTER, A. (1990). Computer learning. *The American School Board Journal, 177,* 12–18.

TRYBUS, R. (1985). *Today's hearing impaired children and youth: A demographic and academic profile.* Washington, DC: Gallaudet Research Institute.

TURNBULL, A. P., & TURNBULL, H. R. (1990). *Families, professionals and exceptionality: A special partnership.* Columbus, OH: Merrill.

TURNBULL, H. R. (1986). *Free appropriate public education: The law and children with disabilities.* Denver: Love Publishing.

TUTTLE, D. W. (1984). *Self-esteem and adjusting with blindness.* Springfield, IL: Charles C Thomas.

TUTTLE, D. W. (1986). Education programming. In G. T. Scholl (Ed.), *Foundations of education for blind and visually handicapped children and youth: Theory and practice.* New York: American Foundation for the Blind.

UMBREIT, J. (Ed.). (1983). *Disabilities and health impairments: An introduction.* Columbus, OH: Merrill.

UNDERWOOD, J. D., & UNDERWOOD, G. (1990). *Computers and learning: Helping children acquire thinking skills.* Oxford: Basil Blackwell.

UNITED STATES DEPARTMENT OF EDUCATION. (1988). *Tenth annual report to Congress on the implementation of the Education of the Handicapped Act.* Washington, DC: Office of Special Education Programs.

UNITED STATES DEPARTMENT OF EDUCATION. (1991). *Thirteenth annual report to Congress on the implementation of the Individuals with Disabilities Education Act.* Washington, DC: Office of Special Education Programs.

UNITED STATES GENERAL ACCOUNTING OFFICE. (1990). *Special education: Estimates of handicapped Indian preschoolers and sufficiency of services: Briefing report to congressional requesters.* Washington, DC: Author.

UNITED STATES OFFICE OF EDUCATION. (1977). Implementation of Part B of the Education of the Handicapped Act. *Federal Register, 42,* 42474-42518.

UTLEY, C. A., LOWITZER, A. C., & BAUMEISTER, A. A. (1987). A comparison of AAMD's definition, eligibility criteria, and classification schemes with state departments of education guidelines. *Education and Training in Mental Retardation, 22,* 35–43.

VANDYKE, D. C., & FOX, A. A. (1990). Fetal drug exposure and its possible implications for learning in preschool and school age populations. *Journal of Learning Disabilities, 23,* 160–163.

VANORNUM, W. (1990). Foreword. In J. Gertdz & J. Bergman, *Autism: A practical guide for those who help others.* New York: Continuum.

VAN RIPER, C., & EMERICK, L. (1990). *Speech correction: An introduction to speech pathology and audiology* (8th ed.). Englewood Cliffs, NJ: Prentice-Hall.

VANTASSEL-BASKA, J. (Ed.). (1988). *Comprehensive curriculum for gifted learners.* Boston: Allyn & Bacon.

VAUGHN, S., & BOS, C. S. (1987). *Research in learning disabilities: Issues and future directions.* Boston: College Hill.

VERNON, D. (1967). Relationship of language to the thinking process. *Archives of Genetic Psychiatry, 16,* 325–333.

VIADERO, D. (1991, March 27). Law to aid handicapped infants faces critical test. *Education Week,* (10), 27, 28.

WADSWORTH, B. J. (1989). *Piaget's theory of cognitive and affective development* (4th ed.). New York: Longman.

WAGNER, M. (1972). Environmental interventions in emotional disturbance. In W. C. Rhodes & M. L. Tracy (Eds.), *A study of child variance: Vol. 2. Interventions.* Ann Arbor: University of Michigan Press.

WALDROP, M. (1990). Can computers think? In R. Kurzweil (Ed.), *The age of intelligent machines.* Cambridge: MIT Press.

WALKER, J. E., & SHEA, T. M. (1988). *Behavior management: A practical approach for educators* (4th ed.). Columbus, OH: Merrill.

WALKER, J. E., & SHEA, T. M. (1991). *Behavior management: A practical approach for educators* (5th ed.). New York: Merrill/ Macmillan.

WANG, M. C., & WAHLBERG, H. J. (1988). Four fallacies of segregationism. *Exceptional Children, 55,* 128–137.

WARREN, D. (1984). *Blindness and early childhood development* (2nd ed.). New York: American Foundation for the Blind.

WATSON, G. (1989). Competencies and a bibliography addressing student's use of low vision devices. *Journal of Visual Impairment and Blindness, 83,* 160–163.

WAYMAN, K. I., LYNCH, E. W., & HANSON, M. J. (1991). Home-based early childhood services: Cultural sensitivity in a family systems approach. *Topics in Early Childhood Special Education, 10,* 56–75.

WEBER, M. C., & BINKELMAN, M. (1990). Legal issues in the transition to public school for handicapped infants and children. *Journal of Law and Education, 19,* 193–206.

WEBSTER, A., & WOOD, D. (1990). *Special needs in ordinary schools: Children with hearing difficulties.* London: Cassell Educational.

WECHSLER, D. (1967). *Wechsler Preschool and Primary Scales of Intelligence.* San Antonio, TX: Psychological Corporation.

WECHSLER, D. (1974). *Wechsler Intelligence Scale for Children—Revised.* San Antonio, TX: Psychological Corporation.

WECHSLER, D. (1981). *Wechsler Adult Intelligence Scale—Revised.* San Antonio, TX: Psychological Corporation.

WEHMAN, P., KREGEL, J., BARCUS, J. M., & SCHALOCK, R. L. (1986). Vocational transition for students with developmental disabilities. In W. E. Kiernan & J. A. Stark (Eds.), *Pathways to employment for adults with developmental disabilities.* Baltimore: Paul H. Brookes.

WEISS, G. (1964). *Cluttering.* Englewood Cliffs, NJ: Prentice-Hall.

WEISS, G. (1981). Controversial issues of pharmacotherapy of the hyperactive child. *Canadian Journal of Psychiatry, 26,* 385–392.

WHELAN, R. J., & GALLAGHER, P. A. (1972). Effective teaching of children with behavior disorders. In N. G. Haring & A. H. Hayden (Eds.), *The improvement of instruction.* Seattle: Special Child Publications.

WHITE, K. R., BUSH, D., & CASTRO, G. (1986). Let the past be prologue: Learning from previous reviews of early intervention efficacy research. *Journal of Special Education, 19,* 417–428.

WHITE, K. R., & CASTRO, G. (1985). An integrative review of early intervention efficacy studies with at-risk children: Implications for the handicapped. *Analysis and Intervention in Developmental Disabilities, 5,* 7–31.

WHITE, K. R., MASTROPIERI, M., & CASTRO, G. (1984). An analysis of special education early childhood projects approved by the Joint Dissemination Review Panel. *Journal of the Division of Early Childhood, 9,* 11–26.

WHITMORE, J. R. (1985). *Characteristics of intellectually gifted children.* Reston, VA: Council for Exceptional Children. (ERIC Digest No. 344)

WHITMORE, J. R., & MAKER, C. J. (1985). *Intellectual giftedness in disabled persons.* Rockville, MD: Aspen.

WICKMAN, E. K. (1929). *Children's behavior and teacher's attitudes.* New York: The Commonwealth Fund.

WIDERSTROM, A. H., MOWDER, B. A., & SANDALL, S. R. (1991). *At-risk and handicapped newborns and infants: Development, assessment, and intervention.* Englewood Cliffs, NJ: Prentice-Hall.

WIEDERHOLT, J. L. (1974). Historical perspectives on the education of the learning disabled. In L. Mann & D. Sabatino (Eds.), *The second review of special education.* Philadelphia: JSE Press.

WIIG, E., & SEMEL, E. (1984). *Language assessment and intervention for the learning disabled.* Columbus, OH: Merrill.

WILCOX, S. (1989). *American deaf culture.* Silver Springs, MD: Linstok Press.

WILCOX, S., & CORWIN, J. (1990). The enculturation of Bomee: Looking at the world through deaf eyes. *Journal of Childhood Communication Disorders, 13,* 63–71.

WILDER, L. (1986). *Professionally speaking: Getting ahead in business through effective communication.* New York: Simon & Schuster.

WILL, M. (1984). *OSERS programming for the transition of youth with disabilities: Bridges from school to working life.* Washington, DC: Office of Special Education and Rehabilitative Services.

WILL, M. (1986). Education of children with learning problems: A shared responsibility. *Exceptional Children, 52,* 411–415.

WILLIAMS, G. H., & WOOD, M. M. (1977). *Developmental art therapy.* Baltimore, MD: University Park Press.

WILLIAMS, R. L. (1972). *The BITCH test: Black intelligence test of cultural homogeneity.* St. Louis, MO: Williams & Associates.

WING, L., & ATWOOD, A. (1987). Syndromes of autism and atypical development. In D. J. Cohen & A. M. Donnellan (Eds.), *Handbook of autism and pervasive developmental disorders.* New York: Wiley.

WINTER, R. J. (1983). Childhood diabetes mellitus. In J. Umbreit (Ed.), *Physical disabilities and health impairments: An introduction.* Columbus, OH: Merrill.

WINTON, P. (1986). Effective strategies for involving families in intervention efforts. *Focus on Exceptional Children, 19,* 2–12.

WITT, J. C., ELLIOTT, S. N., GRESHAM, F. M., & KRAMER, J. J. (1988). *Assessment of special children: Tests and the problem solving process.* Glenview, IL: Scott, Foresman.

WITTY, P. A. (1951). *The gifted child.* Lexington, MA: Heath.

WOLERY, M. (1989). Transitions in early childhood special education: Issues and procedures. *Focus on Exceptional Children, 22,* 1–22.

WOLFE, D. A. (1985). Child-abusive parents: An empirical review and analysis. *Psychological Bulletin, 97,* 462–482.

WOLFENSBERGER, W. (1972). *The principle of normalization in human services.* Toronto, Canada: National Institute on Mental Retardation.

WOLFORD, B. I. (1987). Correctional education: Training and educational opportunities for delinquent and criminal offenders. In C. M. Nelson, R. B. Rutherford, & B. I. Wolford (Eds.), *Special education in the criminal justice system.* Columbus, OH: Merrill.

WOOD, J. W. (1989). *Mainstreaming: A practical approach for teachers.* Columbus, OH: Merrill.

WOOD, J. W., & MIEDERHOFF, J. W. (1988). Bridging the gap. *Teaching Exceptional Children, 21,* 66–70.

YATES, J. R. (1988). Demography as it affects special education. In A. Ortiz & B. Ramirez (Eds.), *Schools and the culturally diverse exceptional student: Promising practices and future directions.* Reston, VA: Council for Exceptional Children.

YELL, M. L. (1988). The effects of jogging on the rates of target behaviors of behaviorally disordered students. *Behavioral Disorders, 13,* 273–279.

YOSHINAGA-ITANO, C., & SNYDER, L. (1985). Form and meaning in the written language of hearing impaired children. *Volta Review, 87,* 75–90.

YURKOWSKI, P., & EWOLDT, C. (1986). Semantic processing of the deaf reader. *American Annals of the Deaf, 131,* 243–247.

ZAMETKIN, A. J., NORDAHL, T. E., GROSS, M., KING, A. C., SEMPLE, W. E., RUMSEY, J., HAMBURGER, S., & COHEN, R. M. (1990). Cerebral glucose metabolism in adults with hyperactivity of childhood onset. *New England Journal of Medicine, 323,* 1361–1366.

ZERKEL, P. A., & STEVENS, P. L. (1986). Commentary: The law concerning public education for the gifted. *West's Education Law Reporter, 34,* 353–367.

ZILBOORG, G., & HENRY, C. (1941). *A history of medical psychology.* New York: Norton.

ZIRPOLI, T. J. (1990). Physical abuse: Are children with disabilities at greater risk? *Intervention in School and Clinic, 26,* 6–11.

ZWEIBEL, A., & MERTENS, D. (1985). Factor-analytic study of intellectual development in deaf and hearing children. In D. Martin (Ed.), *Cognition, education, and deafness: Implications for research and instruction.* Washington, DC: Gallaudet University Press.

NAME INDEX

Abroms, K. K., 97
Achenbach, T. M., 165
Adams, J., 251
Addis, G., 151
Alber, M.B., 295
Albertini, J., 247
Aleman, N., 463
Algozzine, B., 46, 163
Algozzine, R., 163
Allen, H., 238, 387
Alper, A. E., 160
Als, H., 397
Alvino, J., 497
Ammerman, R. T., 181
Anderson, E., 287
Anderson, W., 483, 485
Apgar, V., 397
Aram, C., 218
Armbruster, V. B., 411–415
Armstrong, R. W., 313
Arnold, K. M., 239
Ashby, J. E., 59
Atwood, A., 183
Azrin, N. H., 115

Baca, L., 455, 468
Badarak, G., 146
Bagnato, S. J., 412
Bailey, D. B., 381, 403, 404
Baker, B. L., 488, 492
Balik, B., 322, 333
Balow, B., 164
Banaga, N., 271, 272, 275, 295
Banbury, M. M., 484
Bandura, A., 174
Banmeister, A. A., 382
Barcus, J. M., 438
Barr, M. W., 86
Bartholome, W. G., 330, 331

Bayer, D., 326
Behrman, R. E., 336
Beirne-Smith, M., 94, 98, 99, 102, 111, 112, 114, 117, 427, 438, 480
Bell, A. G., 7, 230
Bennett, J. W., 97
Bentzen, F., 128
Berg, F. S., 253
Bergman, J., 182, 183
Berkell, D. E., 426, 434
Berman, A. L., 186
Bernstein, D. K., 198
Bettelheim, B., 159
Betts, G., 366, 367, 369
Bickel, W., 386
Biemer, C., 218
Bierman, C. W., 329
Bigelow, A., 278
Bigge, J. L., 310, 319, 321, 323, 324, 326, 328
Biller, E. F., 434
Binkelman, M., 411
Birch, J., 238
Black, T., 387
Blaesus, Balbus, 196
Blair, J. C., 260
Blaloch, J., 218
Blankenhorn, D., 477
Blasch, B. B., 304
Blaylock, A. W., 464
Blockson, R. H., 374
Bloom, B., 369
Bochner, J., 247
Bodner-Johnson, B., 239
Bondeau, R., 238
Boothroyd, A., 258
Borkowski, J. G., 101
Borland, J. H., 348, 358, 371
Borthwick, S., 108
Boss, C. S., 419

Boston, J. B., 360, 362, 364, 370
Bower, E., 162–164
Braille, L., 267
Brandwein, H., 96
Bratton, S., 46
Brazelton, T. B., 397
Bredekamp, S., 203, 415
Brewer, D. W., 210
Bricker, D. D., 333, 382
Brightman, A. J., 488, 492
Brody, E. B., 407
Brody, G. H., 181
Brolin, D., 438, 442
Bronfenbrenner, U., 382
Brooks, M. B., 319
Brooks, P. H., 382
Brostrom, G., 442
Brown, J., 426, 434
Brown, S., 251
Browning, L., 251
Brutton, M., 237
Bryant, D. M., 406, 408
Bryson, S. E., 92
Buchanan, M., 149
Bursick, B., 180
Bush, D., 384
Butler, J. A., 483
Buttrill, J., 218

Campbell, P., 74, 76, 77
Capute, A. J., 314
Carta, J., 415
Carter, D. J., 69
Cartledge, G., 240
Castro, G., 384, 385
Cervantes, H. T., 455, 468
Chace, M., 174
Chadsey-Rusch, J., 448
Chalfant, J., 128

SUBJECT INDEX

PHOTO CREDITS

Chapter 1

2, Bob Daemmrich/Stock, Boston; **5,** (left) Catherine Green, (right) Laima Druskis/Photo Researchers, Inc.; **11,** James L. Shaffer; **17,** Skjold Photos; **21,** (top) Mary Langenfeld, (left & right) Jim West.

Chapter 2

24, Martha Tabor/Working Images Photographs; **29,** Gail Meese/Meese Photo Research; **34,** Michael Siluk; **39,** James L. Shaffer; **41,** James L. Shaffer; **47,** Mike Penney; **48,** Ray Baltar Photography; **50,** Gail Meese/Meese Photo Research.

Chapter 3

52, Virginia Blaisdell; **71, 74,** courtesy, IBM; **75,** Barry Staver; **76,** courtesy, Sabolich Prosthetic and Research Center; **78,** courtesy, Adaptive Communications Systems; **80,** MacDonald/Envision.

Chapter 4

84, Sunrise/Trinity Photos; **89,** Gale Zucker; **93,** Martha Tabor/Working Images Photographs; **95,** Gail Meese/Meese Photo Research; **100,** Spencer Grant/Stock, Boston; **108,** James L. Shaffer; **113,** (left) Jackie Bacho, (right) James L. Shaffer; **114,** Hazel Hankin/Stock, Boston.

Color Insert: Preparation For Independent Living

p. 1, (top) Gail Meese/Meese Photo Research; (bottom) author-supplied photo; **p. 2,** (top) Paul Conklin; (middle and bottom) Gail Meese/Meese Photo Research; **p. 3,** (top) Paul Conklin; (middle) author-supplied photo; (bottom) Gail Meese/Meese Photo Research; **p. 4,** (top) Gail Meese/Meese Photo Research; (bottom) author-supplied photo.

Chapter 5

120, Gale Zucker; **125,** James L. Shaffer; **129,** Michael Weisbrot/Stock, Boston; **136,** Virginia Blaisdell; **141,** courtesy, IBM; **145,** (all) James L. Shaffer; **146,** Martha Tabor/Working Images Photos; **149,** ©Jeff Slocomb/Outline Press.

Chapter 6

154, Paul Fortin/Stock, Boston; **157,** Varone/Envision; **161,** Frances M. Cox/Stock, Boston; **166,** Billy E. Barnes/Stock, Boston; **171,** Gail Meese/Meese Photo Research; **173,** James L. Shaffer; **177,** Dorothy Littell/Stock, Boston; **187,** Allen Zak; **191,** Gail Meese/Meese Photo Research.

Color Insert: Behavior Disorders: Troubled Youngsters/Troubling Behavior

p. 1, (top) Steve Bourgeois/Unicorn Stock Photos; (bottom) Eric R. Berndt/Unicorn Stock Photos; **p. 2,**